NATHANIEL
HAWTHORNE

Nathaniel Hawthorne, 1850; portrait by Cephas Giovanni Thompson. Courtesy of the Library, Grolier Club of New York

NATHANIEL HAWTHORNE

A Biography

ARLIN TURNER

NEW YORK   OXFORD

OXFORD UNIVERSITY PRESS

1980

Copyright © 1980 by Oxford University Press, Inc.

LIBRARY OF CONGRESS CATALOGING IN PUBLICATION DATA
Turner, Arlin.
  Nathaniel Hawthorne, a biography.

  Includes index.
  1. Hawthorne, Nathaniel, 1804-1864—Biography.
2. Novelists, American—19th century—Biography.
I. Title.
PS1881.T79   813'.3 [B]   78-21988
ISBN 0-19-502547-4

Printed in the United States of America

Preface

One of Nathaniel Hawthorne's college-mates, Jonathan Cilley, declared great affection and admiration for him, but continued, "He lives in a mysterious world of thought and imagination which he never permits me to enter." After attending Hawthorne's funeral, Ralph Waldo Emerson wrote in his journal that he had thought he "might one day conquer a friendship" with the author and neighbor he had known more than twenty years, and added, "Now it appears that I waited too long." Hawthorne's widow said after his death that she wished "no one would try to write about him, for no one can know enough to do it." After generous portions of his notebooks and letters had been published, and after members of his family had put large amounts of other biographical information into print, he still retained among his biographers much of the enigmatic—or contradictory—character that he had among his contemporaries. The inclination toward solitude, which stayed with him even among his gregarious and garrulous neighbors at Concord, has not been easy to reconcile with his activities in the world about him—few, if any, of our major authors have been as extensively and significantly involved as he was in the affairs of his time.

My plan in this biography is to present the rich variety of Hawthorne's personality, and the individuality and complexity of his thought. From his boyhood onward, those about him recognized the distinctive quality of his mind. His habitual independence of thought and action, his skeptical outlook, and his unshakable reliance on his own convictions were in the minister's awareness when he asserted at Hawthorne's funeral, "All who knew him, knew that his thought was his own, his fame his own, his work his own." Hawthorne's intellectual and artistic integrity was such that whatever he did and whatever he wrote would bear the imprint of his mind. To recognize his life and his writings as the components of a consistent whole is to clarify much that otherwise might be puzzling in one or the other.

I want also to record Hawthorne's lifelong efforts to know the land and the people of his region, to understand the nature and the meaning of the American experience, from the first settlement onward, and in the full diversity of the people. He once remarked that he had "an appetite for the brown bread and the tripe and sausages of life, as well as for its nicer cates and dainties." Prepared by observations recorded in his mind and in his notebook during repeated travels in New England and New York, and by an intimate familiarity with American history, he undertook to know the character of the new nation, and to foresee its future. His findings and his conclusions are woven into his sketches, tales, and romances.

My plan, further, is to introduce Hawthorne's works into the biographical narrative with the prominence they had in his life. From the time he graduated from Bowdoin onward (if not indeed from the time he was preparing for college), he was unwaveringly dedicated to authorship. He is one of the most autobiographical of our writers—in his particular way. No work of his, to be sure, traces out its author's experiences as closely as do some of Herman Melville's, nor does any work of his re-create his own way of life as closely as do some of Henry James's novels. The autobiographical quality in Hawthorne's fiction derives from the consistency of his mind, which produced a steadiness of purpose and outlook that shaped everything he wrote. My intention is not to offer critical evaluations of individual tales and romances, or to apply one critical method or approach, or to survey the library of Hawthorne criticism; nor is it to press Hawthorne's mind and temperament within the confines of a particular pattern or formula. My intention is rather to place Hawthorne's works, a good portion of them, in the context of his life, characterizing his works and reporting his life in such terms as he might have used himself, and leaving readers, as he indicated many times was his preference, to supply their own interpretations and applications. It is my hope that others writing on Hawthorne will find materials in this volume that prove useful in their criticism of his works and in their speculations about aspects of his biogra-

phy. The character Hilda in *The Marble Faun* may be taken as speaking for
the author when she says that a reader should "find a great deal more" in a
poem than the poet "actually expressed." And what Hawthorne said about
a painting by Michelangelo, that for any "profound picture, there are
likely to be as many interpretations as there are spectators," he might have
applied also to literary works, for to him a profound poem or a romance
would be, like a profound painting, "a great symbol, proceeding out of a
great mind."

I quote Hawthorne freely on the following pages, allowing him to reveal in his own language, particularly in his letters and notebooks, the
contours and the texture of his mind. His prefaces, his sketches, and also
his fictional works add to what can be known about his view of himself
and his writings, and about his response to the events, the social ferment,
and the intellectual currents of his time. His habits of thinking and speaking in metaphor appear in his letters as well as in his imaginative works, as
do also his distinctive ways of seeing and saying things; for with him the
style is indeed the man himself.

San Marcos, Texas   A.T.
November 1979

Acknowledgments

It is pleasant to acknowledge my appreciation of the help I have received from many sources. First, I would name Professor Killis Campbell, who guided my first study of Hawthorne and who, by precept and his own example, made responsible literary research and effective writing seem to be goals worth pursuing. Next, I would name the late Randall Stewart, Norman Holmes Pearson, Claude Simpson, and William Charvat, to whom all students of Hawthorne are indebted. I owe particular debts to them because of their friendship as well as their scholarly assistance over the years, and to Manning Hawthorne, generous and scholarly representative of the Hawthorne line in our time. L. Neal Smith has given me the benefit of two storehouses of information on Hawthorne: his own knowledge and the materials assembled at the Ohio State University Center for Textual Studies. He has read this biography in manuscript, as have Manning Hawthorne and Buford Jones. Raymona Hull has read the chapters on Hawthorne's years in Europe and has permitted me to read the work on those years she has in preparation. I have also read in manuscript James O. Mays's study of Hawthorne as consul. C. E. Frazer Clark, Jr., has been generously helpful in a variety of ways.

Others to whom I am indebted for direct assistance or for their published writings are John H. Byers, Jr., Herbert T. F. Cahoon, Robert Cantwell, B. Bernard Cohen, J. Donald Crowley, Edward H. Davidson, Richard H. Fogle, Wayne Allen Jones, David B. Kesterson, John J. Mc-

Donald, Terence Martin, Arthur Monke, Barbara Mouffe, Mrs. Andrew Norton, Lola Szladits, Hyatt H. Waggoner, and Thomas Woodson. Something of what I owe to these and others will be indicated in my notes. A number of my former graduate students will find on the pages of this book matters of information or interpretation to which they have contributed. The preparation of the manuscript has gained at various stages from the skill and the care of Virginia Bossons, Anne Durden, Dorothy Roberts, and Julie Johnson. The proofreading and the making of the index have profited greatly from the assistance of Debra Harper.

I am indebted to the following for access to Hawthorne manuscripts and other materials and for permission to quote passages: Manning Hawthorne, C. E. Frazer Clark, Jr., the Berg Collection and the Manuscript Division of the New York Public Library, the Hawthorne-Longfellow Library of Bowdoin College, the Bancroft Library of the University of California, Berkeley, the Boston Public Library, the Center for Textual Studies at Ohio State University, the Duke University Library, the Essex Institute, the Henry E. Huntington Library, the Houghton Library, Harvard University, the Massachusetts Historical Society, the Pierpont Morgan Library, the Princeton University Library, and the Yale University Library.

Support for the research and writing of this biography has come through a National Endowment for the Humanities Senior Fellowship, a Huntington Library–National Endowment for the Humanities Fellowship, an American Council of Learned Societies grant, and grants from research funds at Duke University.

In a full sense, my wife, Thelma Sherrill Turner, has been my partner in the writing of this biography.

Contents

Illustrations

NATHANIEL HAWTHORNE

1

The Hawthorne Beginnings

Nathaniel Hawthorne was born in Salem, Massachusetts, on Union Street, July 4, 1804. His birth on the birthday of the young nation and on a Union Street might be taken to forecast the author who would find materials for his tales and romances in the America of his own time and earlier, who would seek to understand the special character and meaning of America, and whose works would stand high in the national literature as it won a place among the literatures of the world.

Few authors have identified themselves in their minds and in their works so fully as did Hawthorne with a region and a heritage. He once said New England was "quite as large a lump of earth" as his heart could take in; and during the Civil War, he said at least half seriously that he would like to see New England a separate nation.[1] Conscious of the "deep and aged roots" his ancestors had struck into his native soil, he felt it almost a matter of destiny to make his home in Salem, and he had a feeling for the town which, he said, for lack of a better word he would call affection. Yet he was "invariably happiest elsewhere," and he had never found there "the genial atmosphere which a literary man requires, in order to ripen the best harvest of his mind."[2] This affair of affection and estrangement was lifelong with Hawthorne, even while he filled major national and international roles and lived abroad. In his fictional writings, he gave his home region a fuller and more searching portrayal than any other part of the nation has received in the work of a major author. In those fictional works he nevertheless succeeded, to a degree achieved by only a few authors, in reaching beyond the immediate and the particular.

Various elements in Hawthorne's origin and early years invite designation as symbols such as occur on his own pages. He was born in a house that dated from the era of his first American ancestors and had been remodeled at intervals to meet the fashions and the needs of new times. The house was not on Washington Square or Essex Street or Derby Street, where the families having both station and wealth had built their mansions, but it was near the square and between those two streets. The household included a grandmother, widow of a sea captain who had entered folk tradition as a hero of the Revolution. On the day Hawthorne was born, his father, Nathaniel Hawthorne,[3] also a sea captain, was bound homeward from the Far East—on one of many voyages by Salem ships that so dominated trade with the Orient as to make Salem the leading American port for the Eastern trade and to place its sea captain–merchants among the wealthiest in the country. Four years later his father died of yellow fever on a voyage to Surinam, leaving a young widow and three small children, in a pattern that was familiar in Salem and other port towns.

Report has it that when word reached the house on Union Street, the mother called to her room the two oldest of her three children, Elizabeth and Nathaniel, six and four years old, and told them their father was dead.[4] It would have been in character for her, apparently—and surely in character for many such "wives of the dead" as Nathaniel Hawthorne later portrayed in one of his stories—to accept with stoicism the actuality she had known as a possibility through the silences of her husband's long voyages, and to introduce the children to the same actuality, at once and bluntly. Whether young Nathaniel learned of the event in this way or in a way less dramatic, he grew from childhood onward into a sharpened realization of what consequences the death of his father at the age of thirty-three had for the widow and the children. There would be reminders at least during the forty years his mother spent in some manner and some degree of mourning. The questioning mind of the later Hawthorne would attempt—at his mother's death-bed, for example—to understand these consequences, against the history of the young nation and among his speculations about the nature and the destiny of man.

Hawthorne was born eight years after the death of his grandfather Hawthorne, the Revolutionary War hero, and he could remember little about his father; but through local tradition and the recollections kept alive by his mother and his grandmother Hawthorne, he came to know experiences that were commonplace among sea-going families of the region and the time. The extent to which he sensed the qualities of seafaring life, in a household containing the widows of two sea captains and within shouting distance of some of the busiest wharves in America, is suggested by his boyhood thought of going to sea, his reluctance afterward to live inland, his fondness for sea travel, his lifelong response to legends of the sea, and his recognizing the literary possibilities of loss and the fear of loss at sea, as in his story "The Wives of the Dead" and in the Agatha story that he and Herman Melville both considered but neither wrote.

In later years when Hawthorne, a college graduate dedicated to a literary career, began searching local history for the materials of fiction, he was to discover that before his father and grandfather, stretching back to the founding generation in New England, were ancestors of his who embodied significant and distinctive elements of the earlier history. On further reading, he saw how fully the history of his own family was interwoven with the history of its American home, Salem. While he was most assiduous in this reading, from 1825 to 1835, he witnessed a reassessment that dealt harshly with the Puritan forces in early New England; and he was aware that his contemporaries identified his early ancestors with those forces no less explicitly than he did. He was aware also that the era of fabulous trading voyages to the Orient was receding into history and was also being reassessed. The history he read—whether national, regional, or ancestral—received the questioning analysis that was normal to the working of his mind.

Daniel Hawthorne (1731–96), the novelist's grandfather, in the fourth generation of the family in America, was a master and owner of ships before the Revolution, and was associated with Richard Derby, Sr. (1712–83), whose family in the next generation was to hold greatest prominence among the sea captain–merchants of Salem. As a privateersman in command of the *True American*, he was wounded in an engagement on October 28, 1776, when three members of his crew were killed and ten wounded.[5] He gained a modest place in patriotic lore through a ballad of twelve quatrains entitled "Bold Hathorne," written by the ship's surgeon.[6]

Daniel Hawthorne had been married in 1756 to Rachel Phelps, one of the twelve children of Jonathan Phelps, a blacksmith.[7] He brought from Liverpool in 1767 a young Irishman, Simon Forrester, who later married his oldest daughter, Rachel, became a sea captain and a privateer, and accumulated one of the largest fortunes among the Salem merchants. Forrester lived until 1817, his wife until 1823; they had eleven children.[8] Two other daughters of Daniel Hawthorne, Eunice and Ruth, remained unmarried; Judith married George Archer, a ship captain and merchant; Sarah married John Crowninshield, who belonged to one of the prominent maritime families; the older son, Daniel, went to sea and early became master and owner of ships.[9] These multitudinous uncles and aunts and their families were continuous reminders to Nathaniel Hawthorne that his paternal lineage was woven into the fabric of his native town.

Nathaniel Hawthorne, son of Daniel and father of the novelist, is a figure of hazy outline in the records that have been preserved. His career as a mariner was in many ways typical, but with a special shading of disappointment and pathos. He was born on May 19, 1775, went to sea early, and at the age of twenty sailed on the *America*, commanded by Jacob Crowninshield. The owner of the ship was Elias Hasket Derby, perhaps the most daring and surely the most successful owner of ships in the Oriental trade.[10] In Hawthorne's sketch "The Custom-House," he is the "old King Derby" who is named with "old Simon Forrester" among the "princely merchants of Salem." On the homeward voyage from Calcutta on the *America* in the winter of 1795 Nathaniel Hawthorne kept a journal (now at the Essex Institute, Salem) that was later in the hands of his son. After seven months at home he sailed aboard the *Perseverance*, owned by his brother-in-law Simon Forrester, on a voyage of a year and a half to Batavia, Manila, and China, and kept a journal in the same book. He made no entries when the ship was in port, but during the stay of the *Perseverance* in Manila he wrote in the journal a quatrain invoking the time when "Lowering Clouds appear/And angry Jove deforms the inclement Year." On a loose sheet in the journal are couplets in which he says that during storms at sea he will think on his dear Betsey's charms. The Betsey of these lines presumably was Elizabeth Clarke Manning, who lived in the next street to the Hawthornes in Salem. It can be presumed also that thought on her charms prompted a series of entries in the journal setting down day after day the homeward course and the distance yet to be traversed.

A third journal kept by Nathaniel Hawthorne records a voyage of the *Herald*, commanded by Captain Nathaniel Silsbee, from Boston to the Orient, February 3, 1800, to the next January 23 (now at the Huntington Library). The last paragraph of the journal was copied lower on the page by the future novelist, whose scribblings and signatures, with the date 1825, appear on several pages. Inside the front cover the novelist's son

Julian wrote on March 3, 1908, that this journal was the companion of Hawthorne's childhood and boyhood, and that he was particularly interested in the fight with a French privateer on November 3–4, 1800. Even the report of the fight in the matter-of-fact log of Nathaniel Hawthorne was one to give the son pride in his father and in America. Bound home from Calcutta, the *Herald* led the other four American ships sailing in its company in an attack that saved a British ship from a French privateer.[11]

On August 2, 1801, Nathaniel Hawthorne was married to Elizabeth Clarke Manning. The ceremony was performed by William Bentley, pastor of the East Church of Salem, which the Manning family attended.[12] Nancy Forrester, daughter of Simon Forrester and Rachel Hawthorne and eleven years old at the time, remembered in old age that the bride was "a beautiful woman, with remarkable eyes, full of sensibility and expression, and that she was a person of singular purity of mind."[13]

Nathaniel Hawthorne probably sailed for the Orient again late in 1801 or early the next year, possibly in command of the *Astrea*.[14] A daughter, Elizabeth Manning, was born on March 7, 1802. In the spring of 1803, he sailed to St. Petersburg, Russia, as mate on the *Hannah*. After returning in September, he embarked on December 16 for the Orient, aboard the *Mary and Eliza*, with Henry White master. The ship was home the next October—with Hawthorne in the role of captain. Upon reaching home, Captain Hawthorne discovered that on July 4, 1804, his second child had been born, a son, to bear the name Nathaniel, in the fifth of successive American generations in which the name had appeared.

Following his voyage as master of the *Mary and Eliza*, Nathaniel Hawthorne was voted on November 7, 1804, into the Salem East India Marine Society, of which his older brother, Daniel, had become a member at its founding in 1799. Its members, now numbering fifty-eight, had served as captains or supercargoes on voyages by way of either Cape Horn or the Cape of Good Hope. Late in the summer of 1804, this Captain Daniel Hawthorne was lost with his ship on a voyage to the Azores. On November 23, after only a month at home, Nathaniel Hawthorne sailed for the West Indies as captain of the schooner *Neptune*. Later voyages on this ship took him to Bordeaux in April, 1805,[15] to Nantes in October, 1806, and back to Salem by February 28, 1807. As captain of the *Nabby* he sailed for Cayenne, French Guiana, at the end of June and was home October 14.[16] Late in 1807, threats to foreign trade reached a climax, with both England and France seizing American ships and pressing seamen into military service. In December Congress passed the Em-

Hawthorne's Birthplace, Union Street, Salem. Courtesy of the Essex Institute, Salem, Mass.

bargo Act, which would strike back at the belligerents by forbidding nearly all foreign trade. In haste to leave port before the embargo became effective, Captain Hawthorne sailed again for the West Indies on December 28. Less than a fortnight later, on January 9, 1808, his third child, Maria Louisa, was born.

The *Nabby* was at Surinam (Dutch Guiana) on January 28. Before it could be cleared for home, yellow fever struck its crew, and when it did sail on March 14, the first mate was in command. The *Salem Register* of April 9 and the *Salem Gazette* of April 15 announced that Captain Hawthorne had died. On Sunday, April 10, the Reverend William Bentley received from the widow's father a request for prayer for Captain Hawthorne (always spelled "Harthorne" in Bentley's *Diary*). The steps required to close the record of Captain Hawthorne were simple. After the

Nabby returned, his clothes and other belongings were to be claimed; the widow was appointed to administer the estate; and the ship owners rendered on August 1 the final statement of his account and paid the balance due, $573.40.[17] The list of the expenses in Surinam could not fail to actualize for the widow—and perhaps her son later—the loneliness and the misery of Captain Hawthorne's last hours: amounts for washing clothes, board, porter, sundries, the physician, the coffin, "permission to bury Capt. Hathorne," the digging of the grave, the minister, and money advanced by a local broker for incidental expenses.

Although the novelist could have had in after years only hazy recollections of his father, mementoes enough remained (a tea service brought from China, a punch bowl and a pitcher from India, a gun that would be his later), along with the memories of his mother and grandmother and aunts, to give his father a presence within the family. The son's signature and a stamp of his name appear several times in the journals his father kept on the *America* and the *Perseverance;* his scribbling and signatures are plentiful in the *Herald* journal. Dates in the volumes show that they were in his hands in 1820 and 1825, and his son Julian dates some of the marks as late as 1835. Most of the marking is simply playful imitation of his father's ornamental script, but some of the marks seem to allow glimpses into the mind that prompted them. The couplets to "dear Betsey" and the other verses in the *Perseverance* journal are copied on the same pages, with corrections in spelling, capitalization, and punctuation that suggest a boyish intolerance. At the end of the same volume is a partial record for August 15, 1820, in which the writer, presumably Hawthorne, played at writing a ship's log. His interests and his outlook in the year 1820, when he was in Salem preparing for college—and was writing and publishing his hand-lettered newspaper the *Spectator*—well might have prompted such an attitude as the marks in the journals seem to reflect: a curiosity to know his father, to imitate and to experience vicariously his career, and yet to add an ironic, critical touch of his own.

Captain Nathaniel Hawthorne, father of the novelist, described himself as five feet ten and a half inches tall and of light complexion.[18] That the son in maturity resembled his father is suggested in the report that a sailor stopped him at the Salem custom-house when he was past forty years old and asked whether he was not related to the sea captain. The novelist said of an engraving made from his portrait painted by C. G. Thompson in 1850 that in the expression there was "a singular resemblance" to a miniature of his father.[19] Captain Hawthorne came down in family tradition as a reserved man, fond of reading, and subject to melancholy, but kindly and partial to children. His son once wrote that his own "natural tendency toward seclusion" had come from the paternal side.[20] Captain Hawthorne's sea journals show him careful in record-keeping and in penmanship. He used tobacco, and the large number of yards of it charged to his account with the Salem merchant John Scrobie suggests that he used more than a moderate amount.

Captain Hawthorne may have appeared to his son a failure, at least when viewed alongside those mariners of his time, including relatives, who sailed their own ships, accumulated fortunes, and built mansions in Salem. It might have occurred to the son to compare his father with Nathaniel Silsbee, master of the *Herald* on its voyage to the Orient in 1800. Silsbee, twenty-seven years old at the time (two years older than Hawthorne), thought that after one more voyage on the *Herald*, in which he owned a one-fourth interest, he would be able to retire from the sea. He afterward built a house on Washington Square in Salem; he served in the state government and later in the United States Congress. It was his daughter Mary on whose account the young story-writer Nathaniel Hawthorne was ready in 1838 to fight a duel. His son and namesake was one of the Whig politicians who in 1849 forced Hawthorne out of his office in the Salem custom-house.

Until his death, Captain Hawthorne and his wife and children lived in the crowded house of his mother. Not until his final two voyages, apparently, was he a regularly assigned captain. That he had left his widow and children all but penniless was of course known to the children as they grew up. It would be surprising if the captain's son, in his boyhood, during his debate later as to what calling he would follow, and still later when as a dedicated author he dreamed in what he called the "chamber under the eaves" in Salem—it would be surprising if he did not puzzle over the character and the fortune of his father. He would have kept in mind, surely, that his grandfather and his father had engaged in the same maritime ventures that had brought wealth and prominence to the Derbys, the Crowninshields, the Grays, the Ropeses, and the Silsbees. He would have remained aware that a great-grandmother of his was a Bowditch, of the family which had as one member the famous mathematician and navigator Nathaniel Bowditch. He would have been aware also that his grandfather's sister Ruth Hawthorne had married a Ropes and his aunt Sarah Hawthorne had married a Crowninshield; also that, among other Hawthorne relatives, his aunt Judith Archer, his aunt Rachel Forrester, and their children possessed wealth in the Salem of his own time.

The sparse records left by Captain Nathaniel Hawthorne invite speculation. In his journals he noted the fish and birds sighted at sea, in addition to the mariner's essentials of weather, currents, and coastal hazards. His poetic scribblings were not restricted to yearnings for his absent Betsey, and he lavished care in ornamenting the script of his journal. It would be surprising if Nathaniel Hawthorne did not recognize, even in the faintly delineated portrait of his father available to him, a spirit kindred to his own. If a choice had been open to his father, might not he too have passed over the professions and trades and business, and the possibilities of wealth, and chosen instead the realms of thought, dreams, speculation, and creative imagination?

Something of distance and coolness existed between the populous families among the Hawthorne kin and Captain Hawthorne's widow and children. The widow was retiring, it is clear, and she may have held back out of sensitivity or pride. It is worth noting that, on the evidence of letters that have been preserved, sisters of hers, particularly Aunt Mary Manning, were more persistent than she was in urging the captain's children to visit or write to their Hawthorne relatives.[21]

The novelist's birthplace, 27 Union Street, was built at some time before 1685; it passed in 1745 to Jonathan Phelps and later to Captain Daniel Hawthorne, his son-in-law.[22] It was constructed on a plan common in early Salem: a rectangular frame structure of two stories and additional rooms under the gambrel roof, with shingle roof and wood siding, and fireplaces on all floors. With its small rooms and low ceilings, and with the uncovered entrance only slightly above ground level, the house epitomized compactness, economy, and solidity.[23]

The household in which Nathaniel Hawthorne was born contained his grandmother, seventy years old in 1804, his mother, waiting through long absences of her seafaring husband, his uncle Daniel Hawthorne, and two unmarried aunts. It was a household of women, only rarely and temporarily invaded by the father or the uncle between voyages. At the death of Captain Hawthorne in 1808, his widow may have felt that she and her children could make less claim on the resources of the household than the grandmother and the two maiden aunts, or that she would be more comfortable in the home of her own parents; she would have known that the resources there were more adequate. When she left the Hawthorne house to live with her parents, about July 1, 1808, her move was only next door, but it substituted the Mannings for the Hawthornes in her children's close relationships; and consequently her son Nathaniel did not discover his early paternal ancestry until he had graduated from college and had begun reading colonial New England history in search of materials for literary use.

2
The Manning Years

When Captain Nathaniel Hawthorne's widow took her children to live with her parents, she entered a household more populous than the one she was leaving. The Manning house was on Herbert Street, on a lot extending through to Union Street on the south side of the Hawthorne lot. It was a plain rectangular frame house of three stories, with an additional room at each end of the attic, lighted by a gable window. One end of the house stood flush with the street; an open yard-space in front separated it from the next house to the south.

Richard Manning, Jr., and Miriam Lord Manning had nine children, ranging in 1808 from seventeen to thirty-one years of age, all unmarried except for Elizabeth Hawthorne. Three of the others married later: Richard in 1815, Priscilla in 1817, and Robert in 1824; but only Robert had children, the first of them not born until 1826. The Hawthorne children grew to maturity, therefore, with no other children to share the interest of their Manning uncles and aunts, who maintained uncommonly close ties within the family. Letters between family members in Salem and others temporarily elsewhere leave no doubt that the children were much in their minds, and that Nathaniel was a favorite. Because the estate of Richard Manning, Jr., remained undivided more than twenty years after his death, common financial interests tended to hold the family together. Elizabeth Hawthorne and her children gained from this circumstance, for the resources available for their support were not limited strictly to what would have been hers as one of the heirs.[1]

Although the move to the Manning house covered only a few yards, in ways not readily apparent the distance was considerable. It was a move from one heritage to another and from one current orientation to another. As Nathaniel would know later from reading colonial history, the early Hawthornes in America filled important roles in the transplanting of European culture and the shaping of the new society; and in the times of his father and his grandfather, when the beauty and the wealth of the Orient were being unloaded at the Salem wharves, the Hawthornes moved in the fringes of prominence and touched elbows, at least, with the merchant princes who brought modern-day treasures from remote shores and furnished the three-story and four-story mansions designed by the native architect Samuel McIntyre (1757–1811). Even though Hawthorne daughters had married into some of these patrician families, and Nathaniel grew up among their descendants, he did not draw close to any of them, and he made only slight references to his father and his grandfather. When he later encountered the first two colonial ancestors in his reading, he saw them as the most illustrious of the Hawthorne line in America; and more than once he remarked in playful self-depreciation that after them the line had dimmed steadily until it approached oblivion with him. From the time he was four, Hawthorne's world was the world of the Mannings. The report has come down that he would go next door on Sunday afternoons and read in Grandmother Hawthorne's room—chiefly *The Pilgrim's Progress*, a book acceptable for Sunday reading. His father's sea journals were in his hands about 1820.[2] But it was ten years later that he first showed himself aware of his paternal heritage.

The Mannings were tradesmen and businessmen, active in the workaday affairs about them, for the most part practical, energetic, and enterprising. The only one in the immediate family to choose a different course was the second youngest son, John, who went to sea in 1812 and never returned. In a notebook entry for June 30, 1854, Hawthorne said that, even to that day, he never saw his name "without thinking that this may be the lost uncle."[3] He gave Hepzibah Pyncheon in *The House of the Seven Gables* (Chapter 4) an uncle who "had sailed for India, fifty years before, and never been heard of since." The grandfather of Nathaniel Hawthorne, Richard Manning, Jr., came from his native Ipswich and at the age of nineteen, in 1774, was established in Salem as a blacksmith. His wife was Miriam Lord, who William Bentley said came from an ancient and venerable family in Ipswich. Manning prospered as a blacksmith and by 1784 was in the livery-stable business on Union Street. He next established a stagecoach line to Boston, which soon after 1800 he relinquished to his sons. He had begun before 1800 buying land in the vicinity of Raymond, Cumberland County, Maine, on the shores of Lake Sebago, and afterward devoted himself to land trading and development.[4] He spent much of his time in the new region, which was called in his family "the land of promise." On his way from Salem to Raymond on April 19, 1813, he died of an apoplectic stroke at Newburyport. (Another grandparent of the Hawthorne children, the widow of Bold Daniel Hawthorne, died on April 16.)

Manning left no will and no adequate account of his property. Since his widow, his nine children—except the oldest son, William—and his three grandchildren lived on Herbert Street as a family unit, they left the estate undivided. Arrangements were made for the widow to administer the estate, for Robert, the third of the sons, to serve as her chief agent, and for Richard, the second son, to manage the Maine land, for a fee of $100 a year. Richard settled permanently on the land, being known afterward as Richard Manning, 3d, or Richard Manning of Raymond, to distinguish him from his father, who had been Richard Manning of Salem. An inventory of the estate prepared by Richard listed for Salem the family residence and a store on Herbert Street, a house and stables on Union Street, and three lots on Derby Street. The list showed nearly 10,000 acres in Maine, with enough notes and mortgages and other property to bring the worth of the total estate past $54,000—a considerable fortune. Account books kept by Richard Manning, Jr., and by his sons Richard, Robert, and Samuel are preserved at the Essex Institute. It is unlikely that Nathaniel Hawthorne spent as much time with these books as with his father's sea journals, but if he had looked into the accounts his grandfather kept through much of his life, he would have found a sequence not uncommon in early America. Beginning as a tradesman, Richard Manning had applied energy, initiative, and a measure of business daring, and he had turned in his last years to the new lands being opened up as the nation expanded. In his grandfather's records, Nathaniel Hawthorne would have met the names of the sea captains and merchants who had caused Salem to stand, among the New England towns, second in population only to Boston, and first in wealth relative to size. The captains and merchants were Manning's customers. With the increased wealth and the consequent accumulation of artistic and cultural artifacts from Europe and the Orient, many family names handed down from the early settlements gained new luster, and at the same time new names appeared beside them, having only short histories to recount, and those histories telling mainly of initiative and daring and shrewdness and good fortune in foreign trade or in enterprises that grew as the population expanded inland. Manning's account books might be used to call the roll of both old and new names among the notable of Salem. Five sea captains named Derby and four named Crowninshield were customers, as were "Capt. Daniel Harthorn" (probably Nathaniel Hawthorne's grandfather first and his uncle later), Captain Simon Forrester and Captain George Archer (both uncles of Nathaniel Hawthorne), the Reverend William Bentley, Benjamin Lynde Oliver (who later was to tutor Nathaniel Hawthorne for college), and Thomas Manning (brother of Richard Manning, Jr.), who brought up a large family in Salem.

In the account books of his Uncle Robert Manning, Nathaniel would have seen the record of a man who relied on self-education, intellectual curiosity, and imagination to move on from the business foundations provided by his father, into activities that were scientific as well as promotional. At his death in 1841 Robert Manning was known internationally for his achievement in the development and distribution of fruit trees suited to his region. The account books of Nathaniel's Uncle Richard Manning would have revealed a man at home in the new lands "down east," who from the time he went to Raymond in 1813 did not return to Salem or want to return, he said, even for a visit, during the remaining eighteen years of his life. He served as justice of the peace and worked for the progress of the region; but his interests reached far beyond his community, and included an interest in literature. A constant reader of newspapers and magazines, he ordered new books, ranging from practical guides for stockmen and farmers to history and biography, and not excluding novels. Even in letters weighted with details of land transactions he showed now and then a gift for turning phrases and ideas, a touch of genial wit, and a frank, open personality. He was alive to the beauty no less than the hardship of what he called the wilderness, a wonderland of hunting and fishing and exploring the forests and the shores of Lake Sebago, which Hawthorne knew for some months and remembered with nostalgia in later years. Richard Manning kept scrupulously accurate records of all transactions for the estate, neatly written and accented with flourishes of language and pen, and provided an extra copy as a precaution against loss.

Details from a variety of sources contribute to the record of Hawthorne's boyhood. His sister Elizabeth (Ebe) and Elizabeth Palmer Peabody, both possessively interested in his career, outlived him by two decades and recorded late in life their recollections of his early years. Biographers within his family, especially his wife, his daughter Una, his son-in-law George Parsons Lathrop, his son Julian, and his daughter Rose, modified the accounts dating from his lifetime with their own recollections and their own attitudes. Hawthorne's own statements about his childhood may take liberties with fact, but they may be important in revealing how the events of his early life appeared to him at the time they occurred and also later—thus affording a double view of the occurrences and of the mind that interpreted them. Most useful of all are the casual and unself-conscious revelations in Hawthorne's boyhood letters and in the letters exchanged among the Mannings.

Anecdotes of his childhood show him to have had early a distinctive personality and a disposition by no means retiring.[5] He was playful and imaginative and seems to have dominated his playmates. His fondness for cats did not prevent him from teasing them. To a reprimand after he had thrown a cat over a fence, he supposedly countered, "Oh, she'll think it was William," a playmate. At another time he had kicked a dog and remarked that the dog would think his grandmother did the kicking. His sister Elizabeth remembered that he once had a pet monkey that died and was buried in the garden, and that at another time, when a cat was buried, he wrote a quatrain for the occasion.[6] She quoted him as saying that he quarreled with one John Knights at school because he was "a boy of very quarrelsome disposition." A sense of the dramatic and a relish of the odd are suggested in her report that once in the country, presumably in Maine, he refused to take money offered him and explained that there were no stores where he could spend it. Another report of hers, that he refused to accept a five-dollar bill his uncle Simon Forrester offered him, probably combines some event of his boyhood with her memory of the distaste she and he both had for Forrester. Hawthorne would often remark, report has it, that he was going away to sea and would never come back; and he was fond of quoting the line from Shakespeare's *Richard III*, "Stand back, my lord, and let the coffin pass." The assertion he is reported to have made many times as a youth, that he expected to die before the age of twenty-five, probably signifies only that he indulged in youthful self-pity, but it is worth noting that his mind ran to such prospects.[7]

The Manning correspondence shows the Hawthorne children receiving abundant attention from their uncles and aunts, who were affectionate (though not demonstrative), generous, solicitous of "the little ones," and for the most part proud of "our children." Again and again the Mannings showed a greater deference for Nathaniel than a boy of his age might have expected. When he was seven or eight years old, his uncles Robert and Samuel took him along on a trip into New Hampshire, giving him a fore-taste of the journeys he would take with one or the other of them or alone in later years. His boyhood letters indicate that he liked and took for granted the attention he received. He could tease with impunity, he knew, but he seems to have accepted direction with no more than playful objec-tion. His elders recognized special qualities in his mind, and when the time came they were eager to see him educated. Robert urged the children to write him when he was away, and Nathaniel's earliest letter that has been preserved was written to him, December 9, 1813. Robert answered at once, and a year later sent word to Nathaniel and Ebe that he would "give them a schooling" if they did not write him.

An accident in Nathaniel's ninth year, causing extended lameness, seems to have had important effects on his future. The restrictions on his activities probably turned him toward reading, and possibly encouraged habits of seclusion and introspection. His lameness no doubt drew atten-tion and sympathy from his uncles and aunts and thus may have con-vinced them more firmly that he had gifts worth cultivating. He had been hit by a ball while playing, about November 10, 1813. A doctor was con-sulted, and after a month's absence from school and no improvement, a second was called in.[8] A cure in a week or two was expected, but on the next January 12 Ebe sent Uncle Robert a frantic note: He must come home, for Nathaniel would not walk on his foot, as the doctor said he should. In May Nathaniel was too lame to go for the visit to Raymond he had been promised; and on July 4 he lamented his confinement, for he had to miss the celebration. His Aunt Priscilla probably reflected a family rec-ognition of his talents, when she asked Robert to advise him to practice his writing and get his other lessons regularly. "However rich the soil," she added, "we do not expect fruit, unless good seed is sown, and the plants carefully cultivated."[9]

Nathaniel had been attending the school of Joseph Emerson Worcester (1784–1865), who, report has it, came to Herbert Street to hear his lessons while he was lame.[10] Among the receipts that have been preserved, one shows that Mrs. Hawthorne paid Elizabeth Carlton a quarter's tuition for Nathaniel and Elizabeth on July 11, 1808. If Nathaniel's instruction began on April 11, as this receipt indicates, three months before he was four years old, two or three days after word of his father's death reached

Salem, and a month after the birth of the third child, Maria Louisa, the arrangement was probably made to relieve his mother in her distress, and it may have reflected the transfer of responsibility for the mother and her children from the Hawthorne family to the Manning family.[11] On January 20, 1815, Mrs. Hawthorne wrote her brother Richard that after fourteen months Nathaniel walked without his crutches as well as ever; but he seems not to have been able to attend school regularly until February, 1816, two years and four months after his accident. When early June of that year brought another opportunity to go to Raymond, he went with his mother and sisters. According to family tradition, one of the doctors consulted about his foot was Dr. Nathaniel Peabody who became his father-in-law twenty-five years later.[12]

For ten years after the death of Richard Manning, Jr., the question was debated whether the family would move to Maine. Both the children and their elders felt the attraction of the wild land on the shore of Lake Sebago. They often said in their letters that they disliked Salem. Perhaps they were merely disparaging the near in comparison with distant pastures, but perhaps too they were aware that at Raymond the Mannings had the more elevated station of founders and developers. Twice Mrs. Hawthorne moved tentatively to Raymond with the children, and her son declared in later years that he spent the happiest days of his life "savagizing" in the Maine woods.

The land at Raymond was not sold quickly, but in a way to assist and to profit from the development of the region. After a dozen years 5,000 acres remained. Mrs. Hawthorne, as one of the heirs, was entitled to her portion of the yield from the "undivided" estate, and it is clear that support of her children was taken for granted. In the summer of 1814 she had considered moving to Raymond with her children and her sister Mary. Fearful in September that the British would occupy Salem, she considered moving to Ipswich, but Nathaniel protested that he wanted to stay and see the British. In November she and Mary began plans to take over a farm the estate owned at Bridgetown, twenty miles north of Raymond, where there would be a church and a school for the children. When the Hawthorne family at last visited Raymond in June, 1816, the children were as pleased as they had expected to be. In addition to fishing for salmon trout, Nathaniel may have been allowed to use his father's fowling piece, which was to become his. Grandmother Manning and Aunt Mary came for a visit and stayed until early December. In August Robert began insisting that Nathaniel be sent to Salem for school, but not until late October was he sent. His mother and sisters remained at Raymond, expecting to stay permanently, but his mother was sick during the winter, and they returned to Salem the next spring.

The question of a permanent move to Maine remained undecided. Mary favored moving the entire family; Priscilla, youngest of the daughters, was opposed, both before and after she married John Dike in 1817. Maria, the third oldest daughter, had died on May 20, 1814, at the age of eighteen. Samuel went to Raymond in 1816 and stayed two years. In 1817 Robert began planting at Raymond the fruit trees he was developing. Richard had built a new house and had married Susan Dingley, a daughter in the family with whom he and his father before him had made their headquarters in Maine. Early in the year 1818 it was decided that at least some of the family would move. Richard completed a store building and began a new house for them. The Hawthornes prepared to move in the summer, but were delayed until October for the completion of the house—to Nathaniel's pleasure, for he was reluctant to leave dancing school.[13] The new house at Raymond, a plain rectangle in plan, with two stories and a one-span roof, and a window in each end of the attic, had been built large enough for all members of the family who might decide to move from Salem.

Allowing Nathaniel only six weeks in the region he had remembered fondly since the summer of 1816, Uncle Robert took him away on December 16, along with Jacob Dingley, brother to Uncle Richard's wife, to the boarding school the Reverend Caleb Bradley (1772–1861) held at Stroudwater, a suburb of Portland. A man of firm views, eccentric in manners and speech, Bradley might win interest but hardly tolerance from such boys as Nathaniel.[14] The report has come down that afterward Nathaniel would recite at home for the amusement of the family the blessing he said Bradley repeated invariably at the table. His residence in the Bradley family is reflected in his tale "The Vision of the Fountain." When the two boys carried out a threat and came home in February without permission, Uncle Robert sent Nathaniel back to finish the term, and began thinking of sending him to Salem for school.

A series of notebook entries published by Samuel T. Pickard first in the *Portland Transcript* (1870–73) and later as *Hawthorne's First Diary* (Boston, 1897) furnish a close-hand account of the scene and the activities of Hawthorne's boyhood at Raymond. The entries were printed, not from the original diary, but from copies received by such a mysterious route as to leave their authenticity uncertain. Nevertheless, the circumstances and the events reported in the diary square fully with information from other sources, and in outlook and interests the diarist is enough like the Hawthorne of the later works to argue that he was the diarist. There is evidence, however, that changes were made by another hand, no doubt that of William Symmes, who was Hawthorne's companion at Raymond and who furnished the copy from which the diary was printed.[15] As published, the diary opens with this note, dated at Raymond, June 1, 1816: "Presented by Richard Manning, to his nephew Nathaniel Hathorne, with the advice that he write out his thoughts, some every day, in as good words as he can, upon any and all subjects, as it is one of the best means of his securing for mature years, command of thought and language." It would have been in keeping with Richard's mind for him to duplicate Robert's urging his nephew to write. A Hawthornesque fusion of the actual and the imaginative is characteristic of the diary. The episodes are narrated in a way to indicate, as is regularly true of Hawthorne's early notebooks, that they are being tested for literary use. To the most troublesome of all the questions, whether Hawthorne could have produced by his fifteenth year the mature writing of the *First Diary*, the answer may be that Symmes touched up the entries. A more likely answer may lie in the comparable maturity, if not indeed sophistication, of the writing in Hawthorne's boyhood letters and in the *Spectator*, which he wrote only a year after the diary was supposedly written.

He had spent, all told, no more than nine months at Raymond; yet he believed his experiences in the Maine woods gave him attitudes and habits that remained with him. He told James T. Fields in 1863 that he lived in Maine "like a bird of the air," but that there he first got his "cursed habits of solitude."[16] A sketch he wrote in 1853 shows how he remembered his boyhood in Maine:

> here I ran quite wild, and would, I doubt not, have willingly run wild till this time, fishing all day long, or shooting with an old fowling-piece; but reading a good deal, too, on the rainy days, especially in Shakspeare and "The Pilgrim's Progress," and any poetry or light books within my reach. Those were delightful days; for that part of the country was wild then, with only scattered clearings, and nine tenths of it primeval woods. . . . I would skate all alone on Sebago Lake, with the deep shadows of the icy hills on either hand. When I found myself far away from home, and weary with the exhaustion of skating, I would sometimes take refuge in a log cabin, where half a tree would be burning on the broad hearth. I would sit in the ample chimney, and look at the stars through the great aperture through which the flames went roaring up. Ah, how well I

recall the summer days, also, when with my gun I roamed at will
through the woods of Maine![17]

His sister Elizabeth recalled taking long walks with him, once three miles
on the frozen Lake Sebago under a full moon, at other times along the
craggy shore of the lake.[18] Julian Hawthorne remembered his father's
telling him of once tracking a bear, armed with his fowling-piece, but
never overtaking it.[19] It was a boy's paradise as the grown man remembered it, and much of what he remembered had been close to actuality.
Henry Wadsworth Longfellow visited the Lake Sebago region more than
half a century later and wrote of it: "If 'Long Pond' were called Loch
Long, it would be a beautiful lake. This and Sebago are country cousins
to the Westmoreland lakes in England, quite as lovely, but wanting a little
more culture and good society."[20] Hawthorne would have felt less than
Longfellow the want of culture and good society—surely less in boyhood,
and probably less afterward as well.

Hawthorne wrote Uncle Robert on May 16, 1819, that he had shot a
partridge and a hawk and had caught eighteen large trout. It is not surprising that he said in the same letter, "I am sorry you intend to send me
to school again."

3

Preparing for College

Following his unsatisfying term in Caleb Bradley's school, Hawthorne might plausibly have stayed at Raymond, where he wanted to be and his mother and sisters presumably would live. With schooling already equal to that of his uncles, and beyond the normal for the region, he might have slipped comfortably into the life of the down-east community. But his Uncle Robert Manning was no less determined in 1819 than three years earlier to see him educated and, as the acknowledged head of the household, took responsibility in this as in other matters. How much weight Nathaniel's mother had in decisions about his future is not clear, but she no doubt deferred to Robert. The divided authority Hawthorne knew in his early years may have encouraged him toward the seclusiveness, the independence of mind, and the reliance on his own convictions that characterized his mature years. Here may have originated his reluctance to discuss personal matters with his mother and sisters, such as his engagement to be married twenty years later.

The decision to give Nathaniel further education reflected a confidence in his ability and an awareness that in America it was possible to rise through the application of talent and initiative. Grandfather Manning had been designated "yeoman" in the documents naming his widow to administer his estate. The Reverend William Bentley had listed him on the church roll in 1792 as "blacksmith," when he listed as "esquire" another Richard Manning in his congregation, who was a sea captain and merchant. The route to the professions was normally through one of the colleges. Now and then Nathaniel made teasing references to the plans to educate him. He once wrote Robert, for example, "You ordered me to write as well as I could," and continued, "but this is bad paper. I am writing with a bad pen, and am in a hurry as I am going to Portland at noon with Mr. Leach." When plans to send him to school became definite, he informed Robert, "Mother says she can hardly spare me." Late in June he left for Salem, not to return to Maine or see his mother for two years, and to know Raymond afterward only on a few brief visits.[1]

Aunt Priscilla had already arranged for him to enter Samuel H. Archer's School on Marlboro Street. He could find no fault with the school, he wrote Uncle Robert, "except [its] not being dear enough . . . and not near enough"; and he wrote his sister Louisa, "I now go to a 5 dollar school, I, that have been to a 10 dollar one. 'Oh Lucifer, son of the morning, how art thou fallen!' " The ten-dollar school probably was Caleb Bradley's. How much preparing Nathaniel for college had become a family mission is indicated in letters sent to Raymond by Aunt Mary, who managed the household on Herbert Street. In reporting Nathaniel's arrival, she said she would do her best "for the benefit of the whole concern." She already had taken him to visit a childhood playmate, Benjamin Foster, on familiar ground, in an astute move to dilute his longing for Maine.[2] He experienced a solitary Fourth of July and birthday, and in addition had a painful swelling in his left cheek and eye. Aunt Mary reported, "he bears it as patiently as can be expected, but he sighs for the woods of Raymond, and yet he seems convinced of the necessity of preparing to do something." He did not enter school until July 7, because his aunt had not had time to finish the clothes he needed. She could report after a month that, since Nathaniel began school, she had not heard him say he wished he were at Raymond. She begged that Robert not hurry to Salem on Nathaniel's account. "We think ourselves capable of taking care of one Boy." Aunt Priscilla also took the role of advocate, saying in one letter that he seemed to like the language study and intended to puzzle Louisa with a letter in Latin. What he studied besides the languages is not recorded. A copy of B. Shey's *The American Book-Keeper* that has been preserved, bearing his signature and the date October 25, 1819, among signatures with later dates, may signify that he was studying bookkeeping to prepare for work in his uncles' stagecoach office.

In the new year Nathaniel's future was still under discussion. On January 11, 1820, Robert allowed him to postpone writing a letter to Ray-

The Manning House, Herbert Street, Salem: "Castle Dismal," containing the "Chamber under the Eaves." Courtesy of the Essex Institute, Salem, Mass.

mond rather than miss an evening of study. Two weeks later his mother hoped he had given up the thought of going to sea, "for some years at least." Near the end of his last quarter of school in February, Robert doubted that suitable work could be found for him, and added, "as a last resort we can bind him for 7 years to turn a cutler's wheel and perhaps better." The fact that this letter was addressed to Louisa, thirteen years old—though of course intended for all members of the family at Raymond—may mean that the idea of Nathaniel at a cutler's wheel was meant as a joke. In a letter of February 29 Aunt Mary took a firm position in regard to the "one boy" she felt she was capable of looking after. Expectations should not be too great, but his teacher wanted to see him go to college, and she believed the prospect for his making "a worthy and useful man" was "better in that way than in any other." Uncle Robert would send him to college if he thought he could easily meet the expenses. She would give a hundred dollars. That might be only a drop, but it would be "a great drop," and if every one of his relatives as near to him as she would put in as much, "his bucket would be full." The other relatives as near as she were five Manning uncles and aunts and five aunts on the Hawthorne side, including some who could afford much more than her hundred dollars. No record has come to light of any contribution by Hawthorne relatives toward Nathaniel's education.[3]

Aunt Mary's idea about Nathaniel prevailed, and he could write his mother on March 7, "I have left school, and have begun to fit for College under Benj^m L. Oliver, Lawyer. So you are in great danger of having one learned man in your family. . . . After I have got through College I will come down and learn Ebe [.] Latin and Greek." This long letter shows a youngster excited and grateful but in boyish fashion determined to conceal his feelings. He asks his mother, "Shall you want me to be a Minister, Doctor or Lawyer? A Minister I will not be." He then confesses his uneasiness and awe at the prospect before him. "Oh how I wish I was again with you, with nothing to do but go a gunning. But the happiest days of my life are gone. Why was I not a girl that I might have been pinned all my life to my Mother's apron."

Nathaniel studied his lessons at home and went for recitation at seven in the morning to the Lynde mansion at Essex and Liberty streets, where Benjamin Lynde Oliver (1788–1843) lived.[4] The confidence of Oliver that Nathaniel would be ready to enter college the following October supported the judgment the Mannings had formed earlier. But Robert, wanting to make sure that his nephew did not enter under a handicap, had him extend his preparation another year. Besides his study with Oliver, Nathaniel began other activities appropriate to the learned man he would become. He attended on March 14, 1820, a concert by the Handel Society of Salem, on May 3 Kotzebue's sentimental drama *Lovers' Vows*, the next March 5 Edmund Kean's performance of *King Lear* in Boston, and on May 28 a performance of John Home's Gothic play *Douglas* in Salem.[5] In letters to Ebe he said more about literature, quoting from his favorite poems, sending some of his own verses, and reproaching her for not reciprocating. He had read all of Sir Walter Scott's novels except *The Abbot;* he liked *The*

Lord of the Isles as well as any of Scott's poems. Next to Scott's romances, he liked William Godwin's *Caleb Williams.* He had read also Godwin's *St. Leon* and the travels of Sir John Mandeville.

Returning on June 1, 1820, from a visit to Raymond, Aunt Mary brought Louisa with her, to further her own education and to keep Nathaniel company. He had asked earlier for Ebe to be sent, for he had no one to talk to but his grandmother, Aunt Mary, and Hannah Lord, the maid. He and Louisa played shuttlecocks and battledores together; she heard the orations he practiced as school assignments; both attended Turner's Dancing School, and both went to the end-of-term ball on October 26. Uncle William sponsored Louisa's dancing lessons, which Aunt Mary thought a waste of money and effort, and Aunt Rachel Forrester gave her a dress to wear to the ball. After the close of Turner's school, Nathaniel attended the dancing school of Monsieur Bosseux. The children's mother evidently supported their wish to take dancing lessons, and at about the same time her quiet voice seems to have prevailed in letting Louisa stay in the school she liked, against Aunt Mary's plan to move her to another. After a month in Salem, Louisa wrote that only once or twice had Nathaniel laughed at her, quarreled with her, or pestered her. They formed on June 10 the Pin Society, which met every Saturday, had by-laws, dues (one pin)—and two members. The proceedings, which Nathaniel kept in a notebook that has been preserved, suggest that congenial relations existed between the two members, and that he enjoyed the playful turning of ideas and phrases appropriate to the organization. The society was discontinued after August 25, 1821, a month before Nathaniel was to depart for college, because, according to the minutes, "a large proportion of the Members were absent from town; and those who remained were unwilling to meet without them."[6] Louisa had returned to Maine.

The *Spectator* was also a joint enterprise, though the editor was announced as "N. Hawthorne" and he alone printed the numbers by hand lettering. Louisa contributed poetry (one poem of five lines bearing her name), and she publicized the paper in her letters to Raymond. Six dated numbers were printed, beginning with August 21, 1820, preceded by an undated issue which included a prospectus.[7] The neatly lettered sheets and the care exhibited in the contents evidence perseverance, if not indeed a determination to pursue literature. The *Spectator* included the full range of departments, types of news, advertisements, and editorials; and the editor infused humor and irony throughout. In apologizing for inaccuracies in the paper, for example, he cited the number of offices he had to fill: "In the first place, we study Latin and Greek. Secondly we write in the employ of Wm. Manning Esq. Thirdly, we are Secretary, Treasurer, and Manager of the 'PIN SOCIETY.' Fourthly we are Editor of the Spectator. Fifthly, sixthly and lastly, our own Printers, Printing Press and Types." (He was writing afternoons in Uncle William's stagecoach office, for which he received a dollar a week and expected William to give him also a suit of clothes.) Lest any reader take offense at anything he wrote, he warned that he intended to take fencing lessons, begin target practice, and meanwhile carry "a stout oaken cudgel." The titles of the essays announce them to be of a kind appropriate to a paper named for the *Spectator* of Addison and Steele: "Solitude," "Industry," "Benevolence," "Wealth," "Hope," "Courage." The "melancholy season autumn," he said, reminds us that youth must fade and we must "go down to the silent grave"; only the thought that "the soul can never die . . . can cheer us as we travel towards the Grave." As poet the editor warns that youth is fleeting and that in "the dark dread sleep of death" neither fame nor glory "can ever wake your spirits," but only the certainty that "There is a God, in Heaven enthron'd."

These contents of the *Spectator* may be dismissed as exercises imitating conventional pieces, in the manner of the early English Romantics and their followers in America. But they show the interests and the special ways of seeing and saying things that characterize the later Hawthorne. The essay on solitude notes the duality in man's nature, the social being and the recluse, that his mature works would explore many times. Here the weight is thrown on the side of the active life, against "the cold calmness of indifference."

The editor says that the publisher of the *Spectator* has died of starvation; "any number of indigent POETS and AUTHORS" will be employed; the editor will publish a new edition of the MISERIES OF AUTHORS, with a sequel drawn from his own experience. He speaks of himself as a literary man, and remarks in passing that "wealth does not lie in the path of literature." He declares in his prospectus that he hopes to "reform the morals, and instruct and amuse the minds" of his readers, "advance the cause of Religion, and give to truth and justice a wider sway." The tone is that of the eighteen-century periodical essay, and Hawthorne may have known such later works as Washington Irving's *Letters of Jonathan Oldstyle* (1802).

Other prominent themes of Hawthorne's later works appear in the *Spectator*. A wanderer finds after an absence of a few years that all is changed and he "looks to the Grave, as his only resting place"; the narrator of a poem leaves his father's fields in pursuit of glory and, having won it, sighs for the cottage of his childhood; another poem affirms that if one could raise the veil and see what the future holds for him, he would not dare "cast one look." Courage and cowardice may be ironically confused; a schoolboy blunders into the enemy's ranks during a snowball fight and, after fleeing back to his own lines, is praised for bravery; perhaps braving the disapproval of the world "in a good cause" is the "noblest species of courage"; a "duellist may with much more propriety be called a coward, than he who refuses a challenge." This last statement has special interest in view of the editor's own experiences eighteen years later when he was ready to challenge his friend John Louis O'Sullivan and his college-mate Jonathan Cilley was killed in a duel.

The *Spectator* reflects a mind of the same turn and the same quality that remained with Hawthorne the rest of his life. The contents suggest the closeness and the understanding within the Manning family, and the author's assumption that his wit and irony and his subtlety would not be lost on his readers. He felt at liberty to tease his uncles and aunts—and to lecture them mildly. The weekly numbers were in effect letters to Raymond, announcing Salem news and commenting on affairs in Maine, all turned to a humorous purpose. Announcements of marriages and engagements were concocted as a way of teasing his relatives and friends. One item reads: "Births. The Lady of Dr. Winthrop Brown a SON and HEIR. Mrs. Hawthorne's cat SEVEN KITTENS. We hear that both of the above ladies are in a state of convalescence." (Dr. Brown was unmarried.) Aunt Mary seems to have been as tolerant of the children in her charge as her devotion to duty and morality would allow. She probably enjoyed this item: "WANTED, A HUSBAND, not above seventy years of age. None need apply unless they can produce GOOD REC[C]OMMENDATIONS or are possessed of at least TEN thousand DOLLARS. The Applicant is YOUNG, being under FIFTY years of age, and of GREAT BEAUTY. MARY MANNING, Spinstress." The editor reported that on a visit to Raymond his Aunt Priscilla had killed "two enormous and horrifick striped Serpents," and added, "This is true Courage." The same number printed an essay on courage. His denial that the people of Maine were obliged to eat shoe-leather, as had been reported, belongs to a sequence of bantering exchanges on weather and crops that appeared in the letters of half a dozen family correspondents and were skillfully adapted in the *Spectator*. A number of items in the *Spectator* reflect the moral slant that is evident in much of Hawthorne's later work, and his viewing of the immediate and the literal in broad contexts.

In generalizing that the older we grow and "the shorter time we have to enjoy our riches, the more we wish to amass them," he echoed an earlier protest to Uncle Robert that his grandmother and Aunt Mary hoarded the foods that he liked best; and he may have had in mind his Uncle Simon Forrester, Old King Derby, and others he named later in "The Custom-House" as foolish hoarders of wealth.

On June 7, 1821, Elizabeth arrived from Maine; Nathaniel had not seen her for nearly two years and at first did not recognize her. Louisa soon went to Raymond. The congeniality of his relations with Louisa was never possible with Elizabeth, but she could furnish companionship in learning and might help in his final preparation for college.

Nathaniel still longed for the Maine woods; and as the time to leave for college approached, he urged his mother to stay in Raymond so that he could spend every vacation there with her; it would be "a second Garden of Eden." Such declarations often have a note of self-pity that he enjoyed, as in a letter to Ebe on October 31, 1820: "I have almost given up writing Poetry. No Man can be a Poet & a Book-Keeper at the same time. I do find this place most horribly 'dismal.' And have taken to chewing 'tobacco' with all my might, which I think raises my spirits." At other times, he lamented working in Uncle William's stagecoach office, but took pride in the employment and the salary. It was a habit of his to disparage his own accomplishments, educational and others, in half-truths stated for humorous effects. In 1853, for example, he wrote: "One of the peculiarities of my boyhood was a grievous disinclination to go to school, and (Providence favoring me in this natural repugnance) I never did go half as much as other boys, partly owing to delicate health (which I made the most of for the purpose), and partly because, much of the time, there were no schools within reach."[8]

The one probably due most credit for overcoming his "disinclination to go to school" was Aunt Mary, while she had charge of the Hawthorne children in Salem. Mrs. Hawthorne had long been closer to Mary than to any other of her brothers and sisters. They had moved together in 1806 from the Unitarian East Church attended by the Mannings to the Congregational First Church of the Hawthornes. Mrs. Hawthorne's waiting five years to join her husband's church suggests that during his absences she preferred going with members of her own family to a familiar church, and that she had not developed close relations with her husband's mother and sisters. She was proposed for communion in the First Church on April 6, 1806; Mary, six weeks later. Both were baptized on May 29; the next day Elizabeth and Nathaniel, four and two years old, were baptized.[9] The children had not been baptized at the customary early age, probably because their parents belonged to different churches. Their father had been absent more than a year, and their mother had decided, it seems, to change her church membership and avoid further delay of the children's baptism. Both Mary and Mrs. Hawthorne welcomed the stricter doctrine of the First Church, and they shared an interest in its missionary programs.

Aunt Mary visited the Hawthorne children's three aunts on Union Street and the women of Rachel Forrester's family, regularly passing along greetings and news and urging Ebe and Louisa, when they were in Maine, to write their Hawthorne aunts and cousins. Their mother asked them to visit their paternal connections, but she asked with the reserve she displayed in other matters.

Aunt Mary's was a voice of caution—warning Nathaniel about his gun, for example—and hence often negative. It was a voice urging morality, duty, responsibility, and faithful work, a voice not likely to endear her to children. In letters to Raymond, Nathaniel cited Aunt Mary as the chief source of his misery, but with a half-seriousness and a tolerance hardly to be expected in a boy his age. With her strictness she had reliability and integrity, and also kindness and generosity—qualities he would have denied that she had, conscious that she and others as well would know he nevertheless was fond of her. A paragon maiden aunt, she had the stern virtues that would gall a boy assigned by fate to her care, but had in addition the softer virtues that would win his affection. In writing his mother that he had "begun to fit for College," Nathaniel complained that Aunt Mary and his grandmother continually scolded him, then added, "One good effect results from their eternal finding-fault. It gives me some employment in retaliating, and that keeps up my spirits." In an earlier letter to Robert, he had spun out his feigned grievances in a similar tone: "There is a pot of excellent guaver jelly now in the house and one of preserved limes and I am afraid they will mould if you do not come soon for it's esteemed sacrilege by Grandmother to eat any of them now because she is keeping them against somebody is sick and I suppose she would be very much disappointed if everybody was to continue well and they were to spoil. We have some oranges too . . . which are rotting as fast as possible and we stand a very fair chance of not having any good of them because we have to eat the bad ones first as the good are to be kept till they are spoilt also."[10]

Nathaniel's comments on Aunt Mary in letters and in the *Spectator* were in the nature of affectionate teasing intended for her no less than others to see. The teasing continued long after he had escaped her control. In what appears to be his only letter to her that has been preserved, dated November 26, 1824, when he was at college, he pretended to have learned that she was going to be married to Charles W. Upham, minister of the First Church. She and others reading the letter at Salem would enjoy this joke, as they would his thrust at Aunt Mary's zeal in her missionary society and his assuring her that in cold weather he kept excellent fires and did not stir from them, unless it was absolutely necessary. What more could a fond aunt ask than his concluding declaration that he wished he could be at home Thanksgiving, for he thought her puddings and pies and turkeys "superior to anybody's else"?

Aunt Mary died in 1840, at the age of sixty-three. Nathaniel had been a member of the same household with her during her last thirty-five years, as she lived out a pattern not uncommon among unmarried women of the time—narrow in her own activities but rich in the affection, the solicitude, and the service she offered those around her. He saw how she lent her strength to support her widowed sister and to advance her nephew toward the education and fulfillment she perceived early would be possible for him. He would have seen in her also the absolute integrity he came to demand.

In the Manning correspondence, stereotyped moralistic phrasing occurs with some regularity, especially in the letters of Mary and the youngest daughter, Priscilla, but much less in the letters of Mrs. Hawthorne. She was matter-of-fact and practical, as a rule, avoiding extravagance of sentiment and language, restrained, in comparison with Mary and Priscilla, in passing judgment or offering opinions. Her reticence in regard to plans for the children's education was the greater, in part perhaps because others must pay the special costs, but in part, surely, because she had already an inclination toward the retirement that was to deepen through her remaining years.

4

Bowdoin College

The decision to send Nathaniel to college came only after full discussion in the Manning family; the choice of Bowdoin College seemed to require no discussion. Nathaniel hoped that Maine, after becoming a state in 1820, would be more than the land of promise the Mannings had called it. He was pleased that Brunswick, the seat of the college, was within easy traveling distance of Raymond. He and Uncle Robert left Salem on Friday, September 28, 1821; and, although he had not seen his mother for two years, they stopped less than a full day at Raymond and were at Brunswick Tuesday morning by eleven. Even before returning to Raymond, Robert wrote members of the family in Salem a step-by-step account of this new adventure.[1] No member of the family had gone to college before.

After Nathaniel had presented the letter he had brought from Benjamin Lynde Oliver and the entrance examination had been set for two o'clock, he had lost his earlier assurance and felt so sure he would not pass that he asked Robert to stand ready to take him home at once. Within an hour, though, he had been admitted and assigned a roommate. There being no dormitory rooms available, he and his "chum" rented a room in the home of Professor Samuel Phillips Newman. Together they bought furniture for the room, and Nathaniel said he had never before done so much trading on his own. Since Robert had not counted on the need to buy furniture and books, he had to leave Nathaniel barely enough money for immediate incidental expenses. A shortage of funds would continue to his graduation day.

In less than a week Nathaniel wrote his Uncle William that the college laws were not too strict and he did not have to study as hard as in Salem. In this letter, as in letters to his mother, and especially in those to his sister Elizabeth, there is a degree of posing. He had done as well as "most of the Candidates" on the entrance examination. "My Chum . . . has money enough, which is perhaps unfortunate for me, as it is absolutely necessary that I should make as good an appearance as he does." In saying that by his ability and his learning he had won entrance to the company of such as Alfred Mason, he was implying that those supporting him had an obligation to perform up to a similar level. Mason had been prepared for college at Phillips Academy, Exeter. His father, Jeremiah Mason of Portsmouth, was a famous lawyer and a friend of Daniel Webster.

Bowdoin was a young college, in comparison with Harvard, Yale, and Dartmouth; it was small, rural, and primitive in its facilities, having opened in 1802, with an entering class of eight. The first building, Massachusetts Hall, was ready in 1802, Maine Hall in 1807. In 1821 there were also the small wooden chapel and near it the president's house; the enrollment was 114. Brunswick was a village thirty miles from Portland, located at the point where the Androscoggin River swings eastward to join the Kennebec River. The village owed its existence mainly to lumbering, and the Bowdoin students remembered afterward the wild scene when spring floods hurled great logs down the rapids and over the falls at the foot of Maine Street. The college grounds, on a sandy plain, level as a floor, at the south edge of the settlement, were enclosed on three sides by uncut forest that reinforced the sense of isolation and quiet. The favored off-campus haunts of the students were Paradise Spring,[2] near the Androscoggin, a brook where fish could be caught, and a grove of pines that furnished as deep seclusion as Nathaniel had known at Raymond.

Nathaniel probably wrote home more often in his first than in his last three years, though little can be said with certainty, for according to his sister Elizabeth he would destroy his letters when he went home to visit. The record supplied by his letters is supplemented in a book by his classmate Horatio Bridge, *Personal Recollections of Nathaniel Hawthorne*, which furnishes details and impressions that ring true, even though they were not written until Bridge's college days had receded almost seventy years.

During his first term, Nathaniel said over and over that he looked forward to vacation and a visit to Raymond. Beginning with the second term, his letters say little about getting home. It is likely that his vacation, mid-December to early February, had proved disappointing. Two and a half years had passed since he lived at Raymond, and he had been enlarged by his study at Salem and his term at college. On May 22, 1822, after his second vacation, his mother moved back to Salem, permanently, as it turned out, taking Louisa to join Ebe there. Even with her brother Richard as a neighbor and the resources of the estate to help her operate the farm with hired labor, she abandoned the undertaking after four years. She returned to Raymond in the summer of 1824, but only to have her furniture sent to Salem.[3] In Nathaniel's final vacation before graduation, in the spring of 1825, he again visited Raymond and afterward wrote Ebe that he got but little pleasure from the visit and had no desire to return. Now, at the age of twenty-one, he had passed beyond the fascination with Uncle Richard's "wilderness," as she had done earlier. Convinced that he would not go back to Raymond if he could, he turned in other directions, without regret but grateful for the Wordsworthian exhilaration of his experience there and his recollection of it. Whatever plans he might lay for the future, his boyhood idyll of the Maine woods would have no place in them.

Early in his first term at Bowdoin, Nathaniel and his chum moved into Maine Hall, Room 19. On the afternoon of March 4, 1822, the hall was burned out, and until it was restored the next autumn, they rented rooms in the house of Mrs. Adams, adjoining the campus, where they had boarded since February. Other students lost heavily in the fire, but since it started on the third floor, Nathaniel, on the second, had no damage except for a tear in an old coat. He and Mason returned to Room 19 for their sophomore year and lived "together in the greatest harmony," he wrote his mother. During his junior and senior years he had a room alone in the home of Mrs. Downing on Federal Street, some two blocks north of the campus.

Greek and Latin and mathematics, as at other colleges, occupied greatest space in the Bowdoin curriculum. Grammar and rhetoric were included in the first two years, and there was practice in composition in these and also in the Latin and Greek courses. Modern languages and literatures and modern history had no place in the curriculum. The study of moral and mental philosophy was weighted toward the moral and had its base in the rationalism of the preceding century. A large portion of the faculty had been trained for the ministry; students were required to attend morning and evening chapel services.

Looking back from old age, Horatio Bridge said that in quality the faculty at Bowdoin was "probably as high as that of any other young college."[4] The president, William Allen, had published in 1809 a work which he enlarged in two later editions, *American Biographical and Historical Dictionary*. Parker Cleaveland, who taught chemistry and mineralogy, was the most distinguished faculty member and perhaps the one friendliest to the students. Henry Wadsworth Longfellow, a classmate of Hawthorne's, wrote a sonnet in tribute to Cleaveland on the fiftieth anniversary of their graduation. Samuel Phillips Newman was the professor of ancient languages until 1824, and after that professor of rhetoric and oratory. He published a book on rhetoric that went through many editions. Alpheus S. Packard, a tutor from 1819 to 1824 and later professor of Latin and Greek, is addressed in Longfellow's poem "Morituri Salutamus," written for the fiftieth anniversary, when Packard was the only teacher of the class of 1825 still living. Thomas Cogswell Upham, who came to Bowdoin a year before Nathaniel graduated and later was professor of mental and moral philosophy, published widely in religion, philosophy, and psychology. No doubt Hawthorne knew his influential work, *Elements of Mental Philosophy*, when it appeared in 1831.

Tuition was eight dollars a term, and, omitting clothes, travel, and unusual personal expenditures, a student's expenses for a year would not greatly exceed a hundred dollars,[5] the sum Aunt Mary had offered to provide for Nathaniel. He had special expenses when, early in the first term, he had the measles, was taken into a private home for care, and had the doctor five times. Upon first enrolling, he furnished a bond for a hundred dollars signed by three of his uncles, guaranteeing payment of his fees and any assessments for damages. With the college holding this bond, Robert probably did not feel required to pay the bills promptly each term, but Nathaniel thought the matter more serious. On October 1, 1824, he wrote Ebe that his term bills were unpaid for more than a year past and cited the regulation that a student in arrears "*may be dismissed from College.*" Another term passed before Robert furnished him seventy-five dollars to pay his bills. Uncle Robert had taken responsibility for sending Nathaniel to college; Uncle William and perhaps others of the Mannings helped with small sums; and Mrs. Hawthorne drew money against her account with the estate on several dates close enough to term openings to suggest that the cash was for Nathaniel's return to Bowdoin.

Robert may have been slow in paying the term bills in part because of dissatisfaction with the reports from Bowdoin. Since course grades were not given, the only reports forthcoming were on disciplinary matters. The Laws of Bowdoin College established such a thicket of prohibitions that some students probably felt challenged to violate them. In his second term Nathaniel was fined a dollar for missing recitations and Sabbath services. He wrote Louisa that he had narrowly escaped being caught playing cards and meant to be more careful in the future. On May 29 President Allen wrote Nathaniel's mother that the faculty had voted to fine him fifty cents, along with six others, for playing cards for money.[6] Nathaniel wrote his mother the next day, "If I am again detected, I shall have the honour of being suspended. When the President asked what we played for, I thought it proper to inform him it was 50 cts. although it happened to be a quart of wine, but if I had told him of that he would probably have fined me for having a blow. There was no untruth in the case, as the wine costs 50 cts." He had not played cards since, and would not drink wine until the last week of the term. His mother could take little assurance from the casuistry of his dialogue with the president or his promises for the future. It is unlikely that the matter was kept secret from Uncle Robert, or that he was prepared to read with equanimity the postscript, "I must have some money."

Writing on May 31 to a friend at Raymond, Mark Leach, Nathaniel said he had been "much more steady" recently, fearing that Uncle Robert would take him out of college or that he would be suspended. On August 5 he wrote Ebe, with the teasing and belligerence usual in his letters to her, saying that since his "foolish scrape" he had been "as steady as a Signpost, and as sober as a Deacon." The president's suggestion that he had been led away "by the wicked ones" prompted him to add, "I have a great mind to commence playing again, merely to show him that I scorn to be seduced by another into anything wrong."

Taking the risk of detection in breaking the rules was a game of chance especially inviting at the isolated college governed by abundant rules; the game was more inviting when the rule broken was especially resented. Required attendance at religious services was particularly galling because the students disliked the minister, Parson Mead. Nathaniel assured his family, May 4, 1823, that he had taken no part when Mead was hanged in effigy. His fines in his sophomore year totaled $5.40, including $1.00 for being at a tavern on a Saturday night; in his junior year, $11.63[7]—a considerable sum when tuition was $24 a year and the rent and cleaning of his room cost $11.22 a year. Nathaniel seems to have expected to be disciplined by his family on account of the fines. The tolerance of the Mannings is evidence that they had confidence in him and generosity of spirit as well.

During his first two years, Nathaniel's infractions of rules suggest high spirits and boyish assertiveness. In his third year, he was fined for academic delinquencies. Reading the literary works he mentioned in letters to Ebe, mainly recent fiction such as they had read before he left Salem, no doubt occupied time stolen from class preparation. His failure to turn in compositions assigned, although the ones he submitted were excellent, may be taken to forecast the necessity he avowed in later years to wait for the proper mood and the proper conditions for writing. The absence of fines in his senior year may mean that he feared being suspended or having his funds stopped, but may mean also that he felt himself already beginning his career, and saw following regulations as the way to avoid interference with his purpose. The genial teasing of his boyhood letters carried over into the letters he wrote from Bowdoin. He liked to realize the effects he could achieve by turns of idea and phrase, as in asking Louisa late in his junior year for an excuse that would gain him a week's leave of absence.

> If you are at a loss for an excuse, say that Mother is out of health, or that Uncle R. is going a journey on account of his health, and wishes me to attend him, or that Elizabeth is on a visit at some distant place and wishes me to come and bring her home. Or that George Archer [his cousin] has just arrived from sea, and is to sail again immediately, and wishes [to] see me before he goes. Or that some of my relations are to die or be married, and my presence is necessary on this occasion. And lastly, if none of these excuses will suit you, and you can think of no other, write, and order me to come home without any. If you do not, I shall certainly forge a letter, for I *will* be at home within a week. Write the very day that you receive this.[8]

When his mother read the letter, as he of course intended, she might have wished for assurance that the threat to forge a letter was in fun.

Nathaniel's antipathy for declamation produced some of his fines, and deprived him of a part in the graduation exercises. He had practiced declaiming while preparing for college, and on one occasion he delivered a Latin dissertation at an exhibition in the chapel, about which he wrote one of his sisters that he had made "a very splendid appearance in the chapel . . . before a crowded audience."[9] Of the fifteen performers on the occasion, only he and Henry Wadsworth Longfellow spoke in Latin. His taking part in the program is evidence that he ranked high in Latin and also that, as his senior year opened, he was willing to carry out college assignments, even including declamation, but probably only this one time. In a letter of November 4, 1852, declining an invitation to lecture before the Rochester Athenaeum, he said he had never appeared before a public audience, except once in his college days. Horatio Bridge remembered Hawthorne's telling him that once when he declaimed in school at the age of twelve or thirteen he was ridiculed by older boys. Whether or not his antipathy originated in such an incident, it was undoubtedly genuine. As consul at Liverpool thirty years later he made the after-dinner speeches required of him, and with success that surprised him, but he vowed that after leaving office he would never again raise his voice "so as to be heard by more than six people, nor to speak more than a hundred words together."[10]

Hawthorne gave little attention to other studies than ancient languages and biblical and classical literatures—with one exception. In his last year he paid an extra fee to attend a term of lectures on anatomy and physiology given by John Duncan Wells in the medical school.[11] Henry Wadsworth Longfellow has been cited as speaking of the "graceful and poetic translations" Hawthorne gave from Latin authors.[12] Professor Newman is reported to have been "so impressed with Hawthorne's powers as a writer" that he would read his compositions aloud for the enjoyment of his family and to have remembered distinctly "Hawthorne's reluctant step and averted look, when he presented himself at the Professor's study, and with girlish diffidence submitted a composition which no man in his class could equal." The report comes through a Bowdoin graduate of 1866, who probably had his information directly from Newman; but it would be surprising if it did not owe more to Hawthorne's subsequent literary fame than to what Newman remembered after more than forty years.[13]

Professor Alpheus S. Packard remembered, after almost sixty years, Hawthorne as he sat in a recitation-room of Maine Hall, "with the same shy, gentle bearing, black, drooping, full, inquisitive eye, and low, musical voice that he ever had." Packard quoted from an unidentified classmate who said that Hawthorne dwelt "in unrevealed recesses which his most intimate friends were never permitted to penetrate," and that among his associates

> he never told a story or sang a song. His voice was never heard in any shout of merriment; but the silent, beaming smile would testify to his keen appreciation of the scene and to his enjoyment of the wit. He would sit for a whole evening with head gently inclined to one side, hearing

every word, seeing every gesture, and yet scarcely a word would pass his lips. But there was an indescribable something in the silent presence of Hawthorne which rendered him one of the most desired guests on such occasions. Jonathan Cilley was probably his most intimate friend in the class; and yet his discrimination would lead him to say, "I love Hawthorne; I admire him; but I do not know him. He lives in a mysterious world of thought and imagination which he never permits me to enter." [14]

The assertion that Cilley was probably Hawthorne's most intimate friend in the class has support in the frankness of their talk, as Hawthorne recorded it in his notebook, when he visited Cilley in 1837. In the sketch Hawthorne wrote after Cilley's death the next year, he said that Cilley had been like a brother to him in college. It was with Cilley that Hawthorne, on November 14, 1824, wagered a barrel of "the best old Madeira wine" that he would not be married within the next twelve years. When reminded that he had lost the bet, Cilley said that he had misjudged Hawthorne "in the line matrimonial," but not in the literary line. [15]

Cilley belonged to the six-member Pot-8-O Club, one of the three clubs Hawthorne joined at college. Its name was chosen to reflect the abundance of potatoes grown in Maine and the common reference to potatoes as a staple food in the state. At weekly meetings the members dined on roasted potatoes and cider or some other mild drink, presented a poem or an original dissertation of at least fourteen lines, or paid a fine of a peck of potatoes. [16] Another member of the club was David Shepley, who recalled in 1875 that Hawthorne's neglect of the regular studies did not disturb him or lessen the respect of teachers or classmates, who realized that, "already an accomplished scholar," he could not be judged by normal standards. "He was near," Shepley said, "yet distant; had intimacies, but intimates knew him only in part"; and yet his "marvellously magnetic," silent presence was "eagerly sought." [17]

If Horatio Bridge was not Hawthorne's closest friend at Bowdoin, he became soon afterward and continued until Hawthorne's death. He held the signed document in the marriage wager of Cilley and Hawthorne and with them belonged to the Androscoggin Loo Club, whose members would take "a keg of wine and a liberal amount of provender . . . for a week end in the forest." [18] Bridge says that the club existed about two years and that "the stakes . . . were, of course, small." He tells of the Navy Club, which was organized in the final term by the fourteen class members who had no part in the commencement exercises. Hawthorne was elected Commander, and everyone else had a title, "from Commodore to Cook." They met weekly at Ward's Tavern for supper. Bridge's reports of the episodes may lack something in exact detail, but they help to fill out the portrait of Hawthorne at Bowdoin. He and Hawthorne went several times to call on John Brown Russwurm in the room he occupied at the edge of town. A mulatto, Russwurm identified himself with the colonization movement and in 1836 became governor of the Maryland Colony at Cape Palmas. They also visited together an aged fortune-teller in her cabin near the river.

Hawthorne frequently quoted poetry "in his deep, musical tones," Bridge remembered. One of his own poems he recited was "Moonlight," in which the poet says that in the moonlight "we may meet that shadow band, / The dead of other years"; another was "The Ocean," similar in thought and tone. Hawthorne said he had written "Moonlight" earlier, and Bridge believed he wrote no poetry after entering college.[19] In years past, poetry-writing had occupied him and his sisters considerably. After quoting three pieces of verse in a letter to Louisa on September 28, 1819, he said, "I am full of scraps of poetry[,] can't keep it out of my brain. . . . I could vomit up a dozen pages more. . . . Tell Ebe she's not the only one of the family whose works have appeared in the papers." The next year he included nine poems in the *Spectator*. "The Ocean" and "Moonlight" were published in newspapers within two years after his graduation;[20] two drinking songs from his pen were printed in *Fanshawe;* a song of two quatrains appeared in the first publication of "The Three-Fold Destiny" in March, 1838, but was dropped afterward. It was Hawthorne's habit in later years to say that he did not write poetry—and that he read little current poetry.[21] In dedicating *The Snow-Image and Other Twice-Told Tales* to Bridge in 1851, Hawthorne recalled, through the coloring of pleasant memory, that, when they were "lads together at a country college," it had been Bridge's "prognostic of" his "friend's destiny, that he was to be a writer of fiction."

Another college-mate, a year ahead of Hawthorne and destined to play an important role in his future, was Franklin Pierce. In the campaign biography Hawthorne wrote when Pierce was a candidate for the presidency in 1852, he told how Pierce, not "distinguished for scholarship" his first two years, called upon his characteristic determination and at graduation "took a highly creditable degree." Pierce organized a military company, in which Hawthorne was a private.[22] They were associated, along with Cilley and Bridge, in the Athenean Society, in which Pierce was the chairman of a standing committee, with Hawthorne as a member. Hawthorne wrote Ebe with some pride that the Athenean library contained 800 volumes. He joined with others to donate books, including Percy's *Reliques* and sets of the works of Samuel Johnson and Jonathan Swift. It is probably not amiss to relate the choice of Johnson's works to the interest in Johnson that Hawthorne showed in later years. The Athenean Society was reputed to be more democratic than its rival, the Peucinian Society, in activities and in political orientation. Hawthorne and his close friends among its members supported Andrew Jackson against John Quincy Adams in the presidential election of 1824. The Peucinian Society was considered the more scholarly, and its members were likely to be Whigs. Henry Wadsworth Longfellow was a Peucinian. Perhaps it was for that reason, and also because he did not come to Bowdoin until his sophomore year, that he and Hawthorne did not become close friends. Hawthorne seems to have seen less of Henry, a model student, than of his brother, Stephen, a careless student who at one time was suspended.

The reports of Hawthorne at Bowdoin picture him as quiet, thoughtful, and to a degree mysterious, yet genial and friendly, a welcome member of organized clubs or extemporaneous social gatherings. His classmates and his teachers left ample testimony that in appearance he was impressive. They spoke of his strong, athletic build, but they were impressed most by his eyes—as were many others after them. Bridge remembered him at Bowdoin as "a slender lad, having a massive head, with dark, brilliant, and most expressive eyes, heavy eyebrows, and a profusion of dark hair."[23] According to two reports Hawthorne's classmates had reason to know that his habitual mildness might disappear when occasion demanded. Calvin Stowe (1802–86), who graduated in 1824, recalled once seeing Hawthorne holding an umbrella that the wind had turned inside out as he walked across the campus. Stowe remembered "the silent but terrible and consuming wrath with which Hawthorne regarded the implement."[24] Bridge tells of Hawthorne's once being made the butt of a joke in a group of friends. When he decided that the joke was being carried too far, "Hawthorne singled out the one among us who had the reputation of being the best pugilist, and in a few words quietly told him that he would not permit the rallying to go further. His bearing was so resolute, and there was so much danger in his eye, that no one afterwards alluded to the offensive subject in his presence."[25]

Hawthorne in 1853 wrote about his college years: "I was an idle student, negligent of college rules and the Procrustean details of academic life, rather choosing to nurse my own fancies than to dig into Greek roots and be numbered among the learned Thebans."[26] It was not his habit to disparage the country college he attended or to call his four years wasted. He realized that his college-mates included a remarkable group of young men—some of whom would rise to distinction in various professions; he had won their respect and had made lifelong friends among them. He had come to Bowdoin from a background that included little beyond the members of his family and the tutor who prepared him for college, had excelled in those areas that interested him in competition with some of the best minds in the country, and had reached levels of understanding in political, social, and cultural areas that would foster additional growth. He seems to have valued most at Bowdoin the reading, thinking, and dreaming he did on his own responsibility. The college provided—or allowed— the solitude and the freedom required for his own development, in the presence of classmates, teachers, and library. He formed at college the pattern of imaginative composition that would produce the sketches, tales, and romances of his mature years.

Through his four years at college, Nathaniel wrote letters to Ebe in the world-weary, bantering tone fitting to the pose he liked to assume before her. Once he told how he had been sought out by a new freshman, Gardiner Kellogg, whose family were acquaintances of the Mannings, and how he responded to Kellogg "with that condescending affability" which was one among his "many excellencies."[27] At another time, he said he flattered himself that, with his cane, white gloves, and gold watch-chain, he had made "a most splendid appearance in the eyes of the pestilent little freshmen."[28] A further posing appears in his report that he had seen in Portland his cousin Thomas Healey Forrester, who was drunk, "in as delectable a state as could be well imagined," and that fortunately he was not recognized.[29] Before closing this letter, he lamented, "I am tired of college, and all its amusements and occupations. I am tired of my friends and acquaintances, and finally I am heartily tired of myself. I would not live over my college life again, 'though 'twere to buy a world of happy days.' "

In writing Ebe again as graduation day approached, Nathaniel showed himself sobered as he looked past graduation. His family had expectations of him he could not realize, except that Uncle Robert never expressed by his deportment, he said, a very high estimation of his abilities. Whatever may have prompted him to cite in this way the uncle who had sent him to college, his remark reflected a mixture of self-blame and pique with Rob-

ert that at the moment he found satisfying. He went on to tell of an interview with President Allen about the commencement exercises: "He called
me to his Study, and informed me that though my rank in the class entitled me to a part, yet it was contrary to the laws to give me one, on account of my neglect of Declamation. . . . I am perfectly satisfied with
this arrangement, as it is sufficient testimonial of my scholarship, while it
saves me the mortification of making any appearance in public at commencement." Ebe must send him a copy of any letter the president might
write his mother, and she must let him know what were the sentiments at
home.[30] In this letter, the last preserved from his college years—the last
for another four years—he was looking backward and forward at a serious
point in his life. What members of his family thought of him and his doings, even what Elizabeth thought, now seemed important. Perhaps he
realized that those who had made going to college possible must continue
their support if he were to pursue authorship as he hoped to do.

Commencement took place on September 7, 1825. Seemingly no
member of Hawthorne's family attended. He was ready to go home, even
to Salem—or perhaps especially to Salem. But first there would be the hi-
larity and the sadness of the graduation period.[31] Hawthorne's rank was
eighteenth in the class of thirty-eight, including Gorham Deane, brilliant
scholar and prodigious worker, who had died on August 11. The title of
Jonathan Cilley's speech was "The Effects of Fictitious Writing on
Morals." Henry Wadsworth Longfellow's speech was entitled "Our Native Writers"; he was elected to membership in the Phi Beta Kappa Society, of which a Bowdoin chapter was being established that year. (Hawthorne was elected to membership on September 18, 1842.) When the
graduating class held its farewell meeting in Cullen Sawtelle's room,
Longfellow read a poem he had written for the occasion. Two of the most
gifted literary authors of their time had touched elbows almost daily for
three years and yet were barely acquainted. The friendship that was generous and satisfying to both did not begin until Hawthorne had spent
twelve years of literary apprenticeship at Salem in "the chamber under the
eaves."

5

The Chamber
under the Eaves

Hawthorne came back to Salem after graduation, sure he wanted to be a writer but uncertain as to what he would write or how he would live while proving his talent. His wager that he would not be married before 1836 indicates that he had in mind a long apprenticeship. Being sent to college, he knew, meant being taken from his background and thrust toward a higher status; but he knew also that in rejecting the usual professions he risked forfeiting the normal advantages of a college education.

His preference for a career in literature seems to have met no opposition from his mother or the Mannings; and he might have found encouragement in the insistence of both Robert and Richard that he write often and as well as he could. In a letter to his mother on March 13, 1821, he recorded his thinking about the professions, and at the same time consciously displayed his adeptness in prose composition.

> The being a Minister is of course out of the Question. I should not think that even you could desire me to choose so dull a way of life. Oh no Mother, I was not born to vegetate forever in one place, and to live and die as calm and tranquil as—A Puddle of Water. As to Lawyers there are so many of them already that one half of them (upon a moderate calculation) are in a state of actual starvation. A Physician then seems to be "Hobson's Choice," but yet I should not like to live by the diseases and Infirmities of my fellow Creatures. And it would weigh very heavily on my Conscience if in the course of my practice, I should send any unlucky Patient "Ad inferum," which being interpreted, is "to the realms below."

Oh that I was rich enough to live without a profession. What do you think of my becoming an Author, and relying for support upon my pen. Indeed, I think the illegibility of my handwriting is very authorlike. How proud you would feel to see my works praised by the reviewers, as equal to the proudest productions of the scribbling sons of John Bull.[1]

At the end of his college years, Hawthorne's thoughts about a profession were inseparable from his awareness of how much his relatives expected of him. He had finally come to the conclusion, he wrote Ebe on July 14, 1825, that he would "never make a distinguished figure in the world," and wished only "to plod along with the multitude." It comes through clearly in the letters of the Mannings that Robert, Richard, Mary, and Priscilla believed Nathaniel possessed special gifts. Whether they thought those gifts lay in literary composition, they and his mother were willing, it seems, to let him plot his own course and to await the result. Horatio Bridge said long afterward that Hawthorne "formed several plans of life," in his first ten years out of college, and once had settled on "entering his Uncle Manning's counting-house."[2] But if Hawthorne seriously considered or was urged to consider any other than a literary career, no evidence has come to light. The records of his life during those years are sparse. No letter of his dated within four years of his graduation has been recorded; and the Manning correspondence thinned out, because there came to be little family business and little passing between Salem and Raymond.

There was so little passing that in 1826 Richard Manning sent word to Salem that he had accumulated $1,000 belonging to the estate and would send it by anyone who came for it. Hawthorne went to Raymond on September 20 and took back to Salem $1,400, which was charged to his mother's account. He made only a brief visit, and left it for Aunt Priscilla to write Uncle Richard that he had enjoyed his visit and had reached home safely. He now had more important interests than the Maine wilderness. After Grandmother Miriam Manning's death on December 19 of that year, steps were begun toward dividing the Manning estate. Richard estimated in 1828 that the 5,000 acres still owned in Maine were worth $10,000 and mortgages another $10,000. After his death in 1831 the accounts of the remaining heirs were summed up, with six percent interest through the year 1831 added to each withdrawal. Most withdrawals had been made since 1826, including one withdrawal of about $2,000 by each of the heirs. In addition to the $1,400 in 1826, Mrs. Hawthorne had drawn small amounts at intervals over several years, making a total of

$6,500, including interest. Her account shows nothing charged to board and lodging for her or her children during the period covered, November, 1818, to the end of 1831.[3]

In the sketch Hawthorne gave Richard Henry Stoddard in 1853, he spoke of a "slender means of support" that had allowed him an apprenticeship to writing. He probably meant the $1,400 he brought from Raymond in 1826, with later additions from the Manning family. By Uncle Richard's will in 1831 he received $300, and by Uncle Samuel's in 1833 $100, as did each of his sisters in both instances. In addition to her own share of the estate, Mrs. Hawthorne had been willed one-half of her sister Maria's share at her death in 1814, one-third of Richard's in 1831, and one-half of Samuel's in 1833. As the estate was liquidated, the heirs received money from property sold and also from current income, such as the $20 a month paid to Mrs. Hawthorne in 1830 and 1831 as rental on stables belonging to the estate. After Mary Manning became owner of the house on Herbert Street in 1827, Mrs. Hawthorne received free rent in payment for boarding her.[4] Thus she seems to have had funds enough to support herself and her three children, leaving her son's "slender means" for travel and other personal expenses.

Robert Manning was married in 1824 to Rebecca Burnham, a second cousin whose grandmother was a sister of Grandmother Manning. After Richard Manning had met his sister-in-law five years later, he sent Robert a letter that suggests the way the population of Salem appeared to the Mannings—and to Hawthorne as he grew up. He said Robert had a greater treasure in Rebecca than if he had married one of the "proud and haughty heiresses of Salem," whom others in the family would hardly have dared to speak to. Robert built a house on Dearborn Street, beyond the North River, where he laid out orchards for his fruit trees. Late in 1828 he built beside his house one for the Hawthornes, where they lived from early 1829 until they moved back to the Herbert Street house at the end of 1832.[5]

Hawthorne owed his ten unencumbered years for writing to his Manning relatives as well as his mother, for directly or indirectly they contributed to his support. When he wrote about his slight achievements in those years, as he often did in tales, sketches, notebooks, and letters, and about the folly of pursuing fame, he was no doubt indulging in a show of feigned modesty, but he probably remembered with special irony the expectations and the confidence of his relatives.

Hawthorne implied in his 1851 preface to the *Twice-Told Tales* that

Bridge encouraged him in writing fiction while they were in college; teachers and other classmates said in later years that they knew literary beginnings of his at college, and his sister Elizabeth remembered his writing her from Bowdoin that he had "made progress" on his novel. *Fanshawe*, published three years after his graduation, is set at a remote college which in itself and in its surroundings is identifiable with Bowdoin. The village located on a river in the virgin forest; the college buildings, the curriculum, the rules for conduct, and "the deep and awful sense of religion"; the composition of the student body and the habits of breaking regulations—in these details Hawthorne was recording his college years, while on the ground or while his memory was still fresh. He achieved a convincing actuality, enlivened by comical and farcical scenes: Dr. Melmoth, the college president, and his shrewish wife, for example, and the students writing love poems in Latin and Greek.

Into a college scene—into Bowdoin College, in effect—comes a character of mystery and evil borrowed from the Gothic romances. The scheme of the villain is contrived, and his villainy remains only half explained. The materials from the author's own observations are not adequately fused with the machinery drawn from the romances he had been reading. In the character Fanshawe the romance and the commonplace elements are brought closest together; the profound scholar, doomed to die early, proves first his courage and afterward his nobility of character in renouncing his love. Fanshawe was modeled on Hawthorne's classmate Gorham Deane, who died a few weeks before graduation.[6] The other characters are suited to the comedy-of-manners portion of the story; in the romance of mystery and midnight abduction they are little more than pawns to be moved about as required by the plot.

The plot of *Fanshawe* is blocked off well and remains in the author's control, but the work suggests a scenario rather than a full-blown novel; the narrative method is more to state than to reveal. In comparison with Hawthorne's later works, it shows him with little to say, with no overarching idea to control the characters and the plot. But a few passages reflect the turn of his mind, as it had already appeared in his letters and in the *Spectator*. The final sentences, for example, have an ambiguity and an irony that would not be out of place alongside his later treatments of fame. When the heroine, four years after Fanshawe's death, was married to "the poet of his class," she drew him "away from the passions and pursuits that would have interfered with domestic felicity; and he never regretted the worldly distinction of which she thus deprived him. Theirs was a long life of calm and quiet bliss; and what matters it, that, except in these pages, they have left no name behind them?"

The author of *Fanshawe* had his eye on the formula of the Gothic romance. (The name of Dr. Melmoth came from Charles Maturin's *Melmoth the Wanderer*, 1820, and a quotation from Maturin heads Chapter 8.) But he modified the formula freely. He was less interested in horror and the weird and the remote than in the circumstances of the life he knew at Bowdoin College. He was inclined toward a genial humor and satire that would be lost in a Gothic scene, and already he showed adeptness with dramatic scenes and subtlety in character delineation.

Hawthorne's sister Elizabeth dredged her memory to furnish information for three biographers after his death: James T. Fields, George Parsons Lathrop, and Julian Hawthorne. Her recollections seem largely dependable, though differences appear in the details as the biographers printed them. In Julian Hawthorne's statement, the fullest and most circumstantial, she remembered that, besides starting a novel at college, Hawthorne wrote some tales, which she read in the summer of 1825 and thought contained more of "his peculiar genius" and were better than *Fanshawe*. They were to be called "Seven Tales of My Native Land" and to have a motto from Wordsworth, "We are Seven." She recalled that one was "a tale of witchcraft,—'Alice Doane,' " and another was "Susan Grey."[7] According to Fields,[8] Hawthorne wrote the tales after leaving college; according to Lathrop,[9] he read the stories to his sister, and among them were stories of pirates and privateers, one of which contained a poem beginning with the line "The Pirates of the Sea; they were a fearful race." Since Hawthorne was in Salem during the free period before his graduation early in September, 1825, Elizabeth might have read the tales then. It is easy to believe that during his senior year and perhaps part of his junior year, when he roomed alone, he wrote fiction in some of the time he might have given to his studies.

Julian Hawthorne reports, from Elizabeth, that one publisher, after keeping the tales a long time, returned them without reading them. According to Lathrop, Ferdinand Andrews, one of the owners of the *Salem Gazette*, agreed to publish the tales, but delayed "so long that the author, exasperated, recalled the manuscript. Andrews, waiting only for better business prospects, was loath to let them go; but Hawthorne insisted, and at last the publisher sent word, 'Mr. Hawthorne's manuscript awaits his orders.' The writer received it and burned it, to the chagrin of Andrews, who had hoped to bring out many works by the same hand." In Julian

Hawthorne's account, Hawthorne decided to write a short book, with the hope of publishing it while he continued seeking a publisher for the larger book of tales. He paid Marsh and Capen of Boston $100 to publish *Fanshawe*, but afterward destroyed every copy he could lay his hands on. He took back, and no doubt burned, the copy he had given Elizabeth, and instructed her "to keep the authorship a profound secret." Bridge reports that he destroyed his copy on Hawthorne's instructions.[10]

Elizabeth Palmer Peabody, Hawthorne's sister-in-law, is another source for information on his first writings. She remembered him as a child, when their families were neighbors. She took such a lively interest in him later, and so earnestly undertook to shape his career, personal as well as literary, that when she recalled his early years after half a century had elapsed, she may have been recalling a young author created in her mind, rather than the actual man. She said in 1875 that before publishing *Twice-Told Tales* Hawthorne had destroyed "the manuscripts of more romances than he ever wrote afterwards." She said he told her that "Young Goodman Brown" was one of the tales escaping the fire, and told another friend "he thought that he never afterwards accomplished such 'tours de force,' as in these self-condemned tales."[11] She quoted Hawthorne further (in language that sounds much like her but little like him) as saying that he burned the stories because they were "not entirely true," having been written in a morbid mood caused by his isolation from a "healthy tone of real life, and actual nature."

These accounts of Hawthorne's first writings are partially corroborated by Horatio Bridge, a regular correspondent of his during these years, who said that Hawthorne "peremptorily demanded the return of the manuscript" of the "Seven Tales" even though Andrews offered to go ahead with publication at once, and burned it "in a mood half savage, half despairing." Bridge said also that Hawthorne wrote him afterward that he had been too severe in dealing with Andrews.[12] Writing in 1893, Bridge could hardly have kept his own recollections separate from the reports originating with Elizabeth Hawthorne and Elizabeth Peabody. All three of them, it is to be noted, had to recall what Hawthorne had told them fifty years or more earlier. More important, before any of their recollections were published, Hawthorne had said enough in print about the burning of manuscripts to influence the memories of others. He never mentioned *Fanshawe* in any record that has been preserved, and, when James T. Fields once asked about it, instructed him never to speak of it again.[13] But he dealt several times with the burning of stories.

Characters in three of the early tales burn manuscripts in symbolic action that represents self-blame for failure and for the folly of pursuing fame, and represents also a protest against publishers and readers. The narrator of "Alice Doane's Appeal" (1835) reads aloud a story that, with one other, he says, had escaped destruction; but "one great heap had met a brighter destiny: they had fed the flames." In "The Devil in Manuscript," published the same year, the character Oberon, whose name is one Hawthorne had signed in writing Horatio Bridge after they left Bowdoin, burns the tales he has been unable to publish and exults in bitter irony when sparks from the fire ignite the roofs of neighboring houses.[14]

Any burning of manuscripts would be an act of protest aimed outwardly or inwardly or both. Oberon has been told that "no American publisher will meddle with an American work, seldom if by a known writer, and never if by a new one, unless at the writer's risk"; but he turns inward and declares that he has been drawn "aside from the beaten path of the world, and . . . into a strange sort of solitude." In a final reversal he predicts for himself a long repentance for burning his manuscripts. "Fragments from the Journal of a Solitary Man," published in July, 1837, but no doubt written at about the same time as "The Devil in Manuscript," has as chief character a disappointed author, also named Oberon, who says he has published enough and leaves instructions for all his papers to be burned after his death.

On December 22, 1841, Hawthorne answered a request from Evert A. Duyckinck and Cornelius Mathews for contributions to their magazine, the *Arcturus*, by saying that he had burned quires of manuscript stories. Ten years later, in the preface to a new edition of *Twice-Told Tales*, he spoke of works he had burned "without mercy or remorse" and, moreover, said he had marveled "that such very dull stuff . . . should yet have possessed inflammability enough to set the chimney on fire!" The burning of the "Seven Tales" was in Hawthorne's mind when he fictionized the episode no less than when he referred to it in the letter or the preface. Fact and fiction, the actual and the imagined, the author and Oberon had become one.[15]

Manuscript burning, in fact or fiction, dramatizes an author's protest that his works are not accepted by the world around him. William Cullen Bryant, Ralph Waldo Emerson, Edgar Allan Poe, William Gilmore Simms, Herman Melville, Evert Duyckinck, and others of the New America group lamented the failure of American readers and publishers to give native authors their due alongside foreign authors; and Hawthorne declared in his tale "The Artist of the Beautiful" that an artist finds his reward, not from society, but within himself. His character Oberon noted the irony that fame—or success—came only with the destruction of the manuscripts and, by implication, the thwarting of the artist's highest purposes. It was a Hawthornesque touch for him to say that the works he and his character burned were "very dull stuff" and were destroyed without regret. If he published *Fanshawe* while still hoping to see his volume of tales in print, as his sister remembered, he probably decided to withdraw the novel and the manuscript tales at the same time and for the same reason. If he had not grown dissatisfied with the tales, he probably would have let Andrews go ahead with publication.

The tales of witchcraft and pirates and privateers that Elizabeth remembered probably had, like *Fanshawe*, American settings. Hawthorne had heard Longfellow's commencement address on "Our Native Writers," and it is likely that both he and Longfellow had been encouraged in their thinking by one of the Bowdoin teachers, Thomas Cogswell Upham. In his introduction to a volume of poems, *American Sketches*, published in 1819, Upham calls for a national literature. A nation should "encourage and reward" its authors, and they should rely confidently on their own resources and observations. America lacks the ruins of Europe, to be sure, but it possesses its own rich materials: the early explorers, the first settlers, the missionaries, the Indians, and the frontier villages. Two of the examples he cites, Father Ralle and King Philip, appear in Hawthorne's writings,[16] and poems in his volume probably contributed to two of Hawthorne's early stories, "Roger Malvin's Burial" and "The Gray Champion."[17]

The early tales were cut to the Gothic pattern but adapted to the New World, as were the romances Charles Brockden Brown had published at the turn of the century. The "Alice Doane" named by Elizabeth was likely an earlier version of "Alice Doane's Appeal" (1835). In the story as published, the narrator takes from his pocket a manuscript written "years ago" and presents orally, in excerpt and summary, an account of adventure, suspense, mystery, concealed identity, abduction, murder, incest, wizardry, and a family divided between the Old World and the New. The focus is not on the Gothic extravagances or the resolution of the plot, but on the effects produced on the narrator and his two women companions, as evening falls on Gallows Hill, where the witches were hanged in 1692. Subtlety and depth not inherent in the story being read are achieved through authenticity of the scene, the response of characters in the presence of evil and the supernatural, and the interplay of human forces. An authorial statement on Scott in a later story, "P.'s Correspondence" (April, 1845), gives in summary the conclusion Hawthorne had reached: "The world, nowadays, requires a more earnest purpose, a deeper moral, and a closer and homelier truth than he was qualified to supply it with."[18] The transformation of the earlier into the later story of Alice Doane shows the author turning from conventional stories of action and excitement toward fiction that explores human character and human destiny in the context of important moral issues. This transformation gave Hawthorne a creative direction and an impetus that would continue through the rest of his life, resulting immediately in tales and sketches that fit comfortably among his later works.

Hawthorne matched his firmness in condemning *Fanshawe* and the "Seven Tales" with equal firmness in marshaling his efforts, including his reading, in the new direction. From boyhood he had read standard English authors: Spenser, Shakespeare, Bunyan, Scott, and the Gothic romancers. But he had overlooked one lesson he might have learned from them, particularly from Scott: the value of place and history in fiction. Even in *Fanshawe* he had not achieved full reality of place and time. He now recognized a need to know the land, the people, and the history of the region of his fiction as intimately as Scott knew his Highlands. He must fill blanks left by his college studies in the geography, history, and lore of his home town and region. On the Salem Athenaeum Library card that came to him through his Aunt Mary Manning he borrowed histories, magazines, and newspapers. In old newspapers he sought ideas for stories and such factual items as fill the three sketches in "Old News" (1835). A parallel and essential source would be his observations, close at hand or on travels away from home. His letters and the notebook he began keeping by 1835 show him recording, in memory and on paper, scenes that were notable in either history or nature.

In 1829, at about the time Hawthorne was making a new start, he sent a tale to Samuel Griswold Goodrich, author, editor, and literary entrepreneur, who was thirty-six years old and would have an important role in his early literary career. Goodrich said later that he had taken the initiative, after learning that Hawthorne was the author of "some anonymous publication" which seemed "to indicate extraordinary powers."[19] When Goodrich had read the story and had offered to help find a publisher, Hawthorne sent him more tales in December, along with his earliest self-criticism that has come to light. These stories, he said, had been completed considerably earlier except for giving them titles. If he finished two or three others not yet ready to be sent, they would be "about on a par with the rest." He described one of the tales, perhaps "Young Goodman Brown," in a way to show that he thought it distinctive and was pleased with it, even while seeming to doubt its worth. Founded on local superstitions, it was "certainly rather wild and grotesque, but the outlines of many not less so might be picked up hereabouts." Goodrich had mentioned shorter pieces, presumably meaning the length he wanted for his annual, *The Token*. Hawthorne said that, if he wrote any, he would send them; but, he added, "I think I shall close my literary labours with what I have already begun."

Goodrich wrote in January that he would try to locate a publisher who would give the collection "a fair chance of success," adding that he believed *Fanshawe* would have paid a profit if it "had been in the hands of more extensive dealers." He particularly liked "The Gentle Boy" and "My Uncle Molineaux" (published later as "My Kinsman, Major Molineaux"). He was doubtful the public would approve of "Alice Doane," and he would return a fourth story, "Roger Malvin's Burial."[20] Hawthorne declined Goodrich's offer of $35 for permission to print "The Gentle Boy" in the *Token*, but he wrote on May 6 that he was sending two short pieces. He wanted them attributed to the author of *Provincial Tales*, which he proposed as the title of his volume, even though it might never be published. He added, "An unpublished book is not more obscure than many that creep into the world, and your readers will suppose that the Provincial Tales are among the latter." One of the new pieces was "Sights from a Steeple," printed in the *Token* for 1831, which came off the press the preceding autumn to catch the Christmas market.

"Sights from a Steeple" is a descriptive and speculative sketch presenting the scene and the people in it—all observed by a reporter who thinks that "The most desirable mode of existence might be that of a spiritualized Paul Pry, hovering invisible round man and woman, witnessing their deeds, searching into their hearts, borrowing brightness from their felicity, and shade from their sorrow, and retaining no emotion peculiar to himself." But since he cannot "know the interior of brick walls, or the mystery of human bosoms," he creates histories, intentions, and emotions for the people he observes. The one describing the scene may say that he reveals no more emotion than would Paul Pry, but alongside his impersonal role which allows free scope to speculation and fancy, there is the authorial role in which Hawthorne and the observer are one. The sketch is of a type Hawthorne was to repeat many times; and he feared—or pretended to fear—that he would himself become the cold observer of his fellowmen that he portrayed in the Paul Pry of this sketch.[21]

Two tales and three biographical sketches by Hawthorne appeared in the *Salem Gazette* late in 1830, within a few weeks of the appearance of the 1831 *Token.* These pieces, published separately while he sought to bring out a collection for which he was reserving the tales he thought best, show him testing literary methods and extracting from the history of New England materials to illustrate the human and moral problems that had come to interest him most. The two tales, "The Hollow of the Three Hills" (November 12) and "An Old Woman's Tale" (December 21), no doubt had belonged to the "Seven Tales," perhaps in earlier versions. In the first, scenic details are presented concisely and fully; but for all the concrete details, the hollow is more fantasy than reality, appropriate to the revelation of guilt and shame that is the more effective for the half-light of the evening that blurs alike the features of the hollow and the happenings being suggested, not through sight, but through sound, attenuated by time and distance. In this, the earliest published tale known to be Hawthorne's, the economy, the restraint, the interlocking of narration and description, the achievement of effects through tone of language, indirection, suggestion, understatement, and metaphor—all testify to conscious management and an adept pen. This story of less than 2,000 words introduces the author's lifelong puzzlement over human guilt and the ramifications of its effects.

"An Old Woman's Tale" experiments with the handling of scene behind a haze. The village street is real at moments, but as reflected through the minds of the two characters who view it in a dream, or a waking dream they both share, the outlines blur—as is appropriate while the street is filled on a moonlit night by occupants of the village graveyard. The story closes with a playful uncertainty as to what has happened. A frame story, it opens with the narrator telling of an old woman in the house where he was born, whose "personal memory included the better part of a hundred years," and who "had strangely jumbled her own experience and observation with those of many old people who died in her young days." He would re-tell one from the thousand traditions he had heard from her. "Her ground-plots, seldom within the widest scope of probability, were filled up with homely and natural incidents"—thus the narrator states the formula that Hawthorne had evolved for interweaving in fiction the homely and the fantastic to produce the desired "garb of truth." It might be supposed that this old woman, who the narrator says deserves a listener far more than he does, was Grandmother Rachel Phelps Hawthorne; but an exact identification cannot be expected, for in this introduction, hardly less than in the story itself, fiction and fantasy are interfused. It became a habit of his to base a character on an actual model and to modify it freely to serve his fictional purpose. If "An Old Woman's Tale" was one of the "Seven Tales," it may have included then only the inner narrative of the present story, in which the residents of the graveyard return to the streets and houses they once knew, and show a young couple, too poor to marry (the observers in the final version), where to dig for buried treasure. No longer satisfied with such a plot as this, Hawthorne, it can be assumed, converted it into a dream, adding the whimsical introduction and giving the story proper an airy uncertainty and a movement back and forth between commonplace reality and fantasy. The conclusion leaves no doubt that Hawthorne's interest was in something besides a conventional plot. The young man, David, had been digging at a spot where a character in the dream had dug. "Suddenly he poked his head down to the very bottom of the cavity," and cried, " 'Oho!—What have we here?' " In this tale, as in "Alice Doane's Appeal," emphasis is not on the tale itself but on the narrator and his telling of it. In both tales, as in the later story "Main Street" (1849), the reader takes a position beside the author to observe the narrator in the telling of his story, and to become, along with him, a critic and speculator on the methods and purposes of fiction.

The three biographical sketches printed in the *Gazette* in the same period as the two tales—"Sir William Phipps" (November 23); "Mrs. Hutchinson" (December 7); and "Dr. Bullivant" (January 11)—testify that in searching New England history for literary materials, Hawthorne had an eye to the definition and growth of the national character and to broad human and moral problems as well. The sketches evidence an easy familiarity with public figures and events in colonial New England, and an attempt to understand the flavor of life and the mind and character of the people. Dr. Bullivant, the "gay apothecary," who was an associate of the corrupt royal governor in the reign of Charles II and helped to loosen the dominance of the first generation, leads Hawthorne to conclude that "we are perhaps accustomed to employ too sombre a pencil in picturing the earlier times among the Puritans." He nevertheless says that "a prevailing characteristic of the age was gloom, . . . and its long shadow, falling over the intervening years, is visible, though not too distinctly, upon ourselves." But he qualifies again, saying that the gloom was not a "material detriment to a deep and solid happiness." He had been reading the London bookseller John Dunton's account of visiting Boston and Salem in 1686 and finding gloom no more conspicuous than in London.[22]

Puritan sternness and narrowness were epitomized in John Endicott, who, as Hawthorne remarked in the sketch of Mrs. Hutchinson, "would stand with his drawn sword at the gate of heaven, and resist to the death all pilgrims thither, except they travelled his own path." Endicott was prominent in the expelling of Anne Hutchinson from Massachusetts, an event that prompted the kind of ironic analysis that would characterize Hawthorne's study of history and the affairs of his own time. In the first chapter of *The Scarlet Letter* Anne Hutchinson is called "sainted," but in this early sketch her saintliness is qualified by reference to "a flash of carnal pride half hidden in her eye," which led her to prove by her own mouth the accusations against her. The decision to expel her was inevitable, moreover, in a time when "religious freedom was wholly inconsistent with public safety. . . . Unity of faith was the star that had guided these people over the deep; and a diversity of sects would either have scattered them . . . , or, perhaps, have excited a diminutive civil war among those who had come so far to worship together." In the story "The Gentle Boy" as first published in 1832, the author again offered partial extenuation for the Puritans' severity against the Quakers by saying that the first generation in Massachusetts saw the enforcement of discipline in affairs of both church and state to be a necessity for survival.

An introduction to the sketch of Anne Hutchinson is a short essay on public women in the author's time, wavering in tone from seriousness to whimsy. Changes are taking place, the author says, which seem to threaten "posterity with many of those public women, whereof one was a burden too grievous for our ancestors." He fears that there will be added "a girlish feebleness to the tottering infancy of our literature," and that "the ink-stained Amazons will expel their rivals by actual pressure, and petticoats wave triumphantly over all the field." Such remarks would occur over and over in his letters and other writings of the future, at times alongside serious comments on literature, especially after Sophia Peabody had become his wife and had drawn more closely into his orbit Elizabeth Peabody, Margaret Fuller, and others who were in some degree advocates of women's rights.

The author of these biographical sketches is consciously shaping them for literary purposes. Biography is normally lifeless, he remarks in opening the sketch of Phipps, but remedy is possible "without an absolute

violation of literal truth. . . . A license must be assumed in brightening
the materials which time has rusted, and in tracing out half-obliterated
inscriptions on the columns of antiquity: Fancy must throw her reviving
light on the faded incidents that indicate character." Accordingly he
passes briefly over the facts of Phipps's early career, in order "to picture
forth a day" while he was governor.[23] Similarly in the sketch of Dr.
Bullivant we "suppose ourselves standing" before the apothecary shop
through a representative day. The sketch of Mrs. Hutchinson looks
"around upon the hearers" at her trial and gives an imaginative recreation
of the happenings.

The sureness of presentation these sketches display and the discussion
of purposes and means argue that the author had indeed written and destroyed quires of tales and sketches. They drew on seventeenth-century
history, in which the coming of the Quakers and the witchcraft delusion
held greatest interest for Salemites of Hawthorne's time. Because his ancestors were prominent in those episodes, he came to have overlapping
historical, personal, and literary interests in them that bore fruit in his
tales and novels.

6

Of Puritans, Quakers,
and Witches

In reading New England history, Hawthorne discovered paternal ancestors of his from the founding of the Massachusetts Bay Colony onward, and learned that in the first two American generations they stood prominent in church and state. William Hawthorne, earliest of the line in America, pronounced sentences on the Quakers; his son John was a magistrate conspicuous in the witch trials of 1692. Although Hawthorne said he took shame upon himself on account of these progenitors, he also pointed to them as men of station and accomplishment, and he said again and again that his achievement was slight in comparison with theirs. His race had lived at Salem two centuries "in respectability," he wrote in his sketch "The Custom-House" with obvious pride, never, so far as he knew, "disgraced by a single unworthy member."

The English seat of the family was at Bray, in Berkshire, where Hawthorn Hill was prominent on the landscape.[1] William Hawthorne (1606 or 1607–1681) was born in England, and after being converted to Puritanism, came over soon after the Massachusetts Bay settlement in 1630, along with his brother John and his sister Elizabeth. He settled first at the village of Dorchester, and by 1634 had become a freeman and a member of the General Court of the colony.[2] A man of initiative and varied abilities, he moved quickly into prominence. In 1636 he moved to Salem, and during more than forty years shouldered responsibility in town, county, and colonial governments. Relying on the Bible and the sword, which his descendant the novelist saw as emblems of his character, William Hawthorne left firm marks in the history of relations between the colony and the mother country. Once he spoke out so firmly advocating colonial authority that the General Court and the governor removed him from his military command and required him to deliver a public apology.[3] The king commanded that representatives be sent to London to answer charges against the colony, and specified that William Hawthorne and Governor Richard Bellingham be included. A letter and a gift of two ship masts were sent instead; and soon afterward, October 26, 1666, another letter was sent, signed Nadnorth and presumably by Hawthorne, offering much the same defense as the official letter. Almost two hundred years later, on July 24, 1856, Nathaniel Hawthorne received a copy of this letter from the State Paper Office in London.[4]

It was as a magistrate pronouncing judgment on the Quakers that William Hawthorne gained special prominence in history and in the awareness of his descendant the novelist. When the first Quakers appeared in the Massachusetts Bay Colony in the summer of 1656, they were expelled, but they returned. After cumulatively harsher sentences had proved of no avail, and with converts joining the sect, the General Court passed a law applicable to both foreigners and natives who would not abandon Quakerism or leave the colony. It provided for banishment on pain of death.[5] In the minds of those who had expelled Roger Williams and Anne Hutchinson because of divergences on small points in a large corpus of belief they held in common, the Quakers could not be tolerated, asserting as they did that the light within had as great authority as biblical revelation, insisting on their role as emissaries of God called to chastise both church and state, and refusing to accept civil authority.

On October 27, 1659, William Robinson and Marmaduke Stevenson were hanged at Boston. Mary Dyer, under the same sentence, was pardoned at the scaffold and sent out of the country; she returned and was executed on June 1, 1660. William Leddra was executed the next March 14. During Leddra's trial, Deborah Wilson went naked through the Salem streets.[6] Afterward twenty-eight were freed from prison and conducted out of the colony; late in 1661 an order from Charles II required that all Quakers condemned or imprisoned be sent to England.

In "The Custom-House" the novelist says that William Hawthorne, "this grave, bearded, sable-cloaked, and steeple-crowned progenitor,— who came so early, with his Bible and his sword, and trode the unworn street with such a stately port, and made so large a figure, as a man of war

and peace,—" gave him "a sort of home-feeling with the past." His ancestor had "all the Puritanic traits, both good and evil," and was "a bitter persecutor; as witness the Quakers, who have remembered him in their histories, and relate an incident of his hard severity towards a woman of their
sect, which will last longer, it is to be feared, than any record of his better
deeds, although these were many." This reference probably was to William Sewell's *History of the Quakers,* which reports that William Hawthorne
ordered "Anne Coleman and four of her friends" to be "whipped through
Salem, Boston, and Dedham."[7] In the story "Young Goodman Brown,"
Brown's companion on the forest trail says, "I helped your grandfather,
the constable, when he lashed the Quaker woman so smartly through the
streets of Salem." And in *Grandfather's Chair* (1841) the Quaker persecu-
tions are recounted briefly, with the victims named.

These references are casual, almost playful; in "Main Street" (1849),
there is only a brief statement, but it suggests the complexity involved.
Hawthorne names Anne Coleman and his ancestor and continues, taking
from William Sewell's account the whip of knotted cords and the blood
drawn by the lashes, "The crimson trail goes wavering along the Main-
street; but Heaven grant, that . . . there may have been a dew of mercy
to cleanse this cruel blood-stain out of the record of the persecutor's life!"
Earlier in the story he tells of a Quaker woman wildly denouncing a minister on the steps of the meeting-house, and of listeners who wept, thinking
that if such blasphemies are allowed, "we have brought our faith across
the seas with us in vain." Long before writing these passages, Hawthorne
had puzzled over the Quaker episode, for its meaning in the history of his
family, his town and region, and the nation. The course of his thinking on
the episode can be traced out in "The Gentle Boy," a tale sent to
Goodrich in 1829.

The author of this story takes care to lay out the situation and the issues. He leaves no doubt that he has read accounts from both oppressed
and oppressors (though he does not cite either William Sewell or Daniel
Neal or name the historical persons to whom he alludes), and that he has
striven to assess the error and the guilt on each side, and to understand the
causes, the motives, the spiritual and the psychological aberrations involved. In such a pairing of forces as this, sympathy normally flows to the
oppressed, and the phrasing employed to report the events reflects sympathy with the Quakers; but the tale portrays the Quakers as "wandering en-
thusiasts" who were "eager to testify against an oppression which they
hoped to share." They harbored "revengeful feelings," engaged in "in-

decorous exhibitions," and invited martyrdom by persisting in the role they assumed as agents of God's will. Catherine, mother of the gentle boy, was "a woman of mighty passions, and hatred and revenge now wrapped themselves in the garb of piety," as she climbed to the pulpit and pronounced a curse on the Puritans—"Woe to them in their death hour, whether it come swiftly with blood and violence, or after long and lingering pain!" The scene is portrayed with a masterly pen, enforcing the view that on both sides strident error, bigotry, and fanaticism prevailed, with sympathy and tolerance surfacing only at brief intervals. As Catherine rose to depart on her wanderings, abandoning her child again, the men stationed at the door to arrest her—for she had returned to the colony after expulsion on pain of death—"suffered her to pass. A general sentiment of pity overcame the virulence of religious hatred."

Through the course of the narrative, the Quakers and the Puritans have both shown themselves fanatical bigots, with only small portions of tolerance and sympathy. The final sentences turn an ironic light on the resolution of the conflict. After the gentle boy had died, the king's order had ended the persecution, Catherine had made her home with the Piersons, and "a more Christian spirit . . . in regard to the persecuted sect" prevailed, those in the dominant faction felt for those who had suffered only such pity and kindness and sympathy as are decent and not painful. All spoke of Catherine "with that degree of pity which it is pleasant to experience; every one was ready to do her the little kindnesses which are not costly, yet manifest good-will; and when at last she died, a long train of her once bitter persecutors followed her, with decent sadness and tears that were not painful, to her place" beside the grave of the gentle boy.

In the 1832 version of this tale Hawthorne apologized for the Puritans, repeating what he had said in the sketch of Anne Hutchinson: they feared that admitting divergent religious sects would destroy the unity that would be necessary for their survival. In reprinting the tale, he cut out this apology and several shorter passages, including the final statement that the outcome gave him a kindlier feeling toward his ancestors. He thus improved the tale; for the deleted passages had brought the author awkwardly between his reader and the story, or they had used direct rather than indirect presentation.[8] These authorial passages had grown from Hawthorne's wish to understand his ancestor who transported the family to the new land and helped plant the new nation. To understand his ancestor of the second American generation, he brought the witchcraft delusion of 1692 into his fictional works. Again a segment of the past furnished

OF PURITANS, QUAKERS, AND WITCHES

him impressive materials for examining complex moral dilemmas. The witchcraft episode was more puzzling and more tragic and richer in symbolic materials than the Quaker episode, and consequently appears more often and serves more diverse functions in his fiction.

Witches were executed in America before 1692 and afterward; but in Salem the methods of accusation and trial that evolved were such as to allow—or to encourage—riotous fear and hatred that came to dominate even the courtroom, with the result that only an agency outside the colony could stop the hangings—but only after nineteen had been executed. The lore of the witches' Sabbath or the black mass had lost no force in coming from the Old World to the New; the rituals and the paraphernalia of the devil's band were well known: forest meetings with the black man, baptism, the black book in which converts signed with an iron pen dipped in blood, pain inflicted by invisible means. Thus when the children of the Reverend Samuel Parris of Salem Village were noticed performing strange antics and were asked for an explanation, they replied, either from fear or in enjoyment of their play-acting, that they were being tortured by a family servant, an aged crone named Tituba—and the children were believed. Joined later by others, they added one name after another to the list of accused. The entire cast of the drama enacted in Salem Village—the accusers, the magistrates, the jurors, the observers and even the ones accused—found it difficult to keep separate what had happened to them, what they had seen happen, what they had been told happened, and what they had been taught to believe happened in the province of witches. Leading questions and intimidation were normal at the hearings and at the trials; charges were supported mainly by spectral evidence. The assumption was that the accused had willingly entered into a pact with the devil; to allow a possibility that the devil might act through the specter of an unwilling agent would remove the stigma of guilt, and hence would alter the basic purpose and procedures of the trials. It developed that one who had been accused could have little hope of escaping death except by confessing and naming colleagues in the service of the black man. Before the trials were closed, prisons held about fifty who had confessed themselves bewitched and had accused others; included were children whose testimony had sent their parents to the gallows. Among those executed were a beloved minister; even the wife of the popular Governor William Phipps was accused.

The annals of the witchcraft delusion would have interested Hawthorne as a record of error and suffering, religious enthusiasm and psychological aberration; he was doubly interested because an ancestor of his was a prominent actor in the sad drama. John Hawthorne (1641–1717) assumed prominence in public affairs according to a pattern common in early New England. It was hardly that he was chosen or that he put forward a claim; rather, prominence was his because his family heritage gave him station, prestige, education, and presumed ability. He was the fourth child of William Hawthorne; but his brothers, Eleazer (1637–80) and Nathaniel (1639–81) and William (1645–78), died before their father, leaving him to take up the public responsibilities of the first William. He entered colonial politics just as a period of uncertainty and turmoil began. Edward Randolph, commissioner of the king who earlier had singled out William Hawthorne for censure and in 1684 succeeded in having the colonial charter revoked, saw John Hawthorne as a stubborn defender of the earlier colonial authority, and in 1686 cited him to the king for disloyalty.[9] John Hawthorne resumed important positions in the government after William and Mary came to the throne in 1689.

As a magistrate both for the county and for the colony, John Hawthorne had a part in the witchcraft episode, from the first hearings, in which on March 1, 1692, he and Jonathan Corwin received charges against Tituba and two ancient and infirm women, Sarah Good and Sarah Osborn, and on March 7 ordered them held for trial. The histories of New England that Nathaniel Hawthorne read during his twelve years in the chamber under the eaves were for the most part interpretative rather than documentary, each historian shading the witch episode according to his own view. John Hawthorne appeared in these accounts as a stern, relentless prosecutor. Yet his descendant the novelist might see him as a man who could be respected, dignified and business-like, capable of hewing to lines of doctrine and procedure that proved unacceptable in later times but were not challenged among his contemporaries in America or Europe. Believing that Satan enticed followers into his service and used them in his special warfare against New England, John Hawthorne saw it his duty to discover any who had joined the devil's band and to extract a confession, for a major purpose in the preliminary hearings was to accumulate evidence that could be introduced at the trials later. Yet he seemed at times to seek not so much confirmation of the charges as an explanation for the sake of his own understanding. In questioning Rebecca Nurse, he seems to have dropped a hint of sympathy, noting that the accusers present cried out that she hurt them and asking her simply for an upright answer. The records show that John Hawthorne was earnest and unyielding, but seemingly without the harshness of the judges before whom the accused were later tried, and without the vindictiveness and cruelty displayed, for example, by others following Rebecca Nurse's trial four months after the hearings. The jury voted her not guilty; but after the accusers and others had protested, and Judge William Stoughton, presiding over the trial, had called the jury back to reconsider the evidence, the jury found her guilty. Governor Phipps granted her a reprieve but withdrew it in deference to urging he received from Salem. After she was under sentence to be hanged, the Reverend Nicholas Noyes, minister of the First Church of Salem, had her brought in shackles before the congregation on July 3 and secured a unanimous vote of excommunication.

Although Noyes had no official role at the hearings, he often interrupted the proceedings to inject charges or opinions of his own.[10] It is recorded that at the execution of Sarah Good earlier, he said to her that she knew she was a witch, and had her reply that she was not, and that, if he took her life, God would give him blood to drink. This curse appears in *The House of the Seven Gables*. To Hawthorne's mind it was an apt symbol, as he indicated when he appropriated it in referring to his first two American ancestors in his sketch "The Custom-House": "I, the present writer, as their representative, hereby take shame upon myself for their sakes, and pray that any curse incurred by them—as I have heard, and as the dreary and unprosperous condition of the race, for many a long year back, would argue to exist—may be now and henceforth removed." The Reverend Parris was also on hand constantly at the hearings, coaching his daughters and other accusers, and in some instances interrogating witnesses himself. A third minister attracted to the witch trials was Cotton Mather, who came from Boston to be present. His role at the hanging of the minister George Burroughs suggests his influence on the course of events. Burroughs made a speech on the ladder at the scaffold that so affected the listeners that, after he had been turned off, Mather felt the need to ride forward on his horse and sway the crowd back to support of the executions. Five were hanged that day.[11]

During the years when Hawthorne was reading colonial New England history, others in Salem were learning that history with particular attention to the hanging of the witches. A new edition of Robert Calef's *More Wonders of the Invisible World*, first published in 1700 and reprinted at Salem in 1823, gave them an uncompromising condemnation of Mather and the others responsible for the witch trials. Charles W. Upham, minister of the First Church, delivered at Salem two lectures on the witchcraft delusion and published them at Boston in 1831 with the title *Lectures on Witchcraft*. He presented a severe indictment of the witch persecutors, and was severest on the three ministers Cotton Mather, Samuel Parris, and Nicholas Noyes as purveyors of superstition and vindictiveness. In a lecture at Salem in 1828, Joseph Story, justice of the United States Supreme Court, offered an opposing view, saying that behind the dark saga of the witches were beliefs "which had the universal sanction of their own and all former ages; . . . which the law supported by its mandates, and the purest judges felt no compunctions in enforcing."[12] Perhaps statements of this kind encouraged Hawthorne toward the view he came to reflect in his fictional works. The error of belief in witchcraft, he concluded, resulted from natural fears and superstitions; the error grew into the awesome black flower of 1692 because the uncertainties and fears produced in the struggle to found a new society were fed by the intolerance inherent in the Calvinistic beliefs and strengthened by a group of narrow and bigoted, though learned, ministers who were guardians and enforcers of those beliefs. Thus Cotton Mather became to Hawthorne, as he was to Robert Calef and Daniel Neal and Charles W. Upham, the one most responsible for the hanging of the witches, with Nicholas Noyes and Samuel Parris responsible to lesser degrees. When viewed beside these ministers, John Hawthorne stands as a faithful public servant, strict and uncompromising, but without the emotional defense of preconceptions so prominent in these learned ministers.[13] Nathaniel Hawthorne would have noted that his ancestor did not serve as a judge at the trials, perhaps choosing to continue with the preliminary hearings, and that he did not join William Stoughton and Samuel Sewall in endorsing Cotton Mather's book on the witch trials, *The Wonders of the Invisible World*, although he had met with Mather and others when the book was being planned.[14]

   The witchcraft episode is echoed again and again in Hawthorne's works. It furnished him abundant symbols, and it was especially useful because the lore of witchcraft was familiar to his readers and incorporated major elements of human nature and experience. Often there is only a passing reference to the province of witchcraft. The sculptor in "Drowne's Wooden Image" is said to have "sold his soul to the devil"; it is reported that the darkened portrait in "Edward Randolph's Portrait" was "of the Evil One, taken at a witch meeting near Salem"; the narrator in *The Blithedale Romance* (Chapter 25) could see in Hollingsworth "all that an artist could desire for the grim portrait of a Puritan magistrate, holding inquest of life and death in a case of witchcraft." In two stories Hawthorne pictures a procession to Gallows Hill. In "Alice Doane's Appeal" the narrator tells how, on the day George Burroughs and others, like him not named but identifiable, were hanged, the procession was followed by "Cotton Mather, proud of his well won dignity, as the representative of all the hateful features of his time; the one blood-thirsty man, in whom were concentrated those vices of spirit and errors of opinion, that sufficed to madden the whole surrounding multitude." In the second story, "Main Street," the procession is that of August 19, 1692, when five witches were hanged, including two who are associated particularly with Cotton Mather. The author cites Mather's calling Martha Carrier a "rampant hag" whom the devil had promised she would be queen of hell, and tells of his addressing the crowd after George Burroughs had been hanged. Hawthorne's habit was to cite Cotton Mather as the most despicable figure of the witch era. In the sketch "Time's Portraiture," Father Time and Cotton Mather "hung the witches"; in the sketch "Hannah Duston," Mather was a "hard-hearted, pedantic bigot"; in *Grandfather's Chair*, Mather was the chief agent of the mischief of the witchcraft delusion.

Mistress Hibbins, a historical figure who in 1656 was hanged in Boston as a witch, brings the suggestive presence of witchcraft into *The Scarlet Letter*, as Matthew Maule brings it into *The House of the Seven Gables*. But Hawthorne's fullest display of witch lore is in one of the first tales he wrote, "Young Goodman Brown." In it several of the witches hanged in 1692 appear and are named; the black man, presiding over a meeting of his subjects in the forest, administers the sacraments and proclaims the common bond of all in sin. One of the subtlest and most effective to come from Hawthorne's pen, this story illustrates in brief compass the elements he found in the witchcraft tradition appropriate to the moral questions and the special aspects of colonial history he wanted to explore in his fiction. Goodman Brown's experience illustrates the universality of sin, the effects of sin, perhaps the effects of a belief in the universality of sin; it also opens up questions about the human and social implications of Calvinism in general and of the Puritan era in early America.

The histories Nathaniel Hawthorne read had little to say about his ancestors who followed the illustrious first two. Joseph (1692–1762), tenth of John Hawthorne's thirteen children, fourth of those who reached maturity, became a sea captain and won local fame in 1724 when his ship, severely disabled on a voyage to the Azores, saved the captain and crew of another Salem vessel.[15] Three brothers of his moved to England, possibly fleeing the ill fame that had come to their father after the witch trials. One of them, Ebenezer, was recorded as master of a ship which in the summer of 1711 brought smallpox to Salem.[16] Another brother, Benjamin, was lost with his ship and crew in 1732.

Captain Joseph Hawthorne had married in 1715 Sarah Bowditch, from a seafaring family that two generations later was to include the Nathaniel Bowditch who won fame as mathematician and author of navigation tables. He left the sea and became a farmer. Of his ten children only one made a public mark, his son Daniel, grandfather of the novelist, who was memorialized in the ballad "Bold Hathorne." Two others, by their choice of wives, called the attention of fellow townsmen to their grandfather, the witch judge. William, the eldest son of Joseph, married Mary Touzell, and the third son, John, married Susannah Touzell. Both wives were granddaughters of Philip English, a merchant and ship owner of Salem, who had been arrested in 1692 on a warrant signed by John Hawthorne and George Corwin charging him and his wife with witchcraft. English and his wife escaped from prison and avoided trial but had their property confiscated. It struck Hawthorne's sense of the ironic that, since Philip English had legitimate daughters but only illegitimate sons, "all the legitimate blood of English" was in the Hawthorne family (VIII, 74–75). He might have noted a further irony, that the heritage of the early American Hawthornes—property, mementoes, traditions, and information—had been handed down in the branches of the family descended from Philip English. In his own time the chief bearer of the traditions was his distant cousin Susan Ingersoll, a granddaughter of John Hawthorne and Susannah Touzell, with whom he had closer association than with any others of his Hawthorne kin.

7
"The Story-Teller"

In publishing several pieces in the *Salem Gazette* and the *Token* at the end of 1830, Hawthorne held back major tales that he hoped to bring out as a collection. Seeing no likelihood of publishing the "Provincial Tales," he allowed Goodrich in the spring of 1831 to choose among the tales for the *Token*. Goodrich said of the four he published in the 1832 issue that they were as good as anything he got, if not better, and that, since they were to be anonymous, as was customary in the *Token* and generally in newspapers and magazines, readers would not know that one author wrote all four. In January of 1832, Hawthorne offered something from the abandoned collection to another annual, the *Atlantic Souvenir*, which later in the year was combined with the *Token*.

As suggested by the title, the "Provincial Tales," no less than the "Seven Tales," were American, with ties to the land and the history. One of the four chosen by Goodrich was "The Gentle Boy." Another was "The Wives of the Dead," which tells the perennial story of the wives of mariners and militiamen in such towns as Salem, but goes beyond the matter of loss or possible loss at sea and in Indian warfare to report waking dreams such as Hawthorne explored again and again in fiction and in sketches like "The Haunted Mind." Another tale, "My Kinsman, Major Molineux," moves back into colonial times and offers a panorama of realistic though only half-lighted or luridly lighted scenes a boy from the country views on his first visit to the city. The rich texture of imagery and

suggestion may be applicable, ambiguously but invitingly, to an individual, as the boy gains experience and perhaps maturity, and applicable also
to society or the colony, as the bearer of royal authority, the boy's uncle,
is tarred and feathered. "Roger Malvin's Burial," the fourth story in the
Token for 1832, suggests that the circumstances of Lovell's Fight, in 1725,
were not creditable to the colonists; but the fight serves only to produce a
situation in which the author puzzles over the source, the nature, and the
effects of guilt, opening up a subject that would recur many times in his
future work.

The *Token* for 1833 contains a biographical sketch of another historical
figure, Sir William Pepperell, and two stories derived from autobiographical rather than historical sources: "The Canterbury Pilgrims," based
on the author's visit with his Uncle Samuel Manning to the Shaker community at Canterbury, Vermont, in 1831, and "The Seven Vagabonds,"
based also on his summer travels. In the sketch "Sights from a Steeple" he
had explored the autobiographical mode, discovering that he could use his
own experiences, thought, and character as freely as he had used history
to achieve the fusion of reality and fantasy, the literal and the speculative,
most congenial to his mind. From the early 1830's onward, he undertook
to supply his creative imagination from observation, especially in summer
travel, as well as from reading.

By the summer of 1832, when the *Token* for the next year had gone to
press, Hawthorne could take satisfaction in the dozen tales and sketches
he had published. They were of the kind he had chosen to write after destroying his early works, and he realized, surely, that three or four of the
tales were of a high quality. But he had been reluctant to see the pieces
appear separately; and, although he knew that collections of stories did not
sell, he was ready to begin on a third collection, this one with a more
complex plan. In it he would embed the tales and sketches in a framework
narrative that would draw on his travels in New England. Besides solitary
walks near home—to Gallows Hill, along the Swampscott beach, and
through the old streets of Salem, Beverly, and Danvers—he had gone farther afield at least as early as 1828. In October of that year he was in Con-
necticut with his Uncle Samuel, who traveled to seek relief for his tuber-
culosis and to buy horses for the stagecoach business. At New Haven he
encountered Horace Conolly, a student at Yale who in Salem afterward
would touch his life in important ways. He also visited the Judge's Cave,
where the regicides William Goffe and Edward Whalley supposedly lived
in hiding. The visit would have recalled to his mind the historical episode that suggested his story "The Gray Champion."[1]

On the road with Samuel again probably the next year, he wrote home that he had "met with many marvellous adventures."[2] At one place he was told he "bore a striking resemblance" to a prominent local family, and at another he was taken for a lawyer in search of a place to settle. He continued, "Moreover, I heard some of the students at Yale College conjecturing that I was an Englishman, and to-day, as I was standing without my coat at the door of a tavern, a man came up to me, and asked me for some oats for his horse." He was telling a joke on himself, a consciously shaped anecdote, rising through three steps and then stumbling in a deflating fourth step. He was modifying facts to produce a narrative that would be true fictionally, whether true literally or not. Alert to what might be distinctive or significant, he continued to practice the manipulation of thought and expression that had begun in his boyhood letters. It "was (of course) very grievous" to both Samuel and him, he wrote, not to be able to attend service on Sunday.

A long letter Hawthorne wrote Louisa while traveling with Uncle Samuel again in 1831 leaves no doubt that he was consciously storing his mind and was turning ideas and phrases to produce effects. At Concord, New Hampshire, they had the door of a cell at the state prison barred upon them, but made their escape. Uncle Samuel was everywhere surrounded by a troop of horse-dealers, who all seemed to know him by instinct. Since his uncle had begun to exhibit symptoms of homesickness, Hawthorne doubted that they would see Canada this trip. After reporting the "ridiculous capers" and "ridiculous ceremonies" he had observed at the Shaker church in Canterbury, Hawthorne said, as if it followed in logic, "I spoke to them about becoming a member of the Society, but have come to no decision on that point." He concluded with an acknowledgment that he thought of the letter as a literary composition: "This is not intended for a public letter, though it is truly a pity that the public should lose it."[3] He visited other Shaker villages and in 1838 wrote a second story about the sect, "The Shaker Bridal."

The trip Hawthorne planned for the summer of 1832 was to be longer than any he had yet taken, and it may have been his first extended trip alone. He would travel by way of New York and Albany to Niagara, he wrote Franklin Pierce on June 28, then to Montreal and Quebec, and return through Vermont and New Hampshire. "I am very desirous of making this journey on account of a book by which I intend to acquire an (undoubtedly) immense literary reputation, but which I cannot commence writing till I have visited Canada." He had in mind a collection of tales to be narrated by an itinerant author who would follow such a route as his and would recite his tales to audiences along the way. An outbreak of cholera in Canada, with cases in Boston and elsewhere, altered his plans. At Burlington, Vermont, on September 16 he wrote his mother about spending two nights at Ethan Crawford's house in the White Mountains and climbing Mt. Washington. If he wrote out further accounts of this journey in letters or notebooks, they have not come to light; but the extent of his travel and the store of materials he gathered can be estimated from the fragments of the frame narrative he wrote for the collection entitled "The Story-Teller."

Elizabeth Peabody recalled in old age what Hawthorne had told her about the fate of the "Story-Teller" collection. She said that, when the two-volume manuscript was finished, he sent it to Goodrich, who declined to undertake publication but offered to buy some of the stories for the *Token* and to pass others along to be published in the *New-England Magazine*. "So they tore up the book and Hawthorne said he cared little for the stories afterwards, which had in their original place . . . a great degree of significance." She recalled his saying also that, since the tales paid him little, published in this way, and did little to introduce him into the world of letters, "It was like a man talking to himself in a dark place."[4] Although hazy as to particulars, Elizabeth Peabody's account provides a frame into which details from other sources can be fitted and thus makes it possible to fill out the following history of "The Story-Teller" with some completeness.

The manuscript was in Goodrich's hands at least by early 1834, and soon was judged not publishable as a book. After selecting two tales for the *Token* of 1835, which appeared as usual late in the preceding year, and perhaps others for later issues, Goodrich gave the remainder to the *New-England Magazine*, which in November printed the opening sections of the frame narrative and in December the first tale, "Mr. Higginbotham's Catastrophe," both under the title "Passages from a Relinquished Work." The owner and editor, Joseph Tinker Buckingham, would seem to have had in mind serializing the remainder of the manuscript. Late in 1834, however, he sold the magazine to John O. Sargent and Samuel G. Horne, and with the number for March, 1835, Park Benjamin became editor. Selections from "The Story-Teller" continued to appear, but separately and without mention of the collection to which they had belonged. Since Benjamin had become associated with the magazine before he was editor, he may have been involved in publishing the first selections, but more likely the initial plan for serialization was Buckingham's and the plan to change it was Benjamin's. Hawthorne wrote Elizabeth Peabody more than twenty years later that "it was Park Benjamin, not Goodrich, who cut up" the "Story-Teller."[5] At the close of 1835 the *New-England Magazine* was merged into the *American Monthly Magazine*, in New York, which had Benjamin as editor and printed additional selections from the manuscript. One story probably from the collection, "Little Annie's Ramble," was published in the *Keepsake* for 1835, an annual having Benjamin as editor and the same publisher as the *New-England Magazine;* and Hawthorne published "An Ontario Steamboat" in the *American Magazine of Useful and Entertaining Knowledge* for March, 1836, while he was its editor.

Although parts of "The Story-Teller" were published in at least three magazines and two annuals, it is possible to re-assemble portions of the framing narrative, to identify a few of the enclosed tales and sketches with certainty, and to name others with moderate assurance. The reconstructed work reveals much about Hawthorne's growth as an author, and it seems to have had genuine merit, in both plan and execution. It included some of Hawthorne's best tales. The autobiographical frame followed the Story-Teller along the routes of Hawthorne's summer wanderings, reporting such experiences, observations, and impressions as he had in mind when he set out from home in September, 1832.

Hawthorne would have known Washington Irving's *Sketch Book*, *Bracebridge Hall*, and *Tales of a Traveller*, each of which contains a loose gathering of stories, sketches, essays, and autobiographical accounts. They may have been models for the first two collections he assembled, but in "The Story-Teller" he planned a tighter frame, which would be a continuous narrative, having a plot of its own, with the Story-Teller serving as both narrator and character, and with the setting moved from one to another of the natural and historical attractions in the region traversed. The Story-Teller would be a fictional personality, presenting through his own mind the scenes and the stories and the enclosing narrative, and in turn revealing his own evolving character.

In the *New-England Magazine* for November, 1834, appeared the opening sections of "The Story-Teller," in which the narrator leaves home, meets an itinerant preacher, and travels on in his company. He identifies himself with the narrator of "The Seven Vagabonds," who had vowed to "become an itinerant novelist." (That story had gone to Goodrich, for the 1833 *Token*, at about the time Hawthorne settled on his plans for his new collection.) With each specimen to be included, he says, will be given "a sketch of the circumstances in which the story was told. Thus my air-

drawn pictures will be set in frames, perhaps more valuable than the pictures themselves, since they will be embossed with groups of characteristic figures, amid the lake and mountain scenery, the villages and fertile
fields, of our native land." The question raised here whether the frames
may be more valuable than the "air-drawn pictures" they enclose was one
that Hawthorne never resolved—at least said he never resolved. The
frames in "The Story-Teller" take their value, he meant, from the closely
observed and accurately portrayed life and scene which they include; but
in the collection as a whole the actual is infused with the fanciful, and the
total value inheres mainly in the product of the fusion. Hawthorne was
thinking of the distinctive quality he was to achieve later in the au-
tobiographical-imaginative sketch "The Old Manse." In a similar sketch,
"The Custom-House," he wrote that in the day-to-day life around him
was a better story than the one he had written, *The Scarlet Letter*. In "The
Story-Teller" he illustrated the divergence of romance from realistic fiction which he would return to in connection with each of his four major
romances.

The opening sketch of the frame narrative glances forward to the end of
the journey and forecasts the failure of the story-telling venture, when it
will be "too late for another trial." The narrator, "being heir to a moderate
competence," has decided not to enter a profession and to remain "aloof
from the regular business of life." At his return home, in the concluding
episode of the frame narrative, which Benjamin published in the *American
Monthly Magazine* for July, 1837, with the title "Fragments from the Journal of a Solitary Man," he is known as Oberon and has shown himself
closely akin to the Oberon of "The Devil in Manuscript." He dies after
directing that all his unpublished works be burned. Fragments from his
journal being published combine world-weariness and self-accusation.
The Story-Teller, sobered by disillusionment and awareness of approaching death, pictures himself as a dreamy recluse, lacking a sense of
brotherhood, one of "the busy idlers," without "sufficient energy or will
to return into the world." He has published works from his pen but has
never discovered the secret of his powers. He would teach any youth who
might think of imitating him that "the world is a sad one for him who
shrinks from its sober duties," and would "warn him to adopt some great
and serious aim." He would beseech such a youth not to step aside from
the highway of human affairs or relinquish his claim on human sympathy;
and "often, as a text of deep and varied meaning," he would "remind him
that he is an American."

The Story-Teller reiterates what Oberon says in "The Devil in Manuscript" about literary fame and "the miseries of authors," and what Hawthorne had said as early as the *Spectator*. In this regard he is akin to the artist as conceived in the Romantic tradition and to Owen Warland in Hawthorne's tale "The Artist of the Beautiful." But his outlook is exaggerated so farcically in the early episodes and so whimsically throughout that he cannot be taken as a spokesman for the author.

The closeness with which Hawthorne bound the tales and sketches into the enclosing narrative is suggested in the December installment, in which "Mr. Higginbotham's Catastrophe" appears, along with an appropriately farcical account of its presentation. The "mimicry and buffoonery" of the Story-Teller drew such a "tumult of approbation, that, just as the story closed, the benches broke . . . and left a whole row" of his admirers on the floor."[6] A story printed in the *New-England Magazine* for August, 1835, "The Vision of the Fountain," makes no reference to "The Story-Teller," but statements in the text addressed to "fair ladies" and "sweet maids" are evidence that the story was supposedly told to an audience of young ladies.

When the manuscript of "The Story-Teller" was cut up, the links and explanations were likely to be superfluous or confusing, but without them, as "The Vision of the Fountain" illustrates, the author's purpose may be defeated. In its original setting, including two introductory paragraphs that were kept in the magazine but dropped in later printings, this story was told to an audience of girls sixteen years old by a man of middle age who gave "a sigh to the memory of Rachel," whom at fifteen he had seen fleetingly reflected in a fountain. The boy of fifteen "had lofty, sweet, and tender thoughts, and dim, but glorious visions," and if he could now look into the eyes of his listeners, "like a star-gazer," he "might read secret intelligences."[7] The reader, aware of the Story-Teller and his audience, would have read the framework and the story as a unit in which the author's purpose was to harmonize action, character (including narrator and listeners), tone, and situation, in the story and in its presentation. With its frame cut away except for vestiges, the story is awkward and sentimental.[8]

In the *New-England Magazine* for November and December, 1835, Benjamin published under the title "Sketches from Memory" seven descriptive and narrative passages that can be related to other pieces from "The Story-Teller," and can be located on the itinerary followed by Hawthorne and his Story-Teller. Benjamin included each month a short laudatory introduction, no doubt from his own pen. The two selections printed in November, "The Notch of the White Mountains" and "Our Evening Party among the Mountains," fictionize the account Hawthorne wrote his mother in September, 1832, of his journey through the White Mountains. Following a reference in the first sketch to "the red pathways of the slides," it is safe to assume "The Ambitious Guest" appeared in the manuscript. (Here and at other points in the segments Benjamin published from the manuscript, he indicated omissions, which may be taken as guides to the location of selections to be included, as Hawthorne had laid out the work.) The origin of this tale was in an occurrence on August 28, 1826, when the Willey family, fearing destruction of their house by a landslide, rushed out at night to a tent prepared for such an occasion, and were buried by the slide. Traveling to Raymond a few days later, Hawthorne would have felt something of the immediacy he gives the tragedy in his story. The fact that visitors were present and not all of the bodies were recovered gave Hawthorne his ironic conclusion. In his story the youthful guest for the night had told of his ambition to gain such fame that a monument would be raised to his memory; those who came to search after the slide could do no more than wonder whether a guest had occupied the extra chair before the fireplace.

In the second of these sketches, an assortment of guests at Crawford's inn, such as appear in the story "The Great Carbuncle," hear the legend of the Great Carbuncle and tales about those who have searched for it. The narrator adds, "On this theme, methinks I could frame a tale with a deep moral," no doubt introducing "The Great Carbuncle." In the final sentence of that story, the narrator says that many miles from the Crystal Hills he saw "a wondrous light around their summits, and was lured by the faith of poesy, to be the latest pilgrim of the GREAT CARBUNCLE." The narrator thus identifies himself with the Story-Teller and prepares for the continuation of the frame narrative. In the December *New-England Magazine* the editor wrote a note to introduce five sketches as Part II of "Sketches from Memory"; he printed independently three additional pieces that no doubt also belong to the narrative of the Story-Teller's travels: "My Visit to Niagara," "Old Ticonderoga," and "An Ontario Steamboat." When Park Benjamin moved to New York to edit the *American Monthly Magazine*, very little of "The Story-Teller" remained in manuscript. He had published in the *New-England Magazine* a dozen sketches and tales and five installments from the frame narrative, and one tale in the *Keepsake*. Goodrich had included two pieces in the *Token* for 1835, three more the next year, and had eight in hand for 1837. After printing "Old Ticonderoga" in the *American Monthly* for February, 1836, Benjamin assembled other scraps into "Fragments from the Journal of a Solitary Man" for the issue of July, 1837.[9] The Story-Teller, who is the friend and literary executor of Oberon, provides explanations needed to accompany a number of selections from Oberon's journal. It is not difficult to believe that Hawthorne had little interest in this gathering of snippets.[10]

From the portions of the frame that can be identified and what can be known from other sources, Hawthorne's summer travels in the early 1830's can be traced with some certainty. After spending two nights at Crawford's Notch in 1832, he was at Burlington, Vermont, on September 16 (letter to his mother, "An Inland Port"). Deciding not to go to Canada, he probably dropped back south and traveled westward on the Erie Canal ("The Canal Boat"). At Rochester he seems to have left the canal and gone by way of the lake and the St. Lawrence as far east as Ogdensburg before taking a steamboat to the western end of the lake ("Rochester," "An Ontario Steamboat"); after leaving Lake Ontario at Lewiston, he was at Niagara Falls on September 28 (certificate of visit to Termination Rock;[11] "My Visit to Niagara"). After going by steamboat to Detroit ("A Night Scene"), he visited Ticonderoga on his return eastward ("Old Ticonderoga"). If some of the travels reflected in these sketches occurred, not in 1832, but in the following summer, they would have been in time to furnish materials for "The Story-Teller."

The Story-Teller of these fragments resembles Hawthorne in the places he visits, his love of the sea, his fondness for conceits and fancy, his habit of seeing meaning in objects or actions or features of a scene, his telling of anecdotes in which he is himself the sufferer, his decision against various professions in favor of literature, his having a guardian rather than his father to deal with in choosing a career, and his burning of manuscripts. In addition, he incorporates several of Hawthorne's poses: the expectations of an early death, the ability to perceive the inner beings of those around him, self-depreciation, and the disparagement of fame. In the framing narrative, moreover, occur several ideas that appear elsewhere in Hawthorne: England as the ancestral home; Americans compared to foreigners, especially the English; the possibility of an elixir of life and the role of death in man's experience; the social and moral effects of America on immigrants; isolation, as in the stepping aside from the currents of life and waiting to be called forth.

In conspicuous ways, however, the Story-Teller is not the author.

Hawthorne is one of our most autobiographical authors—but in a special way, which he clearly recognized. Near the end of a later sketch, "The Old Manse," he exclaims, "How little have I told!—and, of that little, how almost nothing is even tinctured with any quality that makes it exclusively my own! . . . So far as I am a man of really individual attributes, I veil my face." At another time he said he wrote about his own experiences because he owned them and knew them best. Thus, he gave the Story-Teller his own travels and observations and made him the disillusioned author that he thought he was—or pretended to think he was. It was Hawthorne's habit to see himself and his own experiences as symbolic, and hence usable for representational purposes in his imaginative writings. He traveled in the summer of 1832 for the deliberate creation of literary materials, but where he used those materials, in the frame narrative of "The Story-Teller," his face remains veiled, and can be discovered only in a tracing out of shadowy lineaments.

To the Story-Teller, seeing Niagara Falls is the climax of his travels, anticipated in advance and remembered afterward. "My Visit to Niagara" contains an extended analysis of the observer's sensations and, in satiric over-simplification, a summary of current approaches to the natural sub-lime. A mother is so earnestly protecting her child that she ignores the Falls; a businessman envisages the Falls harnessed for water power; an-other observer is busy adjusting the Falls to the description in a book in his hand; another views it through a poem he is reading; one man is so awed that he drops his staff over the precipice. At the close of his last day at the Falls, the narrator eschews the other visitors present and all records others have left in art and literature, in order to experience the Falls "in the simplicity of his heart." Thus he achieves a satisfying culmination and a purification of the emotions he felt before he arrived at Niagara and when he lay awake in the middle of the night after his first glimpse.

The first installment printed from the manuscript, in November, 1834, draws a careful portrait of the Story-Teller at the time he leaves home. "Mr. Higginbotham's Catastrophe," the initial story in the collection, ap-peared a month later in its complete setting in the framework. "Fragments from the Journal of a Solitary Man," published in July, 1837, pictures the Story-Teller, disillusioned and world-weary, at the end of his travels re-turning home to die. If the narrator had an equally detailed and careful portrayal through the intervening years, and if the other selections had settings as full as that of "Mr. Higginbotham's Catastrophe," the frame narrative was a work of considerable scope. Understandably Hawthorne was unhappy to see the collection dismantled and a large part of the contents rendered unusable by the separate publication of selections from it.

From the beginning of his travels late in 1832, Hawthorne concentrated on the "Story-Teller" collection, producing the narrative framework and adding enough stories and sketches to those already on hand to make two volumes. By the summer of 1834 the plan for book publication had been abandoned. It was this period of enthusiasm and intense productivity, followed by disappointment greater than he had felt on account of *Fanshawe*, the "Seven Tales of My Native Land," or the "Provincial Tales," that Hawthorne had in mind when he spoke bitterly of his years in the chamber under the eaves, waiting for the world to call him forth. Late in the year 1836, he wrote in his notebook, "In this dismal and squalid chamber, FAME was won." Falling within a series of ideas for stories and observations recorded for possible literary use, this entry presents an irony that seems to have been much in his mind. In the eleven years since his graduation from college, he had given himself totally to literature—reading, thinking, musing, dreaming, writing, and destroying much of what he wrote. Three times he had prepared collections of tales and sketches for book publication, and each time had seen the collection dismantled and only a few of the tales published separately—and anonymously. But he was so firmly committed to writing that, following the brief sarcastic reference to the fame he had won, he continued filling his notebook with the materials of literature.

8

Twice-Told Tales

Hawthorne could take some satisfaction in seeing almost the entire contents of "The Story-Teller" published, and in having Goodrich and Benjamin ask for more of his work, but publication in an annual or in a magazine could provide neither satisfactory income nor recognition. As if taking to heart Benjamin's lament in the *New-England Magazine* of October, 1835, that an American author could not live by his pen, he accepted appointment to edit the *American Magazine of Useful and Entertaining Knowledge*, which had been founded in 1834 on the model of the London *Penny Magazine of the Society for the Diffusion of Useful Knowledge*. Goodrich was connected with the publishers, the Bewick Company of Boston, and apparently caused the preceding editor, Alden Bradford, to be removed and Hawthorne to be appointed.[1] Bridge wrote that it was no small matter for Hawthorne to get out of Salem, and added, "You are now fairly embarked with the other literary men, and if you can't sail with any other, I'll be d——d."[2] Pierce sent congratulations and noted that he had been trying to secure employment for Hawthorne with Francis Blair of the *Washington Globe*.

When Hawthorne went to Boston at the middle of January, 1836, to begin preparing the March issue of the magazine, his first letters home reflected excitement and a sense of adventure, but before long disappointment was apparent. He wrote Louisa on February 15 that he had not yet received the $45 which he was still due for three stories in the 1836 *Token* and which Goodrich had promised to pay on his arrival. He had found Goodrich "a good-natured sort of man enough; but rather an unscrupulous one in money matters, and not particularly trustworthy in anything." He had no doubt that Goodrich was authorized to hire him for $600, rather than the $500 he was to be paid. The added statement that the world was as full of rogues as the family cat, Beelzebub, was of fleas, is in the tone Hawthorne often used in writing his sisters, and suggests that other parts of the letter are similarly playful overstatement. Five days earlier he had called the Bewick Company "a damned sneaking set." Ebe and Louisa would appreciate also his playful boasting that he had declined an invitation to a literary party "holden weekly by two blue-stockings," but would go "by and by." After reading Henry Chorley's notice of his tales, he wrote, "My worshipful self is a very famous man in London—the Athenaeum having noticed all my articles in the last Token, with long extracts."[3]

Hawthorne wanted Louisa to send him two or three dollars; for out of the five dollars borrowed from Uncle Robert when he left Salem, only thirty-four cents remained. It had all gone for "absolute necessaries," except that on his first day in Boston he had spent six cents for a glass of wine and three for a cigar. This accounting would not be comforting to his mother, but she had learned that what he wrote to Herbert Street during his absences could not be read always as sober fact. The money from Louisa had come by February 17, and at about the same time the $45 came from Goodrich, along with a letter saying he had been "hoping several days to see" Hawthorne's face. If there had been any estrangement between them, it soon ended, for Hawthorne undertook immediately to review a new volume of Goodrich's poems for the Boston Atlas and to give the editor of the Salem Gazette another copy for review. It can be assumed that he then paid his first visit to Salem since coming to Boston. His review was in the Atlas on February 23; the review in the Gazette, probably by his friend Caleb Foote, was out on February 26; both reviews were favorable.[4] Not until May 7, after four months in Boston, did Hawthorne receive anything on his salary, and then only twenty dollars. Unless he was paid "the whole amount shortly," he wrote Elizabeth, he would return to Salem and stay until he was paid.

There had been other difficulties from the outset. Since the Bewick Company was an engraving firm, the editor had to provide copy to accompany illustrations he did not select, and seldom had more than a day or two's notice of the engravings chosen. He provided most of the contents by compiling, quoting, and paraphrasing from books and magazines; but he was handicapped because the publishers did not provide membership in the Boston Athenaeum Library to enable him to check out books. His letters to Salem carried urgent requests for books to be sent—along with equally urgent requests for clean shirts and collars and socks. He asked Elizabeth repeatedly to send extracts and her own concoctions, prose and poetical. "I make nothing of writing a history or biography before dinner. Do you the same." She began a sketch of Alexander Hamilton, but, since an engraving of Hamilton had been scheduled for the May number, he had to complete it himself and, as he wrote her on March 22, had also to correct some of her "naughty notions about arbitrary government." He could not endorse the arguments for a strong central government[5] that she had retained from her source. She remembered in old age that she and her brother often argued politics, "he being a Democrat, and I of the opposite party."[6]

In spite of the vexations, Hawthorne was not altogether displeased, and he was a successful editor. He printed several of his own sketches in the first three numbers; he may have had no more ready for the later numbers, or he may have been unwilling to put them into the magazine. Some of the historical and biographical topics interested him; and in his sketch of John Adams he followed the pattern of earlier sketches of Anne Hutchinson and others, selecting Adams's interview with King George soon after the Revolution and filling it out with details to carry the symbolic and ironic import he saw in it. A long account of the Boston Tea Party prepared him to write on the same subject later in *Grandfather's Chair*. Some of the architectural engravings led Hawthorne to historical sources that furnished him information for later use. Even the least promising illustration could incite his customary play of idea and language, and make him for the nonce a personal essayist drawing his reader along in an excursion of free association. The Suffolk Bank Building in Boston looked down on the site of the Boston Massacre. It would have been in character, Hawthorne said, for New England to erect an "architectural or sculptural device" at the spot, thus to associate the memorial "with the daily business of the people, and to consecrate even the Exchange" to this event of the past. A picture of the New York University building prompted him to write a disquisition on a liberal education, in which he said, "All really educated men, whether they have studied in the halls of a University, or in a cottage or a workshop, are essentially self-educated."

A shot tower on Manhattan Island held some interest for him because of its use, but it suggested a path he often followed in thinking about the literary author in America: "The tower needs nothing but antiquity, and a mantle of clinging ivy, and above all, the charm of legend and tradition, in order to afford as good a subject for the pen of the poet or novelist, as it already does for the pencil of the artist." Beyond the pieces required by the engravings, Hawthorne could follow his own interests. He searched magazines and newspapers, early as well as contemporary, for such bits of odd information as appear in his notebooks and in his sketch "A Virtuoso's Collection" (1842). His was an omnivorous curiosity, and rarely did he cite an item from art, literature, science, medicine, nature, geography, industry, history, mythology, or popular lore without adding a figurative or an ironic touch; it was his habit to look for meaning, and to suggest what he found.

In the few pieces of literary comment Hawthorne printed in the magazine, he gave hints of his preferences and beliefs, as in notes written to accompany excerpts from *The Life and Death of Mr. Badman* by John Bunyan. He wondered "whether the present generation has not lost more than it has gained, by the philosophy which teaches it to laugh, rather than tremble, at such tales as these" narrated in *Badman*. *The Pilgrim's Progress* would remain popular because of "the human interest with which the author has so strongly imbued the shadowy beings of his allegory." In this, Hawthorne was stating a principle he had followed in his tales and later was to state in the prefaces to his romances and elsewhere: to endow his allegorical characters with convincing human traits, and to place them in a neutral land between reality and fantasy. His longest literary comment in the magazine is a tribute to Thomas Green Fessenden, in whose home he was living.[7]

In his first employment, at the age of thirty-two, except for bit-work in his uncles' stage coach office while preparing for college, Hawthorne met his responsibilities and, in spite of handicaps, produced a remarkably good magazine for its type. As editor, he continued the reading and storing of his mind he had done since leaving Bowdoin; writing for the magazine was not far different from writing in his notebooks. If his salary had been paid and he had been given control over the engravings, and if the drudgery of hand-copying extracts for the printer had been eliminated, the editorship might have provided the income he needed while he continued his own writing. All the employment he took afterward led him away from literature and all but paralyzed his creative pen.

Hawthorne asked on June 3 for something beyond the $20 he had received on his salary, but the Bewick Company was in bankruptcy. After preparing copy for the August number, he returned to Salem. In an Editorial Notice he said this number would probably be his last, but that he expected the difficulties impeding "the prosperity of the concern" to be removed. He noted, as his predecessor had done also, that he had not had full control over the contents, since others had selected the embellishments; but he cited no other objections. No magazine was issued in September, because of a fire at the printer's; publication resumed in October, with Alden Bradford again the editor. Letters from Horatio Bridge show that Hawthorne wanted to continue as editor and that Bridge thought he would.[8]

Hawthorne and Goodrich continued business relations and much of the time stood each ready to do the other a favor. Hawthorne commended a book by Goodrich, *A System of Universal Geography*, in his last number of the magazine, and he had already agreed to contribute to Goodrich's Peter Parley series for children, and had asked Elizabeth to help, offering her the entire fee of a hundred dollars. The work that resulted, the two-volume *Peter Parley's Universal History on the Basis of Geography*, passed through many editions in the following decades. Although little choice in selection or treatment was allowed him, Hawthorne's special way of seeing and of saying things appears now and then. His preface announces a principle that would guide him in this and also in his later writing for children: "A large part of the actions of men, as related by the historian, are evil. . . . The master spirits generally stand forth as guided only by ambition, and superior to other men in wickedness as in power. . . . It is necessary that history should be known, that we may learn the character and capacity of man; but in telling of the vices and crimes that soil the pages of the past, I have taken advantage of every convenient occasion, to excite hatred of injustice, violence and falsehood, and promote a love of truth, equity and benevolence."

When Goodrich proposed on December 17 a Peter Parley volume of six hundred pages on "the manner, customs, and civilities of all countries,"[9] for which the pay would be $300, Hawthorne declined, no doubt with an eye to his improved financial prospects. He had been paid $108 for eight of his pieces printed in the 1837 *Token*, and two or three were wanted for the next year. Goodrich also was arranging publication for a collection of his tales. Hawthorne did not know until afterward that Horatio Bridge was responsible for this new brightening of his literary horizon. Bridge had suggested in September that Hawthorne try again to publish a book of tales—and that he put his name on the title-page. He would with great pleasure raise anything needful "in a pecuniary way." [10]

Bridge burned Hawthorne's early letters to him, as he was instructed to do, but it can be surmised from his own letters and his published recollections that in the last quarter of 1836 Hawthorne was disturbingly depressed. On October 16 Bridge urged Hawthorne not to give up to the blues, "for God's sake and your own, and mine, and everybody's." He asked permission to publish a piece he had written for the Boston *Post*, in which he named Hawthorne as author of the pieces in the 1837 *Token*, and called him "one of the very best" American writers. On October 22 he answered a letter just received: "There is a kind of desperate coolness about it that seems dangerous. I fear that you are too good a subject for suicide, and that some day you will end your mortal woes on your own responsibility. However, I wish you to refrain till next Thursday, when I shall be in Boston." Thursday was the day Bridge was to put up the money needed to get the volume of tales published. Goodrich had written him on October 20, replying to his offer, that the book would cost about $450 and would require a guarantee of $250, adding that he was confident Bridge would get his money back. Bridge stipulated that his part in the transaction be kept from Hawthorne. [11]

The publisher was the American Stationers' Company of Boston, recently organized to advance American literature by bringing out books that otherwise might not appear. On November 7 Goodrich wrote Hawthorne that arrangements were being concluded; his suggestion that the book be entitled "The Gray Champion, and Other Tales" may have led to the choice of that story to open the volume. Ten days later Bridge urged Hawthorne not to dedicate the book to Goodrich, saying that a dedication would bring "the two parties into a false attitude toward each other." While critical of editors as a rule, Bridge had advised Hawthorne to cultivate them—to write for the New York *Mirror* and for the *Knickerbocker* (in which he had stories in 1837), and not to break with Goodrich or Benjamin, though he once said that he would like to see Hawthorne "thoroughly angry and pouring it into" Benjamin. [12] Now he had no doubt of Goodrich's selfishness in regard to Hawthorne. "The 'Token' was saved by your writing," he said. "Unless you are already committed, do not mar the prospects of your *first* book by hoisting Goodrich into favor." The book appeared without a dedication. The next February 1 Bridge wrote that he was glad Hawthorne and Benjamin were reconciled, though he believed Benjamin and Goodrich to be selfish and unscrupulous, particularly Goodrich.

After graduating from Washington College at Hartford and studying law at Harvard and Yale, Benjamin had turned to literature, and by 1834 had begun a career as magazine editor. In that capacity he turned his hand to bringing Hawthorne before the public. In reviewing the 1835 *Token* in the *New-England Magazine* for October, 1834, he called the author of "The Gentle Boy" a "writer of some of the most delicate and pleasant prose ever published this side of the Atlantic"; the next April he praised the "originality and graphic freshness of coloring" in Hawthorne's work. In reviewing the 1836 *Token*, he called Hawthorne "the most pleasing writer of fanciful prose, except Irving, in the country"; and the next year he named Hawthorne as the author of eight tales in the *Token*, perhaps wishing to compliment Hawthorne and perhaps also to embarrass Goodrich by exposing his reliance on one author for so many pieces in one issue. He was carrying on a vituperative literary war with Goodrich and now proposed that Hawthorne be asked to write the next year's *Token* entire. If "this voluntarily undistinguished man of genius," he said, would issue a collection of his tales and essays, "their success would be brilliant—certainly in England, perhaps in this country."[13] Benjamin had in mind the lament that American publishers and readers favored literary works from across the Atlantic and left native authors without the support they deserved—a lament that was growing more insistent and the next year received a notable statement in Emerson's essay "The American Scholar."

Bridge wrote Hawthorne on April 27, 1837, that he had talked with Goodrich and liked him, though he seemed to take too much credit for discovering Hawthorne and bringing him forward. Twenty years later, when Elizabeth Peabody proposed to write something correcting what Goodrich had said in his recently published *Recollections* about his relations with Hawthorne, he replied with a firm rebuff and an assessment of Goodrich that probably had varied little since their first acquaintance. The letter reveals something about his relations with Elizabeth Peabody as well as his relations with Goodrich.[14]

> . . . It is funny enough to see him taking the airs of a patron; but I do not mind it in the least, nor feel the slightest inclination to defend myself, or to be defended. . . . So pray do not take up the cudgels on my behalf; especially as I perceive that your recollections are rather inaccurate. For instance, it was Park Benjamin, not Goodrich, who cut up the

"Storyteller." As for Goodrich, I have rather a kindly feeling towards
him, and he himself is a not unkindly man, in spite of his propensity to
feed and fatten himself on better brains than his own. Only let him do
that, and he will really sometimes put himself to some little trouble to do
a good-natured act. His quarrel with me was, that I broke away from
him before he had quite finished his meal, and while a portion of my
brain was left; and I have not the slightest doubt that he really felt himself wronged by my so doing.

Even with assurance late in 1836 that his book would be published,
Hawthorne remained blue, judging from Bridge's side of their correspondence: "The bane of your life has been self-distrust," Bridge wrote on
Christmas Day. "I have been trying to think what you are so miserable
for." On the next February 1 he said, "I wish to God that I could impart
to you a little of my own brass. You would dash into the contest of literary men, and do honor to yourself and country in a short time. But you
never will have confidence enough in yourself, though you will have
fame." Another Bowdoin classmate, Jonathan Cilley, rejoiced that Hawthorne had become "a writer of great repute." He had not mistaken his
friend "in that particular," though he had mistaken him "in the line matrimonial." He was writing on November 17, 1836, to acknowledge that he
had lost the wager he had made at college that Hawthorne would be
married within twelve years.[15]

Twice-Told Tales was published on March 6, 1837, in an edition of a
thousand, between 600 and 700 copies of which had been sold in three
months. It sold for a dollar, and the author received the usual royalty of
ten percent. The American Stationers' Company closed down early in
1838; a year later the remaining copies of the edition, fewer than 100, were
being sold.

A review in the *Salem Gazette* on March 14, 1837, had the obvious purpose of recommending the book of a local citizen, but several phrases mark
the reviewer as a thoughtful reader. The same number reprinted "Fancy's
Show Box." Another Salem paper, the *Essex Register*, reprinted a review
from the Boston *Daily Advertiser*. Bridge wrote articles for the *Age* of
Augusta, Maine, March 21 and April 5, citing the originality of the tales
but adding that they were "too ideal and refined to please the great mass
of readers."[16] The reviewer in the *Knickerbocker Magazine* for April, likely
Lewis Gaylord Clark, found in the book reminders of Washington Irving,
Henry Wadsworth Longfellow, and Charles Lamb, and said that "in quiet
humor, in genuine pathos, and deep feeling, and in a style equally un-

studied and pure, the author . . . has few equals, and with perhaps one
or two eminent exceptions, no superior in our country." Bridge said that
some of his acquaintances did not buy the book because the tales were
twice-told, but he was confident that if the *North American Review* published a review, it would be worth more than all the other reviews combined. The *North American* did publish a review in July—by Henry Wadsworth Longfellow.

The day after *Twice-Told Tales* was issued, Hawthorne addressed a letter
to Longfellow, apparently the first word passed between them in the dozen
years since their graduation at Bowdoin, saying that the publisher would
send him a copy of the new book. He wrote in modesty and deference.
"We were not, it is true, so well acquainted at college, that I can plead an
absolute right to inflict my 'twice-told' tediousness upon you; but I have
often regretted that we were not better known to each other, and have
been glad of your success in literature, and in more important matters. I
know not whether you are aware that I have made a good many idle attempts in the way of Magazine and Annual scribblings." Longfellow's
review in the *North American Review* included, besides other quotations,
"A Rill from the Town Pump" entire. The comment is general but highly
laudatory, and is itself more a literary work than a review. The tales,
Longfellow said, were written by a man of genius, in a "bright, poetic"
style, "soft and musical." They were national in character, discovering the
materials of story and romance in the "puritanical times" of New England.
After reading the review "with huge delight," Hawthorne wrote Longfellow on June 19 that he had hoped his friend would write a review, but
had not "anticipated how very kindly it would be done." He continued,
"there are at least five persons who think you the most sagacious critic on
earth—viz. my mother and two sisters, my old maiden aunt, and finally,
the sturdiest believer of the whole five, my own self. If I doubt the sincerity and correctness of any of my critics, it shall be of those who censure
me."

Hawthorne had sent Longfellow on June 4, before the review appeared,
a letter that offers little exact detail, but is one of the most remarkable instances of self-revelation and self-analysis in our literary archives. This letter reveals that, for Hawthorne, author of moral romances and studies of
human character, the important consideration was not what an event or a
situation was, or even what he thought it was, but rather what his creative
imagination conceived it to be. To him, every object, act, or person,
including himself and his activities, was less significant in itself than in

what it could be taken to represent. His dwelling might be pictured as an owl's nest, he said,

for mine is about as dismal, and, like the owl, I seldom venture abroad till after dusk. By some witchcraft or other—for I really cannot assign any reasonable why and wherefore—I have been carried apart from the main current of life, and find it impossible to get back again. Since we last met . . . , I have secluded myself from society; and yet I never meant any such thing, nor dreamed what sort of life I was going to lead. I have made a captive of myself and put me into a dungeon; and now I cannot find the key to let myself out—and if the door were open, I should be almost afraid to come out. You tell me that you have met with troubles and changes. I know not what they may have been; but I can assure you that trouble is the next best thing to enjoyment, and that there is no fate in this world so horrible as to have no share in either its joys or sorrows. For the last ten years, I have not lived, but only dreamed about living. It may be true that there have been some unsubstantial pleasures here in the shade, which I should have missed in the sunshine; but you cannot conceive how utterly devoid of satisfaction all my retrospects are. I have laid up no treasure of pleasant remembrances, against old age; but there is some comfort in thinking that my future years can hardly fail to be more varied, and therefore more tolerable, than the past.

You give me more credit than I deserve, in supposing that I have led a studious life. I have, indeed, turned over a good many books, but in so desultory a way that it cannot be called study, nor has it left me the fruits of study. As to my literary efforts, I do not think much of them— neither is it worth while to be ashamed of them. They would have been better, I trust, if written under more favorable circumstances. I have had no external excitement—no consciousness that the public would like what I wrote, nor much hope nor a very passionate desire that they should do so. Nevertheless, having nothing else to be ambitious of, I have felt considerably interested in literature; and if my writings had made any decided impression, I should probably have been stimulated to greater exertions: but there has been no warmth of approbation, so that I have always written with benumbed fingers. I have another great difficulty, in the lack of materials; for I have seen so little of the world, that I have nothing but thin air to concoct my stories of, and it is not easy to give a lifelike semblance to such shadowy stuff. Sometimes, through a peep-hole, I have caught a glimpse of the real world; and the two or three articles, in which I have portrayed such glimpses, please me better than the others.

I have now, or soon shall have, one sharp spur to exertion, which I lacked at an earlier period; for I see little prospect but that I must scribble for a living. But this troubles me much less than you would suppose. I can turn my pen to all sorts of drudgery, such as children's books &c, and by and bye, I shall get some editorship that will answer my purpose.

Frank Pierce . . . offered me his influence to obtain an office in the Exploring Expedition. . . . If such a post were attainable, I should certainly accept it; for, though fixed so long to one spot, I have always had a desire [to] run round the world.

. . . I am glad to find that you had read and liked some of the stories. To be sure, you could not well help flattering me a little, but I value your praise too highly not to have faith in its sincerity.

I intend, in a week or two, to come out of my owl's nest, and not return to it till late in the summer—employing the interval in making a tour somewhere in New-England. You, who have the dust of distant countries on your "sandal-shoon," cannot imagine how much enjoyment I shall have in this little excursion. Whenever I get abroad, I feel just as young as I did ten years ago. What a letter am I inflicting on you! I trust you will answer it.

The main outline of this self-portrait Hawthorne repeated again and again—in letters to his fiancée two years later, in prefaces to later volumes, and in sketches that seem to invite reading as autobiography. The letter provides a portrait, not a photographic reproduction. His term as magazine editor would refute any literal reading of the statements that he could not get back into the world and would be afraid to if he could. But such details do no harm in metaphoric reading, in a symbolic portrait. The "one sharp spur to exertion" which he had then, the necessity to "scribble for a living," probably means that the funds from the Manning estate which had supported his twelve-year apprenticeship had been exhausted. An editorship would meet his need, or the office in the South Seas Exploring Expedition his friends were at the time seeking for him.

9

Duels:
Comic and Tragic

With *Twice-Told Tales* in print, Hawthorne still needed a salary, and in the spring of 1837 Franklin Pierce undertook to have him appointed historiographer on the South Seas Expedition to be commanded by Lieutenant (later Commodore) Charles Wilkes. After conferring with Hawthorne, he sent J. N. Reynolds, who was to be in charge of scientific investigations, a sample of Hawthorne's writings, along with a firm recommendation and a suggestion that the salary be at least $1500. Hawthorne, he wrote, is "extremely modest, perhaps diffident,—a diffidence, in my judgment, having its origin in a high and honorable pride; but he is a man of decided genius, without . . . any of those whims and eccentricities which are supposed to characterize men of genius, and which might disqualify him for any solid and steady business. . . . I know Hawthorne's worth, and am sure you would admire him as a man of genius, and love him as a companion and friend." He told also of Hawthorne's editing the *American Magazine* "with great diligence and success." Bridge said he would himself "answer for the whole Maine delegation," and solicited the help of George Bancroft and Jonathan Cilley, now a congressman. But nothing came of the efforts; the chaplain on the expedition was designated to serve as historiographer.

Bridge remained confident; he was sure Pierce could get Hawthorne an editorship or a clerkship in Washington; "I tell you that you will be in a good situation next winter, instead of 'under a sod.' " Meanwhile he invited Hawthorne to visit him at Augusta all summer and write.[1] Hawthorne arrived on July 3 and three days later began a detailed notebook account. His earliest notebook that has been preserved opens on May 28, 1835,[2] in the pattern he would follow in future notebook writing. He wrote down his observations carefully, not necessarily on the spot, but soon enough for him to recall full details. One purpose was to practice writing, but he wanted also to set down observations and thoughts that could be mined later for literary use. He also jotted down, from his reading and other sources, ideas and materials for stories.

He stayed a month with Bridge, and on the evidence of his notebook (VIII, 32–65) he enjoyed the leisurely, carefree existence. Bridge kept bachelor quarters in the family mansion and was engrossed in the construction of a mill-dam that was half completed. He realized that the undertaking was a gamble, with bankruptcy ahead if he failed. He lost the gamble afterward, when flooding swept the dam away before it was completed, but during Hawthorne's visit he was optimistic and a pleasant, restful host. Hawthorne recorded a judgment in his notebook that he probably would have endorsed as long as he lived: that Bridge combined "more high and admirable qualities, of that sort which make up a gentleman," than any other he had known. They took walks or they rode farther afield, once staying away overnight. Bridge fished and Hawthorne bathed in the streams. Drinkables were in good supply, Hawthorne noted, but he and his friend were not "such thirsty souls" as they once were. He was attracted by the vivacity and mirth of a Frenchman named Schaeffer living in the Bridge mansion, who gave him lessons in French pronunciation and "frenchified" their names, producing "M. du Pont" and "M. de L'Aubépine," a name Hawthorne was to use afterward.

On July 28 Hawthorne saw Jonathan Cilley for the first time since they left college, and on August 5 took the stage to visit him at Thomaston, on the coast thirty-five miles southeast of Augusta. Hawthorne put into his notebook an analysis of Cilley's mind and character, concluding, "Upon the whole, I have quite a good liking for him" (VIII, 63–65, 70). He could not know that after a few months he would be writing a memorial to his friend and would make use of these notes.

Two mansions Hawthorne saw invited the kind of rumination that was a lifelong habit with him. The new mansion being erected by Robert Hallowell Gardiner south of Augusta would probably become known as Gardiner's Folly, he thought, since construction had ceased for lack of funds, and the windows were boarded up. It offered Hawthorne "hints of copious reflection, in reference to the indulgence of aristocratic pomp among democratic institutions" (VIII, 42). He visited also the ruined mansion of General Henry Knox, whose attempt to establish a feudal domain was, to Hawthorne's mind, "an illustration of what must be the result of American schemes of aristocracy" (VIII, 67). On Knox's land he now saw the American pattern of small towns and neat houses occupied by the families of farmers or mechanics, which left no traces of the pretentious Knox estate, except for the ruined mansion.

The notebooks show Hawthorne alert to any class or type of people unfamiliar to him, such as the Irish families, with their abundant children and their habitual quarreling between families and between husband and wife. One scene was worth recording in detail, as an example of what Hawthorne called moral picturesqueness. A "simple-looking fellow" inquired at a tavern where he might find his wife, known as a prostitute to some of the group. Hawthorne would have liked to witness the man meeting his wife; but he saw more than mirth in the scene—"a man moved as deeply as his nature would admit, in the midst of hardened, gibing spectators." He added, "it is worth thinking over and studying out." This character joins others set down in his notebook from observation in taverns and on steamboats, characters such as might appear in his fiction, acting out their roles while he stands by puzzling out questions of human nature and human destiny, his task to perceive and record, not to proclaim— though possibly to suggest—sympathy, pity, or condemnation.

The notebook Hawthorne kept in Maine records more than casual observations of several young women: at the Bridge mansion, the "pretty, black-eyed intelligent servant-girl," "la belle Nancy" at Robinson's Tavern, the "very tall woman, young and maiden looking," who served dinner there; and at the tavern in Thomaston, the "frank, free, mirthful daughter of the landlady, about twenty-four years old, between whom and myself there immediately sprung up a flirtation, which made us both feel rather solemncholy when we parted on Tuesday morning. She is capable, I know, of strong feelings," he continued, "and her features expressed something of the kind, when we held out our hands for a parting grasp." At the same tavern, there was "a rather pretty, fantastic little devil of a brunette," who walked "by jerks, with a quiver as if she were made of calves-feet jelly." This long entry concludes, "I talk with everybody—to Mrs. Trott, good sense—to Mary, good sense with a mixture of fun—to Mrs. Gleason, sentiment, romance, and nonsense" (VIII, 65–66).

Hawthorne's sister Elizabeth remembered in her old age that he once returned from Swampscott, a coastal village south of Salem, "captivated, in his fanciful way, with a 'mermaid,' as he called her," a fisherman's daughter, who kept a little shop. He brought home a pink sugar heart in memory of her, kept it a while, and then ate it. According to Elizabeth, the "mermaid" became Susan in "The Village Uncle," which had the title "The Mermaid; A Reverie" when it was published in the *Token* for 1835. The sugar heart appeared in this first printing: "Oh, Susan the sugar heart you gave me, and the old rhyme—'When this you see, remember me'— scratched on it with the point of your scissors! Inscriptions on marble have been sooner forgotten, than those words shall be on that frail heart." But when the story was included in the 1842 edition of *Twice-Told Tales* the sugar heart was omitted—significantly, perhaps, because Hawthorne was engaged to be married soon afterward. His note on the landlady's daughter at Thomaston suggests that this was not the only instance in which he created in his imagination a romance that he thought or pretended to think not altogether fictional. He "had *fancies* like this whenever he went from home," Elizabeth said. In the spring before going to Augusta he had divulged so much about matrimonial ideas that Bridge asked him twice in April whether he was thinking of getting married.[3]

On his return from Maine the second week in August, Hawthorne had the longest sea voyage he had yet taken, on the overnight steamer to Boston from Owl's-Head, near Thomaston. Within a few weeks he had written full notebook entries about visits to the Essex Historical Society, on the outskirts of Salem, and trips to Boston, Thompson's Island, and the Boston Navy Yard with Jonathan Cilley. In Boston he called on his relative Eben Hawthorne, whose hobby was pride of ancestry, to learn what he could on the spelling of the family name; but Cousin Eben "kept telling stories of the family, who seemed to have comprised many oddities, eccentric men and women, recluses, etc." (VIII, 74–75).

Early in his visit with Bridge, Hawthorne had written in his notebook, "fate seems to be preparing changes for both of us. My circumstances, at least, cannot long continue as they are and have been; and Bridge, too, stands betwixt high prosperity and utter ruin." He was thinking of Bridge's risk in building the mill-dam. As for himself, he must have some means of livelihood, and would not resume his former seclusion. A letter he had received in April encouraged the hope that his pen could yield greater income than in the past. John Louis O'Sullivan had written soliciting "frequent contributions" to a "literary and political monthly" he was founding in Washington, the *United States Magazine and Democratic Review*, which would pay contributors from three to five dollars a page. Hawthorne furnished "The Toll-Gatherer's Day" for the October number and beginning in January had eight contributions in the next thirteen issues. Of his three dozen tales and sketches published from 1838 through 1845, two dozen of them appeared first in the *Democratic Review*.

"The Toll-Gatherer's Day: A Sketch of Transitory Life" presents the flow of travel over the bridge between Salem and Beverly, during a day when the narrator sits on a bench and fancies that the earth shifts its scenes before him. The preserved notebooks contain no record of such a day, but in writing "Foot-prints on the Sea-shore," in the *Democratic Review* of January, 1838, Hawthorne had a notebook account open before him and took from it not only items in the scene and his responses to them, but also exact phrasing.[4] These two sketches reinforce the suggestion that in another province Hawthorne may have expected his circumstances to change, for in them young women have even greater prominence than in the notebook. In "The Toll-Gatherer's Day," the narrator sends his blessing after a bride and groom and refers to the toll-gatherer's "queer parting smile" at the thought of their wedding night.[5] In "Foot-prints on the Sea-shore," the only human intrusion on the narrator's communion with the sea and the beach, and with his dreams, is caused by three young girls who come in and out of view during his walk. Letting his "mind disport itself at will," he writes, "Here can I frame a story of two lovers, and make their shadows live before me. . . . Here, should I will it, I can summon up a single shade, and be myself her lover." And when he is invited to join the fishing party to which the girls belong, he confesses that, after all his solitary joys, "this is the sweetest moment of a Day by the Sea-Shore." If the author who wrote these sketches and who also had a flirtation with the landlady's daughter at Thomaston had not already found one young woman particularly attractive to him, he would soon.

On April 12, 1838, Hawthorne wrote to Catherine Calista Ainsworth, a niece of Thomas Green Fessenden who had lived in the household while he was a boarder in 1836, "I have heard recently the interesting intelligence that I am engaged to two ladies in this city. It was my first knowledge of the fact. I do trust that I shall not get married without my own privity and consent."[6] He wrote Mrs. Fessenden the same day, "What a pity that I did not hearken to your good counsel, and spend the winter in Boston! It has been a winter of much anxiety and of very little pleasure or profit."

The winter had brought him an affair of the heart with Mary Crowninshield Silsbee that led him to the point of challenging a friend, John Louis O'Sullivan, to a duel, and it had brought the death of another friend, Jonathan Cilley, in a duel. The winter had brought him also the acquaintance of Elizabeth Peabody, who was to have a major influence on his career, Mary Peabody, and their sister, Sophia, who was to become his wife. The sequence of events can be discovered only by tracing out faint lines and relying on surmise to establish points of intersection; but the total design becomes clear.

O'Sullivan said it was Cilley who first interested him in Hawthorne.[7] That would have taken place before April 19, 1837, when he invited Hawthorne to contribute to the *Democratic Review*. By the end of the year Hawthorne had placed three sketches with O'Sullivan. Mary Silsbee (1809–87) was the daughter of Nathaniel Silsbee, captain of the *Herald*, on which Hawthorne's father sailed to the Orient in 1800–1801. O'Sullivan may have met her in Washington, where her father was a member of Congress until 1835, or in Boston; he presumably saw her in Salem afterward, and may have introduced her to Hawthorne.

On February 8, 1838, Hawthorne wrote Horatio Bridge:

> It is my purpose to set out for Washington, in the course of a fortnight or thereabouts—but only to make a short visit. Would it be utterly impossible, or extremely unadvisable, for you to come to Boston or this place, within that interval? Not that you can do me the least good; but it would be a satisfaction to me to hold a talk with the best friend I ever had or shall have (of the male sex)—and there may be cause for regret on your part, should we fail of a meeting. But I repeat that you cannot exercise the slightest favorable influence on my affairs—they being beyond your control, and hardly within my own. Perhaps you have been thinking of a visit to Boston, and this letter may merely hasten it. If so, I shall be glad. Do not come, if it will put you to serious inconvenience.
>
> God bless you and
Your friend, Nath..
>
> Be mum!

This letter has several lines cut out, no doubt by Bridge, who had instructions from Hawthorne to burn all his early letters. (It is the only one of the letters to Bridge earlier than March 23, 1843, that has come to light.) The excised portion no doubt indicated that an affair of the heart had disturbed the dull way of Hawthorne's life, and had not terminated, for Bridge was his best friend only "of the male sex." When Hawthorne wrote this letter, he had decided to champion Mary Silsbee on account of wrongs he believed she had suffered; at about the same time he wrote O'Sullivan demanding an explanation. O'Sullivan's explanation was satisfactory, and a full reconciliation between them resulted.

Sixteen days after Hawthorne wrote Bridge, Jonathan Cilley was killed in Washington. Serving his first term in Congress, he had reluctantly accepted a challenge and had fallen in a duel with William J. Graves, congressman from Kentucky. Graves had brought Cilley a note from J. Watson Webb, owner and editor of the *New York Courier and Exchange*, questioning a statement Cilley had made about that paper in the House of Representatives. When Cilley refused the message from Webb, Graves took the position that his own honor had been questioned, and persisted in his challenge although Cilley asserted that he had meant no disrespect to him. At the third exchange of rifle shots on February 24, Cilley was hit and within a few minutes was dead.

Julian Hawthorne published a "little story" about Hawthorne and two others he said he would designate Louis and Mary, drawing on what his Aunt Elizabeth Peabody had told him from her recollections after forty-five years. The notes he made during his conversation with her indicate how freely the story was elaborated at both stages of its composition. Miss Peabody described Mary as a coquette whose "Armida wiles" were sufficient to entrap others as well as Hawthorne. She said that Cilley's decision to fight Graves was influenced by Hawthorne's "example in having challenged O'Sullivan," and that Hawthorne "felt in a way responsible for" Cilley's death. Julian Hawthorne filled in the story with details appropriate to a piece of fiction.[8]

When Julian Hawthorne asked Bridge in 1882 for information "about the duel which was at one time imminent" between Hawthorne and O'Sullivan, Bridge avoided the question, but a decade later he broached the topic in his *Personal Recollections of Nathaniel Hawthorne*, in order to correct the account already in print. Hawthorne meant to challenge O'Sullivan, Bridge said, "and it was only after ample explanations had been made, showing that his friend had behaved with entire honor, that Pierce and Cilley, who were his advisers, could persuade him to be satisfied without a fight."[9] Bridge was mistaken in saying that Hawthorne went to Washington at the time, for in 1852 Hawthorne said that his trip to Washington then was his first. After Cilley's death, O'Sullivan spoke of talking with him recently, supporting Bridge's statement that Cilley was one who interceded to prevent a duel between Hawthorne and O'Sullivan.[10] Bridge recalled also being in Washington a month after Cilley's death and in the company of Franklin Pierce and others who had been close to Cilley. "I never heard, at that time nor afterwards, that Cilley was in any way influenced by Hawthorne's example. Nor did Hawthorne ever intimate to me, by word or letter, that he considered himself at all responsible for Cilley's course in accepting Graves's challenge."[11] The folly of Hawthorne's proposing to challenge O'Sullivan and the generally pleasant farce that resulted might have been expected to influence Cilley to reject rather than accept Graves's challenge. Cilley being a Democrat and Graves a Whig, the heated editorial comment the duel provoked as a rule lamented the death, condemned dueling, and placed blame according to each editor's party affiliation.[12]

O'Sullivan had an essay on the duel in the *Democratic Review* for March, and by March 15 Hawthorne had agreed to write a memorial essay. He and O'Sullivan were again friends, and in their correspondence afterward they spoke frankly about the affair. Hawthorne made a wry confession of his error in accusing O'Sullivan, and they both gave evidence of the understanding and generosity that would underlie their friendship the rest of Hawthorne's life. In asking Longfellow on March 21 for reminiscences of Cilley, Hawthorne said the memorial would be "a thorny affair to handle." He avoided one thorny aspect by saying little about the political background for the duel. Although a congressional committee was still investigating it, Hawthorne, like the public at large, had formed his opinion on the evidence already available—that the killing of Cilley was murder. "A challenge was never given on a more shadowy pretext; a duel was never pressed to a fatal close in the face of such open kindness as was expressed by Mr. Cilley; and the conclusion is inevitable, that Mr. Graves and his principal second, Mr. Wise, have . . . overstepped the imaginary distinction, which, on their own principles, separates manslaughter from murder." He would spare himself "the details of the awful catastrophe," he said, "for I write with a blunted pen and a head benumbed, and am the less able to express my feelings as they lie deep at heart, and inexhaustible." Cilley had been "almost as an elder brother" to him in their college days.[13]

Upon seeing Cilley in Maine the previous summer, Hawthorne had written in his notebook (VIII, 61–63) an analysis so finely drawn and clinical as to suggest the portraits of characters in his major works. Cilley had succeeded over great handicaps, because he was "shrewd, crafty, insinuating, with wonderful tact" in using other men for his purposes. He had seen "the thorough advantage of morality and honesty," and was as honest as "the great sun of the world—with something even approaching high mindedness." Bridge would have known, as perhaps Longfellow and Pierce did too, that Hawthorne's habitual close scrutiny of his acquaintances, no less than his fictional characters, was an additional reason he found writing the memorial sketch "a thorny affair." In the essay, Cilley's character is far less subtly analyzed than in the notebook. The essay mentions his harsher traits, but it stresses his "companionship with the yeomen of the land" and the absence in his personality of the "aristocratic stateliness" common among politicians. Hawthorne may have remembered what Cilley wrote him on November 17, 1836, not to turn up his "aristocratic nose," for politics was "a pathway to fame and honor, as well as the course" Hawthorne had chosen. The Manning background from which Hawthorne went to college identified him with the yeomen of the land. He was a Jacksonian and often pointed to the folly of attempting to plant European aristocracy in America. Cilley nevertheless spoke of his "aristocratic nose," probably having in mind not the prestige of his paternal line, but the qualities of mind and character that impressed his associates from his college years onward.

No clear attitude toward dueling appears in the sketch of Cilley. Hawthorne had spoken on the subject several times in the *American Magazine*, once stating it as a fact that neither law nor public sentiment can eliminate dueling (August, p. 515), and another time (May, p. 356) that Alexander Hamilton can be "absolved from the guilt of duelling" because he had determined not to return the fire of his antagonist, Aaron Burr. A notebook entry, written between December 6, 1837, and the next June 15, tells how a Lieutenant Finch was unjustifiably forced to fight Lieutenant Frank White, "an inveterate duellist and an unerring shot." Finch received training from his second, made sure he fired first, and shot White through the heart. The entry concludes on a note of exultation in the justice of the outcome: "White, with a most savage expression of countenance, fired, after the bullet had gone through his heart. . . . His face probably looked as if he were already in the Hell, whither he went at this same instant. But afterwards it assumed an angelic calmness and repose."[14] The use of different ink in the last sentence may mean that the author had a particular interest in this item and returned to it after first writing it. The combination of moral certainty and personal feeling inspiring this note is rare in Hawthorne, and suggests that he wrote it while his mind was fixed on challenging O'Sullivan. In the memorial essay he said that, while true to the character of his region in all things else, Cilley, by engaging in a duel, had swerved "from his Northern principles in this final scene." He never-theless concluded that even the most rigid might forgive Cilley; his "error was a generous one, since he fought for what he deemed the honor of New England." Hawthorne mailed his essay on April 15, but it was held up until September, awaiting a satisfactory portrait of Cilley to include.

In a letter of November 5, 1838, answering one of October 29 from O'Sullivan, Hawthorne first disposed of business matters between author and editor, and then turned to a discussion already in progress on the Mary Silsbee affair. This is by no means an ordinary letter; the writer had recently been ready to challenge the recipient to a duel, and the subject was the one over whom the duel would have been fought. Mary had trav-eled southwest with her father and her sister from May 31 till August 21, and Hawthorne had been absent and out of communication from July 23 to September 24.

> As touching other matters—in accordance with your exhortations, I have seen our fair friend. Her manner of receiving me was incomparably good—perfectly adapted to the circumstances—altogether beyond criti-cism. It might seem that I should have had the vantage-ground in such an interview—having been virtually invited to it by herself, after expressing a desire and determination to break off all intercourse—and having ex-pressly stated, moreover, that any future intercourse should not be on the ground of friendship. But it was no such thing. All the glory was on her side; and no small glory it is, to have made a wronged man feel like an offender—and that, too, without permitting any direct allusion to the matter in dispute—and to have put on just so much dignity as to keep me precisely at the distance she chose, tempered with just so much kindness that I could not possibly quarrel with her. She was dressed in better taste and looked more beautiful than ever I saw her before; and she, and her deportment and conversation, were all of a piece, and altogether consti-tuted a perfect work of art—meaning the phrase in no bad sense.
>
> Yet the interview has not produced the effect that she anticipated from it. I came away with, I think, the most dismal and doleful feeling that I ever experienced—a sense that all had been a mistake—that I never really loved—that there was no real sympathy between us—and that a union could only insure the misery of both. Surely, having this feeling, it is my duty to stop here, and to make her aware that I have no further aims.
>
> It is fit that I do her all manner of justice, as respects her treatment of me. Looking back at her conduct, with the light that her last letter has given me, I am convinced that she has meant honorably and kindly by me,—that I have nothing to complain of in her motives, though her ac-tions have not been altogether so well-judged. I now put a different in-

terpretation on the "secret spring," which I was to discover "soon, or
never." It cannot be her father's disapprobation; for I had reason to suppose that he knew something of the affair, and sanctioned it. That
"spring" was within her own heart, and I was to discover it by reflecting
on something that she had formerly revealed to me. I have reflected, and
think that I have penetrated the mystery.

Yes—I will stop here. . . .

If Elizabeth Peabody's statement to Julian Hawthorne is to be trusted,
that Mary Silsbee said she would marry Hawthorne when he had an income of $3,000,[15] the "secret spring" would seem to have been a require-
ment that her husband have such an income as was unlikely for Hawthorne.

In the same letter Hawthorne asked O'Sullivan not to be "one whit the
less zealous" to help him get the Salem postmastership, for the salary
would "purchase other comforts as well as matrimonial ones." Finally he
mentioned a review of *Twice-Told Tales* and remarked, "It makes me smile
to see what a mild, gentle, and holy personage the reviewer makes of
me—living, one would think, in a heaven of peace and calm affection. I
fear you would take rather a different view of me." To such an extent had
understanding and sympathy developed in a few months between the potential duelists.

Hawthorne's readiness to challenge O'Sullivan was out of character for
one with his skeptical outlook, his impatience with enthusiasm, and his
usual insistence that appearances may be deceiving. It may appear less so,
however, when the circumstances and his particular traits of mind and
character are considered. He was in love with Mary Silsbee—or thought
he was—and Mary was both fond of intrigue and adept at achieving her
goals (on the testimony of Elizabeth Peabody). With Hawthorne convinced that O'Sullivan had wronged Mary Silsbee and that dueling had a
role in society beyond the reach of both law and public attitudes, and with
his customary readiness to accept obligations, his action is in a degree un-
derstandable.

He did not stop seeing "our fair friend" entirely. The following January
1 he wrote Longfellow he had been at Miss Silsbee's "some time since";
and on May 19, after she had become engaged to Jared Sparks, he wrote
O'Sullivan, enclosing what she said was the last of O'Sullivan's letters to
her. She had burned Hawthorne's letters, at his request. The last knot of
their entanglement was loosed, he said. "She is to be married, I believe,

this week—an event which, I am almost sorry to think, will cause a throb
in neither of our bosoms." His visits to Salem had been so short that he
had found no time to call on her for the past three months; but, he concluded, "I understand that I am still in good odor with her. As for me, I
have neither resentment nor regrets, liking nor dislike—having fallen in
love with somebody else."

10

The Peabodys

When Hawthorne told John Louis O'Sullivan in May, 1839, that he had no regrets at the marriage of Mary Silsbee, "having fallen in love with somebody else," he meant Sophia Amelia Peabody, whom he had known since November, 1837. During the intervening year and a half, Sophia's sister Elizabeth had declared among her acquaintances and in print that Hawthorne was a genius; and it came to be thought by some—perhaps including Elizabeth—that he and Elizabeth would be married. Eventually it developed that Sophia was the one who had gained his heart—during the months in which he proposed to fight a duel on Mary Silsbee's account and in which he discovered that he had only thought he loved Mary. The ironic reversals in these developments would not be out of place on Hawthorne's fictional pages.

While Nathaniel and his sisters were growing up on Herbert Street, the Peabody family lived close by on Union Street. The father, Nathaniel Peabody (1774–1855), was a dentist; his wife, Elizabeth Palmer (1778–1853), was a teacher. There were three sons: Wellington (1816–38), who died in New Orleans; George Francis (1813–39), who died at home after a lingering illness; and Nathaniel Cranch (1811–81), a pharmacist who brought up a family in Boston and the vicinity. The oldest of the daughters, Elizabeth Palmer (1804–94), remembered playing with the Hawthorne children and studying her lessons with Elizabeth Hawthorne. She began teaching early; her sisters, Mary Tyler (1806–87) and Sophia

The Peabody House, Charter Street, Salem; Dr. Grimshawe's House and Charter Street Graveyard. Courtesy of the Essex Institute, Salem, Mass.

Amelia (1809–71), were among her pupils and themselves became teachers. When Sophia was ten years old, Elizabeth more or less formally accepted responsibility for her education, and the rest of her life took pride in Sophia's development. She told Julian Hawthorne in old age that she had intended to write an account of his mother, "the rarest specimen of woman" she had ever known.[1]

After living in Boston from 1824 to 1828, the Peabody family returned to Salem and settled in 1835 beside the Charter Street Cemetery, where John Hawthorne and other early Hawthornes were buried. Sophia suffered from severe headaches and was particularly affected by noises. When Mary was employed in 1833 as tutor in a Cuban family, Sophia accompanied her, hoping to benefit from the climate. She kept a descriptive and narrative journal which reached home in installments, was carefully preserved, and was known as her "Cuban diary." Returning to Salem in

1835, she began a routine that her family, particularly her mother, considered essential for her. She spent much of the time in her upstairs room, often in bed, reading, writing, and drawing when she felt able, shielded from noises and all unpleasantness that could be kept from her, and repeatedly the object of medical attention and experimentation. At intervals she left her room, occasionally went out, and even visited in Boston. The fact that she experienced no recognizable ill effects from these violations of her invalid's routine—and seems to have experienced none in Cuba—suggests parallels between her case and that of Elizabeth Barrett. The question of additional parallels would have to await the appearance of a counterpart to Robert Browning.

Before rejoining her family at Salem in 1837, Elizabeth Peabody had won a place on the Boston intellectual and literary scene. She had served as secretary to William Ellery Channing (1780–1842), the distinguished Unitarian theologian, and would publish her reminiscences of him in 1877. She had been associated with Amos Bronson Alcott (1799–1888) in his experimental school and, with assistance from Sophia, had recorded and published the proceedings of the school, A Record of a School (1835). Initiative and unconventionality were lifelong traits of hers. James Freeman Clarke said that she "was always engaged in supplying some want that had first to be created"; Van Wyck Brooks, looking back from another age, called her "one of the old reformers who never lost her zest."[2] In opinions attributed to Ralph Waldo Emerson, "her journals and correspondence would probably be a complete literary and philosophical history of New England during her long life," and "her recollections and correspondence would comprise the spiritual history of her time."[3] She concluded that the discovery and encouragement of a literary genius such as Nathaniel Hawthorne was a cause worth her efforts, and she supplied his early biographers freely from her recollections.[4] She said that after taking note of "The Gentle Boy" and other sketches and tales published anonymously in the early 1830's and being told that Nathaniel Hawthorne was the author, she thought first that the name was assumed and afterward that the author was Elizabeth Hawthorne, who as a child had seemed to her a genius. During a call on Herbert Street, she learned from Louisa that not her sister but her brother was the author. To her declaration, "But if your brother can write like that, he has no right to be idle," the reply was, "He never is idle."

After a year, as Elizabeth Peabody remembered, she received a copy of Twice-Told Tales, inscribed to her "With the respects of the Author." She invited Hawthorne and his sisters to call, using the pretext that she wanted to ask him about the rates paid by the *Democratic Review*. On Thursday, November 16, Mary Peabody wrote her brother George, then in New Orleans, that Hawthorne had come the preceding Saturday evening and, although he had "lived the life of a perfect recluse till very lately" and suffered "inexpressibly in the presence of his fellow-mortals," had promised to come again. In Elizabeth Peabody's memory, Hawthorne's first visit had taken on momentous and romantic qualities by the time she described it for Julian Hawthorne forty-five years later: "a great ring came at the front door. I opened it, and there stood your father in all the splendor of his young beauty, and a hooded figure hanging on each arm." While the callers were looking into some new volumes of Flaxman's drawings, she ran upstairs and told Sophia she must dress and come down; " 'you never saw anything so splendid—he is handsomer than Lord Byron.' " Sophia said it would be ridiculous to get up, and added, "If he has come once he will come again."[5]

Elizabeth Peabody was never slow in promoting a good cause, such as drawing her new acquaintance out of his seclusion. According to her account, she elicited for him the next day a dinner invitation from Frederick Howes, whose sister-in-law, Susan Burley, presided over something of a literary salon where Saturday evening meetings were held and where Hawthorne became a regular attendant. She recalled also a dinner at the home of his friend Caleb Foote, editor of the *Salem Gazette*, after which Hawthorne escorted her home and talked about the way his family lived on Herbert Street. She quoted him as saying, "we do not live at our house, we only vegetate. Elizabeth never leaves her den; I have mine in the upper story, to which they always bring my meals, setting them down in a waiter at my door, which is always locked. . . . My mother and Elizabeth each take their meals in their rooms. My mother has never sat down to table with anybody, since my father's death. . . . It has produced a morbid consciousness that paralyzes my powers." The extent to which Elizabeth Peabody's memory adjusted itself to a view she held is suggested in her remembering that Hawthorne told her on this occasion that he had not seen his sister Elizabeth for three months—a few days earlier, by her own account, he and both his sisters had called together at her house. In reproducing this conversation Elizabeth Peabody was reaching back in memory almost half a century. Much closer to her were Hawthorne's several prefaces and his *American Notebooks* in which had been included selections from letters to his fiancée exaggerating his earlier isolation as a way of declaring his happiness in his new love. Julian Hawthorne as a rule allowed her creative recollections to stand or modified them further on his own.

When Hawthorne was introduced to Sophia on his second visit, as Elizabeth Peabody recalled for Julian Hawthorne in 1882, "he rose and looked at her—he did not realise how intently"; and when she spoke afterwards, "he looked at her with the same intentness of interest. I was struck with it, and painfully. I thought, what if he should fall in love with her; and I had heard her so often say, nothing would ever tempt her to marry, and inflict upon a husband the care of such a sufferer."

Hawthorne's daughter Rose gives a delightful version of his "capture by the admiring enemy," the Peabody sisters.[6] The pursuit seems to have progressed slowly at the beginning because of competition for Hawthorne's attention. It was three months after he first met the Peabodys that he championed Mary Silsbee, and a full year before he decided to make her aware that he had "no further aims." Early in 1838 Elizabeth Peabody borrowed the *American Monthly Magazine,* in which she liked Hawthorne's sketch of Fessenden more than she had expected. She borrowed *Twice-Told Tales,* since her copy had been sent to her brother in New Orleans, for Sophia planned to make drawings suggested by the tales and wanted to begin at once, Elizabeth wrote. In a postscript she invited Hawthorne to tea.

The notebook Hawthorne kept in the winter of 1837–38 contains abundant items on young women and love. No dates appear between December 6, 1837, and the next June 15, but the notes are in the order of composition and can be read for rough parallels to the Mary Silsbee affair and his growing interest in the Peabody sisters.[7] Two early notes read, "Love 'wisely but not too well' "; and "In love-quarrels a man goes off on stilts, and comes back on his knees." A story might be written "to show how we are all wronged and wrongers, and avenge one another; as a man is jilted by a rich girl, and jilts a poor one." An entry on the following page suggests that he was thinking of O'Sullivan under Mary Silsbee's accusation, "A man living a wicked life in one place, and simultaneously, a virtuous and religious one in another." Next is the report of the White-Finch duel, already cited, on which Hawthorne had obviously strong feelings. At this point is summarized a report on "Elizabeth P. Peabody's great-grandmother," the first mention in the notebook of anyone in the Peabody family.

Three pages farther on are a series of references to the Peabodys, including several quotations from Sophia's Cuban diary. These notes were written after the death of Cilley on February 24, when visiting between the two houses had become frequent. One letter Elizabeth Peabody wrote Ebe has as its subject a recent Thursday evening they had spent together, probably March 1, following Cilley's death.[8] Seeing how much Hawthorne was suffering, she had been loquacious, so as not "to seem to claim entertainment" from him, and had thought it would be good "if he could divert himself with the German." (For several months the possibility of studying German was under discussion; on March 21 Hawthorne asked Longfellow to recommend a German grammar.) If he should take government employment in Washington (which he was still considering more than a month later) she hoped he would remain "free to return to freedom." Before closing her letter, she unabashedly declared Hawthorne a genius, in Emersonian language: "he is one of Nature's ordained priests, who is consecrated to her higher biddings"; he "has been gifted and kept so choice in her secret places by Nature thus far, that he may do a great thing for his country." In government employment, he would be associated with men unable "to appreciate the ambrosial moral *aura* which floats around our ARIEL,—the breath that he *respires*. I, too, would have him help govern this great people; but I would have him go to the *fountains* of greatness and power,—the unsoiled souls,—and weave for them his 'golden web,' . . . —it may be the *web of destiny* for this country."

At about the time of this letter Elizabeth Peabody wrote an essay-review of *Twice-Told Tales* for the *New-Yorker* of March 24. In the *American Monthly Magazine* for March was a favorable review of moderate length and considerable perception. Since Park Benjamin, an acquaintance of the Peabodys for several years, was editor of the *American Monthly* and had editorial connections with the *New-Yorker*, he no doubt was to some degree responsible for both of these reviews. In her essay of more than three thousand words, Elizabeth Peabody assessed Hawthorne's work in much the same tone and language she had used in writing his sister. If his genius preserves "the sweetness and purity of its fountains, far up in the solitudes of nature," she wrote, "he will take his place amongst his contemporaries, as the greatest artist of his line; for no one of our writers indicates so great a variety of the elements of genius."[9] She found him Wordsworthian—and in her estimation she could offer no higher praise; she quoted from Emerson and left no doubt that she read Hawthorne as a Transcendentalist.

By March 3, 1838, Hawthorne had revealed to the Peabody sisters much about his plans, his disappointments, and his hopes—both literary and personal. On that day Elizabeth wrote in his behalf to Horace Mann (1796–1859), whom her sister Mary would marry in 1843. Since Mann was secretary of the Massachusetts Department of Education and was planning to launch a series of innovative schoolbooks, she wanted to tell him about the author of *Twice-Told Tales*, "a man of first rate genius," who wanted to take up "some serious business for his life," she said, and had in mind a "great moral enterprise . . . —to make an attempt at creating a new literature for the young. . . . He says that were he embarked in this undertaking he should feel as if he had a right to live." She had persuaded him not to give up the idea, and wanted Mann to recommend him to the publisher Nahum Capen as a writer for the young. Mann looked into *Twice-Told Tales*, but concluded that the need in children's schoolbooks was for something "nearer home to duty & business."[10] Hawthorne was at the time discussing with Longfellow a plan for collaboration in writing for children.

During much of the year 1838 the three Peabody sisters cultivated social relations against a frustrating reluctance of the Hawthornes, particularly Elizabeth, whom they found shy and uncommunicative and unpredictable. Elizabeth Peabody was convinced that, for Hawthorne's own good, the good of literature, and in turn the good of the nation, he needed to be drawn out of his owl's nest, and was not put off by Ebe's aloof or cool responses to invitations to visit or go walking. Notes, books, flowers, and felicitations were exchanged. Invitations to walk sent from Charter Street to Louisa or Ebe regularly had appended, "Don't forget to ask your brother." Although Sophia did not venture out when there was an east wind, she was a vicarious presence on all the excursions.

The death of Jonathan Cilley was much in Hawthorne's mind during the spring of 1838. He met Bridge in Boston on March 17, doubtless to consult with him on the memorial essay he was to write. Meeting on the street, he and Longfellow arranged to dine together the next day, but a snowstorm prevented Longfellow from coming in from Cambridge. Longfellow called on Hawthorne in Salem on March 25, continuing their talk about writing a children's book together. After finishing the memorial essay on April 19, Hawthorne went to Augusta on May 3, when Cilley's remains were brought there from Washington for burial. Discussion of the duel continued months longer in Congress and in the newspapers. In the spring and into summer, the Peabody sisters were much in Hawthorne's company and in his mind, perhaps welcomed in part because of the distress he felt over Cilley's death and over the affair of Mary Silsbee. It was during those months that he decided he did not love Mary, and solved the puzzle—by a route most of the way uncertain and often disturbing—as to how Elizabeth and Sophia Peabody stood in his affections.

After his first call on Charter Street in November, 1837, Hawthorne probably wrote O'Sullivan in behalf of Elizabeth Peabody, for her essay on Emerson appeared in the *Democratic Review* for the next February. He wrote again on April 19, asking O'Sullivan to consider a second essay of hers. He noted that her article on Emerson was "particularly poor," and added, "She is somewhat too much of a theorist, but really possesses knowledge, feeling, eloquence, and imagination." The new article, "On the Claims of the Beautiful Arts," which O'Sullivan accepted for the November *Democratic Review*, argues that funds, both private and governmental, should be provided for the training and support of artists, for they are "a natural priesthood of the race" and "perpetual symbols of the Divine in human nature." She was speaking about painters and sculptors but might have applied the same terms to literary artists, as she had done in reviewing *Twice-Told Tales*.

In the middle of April, 1838, Elizabeth Peabody went to West Newton and stayed through the summer with her brother Nathaniel. She and Hawthorne corresponded, sending letters in the packets she exchanged with her family. He had set the condition that she "never show his letters." Sophia, keeping her informed on the news of Salem, wrote from the assumptions that she and both her sisters had feelings close to reverence for Hawthorne, and that his chief interest was in Elizabeth. She could write the more freely because she and others assumed that, being an invalid, she could never think of marriage, though once she spoke of a possible husband, and hastened to add that she had forgot. Every letter showed frank adoration of their new friend: he had been "very brilliant" or "brilliantly *rayonnant*"; she saw in his "celestial expression . . . a manifestation of the divine in human"; his smile had "the innocence and frankness and purity of a child's soul in it"; once when he came and she could not go downstairs, she "must needs dream about him all night." Remembering the mission to draw him out of his seclusion, she exclaimed, "Only think what progress! To come and propose a walk at mid-day!" [11]

Sophia revealed, perhaps consciously, Hawthorne's growing attention to her. Once when he took her for a Saturday evening at Miss Burley's, "He was exquisitely agreeable, and talked *a great deal*, and looked serene and happy and exceedingly beautiful." He so admired a forget-me-not she had painted that he had it mounted in a pin and said it was too fine for him to wear. His notebook bears testimony that Sophia was increasingly in his mind. With the Cuban diary in his room, he copied out several passages, including Mary's description of Sophia "stretched in a calm and deep slumber, unconscious of all that may be going on,—and then waking up as if she were just made." Several items he indicated were written by Sophia; and his note "Cleaning an obscure old picture," related to her diary account of cleaning and restoring a portrait in Cuba, furnished the central episode in his tale "Edward Randolph's Portrait."[12] She wrote her sister that he thought he could make many stories from her "works," and later she said, "To be the means in any way of calling forth one of his divine creations is no small happiness—is it? How I do long to read it." When Elizabeth was expected home for a visit on May 13 but failed to come, she may have detected something of a role being over-played in Sophia's extravagant report of Hawthorne's disappointment, and in the statement in another letter, "I don't think he wants to come now you're gone."[13] When Elizabeth had questioned whether her interests were being overlooked when Hawthorne came to Charter Street, Sophia answered, "I am diverted at the idea of our cutting *you* out, of all things. Mr. H's coming here is one sure way of keeping you in mind, and it must be excessively tame after the experience of your society and conversations, so that I think you will shine more by contrast."[14]

As Elizabeth Peabody recalled for Julian Hawthorne the courtship and engagement of his parents, she pictured herself as the confidant of both and seems to have believed that she herself, by implication deliberately, had brought about "their heaven made union." There are clear hints in her recollections, however, that she was surprised and disappointed when they became engaged. After telling how she had corresponded with him while she was in West Newton in the spring and summer of 1838, she continued, "And while this was going on, he saw a great deal of your mother, who, having grown up with the feeling that she was never to be married, looked upon herself as a little girl." But her letters show her disappointed in her correspondence with Hawthorne. When a letter she expected did not come, she instructed Sophia late in May, to tell him she "could only be consoled by having one *very soon.*" She continued, "His last letter was queer—and written in some sort of excitement—when he was fighting with some unhappiness I know. He said in it he had written me quite a different sort of letter which he had concluded not to send and I wrote to him to send it by all means."

Perhaps Hawthorne was displeased to have it reported that he was engaged to two women, meaning Elizabeth Peabody and Mary Silsbee; perhaps his interest in Sophia made his relations with Elizabeth uncomfortable. More likely, the unhappiness Elizabeth detected had grown from his distress early in the year and his uncertainty about his future in other areas as well as in love. He was uncomfortable, surely, because, during the time his interest in Sophia was growing, she and Mary Silsbee exchanged visits often. Two ideas for stories written out in his notebook, probably in May, suggest that he was trying to make up his mind about Mary Silsbee. One story would picture a woman able to sympathize with all emotions but having none of her own. Another would "look at a beautiful girl, in her chamber or elsewhere, and picture all the lovers, in different situations, whose hearts are centered on her." He continued writing Elizabeth, but with what she thought disturbing hiatuses. He was not seen much on Charter Street, Sophia said, since "the *furor scribendi*" had been upon him. He had vowed to begin on May 1 rising at dawn; and his notebook furnishes evidence that he had resumed authorship in earnest; he wrote full reports on his visit with Bridge in Boston on June 16, the crowds on the Salem streets July 4, the Charter Street graveyard, an exhibition of wax models, and an all-night excursion off Salem harbor.[15]

On July 23 Sophia wrote Elizabeth of reading in the *Gazette* "an exquisite production about the moon which I am sure he wrote after that night upon the sea. It combines the wit, humor, pathos, wisdom and grace of his style and matter." Her reference was to a sketch entitled "Journey of the Moon on a Summer's Night," signed Jonathan Oldbuck, which appeared in the *Salem Gazette* on July 20, reprinted from the New York *Mirror* of July 14. Hawthorne's "night upon the sea" was the night of July 7, which he had spent on a boat outside the Salem harbor and had recorded in his notebook. The sketch chronicles a night's journey of the moon, accompanied by a little star and a comet, describing its effects on various earth creatures and the spectrum of blame and praise elicited from them. It is an allegory worthy of Sophia's characterization, illustrating the rewards of attention to duty, in the face of misunderstanding and condemnation. Hawthorne had left Salem the day Sophia read the sketch, but she vowed to find out from his sister Elizabeth whether he had written it. She saw Elizabeth later in the day, but no evidence has come to light that Hawthorne was indeed the author.[16]

Writing in his notebook between July 10 and 13, 1838, Hawthorne referred to the character Ladurlad in Robert Southey's metrical romance *The*

Curse of Kehama, who had relief from the tormenting fire in his heart and brain while visiting a celestial region, but had it rekindled when he returned to earth. "So may it be with me in my projected three months seclusion from old associations." Two additional notebook entries make clear what his purpose was in breaking away more thoroughly this summer from his normal associations than ever before. In one he supposes that a person imputes "to various persons and causes" a series of events that have destroyed his happiness, but "finds out that he is himself the sole agent. Moral, that our welfare depends on ourselves." An entry on the next page supposes that one is able for a moment to perceive his own "mental and moral self, as if it were another person." When this happens, "the observer sees how queer a fellow he is."[17] Sophia reported to Elizabeth that he was determined to be let alone. He would not tell his mother where he would be, and thought of changing his name, "so that if he died no one would be able to find his gravestone." He first said he would write nothing, but then decided to keep a journal for the benefit of future stories.[18]

Following the last entry quoted above, Hawthorne wrote the words "other book," meaning that for the record of his summer travels he would resume the notebook he had used in Maine the preceding summer and on three trips to Boston afterward. He left for Boston by stage on July 23, boarded the afternoon train for Worcester, put up there at the Temperance House, and the next morning took the stage for Northampton. Leaving Northampton between one and two in the morning, he reached Pittsfield in the afternoon and, arriving at North Adams a day later, July 26, decided to remain for a while. Breaking his resolution to let no one know his whereabouts, he wrote his friend David Roberts in Salem, asking him to forward any letters arriving for him and to pass along any news there might be, but to tell no one of hearing from him. He expected to move into New York State after two or three weeks and to be home "in the course of six months." As it turned out, he stayed at a North Adams tavern until September 11 and reached Salem on September 24, after an absence of two months.

On his second day at North Adams, Hawthorne began what would be his fullest and most extended notebook record up to this time. He described scenes, narrated episodes he observed or heard about, noted ideas and materials for stories; but he was most alert to the people he encountered. One day's entry opens "Remarkable characters:—" and by the time he left North Adams, he had accumulated a gallery of characters, so fully and carefully presented that they could be transferred a dozen years later, with but slight changes, into the story "Ethan Brand." He followed the roads and paths over the hills; again and again he bathed in the streams; he visited a lime kiln; and he narrated episodes of a dog chasing its tail, a showman with his diorama, an old man telling of a daughter who had been lured away from home and into some undefined life of shame. He attended commencement at Williams College and was present at two funerals, once walking in the procession behind the corpse.[19] In his portraits of those he met in the stagecoaches, in the tavern, on the village streets and country roads, he is a fiction writer, seeking to understand and reveal, with the tolerance of a creator rather than a judge. The evidence of the notebook is that, like Ladurlad, he had found relief from the burning within his heart and mind; but events following his return home indicate that his internal fires were not rekindled, as were Ladurlad's.

During Hawthorne's absence Elizabeth asked Sophia, July 25, to persuade Ebe to write her, on the promise that she would burn the first letter; they then "could make a bargain about the rest of the correspondence." Writing to Ebe later in the summer, she indicated a skein of misunderstandings between her and Hawthorne for which she thought Ebe responsible. She had told Ebe earlier that in Hawthorne's letters of the last spring "were evidences of his 'unequal spirits,' " and when she suspected Mary Silsbee to be coquetting, she had interpreted the letters in that light. But she had not "meant to say those letters were an outpouring of distressed feelings in a confidential way. . . . They were not confidential at all"—the fact that they were not as confidential as she had expected made her more certain he had something to conceal. "You cannot think how ridiculous it makes me appear in his eyes," Elizabeth said, because he thought she had cited his letters as proof that he was sentimental. She "could not tell him the *truth*," she continued, "without seeming to contradict his sisters point blank—a thing which he could not bear.—So it must remain with you—to undo this mischief." She desperately feared she would lose his confidence and his correspondence, "his sensitiveness to ridicule being perhaps the most active principle that regulates his conduct."

In her earnest attempts to discover what caused Hawthorne's "unequal spirits," Elizabeth Peabody had speculated in ways that Ebe did not understand or did not approve. She felt a need also to write Sophia on July 31 a long explanation that is not fully clear and concludes by asking that they not discuss the subject again. In saying, finally, that she had not been honest in not claiming or asking for what she desired, she seems to mean that she had not revealed the nature and the extent of her interest in Hawthorne. When he reached home from North Adams, Elizabeth Peabody had returned from West Newton and was preparing to continue promoting his literary career and her own interest in him. She delayed a week in sending word of his return to Sophia, who was in Boston studying modeling with the sculptor Shobel Vail Clevinger (1812–43), wanting it to be a surprise to her, she said. The first Sunday he was home, September 30, she invited him and Ebe for a walk, which produced an adventure. Ebe became separated from the others, and all three had grown frantic before she was found. Hawthorne must idealize the adventure, Elizabeth wrote Ebe the next day, picturing Ebe as a coquettish girl who was being punished for tormenting a faithful swain; further, "I must figure in it as some old aunt." She asked Ebe to tell her brother that she wanted him to take her to Miss Burley's.

Hawthorne had returned to much the same relations with the Peabodys he had left in July. All assumed, it seems, that his interest was in Elizabeth rather than Sophia, and some thought there was already an engagement. But in the pursuit of Hawthorne's affection, Sophia's success was growing. Because he liked her Cuban diary so much, she dedicated the last portion of it to him, "inscribed by his true and affectionate friend."[20] He paid her a compliment in his preface to the separate edition of "The Gentle Boy" which included her drawing of Ilbrahim. After she had begun a drawing of Hawthorne on December 5, she wrote him the following day, "I had never beheld your face before I tried to produce it. Now I shall recognize it, I am certain, through all Eternity." An entry in his notebook reads, "S. A. P.—taking my likeness, I said that such changes would come over my face, that she would not know me when we met again in Heaven. 'See if I don't,' said she, smiling. There was the most peculiar and beautiful humor in the point itself, and in her manner, that can be imagined." At the top of the next page, he wrote "Decr 12th, 1838," and marked it with double lines before, after, and beneath; on the same line he wrote "Do. [Ditto] 29th," similarly marked.[21] It can be supposed that he was marking those as memorable days in his love affair.

On January 5, 1839, when Sophia was in Boston again to study modeling, Mary Peabody wrote her a cryptic letter. Mary Foote, Sophia's close friend and now wife of Caleb Foote, had been asked what she "thought of the *report*—and whether she thought it ever *would be true.*" Mary Foote's reply was that she did not think so, and was "quite possessed with another idea, and dreamed that dream again last night." Mary Peabody added, "I did not tell her I agreed with her, though I do in my heart." Both of them believed—and wanted to believe—that an engagement likely to develop would involve Sophia rather than Elizabeth. Whether Elizabeth then had a similar belief is not revealed, but since her efforts to further Hawthorne's career continued after she knew he and Sophia were engaged, perhaps her affection for her sister and her dedication to the support of genius were enough to overcome any jealousy and hurt she may have felt.

In later years, reports were repeated and refuted over and over that Hawthorne had been engaged to Elizabeth Peabody before becoming engaged to Sophia. Robert and Elizabeth Barrett Browning were cited as a source of the report in Italy, and it was said that Mrs. Browning's poem "Bertha in the Lane" was a retelling of the episode, but the parallels are slight.[22] It is clear that Elizabeth wanted closer ties with Hawthorne, thought the ties were closer than they were, and did not hesitate to enlist Sophia and Ebe to help her cause. In writing O'Sullivan on May 19, 1839, that he had fallen in love with someone besides Mary Silsbee, Hawthorne said of Elizabeth, "She is a good old soul, and would give away her only petticoat, I do believe, to anybody that she thought needed it more than herself." He continued to value her generosity and her help, and once said he appreciated her true worth more than anyone else; but he was exasperated by her habit of taking command and of instructing those around her. Hawthorne appointed Elizabeth Peabody "his future biographer"; so she wrote Louisa on November 9, 1838, in a letter in which she said that she wanted him to come for tea and to accompany her to visit Mary Pickman. The next day she asked Louisa to give her brother a note when he came down to dinner, adding, "He said he was going to write today. . . . We will not interrupt the bird in his song. I *wonder* what sort of a preparation he finds an evening of whist, for the company of the Muse!" Her reference was to the card games Hawthorne played occasionally. The players assumed names which appeared regularly in their correspondence for years afterward: Hawthorne was Emperor; Louisa, Empress; Susan Ingersoll, Duchess; Horace Conolly, Cardinal; and David Roberts, Chancellor. Once Elizabeth Peabody wrote Ebe from the Peabody house that Mary Silsbee had come for a visit and was ill downstairs. She added, "nevertheless I guess your brother would not be refused if he were to send in his name—and very likely it would be a pleasure that would help on her recovery—especially if he contradicts her all the time in the *piquante* man-

ner of an *accomplished coquette.*" The two Elizabeths could speak casually—
and sarcastically—of the Mary Silsbee affair.

If Elizabeth Peabody failed to gain the personal relations with Hawthorne she wished, she did not fail to find the employment she thought he
should have. In the spring of 1838 she had spoken about him to the publisher Nahum Capen, following up herself the suggestion she had written
Horace Mann. Convinced that the government must provide for its artists,
and that Hawthorne must have employment that would leave him time for
writing, she wrote about him in October to her friend Orestes Brownson,
who had been appointed steward of the Chelsea Marine Hospital, at the
good salary of $1,600 a year and with only slight duties to perform.
Brownson consulted the official responsible for his own appointment,
George Bancroft (1800–81), historian and politician, now collector of the
Port of Boston. Bancroft had supposed Hawthorne would not accept an
appointment but would be delighted to give him a place, so Elizabeth
wrote Ebe in October. Her own opinion was that Hawthorne would never
be happy in Salem, that he should be in Boston. She would write Brownson again, telling him all "the *immunities* the office must have."

She told Bancroft herself, and also wrote his wife, that Hawthorne
needed an income but must have time for writing. A clerkship would not
do, for he "would not like a master." Hawthorne wrote O'Sullivan on
November 5 that Bancroft had offered him "the post of Inspector in the
Custom-House, with a salary of $1,100," and he thought he would accept
it, but he was still interested in the Salem post office. If Mary Silsbee had
dropped out of his matrimonial considerations, she had been replaced by
Elizabeth or Sophia Peabody—or perhaps both of them as yet. Their presence in Salem and the presence of his whist companions and the "Hurley
Burley," as Susan Burley's literary Saturday evenings were called, might
combine to make him prefer the Salem post office to the Boston custom-
house. At the end of the year 1838 he might have predicted, with more
certainty than while visiting Bridge a year and a half earlier, that his fortune was due to change.

11

Port-Admiral

For the opening of the year 1839, Hawthorne wrote "The Sister Years," a New Year's address by the newsboy to his customers, to be published by the *Salem Gazette* on a broadside and in its regular issue. He had written "Time's Portraiture" as the address of the preceding year. Sophia read this new address on the train to Boston with Elizabeth and afterward wrote her father it was "so full of wisdom and so illuminated with wit." She and Elizabeth met George Bancroft at tea, and back in Salem on January 4, Elizabeth told Hawthorne that he was to have an inspectorship in the Boston custom-house. "He *felt very bad* when he found he actually got it," Mary Peabody wrote Sophia the next day; but in his notebook he entered the date in large capital letters. On the same page he quoted Sophia: "There is no Measure for Measure in my affections. If the Earth fails me in love, I can die and go to GOD"; [1] and on the next page he quoted her again. He may have felt bad about going to Boston because he would be leaving her in Salem.

In writing Bancroft his acceptance on January 11, he postponed deciding between an ordinary inspectorship and one "more laborious and responsible" that was also available. The next day he wrote Longfellow that he was going to accept the post, having as much confidence in his "suitableness for it, as Sancho Panza had in his gubernatorial qualifications." He would be "a sort of Port-Admiral, and take command of vessels after they enter the harbor, and have control of their cargoes." Understanding that he would have considerable free time, he meant to employ it in sketches with such titles as "Passages in the life of a Custom-House Officer"—"Scenes in Dock"—"Voyages at Anchor"—"Nibblings of a Wharf-Rat"—"Trials of a Tide-Waiter"—"Romance of the Revenue Service." He would write also an ethical work on Duties, and already he had begun to think import duties much more important than moral and religious duties. That he expected to do more serious writing than the works he listed for Longfellow is indicated by the full notebook entries he began at once. He thought he could furnish within a year or less five articles requested by George P. Morris of the *Mirror*. In a letter of January 17 to the secretary of the treasury, Bancroft identified the appointee as "Biographer of Cilley," and hence a member of the Democratic Party.

A note Elizabeth Peabody sent Ebe, probably the day before Hawthorne left for Boston, suggests how earnestly she undertook to preside over developments. She would spend the evening on Herbert Street while Hawthorne attended a smoking party, and he would come home between ten and eleven to escort her home. Not feeling well, she stayed at home, but sent a drawing for Ebe to keep "until Post Office time when Nathaniel must bring it round to me. . . . Pray write me whether you are reconciled to N's going to Boston." Earlier she had told Ebe that he could come to see them often on the train. (The railroad between Salem and Boston had opened late in August.)

Hawthorne went to Boston January 16, was entered on the payroll the next day, and soon was at work on the wharves. On February 6 he was aboard the *Thomas Louder*, a schooner unloading coal from New Brunswick, and began keeping a notebook account. Spending the first day on deck, he suffered from the cold; the next day, seated before a fire in the cabin, "the rudest and dirtiest hole imaginable," he could count the tubs of coal being craned out of the hold, and was comfortable; but on reaching home, he found that he had "swaggered through several thronged streets with coal streaks" on his visage. Four entries dated from February 7 to 19, 1839 (VIII, 187–95), constitute the only notebook record of his two years in the Boston custom-house. He soon realized that in an occupation "so alien to literature" the writing he had expected to do was impossible. In writing Longfellow on May 16 that he thought of publishing a second volume of tales, he said, "If I write a preface, it will be to bid farewell to literature; for, as a literary man, my own occupations entirely break me up." His duties were not laborious, but he was cramped by a sense that he was not master of his own time and motions. The habits of composition he had formed during his twelve years under the eaves allowed no interference. A few months later, on November 17, he wrote Sophia Peabody that his thoughts sometimes wandered back to literature and he had "momentary impulses" to write stories. But for the present he could do no more than record for future use aspects of the life he was leading and the people he observed. His letters to her furnish much of the record he might have put into his notebook. When *Passages from the American Notebooks* was first published, the letters were in fact inserted to cover this period and his period at Brook Farm.

One task Sophia had in Boston in January, 1839, was to have a new engraving made of her drawing of the character Ilbrahim in "The Gentle Boy." Elizabeth Peabody recalled long afterward that when Sophia showed Hawthorne the drawing and asked whether her figure looked like his Ilbrahim, the answer was, "He will never look otherwise to me!"[2] Susan Burley paid for a separate edition of the story, with Sophia's drawing as a frontispiece and with a preface by the author that speaks first of the tale with his usual modesty and then of the drawing, "a creation of deep and pure beauty," which had received "the warm recommendation of the first painter in America," Washington Allston. *The Gentle Boy:A Thrice-Told Tale* was announced in December but bore the date 1839. The engraver, Joseph Andrews, had "changed the position of the eyes of Ilbrahim—darkened the brows—turned the corners of the mouth down instead of the original curve—enlarged the under lip—and indicated the chin" (IX, 567). Sophia wrote out exact directions for restoring the drawing, and a new engraving was included in later copies. Caleb Foote in the *Salem Gazette* and Park Benjamin in the *New-Yorker* and in the *New York Review* divided their praise between the author and the illustrator.[3]

Soon after Hawthorne arrived in Boston, he was calling regularly on Sophia at the Samuel Hoopers'. In early February he paid her a two-hour visit, according to her diary letter home; he called each of the next two days; the fourth day he came in the morning and later in the day to escort her in making a call, but instead they "walked round the common and saw the sunset."[4] After Sophia had returned to Salem, he saw her there March 3. Three days later he wrote:

> Do grow better and better—physically I mean, for I protest against any spiritual improvement, until I am better able to keep pace with you—but do be strong, and full of life—earthly life—and let there be a glow in your cheeks. And sleep soundly the whole night long, and get up every morning with a feeling as if you were newly created; and I pray you to

lay up a stock of fresh energy every day till we meet again; so that we may walk miles and miles. . . . Am I requiring you to work a miracle within yourself? Perhaps so—yet not a greater one than I do really believe might be wrought by inward faith and outward aids.

This is the earliest of Hawthorne's letters to be preserved and published as "love letters," but it was not the first that passed between them. In it he replied to her query whether she was writing too often. They had agreed to write every two weeks, and she was to expect his letters on alternate Saturdays. Her letters did not interfere with his "worldly business," he assured her, adding, "I keep them to be the treasure of my still and secret hours, such hours as pious people spend in prayer; and the communion which my spirit then holds with yours has someting of religion in it." As if anticipating the urging of this letter, she had undertaken to convince others—and herself—that her health was improved. In January, she had written home how well she felt and how one after another of her friends exclaimed that she had a "beautiful appearance," "had gained flesh," and was "less of a wraith" than last October.

A letter from Mrs. Peabody at about this time shows that she sensed a change in Sophia's outlook and was frightened by it. In a reiterated sermon on prudence, she mentioned her daughter's "confiding affection," her "sensitive nature," "shattered nerves," and "precarious health," and begged her to arm herself "at all points for disappointment, or rather to prevent disappointment." "Be strong of faith," she said, "—be candid— anchor your soul on domestic love." Prudence "will tell you that the love which settles down upon the household circle 'tho more quiet, is deeper, steadier, more efficient than any other love."

Hawthorne's letters in April show that he and Sophia had been certain of their love for some time, whether avowedly engaged or not. Because it was assumed that her health would not allow her to marry, they seem not to have considered themselves engaged until near the middle of the year. On the day Hawthorne wrote O'Sullivan that he was "in love with somebody else," not Mary Silsbee, May 19, 1839, Sophia wrote her sister Elizabeth a letter showing that both sisters knew Sophia was the object of Hawthorne's love. Both could still share unreservedly their adoration of Hawthorne and his writings, and Elizabeth was as diligent as ever in striving to brighten his literary future. While visiting the Emersons at Concord, she wrote Sophia on June 23 to report "down in Herbert Street" that Bancroft had called Hawthorne "the most efficient and best of the Custom House officers." Noting that Emerson had not read any of

Hawthorne's writings, she added, "He is in a good mood to do so, however, and I intend to bring him to his knees in a day or two, so that he will read the book, and all that Hawthorne has written." A letter of Sophia's a week later indicates that there had been moments of strain between the two sisters. She reported that on a recent Saturday when Hawthorne came to Salem and the wind kept her from going out, they "were both so virtuous that he went alone to Miss Burley's." If Elizabeth could know what a sacrifice that was, she continued, "you would never again accuse either of us of disregard of the claims of others." Sophia wrote on July 5, "My wildest imaginations, during my hours of sickness in the past, never could have compassed such a destiny. . . . Now I am indeed made deeply conscious of what it is to be loved."[5] She spoke of her "sickness in the past," not in the present.

On November 25, 1839, Hawthorne asked Sophia to remember a year back. He had forgotten how far they had then "advanced into each other's hearts." Now they knew they had found "all that life has to give—and a foretaste of eternity." The earliest love letters dwell largely on spirit. Answering on April 30, 1839, doubts of hers about the continuance of their "earthly and external connection," he wrote, "Let us trust in GOD for that. . . . Pray, for my sake, that no shadows of earth may ever come between us, because my surest hope of being a good man, and my only hope of being a happy man depends upon the permanence of our union." Late in the spring suggestions of physical being appeared more often. A letter of May 26, written after Sophia had visited nearly a month in Boston, has three lines cut out, the earliest of many letters with excisions made by Sophia before leaving them to pass into other hands after her death. In addition, references to bosoms, kisses, and the like were inked out and omitted from the printed *Love Letters*,[6] but most of them have since been deciphered and restored. Hawthorne never read her letters without washing his hands, he wrote her, and he thought them "too sacred to be read in the midst of people."[7]

His letter of July 24 declared that God had married her soul to his. "We *are* married! I felt it long ago." When their lips last touched, was it not the symbol of a bond between their souls, infinitely stronger than any "external rite could twine around" them? "The world might, as yet, misjudge us; and therefore we will not speak to the world." Soon they called each other husband and wife, and they both enjoyed writing "Sophia Hawthorne." Excisions are more frequent in his letters, as are marked-out but decipherable passages speaking of the time when they would sleep on the same pillow and he would awake with her in his arms. In September Hawthorne wrote to a dual person, his Dove and Sophie Hawthorne, and on October 23 he wrote that, when he fancies his Dove breathing gently in his arms (inked out), "lo and behold! there is the arch face of Sophie Hawthorne peeping up" at him, and he meditates "what sort of chastisement would suit" the misdemeanors of his "little Wild-Flower." But, "Methinks a woman, or angel (yet let it be a woman, because I deem a true woman holier than an angel)—methinks a woman, then, who should combine the characteristics of Sophie Hawthorne and my Dove would be the very perfection of her race." He loves "each best, and both equally," but has "reason to apprehend more trouble with Sophie Hawthorne" than with his Dove.

Hawthorne lived at 8 Somerset Place until George Hillard, a young lawyer with literary interests, invited him in October, 1839, to occupy a parlor and bedroom in a house he was taking at 54 Pinkney Street. He hung two of Sophia's paintings, added furniture of his own, and bought volumes of Milton and of Coleridge, the first from a list of books he and Sophia would want.

Even in vowing his devotion to the composite spiritual Dove and naughty Sophie Hawthorne, he left no doubt that his individuality, his personal integrity, would remain intact. He told her about declining social invitations he knew she would have liked for him to accept: Bancroft's for dinner with Margaret Fuller December 4, 1839, when Providence had given him "some business to do," for which he was very thankful; and twice to Dr. William Ellery Channing's. Once he wrote, "What possible good can it do for me to thrust my coal-begrimed visage and salt-befrosted locks into good society?"[8] When Sophia proposed to send him a ticket to a series of lectures by Emerson, he declined, saying that he did not profit much from attending lectures. The question whether to go hear Father Taylor preach was not answered at once and prompted him to forewarn his Dove on such matters. After ten years at sea, Edward Thompson Taylor (1793–1891) entered the ministry of the Methodist Episcopal Church and became minister of the Seamen's Bethel Church in Boston, where he was supported by William Ellery Channing and Ralph Waldo Emerson, and was acclaimed a genius by Elizabeth Peabody. He was Melville's original for Father Mapple in *Moby-Dick*. On March 15, 1840, Hawthorne asked Sophia whether she had expressly commanded him to hear Father Taylor, saying that she knew how difficult it was for him "to be touched and moved, unless time, and circumstances, and his own inward state, be in a 'concatenation accordingly.' " Two weeks later, he begged her to "grant him indulgence for one more Sabbath." Their sympathy was broad and general enough, he said, to secure their bliss, without their "following it into minute details." Although doubtful that he would appreciate this "Son of Thunder," he made her a promise: "at some auspicious hour, which I trust will soon arrive, Father Taylor shall have an opportunity to make music with my soul. But I forewarn thee, sweetest Dove, that thy husband is a most unmalleable man;—thou art not to suppose, because his spirit answers to every touch of thine, that therefore every breeze, or even every whirlwind, can upturn him from his depths."

On a Sunday afternoon walk in Boston two months later Sophia asked why he was so grave and two days later received further self-analysis and warning: "Lights and shadows are continually flitting across my inward sky, and I know neither whence they come nor whither they go; nor do I inquire too closely into them. It is dangerous to look too minutely at such phenomena." If there should be at any time "an expression unintelligible" from one of their souls to the other, they would not "strive to interpret it into earthly language, but wait for the soul to make itself understood." It was not that he loved mystery, but that he abhorred it, and felt that "words may be a thick and darksome veil of mystery between the soul and the truth which it seeks." He apologized for this "misty disquisition," but the sermon had created itself for her, and he had no right to keep it back.[9] He no doubt saw that it stated the terms which must govern his relations even with his wife. It implies a reason for his lifelong reticence in social conversation and suggests a meaning for the "eloquent silence" that impressed associates from his college days onward.

Two years later, on February 27, 1842, Hawthorne wrote Sophia again on the same subject. After explaining "the strange reserve, in regard to matters of feeling, . . . this incapacity of free communion" within his family that kept him from telling his mother and sisters about his engagement, he continued,

> I tell thee these things, in order that my Dove . . . may perceive what a cloudy veil stre[t]ches over the abyss of my nature. Thou wilt not think that it is caprice or stubbornness that has made me hitherto resist thy wishes. Neither, I think, is it a love of secrecy and darkness. I am glad to think that God sees through my heart; and if any angel has power to penetrate into it, he is welcome to know everything that is there. Yes; and so may any mortal, who is capable of full sympathy, and therefore

Nathaniel Hawthorne, 1840; portrait by Charles Osgood. Courtesy of the Essex Institute, Salem, Mass.

worthy to come into my depths. But he must find his own way there. I can neither guide him nor enlighten him. It is this involuntary reserve, I suppose, that has given the objectivity to my writings. And when people think that I am pouring myself out in a tale or essay, I am merely telling what is common to human nature, not what is peculiar to myself. I sympathize with them—not they with me.

He wanted it understood that, at the level of day-to-day affairs also, his individuality and independence must be inviólable. He would take her for his "unerring guide and counsellor in all matters of the heart and soul," and he would "never transact any business without consulting" her, but she must expect him at times to follow his own follies and have his "own way, after all." [10]

When Hawthorne wrote Longfellow on November 20, 1840, that he had been "occupying Grandfather's Chair, for a month past," he knew his meaning would be understood, for they had discussed writing for children, possibly in collaboration, and now his first book for children, except for *Peter Parley's Universal History*, was near completion. With reduced shipping and consequently less time required on the wharves as winter approached, he had begun a writing program that he hoped would provide the income he needed. Over the past three years he had cited children's books as one kind of drudgery to which he might turn his pen. Convinced that he felt a genuine mission in writing for children, Elizabeth Peabody had succeeded in interesting the publisher Nahum Capen in him; and late in 1839 he wrote Sophia that Capen wanted him to "manufacture" a book. [11]

When Longfellow first broached the subject of collaboration on a book of fairy tales in March, 1838, Hawthorne encouraged the idea, proposing that he appear as contributor and Longfellow as editor. He had considered "overtures from two different quarters, to perpetrate children's histories and other such iniquities," but with this book they might "make a great hit, and entirely revolutionize the whole system of juvenile literature." He went on, "I think that a very pleasant and peculiar kind of reputation may be acquired in this way . . . ; and what is of more importance to me, though of none to a Cambridge Professor, we may perchance put money in our purses." On March 25 Longfellow went to Salem and had a long talk with Hawthorne, whom he called in his journal "a man of genius and a fine imagination." When Hawthorne was back from North Adams, he wrote that he thought the "Boy's Wonder-Horn" could be finished in a short time. Longfellow did not want to go ahead with the collaboration, it seems, for Hawthorne wrote on January 12 of not being allowed to "blow a blast upon the 'Wonder-Horn' " and threatened "to set up an opposition—for instance, with a corn-stalk fiddle, or a pumpkin vine trumpet." He added that he meant to write for children, either in his own book or in the series planned by the Board of Education, to which he had been invited to contribute. [12]

In his letter to Longfellow on January 12, 1839, Hawthorne opened discussion of another collaborative project. He had learned that Longfellow
was "thinking of a literary paper," and wrote, "Why not? . . . And whatever aid a Custom-House officer could afford, should always be forthcoming." The subject probably had further discussion after his move to Boston, and on August 31 he asked his friend Caleb Foote for estimates of
costs and advice on arrangements for a daily which he and Longfellow, he
said, contemplated establishing in Boston. Longfellow continued for at
least two years to think of editing a newspaper, but he and Hawthorne
seem not to have pursued further the idea of a joint undertaking.[13] During
the years 1839 and 1840 they had literary discussion often, at dinner or in
the evening. The letters and notes they exchanged show a consistent geniality and mutual regard.

Late in November, 1840, appeared *Grandfather's Chair*, the first of three
small books for children; *Famous Old People* was out early the next year,
and *Liberty Tree* a few weeks later. Elizabeth Peabody was the publisher.
The Peabody family had moved to Boston in July and settled at 13 West
Street, where Elizabeth opened a bookstore specializing in foreign books,
and also published books and the journal of the Transcendentalists, the
Dial. Hawthorne's prefaces to these volumes were modest but showed that
he had worked with a clear purpose and believed he had succeeded. As
was his habit, he disparaged the books in writing Sophia; he imagined
himself bearing the unsalable remnant of the first volume on his back, as
Christian bore his burden. Thinking of the income they would need to be
married, he had a motive that should draw out his whole strength, he said;
yet, he must keep such considerations out of his mind, because external
pressure disturbed rather than helped him.[14] In late 1840, he hoped to
edit for the publisher Munroe a "Grandfather's Library," which would
reprint books of his own and also works he would choose by other authors. He sent enthusiastic suggestions for drawings Sophia would make
to illustrate new editions of his three little books. Nothing came of the
plan, but Munroe contracted to publish a new edition of *Twice-Told Tales*
with a second volume added (1842).

Late in 1840 Hawthorne began to savor in advance the freedom he
would gain when he escaped from the custom-house. He lamented the
time he had lost, but was pleased to be "entitled to call the sons of toil" his
brethren and to know how to sympathize with them. The experiences he
had acquired might in the future "flow out in truth and wisdom." If
Sophia were with him on his salt-vessels and colliers, she might describe

or draw pictures that he could weave into works of his own when he was "again busy at the loom of fiction." The letters to Sophia paint a steadily darkening picture of the custom-house and work aboard the ships, especially dark when he thought of being exiled from his writing desk. But he reminded himself at intervals that this passage would be important in the sum of his real existence. He had gained worldly wisdom in "this earthy cavern," and also wisdom "not altogether of this world"; he had gained a stronger sense of "power to act as a man among men." Nevertheless his Dove must not pride herself too much in her husband's utilitarianism; "he is naturally an idler, and doubtless will soon be pestering thee with his bewailments at being compelled to earn his daily bread by taking some little share in the toils of mortal man." His habit of looking at himself with a wry smile produces often such a note as this, on May 29, "I am convinced that Christian's burthen consisted of coal; and no wonder he felt so much relieved when it fell off and rolled into the sepulchre. His load, however, at the utmost, could not have been more than a few bushels; whereas mine was exactly one hundred and thirty-five chaldrons and seven tubs."[15]

Hawthorne was a dependable customs officer and took satisfaction in doing his work well. He reported that once when his authority was "put in requisition to quell a rebellion of the captain and 'gang' of shovelers aboard a coal-vessel," he "conquered the rebels, and proclaimed an amnesty." It was on this or a similar occasion that a ship captain, report has it, undertook to interfere with his management of the ship during the unloading and provoked "such a terrific uprising of spiritual and physical wrath, that the dismayed captain fled up the wharf and took refuge in the office, inquiring, 'What in God's name have you sent on board my ship as an inspector?'"[16] More than once when Colonel Joseph Hall, supervisor of the measurers, was ill, Hawthorne substituted for him. Fretting on one such occasion, because he could not visit Sophia as he had expected, he wrote her of continued absences among the other measurers, "so that if thy husband were to be as careless of his duty as they, the commerce of the United States would undoubtedly go to wreck."[17]

When O'Sullivan wrote suggesting a clerkship in Washington, Hawthorne replied on March 15, 1840, that he would consult Franklin Pierce, but that the move he would most welcome would be a move out of governmental employment. "There is a most galling weight upon me—an intolerable sense of being hampered and degraded; and I am afraid I should feel it much more in the situation which you recommend, than in my present one." If he stayed in his present office until May, 1841, as he intended, he would be paid $2,000 and was resolved to save at least half of it. He could write nothing for the *Democratic Review*, he had written O'Sullivan after a few weeks in the custom-house, and must declare himself "no longer a literary man." In a letter of April 20, 1840, he returned to the subject and indicated that he was not likely to stay in the custom-house another year. He lamented that he had spent every golden day of the last summer "in one filthy dock or another," without any of the travel that had been habitual with him. "What a miserable sort of thrift is it, to give up a whole summer of this brief life for a paltry thousand or two thousand dollars! I am a fool."

A walk into the country with Hillard on June 21 was but a taste of the freedom he hoped to regain, and to share with Sophia. She had been visiting the Emersons at Concord and had sent Emerson's invitation for him to come for a visit. She had told her Concord friends of her engagement. On October 12 Hawthorne invited Longfellow to come in from Cambridge and dine with him, for he had broken his "chain and escaped from the Custom-House." By November 15 he had sent in his resignation, but he wrote Longfellow November 20 that, since Bancroft would be inconvenienced if a replacement had to be appointed before the end of the year, his "good nature was wrought upon to hold the office a'while longer." He nevertheless was not free at the end of the year, and on January 8 he wrote Bancroft, again asking to be relieved. It seems that in consenting to remain in office, he had the understanding, with Colonel Hall if not with Bancroft, that he would have only nominal duties, in the light of extra work he had done while other measurers were absent over the past several months. There had been whispers to others, not to him, "as to the dishonorableness" of his "proceedings"; he explained to Bancroft that he felt no obligation either to return any part of the pay he had received or to work a longer time, but did not want to compromise Bancroft. By January 10 Hawthorne was at last free of the custom-house and went for a week to Salem. He and Sophia had decided, before the end of November, on a future in the communal society to be established at Brook Farm.

12

Mr. Ripley's Utopia

Hawthorne had intended to leave the custom-house as soon as he could secure an adequate income from another source. He once said that, when he had saved $1,500 from his salary, he would retire and get his bread however he could. A letter to Sophia on November 27, 1840, shows that he had already decided to join "Mr. Ripley's Utopia," where he expected to make a home for her. They had been engaged nearly two years.

Elizabeth Peabody's bookstore at 13 West Street was a center for much of the Transcendental discussion and planning. She published the *Dial* there (1840–44); and Margaret Fuller gave there some of the conversations she began in November, 1839, and continued in four series.[1] Elizabeth continued her association with Dr. William Ellery Channing, Ralph Waldo Emerson, and other proponents of the new thought, and joined Sophia in drawing Hawthorne into the social and intellectual ferment of Boston, and in acquainting him with the thinking and the theorizing that directed George Ripley in his plans for the Brook Farm community at West Roxbury.

Brook Farm was a product of social, religious, and intellectual ferment. An application, a manipulation of the "Newness," in the phrasing of the time, inspired by the Transcendentalist view that the divine is present in all, by faith in human and hence social perfectibility, and by zeal for reform, it was rich in the support the "like-minded" afforded each other in the talk and the correspondence that abounded among them. The Brook

Farm Institute of Agriculture and Education had neither the religious affiliation of many communal societies of the age nor the economic and industrial purpose of others. Ripley came to the community from a ministry of fourteen years in Boston, and ministers were so plentiful among the members that Louisa Hawthorne, who had some of her brother's sense of the incongruous, opined that they would be able to have preaching whenever they wanted it. Ministers found readily acceptable the concepts of "thy brother's keeper" and congregational action for common betterment. But at Brook Farm the focus was not on doctrine or morality so much as on the arts, taste, and social discourse. The kinship was less to the church than ·to the lyceum, Elizabeth Peabody's Wednesdays at her bookstore, Margaret Fuller's "conversations," or the Saturday evening meetings Susan Burley held in Salem. The efficacy of concerted activity, especially talking, went without saying.

Elizabeth Peabody directed her usual vigor and dedication to George Ripley's plan. Her statements in letters and in essays printed in the *Dial*, the magazine of the Transcendentalists, suggest the force she brought to bear on those around her. A meeting for all interested in Brook Farm was scheduled at the Peabody house on May 11, more than a month after the members began living at the community. Elizabeth was already certain in her own mind what had to be done: the community must buy the farm; ten thousand dollars would be needed beyond the amount the associates would provide. And "Ripley still relucts from printing even a prospectus," she lamented. In her first essay on the undertaking, "A Glimpse of Christ's Idea of Society," in the *Dial*, October, 1841, Elizabeth Peabody postulates for communal action a broad foundation in religion and social philosophy. Her second essay, "Plan of the West Roxbury Community" (not published until January, 1842, when the community had been an actuality for eight months), asserts with emphasis that the aim is to provide "LEISURE TO LIVE IN ALL THE FACULTIES OF THE SOUL" and that *"labor is the germ of all good."* Ignoring any antagonism between these assertions, she speaks mainly of practical matters: there will be cooperation rather than competition; "none will be engaged merely in bodily labor"; "all labor is sacred" and bodily labor will have the same rate of pay as intellectual; the organization "admits all sects"; and, a favorite theme of hers, "communication is the life of the spiritual life." The founders of the community had by then bought the farm, and she expected them at any moment to "call together those that belong to them." Perhaps having in mind herself and other advocates of the new dispensation who did not join the community, she said: "Ameliorations of present evils, initiations into truer life, may be made we believe anywhere," even among those "not able to emancipate themselves from the thraldom of city life."[2] During the weeks in the summer and autumn of 1840 when Hawthorne was meeting apostles of the "Newness," he was restless at the custom-house, disillusioned with politicians, and above all eager to be married. Even though he lamented the "Babel of talkers" around Sophia on West Street, wished Margaret Fuller would lose her tongue, and recoiled from the veneration of Emerson that prevailed at the bookstore, he was comfortable enough with the broad principles being formulated to cast his lot at Brook Farm, even though most of those proclaiming the new social order did not. Freed from his office at the custom-house in January, he concluded his affairs in Salem and Boston and on April 12, soon after George and Sophia Ripley had moved to the farm, he walked the nine miles from Boston in a snowstorm and the next day addressed a letter to Sophia from his "polar Paradise." Nearly thirty-seven years old, he still had few encumbrances. When he had hung the two drawings Sophia had given him for his room in Boston, he could feel that he had completed the move.

The seriousness of committing his future with Sophia to the experiment at West Roxbury did not dampen his usual playful spirit. Recognizing that he would be leaving familiar grounds and taking up manual labor that he had never known before, he wrote her of his impending "journey to the far wilderness," and continued in a similar tone of fun and banter when he wrote about his arrival at the farm, his severe head cold afterward, his learning to milk a cow, and his endless days of forking manure. A tone of conscious—perhaps determined—acceptance appears also in his early letters from the farm, with overtones of tolerance and optimism, and no more solemnity than in saying, for example, "I trust that thou dost muse upon me with hope and joy, not with repining." He referred to his "perils and wanderings," his "brethren in affliction," and his "gallant attack upon a heap of manure," which he denominated the "gold mine" and said had a fragrance to which he was "peculiarly partial." He felt "the original Adam reviving" within him and one day chopped hay "with such 'righteous vehemence' (as Mr. Ripley says)," that he broke the machine. Among the cows, he reported, was "a transcendental heifer" belonging to Margaret Fuller, "very fractious . . . and apt to kick over the milk pail"; she "hooks the other cows, and has made herself ruler of the herd, and behaves in a tyrannical manner." Sophia knew best, he said, "whether, in these traits of character, she resembles her mistress." Three days later he continued the characterization, which Sophia would of course know how to read: The herd had "rebelled against the usurpation of Miss Fuller's cow," so that she kept close to him, "rather than venture among the horns of the herd. She is not an amiable cow," he said; "but she has a very intelligent face, and seems to be of a reflective cast of character. I doubt not that she will soon perceive the expediency of being on good terms with the rest of the sisterhood."[3]

After Hawthorne had visited Sophia in his second week at the farm, a sober note began to sound in his letters. Only once had he taken a walk; he could not have imagined the depth of the seclusion; he read no newspapers, and hardly remembered who was president. Writing his sister Louisa on May 3 a letter signed Ploughman, he recited with pride the kinds of work he had done, no doubt thinking of the effect his account would have on his mother and sisters. The ten members of the community, including children, ate together, and "such a delectable way of life" had not been seen on earth "since the day of the early Christians." They rose at half-past four, breakfasted at half-past six, dined at half-past twelve, and went to bed at nine. The letter was going to a household where Elizabeth's habit was to read much of the night and sleep till noon, and members of the family rarely took meals together. He wore cowhide boots with two-inch soles, which he said he would wear when he visited Salem. Reports from Mr. Ripley's utopia were readily sent by its members and eagerly received in the world outside. Elizabeth Peabody passed along a report reaching her that Hawthorne, after two weeks at the farm, had taken hold with the greatest spirit "and had proved himself a fine workman." Sophia Ripley wrote at about the same time: "Hawthorne is one to reverence, to admire with that deep admiration so refreshing to the soul. He is our prince—prince in everything—yet despising no labour and very athletic and able-bodied in the barnyard and field."[4]

When Articles of Association were adopted on September 28, 1841, Hawthorne became a trustee and one of the three directors of finance. In telling Sophia of these "august offices," he cautioned her not to "expect that a man in eminent public station will have much time to devote to correspondence with a Dove." He held shares 18 and 19, selling at $500 each, paying five percent interest, and subject to redemption on a year's notice. The Articles, together with the rules adopted on October 30, provided a minimum of organization. Only like-minded members would be voted in by the trustees; all activities except work would be voluntary; reasonableness would prevail. Faith in the innate goodness of all, in the response of generosity to generosity, in the elevating influences of the arts, and in the virtue of remoteness from cities and society left no requirement for compulsions or authority or government.

There was little in Hawthorne's past, or in the social and intellectual outlook mirrored in his writings, to suggest that he would join a social experiment that Emerson and Margaret Fuller thought vague and impractical. The skepticism of social panaceas, the love of solitude, and the independence of thought and action that were paramount with him might have been expected to allow him only slight patience with a scheme that aimed to achieve "the healing of the nations" and the improving of "the race of men" by assembling participants to live in dormitories, eat at community tables, labor in unison, and converse as a major activity. As he looked back on this episode afterward, he declared that his faith in mankind and his belief in brotherhood were strong enough for him to think the scheme worth his best efforts. Such is the view of Miles Coverdale in *The Blithedale Romance*, who on this matter probably speaks for the author. Hawthorne had enough daring and firmness of purpose to take risks that others of greater faith might avoid. He harbored doubts, and he did not join in the verbal crusade launched by Elizabeth Peabody and others; yet he went to Brook Farm at its founding and provided nearly one-fourth of the capital raised for the venture. Within a few weeks he realized that he had made a mistake. Without the element of desperation in his search for a way of life that would allow him to marry and also to follow authorship, he would have known that there would be at the farm less possibility for the thinking, musing, and dreaming required by his writing than at the custom-house. Since Ripley's plan included separate family residences in the future, Hawthorne later made a payment of $500 toward the building of a house. The prospect of life with Sophia in a cottage of their own, with all but total personal freedom beyond the three hours of work a day that supposedly would provide their living, was so inviting that he could look beyond the intervening hardships.

Some of Hawthorne's letters to Sophia before he went to West Roxbury and for a while afterward indicate that he had fallen considerably under the spell of talk at the Peabody bookstore; but as often as not he gave the language an ironic tone. When Ripley brought four black pigs to the farm, Hawthorne called them "four gentlemen in sables," and presumed they were "members of the clerical profession." Ripley had invited them to become members, Hawthorne said, and, in language that Elizabeth Peabody might have written, he added that he could not "too highly applaud the readiness" with which they had "thrown aside all the fopperies and flummeries, which have their origin in a false state of society." In the tone of amused self-depreciation normal to his letters, he noted that these four "looked as heroically regardless of the stains and soils incident to our profession, as thy husband did when he emerged from the gold mine." He concluded by exclaiming, "Ownest wife, thy husband has milked a cow!!!" [5]

His letters to Sophia trace out the changes in his outlook. On May 4 he might have been writing with the pen of George Ripley or Elizabeth Peabody, in telling about "work under the clear blue sky, on a hill side," when it almost seemed that he was "at work in the sky itself." He was working with ore from the gold mine, which "defiles the hands, indeed, but not the soul." He did not believe he could suffer his separation from her, if he "were not engaged in a righteous and heaven-blessed way of life." He was not long in noticing his lack of privacy, and by June 1 he was convinced that this life gave him a greater "antipathy to pen and ink" than he had at the custom-house; his "soul obstinately" refused "to be poured out on paper"; and he was convinced "that a man's soul may be buried and perish under a dung-heap or in a furrow of the field, just as well as under a pile of money." He could never comfort himself "for having spent so many days of blessed sunshine here."

Sophia visited him and on May 30–31 wrote him her conclusions after seeing him among the Brook farmers.[6] More than ever before, she wanted a home, "where but one thing should be going on, instead of twenty things." He, of all men, should have a sacred retreat. She had seen plainly that he was not leading his ideal life and that, "during the various transactions and witticisms of the excellent fraternity," his was the expression of a witness and hearer rather than of comradeship." So distressed was she at the amount of hard work he did that she begged him never to write in weariness, even to send her a brief note. Brook Farm was beautiful, far surpassing her expectations. Most joyfully would she dwell there "for its own beauty's sake," independently of him, and she could not conceive a greater felicity than living with him in a cottage on one of the lovely sites. "Tell me, ye angels, is your Elysium sweeter or more satisfactory than this will be? Cannot we, ye flaming ministers, walk with God on those green hills, as well as on the amaranths of Heaven? . . . Oh how plainly, in some sharp moments of intellectual vision, do I see that our Heaven is wherever we will make it." On the evidence of this example, her love letters were appropriate answers to his, rich in the color and imagery that came natural to her, and with avowals of love in the language of reverence.

The work grew more burdensome, and Hawthorne was no more willing to shirk it than he had been at the custom-house, lest his share fall on others. On July 9, he said in a brief note to Sophia that his brethren would have to work later because of the few moments he was giving her. At haying time, they returned to the field after supper. A month later, he wrote, "Even my Custom House experience was not such a thraldom and weariness; . . . labor is the curse of this world. . . . Dost thou think it a praiseworthy matter, that I have spent five golden months in providing food for cows and horses?" When he would give up a full membership in the community at the end of August and become a boarder, as he planned to do, a greater weight would fall away "than when Christian's burthen fell off at the foot of the cross." With only a week to "remain a slave," he spoke in exasperation of the "troublesome and instrusive people . . . in this thronged household."[7] Meanwhile he had written George Hillard on July 16 that he could not furnish "that infernal story" he had promised, probably for an issue of the *Boston Book* to follow the one Hillard had edited in 1840. "Stories grow like vegetables," he had said, "and are not manufactured, like a pine table. My former stories all sprung up of their own accord, out of a quiet life." He could not write a letter because of a "crop of blisters" on his hands, nor must Hillard "expect pretty stories from a man who feeds pigs." He might have remembered what his sister Louisa had written him as early as May 10, that his hard work passed Elizabeth's comprehension and their mother groaned over it. A month later Louisa asked why he worked all day for his board, instead of the three hours promised, and what was the use of burning his brains out in the sun, when he could do anything better with them. He had not gone home or written since the middle of June. His plans included a week in Salem early in September.[8]

Hawthorne was slow deciding what to do, in part because the future of the community was not clear. Warren Burton withdrew and left in July and Frank Farley's health was in such a state that Hawthorne accompanied him to the seashore. In a letter of July 18 to David Mack, with whom he had talked at Brook Farm a week earlier, he laid out his views: Ripley placed greater importance on physical labor and on the success of the farming venture than Hawthorne and others did. They felt no constraint from Ripley as to the amount of work they did, but they felt constrained nevertheless, for they feared that failure in the immediate undertakings would be "inauspicious to the prospects" of the community. It had been Hawthorne's desire to give his best efforts in the first year's farming, and to give Ripley's "experiment a full and fair trial." His hope of finding a home for Sophia had given him a personal motive for bearing all the drudgery of the summer. He had decided not to spend the winter at the farm unless certain that a house would be ready for him and Sophia in the spring; by late August he had concluded that they must make other plans for a home, for he doubted that Ripley would succeed in buying the farm.

At Salem on September 3 Hawthorne had the feeling that he had been away from Brook Farm twenty years, which he took to be proof that his life there had been "an unnatural and unsuitable, and therefore an unreal one." He wrote Sophia, "It already looks like a dream behind me. The real Me was never an associate of the community; there has been a spectral Appearance there. . . . But be not thou deceived, Dove of my heart. This Spectre was not thy husband." Those who took his brown and rough hands as evidence to the contrary did "not know a reality from a shadow." While away from Brook Farm, he began thinking again about his literary career. He would take up his pen again, freed from the drudgery of the fields, but he expected it to be a long time before he could "make a good use of leisure," either for enjoyment or for literary work. Back in the "queer community" on September 22, after an absence of three weeks, which seemed half a lifetime, he doubted that he could write there the children's book he had in mind. Without "the sense of perfect seclusion" that had always been essential, the best he could do was "observe, and think, and feel," storing up materials for later use.

On one of his walks he discovered a grapevine that had "married against their will" numerous trees and shrubs; he climbed high into a white pine tree and ate purple grapes from a vine that grew nearly to its top. He accompanied William Allen, the experienced farmer of the community, to the fair to purchase four pigs; he stood watching the swine in their pen one day; once he followed a wood-path across a rail-fence and along a stone wall. Although not obliged to work, he one day helped gather apples, and another day helped dig potatoes. He stored in his notebook a detailed account of a young seamstress from Boston. A picnic party on September 27 peopled the woods with masqueraders. Later there were childish games, in which other grown people took part, while he looked on, he wrote in his notebook (VIII, 201–3), for his nature was to be "a mere spectator both of sport and serious business." Emerson and Margaret Fuller joined the assembly, and there "followed much talk." Hawthorne had written Sophia on September 23 about "some tableaux last night," that were "very stupid, (as, indeed, was the case with all I have ever seen)." Placing this judgment beside an earlier one shows how his outlook had changed. He had written her on May 4 about some tableaux, saying that they went off very well, and he would like to see some arranged by her.

When Hawthorne wrote *The Blithedale Romance* ten years later, he had these notebook passages open before him and, as he said in the preface, "ventured to make free with his old, and affectionately remembered home, at BROOK FARM, as being, certainly, the most romantic episode of his own life—essentially a day-dream, and yet a fact." He had written in his notebook about the picnic party, "It has left a fantastic impression on my memory, this intermingling of wild and fabulous characters with real and homely ones, in the secluded nook of the woods" (VIII, 202). He realized, if not at this time, at least by the time he wrote prefaces to his major romances, that such an intermingling was central to his fictional method.

Although Hawthorne had advanced $500 toward the building of a house, and a few days before leaving the farm in November, 1841, had visited the spot on which it presumably would be built,[9] he did not bring Sophia to live in the community, nor return himself, nor recover the money he had furnished.[10] On October 17 of the next year he resigned as Associate of the Brook Farm Institute. In the meantime he had considered joining a community being established by David Mack at Northampton but had decided against it by May 25, 1842, when he wrote, "it is [my] present belief that I can best attain the higher ends of my life by retaining the ordinary relation to society."[11] His excursion into communal living had not provided the home he wanted for Sophia. He was soon to be married, still lacking the assurance of an income he had sought, but trusting to gain a livelihood in some "ordinary relation to society."

13
Eden Revisited

At the opening of the year 1842, Hawthorne determined to alter his way of life. From his college graduation until January, 1839, there had been little outside hindrance to his writing; editing the *American Magazine* may have helped more than it hurt. But in the last three years his writing had come to almost a complete stop. Aside from his three thin books for children, he had published only the story "John Inglefield's Thanksgiving" (March, 1840), which he passed over in making up collections in 1842 and 1846, before republishing it in 1851. It is a slight story of a wayward daughter who returns briefly to her wholesome family and her suitor, before slipping back to her life of undefined "sin and evil passions." There is a suggestion in the last paragraph that the author saw possibilities he might have developed if circumstances had permitted the musing and dreaming his best works required. "Her visit to the Thanksgiving fireside was the realization of one of those waking dreams in which the guilty soul will sometimes stray back to its innocence."

He had a contract for a new edition of *Twice-Told Tales* and invitations to contribute to the *Boston Miscellany* and to *Arcturus;* but he was slow resuming his pen, as he had predicted, and the first piece he turned out, "A Virtuoso's Collection," in the *Boston Miscellany* for May, was assembled rather than created. This sketch collects in a museum kept by the Wandering Jew scores of items from history, the Bible, mythology, literature, and art, along with a compendium of topics that are treated in others of his works: brotherhood, an elixir of life, matter and spirit, the merits of ancient and modern art. The museum of the Salem East India Society provided some of the items and may have given him the idea for the sketch.[1] In the first two weeks of March, 1842, Hawthorne traveled with Colonel Joseph Hall, his friend in the Boston custom-house, to New York City and to Albany, where he conferred with John Louis O'Sullivan on literary matters, including contributions to the *Democratic Review*. Early in April he was sketching another tale, but he saw nothing printed until January of the next year.

In asking Caleb Foote on January 14, 1842, to repay the remaining $500 of a loan, he probably had in mind an early marriage. His letter to Sophia on March 10 indicates that plans for the wedding were being made; she wrote to Mary Foote on April 22 that it might take place soon. The suggestion that they rent the Old Manse at Concord came from Sophia's friend Elizabeth Hoar, who had been engaged to Ralph Waldo Emerson's brother Charles before his death in 1836. Sophia had pleased her and Emerson with a medallion relief she modeled from a portrait of Charles. With the marriage planned for June, Hawthorne and Sophia went on May 7 to Concord, where, she wrote Margaret Fuller four days later, Emerson accompanied them to the parsonage and to Sleepy Hollow, "over violets and anemones, embellishing the way with perennial flowers of thought." Emerson wrote Elizabeth Hoar the next day that he liked Hawthorne well.[2] The owner of the Manse, Samuel Ripley, had made some renovations and would rent it for $100 a year. When Hawthorne met Emerson at the Boston Athenaeum on May 27, he learned that the Manse garden was making fine progress; Henry David Thoreau seemingly had planted it for the new tenants.

Hawthorne still had not told his mother and sisters about his engagement. Only a few people had been told. In her letter of April 22 Sophia traced out for Mary Foote the steps in which the engagement had been divulged. Because Hawthorne "had powerful reason" for keeping the secret, she had not told even favorite relatives and friends until she moved with her family to Boston in July, 1840. Then she told those who might meet Hawthorne often, since he "wished to come every day." Only recently had the secret been known more widely when she answered a friend's direct question. On June 19 she wrote Mary that she expected on June 27 "to disappear from these regions entirely," but the day for the wedding had not been set.

On February 27, 1842, Hawthorne had taken to Salem Sophia's "parting injunction" to tell his mother and sisters. She could not estimate, he wrote her, what a heavy task she had given him: "We are conscious of one another's feelings, always; but there seems to be a tacit law, that our deepest heart-concernments are not to be spoken of. I cannot gush out in their presence—I cannot take my heart in my hand, and show it to them. . . . And they are in the same state as myself." He offered no explanation except that "this incapacity of free communion" was "meant by Providence as a retribution for something wrong" in their early intercourse. Three months later, he had not told his mother and sisters. That task remained for Sophia. He wrote afterward that the letter she had sent them was "most beautiful," and that they would love her, "all in good time." He knew that for the women in his family time would be necessary; Elizabeth Hawthorne had indicated as much, at least for herself, in answering Sophia on May 23:

> Your approaching union with my brother makes it incumbent upon me to offer you the assurances of my sincere desire for your mutual happiness. With regard to my sister and myself, I hope nothing will ever occur to render your future intercourse with us other than agreeable, particularly as it need not be so frequent or so close as to require more than reciprocal good will, if we do not happen to suit each other in our new relationship. I write thus plainly, because my brother has desired me to say only what was true; though I do not recognize his right so to speak of truth, after keeping us so long in ignorance of this affair. But I do believe him when he says that this was not in accordance with your wishes, for such concealment must naturally be unpleasant, and besides, what I know of your amiable disposition convinces me that you would not give us unnecessary pain. It was especially due to my mother that she should long ago have been made acquainted with the engagement of her only son.

Hawthorne wrote Sophia on June 9 that, upon his arrival at home, his mother had come out of her room at once and inquired very kindly about his Dove. He had been fearful, since "almost every agitating circumstance of her life had hitherto cost her a fit of sickness." But she "had seen how things were, a long time ago"; and, although she had been troubled at first, knowing "that much of outward as well as inward fitness" were necessary for his peace, they now had "her fullest blessing and concurrence." His sisters, too, were beginning "to sympathize as they ought." Elizabeth wrote Sophia June 15, saying she regretted that anything in her previous letter had caused Sophia pain, but saying little that would relieve the pain. "I dare say we shall and must seem very cold and even apathetic to you;

but after you have known us a little while it may be that you will discover more warmth and sympathy than is at first apparent." Their mother resembled her son in disposition, she continued, and was "prepared to receive and love" Sophia as a daughter. She and her sister were not "wanting in that sisterly affection" to which they felt she was entitled.[3]

Ebe's frigidity probably grew from a reluctance to admit another to her brother's affection, a belief that a Peabody was unworthy of a Hawthorne, and a particular antipathy for Sophia. In September, 1847, two years after Hawthorne had moved his family to Salem, and had lived part of that time in the same house with his mother and sisters, Sophia said she had seen Ebe only once in the two years. Writing the children of Uncle Robert Manning in her old age, Ebe often spoke unfavorably of Sophia, once saying, "I might as well tell you that she is the only human being whom I really dislike; though she is dead, that makes no difference; I could have lived with her in apparent peace, but I could not have lived long; the constraint would have killed me."[4] Once the engagement was known, the new relationships were accepted but not stated. Within the Hawthorne family, each member had the right and, by implication, the obligation to conceal all feelings.

Mary Peabody went to Concord at the middle of June and hired a helper to put the Manse in order; Sophia went later for an inspection and a visit among Concord friends, and was back home June 24. The first date set for the wedding was July 4. Returning from Salem on June 27, Hawthorne found Sophia ill. Mary Peabody suggested postponement to July 9, and Sophia was put in the care of Dr. William Wesselhoeft, a Boston homeopathic physician. After learning that she had undergone hypnotic treatment, Hawthorne wrote her on June 30 of being "haunted with ghastly dreams" of being himself magnetized, and repeated cautions he had sent earlier: "Dearest, I cannot oppose thy submitting to so much of this influence as will relieve thy headache; but, as thou lovest me, do not suffer thyself to be put to sleep." His feeling on the matter was so strong, he added, that concealing it would wrong them both.

The wedding took place on July 9, at the bride's home on West Street. Hawthorne wanted the ceremony in the morning, "for it would be strange and wearisome to live half a day of ordinary life, at such an epoch. I should be like a body walking about the city without a soul."[5] The Reverend James Freeman Clarke, minister of the Peabodys' church but not known to Hawthorne, performed the ceremony. Sarah Clarke, sister of the minister, and Cornelia Parks attended Sophia. No member of Hawthorne's family was present.

Ready as usual to see manifestations of concealed meanings, both the bride and the groom were alert to emblems forecasting the future. The wedding day "dawned fair after a long session of clouds and rain," Sophia later wrote in the notebook she kept jointly with her husband,[6] and "while the ceremony was proceeding the sun shone forth with great splendor." On the carriage ride to Concord, just as the dust was becoming inconvenient, she wrote her mother the next day, "down came a diamond dropping, the outskirts of a strong shower farther before us, . . . the most enchanting little bedewing of laughing tears" ever seen. In a driving rain later, the thunder seemed like "celestial artillery" greeting them, "instead of the earthly cannon" Hawthorne said would announce their approach to Concord. When they reached the Manse at five o'clock, Elizabeth Hoar ("Spirit-Elizabeth") had filled all the vases with flowers. Sophia wrote the next day, "It is a perfect Eden round us. . . . We are Adam and Eve and see no persons round!" Thus began the Edenic imagery that was to recur again and again in their thought and speech and was to appear in tales and sketches Hawthorne would write at the Manse. He wrote his sister Louisa on July 10: "The execution took place yesterday. We made a christian end, and came straight to Paradise, where we abide at this present writing. We are as happy as people can be, without making themselves ridiculous." He invited her to be their first guest and added, "in taking to myself a wife, I have neither given up my own relatives, nor adopted others."

Knowing that the question of her health weighed heavily with her family in Boston, Sophia wrote her mother that it was miraculous how well she felt, and her husband looked upon her as "upon a mirage that would suddenly disappear." She felt "a clear new life," which she thought "must be like the Phoenix's when it rises from the old ashes." After a month the Phoenix seemed indeed to have risen, and she wrote her mother the letter about the two of them that she had promised in an earlier letter. She knew the need to console her mother, to declare her affection and her gratitude, without seeming to exult in her new strength and new love. Her mother, a woman of will and practicality, wrote her afterward: "When any one reflects how much I have been with you for thirty years, how fully we shared each other's thoughts, how soothing in every trial was your bright smile and ready sympathy, such an one will give me credit for behaving heroically, as well as gratefully for the blessings left." In another letter Mrs. Peabody declared it a vexation and a grief that her son-in-law had to think of making a living. His family and the whole country possessed something in him that could not be replaced. Her estimate of his worth could not fail to please him; but she had also a certainty as to what should be done and a readiness to offer her opinions that he found uncomfortable. He knew before his marriage that she and her daughter Elizabeth were so convinced of his genius and his mission that they felt a moral obligation to advise him. Her letters suggest that her influence on Sophia had been great. Both had a firm optimism based in religious serenity, a determination to invest all their talents, a reverence for intellectual and artistic gifts, and an alertness to the spiritual wherever it might appear. The mother believed that "the grandeur of earth and sky can be seen and felt while usefully employed as well as if Idle," and that good domestic qualities are not "necessarily at war with the soarings of the imagination or the depths of thought."[7] The mind behind these thoughts appears often in Sophia, but with more astute awareness of the spiritual and with flights of more delicate imagery.

Sophia's sisters had lost none of their eagerness to admire and assist Hawthorne. Mary quoted Colonel Pickman, her uncle, as saying that no one could meet him in the street and not think him a genius; and late in July she told how Elizabeth had recommended him for the editorship of the *Boston Miscellany* and, according to her report, had done it with a masterly hand. After replying on August 20 to a request from Robert Carter for more contributions to the *Boston Miscellany*, Hawthorne spoke of learning through Elizabeth Peabody that the publishers desired him to have a more intimate connection with the magazine than as a contributor, and added that although he had almost promised all his articles to the *Democratic Review*, he was confident he would be released from this obligation "in case of anything like an editorial connection" with the *Miscellany*. He noted on September 2 (VIII, 357) that, according to a report reaching Concord, he was to become editor of the *Miscellany*, but nothing materialized.

The Manse was built in 1765 by the grandfather of Ralph Waldo Emerson, the Reverend William Emerson, whose widow married the Reverend Ezra Ripley and continued to live there. Emerson's father was born in the Manse, and Emerson was living there when he wrote "Nature." The Manse had become vacant after Ezra Ripley died in 1841 at the age of ninety. Hawthorne remarked in the essay "The Old Manse" that he was the first lay occupant and that it was "awful to reflect how many sermons must have been written here." To avoid offending that past, he hoped to write during his occupancy a novel that would incorporate "some deep lesson." The accumulated library in the garret and in an outbuilding was heavy with religious tomes, but he felt no less Christian for passing over "all the sacred part" of the library, for these works contained nothing so real as the newspapers and the almanacs scattered among them. "It is the Age itself that writes newspapers and almanacs," he concluded. "A work of genius is but the newspaper of a century, or perchance of a hundred centuries."

With its exterior "a sober greyish hue," Hawthorne wrote in his journal, the Manse looked antique. The approach, through a fenced lane bordered by rows of trees, increased the sense of remoteness. Through one of its windows the first occupant watched the battle of Concord in 1775, and the present occupants could see the battlefield monument. The Concord River, in view from the back windows, gave Hawthorne an ironic and contrasting symbol he was quick to recognize. Although the fish caught from its sluggish waters tasted of mud, the pond-lilies at its edges connotated such purity and beauty as to symbolize his wife. Sophia's thought and language normally reflected the Transcendental outlook. The extent to which she influenced her husband's outlook is suggested by his saying in his notebook, after observing the trees and rocks reflected in the stream, "It is a comfortable thought, that the smallest and most turbid mud-puddle can contain its own picture of Heaven." He was remembering a statement of hers he had copied into his notebook in 1839, that the sky she saw reflected in the mud puddles showed none of "the foulness of the street."[8] He bathed in the river, but concluded that "one dip into the salt-sea would be worth more than a whole week's soaking in such a lifeless tide."

The Manse was rented furnished, but Hawthorne added the furniture from his bachelor quarters in Boston. Three airtight stoves purchased in November prompted a notebook remark: "Stoves are detestable in every respect, except that they keep us perfectly comfortable" (VIII, 364). The sketch "Fire Worship" (December, 1843) begins with the sentiment of this note, and after recounting an imagined day of Dr. Ripley's before the gracious fireplace of the Manse study, it takes up the idea presented in the sketch "Fire Worshippers" in the *American Magazine* (August, 1836) and develops the dual role of fire at the hearth and at the altar, employing the mixture of fantasy and mock-seriousness that came readily to Hawthorne's mind. Another notebook entry grew from the necessity to replace the cistern at the Manse. "Only imagine Adam trudging out of Paradise with a bucket in each hand, to get water to drink, or for Eve to bathe in!" This new Adam would think himself wronged if Providence did not provide a bubbling spring at his doorstep (VIII, 317).

At the ages of thirty-eight and thirty-three, after three years of uncertainty about Sophia's health and the discouraging prospects for a home and a livelihood, they were determined to savor their happiness fully, as is revealed in the notebook they kept, each writing consciously for the other to read. Hawthorne wrote first on August 5, less than a month after their marriage. His wife had banished him to the study, under "strict command . . . to take pen in hand." But what would he write about? "Happiness has no succession of events," being a part of eternity; and they were living in eternity. "Like Enoch," he said, "we seem to have been translated to the other state of being, without having passed through death. Our spirits must have flitted away, unconsciously, in the deep and quiet rapture of some long embrace; and we can only perceive that we have cast off our mortal part, by the more real and earnest life of our spirits" (VIII, 315).

Although Hawthorne's entries were written for the eyes of his "little wife," they were less like his courtship letters than like his earlier journals, in which he recorded scenes, happenings, impressions, and thoughts to be used later. A new Adam, living a new life with his Eve, found Paradise well worth describing, especially the marvels of nature he had never before observed so steadily or at such close range. He often played with double meanings: Since the butcher called twice or thrice a week, they could improve on "the custom of Adam and Eve" by feasting on "a portion of some delicate calf or lamb. . . . Would that my wife would permit me to record the ethereal dainties, that kind Heaven provided for us, on the first day of our arrival! Never, surely, was such food heard of on earth—at least, not by me" (VIII, 316). After noting casually that his Salem friend David Roberts came for a three-day visit, he added, "My wife shall describe him" (VIII, 362). Sophia warmly disliked Roberts. On September 4, a Sunday, Hawthorne wrote: "My wife went to church in the forenoon; but not so her husband. He loves the Sabbath, however, though he has no set way of observing it; but it seldom comes and goes without—but here are some visitors; so this disquisition must rest among the things that never will be written" (VIII, 358). The interrupted disquisition might have been a supplement to his earlier sketch "Sunday at Home." Writing on the same page, Sophia noted that the visitors were Margaret Fuller and Samuel Gray Ward, and added, "O that they had come later."

Sophia's entries normally abound in extravagances of concept and language. On an outing to pick whortleberries, she had displeased him but "could not comprehend why." She had walked ahead, and he had called her to come back, because she "had transgressed the law of right" in trampling the grass. She was "very naughty and would not obey," and he punished her by staying behind. "This I did not like very well," she wrote, "and I climbed the hill alone. We penetrated the pleasant gloom and sat down upon the carpet of dried pine leaves. Then I clasped him in my arms in the lovely shade, and we laid down a few moments on the bosom of dear Mother Earth. Oh how sweet it was! And I told him I would not be naughty again." [9]

Although the Hawthornes valued the seclusion of their Eden, they were aware of the community and had a part in it. On their walks they might meet up with a fisherman on the river bank or in a boat, or Emerson walking in the woods, or Margaret Fuller reclining near a path in Sleepy Hollow, with a book in her hand, reading or meditating. The Emersons called their second day at the Manse, and a few days later, Emerson brought books and a copy of the *Dial*. George Hillard stopped on the second day with a companion, beginning a journey westward, and came with his wife on August 13, the first house guests at the Manse. Hawthorne's sister Louisa, who continued to be his main link to Castle Dismal, as he called the Herbert Street house in Salem, visited at the Manse from August 20 to September 6. A welcome visitor was George Bradford, a fellow-laborer at Brook Farm, whom Hawthorne invited "to become an inmate" of the family. Hawthorne noted, however, that, with all Bradford's "rare and delicate properties, which make him, in some respects, more like a shadow than a substance," it might be better on both sides if he declined (VIII, 347). Bradford now grew vegetables at Plymouth and sold them in the streets from a wheelbarrow. The moral strength required for this means of livelihood, in company with the utmost gentleness, prompted Hawthorne's admiration. Bradford came to visit several months later, still undecided about moving to Concord. Sophia quoted Hawthorne as saying, "we can see Nature through him straight without refraction." [10]

Hawthorne recoiled from the excessive admiration of Margaret Fuller he found in Sophia and her associates, and in Emerson and others at Concord. From the day of his arrival, he noticed the extent to which the community revolved about Emerson. On April 8, 1843, while Sophia was in Boston, he wrote in the joint notebook about a visit from Emerson (VIII, 371). Knowing that she would "demand to know every word that was spoken," he summarized what Emerson had said about Brook Farm and various residents of Concord, and added, "He seemed fullest of Margaret Fuller, who, he says, has risen perceptibly into a higher state, since their last meeting. He apotheosized her as the greatest woman, I believe, of ancient or modern times, and the one figure in the world worth considering. (There rings the supper-bell.)" He could be sure that, in the alertness to symbols he and Sophia had in common, she would not overlook the ringing of the bell.

Some of the opinions Hawthorne recorded in his notebook—and perhaps some of those he published—were penned as counters in an implicit argument with Sophia, who might introduce Emerson into the notebook as "Plato himself" or might cite an aphorism from one of his essays as absolute truth. He found Edmund Hosmer, the Concord farmer idealized by Emerson in print, to be a "man of sturdy sense, all whose ideas seem to be dug out of his mind"; and he feared that Emerson had done Hosmer a disservice by presenting him as an oracle, with the result that, in assuming the oracular manner, Hosmer lost some of his earlier naturalness. Now and then Hawthorne jotted down a notebook entry to tease his wife about her idol. Emerson came to the Manse once while Sophia was away and took his leave, Hawthorne noted, "threatening to come again, unless I call on him very soon." One Sunday morning, Emerson delayed setting out with Hawthorne and George Hillard for a walk to Walden Pond, "from a scruple of his external conscience, . . . till after the people had got into church" (VIII, 335–36, 372).

Sophia put into the notebook on September 24, 1844, a rejoinder in the continuing, half-playful argument about Margaret Fuller, "Queen Margaret," that she and Hawthorne had carried on at least since he went to Brook Farm. She related—perhaps concocted—a story to prove that a child could discern Margaret's virtue. Her infant of six months, Una, at first gazed at Margaret "with earnest and even frowning brow," for she had found "a complex being, rich and magnificent, but difficult to comprehend and of a peculiar kind, perhaps unique." But in Margaret's arms later, Una examined her again, "smiled approvingly," and remained there "with full content by the hour," having detected "her greatness and real sweetness and love and trusted in her wholly."[11]

On September 27 Hawthorne and Emerson set out on a walking tour, spent the night at Harvard, and walked on the next morning to the nearby Shaker village before turning homeward. There is no evidence in their notebook reports that the two days increased the understanding or the appreciation of either for the other. In the joint notebook, Hawthorne recorded that he had slept his first night away from his wife, and that he came home for the first time in his life, never having had a home before. It was his habit not to attempt notebook recording when his observations had lost their freshness, but this entry is so skimpy as to suggest that the tour had meant little to him (VIII, 361–62). Emerson's account is fuller but suggests that the conversation was trivial, even though, in his phrasing, "we could have filled with matter much longer days." If there had been twenty-four hours for theological discussion with the Shakers, he doubted not that he and his companion would have had their own way, although his own "powers of persuasion were crippled by a disgraceful barking cold," and Hawthorne "inclined to play Jove more than Mercurius." [12] It can be supposed that Hawthorne played Jove during most of the journey. It can be supposed also that each was seeking more to approve in the other than previously, and recognized a handicap in his seeking. Emerson did not read fiction and, after Elizabeth Peabody had forced "Foot-prints on the Sea-shore" upon him, "complained that there was no inside in it." [13] Three weeks before the walking tour, he wrote in his journal: "N. Hawthorne's reputation as a writer is a very pleasant fact, because his writing is not good for anything, and this is a tribute to the man." [14] After a walk with Hawthorne on June 6, 1843, he wrote Thoreau that "The Celestial Railroad" has "a serene strength we cannot afford not to praise, in this low life." [15] In Hawthorne's story, Giant Transcendentalist has taken the place of Bunyan's Giant Despair. Emerson had welcomed Hawthorne among the "present kings and queens" at Concord, and praised him as a man, but had not learned to esteem his work.

Early in his residence at the Manse, Hawthorne sent Margaret Fuller a masterly letter declining her proposal that the poet Ellery Channing and his new wife, Margaret's sister Ellen, become boarders at the Manse. It would be a mistake, he said, for two couples with similar interests and activities to be thrown constantly together; and he was determined that Sophia should preserve her frail strength for painting and sculpturing. He felt little warmth for the "gnome, yclept Ellery Channing" (VIII, 316) upon his first visit at the Manse, and after his second visit called him "one of those queer and clever young men whom Mr. Emerson (that everlasting rejecter of all that is, and seeker for he knows not what) is continually picking up by way of a genius." The lad considers himself a genius, he continued, "and, ridiculously enough, looks upon his own verses as too sacred to be sold for money. . . . I like him well enough, however; but after all, these originals in a small way, after one has seen a few of them, become more dull and common-place than even those who keep the ordinary pathway of life" (VIII, 357). When Channing returned in April,

1843, after an absence from Concord, Sophia resumed the notebook discussion by saying she thought him likely to be a better companion than her husband had supposed. "He has to me a pleasanter way of saying things than Mr. Thoreau, because so wholly without the air of saying any thing of consequence."[16] In a later entry penned in Channing's behalf, she said that he seemed "perfectly to idolize" her husband.[17]

Hawthorne was "rather glad than otherwise" to have Ellery return, but found him "a poor substitute" for Thoreau, who was preparing to leave Concord (VIII, 369). Although Thoreau was also an "original," embodying much that was consciously unnatural, he had a pleasing genuineness, "he being one of the few persons . . . with whom to hold intercourse is like hearing the wind among the boughs of a forest-tree; and with all his wild freedom, there is high and classic cultivation in him too." Thoreau was "ugly as sin" but "of an honest and agreeable fashion, . . . a keen and delicate observer of nature," having "real poetry in him," and also "a deep and true taste for poetry"—in sum, "a healthy and wholesome man to know." Hawthorne's admiration for Thoreau's knowledge of the natural world was reinforced by admiration for the skill, if not indeed the witchcraft, with which he rowed the *Musketaquid*, the boat he had built and used on the Concord and Merrimac rivers. On the day Thoreau first dined at the Manse, August 31, 1842, he sold Hawthorne the boat for seven dollars; upon delivering it the next day, he gave the new owner a lesson in rowing the *Pond Lily*, as it would be called afterward (VIII, 353–57). After noting later Emerson's inconvenience from having Thoreau live in his house, Hawthorne said, "It may be well that such a sturdy and uncompromising person is fitter to meet occasionally in the open air, than to have as a permanent guest at table and fireside" (VIII, 371).

Hawthorne's early journalizing at the Manse reflects his happiness and the fanciful turn of mind habitual with him. The descriptive-narrative sketches are hardly less finished in plan and execution than the sketches he published. He lamented on November 8, 1842, that his journal had fallen into neglect, because his "scribbling propensities" were "far more than gratified in writing nonsense for the press" (VIII, 363). The nonsense written for the press included some of the nine tales and sketches he was to publish in the next year. The labor of notebook composition was equally demanding, or nearly so. Two of his essays derived from his residence at Concord, "Buds and Bird Voices" and "The Old Manse," were composed from records in the notebooks, where their chief imaginative qualities were already present.

14
Calm Summer of Heart and Mind

Whatever entered Hawthorne's awareness entered also the alembic of his questioning mind. In his notebook and his published writings, and also in such casual recordings as his letters and his wife's letters and notebooks, the evidence is abundant that his search for meanings was constant and that his view of the literal and the mundane enclosed at the same time the symbolic and the spiritual. At the Boston custom-house and at Brook Farm he savored and tested his experiences in the context of the work-a-day world, but his notebooks and particularly the letters to his fiancée show that he studied and to a degree shaped those experiences with a view to what he could learn about ultimate meanings. At the Manse his opportunity was greater than before to live an experiment and to approach the elemental, pristine existence that he thought would illuminate the concepts he wished to explore. From the time he left his chamber under the eaves, his focus was not on the New England past, but on the current scene. On the wharves of Boston harbor, among his colleagues at Brook Farm, and in his Edenic existence at the Old Manse, he sought the outward manifestations he needed to "body forth," as he phrased it, the moral and psychological aspects of human character that are central in his fiction. This shift has a parallel in the shift from his earlier historical settings to settings that are vaguely contemporary and of little significance to the tales.

He was prepared to create a life of freedom at the Manse, and determined to live to the fullest. After six weeks, he wrote that he had "rather be on earth than even in the seventh Heaven, just now" (VIII, 344). Beginning his notebook writing on August 5, he gave a few days to describing the house and the environs, and then turned to the fruit trees and his garden, which had a reality in supplying food for the table but also a subtler meaning for these new residents of the Garden. Seeing his "own work contributing to the life and well-being of animate nature" gave "a pleasure and an ideality, hitherto unthought of, to the business of providing sustenance" for his family (VIII, 329–30). He welcomed the labor in his garden for what it would yield, and for the initiation it gave him into an experience common to mankind; but he had no tolerance, he said in "The Old Manse," for the venerable apothegm that "toil sweetens the bread it earns," or for Elizabeth Peabody's elevation of physical labor into the realm of the sacred. For his part, "speaking from hard experience, acquired while belaboring the rugged furrows of Brook Farm," he relished "best the free gifts of Providence" (X, 13).

As summer advanced, his grounds yielded such generous "bounties of Providence" that it was "as if the original relation between Man and Nature" had been restored in his case, and whatever he needed to support his Eve and himself would be furnished (VIII, 332). He could imagine that in this isolation he had found the existence which the busy community at Roxbury had sought in vain. A sober note sounded at intervals in his notebook, but his exultation would soon return, as on the day when he had triumphed over the witchery of the *Pond Lily*, and could feel "a power over that which" supported him: "Oh that I could run wild!—that is, that I could put myself into a true relation with nature, and be on friendly terms with all congenial elements" (VIII, 358). One day in September he "made a voyage alone" to a secluded spot on the river where sky, foliage, sunlight, and shade "seemed unsurpassably beautiful, when beheld in upper air." But when he gazed downward, "there they were, the same even to the minutest particular, yet arrayed in ideal beauty, which satisfied the spirit incomparably more than the actual scene. I am half convinced that the reflection is indeed the reality—the real thing which Nature imperfectly images to our grosser sense. At all events, the disembodied shadow is nearest to the soul" (VIII, 359–60). Perhaps he had not yet spent enough time on the river with Thoreau or Ellery Channing and had not accepted enough of Emerson's thought to owe these statements to them directly; but in the company of Sophia and her sisters and friends, and breathing the air of Salem and Boston and West Roxbury and Concord, he could not fail to look about him at times through Transcendental lenses.

Thanksgiving Day had special significance for the Hawthornes, for they had at last found a home, and a new family had been gathered since the year before. Marriage had brought Sophia a new life, physical as well as spiritual. Before marriage she knew nothing about the capacity of this "miraculous form," the human body, she wrote in the joint notebook; "the truly married alone can know what a wondrous instrument it is for the purposes of the heart."[1] Writing to Margaret Fuller on February 1, 1843, Hawthorne said it would be impossible to take Charles Newcomb as a boarder at the Manse, as she had proposed, for "a reason at present undeveloped," but one he trusted time would "bring to light." Soon afterward Sophia was sure she had suffered a miscarriage. The cause had been a fall, probably on the snow and ice, and possibly when she held her husband's arm, as she liked to do, and ran and slid with him as he skated.[2] Her mother came, and after she had gone home, Sophia wrote her on February 24 that her husband had been "like the veiled Prophet," but that it was then "as if some invisible James Clarke" had married them again. On March 31 Hawthorne wrote of their "one grief," about which his wife had written on the preceding pages (cut out of the notebook as preserved), and of their confidence that by and by they would "welcome that very same little stranger" they had expected earlier. From March 9 to 22 he had been in Salem and Sophia in Boston. She seemed stronger than before her accident, and on June 9 she wrote her mother she was again pregnant.

In the "journal of household events" that Sophia kept from December 1, 1843, to the next January 5, her writing is direct and largely unadorned, in contrast to what she put into the joint notebook. Since Hawthorne was rarely out of her company, the result is close to an hour-by-hour record of what he did during five weeks. He was especially solicitous for his wife; he read aloud to her in the evenings; he even asked her at times to sit with him in his study while he wrote. They walked to the village, to get the mail, to call on the Emersons or others, and often to read in the Athenaeum Library. He took an interest in her sewing for her "little fay," and he prepared some of the meals while Mary O'Brien, the maid, was in Boston. "Imagine him with that magnificent head bent over a cooking stove & those star-eyes watching the pot!"[3] Some months later Sophia wrote that "Hyperion" was again the cook, and "officiated even to dish-washing, with the air of one making worlds."[4]

Their child, Una, was born on March 3, 1844. The father wrote his sis-

The Old Manse, Concord, Mass. Courtesy of the Essex Institute, Salem, Mass.

ter Louisa that Sophia had a terrible time, the baby using "ten awful hours in getting across the threshold." He was pleased when Louisa wrote of his mother's "heroic hypothesis" that, if they lived in Boston, she would come to see the baby.[5] When Una was two months old, John Louis O'Sullivan, her godfather, brought her a silver cup and a Newfoundland puppy that was forthwith named Leo, appropriately for Una's companion. She was taken for a visit in Boston late in May, and for ten days in Salem in November, when Sophia saw Hawthorne's mother and his sister Elizabeth for the first time since her marriage. Grandmother Hawthorne was "entirely satisfied with her child," as was Great-Aunt Ruth Hawthorne.[6] Evidence that Una's presence could accomplish wonders appeared on the first day in Salem: Hawthorne dined with his mother for the first time he could remember.

It pleased Hawthorne to record the sale of apples and potatoes and hay in the "economic history" of life at the Manse, but he reserved time for walking, boating, skating, and bathing in the river, and resented anything that encroached on his time for reading, observing, thinking, and musing. As for seclusion, he might walk to the post office and the library and return home without speaking a word to any human being. Sophia respected his periods of composition, protecting him from the intrusions of others and rarely herself violating the sanctity of his study. Once during her pregnancy, in December, when she was provoked in her efforts at painting, she "was obliged" to go up and look at her husband. She was "conscience stricken for interrupting him," and for spoiling his "vein for writing." That was very hard for her to bear, she said, and she "concluded to go to the village, though the weather was so unpropitious."[7]

Not since boyhood, Hawthorne wrote Margaret Fuller, had he experienced such freedom.[8] During the first summer and autumn, he rose at five in the morning to fish or bathe in the river before breakfast, wrote until dinner at two, walked to the post office, read an hour or more at the library, went rowing or walking, and afterward read aloud to Sophia. But it was in character for him to note one October day that he could not "endure to waste anything so precious as autumnal sunshine by staying in the house" (VIII, 361). He remarked after eight months that he might have turned out more tales and sketches, "if it had seemed worth while," but he had thought his savings and a small income from his pen would suffice until he gained the political appointment he was confident he could have. He wrote Hillard on March 24, 1843, that he stood ready to do literary drudgery. He had considered writing one or two mythological storybooks, to be published under O'Sullivan's auspices in New York; but he doubted that juvenile literature would be profitable, and in September he declined an invitation to begin a series in the *Boys and Girls Magazine*, which had published "Little Daffydowndilly" in July.

At the Old Manse, Hawthorne edited two works he might have considered drudgery, but he welcomed the occasions to be generous to friends. In the spring of 1843, before Horatio Bridge sailed for the African coast as purser of the *Saratoga*, Hawthorne had urged him to write a series of letters for magazine publication that later might be made into a book, and had sent him advice that embodied his own principles for notebook writing: not to stick strictly to facts; to allow the "fancy pretty free license, and omit no heightening touches merely because they did not chance to happen" before his eyes; to write down observations before the novelty wears off; to think nothing too trifling. A year later he offered further advice: Bridge should look at things "in a matter-of-fact way," but without excluding "romantic incident and adventure." He was recommending his own habit of mixing the actual and the fanciful.[9] When he had edited Bridge's manuscript, and was recommending it to Evert Duyckinck on March 2, 1845, he said he had done no more than remodel the style as needed, develop the ideas where Bridge had failed to do it, and "put on occasional patches of sentimental embroidery." Duyckinck accepted the work for the Library of American Books he was editing for Wiley and Putnam. Hawthorne had chosen the title, *Journal of an African Cruiser;* he would be shown as editor and would receive a percentage of the royalty. Duyckinck wrote on October 2 that no recent American book had received such good notice in England.

Hawthorne had read the manuscript journal of an American held in Dartmoor Prison during the War of 1812, and in returning it through William Pike, a former associate of his in the Boston custom-house, had said that it "might easily be made very acceptable to the public."[10] The author was Benjamin Frederick Browne (1793–1873), who after the war returned home to Salem and was in business as an apothecary until 1860. A Democrat active in politics and associated with Hawthorne and Pike, he was Salem postmaster from 1845 to 1849. Hawthorne prepared the journal for serialization in the *Democratic Review* (January–September, 1846), leaving it mainly in its original rough form; and he offered to write a preface or an introduction, but failed to get it published as a book.[11]

Although Hawthorne's letters and notebooks suggest that he took a casual and leisurely attitude toward his work, he published twenty pieces during his three and a half years at the Manse. Sophia spoke of his waiting for inspiration, of "the delicacy and tricksiness of his mood" when he was evolving a new work, and of the "fullness of time" before she would know what he was writing.[12] He had often distinguished between work that came through natural growth and work that was forced. Only three tales from his Manse years, "The Birthmark," "The Artist of the Beautiful," and "Rappaccini's Daughter," reach the level of his best work; others are more concoctions than creations; some are experimental in method and hence of special interest. Before going to the Manse, he realized that he would not have again the conditions he had known in his chamber under the eaves. He had written Cornelius Mathews and Evert Duyckinck on

December 22, 1841, that his early works had grown from "quietude and seclusion" which he could not have again; the world had sucked him "within its vortex." To furnish the *Democratic Review* regular contributions and to have any hope of making a living with his pen, he must do a kind of writing less dependent on the dreaming and musing that had produced his early tales and sketches. From the time he left Herbert Street in 1838 and moved into at least the edges of the social, intellectual, and literary life about him, his creative mind had turned more than ever before to the current scene, as if he were attempting to understand and to establish a relation with that scene. The pages of his notebooks filled with descriptions of persons and places; they bore little evidence of his reading; and historical materials had little place in most of what he published in the next ten years. When asked to contribute something to the first number of *Sargent's New Monthly Magazine*, for example, he reworked as "The Old Apple Dealer" a sketch in his notebook for January 23, 1842.[13] From nothing more than external manifestations he observed across the waiting room of the Salem railroad station, he creates for the apple dealer a speculative portrait of a character who is primarily passive and negative.

In the sketch "The Old Manse," written to introduce the collection of his writings at the Manse, Hawthorne wrote: "These fitful sketches, with so little of external life about them, . . . afford no solid basis for a literary reputation." For a large proportion of this collection, this appraisal is not unjust, considering his habit of undervaluing his works. He might have classed as drudgery two children's stories, "Little Daffydowndilly" and "A Good Man's Miracle." Others of the works he later called "makeweights" that might be used to fill out a collection. In many of the sketches his purpose was only to assemble a sequence of items to illustrate a view of man and society. Two of them are slight in length and intention, the playful "Fire Worship" and "The Antique Ring," which elaborates a scene with imaginative detail of character and incident drawn from history. Several other pieces, like "A Virtuoso's Collection," assemble objects, persons, or ideas for the sake of ironic juxtaposition or contrast and for the interest that attaches to the items themselves in the special coloring thrown upon them. Among the simplest of these is "A Book of Autographs," based on a volume of letters from the Revolutionary era which allow Hawthorne to speculate from available evidence, recreating character and incident and through them the spirit of an earlier age.

The narrator of "The Hall of Fantasy" visits a realm of imagination and dream, and playfully speculates on the best proportions of actuality and fantasy in fiction. He is sure that, short of that state when "idea shall be the all in all," neither ingredient would be acceptable alone. In the Hall are statues of great literary figures of the world and an assemblage of current American writers, most of whom are introduced with brief and favorable characterizations, but for some of the author's "old friends of Brook Farm" and others associated with them, there are demurrers that show him wishing to offer more than perfunctory judgments. His omission of this assemblage of authors when he reprinted the sketch in *Mosses from an Old Manse* indicates that in his mind the tale was cumulative rather than organic, and suggests that he was reluctant to see this whimsical excursion into criticism of current authors, some of them close friends of his, take a permanent place in his work.

As Emerson appeared to the visitor to the Hall of Fantasy, he was surrounded by "all manner of Transcendentalists and disciples of the Newness, most of whom displayed the power of his intellect by its modifying influence upon their own. . . . No more earnest seeker after truth than he, and few more successful finders of it; although, sometimes, the truth assumes a mystic unreality and shadowiness in his grasp." The characterization of Jones Very, that he "stood alone, within a circle which no other of mortal race could enter, nor himself escape from," reflects Hawthorne's sympathetic understanding of this tormented poet, whom he had known in Salem in 1838. Although he did not share Sophia's admiration for "our High Priest of Nature," did not hear the mystical voice which Very expected a convert to hear while reading one of his sonnets, and did not become the brother he said Very sought, his patience with Very won commendation from both Emerson and Elizabeth Peabody.[14] Amos Bronson Alcott doubtless had "the spirit of a system in him, but not the body of it." The keeper of the Hall exclaimed when Orestes Brownson was mentioned, "Pray Heaven he do not stamp his foot or raise his voice; for if he should, the whole fabric of the Hall of Fantasy will dissolve like a smoke-wreath! I wonder how he came here?" (Sophia's name for Brownson was "Bull of Bashan," because of his booming voice.)

In the playful manner of this sketch, it is said that Poe had been admitted to the Hall of Fantasy "for the sake of his imagination, but was threatened with ejectment, as belonging to the obnoxious class of critics." In writing Poe on June 17, 1846, Hawthorne drew the same distinction, after referring to Poe's earlier reviews of his works, saying that he admired him "rather as a writer of Tales, than as a critic upon them," and that he often dissented from his critical opinions, but never failed to recognize his "force and originality" in his tales. Hawthorne recorded no comment, it seems, on Poe's essay-review of *Twice-Told Tales* published in May, 1842, in which Poe found high achievement in the tales and, with them as a base, formulated rules by which he wrote his own best stories and by which short stories were written and evaluated for a century or more afterward.[15]

Another tour de force, "P.'s Correspondence," includes a character intended to call Poe to mind, the narrator's "unfortunate friend P.," who suffers from disordered reason and, in the letter which is the body of this sketch, reports on several authors, dead long ago but appearing here in old age, recanting their main works and supporting views far removed from the ones they formerly held. Several American authors still living are listed as dead long since, but not including Poe. The receiver of the letter, a contributor to the *Democratic Review*, can be identified as Hawthorne; the letter writer, as Poe, who, at the time this sketch was written, was in the public mind in just such a mental state as P. The matter of the sketch is consciously Poesque, and there is a crudeness and an unpleasantness that may have prompted Hawthorne not to name but to hint at an author who might be identified.

Another of the sketches constructed by accumulation is "A Select Party," in which are gathered a series of characters appropriate to the dominion "which the spirit conquers for itself" and where "unrealities become a thousand times more real than the earth," including "a Poet, who felt no jealousy towards other votaries of the lyre." Another sketch, "The Intelligence Office," supposes an office to which are brought the hopes and aspirations of many kinds and orders of humanity. One caller at the office was a figure Hawthorne would have said was vaguely autobiographical, "a man out of his right place," who felt "an urgent moral necessity" to find his "true place in the world." "Earth's Holocaust" describes a bonfire of "articles that were judged fit for nothing but to be burned." The result is a survey of reform efforts in Hawthorne's time, an age of reform, which concludes that the efforts of all reformers are futile unless the heart is purified.

Writing Sophia when they had been engaged a year and more, Hawthorne lamented that they were rarely together out of the company of others, and added, "How happy were Adam and Eve! . . . We love [one] another as well as they; but there is no silent and lovely garden of Eden for us." He and his wife had found an Eden in one another's arms, he said, and had become "the Adam and Eve of a virgin earth."[16] Soon after reaching the Manse, Hawthorne wrote "The New Adam and Eve," using the idea for a "half-sportive and half-thoughtful" story written out in his notebook, presumably in 1836: "The race of mankind to be swept away, leaving all their cities & works," and a new pair to work out an understanding "by their sympathy with what they saw, and by their own feelings" during their first day.[17] A light irony runs throughout as elements of current society are satirized; but the tone remains genial, in keeping with the playful, affectionate portrait of his Eve that Hawthorne wanted to present. The progression from one scene to another provides cumulative manifestations of the theme.

"The Celestial Railroad" is another piece from the Manse period that was made rather than created. It is a retelling of *The Pilgrim's Progress*, with the narrator traveling Christian's route by train and his burden checked in the baggage car. Chief among the elements of society being satirized are the churches and related societies which Hawthorne pictured as offering an easy passage to heaven. In Bunyan's cave, Pope and Pagan have been replaced by German-born Giant Transcendentalist, who feeds on "smoke, mist, moonshine, raw potatoes, and saw-dust," and looks "more like a heap of fog and duskiness" than anything else. "The Celestial Railroad" is a delightful story, testimony that Bunyan's allegorical method was congenial to Hawthorne's mind, and that he enjoyed turning his skeptical and whimsical light upon Emerson. He would have had in mind his wife, Elizabeth Peabody, and other idolators of his neighbor; and he would have been aware that he was joining many others, including some Transcendentalists, in telling jokes at their expense. His close tracking of *The Pilgrim's Progress*, including the dream framework, provides a tone appropriate to his purpose.

Three of the tales written at the Manse, "Egotism; or The Bosom Serpent," "The Christmas Banquet," and "Drowne's Wooden Image," reflect important facets of Hawthorne's thought at the time. The idea for "Egotism; or The Bosom Serpent" had appeared in an early notebook, probably in 1836, and again in 1842.[18] The dual symbol—the serpent as a token of inner guilt and also as a means of discovering similar guilt in others—is particularly suitable to Hawthorne's portrayal of human character. Roderick Elliston, tormented by his own guilt, assumes the role of an avenging angel in exposing the serpents in the bosoms of others and once exclaims that there is enough poison in any man's heart "to generate a brood of serpents." Fittingly for the author in the Garden with his Eve, it is Elliston's love for Rosina that redeems him from the "diseased self-contemplation" that has produced and nourished the serpent. Hawthorne published this tale with a note saying that the "physical fact" presented in it had occurred many times, but he also labeled it one of the "Allegories of the Heart." He thus declared the connection of his tale with the actual world and also with the allegorical meaning the serpent has had in Western thought from the Book of Genesis onward.

Another tale from the "Allegories of the Heart," "The Christmas Banquet," includes the characters of "Egotism" in an enclosing frame, and shows the author still attracted to a plan of linked stories such as he had attempted first in the "Seven Tales of My Native Land." The idea of having a man, at the end of a "long life of melancholy eccentricity," leave a provision for a banquet each year "for ten of the most miserable persons that could be found," had appeared in Hawthorne's notebook several years earlier, and may have derived from his uncle Simon Forrester's leaving in his will $1,500 to provide dinners for the poor on Christmas and Independence Day.[19] Suspense and the thesis are borne by the presence of one man in the yearly procession of guests who seems out of place, but finally explains that his is the supreme misery because he has "possessed nothing, neither joy nor griefs." Sophia referred to this tale as "that terrific and true picture of a cold heart,"[20] and the possessor of the cold heart is akin to the man without a place in the real world whom Hawthorne had feared or had pretended to fear he would become. Among those attending the yearly banquet are characters who, with slight modification, appear elsewhere in Hawthorne's works. There are thumbnail forestudies of Hollingsworth, Priscilla, and Zenobia in *The Blithedale Romance*, and there are episodes and characters that echo "The Hollow of the Three Hills," "Fancy's Show-Box," and "The Birthmark." That is to say that Hawthorne repeated himself often, or that he wrote with such consistency of purpose and thought that his writings—with no more than a few excepted—show themselves to be segments of a general design and have discoverable ties with other segments.

The idea presented in "Drowne's Wooden Image"—that an unexceptional carver of ship figureheads may be elevated by love to the level of artistic genius—combines Hawthorne's and Sophia's emphasis on inspiration, or on the efficacy of musing and dreaming, with the spiritual quality they attributed to their love;[21] and the woman who inspires Drowne wears flowers of Eden, suggesting the Eden inhabited by the Hawthornes. The story is set "in the good old times of the town of Boston." When Hawthorne turned from such fabricated pieces as "The Intelligence Office" and

"Earth's Holocaust" to tales organic in nature, even though a slight one such as this, he turned for subject matter away from the commonplace of his own time toward the remote and the fanciful, while also returning from satire on current social affairs to the probing of character.

"Drowne's Wooden Image" touches one aspect of Hawthorne's thinking on the creative artist; other aspects appear in other tales, and a major character in *The Blithedale Romance* is a poet, who is also the narrator and hence reveals himself as an artist. An earlier tale, "The Prophetic Pictures," reflects the author's thinking on the powers and the responsibilities of the artist, in this instance a gifted painter. Questions are raised, but not answered fully, as to whether the painter reads the future and, if so, whether he is responsible for events he has foreseen, whether he influences, or indeed creates, the future of the subjects he paints. In "The Artist of the Beautiful," written at the Manse, Hawthorne treats the artist in relation to the outside world. This phase of the topic came naturally to his attention during a period when he was attempting to extract a livelihood from writing and was aware of the uncertainties of a literary life. In 1841 he had set down the idea for a tale "to represent a man as spending life and the intensest labor in the accomplishment of some mechanical trifle."[22] Later he decided on a mechanical butterfly and elevated its creator, Owen Warland, to idealized artistic achievement. Against the antagonism of characters representing the elements of society, Warland succeeds; even a woman's love does not qualify her to understand and sympathize, nor does the innocence of a child. When "Nature's ideal butterfly" had been crushed in the child's grasp, "what seemed the ruin of his life's labor" was to the artist no ruin. "He had caught a far other butterfly than this. When the artist rose high enough to achieve the Beautiful, the symbol by which he made it perceptible to mortal senses became of little value in his eyes, while his spirit possessed itself in the enjoyment of the Reality." The story asserts for the artist his necessary freedom from all but his own inner compulsions. The conclusion that a lover cannot enter the precinct of the artist might have been thought unacceptable to Hawthorne and his wife, but it was not. Each valued the creative and critical powers of the other, but each regarded artistic creation as an individual process. He had warned her during their courtship that he had depths which not even she could plumb. She wrote her mother on September 3, 1843, "No two minds were ever more completely different and individual than Mr. Hawthorne's and mine. It would be impossible to have intercourse with one another, if our minds ran into one another. Elizabeth is right in saying we preserve our individuality." He said many times that Sophia was his best critic, but as a rule she read, or he read to her, a finished manuscript, for it was his habit to guard his creative integrity against even her criticism.

Sophia often spoke of her husband's demand for perfection and his "wide comprehension and awful insight"—a phrase Ellery Channing had applied to him. He could "seldom commend anything unqualifiedly unless some untouched work of God, such as a flower or a bird." Among the suggestions for stories he put into his notebook in 1837 are these two together: "A person to be in possession of something as perfect as mortal man has a right to demand; he tries to make it better and ruins it entirely"; and "A person to spend all his life and splendid talents in trying to achieve something naturally impossible—as to make a conquest over nature." On another page he spoke of the "infinitely minute perfection" to be found in nature, in contrast to man's finest workmanship. A note two years later fuses these ideas and goes on to suggest the action and the theme of a tale: "A person to be the death of his beloved, in trying to raise her to more than mortal perfection; yet this should be a comfort to him, for having aimed so highly and holily."[23]

That tale, "The Birthmark," was not written for another four years but turned out to be one of Hawthorne's most characteristic and most successful works. It employs impressive materials, the paraphernalia and the concepts of alchemy, and includes dramatic scenes and tableaux. Symbols, labeled as such, are prominent but are commonplace, rather than learned or esoteric; most prominent is the birth-mark in Georgiana's cheek, which to some is a mark of beauty, but to Aylmer, her learned, perfectionist husband, is "the fatal flaw of humanity." Not recognizing the truth that nature "permits us indeed, to mar, but seldom to mend," Aylmer administers, after all his other attempts have failed, a potion that indeed removes the mark. Georgiana, who realizes that Aylmer is driven to seek the ideal, and loves him the more, says, "My poor Aylmer! . . . You have aimed loftily!—you have done nobly! Do not repent, that, with so high and pure a feeling, you have rejected the best that earth could offer." When the mark, "that sole token of human imperfection," has faded and her soul has taken "its heavenward flight," the "hoarse, chuckling laugh" of the earthbound Aminidab is heard. "Thus ever does the gross Fatality of Earth exult in its invariable triumph over the immortal essence, which, in this dim sphere of half-development, demands the completeness of a higher state." Two concluding sentences detract nothing from the loftiness of

Aylmer's purpose or from his wife's understanding and heroism, in saying that Aylmer lacked the "profounder wisdom" that a devotion to the ideal must be tempered with a realization that in "this dim sphere of half-development" the perfection belonging to the celestial sphere is not achievable. In "The Birthmark" an obsession with a noble purpose produces tragic results. Hawthorne probably anticipated that some readers would see the tale as simply a condemnation of idealism or a condemnation of forbidden learning. His purpose here, as in most of his best works, was to draw fine distinctions in human thought and action, and to illustrate the consequences.

Hawthorne found in an alchemist's laboratory license for mixing the actual and the fanciful in "The Birthmark." In "Rappaccini's Daughter" he chose a Renaissance Italian garden to which had been introduced the lore of mysterious poisons and antidotes, and speculations about man's ability to modify nature for his purposes. He likely had encountered the tradition of "the poisoned maid" in more than one source; in his notebook for 1839 he copied from Sir Thomas Browne's *Pseudodoxia Epidemica* a story of "an Indian King, that sent unto Alexander a fair woman, fed with aconites and other poisons, with this intent, either by converse or copulation complexionally to destroy him."[24] In the musing he gave this story, he conceived of an innocent young woman who, in carrying out an experiment of her father's in the control of nature, has imbibed poison from a luxuriant shrub in her secluded garden, and a young man with a quick fancy but not "a deep heart" who discovers her in her seclusion and, only after they are in love, learns that she is poisoned and he also. The rich texture of this tale, the intricate and delicate threads, and the skill with which the pattern is woven combine to show that the author had given himself long and fruitfully to the probing of human nature and experience, and to the methods of symbolic narrative.

Hawthorne said afterward that he had written at the Manse no important work such as he had hoped to produce, that he had nothing to show but a "few tales and essays, which had blossomed out like flowers in the calm summer" of his heart and mind. Yet some of the tales written at the Manse are among his best, and forecast the full-scale romances to come from his pen later.

15

The Expulsion

After a month at the Manse, Hawthorne remarked in his notebook on the idleness he had fallen into. To spend a lifetime thus "might be a sin and a shame," he said, but it would be good to live for a while "as if this world were Heaven," even though "a flitting shadow of earthly care and toil" would soon mingle with his realities (VIII, 334). Looking back on Brook Farm and the Boston custom-house earlier, he was ready to join Thoreau, Emerson, Ellery Channing, and others at Concord in a determined leisure and a semi-religious experience of nature, with his wife an eager companion. Any references he made to needs that might not be met from his garden and the river were likely to be flippant: God knew how he and his wife were to be provided for, but he wished the secret could be divulged to him; he wondered why God kept him so poor.

In time a "shadow of earthly care and toil" did mingle with realities at the Manse. In February, 1843, Hawthorne and Sophia could not go to Boston until payment came for a magazine contribution, and there seems to have been no reluctance to let others outside the family know about their scant means.[1] He wrote Hillard after the birth of Una that becoming a father had brought "a very sober and serious kind of happiness," and his spirit could not "be thoroughly gay and careless again." Having been "a trifler preposterously long," he must allow himself "to be woven into the sombre texture of humanity." Writing stories for magazines was "the most unprofitable business in the world"; and if he spent his time in such composition, his freshness of mind would be lost and there would be a deterioration in the stories. To support himself by his pen, he must turn to what he called literary drudgery. If a Democratic administration was elected next year, he would again favor Uncle Sam with his services.[2]

It was singular, Hawthorne wrote Bridge, that his work yielded him so little income, for "nobody's scribblings" seemed to be "more acceptable to the public" than his own. He felt a particular grievance that money owed him did not come in.[3] He resented "this abominable system of credit—of keeping possession of other people's property—which renders it impossible for a man to be just and honest, even if he so inclined."[4] Even after an urgent request to O'Sullivan, it was not until December that he received $100 on what was due him. James Russell Lowell's *Pioneer* had failed after three numbers, owing him money he feared would never be paid. He had lent money to William P. Loring and John Muzzy, fellow-employees at the custom-house who had been turned off under the Whig administration. When they were returned to office under President Polk and did not repay him, he asked Hillard to enter suit for him.[5] Financial difficulties grew more oppressive, and late in the year 1844, while Sophia and the baby were in Boston and he in Salem to avoid the expenses at Concord, he wrote her that, by remaining in Salem, he gained freedom from the "consciousness of debt, and pecuniary botheration, and the difficulty of providing even for the day's wants."[6]

The first attempt to get Hawthorne the Salem postmastership was made in 1838, and his application remained active, for that office seemed to him and his supporters ideal for his purpose; he would stay in the region of his literary materials and would have both adequate pay and free time for writing. In 1840 the appointment went to Charles Woodbury, a relative of both Levi Woodbury, secretary of the treasury, and Robert Rantoul, a prominent Salem Democrat; under the Whigs, it went in 1842 to Hawthorne's friend Caleb Foote. After Tyler had become president at the death of Harrison and had formed a coalition with members of the Democratic Party, there was hope that a Democrat would replace Foote. Following a visit to Salem late in October, Hawthorne concluded that he would not get the post office; for, if Foote were removed, Woodbury would be appointed again.[7] He was promised a satisfactory appointment within six months, and, after visiting Salem and Boston again the next spring, he told Bridge that the post office might be his after all, as a reward for his "patriotism and public services."[8] It seemed that Rantoul might lose his race for Congress and Charles Woodbury thus lose his claim on the post office. A week later Hawthorne said he was content not to win the appointment (VIII, 367); he would not know for a year or two whether he could make a living with his pen.[9]

In person or by letter, Hawthorne kept in touch with his political friends. O'Sullivan, Pierce, Hillard, and Bridge visited him at Concord, as did Horace N. Conolly and David Roberts, prominent members of the Democratic organization of Salem. Hillard informed his law partner, Charles Sumner, of Hawthorne's needs. O'Sullivan took him to see George Bancroft on August 26, 1843, and on November 24 wrote Congressman Wise in Hawthorne's behalf, suggesting that Wise might welcome an opportunity to make amends for his part as the second of Cilley's slayer.[10] O'Sullivan presented Hawthorne's candidacy to President Tyler, and Hawthorne was informed that Tyler had appointed him and afterward had withdrawn his name;[11] but in August, 1844, Tyler removed Foote and appointed Benjamin Frederick Browne, the apothecary whose papers from Dartmoor Prison Hawthorne would edit. Hawthorne predicted, rightly it turned out, that Browne would not be confirmed, since Foote, a Whig, had been removed simply on political grounds, and also that Tyler would let Browne serve without confirmation, leaving the permanent appointment to the new president. After the election of Polk, Hawthorne suggested that Bridge assist him toward the postmastership by using his influence to prevent Browne's confirmation,[12] and not until June, 1845, was it clear that Browne would not be removed.

George Bancroft, Polk's secretary of the navy, who was in charge of patronage for New England, became the focus of accelerated efforts in Hawthorne's behalf. O'Sullivan was "moving Heaven and Earth," in Hawthorne's phrasing, and gave Bancroft little peace.[13] Several of his letters repeat the note he sounded on May 31, 1844: "It wounds badly that something fitting and worthy was asked in vain for such a man as Hawthorne." Besides the Salem post office, he mentioned the consulships at Marseilles, Genoa, Gibraltar, and in China; and he culled through a variety of possible appointments: at the Smithsonian Institution, the Chelsea Hospital, the Charlestown Navy Yard, the Portsmouth Navy Yard, the Watertown Arsenal, and "the Robinson Crusoe solitude of Santa Rosa Island." Hawthorne should not be offered an unworthy position. He should have an independent position, with no great amount of clerical drudgery, somewhere near Boston. Appointment to a Washington clerkship would be putting "Pegasus in a Yoke" with a vengeance. Of one proposal O'Sullivan wrote that "nothing but the absolute gnawing of hunger, physical and literal," would reconcile Hawthorne to it. He proposed on July 11 that Hawthorne be appointed collector of the port of Salem. Having in mind the advanced age of the incumbent, General James Miller, he said the position must be vacant soon, and if it could be promised to Hawthorne privately, he would "see to his well-being *en attendant*." [14] —The man Hawthorne once proposed to meet in a duel had become his champion in many quarters.

Horatio Bridge, Hawthorne's primary agent in these matters, set powerful forces in motion in the summer of 1845. He took advantage of a visit by Pierce to Boston and accompanied him on May 9 to see Hawthorne at Concord. Sophia wrote her mother the next day that not only did they give her husband "immediate solid hope," but Bridge lent him $100. The three college-mates went to the hotel for an evening of talk, and when they returned, there was "a radiance and relief" in her husband's face that she had not seen for some time. Hawthorne had been chopping wood at their arrival, and when the three emerged from the shed, she noted, "Mr. Pierce's arm was encircling my husband's old blue frock. How his friends love him!" [15] Two days later Pierce wrote to the postmaster general and to Bancroft urging Hawthorne for the Salem post office, whereupon Bancroft wrote to assure Dr. Browne's supporters that he would not be removed. Bridge then invited the Hawthornes for a visit at the Portsmouth Navy Yard, when other guests were Pierce and his wife, Senator Charles Gordon Atherton of New Hampshire and his wife, and Senator John Fairfield of Maine. Hawthorne's notebook entries suggest that he spent the two weeks, July 25 to August 9, mainly in social activities, including boating and fishing. [16] What plans were laid is not recorded, but ten days later he sent word through Bridge for O'Sullivan to tell Bancroft that he would not accept the offer of a clerkship at the Charlestown Navy Yard, and added, "Perhaps it would be well to let O'Sullivan into the whole business of our late canvass, so that he may be aware of the strength with which we shall take the field, at the next session of Congress." But first, the Hawthornes must vacate the Manse.

Following the period late in 1844 when poverty had driven them into separation in Boston and Salem, Sophia headed some of her letters "Paradise Regained," and the spring brought back some of their former joy in sun, flowers, and open air. Their letters and notebooks sounded a sober note, however, suggesting something of regret and sorrow, but more of acceptance and realization that their earlier freedom could not last. References to "my little wife" and "my kingly husband" had thinned out as their carrot-haired child of immortality intruded. (While Una was an infant, her father spoke playfully of her reddish hair, which became auburn as she grew up.) Hawthorne did not lament the close of the Old Manse interlude, and it was in character for him to speak lightly of financial needs. Once when Sophia was mending tears in his clothes, he said he was a man of many rents; and while she was visiting in Boston in the spring of 1844, he wrote her that he went to bed at dark, "out of a tender consideration for the oil-can." But he lamented being poor while money owed him was not paid; and upon learning that Charles W. Upham, after a visit to Concord, had told in Salem "the most pitiable stories" about their poverty, he protested in writing his wife that they had never been "quite paupers, and need not have been represented as such." [17]

They knew in March, 1845, that the owner of the Manse wanted it for his residence, and Hawthorne was confident of gaining an appointment in Salem by the time they were to move, in the autumn. [18] They decided to put up at Castle Dismal until there was a salary. He would have his old room on the third floor; Sophia would occupy a room with Una on the first floor; she would hire a maid to cook for all; and all would share the drawing room. She said that the years at the Manse would always be a blessed memory, for there her "dreams became realities," but she had "got weaned from it," because her husband's perplexities had "made the place painful to him." [19] Hawthorne wrote Bridge for a loan of $150, and to his chagrin had to send a second request, for Bridge was away from home and did not get the first letter at once. He received also $100 O'Sullivan owed him, but after paying his Concord bills and the moving costs, he had only ten dollars left; and he still owed rent on the Old Manse. [20]

Leaving Sophia and Una in Boston for a few days, he proceeded to Salem, where he wrote her on October 7 that he had "already begun to scribble," in the room "whence so many foolish stories" had gone forth. Three days later he wrote Evert Duyckinck in a sober but hopeful mood, from "the old dingy and dusky chamber" where he wasted many good years of his youth, "shaping day-dreams and night-dreams into idle stories—scarcely half of which ever saw the light; except it were their own blaze upon the hearth." His youth came back to him there, and he found himself "pretty much the same sort of fellow as of old." He had taken out his quire of paper and was prepared "to cover it with the accustomed nonsense," as soon as his mind had "deposited the sediment of recent anxieties and disturbances."

When Sophia was again in Boston the next month, she sent her husband important news, supposedly written by Una to her grandmother, which he sealed and threw downstairs from his third-floor room. Later he wrote, "Doubtless, they find it a most interesting communication; and I feel a little shamefaced about meeting them. They will certainly rejoice at the prospect of another baby, and only temper their joy with the serious consideration of how the new-comer is to be provided for." To him, the promised baby would be welcome, "in poverty or riches." The old reticence persisted in Castle Dismal; he had no direct word from his mother or his sisters about Sophia's pregnancy, but in his next letter he could write, "I suspect the intelligence of thy meditated baby is very pleasant to the grandmother and aunts; for Louisa met me at dinner, that day, with unusual cheerfulness, and observed that Thanksgiving was at hand." A wistful note sounded when he said that his friends Pike and Roberts were planning a house for him (he feared it would prove a castle in the air) and that he had gone later to look at the hill they had chosen for his house. He said he would like to come to Boston and help her and Una on their train ride to Salem but would not, unless he received some of the money owed him, for they were "so miserably poor." He added, "Would thou wast safe home again, eating thy potatoes, and glancing sideways at me with thy look of patient resignation." [21]

It had been determined at Bridge's quarters in the summer of 1845 to push Hawthorne for the surveyorship at the Salem custom-house, and concerted strength was soon directed to that goal. The way was cleared when George W. Mullet was persuaded to withdraw his application for the post, and Richard Lindsey to withdraw his application for the office of naval officer, leaving an opening for John D. Howard, who had strong support among the local Democrats for one of these offices. (Mullet and Lindsey were appointed inspectors later.) Recommendations of Hawthorne and Howard were submitted by the Democratic committees of the Second District of Massachusetts, the Town of Salem, the County of Essex, and a number of individuals prominent in the party nationally, including Franklin Pierce and Senators Atherton and Fairfield. Charles Sumner made his appeal to Bancroft's wife and had Bancroft's reply that he had been "most perseveringly" Hawthorne's friend and was pleased to see Sumner, a Whig, "go for the good rule of dismissing wicked Whigs and putting in Democrats." In the Hawthorne household, George Bancroft was called the Blatant Beast, after the many-tongued slanderer of *The Faerie Queene*, and in 1845 Hawthorne was convinced that he could not depend on Bancroft—at least for any post above an unacceptable clerkship. As patronage broker for New England and guardian of Democratic Party unity, and troubled by the split that had occurred after the Whig President Tyler had appointed local Democrats to office, Bancroft would not believe that both factions supported Hawthorne and Howard.[22] Late in December he injected the name of Stephen Hoyt, who had been dismissed for cause at Boston and might be provided for at Salem, his home town; and he delayed the decision through the next February. On March 1 Hawthorne sent Bridge an analysis of the subtle forces at work and proposed an equally subtle resolution. After learning from O'Sullivan that President Polk probably would not remove Nehemiah Brown, the surveyor in office, without the joint support of Hoyt's friends and his own, he feared that only the less desirable post of naval officer would be open for him. To lessen that possibility, he proposed that Hoyt be slated to become naval officer if Howard "could not succeed." If this arrangement would satisfy Bancroft, Hawthorne thought he could persuade Hoyt's supporters to accept it. Thus Bancroft and Hoyt would win a concession from the Salem people, who would still win offices for both of their candidates, Hawthorne and Howard.[23] Hawthorne concluded by saying that he had become "considerable of a politician" in the last few months. A week earlier he had written Bridge, "What a devil of a pickle I shall be in, if the baby should come, and the office should not!" On March 5 Bancroft finally wrote President Polk recommending Hawthorne and Howard. He had decided on Hawthorne early in February and had favored Hoyt until he had conclusive proof that Howard was supported by the local party organization. Hawthorne's commission, dated April 3, appointed him for four years from April 2 at $1,200 a year. He posted bond of $1000 on April 8, took the oath the next day, and was officially installed April 20.

Those recommending Hawthorne for the post office or the customhouse, in letters and other documents preserved in the National Archives, said little about his political qualifications except that he was "a sturdy Democrat," in O'Sullivan's phrase, or "a pure and primitive Democrat," in the words used by the publishers of the *Salem Advertiser*, who, in contrast, described Howard as an "active, ardent, zealous Democrat." Benjamin Frederick Browne said that Howard was "a vigorous and able political writer" in local journals, and that Hawthorne's literary fame was "coextensive with the English language." Senator Fairfield noted that Hawthorne had always been a Democrat "in principle, feeling and action, though never a warm partisan." Personal and literary commendations of Hawthorne were phrased with little restraint: O'Sullivan called him "the

Charles Lamb, the 'Gentle Elia,' of our side of the Atlantic"; Fairfield thought he had "no superior . . . among our best writers"; the publishers of the *Salem Advertiser* said he was "one of the finest, best and most talented of Americans"; Pierce described him as "a man of genius, of great simplicity of character and the exactest worth in all respects"; Atherton said he was "an honor to the literature of the country, a man of unblemished reputation and high sense of honor." Charles Sumner, wanting his statement to account for his endorsing a candidate from the opposing party, said that there was no one "of any party who would not hear with delight that the author of such Goldsmithian prose" as Hawthorne's "had received honor and office from his country."

When the Hawthornes moved to Herbert Street early in October, 1845, they expected to be there only a short time, but they remained through the winter. In March Hawthorne moved his family to 77 Carver Street in Boston. Sophia would be in reach of Dr. Wesselhoeft until her baby was born; when Hawthorne's duties began at the custom-house, he would commute to Salem. Susan Burley sponsored him for a year's privileges at the Boston Athenaeum. On the day his appointment was certain, Sophia wrote her father to order him a suit of clothes; in April she persuaded him to be vaccinated for smallpox. On June 22, 1846, Hawthorne wrote from Boston to tell his sister Louisa that a son, Julian, had been born: "A small troglodyte made his appearance here at ten minutes to six o'clock, this morning, who claims to be your nephew, and the heir to all our wealth and honors."

Also on June 22 *Mosses from an Old Manse*, Hawthorne's second collection of tales and sketches, came off the press. Evert Duyckinck had proposed on March 21, 1845, to include such a volume in a series he was editing for Wiley and Putnam. In agreeing, Hawthorne said that, as soon as he could "find outward quietude enough," he would furnish two unpublished tales, for which he would be advanced a hundred dollars. By May 2 he had decided to write only one new tale; on July 1 he told Duyckinck that he planned to "construct a sort of frame-work, in this new story, for the series of stories already published," and make the scene "an idealization" of the Manse and its surroundings, with "glimmerings" of his own life there, "yet so transmogrified that the reader should not know what was reality and what fancy." This sketch, which he continued to call a story, still refused "to unfold its convolutions" when he moved from Concord to Salem in October, when the plan for the work was expanded in January to two volumes, or when copy for the second volume was ready in February and a title for the work was selected. Finally, on April 15, 1846, Hawthorne sent Duyckinck the introductory sketch, "The Old Manse," saying that nothing would flow out of his pen until recently, when "forth came this sketch, of its own accord," and much unlike what he had intended.

The titles Hawthorne first sent Duyckinck, April 7, 1845, included only one piece not written in the Manse period, "A Virtuoso's Collection," which had appeared two months earlier. Although Duyckinck's initial proposal had included four earlier tales, and seven earlier pieces were in the contents of the two volumes, Hawthorne continued to consider the collection both a product and a record of his life at the Manse.[24]

The year of uncertainty and strain in which Hawthorne struggled to write the introductory sketch had prepared him to look back in nostalgia and genuine fondness on his three years in Concord. "The Old Manse" is a reminiscent, sympathetic essay, in which the author, after being led "from the Old Manse into a Custom-House," calls up his idyllic existence at Concord. In June, 1843, he had published "Buds and Bird Voices," a portrait of nature as he experienced it during his first spring at the Manse. "The Old Manse" similarly recreates life in his new Eden as he had recorded it in his notebook. The earlier sketch was written by a lover of nature; "The Old Manse" was written, in addition, by a thoughtful interrogator of both man and nature, an author accustomed to searching out essences and relating his observations to universals. His delight in nature's generosity, the "free gifts of Providence," invited a judgment on man's labor. His day-to-day existence suggested meanings and significances and challenged him to muse and think and record the intricacies and the imponderables he encountered. Immediate local history belonged to the scene and to the author's awareness as recorded in the sketch: the origin of the Manse, its occupants, and its ghosts; the battle of Concord, remembered in the bridge and in the monument; the grave of the British soldier on the hill back of the Manse, about which Thoreau told a story that entered later into one of the romances Hawthorne was to leave unfinished at his death. The residents of the community enter the sketch, and the author enters, as the author, describing his intentions and his methods, and assessing his achievement—with his usual modesty, but with the assurance as to his achievement and his judgment that is also usual with him.

Moving his family back to Salem in the autumn after Julian was born in June, Hawthorne avoided Castle Dismal and settled at 18 Chestnut Street. He could write Bridge a letter less gloomy than he had written for months past; he had "great reason to be thankful to Providence."[25] He and his

Sophia Amelia (Peabody) Hawthorne, 1847; from an etching. Courtesy of the Essex Institute, Salem, Mass.

wife called on his Aunt Rachel Forrester and saw a book owned by William Hawthorne in 1634; they visited in the home of the Howeses, where in the early days of their courtship they had attended Susan Burley's Saturday evening gatherings and where on this occasion they saw Ralph Waldo Emerson. This was their first evening out, Sophia remarked, since Una was born. Not until September, 1847, did they find a house to fit their special needs, a large three-story house at 14 Mall Street, rented for $200 a year. Sophia's quarters were on the ground floor; Hawthorne's mother and sisters came from Herbert Street to occupy the separate apartment above; and his study was over them, presumed to be above children's noises. He had been a full year in the nursery, Sophia noted, "without a chance for one hour's uninterrupted musing, and without his desk being once opened!" She was pleased that Madame Hawthorne (as Sophia regularly called her) had been won "out of that Castle Dismal, and from the mysterious chamber into which no mortal ever peeped, till Una was born, and Julian—for they alone have entered the *penetralia.*" Now Madame Hawthorne would have the remainder of her life "glorified by the presence" of her son and her grandchildren.[26]

Elizabeth Hawthorne remained "an invisible entity." While Sophia and the children were visiting at Boston in the summer of 1848, Hawthorne joined them on July 4 and wrote the next day about his surprise when he reached home and entered the sitting room near midnight: "Behold! a stranger there. . . . It was Elizabeth!" They greeted each other casually and talked awhile. She asked him to go for a walk the next day, and he went. Two days later, he wrote again about these unexpected happenings and the possibility that occasionally Elizabeth would come down to see them in the evening. Hawthorne was home by one-thirty in the afternoon as a rule and spent considerable time with Una and "bundlebreech," recording what they said and did. He sometimes walked alone in the evening, as had long been his habit; his wife recorded that on June 12 and 17, 1847, he went out in his boat and returned about nine o'clock. Late in 1848 he became corresponding secretary of the Salem Lyceum, and in that capacity arranged for lectures by Emerson, Thoreau, James T. Fields, E. P. Whipple, Horace Mann, Theodore Parker, Louis Agassiz, Charles Sumner, and Henry Colman. Thoreau and Emerson were invited to be house guests when they came, and Ellery Channing came to visit.

When Hawthorne entered the custom-house, he expected his duties would leave him as much time for literature as he could profitably apply, and he thought he would write first a book of mythological stories for children. But he wrote little while in the custom-house, primarily book reviews, one of them composed, he said, "with an interruption every two sentences."[27] After moving to Mall Street, he began on November 1 retiring to his study and writing every afternoon with results he described to Longfellow ten days later: "Whenever I sit alone, or walk alone, I find myself dreaming about stories, as of old; but these forenoons in the Custom House undo all that the afternoons and evenings have done. I should be happier if I could write—also, I should like to add something to my income." Pleased with the review of *Evangeline* Hawthorne had written for the *Salem Advertiser* and remembering that the subject of the poem had come from him, Longfellow urged him to undertake a "history of Acadie." But Hawthorne declined, although Longfellow had made the subject "so popular that a history could hardly fail of circulation."[28]

The phrasing of a letter to C. W. Webber on December 14, 1848, suggests the handicaps Hawthorne had to overcome in imaginative writing while in the custom-house: "At last, by main strength, I have wrenched and torn an idea out of my miserable brain, or rather, the fragments of an idea, like a tooth ill-drawn, and leaving the roots to torture me." The story was "Ethan Brand," subtitled "A Chapter from an Abortive Romance."[29] He hoped that the spell was broken and he could "get into a regular train of scribbling." But perhaps he would not, for he had "many impediments to struggle against." Soon the impediments were greater. Early in March, 1849, he learned that a move was afoot to turn him out of office.

16

"Decapitation"

On June 7, 1849, Hawthorne was removed from the surveyorship of customs at Salem. The removal became the warmest topic in local political circles and had the attention of important figures on the national scene. As a political question it remained unsettled until his successor, Captain Allen Putnam, was confirmed by the United States Senate on September 24, 1850. Publication of "The Custom-House" as an introduction to *The Scarlet Letter* in March, 1850, brought Hawthorne's view of the affair before a wide audience and drew comment from book reviewers and newspaper editors, and from Salemites who wanted to challenge his portrayal of either the town or his associates at the custom-house. From documents, letters, newspaper reports and editorials, and "The Custom-House" can be constructed a narrative that leaves few uncertainties about the episode and makes clear Hawthorne's responses, some of which would be reflected in his later writings.

Though federal offices were as a rule filled by political patronage, the rule had not been applied strictly in the Salem custom-house. General James Miller, a national hero since the War of 1812, had been appointed collector under earlier party alignments and had held office through changes of national administration, past the age when he could carry out his full duties. The secretary of the treasury appointed the collector, the surveyor, and the naval officer; the collector appointed the other officers of the customs. General Miller's practice had been to make appointments from the party of the national administration, but not to sweep out all members of the defeated party. Although the Democratic Party was in the minority in Salem, it had gained local patronage during Democratic administrations, to the displeasure of the Salem Whigs. Moreover, the maneuvering that gained Hawthorne the surveyorship had not pleased all the local Democrats. General Miller decided not to seek reappointment under the Whig administration of Zachary Taylor, and Hawthorne on December 23, 1848, sent Senator Atherton of New Hampshire a petition, to be laid before the president, that Colonel Ephraim Miller, son of General Miller and deputy collector, be appointed collector. Hawthorne reported, in transmitting the petition, that all who had been shown the petition, "nearly the whole body of the mercantile community," had signed it, and that Ephraim Miller had the endorsement of the local Democratic committees, Robert Rantoul, and General Pierce. Thus Ephraim Miller, a Whig, was appointed by the outgoing Democratic administration on the recommendation of Democrats, depriving the Salem Whig Party managers of the patronage they thought due them under the incoming Whig administration in Washington.

Resentful of this appointment and the similar appointment of the Salem postmaster, local Whigs petitioned Ephraim Miller to appoint as deputy collector a Whig of their choice. After Miller had denied their petition, they asked him to appoint Whigs in place of the Democrats in the customhouse, designating in particular Zachariah Burchmore, a Democrat who had been at the custom-house nearly a quarter of a century and was a sore reminder that Democrats had held office through Whig and Democratic administrations alike.[1] On the first day of 1849, Hawthorne wrote a long letter, perhaps to Senator Atherton, praising Burchmore in language that he later echoed in the portrait of Burchmore in "The Custom-House." Hawthorne's interceding for Ephraim Miller was known locally, and probably his defense of Burchmore also. The Whigs next tried, without success, to get the secretary of the treasury to replace the naval officer. They seem not to have considered asking for Hawthorne's removal; but when they had seen all their efforts fail and had concluded that none of the Democrats in subordinate positions would be removed until the secretary of the treasury had made the first removal, and had concluded also, according to statements of the Whigs, that some of the party activity in the custom-house was chargeable to Hawthorne, "a number of gentlemen, who were acquainted with the facts, drew up a paper, asking for the appointment of Capt. Putnam."[2]

On March 5, 1849, Hawthorne wrote George Hillard that a strong effort was being mounted to remove him from office, and enumerated what he thought were adequate defenses: He had not displaced a Whig, had been appointed because of his "literary character," not "as a reward for political services," and had not "acted as a politician since." He thought Hillard, a Whig, might prompt others, such as Rufus Choate, to enlighten members of the national administration so that his name would be separated from "the list of ordinary office-holders." An "inoffensive man of letters," he had "obtained a pitiful little office on no other plea than his pitiful little literature," and had filled the office faithfully and efficiently. He explained to Longfellow on June 5 that he would have written a long notice of his new book, *Kavanagh*, were he not being hunted by "political bloodhounds" who accused him of having an editorial connection with the *Salem Advertiser* and writing political articles for it. If they should succeed in turning him out of office, he would "surely immolate one or two of them." He did not mean "that poor monster of a Conolly, . . . nor any of the common political brawlers"; but if there were among them any in a higher position, he might "select a victim, and let fall one little drop of venom on his heart, that shall make him writhe before the grin of the multitude for a considerable time to come." He had thought there must be "enjoyment in writing personal satire; but, never having felt the slightest ill-will towards any human being," he had "been debarred from this peculiar source of pleasure." He almost hoped to be "turned out, so as to have an opportunity of trying it."

When word of his removal reached Salem on June 8, Hawthorne wrote Hillard that there was no use for lamentation. He must consider what to do next, and spoke of "some stated literary employment" with a newspaper or "some printing-establishment," or a subordinate office in the Boston Athenaeum. He would not stand upon his dignity; "that must take care of itself." In Boston the next day he was told that a petition from thirty Salem Whigs had been sent to Washington recommending Captain Putnam's appointment and stating that the one to be replaced had written partisan political articles. Sophia said he had taken his dismissal "as a matter of course in the way of politics," although both Whigs and Democrats had assured him that he would not be removed. He had learned about the petition only because a Whig who was friendly to him "on literary grounds" had told another Whig, who was his personal friend, probably Hillard. He learned also that officials in Washington were not told that he was the one being removed.[3] It made him sick, Hawthorne wrote Hillard on June 12, to think of trying to regain his office. He had come to feel that he was in a lower moral state and a duller intellectual state, and he hoped to arrive at something better.

In writing Hillard on June 8, Hawthorne said his wife did not yet know of his dismissal but would "bear it like a woman—that is to say, better than a man." Her greatest surprise, she wrote her mother, was that the one who got up the petition was Charles W. Upham, who had "thus proved himself a liar and a most consummate hypocrite," for he had "always professed himself the warmest friend." She said that the papers called Upham "that valiant General 'of the Whig church militant,' " and that Charles Sumner called him "that smooth, smiling, oily man of God!" She identified three other signers of the petition: "The illustrious and highly intellectual Richard S. Rogers, who never had an idea in his life. Nat Silsbee Jr.—a man of smallest scope, narrow and stingy to the last degree. George Devereux, a furious demagogue, and a most rancorous spirit in all points—(and Mr. Hooper told me, venomous against Mr. Hawthorne on account of an ancient family feud between Hawthornes and Devereux!)." Silsbee was the brother of Mary Silsbee, now Mrs. Jared Sparks. Sophia encouraged friends of hers to plead her husband's case, including Samuel Hooper in Boston and Frederick Howes in Salem; she said on June 21 that the country was "up in arms" and her husband's name was "ringing through the land."

John Louis O'Sullivan joined the campaign with his usual color and vigor. He wrote the secretary of the treasury on June 22 that Hawthorne "never wrote a political line" for the Democratic Review, but wrote instead "some of the most exquisite gems of pure literature that adorn the language." He would "as soon have dreamed of applying to a nightingale to scream like a vulture, as of asking Hawthorne to write politics," and he quoted from the Albany Atlas a statement that "the man who would knowingly commit such an act" as turning "the gentle ELIA of our American literature" out of office "would broil a humming-bird, and break a harp to pieces to make a fire." Among the Whigs who supported Hawthorne, some of them at the urging of George Hillard, were Rufus Choate, George Ticknor, Harvard professor and historian of Spanish literature, and Amory Holbrook, who wrote Secretary Meredith that signatures to the petition that resulted in Hawthorne's removal had been secured "almost secretly, certainly very privately," through "very great misrepresentations" of his "political character and services," and that his reinstatement would please the Salem Whigs. He wanted it understood, though, that in defending Hawthorne he was not defending other Democrats in the custom-house. Hillard appealed to Daniel Webster's idealism and his sense of practical politics, and he persuaded Edward Everett, another Whig, to write Secretary Meredith that removing Hawthorne was a mistake; but Everett replied to Hillard that as a Democrat Hawthorne was "on the side of barbarism and vandalism against order, law, and constitutional liberty," and later he withdrew his letter to Meredith, saying he had now learned that Hawthorne had been "the agent of party measures of the most objectionable character." Everett's reversal followed a visit by Upham in his efforts to counter the growing support for Hawthorne. He had brought back to Salem earlier a copy of the petition Hawthorne had submitted endorsing Ephraim F. Miller for the collectorship, and by altering his copy to make the statement more inclusive than it actually was, Sophia wrote her mother, he could use it to impeach Hawthorne's veracity. This deceit showed the "meanness and cunning" of "the Reverend Priest," whom her husband thought "the most satisfactory villain that ever was."

Newspapers took up Hawthorne's dismissal early, and the most partisan of them printed vituperative exchanges. The Boston *Post* reported the dismissal on June 11, in what became a steady defense of Hawthorne. A letter to the editor the next day concludes, "There stands, at the guillotine, beside the headless trunk of a pure minded, faithful and well deserving officer, sacrificed to the worst of party proscription, Gen. Zachary Taylor. . . ." This picture of President Taylor, the guillotine, and the headless surveyor appealed to Hawthorne, and afterward he referred often to his "decapitation." The *Salem Register* of June 11 carried an editorial endorsing the dismissal. While professing "none but the highest feelings toward Mr. Hawthorne," the editor yet took delight in pointing out that the removal had a message for others at the custom-house. "It is simply this: 'If the Surveyor isn't safe, WHEN AM I TO GO?' Wait patiently, gentlemen, and the answer will come." On June 12 the *Boston Atlas* reprinted this editorial, and on June 16 it printed, with editorial endorsement, a communication from Salem stating charges against Hawthorne, all of a political nature. Two days later Hawthorne sent George Hillard a point-by-point refutation of each charge.

He saw no need to refute the accusation that he had been appointed by intrigue and without the approval of the Salem Democrats, but he noted that Bancroft had offered him two offices earlier. The charge that he had replaced a Whig could be refuted by various people, including Nehemiah

Brown, whom he had replaced, and by "a gentleman now very prominent and active in our local politics, the Rev. Charles Wentworth Upham, who told me, in the presence of David Roberts, Esq., that I need never fear removal under a Whig administration, inasmuch as my appointment had not displaced a Whig." As for the political activities charged against him, he had not done a line of political writing; he had never attended a political meeting or convention; and he had never walked in a torchlight procession—he was tempted to add, he said, that he "would hardly have done anything so little in accordance with" his "tastes and character, had the result of the Presidential election depended on it."

Hillard sent this letter to the *Boston Daily Advertiser*, a paper edited by Nathan Hale, in which it appeared on June 21.[4] The *Salem Gazette*, edited by Hawthorne's Whig friend Caleb Foote, reprinted it two days later, along with the earlier communication to the *Atlas* attacking Hawthorne, and remarked that they were being published because the *Gazette* had received many requests for the Boston newspapers. On June 18, a writer in William Cullen Bryant's *New York Post* said he "did not think, before, that there was a man in Massachusetts who would take an office which had to be obtained by the removal of Hawthorne." The *Boston Post* printed on June 22 a letter from Salem answering the communication in the *Atlas* of June 16. The writer, probably Benjamin Barstow, a member of the Town Committee and vice president of the Hickory Club, said that the charges of political activity had been concocted after Hawthorne's removal because a majority of the local Whigs were surprised and displeased by it. He could deny explicitly that Hawthorne had known or approved of being listed as a delegate to the recent state convention, for he had drawn up the list himself. He identified the writer of the *Atlas* article with the writer of the editorial in the *Salem Register* of June 11 "(for there can be but one such in Salem)."

This writer most likely was Upham; the mind and the prose style of these pieces seem to be the same as revealed in writing known to be his. John Chapman, proprietor and editor of the *Register* and a member of the state governor's executive council, was more restrained than Upham—and the editorial—in venom and in language. He was second in importance only to Upham in making and presenting the case against Hawthorne— probably more important than Hawthorne realized. His and Upham's communications to the secretary of the treasury show that they collaborated in assembling evidence, and possibly in presenting it. Chapman's eagerness to assert his respect for Hawthorne as an author led to misunderstandings that required several steps to correct. In writing Secretary Meredith on June 12, Amory Holbrook placed Chapman among other Whigs who opposed the removal; a week later, he wrote again, saying that Chapman still opposed the removal but wanted other Democrats at the custom-house dismissed. On June 30, when Chapman sent Meredith an uncompromising defense of Hawthorne's removal, he seems to have wanted to say that, if he had known at the time of Hawthorne's removal what he knew later, his view of the matter would have been different. It apparently was bitterness because Ephraim Miller would not replace Democrats in the custom-house with Whigs that prompted him to make a case against Hawthorne, finally, in order to accomplish his first purpose. The same explanation may apply to other Salem Whigs, most of whom were following the two determined leaders: Chapman, methodical and persistent, and Upham, emotional and vindictive.

Fearful that support for reinstating Hawthorne was growing, the Whig leaders wrote Meredith on June 25 that they would soon send new evidence and new statements. On that day Hawthorne read a suggestion in a Salem newspaper that he be offered a better office than he had held, and the next day he wrote Horace Mann that, after an absence of two or three days, he found the general feeling in Salem running strongly in his favor and found some who had opposed him earlier now disposed to compromise. He told Mann that, even if there were an office to which he might be appointed without displacing anyone else, he felt that only by reinstatement in his original position would the charges against him be refuted. In writing to Hillard and Longfellow on March 5, he had spoken of false charges being made in order to effect his removal, but he seemed willing to accept dismissal as a normal political occurrence. He remarked in the letter he wrote for Hillard to publish in a newspaper that he had been appointed as a replacement of Nehemiah Brown earlier in a political move that implied no wrongdoing on the part of Brown. He would have been aware, of course, that the appointment of Brown, a Democrat, by the outgoing Whig president, Tyler, was no different from the appointment of Ephraim Miller which he had helped bring about just before the Whigs replaced the Democrats in the recent election. As a solution of the present conflict, he proposed that Captain Putnam be appointed to the office of weigher and gauger, in which the emolument would be greater than the surveyor's, and he promised to accept reinstatement if it were offered.

Upham wrote Meredith on June 29, urging that Captain Putnam's commission be issued at once, and protesting that "certain literary characters, living in other places, and utterly ignorant of the facts of the case," had caused the dismissal not to be carried out. Lest the charges of political activities not prove adequate to support the dismissal, he launched a new attack that had been hinted in the *Boston Atlas* of June 16: "How comes it that his Loco Foco subordinates received some hundred dollars a year more than their Whig associates?" Burchmore wrote Hawthorne on June 29 that Chapman had admitted to one of the customs officers that Burchmore, rather than Hawthorne, represented the Democratic Party at the custom-house, but that "it was necessary just now to lay it at" Hawthorne's door. In a long letter to Secretary Meredith on June 30, Chapman first reviewed the fruitless attempts of the Salem Whigs to gain positions in the custom-house, and then introduced the charges that Hawthorne had assigned extra work to his subordinates in such a way as to give the Democrats "a much larger compensation" than the Whigs, and that in the autumn of 1847 the Democratic officers were taxed for the support of the party. Chapman said he had it from the lips of one who refused to pay the tax that he "was served with a written notice, *signed by Mr. Hawthorne himself*, that *his services were no longer required.*" He said also that one who protested but was not discharged was omitted afterward from extra work.

Unaware of these new charges, Hawthorne sent Horace Mann on July 2 a sheaf of testimonials from several officers of the local Democratic Party that he had not been an active politician while surveyor. Mann forwarded these documents to Meredith on July 5, along with a copy of Hawthorne's own published defense, and said that other Whigs of his acquaintance thought as he did that the administration had been imposed upon, and would rejoice to see Hawthorne returned to office. In addition Mann put the question to the Taylor administration whether, in view of the scant means the government has of encouraging literary merit, an administration that fails to show regard for distinguished literary merit does not "write itself down as barbarian?" He asked also for a copy of any other charges that might have been made. Hawthorne had suggested that this request be made, saying that one or two of his subordinates at the custom-house were helping the Whigs concoct new charges.

Upham could not furnish Secretary Meredith by July 7 the full representation he had promised, but he reported that in meetings on July 3 and 6 the Salem Whigs had voted "hearty approval" of the removal of Hawthorne. The "Memorial," as Upham titled the final document, gave the history of the affair, in the Whigs' view, and then elaborated on the new charges Chapman had made on June 30. It accomplished the purpose intended, leaving no possibility for Hawthorne to be reinstated. It asked again for the removal of Ephraim Miller and the re-appointment of General James Miller as collector, and nominated as naval officer Nehemiah Brown, whom Hawthorne had replaced as surveyor. The memorial contained the statement that it had been accepted by the Whigs on July 6, "after a free discussion"; but the evidence is clear that Upham wrote it after the meetings of the Whig caucus, and did not have explicit endorsement of its contents. One of the three members of the drafting committee, Henry Russell, declined to serve, and the chairman of the caucus, Nathaniel Silsbee, Jr., took his place; the third member, Thomas Tract, was not listed as attending either meeting. On July 6 the drafting committee was instructed to report "the proceedings of the two meetings," and the next day Upham wrote Secretary Meredith that he hoped "to start early next week to present" to him the action taken in the two meetings.

The "Memorial of the Whigs of Salem" reached a climax in explaining the move against Hawthorne: "It was declared in the streets, with triumphant defiance, that the Whig party dared not, and could not remove Nathaniel Hawthorne." The collector and his official associates "planted themselves, as they thought, securely behind him, and actually made his removal necessary before we could advance a step in obtaining our rightful authority over the Custom House. . . . Mr. Hawthorne owes the application for his removal entirely to the folly of his friend, the Collector, and his other advisers, who placed him between themselves and the power of the administration." Upham began the memorial by saying that the Salem Whigs had supposed major officers would be replaced by Whigs and lesser officers would be removed only for "marked and notorious violence of political action" or "participation in the perversion of the public funds to partisan purposes." Since the case against Hawthorne for political action had been rendered inadequate by the "rash and audacious misrepresentations of ignorant intermeddlers," it had become necessary, Upham said, to draw the second arrow, Chapman's earlier accusation of malfeasance. He listed the amounts four Democrats and four Whigs in the surveyor's department received in one year, showing that the Democrats averaged $96 a year more than the Whigs (which he rounded off to "about $130 more"). The practice originated under Hawthorne, Upham continued, for each inspector to "pay back, ostensibly and professedly for the support of 'the party,' " half of his pay for extra work. Whigs were employed under the Democratic administration, in Upham's logic, only so that the number of Democrats could be kept small and "their share of the spoils" would be greater, thus consummating "the corruption, iniquity and fraud with which the transaction is stamped, from beginning to end."

Refining on Chapman's charge and changing several details, Upham said that the notes suspending three inspectors were later withdrawn as inexpedient; but he held to Chapman's earlier charge that one of the three "held out, and has never received from the hands of the Surveyor, an extra job, from that day to this!!" He added two paragraphs of regret that one of "Hawthorne's true manliness of character, . . . one of the most amiable and elegant writers of America," appreciated by all parties, "and none more than the Whigs of his native city," had been duped into playing such a role. The circumstances reported here, the document concluded, "have been stated with no unkind feeling towards him, and with much regret that the interference of strangers, having no justifiable call to meddle in our affairs, has been so far heeded by the government as to require such special and personal representations."

Whether Hawthorne received a copy of these new charges as a result of Horace Mann's request to the secretary of the treasury, or had them from some other source, he wrote out an explanation for Horace Mann on August 8, to put him "in possession of the facts, in case of accidents." The Whigs had received information from subordinates in his department, as he had suspected. The circumstances that had been twisted into a false charge were these: It fell to him to carry out a directive from the Treasury Department to dismiss two temporary inspectors. Hoping to meet the requirement and yet prepare the way for returning them to work later, he held up the notices; but a friend of the two men told them of the possible suspension. Burchmore and the one who had told them were ready to testify in Hawthorne's behalf. Burchmore had been dismissed a week earlier, but the other had not been, and Hawthorne had "no object to attain, worth purchasing at the sacrifice" this inspector would make in testifying for him. He had no expectation or desire to regain the surveyorship; his purpose was "simply to make such a defence to the Senate" as would ensure the rejection of his successor, and thus satisfy the public that he had been removed "on false or insufficient grounds." He added, "Then, if Mr. Upham should give me occasion—or perhaps if he should not—I shall do my best to kill and scalp him in the public prints; and I think I shall succeed."

Hawthorne said to Mann that, knowing "the rigid discipline of Custom houses as to party-subscription," he thought there might have been an effort to use the deferred possibility of suspension "to squeeze an assessment out of" the two inspectors without his knowing about it; but, if such were proved to be the case, he could not see how his defense would be affected. As it turned out, however, he offered no defense either before the public or before the Senate. In closing his letter to Mann on August 8, he vowed as soon as possible to "bid farewell forever to this abominable city; for, now that my mother is gone, I have no longer anything to keep me here." His mother had been buried on August 2, and before another month had passed, he was writing immensely, so his wife phrased it, on the story that became *The Scarlet Letter*.

17

The Scarlet Letter

While Hawthorne's mother was near death, late in July, 1849, Sophia stayed with her much of each day, leaving her husband to look after the children. For more than a year he had recorded occasionally what Una and Julian did and said. On July 29 his notebook record begins at nine-thirty in the morning, with Una crying for her mother and Julian sad in sympathy. Una's hair has not yet been combed, "everybody being busy with grandmamma." Julian asks to go with his mother to the sick room when she appears for a moment, but must be refused. The children act out various roles in the drama that so impresses them; they talk of "going to die" and "going to God." Their father detects in them hints of under-standing beyond their years.

To Hawthorne it seemed strange that the death of a child is beautiful, though in it Nature betrays her promise and "destroys her prettiest play-things," and that death in old age, "the consummation of life," has "so much gloom and ambiguity about it," as was magnified for him by "these last heavy trobbings—this funeral march" of his mother's heart (VIII, 423–28). At five in the afternoon of July 30 he went to his mother's room for the first time in two days, and was shocked at the change.

I love my mother; but there has been, ever since my boyhood, a sort of coldness of intercourse between us, such as is apt to come between per-sons of strong feelings, if they are not managed rightly. I did not expect to be much moved at the time—that is to say, not to feel any overpowering emotion struggling, just then—though I knew that I should deeply remember and regret her. . . . I was moved to kneel down close by my mother, and take her hand. She knew me, but could only murmur a few indistinct words—among which I understood an injunction to take care of my sisters. . . . I found the tears slowly gathering in my eyes. I tried to keep them down; but it would not be—I kept filling up, till, for a few moments, I shook with sobs. For a long time, I knelt there, holding her hand; and surely it is the darkest hour I ever lived.

Afterward, hearing the children's shouts from the grass plot below, he looked out at Una, "so full of spirit and life, that she was life itself." His notebook record continues:

And then I looked at my poor dying mother; and seemed to see the whole of human existence at once, standing in the dusty midst of it. Oh what a mockery, if what I saw were all,—let the interval between extreme youth and dying age be filled up with what happiness it might! But God would not have made the close so dark and wretched, if there were nothing beyond; for then it would have been a fiend that created us, and measured out our existence, and not God. It would be something beyond wrong—it would be insult—to be thrust out of life into annihilation in this miserable way. So, out of the very bitterness of death, I gather the sweet assurance of a better state of being. [VIII, 428–29]

The working through to this conclusion is a paradigm of Hawthorne's thinking on the problem that his friends Ralph Waldo Emerson and Herman Melville confronted also—as it came to them from the Calvinist heritage they had in common.

Mrs. Hawthorne died in the afternoon of July 31, "after four or five days of pain," Sophia wrote her mother. "At the last she had no suffering,—for eight hours no suffering, but gradually faded as day fades." The funeral was at four o'clock, August 2.

Within a month, Hawthorne was writing nine hours a day, more than twice his normal time at his desk. His wife wrote her mother that he wrote *"immensely,"* and she was almost frightened.[1] She had written him two years earlier, while she was visiting in Boston, that she had suffered for him in her "babydom," that it was important to protect him from the cares of the nursery; for he was born to muse and, "through undisturbed dreams, to enlighten the world."[2] Now that circumstances had freed him from the custom-house, she seems to have been able to free him largely from the nursery. According to published reports, when he told her he had been dismissed, she exclaimed that now he could write his book, *The Scarlet Letter*, and brought out money she had saved from the household

allowance.[3] These reports offer little for the factual record, for what became *The Scarlet Letter* was intended for several months past this date to be
not a book but a tale in a collection with others; but they suggest the state
of Hawthorne's finances and the spirit of his wife. He wrote Hillard on
June 8 that his salary had done no more than support his family and repay
debts he owed. He received $250 a year in quarterly payments, supple-
mented by a portion of the revenue collected at the port, which had
declined as shipping over the Salem wharves fell off. In writing Mary
Mann in 1847, Sophia had used the figure $900 as his annual pay, instead
of the expected $1,200, compared with Horace Mann's $2,000. A nine-
penny calico dress was the best she could afford; her husband urged her to
have a seamstress and provide the clothes she needed, but she could not
"bear to spend a cent till it *must* be spent." It was their hope to furnish a
parlor in the spring, she said, also a guest chamber. There was no carpet
in her husband's study, and he would not consider buying one.[4] She
decorated lamp shades, books, and screens (at $5 and $10 each), some of
them for friends she said wanted to befriend her. When her husband no
longer went to the custom-house, her plan was to give three hours a day to
this work, using the study while he kept the children, after he had spent
nine hours at his desk; but while he was driving his literary pen, he could
give her no help with the children.[5] According to Julian Hawthorne, "the
entire family was prostrated by illness" in the autumn of 1849, and
Hawthorne had "an almost intolerable attack of earache" for several days.[6]
Sophia said her husband suffered from brain fever soon after his mother's
death.

Money for the household bills came from various sources, besides Sophia's earnings. O'Sullivan paid $100 due from the *Democratic Review*, and
John Greenleaf Whittier sent the payment still due for "The Great Stone
Face" in the *National Era*.[7] Sophia's friend Sarah Shaw sent a check she
said was from Francis George Shaw, which she noted was to be repaid
when it was no longer needed, or never.[8] On January 7, 1850, George
Hillard mailed money he had collected among Hawthorne's friends, with
no thought of obligation: "It is only paying, in a very imperfect measure,
the debt we owe you for what you have done for American Literature."[9]
One contributor was Henry Wadsworth Longfellow; another was James
Russell Lowell, who wrote Evert Duyckinck and John Louis O'Sullivan
suggesting that a sum might be sent also from Hawthorne's friends in
New York.[10] When Hawthorne read Hillard's letter in the post office, it
brought tears to his eyes, as his troubles had never done. After declaring

Mall Street House, Salem, where Hawthorne wrote *The Scarlet Letter*. Courtesy of the Essex Institute, Salem, Mass.

in his reply of January 20 that "ill-success in life is really and justly a matter of shame," he concluded, "The only way in which a man can retain his self-respect, while availing himself of the generosity of his friends, is, by making it an incitement to his utmost exertions, so that he may not need their help again. I shall look upon it so,—nor will shun any drudgery that my hand shall find to do, if thereby I may win bread." On December 9,

1853, after two months as consul in Liverpool, Hawthorne repaid the loan through Hillard, $500, "with interest included." Another sum came from an uncommon source. Lewis Mansfield asked Hawthorne's criticism and advice on poetical work he had in progress, and upon receiving a report, sent a payment which Hawthorne decided to accept and to earn as best he could. He declined further payment after sending further criticism; and he declined Mansfield's offer to lend him $1,000, but he accepted a case of champagne later.[11] Hawthorne had a loan from Dr. Benjamin F. Browne; in January, 1851, he sent Browne $100 and said he expected to pay off the remainder of his debt within a year.[12]

Horatio Bridge, as usual ready to turn a hand in Hawthorne's behalf, asked John Jay to suggest Hawthorne as a contributor to *Blackwood's Magazine*.[13] Hawthorne had in mind writing a schoolbook, and it had been his intention for at least a year to publish another collection of tales and sketches. At about this time began his relations with James T. Fields, which became one of the most important author-publisher relationships in the history of American letters. Fields, a brusque young poet who in 1843 had joined William D. Ticknor in the publishing firm that became Ticknor and Company, appeared before the Salem Lyceum while Hawthorne was corresponding secretary. In reminiscences published after Hawthorne's death, he told of visiting 14 Mall Street in the winter of 1849–50, taking home with him a manuscript that turned out to be *The Scarlet Letter*, reading it on the train, returning the next day with great enthusiasm, and arranging for publication of the work. Although Fields was so careful to show himself the discoverer of a great novelist that his report has to be discounted, part of it fits into the record from other sources.[14]

Planning a third collection like *Twice-Told Tales* and *Mosses from an Old Manse*, Hawthorne had four tales recently published or soon to be published: "Main Street," "The Great Stone Face," "The Snow-Image," and "Ethan Brand"; and he could reclaim earlier pieces from magazines and annuals. Again he planned to include one or more unpublished tales, and for that purpose took the idea that had been in the back of his mind at least since he wrote "Endicott and the Red Cross" in 1837, the idea of a young woman sentenced to wear an emblem of guilt. As a second new piece, he planned an autobiographical introduction which would present the background of the tales in his experiences and his surroundings and would prepare the way for the new story of the scarlet letter. By January 8, 1850, Fields had shown an interest in publishing the collection, and on

January 15 Hawthorne sent him the manuscript of "The Custom-House" and the new story, except for the last three chapters. He estimated this story at 200 pages, to which he would add 200 pages from pieces already in print. " 'The Scarlet Letter' is rather a delicate subject to write upon," he noted, but he expected no objections on that score, in his way of treating it. The title of the volume would be "Old-Time Legends; together with *sketches, experimental and ideal.*" Because he wrote "such an infernal hand," he must have proof sheets to revise. After seeing what Hawthorne sent on January 15, Fields suggested that they publish, not a collection of tales, but a single romance, with an autobiographical introduction. Hawthorne replied on January 20 that he preferred Field's choice, "as a matter of taste and beauty," but feared that with only the one long story, the book would be too somber. "I found it impossible to relieve the shadows of the story with so much light as I would gladly have thrown in. Keeping so close to its point as the tale does, and diversified no otherwise than by turning different sides of the same dark idea to the reader's eye, it will weary very many people, and disgust some." He would leave the decision to Fields, and would not be sorry if he decided for separate publication. In that case the title should be *The Scarlet Letter* and, if it would be in good taste, should be printed in red on the title-page.

Hawthorne wrote Bridge on February 4 that he had finished the book the day before, "one end being in the press in Boston," while the other was in his head in Salem. Although his remarks were whimsical, they show that he thought the new book a good one and hoped to have his judgment endorsed by the public. His publisher spoke of it "in tremendous terms of approbation," as his wife did also. When he read her the conclusion the night before, he said, "It broke her heart and sent her to bed with a grievous headache—which I look upon as a triumphant success! Judging from its effect on her and the publisher, I may calculate on what bowlers call a ten-strike!" He later recalled his own emotions in reading the final scene to his wife, "tried to read it, rather," he wrote in his *English Notebooks* for September 14, 1855, "for my voice swelled and heaved, as if I were tossed up and down on an ocean as it subsided after a storm. But I was in a very nervous state, then, having gone through a great diversity and severity of emotion, for many months past. I think I have never overcome my own adamant in any other instance."

The book went through the press at top speed and was released on March 16. Two references in "The Custom-House" to the tales and articles originally intended for the volume are evidence that it was brought out in haste. The first edition of 2,500 copies was sold in ten days, and a second edition of 3,000 copies was printed.

Publication of *The Scarlet Letter* closed an important segment of Hawthorne's life. He had already made plans to leave Salem. During the preceding year, relations with his townsmen had reached an exacerbating nadir that was coincident with the death of his mother; there had followed six months of creativity that he did not equal in intensity or achievement at any other time in his life. In those months, he produced a romance that brought into focus his understanding of sorrow, guilt, and suffering; and in the introductory sketch he delineated the people, the events, and the essential qualities of his experience in the custom-house in a way that enabled him to understand them, and would enable him afterward to leave them behind.

The varieties of personality, motives, and character Hawthorne observed in his efforts to gain and afterward to keep his office were the more fascinating because among those involved were friends and acquaintances of his since boyhood and members of families prominent in Salem, alongside his own, since the founding generation. His years as an officer of the customs showed him the port, once among the busiest in America, now slipping into disuse and decay; the lines of trade extending from the wharves of local merchant-mariners to distant ports; seamen in the varieties common to world trade; and his fellow officers, less varied perhaps and less exotic than the crews of the ships, but no less worth his study. "A better book than I shall ever write was there," he remarked in "The Custom-House"; "leaf after leaf presenting itself to me, just as it was written out by the reality of the flitting hour." That sketch, completed within six months after his removal from office, is a distillation of his life and thought in the preceding three and a half years. In a manner usual with him, it takes materials he knew and through the play of his imagination extracts salient qualities of scene, action, character, and mood, while holding enough of the liberal and factual to gain the semblance of exact portrayal.

The author of "The Custom-House" declares that he had read "(probably in Felt's Annals) a notice of the decease of Mr. Surveyor Pue, about fourscore years ago," and he supposed that the letter and the manuscript he found had been left in the custom-house because "Mr. Pue's death had happened suddenly." The 1827 edition of Joseph B. Felt's *Annals of Salem* (which was a storehouse of information for Hawthorne) records that Jonathan Pue, "surveyor and searcher" of Salem and Marblehead, did indeed die suddenly in Salem on March 24, 1760;[15] Felt's authority, the *Boston Evening Post* of March 31, 1760, reports that Pue died very suddenly the previous Monday. The author says further that the manuscript and the scarlet letter are still in his possession and "shall be freely exhibited" to anyone who desires to see them.[16] The free use of the historical Surveyor Pue illustrates the use the author says he has made of the recovered manuscript; he has followed the story in outline, but has imagined "the motives and modes of passion that influenced the characters" with "nearly or altogether as much license as if the facts had been entirely" of his own invention.

Similarly, and in keeping with Hawthorne's fictional processes, he and the author of the sketch are interfused and yet remain separate personages. Thus he created the "moonlight in a familiar room," the medium he thought "most suitable for a romance-writer to get acquainted with his illusive guests." In this light the objects "lose their actual substance, and become things of the intellect"; and "the floor of our familiar room has become a neutral territory, somewhere between the real world and fairyland, where the Actual and the Imaginary may meet, and each imbue itself with the nature of the other." If there is an anthracite fire that casts a ruddy glow and converts the snow-images of the moonlight into men and women, if the whole scene is observed in a looking-glass and becomes "one remove further from the actual"—if under these conditions "a man, sitting all alone, cannot dream strange things, and make them look like truth, he need never try to write romances."

Besides this glimpse into the author's workshop, and behind it into his conception of the romance, "The Custom-House" embodies the essentials of his experiences as surveyor of customs; and it reveals the meaning and the significance he found in those experiences—provided the sketch is read with an eye to his imaginative coloring. "The Custom-House" records the widely varied patterns of action, thought, and feeling which prevailed among his associates, but which become in the essay a synthesis of universals. In reproducing "the page of life that was spread out before" him, he wrote a portion of the "better book" he had despaired of writing; and in the process he transformed his report of observation into a richly imaginative sketch. Following his habit of mixing the specific and the general, the real and the imagined, the individual and the universal, he could smile at foibles and transgressions among his associates, and could even ignore the persons who had connived to "decapitate" him; he could say about Salem, the entity finally responsible, only that he should have expected less of her. Salem and he were one and the same through the dust of his ancestors over the past two centuries, and through the kinship of all descendants of Adam. Once he had written out the experiences, they took their place among others, indistinguishable as real or imagined, which became the substance of his fictional works. He wrote Fields about "The Custom-House" on January 15: "all political and official turmoil has subsided within me, so that I have not felt inclined to execute justice on any of my enemies." The decapitated surveyor, in becoming a character in a semi-fictional account, had all but ceased to be Hawthorne. Except for the collector of customs, General James Miller, the author's associates at the custom-house are not named; but they can be identified, as they could be also by many of those in Salem who read the sketch when it was published.

Probably none of the customs officers had ever read anything Hawthorne had written, and the only literary discussion he had was with John D. Howard and a young clerk, Joe Waters. To be reminded thus how little his achievements counted outside his own circle was salutary, he wrote in "The Custom-House"; and he took pride in being able to fill a role in the world of affairs. Among his associates in this world was Zachariah Burchmore, who he said was "the Custom-House in himself." He admired Burchmore for his integrity and the efficiency he had shown in nearly twenty-five years of responsible work. Their friendship continued as long as Hawthorne lived. When Sophia first met Burchmore in 1852, she noted his gentleness and his great affection for her husband. For his part, Hawthorne spared no effort to return Burchmore to political employment, and succeeded when the Democrats came to office again in 1853.[17] He had known William B. Pike first at the Boston custom-house and a year after becoming surveyor at Salem brought him into his department as an inspector. He found freer conviviality with Pike and Burchmore than with anyone else at the custom-house. After a few weeks in office, he recommended the removal of two inspectors as incompetent and the appointment of two others, who had been dismissed during the previous administration. One of those reappointed was Captain Stephen Burchmore, brother of Zachariah, identifiable in "The Custom-House" as the one who stirred Hawthorne "to laughter and admiration by his marvellous gifts as a story-teller."

Zachariah Burchmore and John D. Howard wrote to thank Hawthorne for what he had said of them in "The Custom-House," and all of his associates who found themselves in the essay might feel grateful—except one. That one was the permanent inspector, who was recognizable as William Lee, nearing his fourscore years, who had been appointed in 1814. He was "the father of the Custom-House" and "fittest to be a Custom-House officer" of all those the author had known. "He possessed no power of thought, no depth of feeling, no troublesome sensibilities; nothing, in short, but a few commonplace instincts." The nearest he came to mental activity was in calling up "the ghosts of bygone meals" in a manner "as appetizing as a pickle or an oyster." When Hawthorne was asked about publishing his portrait of the permanent inspector in the *Literary World* before *The Scarlet Letter* was released, he replied that, rather than call attention to this severe sketch "in the *alto relievo* of a preliminary abstract, "he would prefer to use instead his sketch of General Miller. He explained, "I shall catch it pretty smartly from my ill-wishers here in Salem, on the score of this old Inspector."[18] Whether Fields or Duyckinck made the decision, his preference was ignored, and the sketch of the inspector appeared on March 16, 1850. The *Salem Register* of March 21 carried a review of *The Scarlet Letter*, no doubt from the pen of John Chapman, the editor. He found in the portrait of Lee the full justification for the removal of Hawthorne that some had not found earlier, and declared that he could not fathom the author's reason for "so rudely and abusively" dragging before the public "a venerable gentleman, whose chief crime seems to be that he loves a good dinner."

The answer to Chapman's query does not come readily. Within the essay itself the portrait of the permanent inspector has a clear purpose and fills it to perfection. He stands for all custom-house employees—and all governmental office-holders; Zachariah Burchmore stands as "the ideal of his class," but stands alone. The portrait of the inspector is like others in Hawthorne's imaginative writings, such as the Old Apple Dealer and some of the minor characters in "Ethan Brand," whom he drew from his observation with only slight changes but made so thoroughly representational that the originals all but dropped out of his awareness. Chapman's defense of William Lee in his review of *The Scarlet Letter* suggests that he was under obligation for help in making up his charges against Hawthorne. George Loring Newcomb, a son-in-law of Lee's, attended the meeting on July 6, 1849, when the Whigs voted to authorize Upham's memorial to the Treasury Department. A comment John D. Howard sent Hawthorne suggests that he knew Hawthorne's reason for drawing the harsh portrait of Lee and considered it adequate: "The 'Old Inspector' was faithfully portrayed, and, as I understand, the galled jade winces, and wishes he was young for your sake!" [19] In his preface to the second edition of *The Scarlet Letter*, dated March 30, Hawthorne said that the local excitement "could hardly have been more violent, indeed, had he burned down the Custom-House, and quenched its last smoking ember in the blood of a certain venerable personage, against whom he is supposed to cherish a peculiar malevolence." A reader acquainted with Hawthorne's prefaces and other semi-autobiographical statements will note that he may seem to say more than he does, as in declaring that reading the essay impresses him with "its frank and genuine good-humor, and the general accuracy with which he has conveyed his sincere impressions of the characters therein described," and that "it could not have been done in a better or a kindlier spirit."

The author of "The Custom-House" says that he was pleased to be thrown among associates far different from "the dreamy brethren of Brook Farm" and his literary acquaintances at Concord and Boston. "Even the old Inspector was desirable, as a change of diet, to a man who had known Alcott." In writing the sketch, Hawthorne gave the episode of his removal a dimension and a form he could manage, and avoided being warped by it. He felt no bitterness toward politicians who had engaged in tactics normal to the political arena, and in time felt little bitterness toward those like Upham and Chapman who had made false accusations to achieve their purpose. Forgiving Upham was difficult for him and his wife because of their friendship in the past, the closeness of which is suggested by Upham's inscribing to Hawthorne a copy of the untitled pamphlet he had written on the death of his son Edward, July 1, 1838.[20] Yet the deceit and the cunning of Upham, seen as traits visited inexplicably but abundantly upon some of the children of Adam, would hardly provoke anger. In a remarkable letter of June 17, 1850, Hawthorne told of discovering, much to his own surprise, he said, that he could forgive a friend of many years who had helped turn him out of office. He was writing to Horace Conolly, the adopted son of Susannah Ingersoll (the Duchess), who had been called the Cardinal among the whist players in the 1830's, and had told Hawthorne, who in turn had told Longfellow, the story that became *Evangeline*. As an officer in the local Democratic Party in 1846, he had recommended Hawthorne for the surveyorship; three years later he was a Whig and supported the move by Upham and others against Hawthorne. Now he wanted Hawthorne to help turn Captain Putnam out of the surveyor's office from which Hawthorne had been removed, hoping to gain the office for himself.

Addressing Conolly as "Ex-Cardinal," Hawthorne answered that he did not "care a damn" who was surveyor at Salem, but that he was determined never again to be any kind of customs officer himself. He had withdrawn his opposition to Putnam and had written Senator James W. Bradbury (1802–1901), a college-mate of his at Bowdoin, that he desired Putnam's confirmation. A year after his appointment as surveyor, Putnam was still serving without confirmation by the Senate. Bradbury had introduced a Senate resolution asking the president for a list of government officers who had been removed, and the resolution had come up for debate several times. If the resolution had passed and the list of dismissed officers, including Hawthorne, had been brought to the Senate floor, confirmation of some of the replacement appointees would no doubt have been denied. Hawthorne wrote that, if he had not interfered, Putnam "must have been rejected to a dead certainty," but now was sure to be confirmed. The remainder of this long letter shows that the writer had a sense of the comic that might appear even when his own discomfiture was great—and that he was capable of great tolerance for such an erring son of Adam as Conolly. "If you had any chance of getting the Surveyorship for yourself," he wrote, "I might take some little trouble to promote it, to reward you for getting me out and to punish you for your misdeeds generally. But as you seem to desire it only from your natural instinct for mischief, you must excuse me for not meddling with the matter." They had met recently in Boston, with a result that was "almost too incredible to put into a romance. . . . You have been slandering and back-biting and stabbing me in the dark for years past, both before and after our breach. You dug me out of office, and did your best to starve me, and at the close of it all, I find myself eating bread and salt and getting corned with you, and just as kindly as if nothing had happened, and kindly and friendly I sit down to write you, with pretty much the same feelings as ten years ago when you used to bother me with your infernal drafts from Philadelphia. There is one Christian in the world and I am he."

But Conolly had blessed where he had meant to curse. Through his "good offices," Hawthorne had been kicked out of the custom-house "just in the nick of time," for, if he had stayed four years longer, he would "have rusted utterly away." As it was, Hawthorne wrote, "I came forth as fresh as if I had been just made, and went to work as if the devil were in me, if it were only to put my enemies to the blush." And what an influence the Ex-Cardinal had exerted on literature! "The seed of Evangeline was yours, and The Scarlet Letter would not have existed unless you had set your mischief-making faculties at work." The letter concludes with the exhortation:

> Goodbye. Imitate my Christian virtues, and as I take nothing amiss which you have done, so do you take in good part all the rough things which my pen lets drop in writing to you as naturally as a bee distils honey. Whatever I may say, I doubt whether anybody (except the Duchess) feels a greater kindness for you, or would be more sorry to have you come to harm.
>
> Try to be a better boy than you have been—say your prayers—leave off cigars—eschew evil, make the most of what good you find in yourself—stick to your friends—forgive your enemies, and leave that wretched old town of Salem the moment you are your own man.[21]

Hawthorne said that Conolly was "a kind of pet serpent and must be allowed to bite now and then, that being the nature of the critter," and that, if they had not met in Boston, he would probably have put him into his next book, "not with any unkindness," but developing both good and evil, and "showing about as queer a combination as the world has ever witnessed." He would "have done the business in a perfectly good natured way," though Conolly probably would not have found the result altogether satisfactory. Since they had now shaken hands, he supposed he could not carry out the plan. Here Hawthorne seems to be describing the method he followed in adapting actual persons, including himself, to fictional use.

Another long-time friend of Hawthorne's present at the Whig meeting on July 6 was Caleb Foote. No doubt Foote had known that Hawthorne was a candidate for the Salem postmastership during his own term in that office, and he might have been expected to engage in similar maneuvers, which are normal in political party activities; but he was a member of the Whig caucus which, to gain political ends, charged Hawthorne with malfeasance in office. Hawthorne might have seen him as a representative of Salem, as one of the reputable citizens who by acquiescence had allowed a blackening of his character to go unchallenged. If he recorded any judgment on Foote in this connection, it has not come to light. Perhaps he thought, as he said of Salem in "The Custom-House," that he should not have expected so much of him.

Hawthorne often remarked that he was eager to leave Salem, and afterward that he had no wish to return. Especially in writing Burchmore and Pike, he spoke of his decapitation and, sarcastically, of the love his hometown had for him. The main thread of "The Custom-House," the author and his native town and the ambiguities involved, is managed with great effectiveness. In the past he has felt inexorably drawn back to Salem, he says, where he has deep roots, but he is now determined that his children shall "strike their roots into unaccustomed soil." He offers a broadly impersonal reason for this decision: "Human nature will not flourish, any more than a potato, if it be planted and replanted, for too long a series of generations in the same worn-out soil." But he mentions with overtones of disapproval the mariner merchants in the time of "Old King Derby," including "old Simon Forrester," and their successors, who scorned their native port and added riches to New York and Boston. The town is "joyless for him," as he thinks of "the old wooden houses, the mud and dust, the dead level of site and sentiment, the chill east wind, and the chillest of social atmospheres." Life at the custom-house is already like a dream; soon he will know the old town only "through the haze of memory." He has not found in the town "the genial atmosphere which a literary man requires," and his townspeople will "not much regret" him; but he confesses that it has been "as dear an object as any," in his literary efforts, "to be of some importance in their eyes," and to win "a pleasant memory in the abode and burial-place" of his forefathers. Finally, "It may be, however,—O, transporting and triumphant thought!—that the great-grandchildren of the present race may sometimes think kindly of the scribbler of bygone days, when the antiquary of days to come, among the sites memorable in the town's history, shall point out the locality of THE TOWN PUMP."

As the custom-house episode receded, Hawthorne came to see it less as a wrong of which he was the victim—though he continued to speak in such terms to Burchmore and Pike—and more as instruction toward an understanding of human nature, and a consequent ability to accept it as man's fate to strive, as Aylmer strives in "The Birthmark," nobly but fatally to escape human imperfection; to discover, as does Owen Warland in "The Artist of the Beautiful," that the artist must find his reward within himself; to find, as in "The Minister's Black Veil," that every heart contains inner secrets that can be revealed to no other; and to face inevitably such consequences of guilt, whether assumed or concealed, as are visited on Reuben Bourne in "Roger Malvin's Burial" and on Young Goodman Brown. This instruction darkened the lenses through which Hawthorne looked, particularly in the months after his decapitation, one result being that *The Scarlet Letter* "lacks sunshine," and is, as he wrote Horatio Bridge on February 4, 1850, "positively a h-ll-fired story," into which he "found it almost impossible to throw any cheering light."

In other ways than in its shadows, *The Scarlet Letter* shows its kinship with the works Hawthorne had published since 1830. Set in early Boston, it drew on the author's long acquaintance with historical characters and events, and on the conclusions he had reached in brooding over the Puritan mind, the new society founded in the wilderness, and the heritage passed from the first and second American generations to those that followed.[22] It interweaves themes from several of the earlier tales: the universality of sin, the effects of concealed sin, the inescapable consequences of all actions, the causes and the effects of isolation, witchcraft, and other manifestations of evil, the ambiguities and contradictions that defeat efforts to reach absolutes and certainties. The main characters have antecedents in earlier works: for Dimmesdale, Hooper in "The Minister's Black Veil"; for Chillingworth, Rappaccini and Baglioni in "Rappaccini's Daughter" and Aylmer in "The Birthmark"; for Hester, the lady in "The Hollow of the Three Hills" and the woman wearing the letter "A" in "Endicott and the Red Cross"; for Pearl, the children in "The Gentle Boy" and the author's daughter Una as he observed her during his mother's final illness.

Hawthorne brought to the writing of *The Scarlet Letter* a clear understanding of his kind of fiction, and a conviction that his tale would fail "unless the speaker stand in some true relation with his audience." In establishing such a relation, "we may prate of the circumstances that lie around us, and even of ourself, but still keep the inmost Me behind its veil," and it is "within the law of literary propriety to offer the public the sketch" presenting himself and his years in the Salem custom-house. When his reader has accompanied him through the sketch, including the report of finding the scarlet letter "A" and the manuscript, and his definition of the type of fiction he is writing, the author will have established the necessary "true relation" with his reader, who then will be prepared for a story that is not literal but representational, in which the embroidered letter, the iron-studded oaken door of the prison, the rosebush beside the door, the holding of a hand over the heart, weeds growing from a grave—a story in which commonplace objects and actions bear symbolic meanings so unobtrusively as to be scarcely recognized and yet are highly effective in the total pattern. It was with a practiced hand that he created dramatic scenes, some of them impressive tableaux such as the three scaffold scenes when the four main characters appear together. The first meeting of Hester and Chillingworth in the prison, their later meeting at the brook-side, Chillingworth's discovery or imagined discovery of the letter "A" on Dimmesdale's breast—these scenes achieve an intensity that proves both the author's technical mastery and the sharpness with which he saw the meaning he wanted to present—and the questions he wanted to pose.

Since *The Scarlet Letter* was planned and partly written as a tale, it may be usefully inspected for indications of Hawthorne's literary methods. His starting point for a piece of fiction was normally an idea, which he presented through varying proportions and arrangements of manifestations in action, character, scene, mood, and imagery. It can be supposed that, as he mused over the main theme, the effects of concealed sin, related or subsidiary themes came to his mind, and along with them additional episodes, and encounters among characters. As the tale grew in its fascination for the author during composition, it grew in length. Thus "The Birthmark" might have been expanded, for example, by more demonstrations in Aylmer's laboratory or by other evidences of human imperfection; and *The Scarlet Letter* might have appeared without the character Mistress Hibbins and without, say, an account of Pearl's relations with the Puritan children. Although Hawthorne's three later romances presumably were not conceived first as tales, they are similarly cumulative in construction, developing their themes through a sequence of episodes and dramatic scenes.

Ironic reversals such as Hawthorne found prevalent in human experience are prominent in *The Scarlet Letter*. The wronged husband, whom society would normally favor, is the one who becomes demonic; it is not from strength but from weakness, physical and psychological exhaustion, that Dimmesdale confesses publicly; he has become a more effective preacher as a consequence of his sin, and many of his parishioners have their faith in him strengthened rather than weakened by his confession; Pearl is to Hester the agent of both torment and salvation. Christian doctrine, the lore of witchcraft and black magic and alchemy, the nature and history of Puritan New England—these are given elements in *The Scarlet Letter;* they are not at issue. They form the substantial background, understood by both author and reader, against which to observe the characters as they confront the questions that are at issue—in this instance the breaking of moral and theological laws belonging to the background. This background serves for Hawthorne the same purpose the fixed social order

of England, France, and Italy serves for Henry James. The initial sin of
Hester Prynne and Arthur Dimmesdale precedes the opening of the first
chapter and is not questioned by the characters or the author. Though
Hester says that what they did had a consecration of its own, it is in her
view a sin nevertheless and its consequences are inevitable. Similarly, in
the final scaffold scene, the reader wanders out of the romance if he asks
whether or not Dimmesdale has won salvation. His tentative answer to
Hester's question whether they will meet in heaven is firmly within the
context of seventeenth-century beliefs in Boston, not beliefs in the author's time or in a reader's time. The romance presents a psychological
study, not a theological study, though the characters move within a pattern of fixed moral and theological beliefs. The integrity of the work
requires this distinction.

The controversy that accompanied the removal of Hawthorne from office appeared so widely in the news that *The Scarlet Letter* was well publicized before it came off the press. The publicity became the more effective
when reviewers cited "The Custom-House" as a report of the author's
misadventures among the Salem politicians. Chapman's attack on the author for his portrait of the permanent inspector would have enticed more
readers in Salem than it repelled. In major journals, moreover, there were
full reviews, most of them favorable and all of them likely to attract
readers.[23]

Evert Duyckinck, in the *Literary World* of March 30, placed "The
Custom-House" beside Hawthorne's earlier sketches composed of "little
cabinet pictures exquisitely painted." He preferred this "Hawthorne of
the present day in the sunshine" to the Hawthorne who is "less companionable, of sterner Puritan aspect, with the shadow of the past over him, a
reviver of witchcrafts and of those dark agencies of evil which lurk in the
human soul." After calling the romance a "perfect creation," Duyckinck
came back to the "less companionable" Hawthorne, saying that "the spirit
of his old Puritan ancestors" lives in him. In *Graham's Magazine* for May,
E. P. Whipple published a review of such understanding that Hawthorne
came to respect his criticism above all others and sought his judgment on
later work. Whipple placed the introductory sketch among the essays of
Addison and Lamb, and he thought the author more powerful than
Eugène Sue, Alexandre Dumas, or George Sand in representing his in-
sights. If *The Scarlet Letter* has a fault, it lies in "the almost morbid intensity with which the characters are realized." Whipple hoped Hawthorne's
next romance would equal this one "in pathos and power," but would be

more relieved by "touches of that beautiful and peculiar humor, so serene and so searching, in which he excels almost all living writers." In the *New York Tribune* of April 1, 1850, George Ripley said he found the character Hester Prynne "surpassing in artistic harmony, and in mystic, thrilling grace, the similar productions of Goethe and Scott" and found Hawthorne's works no less powerful than Poe's but far more acceptable because in them the "elements of terror are blended with . . . solemn and tender relations of the deepest secrets of the heart." Still, Ripley was not comfortable with "the weird and ghostly legends of the Puritanic history," or with the shadows Hawthorne casts over his characters. In saying that "The Custom-House" contains "too sharp touches of the caustic acid, of which the gentle author keeps some phials on his shelf for convenience and use," Ripley may have been recalling Hawthorne's doubts about the prospect at Brook Farm, and his suing later to recover the money he had advanced on a house. The London *Athenaeum* of June 15 carried a review by Henry F. Chorley, who had taken note of Hawthorne's work even before *Twice-Told Tales* appeared. Bowing to current tastes in England, Chorley was not sure "that passions and tragedies like these are the legitimate subjects of fiction. . . . But if Sin and Sorrow in their most fearful forms are to be presented in any work of art," he said, "they have rarely been treated with a loftier severity, purity, and sympathy" than in *The Scarlet Letter*.

On the evidence of the reviews, Hawthorne had indeed made a ten-strike. The reviewers saw the two parts of his book as complementary: in the sketch, humor and sunshine in his delineation of the current scene; in the romance, a remote Puritan past in which guilt and sorrow, fear and retribution are both abstract and human. They might have preferred brighter materials and a lighter tone, but they recognized a power and an artistry that placed the author alongside the masters of American and English literature. Even in the less favorable reviews, he was placed in higher company than ever before. George Bailey Loring, in the *Massachusetts Quarterly Review*, dealt primarily with the Puritan society in which Hawthorne's characters moved, but compared him favorably with Lamb, Richter, Goldsmith, Crabbe, Pope, Scott, and Dickens. A reviewer in the *North American Review* in July, Anne W. Abbott, thought his delineation of scene and character "worthy of the pen of Dickens." Chief of the reviewers who thought the story of the scarlet letter morally objectionable were Orestes Brownson in *Brownson's Quarterly Review* for October and Arthur Cleveland Coxe in the *Church Review* for the next January. Coxe recognized Hawthorne's gifts but thought *The Scarlet Letter* had "already done not a little to degrade our literature, and to encourage social licentiousness." Brownson granted that the romance has "all the fascinations of genius, and all the charms of a highly polished style," but could discover in it "nothing Christian, nothing really moral."

After learning from Fields about Coxe's review, Hawthorne replied that he would like to see it only if it was "really good," and added, "I think it essential to my success as an author, to have some bitter enemies." The author-reader relationship had been a major topic in "The Old Manse" and "The Custom-House," as it was in his prefaces. At about the time *The Scarlet Letter* came off the press, Hawthorne wrote the poet Lewis Mansfield that his poem was not addressed to the world at large, but to "a class of cognate minds," those most capable of understanding him, who might know him only through his work, but would nevertheless know him better than most of those familiar with his face. "It might be, that only one person in the whole world would understand, while all the rest would ridicule you; but it would be worth a life's labor to be understood by that one, while the ridicule of the others would not be worth a thought." In replying to a woman who had written him, Hawthorne returned to the subject of an author and his readers. Her letter had made him sensible "how great a blessing and privilege" it was to be able to hold intercourse with a reader "through the deepest and best of one's thoughts and emotions." If ever anyone offered to point him out to her, he hoped she would turn her head away. She knew him now by the "genuine traits" of his mind and heart. If they were to meet, she would remember him only by "a few superficial features."[24] It was his intention in "The Old Manse" and "The Custom-House" to reveal his heart and mind, preparing his reader for the yet subtler revelation in the fictional works being introduced.

What Duyckinck and Whipple said in print about the gloom of *The Scarlet Letter* Hawthorne had already said to Fields and Bridge. In a letter of March 28, 1850, George Hillard gave the same matter a personal turn. He thought the book would take its place "among the highest efforts of what may be called the Tragic Muse of fiction," but he asked, "How comes it that with so thoroughly healthy an organization as you have, you have such a taste for the morbid anatomy of the human heart, and such knowledge of it, too? I should fancy from your books that you were burdened with secret sorrow; that you had some blue chamber in your soul, into which you hardly dared to enter yourself; but when I see you, you give me the impression of a man as healthy as Adam was in Paradise." He could wish that Hawthorne "would dwell more in the sun, and converse more with cheerful thoughts and lightsome images." This wish became Hawthorne's. At least he said he was determined to write more cheerful stories. The fact that, in spite of his avowed intention, neither he nor his reviewers found his later romances appreciably more cheerful suggests that for him to force such a tone in his writings would be to deny the genuine traits of his heart and mind and to deny the dark side that he found integral to human experience.[25]

18

In the Berkshires

A week after his mother's funeral, Hawthorne vowed that as soon as he could find a suitable residence in the country, he would "bid farewell forever to this abominable city." In spite of his preference for the seashore, where he believed he and his wife both had better health than inland, he traveled to the town of Lenox, in the Berkshires of western Massachusetts, where Samuel Gray Ward on September 25 and W. A. Tappan the next day drove him about in search of a house. Ward had called at the Old Manse in September, 1842, and two years later had settled at Lenox; Tappan's wife was Sophia's friend Caroline Sturgis. Early in April, 1850, Hawthorne engaged a house at Lenox and made plans to leave Salem at the middle of the month.

Moving their household gods from Salem, as Hawthorne phrased it, was a welcome but disturbing event. He could now say he was glad he had been saved from a longer period of stagnation, and in his preface to the second edition of *The Scarlet Letter* he stated that he had composed "The Custom-House" with "frank and genuine good-humor" and no "enmity, or ill-feeling of any kind, personal or political." He had largely overcome his ill-feeling for individuals, Upham included, but he had not forgiven the town or forgotten "the fierce and bitter spirit of malice and revenge" that he had said in "The Custom-House" actuated the Whigs. He had written Bridge the day after he finished *The Scarlet Letter*, "I detest this town so much that I hate to go into the streets, or to have the people

see me. Anywhere else, I shall at once be entirely another man." He returned to the subject of the Salem people in writing Bridge: "I feel an infinite contempt for them, and probably have expressed more of it than I intended; for my preliminary chapter has caused the greatest uproar that
ever happened here since witch-times. If I escape from town without
being tarred-and-feathered, I shall consider it good luck. I wish they *would*
tar-and-feather me—it would be such an entirely novel kind of distinction
for a literary man! And from such judges as my fellow-citizens, I should
look upon it as a higher honor than a laurel-crown." After leaving Salem,
he wrote Zachariah Burchmore, "Please to present my best regards to the
Salem people generally. I presume it to be merely an oversight that they
did not invite me to a public dinner." A month later he said he "would
rather go to any other place in the known world" than Salem. He explained not visiting his sister Louisa before leaving Boston for Lenox by
telling her that he could "not endure the idea of coming to Salem quite
yet."[1] More than a year passed before he set foot in the town again.

   During the month of waiting for the house at Lenox to be ready, Sophia
and the children stayed with the Peabodys in Boston. Hawthorne dined
with Longfellow and Charles Sumner; he visited Bridge at Portsmouth for
a week, and from there wrote his wife that he would not return to the
Peabody house and "add another human being to the multitudinous
chaos" there. He said that hers was a "hard lot in life"; she had done
"much amiss" to marry a husband who could not keep her the way Bridge
kept his wife.[2] Back in Boston by the first of May, he took room and
board near the Peabody house, and used the occasion to put into his
notebook speculative characterizations of his fellow boarders and people
he saw elsewhere. A livery stable across the street, an audience at the National Theater, the room, the displays, and the patrons of Parker's Saloon—these were stored in his notebook (VIII, 487–509) and were later
transferred almost full scale to *The Blithedale Romance* (Chapters 17–22). He
sat for a portrait by Cephas G. Thompson; he visited Professor George
Ticknor, whose three-volume *History of Spanish Literature* had appeared the
year before, to ask whether the tales of Cervantes had been translated—his
sister Elizabeth had in mind translating them. He went to Parker's Saloon
almost every day, hoping to find Burchmore there; he still had friends and
interests in Salem.

   On May 23 the Hawthorne family took the train to Lenox. Renovations
of their house were not complete, but Caroline Tappan had prepared
rooms for them to occupy for a week in her house. Since Hawthorne's

visit to Lenox the preceding September, Ward had moved to Boston and
had leased the Tappans his house, Highwood. At first only a small house
on the estate had been vacant, but Caroline had arranged for the family
occupying a better house, the "red house," to move out and make it available. Although the house was offered rent-free, Hawthorne insisted on
paying fifty dollars a year. Both the Tappans, Sophia wrote her mother,
"have such a feeling about Mr. Hawthorne that they seem to rejoice to
have a chance to do everything for him."[3]

Hawthorne arrived with a cold that confined him several days, but on
June 9 he wrote Burchmore that he had planted enough vegetables to feed
all Salem, had a good tan on his face, and expected to flourish. He lived in
"the ugliest little old red farm-house," which he said was "as red as the
Scarlet Letter."[4] The eight rooms were small and the ceilings were so
low, Sophia said, as to induce a fear of being crushed. A barn as tall as the
house was attached. For the first time in nearly five years, the Hawthornes had a house to themselves. Sophia's delight shows in her first
reports to West Street on the placing of the furniture: "the fairy tea-table,
a Hawthorne heirloom," the "India Box" and the India bowl and pitcher
Hawthorne's father had brought from India, the "ancient Manning chair,"
"the antique ottoman, the monument of Elizabeth's loving kindness," "the
antique centre table which lost one foot on its journey from Salem." In
every room she had statuary and paintings, including her own statue of
Endymion she had once thought of selling for $100. Since Hawthorne's
study upstairs was too tiny to admit a stove in the winter, when cold
weather came, the guest room became the study. The desk that once
belonged to Sophia's brother George was cleaned and refinished and became Hawthorne's writing desk.[5]

What the red house lacked in spaciousness and comfort and beauty, it
made up in its view of water and meadows and woods and mountains,
which local residents said was among the best in the Berkshires. In the
foreground was the Stockbridge Bowl, a lake a mile and a half long, and in
the background wooded hills and craggy mountains. Herman Melville
declared the Berkshires in Indian summer to be unsurpassed anywhere.
Hawthorne knew the region from his sojourn at North Adams in 1838.
Activities at the red house were not unlike those at the Old Manse: gar-
dening, picking fruit, sawing wood, bathing at the lake, walking in the
meadows and the woods, lying on the grass, climbing trees, sledding and
skating in the winter, and reading aloud in the evening; but now the
children—Una six and Julian four—were prominent and in their parents'

minds in most of what took place. All shared a learner's interest in the rabbit Hindlegs, and in the daily and seasonal round of activities at the hen-coop. Sledding down the hill to the lake might produce all the delight and excitement that Hawthorne gave the children who appear in the framework of A Wonder-Book. A spirit of playful adventure seems to have prevailed, no less with the father than with the children. In the days of severe cold and snow blockade, he said they were living in the Zeroic age.

In the first summer at Lenox, Hawthorne consciously deferred work at his desk, while the sun and open air and exercise repaired the damage done by his year of distress. Sophia wrote her mother on August 1 that he had not recovered enough of his vigor even to "seize the skirts of ideas and pin them down for further investigation." His tread was not "again elastic," and he thought Salem was "dragging at his ankles still."

They found themselves now as never before in a stream of talented and interesting new acquaintances, many of them authors and artists. The house occupied by the author of The Scarlet Letter turned out to be within reach of both regular and summer residents. The Tappans, next door, attracted visitors. The Sedgwick family had many branches, "happy as summer days themselves," Sophia said, and delighted to make others happy. A day all four Hawthornes spent with the family of Catharine Sedgwick was memorable, especially for the children, for she presided over a tea party for them in a baby house.[6] Oliver Wendell Holmes and his wife came in summers to his ancestral home near Pittsfield. James Russell Lowell and his recent bride, Maria White, dropped by the red house, on their way to Niagara, with the Scandinavian author Fredrika Bremer. The novelist G. P. R. James was a neighbor; and Fanny Kemble, divorced two years earlier and living near by, sometimes stopped on her black horse, and once took Julian up for a ride.

The framework narrative of A Wonder-Book, written at Lenox, is set in the Berkshires, and specifically at the site of the author's residence. Points on the local scene are introduced by name, as are several authors who lived or visited in the vicinity. A question is asked about "that silent man, who lives in the old red house" and has written "a poem, or a romance, or an arithmetic, or a school-history, or some other kind of book." Since writing the travel narrative as a frame for the Story-Teller collection, Hawthorne had enjoyed intermixing himself into his sketches and narratives so as to make the factual and the imagined indistinguishable; and he realized that the semi-autobiographical sketches "The Old Manse" and "The Custom-House" were among his best writings. He may not have realized that the main attractiveness of these pieces is in the playful but essentially authentic revelation of his mind and personality.

Besides the new acquaintances, many old friends called at the red house. Bridge came at the middle of July and helped Hawthorne build closets and bookshelves and rebuild the hennery.[7] Other visitors were O'Sullivan, with his wife and his mother, Ellery Channing, the poet Lewis W. Mansfield and his wife, E. P. Whipple and his wife, James T. Fields, Frank Farley, and three of Sophia's friends, Elizabeth Hoar, Sarah Shaw, and Anna Greene. Louisa Hawthorne came, as did Sophia's mother and father and her sister Elizabeth. Once Sophia wrote her mother that there must not be another as long as her father's recent visit; her husband must have the quiet and the freedom to muse that was impossible with a guest in the house, especially this little house.

Some of Hawthorne's neighbors found him remote, if not unresponsive. Charles Sedgwick said that he called at the red house five or six times in the first half year after the Hawthornes arrived and that Hawthorne visited him only once, when the entire family was invited for the day. Oliver Wendell Holmes stopped one day to see the view from the red house, leaving his nephew with the horse. When he started back to relieve his nephew and send him to see the view, Hawthorne insisted on holding the horse himself and freeing both to observe the view.[8] It is tempting to see Hawthorne here choosing the company he preferred; the nephew was a son of the Reverend Charles W. Upham. Holmes asked who besides him had ever had the author of *The Scarlet Letter* hold his horse.

The one resident of the Berkshires with whom Hawthorne found time to exchange visits was Herman Melville. He spent far more time with Melville than with any other of his neighbors, and perhaps more than he had ever spent in a comparable period, at Concord or anywhere else, with anyone outside his family. It is true that Melville took the initiative and was persistent in cultivating the acquaintance, and that he later felt he had been rebuffed in his display of affection; but there is abundant evidence that Hawthorne had a high regard for his young neighbor and for his books.

Complex and fortuitous circumstances brought Hawthorne and Melville together early in August, 1850, at a crucial point in the career of each and with important consequences, particularly for Melville—and for American literature. On August 2, Evert Duyckinck and Cornelius Mathews, coming to visit Melville at Pittsfield, met Dudley Field on the train, and they planned a picnic for August 5. Field and his wife, whom the Hawthornes had visited a week earlier, called on August 3 to invite them to the picnic. The next day the Hawthornes dined at Pittsfield with James T. Fields and his bride and visited Oliver Wendell Holmes. On August 5 Fields and his wife came for Hawthorne and drove to Dudley Field's house, where Holmes, Melville, Duyckinck, and Mathews had already arrived. When the party had driven in three vehicles to Monument Mountain and had begun the climb on foot, Hawthorne and Duyckinck walked ahead, talking about *The Scarlet Letter*. A rain shower having come up, "Dr. Holmes cut three branches for an umbrella and uncorked the champagne, which was drunk from a silver mug," Ducykinck wrote his wife the next day. They later "scattered over the cliffs, Herman Melville to seat himself, the boldest of all, astride a projecting bowsprit of rock while Dr. Holmes peeped about the cliffs and protested it affected him like ipecac. Hawthorne looked wildly about for the Great Carbuncle. Mathews read Bryant's poem, entitled "Monument Mountain," which tells the story of an Indian princess who threw herself from a precipice.[9]

There followed at Dudley Field's house a three-hour dinner, "well moistened," Duyckinck said. "Dr. Holmes said some of his best things and drew the whole company out by laying down various propositions of the superiority of Englishmen. Melville attacked him vigorously. Hawthorne looked on." Joined by the historian Joel Tyler Headley, the party went after dinner to the Icy Glen, a cleft in the mountain which Hawthorne said, according to his wife, looked as if "the Devil had torn his way through a rock and left it all jagged behind him."[10]

On August 8 Melville, Duyckinck, and Mathews called at the red house. In a letter to his wife afterward, Duyckinck called Hawthorne "a fine ghost in a case of iron—a man of genius" who "looks it and lives it."[11] After her first glimpse of Melville, Sophia wrote her sister Elizabeth that she found Mr. Typee interesting; and, alluding to the maiden in his first book, *Typee*, she said she could see "Fayaway in his face."[12] In a letter of August 7 Hawthorne had told Horatio Bridge that he liked Melville so much he had invited him to come and spend a few days before leaving the Berkshires. Bridge would have known from this that Hawthorne had an uncommon liking for his new acquaintance. Melville came in the morning of September 3 and stayed five days. He was careful, Sophia wrote her mother, not to interfere with Hawthorne's mornings, walking out or reading, and one morning secluding himself to read Emerson's essays. At times he talked with Sophia about her husband. "He said Mr. Hawthorne was the first person whose physical being appeared to him wholly in har-

mony with the intellectual and spiritual. He said the sunny hair and the
pensiveness, the symmetry of his face, the depth of eyes, 'the gleam—the
shadow—and the peace supreme' all were in exact response to the high
calm intellect, the glowing, deep heart—the purity of actual and spiritual
life." Normally a silent man, he told her, he found that Hawthorne's
"great but hospitable silence drew him out—that it was astonishing how
sociable his silence was."[13]

When Sophia wrote this letter, she had just learned that Melville had
put into print far more extravagant opinions of her husband and his writings—that he was the author of the essay "Hawthorne and His Mosses,"
published in the *Literary World* for August 17 and 24, as written by "a
Virginian spending the summer in Vermont." Melville's copy of *Mosses
from an Old Manse*, inscribed by his Aunt Mary Ann Melvill on July 18,
1850, contains profuse markings in the margins. During the next two days
he was on a wagon tour in the southern part of Berkshire County. He no
doubt wrote the essay on the *Mosses* soon after his return; he told Sophia
he wrote it without any idea he would ever meet Hawthorne. Following
the picnic on August 5, Duyckinck stayed over at Pittsfield another week,
two days longer than he had intended, waiting for Melville to revise and
finish what he had already written, and then rushed the first installment
into print, without taking time for Melville to read proof.[14]

Back in New York, Duyckinck sent Hawthorne the works by Melville
he had not read; and occupants of the red house were reading the books
and the essay on the *Mosses* without knowing they had the same author.
After the second part of the essay had arrived, Sophia exulted in writing
her sister Elizabeth that finally someone had not compared her husband
with Washington Irving, but had said what in her "secret mind" she had
often thought, that he was "only to be mentioned with the Swan of Avon;
the great heart and the grand intellect combined."[15] On August 29 two
letters went into the mail for Evert Duyckinck. In one Sophia said the
Virginian, as yet not identified, was the first person who had "ever in
print apprehended" her husband.[16] In the other, Hawthorne wrote that
the Virginian had "a truly generous heart" and was "no common man;
and, next to deserving his praise," it was "good to have beguiled or bewitched such a man into praising" more than was deserved. As to Melville's books, he said, "No writer ever put the reality before his reader
more unflinchingly than he does in 'Redburn,' and 'White Jacket.' 'Mardi'
is a rich book, with depths here and there that compel a man to swim for
his life. It is so good that one scarcely pardons the writer for not having
brooded long over it, so as to make it a great deal better."

The Hawthornes' surprise and delight can be imagined when they learned, during Melville's visit five days later, that he was the Virginian. There was further delight when Melville drove up one night with the news that he would be their neighbor six miles away. He had bought the estate at Pittsfield he would later name Arrowhead.

Two letters Sophia wrote her mother at this juncture have been praised by biographers of Melville. The one to her mother September 4 caused Raymond Weaver to call her "one of Melville's most penetrating critics."[17] She and her husband had found Melville "a man with a true, warm heart, and a soul and an intellect,—with life to his finger-tips; earnest, sincere, and *modest*." She was not quite sure she did "*not think him* a very great man." The other letter, in which she dwelt on his "great ardor and simplicity," "his truth and honesty," prompted Melville's granddaughter, Eleanor Melville Metcalf, to call it "the most important and perceptive letter any of his contemporaries ever wrote about Melville."[18] At about this time, after James Russell Lowell had called at the red house, Sophia remarked to her mother, September 29, 1850, on the great contrast with Melville: Lowell was superficial, she first wrote; then in her revision, he was unsatisfactory.

It would be a mistake to assume that Hawthorne's and his wife's judgments coincided on any matter; but it would be no less a mistake to suppose that she wrote members of her family opinions not held by her husband. There is no doubt that they had the same fondness for "Mr. Omoo" and the same respect for his mind and his heart. Nor can there be any doubt that Melville knew how he stood with the man of *Mosses*. In a letter to Sophia, on January 8, 1852, six weeks after the Hawthornes had moved away from Lenox, Melville showed himself aware that Hawthorne spared little time for anyone he did not esteem. In jesting about her husband's reluctance to visit among his neighbors, he nevertheless made it clear, as he had done in letters to the master of the red house, that he realized he was the suitor, that he was the one who needed the other more and had more to gain.

Soon after his five-day visit at the red house in September, 1850, Melville moved his family to Arrowhead and took up again the romance of the whale fisheries that had occupied him the past year. Hawthorne began a new romance and soon was staying at his desk until four in the afternoon. When Melville came the next January 22 to invite the Hawthornes for a visit, he took away with him copies of *Twice-Told Tales* in both the 1837 and the 1842 editions, and the promise of a visit to Arrowhead. Four days later Sophia sent him a note, the purpose of which can be inferred from the fact that Hawthorne was only then finishing his romance and would soon begin receiving proof, and from Melville's next letter to Hawthorne, on January 29, in which he said, "That side-blow thro' Mrs. Hawthorne will not do. . . . You, sir, I hold accountable, and a visit (in all its original integrity) must be made." He would not hear of a visit for only a day; and on Wednesday at eleven he would come for the whole family in his sleigh. "Come—no nonsense. If you dont, I will send constables after you." Hawthorne replied on February 3, no doubt postponing the visit until he had finished reading proof on his new romance.

Melville wrote Duyckinck on February 12 that he had driven down to see Hawthorne, "after a long procrastination," and added, "I had promised myself much pleasure in getting him up in my snug room here, and discussing the Universe with a bottle of brandy and cigars." Meantime, he had been reading *Twice-Told Tales,* most of its contents for the first time.

> I think they far exceed the "Mosses"—they are, I fancy, an earlier vintage from his vine. Some of those sketches are wonderfully subtle. Their deeper meanings are worthy of a Brahmin. Still there is something lacking—a good deal lacking—to the plump sphericity of the man. What is that?
> —He doesn't patronise the butcher—he needs roast-beef, done rare,—Nevertheless, for one, I regard Hawthorne (in his books) as evincing a quality of genius, immensely loftier, and more profound, too, than any other American has shown hitherto in the printed form. Irving is a grasshopper to him—putting the *souls* of the two men together, I mean.

When Melville came on March 12 to renew his invitation, Hawthorne accepted for himself and Una. They drove off the next morning in a snowstorm, which continued through the day and kept them at Arrowhead overnight. Unable to go walking, Melville lay on the hay in the barn and Hawthorne sat on a workbench. Melville is reported to have remembered long afterward that Hawthorne proposed to write about their conversation, entitling his account "A Week on a Work-Bench in a Barn," having in mind Thoreau's *A Week on the Concord and Merrimac Rivers,* recently published.[19]

Soon after writing the essay on Hawthorne's *Mosses,* Melville had entered a year of intense application to his romance of the whale fisheries that presumably was already near completion. Meeting Hawthorne, writing his essay on the *Mosses,* and afterward reading *Twice-Told Tales* caused him to plan the story anew, turning it into a symbolic narrative of man's warfare against evil that became *Moby-Dick.* He had found in Hawthorne reinforcement for his own sense of the "blackness" in human nature; and his persistent efforts to see the man of *Mosses* were due in part to his seeking clarification and assurance.[20] Hawthorne had never felt such need for guidance. Amply supplied through reading and observation with ideas and materials for embodying them, he had required simply time for musing, dreaming, and thinking. He may not have realized, therefore, the urgency of Melville's quest—or need—for sympathy and guidance. After getting well into his own new romance, he held his importunate young neighbor at arm's length until writing and proofreading were finished.

Following Hawthorne's long-delayed visit to Arrowhead at the middle of March, Melville called at the red house on April 11 and was given a copy of *The House of the Seven Gables*, on which he wrote five days later a letter in the form of a book review that is in effect an addendum to the earlier essay on the *Mosses*. After speaking of "a certain tragic phase of humanity" which he finds "more powerfully embodied" by Hawthorne than by anyone else, he continues,

> We think that into no recorded mind has the intense feeling of the visible truth ever entered more deeply than into this man's. By visible truth, we mean the apprehension of the absolute condition of present things as they strike the eye of the man who fears them not, though they do their worst to him,—the man who . . . declares himself a sovereign nature (in himself) amid the powers of heaven, hell, and earth. He may perish; but so long as he exists he insists upon treating with all Powers upon an equal basis. . . . There is the grand truth about Nathaniel Hawthorne. He says NO! in thunder; but the Devil himself cannot make him say *yes*.

These sentences were struck from the same mind that at the time was creating Captain Ahab of the *Pequod*. Melville thought this romance of the ancient house in Salem surpassed Hawthorne's earlier works. Inside the house, he said, he had found "a dark little black-letter volume in golden clasps, entitled 'Hawthorne: A Problem.' "

One problem Hawthorne presented Melville was how to be with him more. In this letter Melville renewed his invitation, and concluded, "No nonsense; come." Sophia's letters indicate the trend of her thoughts—and no doubt largely her husband's—on Melville in the spring of 1851. She told how much delight they took in their young friend but indicated that Melville's demands might be greater than Hawthorne would have time or inclination to meet. "The fresh, sincere, glowing mind" spoke its "innermost about GOD, the Devil, and Life." If Melville's "confessions and efforts to grasp" were revealed to one who did not "take in the whole scope of the case," they might appear impious. "Nothing pleases me better than to sit and hear this growing man dash his tumultuous waves of thought up against Mr Hawthorne's great, genial, comprehending silences. . . . Yet such a love and reverence and admiration for Mr Hawthorne as is really beautiful to witness—. . . it is astonishing how people make him their innermost Father Confessor." She wrote later about Melville's pouring out "the rich floods of his mind and experience to him, so sure of apprehension, so sure of a large and generous interpretation, and of the most delicate and fine judgment." She did not imply that Hawthorne enjoyed the role Melville asked him to play, or thought his ministrations effective; she implied, rather, that he would be inclined to draw back from the confessions, the tumult, and the fury which Melville brought with his friendship.[21]

In the letter on *The House of the Seven Gables*, Melville indicated that he had decided on correspondence as a substitute for visiting he was not able to manage; but he wrote later that he would continue his own visiting until told that his visits were "both supererogatory and superfluous." After a long outpouring of the thoughts he wanted to share and explore with Hawthorne, he added, "Don't trouble yourself, though, about writing; and don't trouble yourself about talking. I will do all the writing and visiting and talking myself." He wrote on June 29 that he would drive down to the red house soon. "Have ready a bottle of brandy, because I always feel like drinking that heroic drink when we talk ontological heroics together." On July 22, he had a letter of Hawthorne's to answer, an "easy-flowing long letter," which he said had flowed through him and refreshed all his meadows. After that, he said they must "hit upon some little bit of vagabondism," perhaps climbing Mt. Greylock.

In the longer letters Melville wrote from April onward, he introduced personal and universal topics that were running through his mind, as if preparing an agenda for the sessions of "ontological heroics" he hoped to bring about. In a breathless and largely exclamatory letter written about June 1, he touched on matters he and Hawthorne no doubt had talked about and on others he had in mind for future sessions with his neighbor. "What I feel most moved to write, that is banned,—it will not pay. . . . What 'reputation' H.M. has is horrible." He had heard much praise of Hawthorne's books lately; "the N.H. is in the ascendant." A reference to Hawthorne's story "Ethan Brand" prompted him to say, "It is a frightful poetic creed that the cultivation of the brain eats out the heart. . . . I stand for the heart. To the dogs with the head!" Melville went on, his mind seeming to move at random. He read Solomon more and more. "As with all great genius, there is an immense deal of flummery in Goethe," such as his idea of living in the all, but in this "all feeling" there is at least some truth. "You must have felt it, lying on the grass on a warm summer's day. Your legs seem to send out shoots into the earth. Your hair feels like leaves upon your head." Earlier in this letter, his fancy had taken a more extended flight:

> If ever, my dear Hawthorne, in the eternal times that are to come, you and I shall sit down in Paradise, in some little shady corner by ourselves; and if we shall by any means be able to smuggle a basket of champagne there (I won't believe in a Temperance Heaven), and if we shall then cross our celestial legs in the celestial grass that is forever tropical, and strike our glasses and our heads together, till both musically ring in concert,—then, O my dear fellow-mortal, how shall we pleasantly discourse of all the things manifold which now distress us,—when all the earth shall be but a reminiscence, yea, its final dissolution an antiquity.

These were topics congenial to Hawthorne in his musing and in his speculative moods; and the fantasy in which his neighbor clothed them, along with the richness of the language and the imagery in which he expressed them, would have pleased him. He did not respond in kind, however. When Melville wrote on June 29, not sure when he wrote last or whether he had received an answer, he wanted to persuade Hawthorne to engage in the frank and personal discussions he sought, "though we show all our faults and weaknesses,—for it is a sign of strength to be weak, to know it, and out with it."

Later in the summer, chance provided an occasion for the striking of glasses and heads together. On August 1, while Sophia and Una and the baby, Rose (born on May 20), were visiting in West Newton, Hawthorne and Julian walked to the village and met up with Melville, who came home with them. After supper, they "smoked cigars even within the scared precincts of the sitting-room," and there was "talk about time and eternity, things of this world and of the next, and books, and publishers, and all possible and impossible matters, that lasted pretty deep into the night." Hawthorne then hastened to make the most of what little sleeping time remained. He gave this notebook report a casual tone, for his wife would read it upon her return; but it suggests that the talk was not of his instigation or direction; certainly its duration was not to his liking. While Evert Duyckinck and his brother George were in the Berkshires a week later, Melville brought them to see Hawthorne. They took lunch for a pic-

nic in the mountains, visited the Shaker community at Hancock, and returned for supper at the red house. Melville and the Duyckincks left at ten
o'clock for the six-mile ride to Pittsfield (VIII, 463–68).

On August 30, Melville paid his last visit to the Hawthornes in the
Berkshires. He had not had a visit from Hawthorne since March; and the
phrasing of his various proposals suggests that he had little hope for favorable responses. At the middle of November, however, their association
reached its highest peak. *Moby-Dick* came off the press, dedicated to
Hawthorne and bearing evidence of his shaping influence. The letter
Hawthorne wrote after reading it has not been preserved, but its general
import can be inferred from Melville's reply on November 17, which
sums up—perhaps more by implication than by statement, and in the imagery and language that were customary in his letters to Hawthorne—the
reverence and the affection he had for his older friend in 1850 and 1851.
He had read Hawthorne's "joy-giving and exultation-breeding letter" in
the road where it was handed to him. "In my proud, humble way, a
shepherd-king,—I was lord of a little vale in the solitary Crimea; but you
have now given me the crown of India." The exultation bred by the letter
remained: "I felt pantheistic then—your heart beat in my ribs and mine in
yours, and both in God's. A sense of unspeakable security is in me this
moment, on account of your having understood the book." His pantheistic
feelings left him still with questions: "Whence come you, Hawthorne? By
what right do you drink from my flagon of life? And when I put it to my
lips—lo, they are yours and not mine. I feel that the Godhead is broken
up like the bread at the Supper, and that we are the pieces. Hence this infinite fraternity of feeling."

The "atmospheric skepticisms" had stolen into Melville and made him
doubt his sanity in writing thus. "But the truth is ever incoherent, and
when the big hearts strike together, the concussion is a little stunning.
. . . Lord, when shall we be done growing? As long as we have anything
more to do, we have done nothing. So, now, let us add Moby Dick to our
blessing, and step from that. Leviathan is not the biggest fish;—I have
heard of Krakens." His correspondent need not answer his letter, but he
was not inclined himself to desist. "I should write a thousand—a million—
a billion thoughts, all under the form of a letter to you." Melville was in a
mood for speculation, fantasy, and emblematic representation: "the very
fingers that now guide this pen are not precisely the same that just took it
up and put it on this paper. Lord, when shall we be done changing? Ah!
it's a long stage, and no inn in sight, and night coming, and the body cold.

But with you for a passenger, I am content and can be happy. I shall leave the world, I feel, with more satisfaction for having come to know you. Knowing you persuades me more than the Bible of our immortality."

This is the most comprehensive of Melville's letters in expressing his feeling for Hawthorne through religious, spiritual, artistic, intellectual, and physical images. It sounds, for his relations with Hawthorne, notes of both invocation and benediction. He was aware, it can be assumed, of the inclusive and interwoven imagery of his letter, and no less aware of the meaning behind the imagery. The same awareness can be assumed on the part of Hawthorne. Following this letter, the two met only twice, a year later in Concord and five years later in Liverpool, and the intimately personal element is absent from Melville's subsequent letters. He realized before they parted in the Berkshires that Hawthorne had drawn away from him during the preceding year, and in writing Mrs. Hawthorne on January 6, 1852, making a joke about Hawthorne's reluctance to visit his neighbors, he wanted to hint that he understood the reason. There is evidence through the remaining forty years of Melville's life that he thought he had been rebuffed by Hawthorne, and that he felt a genuine regret for his loss.

19

The House of the Seven Gables

Within three months after being turned out of the Salem custom-house, Hawthorne had given up the thought of regaining his office, and had decided not to oppose the confirmation of his successor as a way of vindicating himself; and he said little more about seeking another office or turning to literary drudgery. He took up the role of author again quickly, and before *The Scarlet Letter* was off the press, he spoke with a pride in his calling and with an assurance that had long been absent from his letters. The readiness with which friends had come forward with avowals of confidence and with funds, by gift and loan, was heartening; the critical reception of the romance gave him assurance as to the quality of his work, and the royalty payments provided income to support him while he continued to write.

After a few weeks at Lenox, he began referring to his next book, and by the middle of June said it would be a romance. Perhaps the picnic on Monument Mountain sent him back to his desk with new energy, for on August 23 he told Fields he might finish writing by November. On October 1 he explained to Fields that the action centered in a house with many gables and an overhanging second story, such as he knew well in Salem; and he sent some titles he was considering, among which were "The House of the Seven Gables" and two alternate versions. Later he added "Maule's Well" and thought of including the word "romance." Not until January 4 was the matter settled, when Fields reported that everybody he asked said the book must be *The House of the Seven Gables*. In telling Fields that all but thirty or forty pages would be set in the present, although the plot would encompass two centuries, he probably had in mind the reviewers' dissatisfaction with the gloom of *The Scarlet Letter* and his own declared intention to move his next work into the sunlight of the present.

Writing this book required more care than *The Scarlet Letter*, Hawthorne wrote Fields on November 3.

> I have to wait oftener for a mood. The Scarlet Letter being all in one tone, I had only to get my pitch, and could then go on interminably. Many passages of the book ought to be finished with the minuteness of a Dutch picture, in order to give them their proper effect. Sometimes, when tired of it, it strikes me that the whole is an absurdity, from beginning to end; but the fact is, in writing a romance, a man is always— or always ought to be—*careening* on the *utmost* verge of a precipitous *absurdity*, and the skill lies in coming as close as possible, without actually tumbling over.

On November 29 he expected to finish in two or three weeks. His hand was trembling from writing all day. Ten days later he was "in a Slough of Despond, having written so fiercely" that he had come to a standstill. He had experienced no such bewilderment as this in finishing *The Scarlet Letter*, and he had not let other writing interfere with the completion of this book. He alerted Fields on January 4 to expect the manuscript soon. On January 12 he said the romance was finished except for "hammering away a little on the roof, and doing up a few odd jobs that were left incomplete." When he had read it to his wife, he would "know better what to think of it." After the reading on January 13 and 14, which stopped with the legend of Alice Pyncheon, his wife recorded her admiration in her journal,[1] speaking of "the inevitable Fate—'the innocent suffering for the guilty' seemingly so dark yet so clear a law—such roundness of line— such complete spherical harmony." After the third reading session, which probably extended through the flight of Hepzibah and Clifford, and, in Chapter 18, the death of Judge Pyncheon, with the gurgling of blood in his throat, according to the curse, Sophia referred to her husband's "awful power of insight," and asked, "Who else so penetrates Life and Death?" She looked forward to hearing him read more of the "miraculous inspirations," but the next day, January 16, she had to note, "behold! he had yet no more to read." The uncertainty he had reported in December no doubt grew from difficulty with the resolution of the plot and caused him to rewrite the concluding chapters.

The House of the Seven Gables. Courtesy of the Essex Institute, Salem, Mass.

By the time Hawthorne began writing *The House of the Seven Gables*, he had grown self-conscious about the gloom in his writing. Friends and reviewers otherwise favorable had said they preferred the Hawthorne of the present day in the sunshine to the Hawthorne who probed the agencies of evil in human nature and experience. At Lenox he had been drawn into the company of literary authors more than ever before, not excluding his years at Concord; and he knew that most of them would have asked him to write more cheerful books. With a congenial theme—the effects of evil passed from one generation to another and borne by the innocent as well as the guilty—and with a pattern of impressive symbols clearly in mind, he at first composed rapidly. He wrote James T. Fields on November 29 that the story darkened "damnably towards the close," but he would "try hard to pour some setting sunshine over it." The character Holgrave serves through the first eighteen chapters as a largely disinterested and cynical commentator on the action. A daguerreotypist and hence an apostle of realistic and scientific thought, and a radical in social views, he foresees impending doom. Near the middle of the book (Chapter 14), he takes on the role of the chorus in Greek drama and remarks that he "cannot help fancying that Destiny is arranging its fifth act for a catastrophe." At this point, the reader cannot help fancying the same kind of outcome.

After ten days spent in rewriting, Hawthorne read his wife the final three chapters on January 26. In preparation she read during the day the chapters she had heard read in the first three sessions. She found in the rewritten conclusion a tone far different from that in the earlier chapters. She now found "unspeakable grace and beauty . . . , throwing back upon the sterner tragedy of the commencement an ethereal light, and a dear home-loveliness and satisfaction." Instead of the dark, Old Testament mood of the earlier episodes, which she admired for their power and their awful insight, she now exulted in the "high tone, the flowers of Paradise scattered over all the dark places, the sweet wall-flower scent of Phoebe's character."[2] In the rewritten conclusion Hawthorne had succeeded amply, for his wife, in pouring "some setting sunshine over" the romance.

After the romance had been finished, Hawthorne showed himself still self-conscious about the proportion of gloom and sunshine in his writings. An engraving from the portrait by Cephas G. Thompson was the frontispiece in the new edition of *Twice-Told Tales,* and it was included in copies of *The House of the Seven Gables* he gave relatives and friends. The engraving was "inflicted with a bedevilled melancholy," he told Fields, but it would do all the better for the author of *the Scarlet Letter.*[3] If it had been ready sooner, he had said earlier, it might have been included with "The Custom-House" as being "the very head that was cut off!"[4] He was pleased with Evert Duyckinck's review of the new romance in the *Literary World* of April 26, but said he could not understand why everything he wrote took "so melancholy an aspect" in Duyckinck's eyes. He had thought this story "rather a cheerful one than otherwise," but perhaps he had been "illuminated" by his "purpose to bring it to a prosperous close; while the gloom of the past threw its shadow along the reader's pathway." He said he thought the new book a more natural and a healthier product of his mind than *The Scarlet Letter* and that he felt less reluctance in publishing it.[5]

Sophia recognized that the revised ending broke the "spherical harmony" she had found in the earlier chapters, but she was pleased to have the earlier gloom lightened. In acknowledging that his purpose had been to give the romance "a prosperous close," Hawthorne implied agreement with her approval of the result. He indicates within the final three chapters, moreover, that he saw the conclusion as breaking the consistency of character and event, and thwarting the fate he had presented in the earlier chapters as inevitable. The action of the conclusion takes place outside rather than inside the ancient house. Sunshine has replaced the storm of the momentous preceding day. Into this outdoor scene of genial and comic humanity, where the commonplace folk now carry on their everyday affairs, enters Phoebe, giving the house again, after a few days' absence, the only cheerful resident it has had in decades. In brief space—both in elapsed time and on the pages of the book—she and Holgrave experience the miracle of love, something that earlier seemed unlikely. "They transfigured the earth, and made it Eden again, and themselves the two first dwellers in it." Clifford and Hepzibah also enter the bright scene, back from their hopeless flight. Word comes that Judge Pyncheon's son has been lost at sea, and things are cleared up instantaneously, as recounted in one sentence: "Clifford became rich; so did Hepzibah; so did our little village-maiden, and through her, that sworn foe of wealth and all manner of conservation—the wild reformer—Holgrave!"

In the abrupt removal of Judge Pyncheon and his son and this hasty, exclamatory apportioning of wealth to all hands, the author means to imply, surely, that the resolution is forced; and in the remaining pages he sounds one note of skepticism after another to show that he knows it is forced. When Phoebe points out the irony of Holgrave's accepting the Pyncheon wealth, and in the further reversal when he proposes to build a house of stone, in order to make more certain the bequests of one generation to the next, his only reply is, "You find me a conservative already! Little did I think ever to become one!" Hawthorne could be sure that thoughtful readers would not understand how the carefully drawn social reformer Holgrave could discard his views so quickly and so casually, even under the prompting of his new love for Phoebe.

Before closing the book, Hawthorne nevertheless reminds his readers of his normal assumption that consequences are inescapable. He remarks once that Judge Pyncheon's "previous steps had already pledged him to those which remained," that after such wrong as Clifford had suffered, "there is no reparation. . . . It is a truth . . . that no great mistake, whether acted or endured, in our mortal sphere, is ever really set right." But he is determined to close the story in the sunshine. As the characters prepared to mount the coach that was to take them to the fine country house that was to be their inheritance and their home, they are described as "chatting and laughing very pleasantly together," and it is said that Clifford and Hepzibah "bade a final farewell to the abode of their forefathers, with hardly more emotion than if they had made it their arrangement to return thither at tea-time." The author allows two of the town residents, who happen to be on hand as the carriage is loading, to speak final words, declaring, for him unmistakably, that the resolution of the story is not to be attributed to an acceptable Providence. Remembering that Hepzibah for many years had earned the small funds she had to live on by keeping a cent shop, one of them said that his wife once kept a cent shop for three months and lost five dollars. He shook his head at the new wealth that had come to the residents of the old Pyncheon house and said to his partner, "If you choose to call it luck, it is all very well; but if we are to take it as the will of Providence, why, I can't exactly fathom it."

In the review of *The House of the Seven Gables* which Hawthorne remarked helped him to see his own work better,[6] E. P. Whipple said (in *Graham's Magazine* for May) that the integrity of conception and execution in the early chapters is weakened as the "movement of the author's mind betrays a slight fitfulness toward the conclusion." From Whipple, Hawthorne had confirmation of what he might have said he had known all along, that he must let a story follow its own logic to the end, as he had done in *The Scarlet Letter*—and as he would do in the two romances he published afterward. Aware that consciousness of guilt is prominent in human history, unable to accept a universe in which consequences could be escaped, Hawthorne found dark tones appropriate to the moral and psychological studies in his fiction. After watching at his mother's deathbed in 1849— during the "last heavy throbbings," the "funeral march" of her heart—he set down in his notebook (VIII, 425, 429) hints of conclusions and assurances that seem to have remained central to this thought. Life, the universe, creation must be rationally acceptable; otherwise men can formulate no usable principles of conduct. To deny that his mother had experienced real sorrow and pain, or to argue that there had been adequate compensation (as Emerson felt that his role of preacher and teacher required him to say), would be a degrading exercise; to see in his mother's life proof that the agent of creation is a fiend, would be to commit man, as a creature worthy of his own respect, to a self-annihilating war with the universe and its creator (as Melville comes close to doing in some of his works). As a consequence, Hawthorne was able to recognize and portray the darker aspects of human experience and still keep an optimistic, though sober, outlook. In his pragmatic view, he could accept the universe and see that man, in his proper course, would hold to his ideals, choose among possibilities, and accept the inevitable. This outlook allowed him, or required him, to feel enveloping sympathy—sympathy for both the agents of evil and their victims, in his fiction and also among his associates and others in his own time. For people and fictional characters alike, descendants of Adam, he seemed to say—or to show—that it would be unrealistic and unjust to expect too much of them.

Although Hawthorne thought the new book better than *The Scarlet Letter*, and once remarked that "The Custom-House" was what gave *The Scarlet Letter* its vogue, he said he was afraid that, with the action brought close to the present, the "romantic improbabilities" would be too glaring against "the humble and familiar scenery."[7] These and other comparisons of the new romance with its predecessor, his asking others for their judgments, and his comments on reviews as they appeared—all suggest that he was testing both theories of fiction and practical rules. Although he had given this romance, on second thought, a bright conclusion, such as Evert Duyckinck and others had called for, he left no doubt that he thought the conclusion inconsistent with the rest of the story and with human experience. In this connection he offers in the book a directly stated precept such as is rare in his fiction: "The better remedy is for the sufferer to pass on, and leave what he once thought his irreparable ruin far behind him."

Hawthorne found ample praise in the reviews of *The House of the Seven Gables*. Fanny Kemble wrote from England that his two romances had caused "a greater sensation" than any book since *Jane Eyre*.[8] Rufus Wilmot Griswold said in the *International Magazine* for May that the new romance was "the purest piece of imagination in our prose literature." Amory Dwight Mayo, writing in the July *Universalist Quarterly*, praised the book enough, Hawthorne wrote Fields,[9] "to satisfy a greedier author" than he was, and pleased him in particular by saying that interest in his characters "is concentrated at the point, in the nature of each, where the battle is raging between human will and spiritual laws." Hawthorne wrote Henry T. Tuckerman that his review in the *Southern Literary Messenger* for June had given him the pleasantest sensation he had ever experienced "from any cause connected with literature," his pleasure being less from the praise than from the fact that Tuckerman understood what he meant.[10] The reviewer had spoken of the "artistic use of familiar materials," the "bits of Flemish painting," the style that "resorts to no tricks of rhetoric or verbal ingenuity," the "touches of humor," the "union of the philosophical tendency with the poetic instinct," and the "perfection of psychological art."

The House of the Seven Gables sold well, against the author's prediction that it would not be as popular as *The Scarlet Letter*. Nearly 7,000 copies were sold in six months.

Among its readers were two descendants of a Judge Pyncheon who lived in Salem at the time of the Revolution. They protested that their ancestor might be identified with the fictional character. Hawthorne proposed inserting in the next printing of the romance an apology, "else these wretched old Pyncheons will have no peace in the other world, nor I in this. . . . Who would have dreamed of claimants starting up, for such an inheritance as the House of the Seven Gables." He left the decision to Fields, and no apology was printed.[11]

Elizabeth Hawthorne wrote her brother quoting Louisa as saying that Judge Pyncheon was supposed to be the Reverend Charles W. Upham, and noting only that she thought there might be "some points of resemblance."[12] More than once since leaving Salem, Hawthorne had said he did not intend to satirize any of his political enemies, no doubt wishing to disown such intentions as he had declared to Longfellow and Horace Mann. He wrote Zachariah Burchmore that the time was past for him to "make war" on his enemies in his fiction, and that "the public would not uphold" him in it.[13] He told Salem friends that there was nothing in the book to stir up the Salemites as *The Scarlet Letter* had done. In creating such a character as Judge Pyncheon, an esteemed public figure, but despicable in his display of beneficence to conceal selfishness and vindictiveness, Hawthorne could not have failed to think of Upham; and, as Henry James remarked, the picture of Pyncheon seems to be "an impression—a copious impression—of an individual."[14] Hawthorne could have been expected to declare that no character in the book was modeled on any person, as he declared when readers identified others of his characters with persons in real life; but he probably would have been willing for readers to identify Upham with Judge Pyncheon.

The author's native town was much in his mind while he wrote, and he could draw upon knowledge he had accumulated since childhood, his reading in local history, and his recent involvement in local affairs. Hepzibah's uncle who had gone to sea "fifty years before, and never been heard of since" (Chapter 4) suggests the author's uncle John Manning. Phoebe owes something to the author's wife, whom he sometimes called by that name, and possibly something to Catherine Calista Ainsworth, whom he knew while living in the Fessenden home in 1836, and whom he was reputed to have told afterward that she was the original for Phoebe.[15]

Hawthorne's notebook furnished a number of details for the portrayal of scenes and characters and for the eastern land claim. On his visit to Bridge in August, 1837, he wrote at length about the ruined Knox mansion at Waldoboro, the Knox family, and the whole affair as "an illustration of what must be the result of American schemes of aristocracy."[16] Within his own family there was the tradition of a title to land in Maine, dating from the second American generation, when John Hawthorne purchased 9,000 acres of land near what later became the Knox estate.[17]

A Hawthorne letter, known only in a version provided by Horace Conolly and therefore of uncertain authenticity, tells how in the spring of 1840 he went with David Roberts to call on Susan Ingersoll in the old house she occupied at the foot of Turner Street. It was this visit, Conolly said, that furnished the idea for *Grandfather's Chair*. With his interest pricked by the phrase and the idea of "seven gables," Hawthorne inspected the entire house, located five gables, and saw marks on the beams indicating where there once had been two others.[18] This house is exhibited in Salem as the House of the Seven Gables.

Hawthorne had encountered the names Pyncheon, Holgrave, Venner, and Maule in the early history of Salem. For Matthew Maule he borrowed more than the names. Thomas Maule, a Salem shopkeeper, was ordered whipped in 1669 for saying that the minister preached lies, and a book he wrote in defense of the Quakers, *Truth Held Forth and Maintained*, was suppressed by order of the General Court. Wishing to relate his fictional Matthew Maule to this Thomas Maule, Hawthorne has his character addressed at his first appearance as "Thomas or Matthew Maule." Thomas Maule was not hanged for witchcraft on Gallows Hill, as Hawthorne's character is, nor is there any record of his pronouncing a curse on an oppressor. For the curse borne by the Pyncheons, Hawthorne went to the witch trials of 1692. As noted in Chapter 6 of this book, he would have learned from various histories that the Reverend Nicholas Noyes, minister of the Salem First Church, urged Sarah Good to confess herself a witch before being hanged, and that she replied, "You are a liar. . . . I am no more a witch, than you are a wizard;—and if you take away my life, God will give you blood to drink."[19] Julian Hawthorne wrote that he had often heard his father "speak, half fancifully and half in earnest, of the curse invoked by one of the witches upon Colonel John Hawthorne and all his posterity, and of the strange manner in which it had taken effect." Thus, in the musing required by Hawthorne for literary creation, he fused external facts with his understanding and his imaginative re-creation of those facts.[20] He was never more explicit about the curse under which the

Hawthornes supposedly suffered than to say that the line had lost the greatness of his early American ancestors.

A new edition of the *Twice-Told Tales* was issued on March 8, 1851; after a few weeks, 1,000 copies had been sold and the new preface, Fields said, was "making a tour of the country" in magazines and newspapers. Hawthorne had thought of writing a sketch similar to "The Old Manse" and "The Custom-House" to introduce this new edition, but while finishing *The House of the Seven Gables* he found time for only a preface. After asserting that an author "would have reason to be ashamed if he could not criticise his own work as fairly as another man's," he gives one of his best characterizations of his early tales.

> They have the pale tint of flowers that blossomed in too retired a shade—
> the coolness of a meditative habit, which diffuses itself through the feel-
> ing and observation of every sketch. Instead of passion, there is sen-
> timent; and, even in what purport to be pictures of actual life, we have
> allegory, not always so warmly dressed in its habiliments of flesh and
> blood, as to be taken into the reader's mind without a shiver. Whether
> from lack of power, or an unconquerable reserve, the Author's touches
> have often an effect of tameness; the merriest man could hardly contrive
> to laugh at his broadest humor; the tenderest woman, one would sup-
> pose, will hardly shed warm tears at his deepest pathos. The book, if you
> would see anything in it, requires to be read in the clear, brown, twilight
> atmosphere in which it was written; if opened in the sunshine, it is apt to
> look exceedingly like a volume of blank pages.

Like all of Hawthorne's self-evaluations, this must be read with an eye to his habitual modesty. When he denies the worth of his writings, he is judging them against a standard he pretends to respect, at least ought to respect, since it has general endorsement. He says, nevertheless, in overtones rather than directly, that his work has an integrity and a worth of its own, and that a work may demand to be read in the proper light.

These sketches, intended to open an intercourse with the world, Hawthorne said had reached only a few readers. It would have jarred the tone of genial modesty if he had remarked, as he had done in writing Lewis Mansfield, that a few readers, or one reader, would be reward enough; but such is his meaning.[21] The author who was, or said he was, "for a good many years, the obscurest man of letters in America" is by no means obscure now; he has achieved critical and popular fame with one romance and is finishing a second, which he can predict will be another "ten-strike." A new edition of his biographical tales was published early in

April, and he was ready to proceed with the new collection of tales and the children's book Fields had proposed.

As Hawthorne set about collecting contents for a new volume of tales, he enlisted his sisters and Fields to help locate copies and at one time was doubtful he would have enough for a volume. *The Snow-Image and Other Twice-Told Tales* came off the press in December in an edition of 2,500, larger than the first printing of any of his books thus far except *The Scarlet Letter*. Of its fifteen pieces, four were major tales first published in the preceding two years: "Main Street," "The Great Stone Face," "The Snow-Image," and "Ethan Brand"; the others had been passed over for earlier collections, some of them dating back to the Story-Teller manuscript. Reprinting the earlier pieces gave the author occasion to glance back over his career, and to write a "Dedicatory Letter" to Horatio Bridge, in which he described his early obscurity in imagery similar to that he had already used: "I sat down by the wayside of life, like a man under enchantment, and a shrubbery sprung up around me, and the bushes grew to be saplings, and the saplings became trees, until no exit appeared possible, through the entangling depths of my obscurity."

Though short and casual, this dedication makes an important statement of Hawthorne's purpose as an author and an implied estimate of his achievement less modest than was usual with him. An introductory essay or preface, he says, helps an author to establish a relationship with his reader by presenting the facts of his own life, arrayed "in a slightly idealized and artistic guise." He is careful himself, though, not to reveal anything "which the most indifferent observer might not have been acquainted with," and warns that one must "look through the whole range of his fictitious characters, good and evil, in order to detect any of his essential traits." As a writer of fiction, he is one who burrows, "to his utmost ability, into the depths of our common nature, for the purposes of psychological romance,—and who pursues his researches in that dusky region, as he needs must, as well by the tact of sympathy as by the light of observation." He might have added that, since about 1830, he had consciously adjusted the romance of adventure and the romance of effect, dominant at the time, to serve his own purpose of psychological delineation.

While assembling the contents of the *Snow-Image* volume, Hawthorne wrote *A Wonder-Book for Girls and Boys*. He first had in mind a series of fairy tales, stories of real life, and classic myths, "modernized and made funny,"[22] but in the plan he followed only classical myths are included, told by a college student who adapts them freely. The intention, as stated in the preface, was to "purge out all the old heathen wickedness and put in a moral wherever practicable," as he had done in *Peter Parley's Universal History*, and substitute for classic coldness "a tone in some degree Gothic or romantic." The book was finished by mid-July, and was published on November 8 (dated 1852). Appropriate illustrations for *A Wonder-Book* would show "wildness of fancy," Hawthorne said, rather than the "grace and delicacy" of the publisher's illustrator, Burrill Billings. But he took satisfaction in the book and, in sending Washington Irving a complimentary copy, said that "it seemed to reach a higher point, in its own way," than anything he had written "for grown people."[23] He was pleased to have reviewers speak of the sunny and happy quality of the book, and to have proved that he could adapt myths for children without writing down to them.

After a year and a half in the Berkshires, Hawthorne was ready to move. The first summer at Lenox had restored his health and equanimity of spirits, and had returned him to authorship. The uncomfortable house, the remoteness, especially when he had to trudge through snow or mud and rain to get the mail and return proof to his publisher, the dependence on others (the Tappans mainly) for transportation of his family and supplies—much that was unsatisfactory could be accepted only temporarily.

An episode in September, 1851, proved that Hawthorne was right when he refused to take the red house rent-free. After an exchange of notes between Sophia and Caroline Tappan had left unsettled the question of rights to the fruit in the orchard-garden at the red house, Hawthorne wrote Mrs. Tappan on September 5 a wonderful letter, "in a spirit of undisturbed good humor and friendly courtesy; and . . . the most perfect frankness." To a question that had been put to his wife, whether he "should not prefer to receive kindness rather than assume rights," he replied that he would "infinitely prefer a small right to a great favor." Continuing in the tone of seriousness lightly stated, he invited Mrs. Tappan to take as many of "the apples of discord" as she wished, in whatever way would "cause them to taste most agreeably"—seizing them on a raid, or receiving them as requital for many past favors, or as a free-will offering. "We have not shrunk from the word 'gift,' " he continued, "although we happen to be so much the poorer of two parties, that it is rather a suspicious word from you to us." Acknowledging "this slight acidity of sentiment" on his part, he concluded that she must take what fruit she needed speedily, "or there will be little else than a parcel of rotten plums to dispute about."[24] In an exchange of notes with Tappan, Hawthorne said he had written this letter "rather to relieve Sophia of what might have disturbed her, than because" he looked "upon the affair in a serious light." He reciprocated Tappan's avowal of good will, and the episode was closed; but it could not fail to increase the Hawthornes' wish to leave the Berkshires. One who knew Hawthorne at Lenox said he "had the look . . . of a banished lord."[25]

Hawthorne said he had never spent a pleasanter winter than at Lenox, but during the summer and autumn he reiterated his protest against the Berkshires: city living was preferable in the summer; he did not feel at home among the hills;[26] he cried out in his notebook against the weather, "I detest it! I detest it!! I de-test it!!! I hate Berkshire with my whole soul, and would joyfully see its mountains laid flat" (VIII, 439); the air and climate he had decided did not agree with his health; and for the first time since boyhood he felt languid and dispirited. Plans had already been made to move from the red house. Hawthorne would take this year Fanny Kemble's house, the Perch, which she had offered rent-free the preceding year, and he would pay the same rent he paid Tappan. Late in September a way of avoiding another winter in the Berkshires presented itself; he would rent the Manns' house at West Newton while Mann was in Washington for the congressional session.

In the summer of 1851, Hawthorne had set his friends to looking for a house he might buy, preferably near the sea. He had word from William Pike about a house at Marblehead Neck, and he inquired about possibilities at Manchester, Squam, and Sandy Bay. "As to Salem," he said, "I hope Providence has no intention of ever bringing me to reside within its limits again. I must be much nearer starving than I think myself now, before I would accept the collectorship. Besides, I am getting damnably out of the beaten track, as regards politics; and I doubt whether I can claim fellowship with any party whatever."[27]

He was never brought to reside in Salem again, and he almost never returned to visit. In less than a year, he found that he could indeed claim fellowship again with the Democratic Party. He took a more active part in politics than ever before and, in an ironic reversal such as might occur in one of his tales, had a determining hand in political affairs at Salem. Three years after being turned out of the Salem custom-house through political action, he was chosen for one of the most lucrative offices in the United States government subject to political appointment. Such develop-

ments as these were far from Hawthorne's expectations when he moved
from Lenox in November, 1851. His expectations were to live temporarily
at West Newton, to settle afterward into a house of his own, and to write
another romance.

20

The Blithedale Romance

The prospect of a second winter in the Berkshires had been only grudgingly acceptable to Hawthorne. The sojourn at West Newton could be for only a few months, but the move was a return to the only region he could consider home, and Sophia and the children would be near her favorite doctor and aging parents. The family rode through a snowstorm to the Pittsfield railroad station on November 21, 1851. The train was decorated in honor of Louis Kossuth, who was on his way to Boston. Later on, all members of the family joined in the tribute America was paying the champion of Hungarian freedom. Sophia was presented to him and Julian showed him a card on which he had printed "God bless you, Kossuth." Hawthorne said he was "about as enthusiastic as a lump of frozen sand" about Kossuth, but was going to hear him "in hopes of warming up a little."[1]

The move broke into Hawthorne's season for writing, which normally began at the earliest frost. After completing *A Wonder-Book* in the summer of 1851, he was undecided what he would write next. If a romance, he wrote Bridge on July 22, he meant "to put an extra touch of the devil into it"; for he feared he would lose ground with the public if he published "two quiet books in succession." Two days later he had decided to "take the Community for a subject" and include some of his experiences at Brook Farm.[2] The next week he borrowed from Caroline Tappan three volumes by Charles Fourier, the French author whose writings on communal societies had furnished the model adopted at Brook Farm after his departure. Only after moving to West Newton was he ready to begin the new romance. The brain-work, as he and his wife phrased it, required in writing tales was far out of proportion to the reward. His usual time for thinking and dreaming lengthened in this instance to four months, followed by an equal time for the writing. While waiting to move from Lenox, he could write the story "Feathertop" (1852) because he had thought it out earlier, probably soon after being turned out of office. His notebook for 1840 contains the suggestion for a story about a scarecrow (VIII, 185); an entry that seems to belong to the summer of 1849 tells how a modern magician makes "the semblance of a human being," with laths for legs and a pumpkin for a head, and how a tailor "transforms this scarecrow into quite a fashionable figure. N.B.—R.S.R." (VIII, 286). The initials stand for Richard Saltonstall Rogers, one of those Sophia identified as active in removing Hawthorne from the custom-house.[3] As with Upham, Hawthorne seems to have put Rogers into a fictional character whose identity might be guessed by knowing readers but would not be suspected by others.[4] He held to the purpose he had stated and wrote no more tales after this one.

Composition of the new romance began early in December; the next April 17 Hawthorne wrote Grace Greenwood that he had been "brooding over a book," had "latterly got under a high pressure of steam," and was then near the end. By May 2 it was finished and had been read by Sophia. In sending the "huge bundle of scribble" to E. P. Whipple, who, in place of Fields, then in Europe, would look it over with his "keen, yet not unfriendly eye," Hawthorne remarked, "After all, should you spy ever so many defects, I cannot promise to amend them; the metal hardens very soon after I pour it out of my melting-pot into the mould." Selecting a title was slow. He first suggested "Hollingsworth" and later added "Miles Coverdale's Three Friends," "The Veiled Lady," "Priscilla," "The Arcadian Summer," and "Zenobia," which he noted William Ware had already used for a novel; then he added "The Blithedale Romance," saying it "would do, in lack of a better."

The book was published in America on July 14. Fields had sold Chapman and Hall the British rights for £200, the first payment Hawthorne had received for works published abroad, either separately or in magazines. He owned English printings of *Twice-Told Tales*, *Mosses from an Old Manse*, *The House of the Seven Gables*, *The Snow-Image*, *A Wonder-Book*, and two editions of *The Scarlet Letter*. Fields reported that 15,000 copies of *The Scarlet Letter* had been sold in Europe.[5]

In writing "Ethan Brand," Hawthorne had turned back to his notebook record of thirteen years earlier. He turned back ten years to fill out the narrative of *The Blithedale Romance* from the notebooks he kept at Brook Farm, transferring some passages almost verbatim. Although he was close enough to walk from West Newton to make fresh observations at Brook Farm, there is no record that he did. Coverdale's arrival at the farm in an April snowstorm and his consequent illness, the milking of cows, the forking of manure, the field work, the trip to the fair, the observation of pigs in their sty, the farewell to the pigs, the dramatic performances in the woods—virtually all that takes place in the book took place while Hawthorne was at Brook Farm. Eliot's Pulpit, the grapevines that climb to the treetops, the residence hall, and the dining room belong to both Brook Farm and Blithedale. The recovery of Zenobia's body from the river follows in close detail the notebook record of July 9, 1845, when Hawthorne was waked by Ellery Channing at the Old Manse and took his boat to join the search for the body of Martha Hunt, who had drowned herself in the Concord River.[6] Coverdale's observations from the boarding-house window in the city and his meeting an "elderly ragamuffin" at the saloon are drawn in similar detail from entries for May 9–16, 1850 (VIII, 494–509).

The author conceded in his preface that he had "ventured to make free with his old, and affectionately remembered home, at Brook Farm," in order to provide a "Faery Land, so like the real world, that, in a suitable remoteness, one cannot well tell the difference, but with an atmosphere of strange enchantment, beheld through which the inhabitants have a propriety of their own." His residence at Brook Farm, being "essentially a day-dream, and yet a fact," served this purpose well. But he declared that the characters of his romance are "entirely fictitious." They "might have been looked for, at Brook Farm, but, by some accident, never made their appearance there."[7] Readers of the time nevertheless sought originals for the characters among residents at Brook Farm, and with varying degrees of certainty found them. Priscilla was modeled on a frail young seamstress, who became the subject of a notebook entry for October 9. Silas Foster derived from three men the author knew: William Allen, chief farmer of the community, William Orange, a neighbor, and Minot Pratt, one of the Brook Farmers. Foster's wife was supposedly based on Mrs. Pratt. Contemporaries found in Hollingsworth traces of Orestes Brownson, George Ripley, and Hawthorne's friend William B. Pike. And many of those who knew Margaret Fuller, or knew of her, identified her with

Zenobia. The two are both authors, gifted as conversationalists and lec-
turers; both are advocates of woman's rights. The author could not have
created Zenobia without having Margaret Fuller in mind, but he drew her
luxuriant beauty from a resident at Brook Farm, Mrs. Amelia Barlow. He
of course knew that Zenobia would be seen as a portrait of Miss Fuller,
and probably for that reason introduced her by name in saying that Priscilla resembles her and that Coverdale receives a letter from her.[8]

Hawthorne embodied much of himself in Coverdale. Besides his activities and observations, Coverdale holds in common with the author most of
his attitudes toward the current interests in, for example, philanthropy,
spiritualism, mesmerism, and woman's rights. The only narrator in
Hawthorne's romances, he also is the chief character, the one of greatest
interest to the author. He is the character that Hawthorne thought, or
pretended to think, he was in danger of becoming: the cold observer, pry-
ing into the hearts of those about him. In the company of others, he is
nevertheless isolated and, without realizing it, is both agent and victim in
the tragedy he sees enacted. It is through his eyes that the reader sees
Hollingsworth's humanitarianism descend into a destructive monomania,
and sees Zenobia thwarted both in the cause to which she is devoted and
in her love. He does realize, finally, the emptiness of his life, but without
fully understanding it.

As a partial self-portrait, Coverdale falls into the company of Oberon in
"The Devil in Manuscript" and "Fragments from the Journal of a Solitary
Man." Although he has given up poetry, and the Blithedale venture has
long since failed, he says that, if three or four of his former associates
were still there, he sometimes fancies that he would turn his "world-weary
footsteps thitherward," for more and more he feels that they "had struck
upon what ought to be a truth." His recollection is that he "once hoped
strenuously, and struggled not so much amiss"; but even before he first
reached Blithedale, as the reader will recall, he was doubtful of its success.
And while declaring his wish for a cause "worth a sane man's dying for,"
he reveals his fatal flaw, without recognizing it. He might offer up his life,
"provided, however, the effort did not involve an unreasonable amount of
trouble." He continues, "If Kossuth, for example, would pitch the battlefield of Hungarian rights within an easy ride of my abode, and choose a
mild, sunny morning, after breakfast, for the conflict, Miles Coverdale
would gladly be his man, for one brave rush upon the levelled bayonets.
Further than that, I should be loth to pledge myself" (Chapter 29). Coverdale has at the opening of the romance doubts about the success of Blithe-

dale that Hawthorne himself stated only after he had been some time at
Brook Farm. His wish to provide a home for Sophia no doubt bolstered
his faith in "Mr. Ripley's Utopia," but he would not have joined the band
of dreamers and invested his money had he not thought the undertaking
worthy and in some degree practical. After he had been disillusioned, he
wrote his fiancée judgments much like those of Coverdale, but without
Coverdale's cynicism and lack of purpose (remarked by Hollingsworth).
Hawthorne's pragmatic outlook allowed him to recognize shortcomings or
flaws or evil in human nature and still avoid misanthropy and antagonism
toward the creator of man. In *The Blithedale Romance*, as was his practice,
he incorporated incidents, attitudes, beliefs, and actual persons—himself
included—but fictionized them so thoroughly that they had an independent existence in the romance.

Reviewers of *The Blithedale Romance* dealt with its author as an un-
doubted genius whose literary artistry was beyond question. Henry F.
Chorley called Hawthorne "the highest, deepest, and finest imaginative
writer whom America has yet produced." [9] George Eliot saw this work as
"unmistakably the finest production of genius in either hemisphere, for
this quarter at least." [10] Orestes Brownson said that Hawthorne had "fully
established his reputation as the first writer, in his favorite line, our American literature can boast." [11] E. P. Whipple, looking first at Hawthorne's
earlier work, pronounced him "inimitable in his own sphere," dweller in
"that 'magic circle' where none can walk" except him. He said that *The
Scarlet Letter*, "the most moral book of the age," had "made a deeper impression on the public mind than any romance ever published in the
United States," and that *The House of the Seven Gables* displayed "the same
far-reaching and deep-seeing vision into the duskiest corners of the human
mind." Recognizing the function of the narrator in *The Blithedale Romance*,
he remarked that the readers are "joint watchers with Coverdale" and
sometimes disagree with his interpretations of the other characters. This
romance was to him "an entirely new product of the human mind." [12]

Reviews noted the Brook Farm connections. George Ripley endorsed
Hawthorne's declaration that Blithedale did not represent Brook Farm,
but spoke of episodes which "may raise a laugh at the expense of the Ar-
cadians of Brook Farm in which probably no one will join more heartily
than the survivors of that motley and mirthful crew." [13] Brownson found
no one of Hawthorne's characters to be purely imaginary, but no one to
have a single original. George Eliot thought that Margaret Fuller "could
not have been absent from the mind of the novelist—nay, must have

inspired his pencil" in his drawing of Zenobia; and she thought the failure to have Zenobia "come out of her struggle in regal triumph" evidences a "lack of moral earnestness" in the author. She joined other reviewers in wanting a more favorable account of the Brook Farm venture.[14]

Hawthorne said that he profited from some criticism of his works and cared little for opinions that did not agree with his. There was ample criticism now to please him, with some of the most favorable coming across the Atlantic. He had achieved what he had imagined in his boyhood: he stood respectably among the scribbling sons of John Bull.

In his search for a place to settle, Hawthorne learned in December, 1851, that the Alcott house at Concord was for sale, and had an invitation from Ellery Channing to make an inspection trip and stay with him a week. "Nobody at home but myself, and a prospect of strong waters. . . . Emerson is gone, and nobody here to bore you. The skating is damned good."[15] But not until the next February 23 did he go to Concord, accompanied by his wife and Julian; two days later the Alcott estate had been purchased, the house and nine acres of land for $1,500.[16] Thirteen additional acres were bought later. Moving was set for early June, and ahead of time Hawthorne wrote his old friend Hosmer to lay in some wood for him and to plow the garden. His wife arrived first with Una and Rose and her maid, and with hired help put things in order, so that when her husband arrived with Julian on June 5, "he had quite a civilized impression of the house at first glance and was delighted with it, not having seen it since his first visit in snow time."[17]

In a few weeks the Hawthornes were fully restored to the community they had left almost seven years earlier. On her first afternoon Sophia met Thoreau and Emerson in the road. When Emerson turned about and walked with her, she said that "his beautiful smile added to the wonderful beauty of the evening sunset." Mrs. Emerson and her children called; Una visited Emerson, and Julian rode the pony of Emerson's son Edward; Elizabeth Hoar took Una home with her and gave her a bouquet of flowers. Ellery Channing stopped by to talk, as did Edward Hosmer. A picnic on July 5 drew Emerson and his wife and children; Una and Julian were included, and on Emerson's invitation, Hawthorne went also.

Sophia's letters to her mother reflect genuine delight at the return to familiar scenes and old friends at Concord. Her assessment of the Concord neighbors may have been more favorable than her husband's, but he had indicated genuine satisfaction from the time he purchased the house, which he said had "picturesque capabilities." In sending a drawing of his residence to accompany an article being published in *Putnam's Monthly Magazine*, he noted that since his marriage less than ten years earlier he had lived in seven houses.[18] After settling into the eighth, he said to more than one correspondent that for the first time in his life he felt at home. On October 1, leaving the baby, called Rosebud, with the maid, the rest of the family went for a walk along Peter's Path and up the hill opposite the Old Manse; returning by way of Sleepy Hollow, they sat down for a while in a secluded spot. The parents had thought to take the walk alone, but the disappointment showing through Una's efforts to conceal it reminded them that, although their enjoyment of the old haunts might be no less than in former years, it would be different. They had realized when they moved to Salem in 1845 that the Old Manse interlude had closed.

Alcott had called the house "Hillside" because of the steep hill behind. Hawthorne re-baptized it "The Wayside," a name which he said seemed to possess "a moral as well as a descriptive propriety."[19] It stood beside the road to Boston, three-quarters of a mile beyond Emerson's house and two miles from the Old Manse. Originally a farm house built before the Revolution, it had passed in 1845 into the hands of Alcott, who made additions that "invested the whole with a modest picturesqueness." Alcott also formed terraces on the hill and built "arbors and summer-houses out of rough stems and branches of trees, on a system of his own." The overall appearance was "the raggedest in the world." Hawthorne said of the hill, which was shaded by locust-trees, elms, white-pines, and small oaks, "I spend delectable hours there, in the hottest part of the day, stretched out at my lazy length with a book in my hand, or an unwritten book in my thoughts."[20] The bathing room of the Wayside had a "long tub," to which a hose could be run from the pump in the large kitchen. Devotee of the cold bath every morning, Sophia saw the pump and the long tub as aids to the daily ritual, and also as some relief from the sea of water she said her husband always created around his tub at Lenox.

Louisa Hawthorne had been expected for a visit at West Newton and later at the Wayside, but had delayed because of her own illness and illness among relatives. After her mother's death, she had lived with her Aunt Rebecca, widow of Robert Manning. She had remained her brother's main link to the family; he had long ago called Elizabeth an impossible correspondent. Louisa had reported on Elizabeth from time to time, how she secluded herself in her room, read much of the night, did not stir until noon, and refused to go anywhere farther than she could walk. During one cold spell, she said Elizabeth was congealed. Writing in 1850 that Elizabeth had gone to live with a family at Kettle Cove, on the coast near Beverly, she had the surprising news that Elizabeth ate at the table with the family, and continued, "What should you say to see her go to church? She actually did go several times while she was here. I was afraid she would forget herself and *speak in meeting*, but she only made up a face at me when I looked at her."[21]

Louisa appreciated her brother's genius. When told about one of his early literary successes, she remarked that nothing about it surprised her. She wrote him on July 1, 1852, of meeting two of their former whist partners. Horace Conolly wanted him to know that he had gone for Pierce in the Democratic convention at Baltimore. Remembering that Conolly had been a Democrat in 1845 and a Whig four years later, she said that "the Democratic Party must flourish if it has many more such converts." David Roberts had recited a list of appointments her brother could choose from if Pierce became president—he might become minister to Russia. She added, "I not by any means thinking office the most desired path to glory for you, very coolly told him I hoped you would have nothing to do with it. I believe he thought I was very ridiculous."

Louisa's expected visit was again postponed in the summer of 1852. Uncle John Dike was going to Saratoga Springs to take the waters for a fortnight, and she was persuaded to go with him, in the greatest undertaking of her life. Hawthorne urged her to come directly from Saratoga to the Wayside. On July 26 she and Uncle Dike boarded the steamboat *Henry Clay* for home by way of the Hudson River and New York City. Before seven on the morning of July 30, William Pike got out of the railroad coach in front of the Wayside. He had left only four days earlier, after a visit. His first words were, "Your sister Louisa is dead," and after he had said that she was lost on the *Henry Clay*, Hawthorne shut himself in his study. When Pike had gone and Sophia was consoling the children with the thought that Aunt Louisa was happy with her mother in another world, Julian went suddenly to the study; "he had the intention of consoling his father with that idea; but his father had gone on the hill."[22]

Approaching New York on July 27, the *Henry Clay* had an explosion and fire midships that forced the passengers to the bow and the stern. Louisa and Uncle Dike were separated; he was rescued, but she jumped into the water and was drowned. At 1:30 P.M. on August 2 William Pike mailed a letter which he understood Hawthorne would receive that evening, saying that Louisa's body had been found and would reach Salem

later that night in the charge of her cousin Robert Manning. But Hawthorne did not receive the letter until the next day, and did not reach
Salem until three in the afternoon. Burial had taken place at ten in the
morning, in the plot at the Howard Street Cemetery, where Louisa's
mother, her Manning grandparents, and other Mannings were buried.
Sophia was glad her husband had arrived too late for the funeral, for "it
would have been so painful to him to go through any ceremony, and to
hear all the Calvinistic thought."[23] He went with Elizabeth to Kettle Cove
for the night and intended to bring her back with him, but she declined.
A dozen years later, after her brother's death, she said she remembered
and enjoyed the thought of his visit in the surroundings so familiar to
her.[24] He reached home August 4, bringing for Una the broach, with the
name of Aunt Rachel Forrester engraved on it, which Aunt Louisa was
wearing when she was drowned. The next day Sophia wrote her mother
that the ghastliness had left her husband's face. "It would be an intrusion
and impertinence to condole with him and attempt suggesting ideas," she
had concluded, for he was "capable of all for himself." And once in a
while he said something that showed her "he was alleviating for himself
the sorrow and loss." While Hawthorne was away for the funeral, she
said, Emerson had sent a note to the Wayside: "But who knows which is
the straightest and most excellent way out of the calamities of the present
world?"[25]

21

"We Are Politicians Now"

On June 17, 1852, Hawthorne wrote Fields that he had meant to write another *Wonder-Book*, but an unexpected task had intervened. Franklin Pierce was the Democratic Party nominee for the presidency and wanted him to write a campaign biography. He had consented, he explained, somewhat reluctantly, for Pierce had "now reached that altitude when a man, careful of his personal dignity, will begin to think of cutting his acquaintance." But he sought nothing for himself "and therefore need not be ashamed to tell the truth of an old friend." When no one of the announced candidates was able to gain a two-thirds majority at the convention in Baltimore, Pierce was put forward as a compromise candidate and on June 5 won out over General Lewis Cass (1782–1866) on the forty-ninth ballot.

Hawthorne did not know of the nomination until June 8, and the next day he wrote Pierce, uncertain whether to congratulate him or not, for it would be absurd to think the office would ever afford him "one happy or comfortable moment." It had occurred to him that Pierce might think of him to write a biography; and he need not say that he was ready to do any service he could. But he said he thought others would perform the task better than he, and suggested, for one, the editor of the *Boston Daily Times*, Charles C. Hazewell. He added, "It needs long thought with me, in order to produce anything good, and, after all, my style and qualities, as a writer, are certainly not those of the broadest popularity, such as are requisite for a task of this kind. I should write a better life of you after your

term of office and life itself were over, than on the eve of the election."
The Wayside was "hardly fit for the reception of a future President," he
said, but he and his wife would be happy to receive Pierce and would
treat him as simply as if he were "a mere country lawyer."[1]

Pierce had already decided to ask Hawthorne to write a campaign biography,[2] and the two probably met when Hawthorne was in Boston June
10–12, sitting for a portrait by George P. A. Healey.[3] Back home on June
13, Hawthorne sent Ticknor a letter to deliver to Pierce. It is likely that
he had taken home the invitation on June 12 and was sending his acceptance after talking with his wife. Twenty years earlier, when Pierce was
running for a seat in Congress, Hawthorne had written him that it was a
pity he was not in a situation to lend the support of his pen, and had envisaged Pierce later as United States senator, minister to England, cabinet
member, "and lastly—but it will be time enough to think of the next step,
some years hence."[4]

When arrangements were made early in July for the book to be published by Ticknor, Hawthorne did not miss the irony—Ticknor was a bitter Whig. Before the end of June, Hawthorne had considerable information in hand, but it was nearly a month before he could begin writing.
Most of the information had to be furnished by others, and it was exasper-
atingly slow in coming. On August 22, when nearly all of the manuscript
had gone to the printer, Hawthorne wrote Ticknor, "I shall send the rest
as soon as they find me materials; and if not finished before the end of the
week, I'll be d——d if I mean to finish it at all." He was ready with the
final copy on August 27, a month after he began the writing, and in that
time he had lost several days at the death of Louisa.

On July 5 Hawthorne had written Pierce about two difficulties he fore-
saw in making the campaign biography a success. Pierce had not made
himself known on the political scene, for, instead of putting himself forward, he had withdrawn into the background. His military career should
be made prominent but should not overshadow him "as a man of peaceful
pursuits." The second difficulty was Pierce's "connection with the great
subject of variance between the North and South." Hawthorne could see
no course worthy of either Pierce or his biographer, "save to meet the
question with perfect candor and frankness, . . . not pugnaciously, and,
by no manner of means, defensively." He concluded, "I sometimes wish
the convention had nominated old Cass! It would have saved you and me
a great deal of trouble; but my share of it will terminate four years sooner
than your own." Pierce visited the Wayside on August 23, four days
before the last manuscript went to the printers.[5]

Hawthorne had the biography off his hands in time to attend the Bowdoin College commencement, which this year celebrated the fiftieth anniversary of the enrollment of the first class. He had responded to the invitation from his former teacher Alpheus Spring Packard that he expected to attend but had not found time to prepare a contribution. He left home August 30 on what turned out to be his longest absence yet from his family, met Pierce at Portland, where the last of the proof was being sent, and on account of rain did not reach Bowdoin until the afternoon of the next day when the ceremonies were nearly over—and luckily, he said, for his "praises had been sounded by orator and poet," and his "blushes would have been quite oppressive." Eight of his classmates were present, "a set of dismal old fellows, whose heads looked as if they had been out in a pretty copious shower of snow." He felt as young as the day he graduated, but each of the others was a mirror in which he saw the reflection of his own age.[6] According to a report that has come down, the toastmaster at the afternoon session, being held in a tent, delivered an elaborate introduction of an alumnus, not named, and when he turned to call on Hawthorne where he had been sitting at the edge of the enclosure, there was only a vacant seat; Hawthorne had lifted the tent wall and slipped out. Because Brunswick was crowded for the occasion, Hawthorne spent the night at Bath, and there some old sea captains insisted on considering him a brother, and calling him "Cap'n Hawthorne."[7]

He and Pierce, who had spoken at the semi-centennial celebration,[8] went to Portland on September 1 and on to Portsmouth the next day. On September 3 Hawthorne took the boat for the Isles of Shoals, taking a letter of introduction from Pierce to Laighton's Hotel on Appledore Island. He found that both were expected and the best accommodations were ready for him. Pierce and his wife came on September 6, but for only a day. Hawthorne's purpose was to stay until he was "saturated with sea breezes." He was following the pattern of his early summer travels: putting up for an uncertain duration in a remote spot and revealing no more of his plans or whereabouts than necessary. He had written Sophia before leaving the mainland that he supposed a letter would reach him, "in case of emergency." He did not write home until September 8; three days later he wrote in his notebook that he was beginning to feel as if he had stayed long enough. On September 13 all the non-residents left the island except him; and he wrote Sophia that he would be home on September 15. On that day Sophia wrote in her notebook, "No dear husband today"; the next day, "I am no longer heroic. I give out entirely.—At one, at five, and at eight we expected papa." When he arrived on September 17, he explained that continuous rain had interfered with passage to the mainland.

The fortnight on the Isles of Shoals was a holiday and also a field trip, as his stay at North Adams had been in 1838. His curiosity led him to every spot of interest on the islands, and he filled his notebook with observations and impressions. He made acquaintances quickly and slipped as unobtrusively as he could into the life of the islands. He played whist at his hotel the first evening. He found two men particularly interesting and satisfying. Thomas B. Laighton, owner of four islands and the hotel, had served in the New Hampshire legislature before moving to the Isles of Shoals in 1839. Ordinarily Hawthorne sat with him in the evening, taking the sea breezes, "puffing a cigar responsive to his pipe—not keeping up a continual flow of talk, but each speaking as any wisdom" happened "to come into his mind."[9] Levi Lincoln Thaxter, holder of college and law degrees, had come to the Isles for an interlude in the preparation he hoped would lead him to a career on the stage, and had been married in 1851 to Laighton's daughter, Celia, who was to become a poet (well known to schoolchildren for "The Sandpiper") and to write the book *Among the Isles of Shoals* (1873). Hawthorne was often in the company of these two and the wife's sister (the four of them meeting "at meal times like one family"), in talk about poetry and the stage; and he recorded from their telling a wealth of the history and the lore of the islands. His last evening he spent with Thaxter, "winding up with *two* glasses of hot gin-and-water"; and Mrs. Thaxter gave him gifts for his three children.

Yet Hawthorne was alone much of his time on the Isles of Shoals. He caught grasshoppers for bait and fished for cunneros off the rocks; he roamed among the huckleberry and barberry bushes along the shore, and heard the sheep bleating; he watched the sailboats lying motionless on the dimpled sea, and at ten o'clock one night he took note of "the sky, and the three-quarters waning moon, and the old sea moaning all round the island."

He said he returned from his two weeks on the Isles of Shoals twice the man he was. His notebook leaves no doubt that he enjoyed the sojourn, that he was not much less carefree than he had been on his summer journeys twenty years earlier. Obviously he had agreeable relations with the families of Laighton and Thaxter. The evidence suggests that with them—dining as a family, telling ghost stories and strange episodes in the history of the islands, socializing in the evening, playing whist, singing, and drinking gin-and-water—he was freer and more relaxed than in most company. There was now, as in his earlier excursions, an element of role-playing which he enjoyed and which made it easier for him to collect literary materials. His careful notebook records show him interested in a variety of matters—the uncertain fates of the two wives the lighthouse keeper had lost, for example; Thaxter's saving the drunken keeper from drifting out to sea, and thus interfering with what might have been the will of Providence; a jumble of rock fragments which suggested by their appearance that they were remnants tossed aside by the Creator when His main work was done; and the records of the church at Gosport, which he received on loan the following November and afterward copied extensively into his notebook (VIII, 544–51).[10] The records told him about Hawthornean characters—people conscious of guilt who sought relief through public confession and the granting of forgiveness by vote of the congregation. The bleak Isles of Shoals, the presence of wind and waves, and the remoteness made the islands an appropriate setting for a romance. In plans for a story to be set on a remote seacoast, the Agatha story, which Hawthorne and Melville both considered during the next few months but neither wrote, they agreed on the Isles of Shoals for the setting.[11]

Before Hawthorne returned from the Isles of Shoals, the *Life of Franklin Pierce* had come off the press, and newspaper comment had begun. He had known that it would mark him as a politician, but he had nevertheless exhorted Ticknor on August 25 to "blaze away a little harder" in his advertising. The author's name should appear prominently in announcements, emphasized by capital letters, such as "HAWTHORNE'S Life of GENERAL PIERCE; SANCTIONED by the General, drawn up from original documents, and with the GENERAL'S OWN JOURNAL, AS WRITTEN IN THE FIELD. . . ." This letter concluded, "Go it strong, at any rate. We are politicians now; and you must not expect to conduct yourself like a gentlemanly publisher." He had known also that to support Pierce was to take a side unpopular among his relatives and his neighbors.

Sophia more than once defended Pierce—and thus her husband also—in writing members of her family, who were uncompromising opponents of both Pierce and Daniel Webster. She said that Horace Mann only hurt himself in flinging innuendoes at Pierce and Webster in one of his speeches. She cited lies she said had been printed against Pierce in the *New York Tribune*, and quoted Hawthorne as saying that Horace Greeley, the proprietor and editor, "must have known they were falsehoods." She noted that the stories of Pierce's intemperance were parallel to the reports her mother had repeated that Webster cohabited with black wenches, and said that since Pierce was no longer guilty of intemperance, the stories would argue in his favor. Her own experience with morphine given her in her girlhood to stop her headaches had left her with "infinite sympathy and charity for persons liable to such a habit." Following Webster's death, she wrote her mother an eloquent tribute to the "grandeur and massiveness in Webster" and, after recalling how severely members of her family judged him, added, "At all events it is a constant source of congratulation to me that He who will weigh him in the balance is God and not Man." She asserted that Pierce had the same views as Daniel Webster on the Fugitive Slave Law and the Compromise of 1850, and was convinced that severance of the Union would doom the slaves' hopes for freedom. Holding views similar to Pierce's, her husband undertook the biography to assist an old friend, aware that "it would subject him to abuse"; but, she added, "provided his conscience is clear, he never cares a *sou* what people say."[12]

After learning that her brother was to write the Pierce biography, Louisa Hawthorne had inquired of her sister whether it was not a shame,[13] probably having in mind the loss of time from his literary work. When the biography was out, Elizabeth sent him newspaper clippings and summarized others in coldly impersonal—or perhaps sarcastic—remarks such as this: The *Puritan Recorder* of Boston "eulogises the book, for you are a favorite with the Orthodox, and especially with the Clergy, and for that reason I think you should judge more charitably of them." She offered to distribute some copies of the book where she lived.[14]

The Democratic newspapers and magazines judged the biography of Pierce a proper and commendable use of Hawthorne's literary pen; the Whig organs as a rule praised his fiction and granted him some literary success in this book, but condemned it as a eulogy of a weak character and unworthy of the author. In the *Literary World* of September 25 Evert Duyckinck concluded that the undertaking was worthy of an author even of Hawthorne's rank and that it would benefit him because it "brought him down from the subtle metaphysical analysis of morbid temperaments . . . to a healthy encounter with living interests." Duyckinck thus continued his argument against the most characteristic qualities of Hawthorne's tales and romances. Caleb Foote's review in the *Salem Gazette* found this "an honest biography of a thorough going, unscrupulous party man," for whom nothing could be claimed above a "respectable mediocrity." The reviewer's real quarrel was with the opinions of Webster, Pierce, and the biographer on the slavery question, which he characterized in the more extravagant language of the abolitionists. His position was similar to that he had taken at the removal of Hawthorne from the Salem custom-house: he would not himself have advanced in 1849 the accusations of malfeasance that caused Hawthorne to be turned out of office; nor would he have originated the charges the abolitionists made in 1852, against Pierce and the writer of the campaign biography; but in each instance Foote took the stand approved by his party. Hawthorne may have seen in this review evidence that he could not expect in 1852 any more generous treatment in Salem than he had received earlier.

On October 18, having the responses to the biography and awaiting the election, Hawthorne wrote Horatio Bridge, whom he had wished to see while he was writing the book—"for the sake of talking over" Pierce's character, as he could not do with anyone else. He thought the biography was "judiciously done," and it was greatly to Pierce's satisfaction. "Without any sacrifice of truth, it puts him in as good a light as circumstances would admit. . . . And though the story is true, yet it took a romancer to do it. . . . I love him; and, oddly enough, there is a kind of pitying sentiment mixed up with my affection for him, just now." Writing Bridge's wife the following May 18, he continued his analysis: Pierce is "often apparently governed by his impulses, but always in such a way that his predetermined ends are forwarded thereby. I never knew or heard of a man at once so warm and so cold, so subtile and so true." In composing the biography of his friend—and that for an important purpose—Hawthorne had slipped into his accustomed role as romancer. And he had achieved in the total portrait of Pierce something of the same warmth and sympathy combined with objectivity that entered his fictional portraits. Furthermore, he had made no compromise in presenting his own and Pierce's views on the growing conflict over slavery and the powers of the Union and the states, and had produced a work that, presumably, won voters for the candidate.

In November, Pierce won the electoral college votes of all states except Kentucky, Massachusetts, Tennessee, and Vermont. Hawthorne found himself at once a sort of "prime minister." Being outside the circle of regular politicians around Pierce, he had acquaintances who would see him as their best link to the source of patronage, and, since he had friends ranging from the president down to ward politicians, his usefulness to job-seekers was assumed to be great. He wished to help his friends whenever possible; and he knew that he would have to decide about an appointment for himself.

22

Prime Minister

When the election of Franklin Pierce in November, 1852, brought Hawthorne into prominence on the political scene, he was by no means a beginner in politics. His tutelage had begun with the efforts of his friends in 1837 to place him on the Reynolds expedition. After that, besides holding two appointments and numbering among his associates politicians on the national level, he had written a memorial essay on a congressman and a biography that helped elect a president. Perhaps more important as preparation for the office of "prime minister" was his experience in the local brawling over post office and custom-house appointments.

Although both his appointments as customs officer were urged on the grounds of his literary achievement, he was associated with political appointees and talked their language from the beginning. While in the Boston custom-house he wrote his fiancée that he wanted "nothing to do with politicians," for in partisan scheming "they cease to be men," and their "consciences are turned to India-rubber—or to some substance as black as that, and which will stretch as much."[1] The object of these remarks was George Bancroft, whom he never felt he could trust. But Hawthorne developed some of his strongest friendships with other political appointees who were also party managers. One such friend was William B. Pike, who derived from tradesmen and was himself a carpenter.[2] Hawthorne once wrote him that there was no man he so much would like to have for a companion, and he valued the thoughtful comment he received each time

Pike read a new book of his. A note of teasing sounds through the letters Hawthorne and Pike exchanged over a period of twenty years, often in reference to their meetings at Parker's Saloon and Restaurant in Boston and to their imbibing of wine and gin-and-water. Late in February, 1853, Pike sent gifts to the three Hawthorne children, not New Year's Day but "President's-day gifts . . . in honor of the new era to open" with the inauguration of Pierce. When Pike became collector of customs at Salem in 1857, Hawthorne purchased a copy of the *New England Primer Improved*, re-titled it "The Collector's Manual," and inscribed it to Pike, from his "Brother in Tribulation" as a "slight token of esteem for him as an officer of the Revenue— . . . intended to counteract in some degree the degenerating influences with which one in official life is constantly surrounded."[3] He told Longfellow that Pike was a "man of no letters, but of remarkable intellect,"[4] and he reminded Pike often that he had wanted him "to do some higher and better thing than other men are able to do." His high regard did not diminish with the years. Looking forward to his return to America after seven years abroad, he wrote Pike, "Perhaps you and I will finally settle down in each other's neighborhood."[5] The number of those whose company he earnestly sought again and again, as he did Pike's, was very small.

The wide differences in "sphere and abilities" that Hawthorne mentions in "The Custom-House" as existing between him and Zachariah Burchmore did not keep them from developing a warm and generous friendship, characterized by greater frankness on Hawthorne's part than his friendship with Pike. His letters to Burchmore refer often to Parker's Saloon in the same teasing way as do his letters to Pike, but he realized that Zack had a weakness for drink and often cautioned him to stay away from it. He once proposed that neither take a glass of spirits until they met again; at another time he urged Burchmore not to drink on weekdays; at still another time, not until after the next election. "I should hate to have you get to be a sot (plain speaking must be excused, in a friend). . . . Do, for God's sake, leave off drinking till you see me again, if no longer."[6] While Hawthorne was at the Isles of Shoals, Burchmore stopped at the Wayside on his way home from a political meeting and told Sophia that he had proposed asking Pierce to appoint Hawthorne to the consulship of Liverpool, but that Hawthorne had threatened to decapitate him if he did. Before leaving, Burchmore said, "Do not let Mr. Hawthorne write again till November. He ought to rest till then." Sophia recorded details of the visit in the notebook Hawthorne would read when he came home. She enjoyed seeing Burchmore's affection for her husband, and could understand the generous reciprocation of that affection.

Hawthorne freely asked favors of Burchmore: to buy and send him clothes, boots, and cigars, and to distribute copies of his new books in Salem. The eight copies he usually sent were for Burchmore (or his daughter or his wife), Pike, Dr. Benjamin F. Browne, Horace Conolly, David Roberts, Ephraim Miller, Louisa Hawthorne, and Uncle John Dike. He spoke to Burchmore in confidence, asking most often for news of local politics, and as a rule he sent his letters through intermediaries because, as he explained, the Salem politicians were watchful of his correspondence with Burchmore. More than once he asked Burchmore not to let it be known that he was furnishing advice or assistance. Since Burchmore could not hope to return to the custom-house during the Whig administration, Hawthorne wrote him again and again not to be hasty in antagonizing those who did not support him and by all means not to make it impossible for Pike and others in the local Democratic organization to support him in the future.

After the election in November, 1852, jockeying for public offices began in earnest. Among the Salem candidates and their sponsors were men who had been Hawthorne's friends a dozen years. He was asked for advice and support, and in the following months he proved his mastery of political manipulation and his understanding of the men involved. He was drawn far deeper into the contests than he had intended, but it was a game at which he knew he was adept, and he enjoyed the success in an arena in which he earlier had been the loser.

Burchmore became a candidate for the naval officer's post at the Salem custom-house without the approval of the local Democratic committees and, as Hawthorne knew well before the election, against the wishes of the party managers. Hawthorne knew also that Dr. George Bailey Loring hoped to replace Ephraim Miller as collector and was sponsored by the chairman of the county Democratic committee, N. J. Lord, who was himself a candidate for the office of district attorney. After talking with Loring, Hawthorne asked Burchmore on December 9 what he would think of "a programme like this": Burchmore to withdraw his claims to the naval office and Loring and his supporters to pledge their influence toward placing him in the Boston custom-house. He thought Loring could be trusted to carry out such a promise, in part because he and his coadjutors wanted to get Burchmore out of the district. As a guarantee that Burchmore would support Loring, Hawthorne drafted a letter for him to copy and present, worded carefully to say that he endorsed Loring over all other candidates for the collectorship, but that his endorsement was "to operate only in case Miller's removal was inevitable." This was the same maneuver Hawthorne had employed in 1846 when he arranged for the Salem Democrats to promise their support to Stephen Hoyt, but only if it turned out that John D. Howard could not be appointed. Hawthorne had not attempted to turn Loring's interest away from the collectorship; he had assumed only the role of agent to facilitate a resolution without taking a position that would appear unfavorable to anyone. A month later, when Loring asked him about the collectorship, he answered only that he was "in an awkward position between two gentlemen," either of whom he would like to benefit. By remaining neutral between Loring and the incumbent, his friend Ephraim Miller, he kept his potential for influence. He added casually that any appearance of disunion in the local party organization would favor the incumbent. Further, he said, he had heard a rumor of a third candidate.[7]

The weight Hawthorne was presumed to have in custom-house appointments was augmented, surely, by the report in the *Salem Gazette* of December 7, 1852, that he might be appointed collector of the Boston custom-house. He wrote Loring the next February 17 that he would help Lord to be elected district attorney, and said again that he would not be quite overcome with grief at the selection of either Loring or Miller as collector. On February 26 he cast his influence firmly for Miller, sending a letter to that purpose for W. D. Ticknor to present to the president. Meanwhile Loring and Lord had recommended Burchmore for a position in Boston, and on March 4 Hawthorne wrote Senator Atherton supporting Burchmore's application to become appraiser in the Boston custom-house, saying that the application had the recommendation of Lord, the whole Democratic influence in the county, and the favorable opinion of Pierce.

Ten days later, complications had arisen. Thinking that Lord and his followers were opposing his application in Boston, Burchmore went to Washington, where Hawthorne wrote, urging him "to try to make friends with the enemy, before proceeding to open war," and giving him explicit directions as to what he should say to Pierce if he had an interview. He concluded the letter, "However, I am no politician, and therefore ought not to pretend to advise you." Convinced that Burchmore had been misled in thinking Loring and Lord were not supporting him in Boston, and learning from Loring that Burchmore was opposing his claims to the collectorship, Hawthorne renewed his efforts to save the initial plan. After considerable correspondence and separate interviews with Lord and Burchmore late in March, he was able to remove the misunderstandings; and on April 4 he wrote Lord a formal and extremely favorable recommendation of Burchmore, with which he enclosed a note Pierce had sent him showing "his high opinion of" Burchmore and suggesting that Hawthorne request the good offices of Lord, the Democratic chairman in Burchmore's home county. Hawthorne conceded that Burchmore sometimes incurred "hostility by his political course," but added that he was "far too useful to be laid aside."

Replying on April 7 to Burchmore's thanks for this intercession, Hawthorne said, "I should have done just the same for you (were it in my power) had you been a Free Soil Whig. So that I do not see how you can impute my zeal to anything but purely personal friendship." When Hawthorne returned home on May 5 after two weeks in Washington, it had been settled that Miller would remain collector and Loring would become the Salem postmaster. Hawthorne told Burchmore that he had met with little encouragement in attempting to get him returned to the custom-house, but had "hopes of finding a soft spot in their gizzards, at all events, if not in their hearts." He would explain to Miller the circumstances of Burchmore's endorsing Loring, and would say that he had himself written the letter of endorsement. Miller "will not question my good will towards him," he said; "for if I did not save him, I should like to know who the devil did." He urged Burchmore to "keep on good terms with Lord—treat Pike as an old friend, and, if occasion serve, let him know that you regret ever having differed with him, and that his good offices would now be most valuable to you." And he warned, "If you declare war against them, and try to fight your way in, I would not give a 'whore's cuss' (to borrow an elegant phrase from the Old General) for your chance of being reinstated."[8]

William Pike had not been turned out of the custom-house with Hawthorne and Burchmore in 1849 and four years later was among the local Democratic Party managers when Burchmore tried to gain appointment as naval officer without their approval. On June 19, 1853, Hawthorne wrote Pike that he was uneasy about "this poor devil Zack," and explained,

> unless you can find in your heart to help him, he is utterly lost. To be sure, he deserves nothing—he is a poor, miserable, broken, drunken, disagreeable loafer, contemptible as an enemy, and only troublesome to his friends; and for these very reasons, I throw him upon your generosity.

> Help him, or he sinks. . . . He is humbled now. . . . He will never
> forget the lesson. But if you really mean to desert him, his fate is ob-
> vious;—he will die a drunkard within two years; and to tell you the
> truth, Pike, I shall not envy you your feelings when you stand over his
> grave and scent the fumes of the rum oozing up through the sods—and
> remember how he was your friend for thirty years, and never differed
> with you until within the last five years of his life, and then only through
> a silly vanity—and how he was once able to do you good, and did it, and
> never did you any harm, even if he desired it—and how, at his pinch,
> you lent him no assistance, merely because he deserved nothing! In
> God's name, which of us miserable sinners does deserve anything?

It would be creditable to all, he thought, if Burchmore "were permitted to
creep back again into his old clerkship." The *Salem Gazette* reported on
November 4 that Burchmore had been appointed "as some sort of Special
Appraiser" in the Salem custom-house, at a salary of $1,200 and that
William Manning had been appointed Superintendent of Repairs. Haw-
thorne had written Lord on May 11 in behalf of his Uncle William.

He could take satisfaction in having saved two of his friends from the
decapitation he had suffered, with Ephraim Miller, a Whig, continuing as
collector under the new Democratic administration, and Burchmore returning to the custom-house in a position comparable to the one he had
lost at the previous change of administration. He had gained these results
against what seemed impossible odds—and in addition had lessened the
enmities among those involved.

A year before Pierce was nominated, Hawthorne had written Burchmore that, although he could not support the Abolitionists, whenever "absolutely cornered," he would "go for New England rather than the
South." The Fugitive Slave Law had cornered him, he said, and he had
favored the Free-Soil Party in its opposition to the extension of slavery
into new territories, well aware that he thus "bade farewell to all ideas of
foreign consulships, or other official stations."[9] The formula adopted in
the Compromise of 1850 presumably would resolve all issues arising over
slavery in the territories. In the campaign biography, Hawthorne supported Pierce's endorsement of the Compromise. He soon was being mentioned in connection with the consulship of Liverpool, which was the
most lucrative post in the foreign service. Writing Bridge as the election
approached, Hawthorne said he had first resolved not to accept any office,
but now he thought it might be "rather folly than heroism" to hold to that
purpose. He could not take a foreign mission, but might take the consulship at Liverpool; and Pierce could not do better either for him or for

the administration, than to appoint him. Pierce owed him something, he said, for the biography had cost him hundreds of friends, who had "a purer regard" for him than Pierce or any other politician had ever gained, and who were dropping off from him "like autumn leaves," in consequence of what he had written on the slavery question. But those were his real sentiments, and he did not regret having them on record.[10]

In December, Hawthorne made inquiries among friends about foreign assignments; and after Pierce had called him for an interview in Boston on February 1 and no doubt had spoken of the consulship at Liverpool, he wrote Frank D. Farley, his fellow at Brook Farm, that if he were offered a post abroad, he thought he would not refuse it. Later in the month he twice suggested that W. D. Ticknor, who would be seeing Pierce in Washington, might do him a good turn by speaking to Pierce about the Liverpool post. By March 21 he knew that the president had made the nomination, which went to the Senate March 23 and was approved three days later. Pierce's agreement to let the incumbent remain until the end of July, filling out his four years, meant that Hawthorne must wait longer for his pay to begin, but the extra time for preparation was welcome. Two staterooms were booked on the Cunard steamer *Niagara*, sailing on July 6.

Early on April 14 Hawthorne left the Wayside in a rainstorm to join Ticknor in Boston and proceed to Washington. They stopped three days in New York, where Hawthorne had a talk with John Louis O'Sullivan, and, he wrote his wife, was to dine with a professor of mathematics and meet Anne Charlotte Lynch, mistress of a famous literary salon. "Why did I ever leave thee, my own dearest wife? Now, thou seest, I am to be lynched." With an appointment to see the president at nine on his first day in Washington, April 21, he expected to be home in three or four days; but his stay in the capital lengthened to two weeks, at Pierce's request. Although his attention was mainly on the interests of others, a tangible gain for himself was the understanding that for the present no consular officer would be appointed to Manchester, leaving the business and the fees from that city to the Liverpool consulate. Besides the puzzles of the Salem custom-house, Hawthorne attempted to work out other appointments. In explaining a delay in writing Pierce in behalf of one office-seeker, he remarked, "there is so much of my paper now in the president's hands, that (as the note-shavers say) I am afraid it will be going at a discount."[11]

To help the young poet Richard Henry Stoddard to an office became a special goal of Hawthorne's. Stoddard had visited at the Wayside and, from notes supplied by Hawthorne, had published a biographical sketch in the *National Magazine* for January, 1853. Hawthorne first thought of taking Stoddard with him abroad as his secretary, and later wrote Senator Atherton and O'Sullivan in his behalf. Stoddard had an interview with Pierce, and afterward was appointed to the Boston custom-house. Hawthorne sent Stoddard a quantity of advice, part of it serious, but most of it genially cynical. "I have had as many office-seekers knocking at my door, for three months past," he said, "as if I were a prime minister; so that I have made a good many scientific observations in respect to them." Politicians are "inveterate guzzlers," he wrote, "and love a man that can stand up to them, in that particular. It would never do to let them see you corned, however." Keep strictly to yourself any deficiencies you may have, his advice continued; if you are discovered to be unqualified for your assignment, you can be transferred to some other post. A final admonition: "A subtile boldness, with a veil of modesty over it, is what is needed." Another of the literary candidates Hawthorne undertook to help was a friend of E. P. Whipple's, Charles Wilkins Webber, who in 1846 had reviewed *Mosses from an Old Manse* with high praise and two years later had solicited a contribution to the *American Whig Review*. He suggested that Whipple secure letters from literary men, which he would pass on to the president, along with whatever recommendation he could add for an appointment that would let Webber "pursue his literary labors somewhere in South America."[12]

Hawthorne reminded Pierce of Horatio Bridge's wish to have a shore assignment, perhaps the consulship at Honolulu (sought also for Herman Melville), and, in assuring Bridge's wife that the president would not go back on his promise, he supplemented the analysis he had written Bridge earlier. Although Pierce might seem to act from impulse, he always acted in a way to advance pre-determined ends. In his own case, he would not have had the Liverpool appointment if Pierce "had not been perfectly sure that he could make no better nor more politic disposal" of it. He held to this original view and wrote Bridge on May 1, 1854, that no other appointment by the president had been so "favorably criticised." His assurance to Bridge's wife proved not too sanguine, for Bridge was ordered to shore duty in Washington as chief of the Naval Bureau of Provisions and Clothing.

Writing his wife on April 28 that the president, "for particular reasons," wanted him again to postpone returning home, he added, "It is very queer how much I have done for other people and myself since my arrival here." In the case of Herman Melville, he was not successful.

In the middle of July, 1852, Hawthorne had invited Melville to visit him in Concord. Since they last met at Lenox the preceding August, each had published a new book and Hawthorne was beginning the biography of Pierce. Melville had been traveling on the New England coast and must stay at home a while, he said; but he had brought back from his travels the material for a story that brought him and Hawthorne together in the ensuing weeks. At Nantucket John Henry Clifford, a lawyer who was to become governor of Massachusetts in 1853, told him of a legal case, involving the settling of an estate, on which he still had strong feelings after ten years. James Robertson, a sailor shipwrecked on the Massachusetts coast, married Agatha Hatch, who had looked after him during his recovery. He left her after two years, when she was bearing his child. He made a new career in Virginia and married a second time. After seventeen years of absence and silence, he visited her and, on the eve of their daughter's marriage, made another visit. When his Virginia wife died, he sent his son-in-law gifts from which Agatha learned of his second marriage. She declined his proposal that she move with him to Missouri but entered no protest when he married a third wife there.

On August 13, Melville wrote Hawthorne a summary of what he called "the Agatha story" and urged him to make use of it. At first he had not seen literary possibilities, he wrote, but later had conceived of "a regular story to be founded on these striking incidents," and still later had thought the story seemed "naturally to gravitate" toward Hawthorne. Melville went to the Wayside early in December and afterward wrote that he greatly enjoyed his visit and hoped his host had "reaped some corresponding pleasure." Noting that Hawthorne was uncertain about undertaking the Agatha story, he said he had decided to write it himself, and asked to have the materials returned, with any suggestions Hawthorne could send. They had agreed that the setting should be the Isles of Shoals and that an "old Nantucket seaman" should be introduced.

Here ends the story of the Agatha story. Leon Howard suggests that Melville saw in the long-suffering Agatha justification for the character Lucy in his new novel *Pierre*, but he observes that little in the story was suited to Melville's interests or capabilities, except the Nantucket seaman.[13] Julian Hawthorne reports that in an interview on August 15, 1883, Melville told him that Hawthorne had not seemed "to take to the Agatha story."[14] That Melville thought his friend might take to the plot is surprising. Although Hester Prynne and the White Old Maid are vaguely similar to Agatha, each of them is far more than a "patient Griselda," a docile victim of another's guilt. The deceiver of Agatha and a second woman and after half a lifetime a third, presumably with no awareness of guilt, was hardly a character for Hawthorne to study. For him the slightest sketch must have an idea at its base; the story of Agatha would seem to be a story of simple, unaccountable pathos.

In all likelihood, political appointments came into the conversation while Melville was at the Wayside in December, 1852, for Hawthorne was already engaged with office-seekers. According to Melville's mother, he had hoped after Pierce's election to receive a consulship, and it was planned that she and her daughters would stay at Arrowhead with the children and his wife would accompany him. "But Herman dislikes asking favors from any one," she wrote his brother Allan, and postpones writing letters.[15] On his way to Washington in April, Hawthorne called on Allan Melville in New York, and a campaign was set in motion. Letters in Melville's behalf collected by his mother, her brother Peter Gansevoort, and Allan Melville were sent on April 22 to Hawthorne in Washington. These recommendations and others stressed Melville's need of a foreign assignment for the sake of his health—hardly the strongest argument for appointment to an important post abroad. All agreed that Melville, like Hawthorne, would be appointed as a literary author, not as a politician, and that Hawthorne would use his influence to secure the appointment. When Hawthorne, returning home from Washington, saw Allan Melville in New York on May 4, he could report that Caleb Cushing, political advisor to Pierce, supported Melville's candidacy, that Pierce had made no promise but might approve an appointment if one were proposed, that Honolulu was not a possibility, and, most important, that the secretary of state, Marcy, controlled the main consular positions. On June 3 Cushing wrote Lemuel Shaw, Melville's father-in-law, that he had presented Melville's case to the president and that Marcy thought it would be arranged, "if Mr M can so arrange as to live at one of the less lucrative consulates in Italy, say *Rome*." Allan Melville checked on the income from the various consulates and declared that none of those in Italy, including the one at Rome, would be adequate, but that if Antwerp were offered, he thought Melville would accept it. Shaw answered Cushing accordingly on June 14, and the matter was closed.

Melville had arrived in New York before Cushing was told that the Roman consulship would not do. It can be supposed that his opinions had been registered in the interval since April 14 and that it was his decision to request the consulship at Honolulu. Still, the candidate himself was astonishingly absent from the interchanges, while his brother, his mother, his uncle, and his father-in-law were busy trying to secure an appointment abroad that would relieve him from the "constant working of the brain, and excitement of the imagination" that they thought responsible for his ill health. Hawthorne probably read two stories Melville wrote in this period: "Bartleby, the Scrivener. A Story of Wall-Street" and "Cock-a-Doodle-Doo!" If so, he might have seen in them evidence of Melville's thinking and the state of his feelings while others bestirred themselves in his behalf and he showed little interest. Each of the stories tells of irrational—at least unexplained—independence which combines with a quiet, absolute pride to produce results that are fatal, but are acceptable to the characters involved. There seems to have been no communication between Hawthorne and Melville until they met in Liverpool in 1856, when Melville was on his way to the Holy Land.

After finishing the biography of Pierce, Hawthorne wrote Bridge on October 18, 1852, that in a day or two he would start a new romance, which he would make more congenial than the last; but he made no progress. The second *Wonder-Book* he had planned to write in the summer was not finished until the next March. It was published on September 20, with the title *Tanglewood Tales*. Fields sold advance sheets to the British publisher Chapman for £50. Three thousand copies were sold at once in America, and a total of seven thousand in ten years. The introductory note, "The Wayside," relates this to the first collection by saying that Eustace Bright has come from the Berkshires to Concord, bringing along six of the tales he has read to the children who listened to the earlier stories. Thus Hawthorne kept the pattern of the tales, but without the linking sessions with the children that might have proved a burden in a second volume. In telling Richard Henry Stoddard that the book was finished, he remarked, "I never did anything else so well as those old baby-stories."[16]

The romance intended to follow *The Blithedale Romance* made no progress while Hawthorne's attention was absorbed by politics on the national scene and among his former associates in Salem, and it could have little place in his thought as he laid plans to spend four years as consul and another year in travel.

23

Return to Our Old Home

In preparing to sail in July, 1853, the Hawthornes planned for an absence of five years. Nathaniel Peabody and his family would occupy the Wayside. W. D. Ticknor, who would serve as Hawthorne's banker, was authorized to pay Elizabeth Hawthorne up to $200 a year. A notebook entry of June 9 records the burning of "heaps of old letters and papers. . . . Among them were hundreds of Sophia's maiden letters—the world has no more such; and now they are all ashes. What a trustful guardian of secret matter fire is! What should we do without Fire and Death!" (VIII, 552). His own letters to her were not burned, and survived to be published half a century later.[1] On June 14 Longfellow gave a farewell dinner party for Hawthorne and invited Emerson, Lowell, Charles Norton, Samuel Longfellow, and the poet Arthur Hugh Clough, who was visiting from England, and in his journal the next day wrote that his old friend seemed "much cheered by the prospect before him," and was "very lively and in good spirits."[2] On July 6 the Hawthorne family took the train from Concord, beginning travels that would extend to seven years.

James T. Fields and Sophia's father came to see them embark, and Ticknor sailed with them. As the *Niagara*, a Cunard Line paddle-wheeler, pulled away from the dock, a salute was fired in honor of the new consul to Liverpool. Julian Hawthorne remembered long afterward that, as he and other children watched the last tip of land disappear, his father intimated that they "should view with regret the disappearance of the land"

they might never see again, but that soon afterward his "gravity lightened." Julian remembered also that a cow and hens were aboard the
steamer, and that except for one squally day the weather was fine
throughout the ten days' voyage. The consul and his wife had places of
honor at Captain Leitch's table. While the ship was docked at Halifax,
Nova Scotia, from eleven to one the second night, they went ashore and
walked into the town. Sir John F. T. Crampton, (1805–86), British minister plenipotentiary in Washington, who had sought out Hawthorne early
in the voyage, left the ship there.[3]

The *Niagara* reached Liverpool on July 16, a cold, rainy day that gave a
foretaste of the weather Hawthorne was to lament many times during the
next four years. He took lodgings first at Waterloo House, a hotel among
the old streets of Liverpool, where the proprietor came regularly to the
consul's table to help serve the soup, and where Hawthorne designated
one of the servants "our Methodist preacher."[4] He soon moved his family
to Mrs. Blodgett's on Duke Street, a favorite of American sea captains,
which his son later called the most delightful boarding-house "that ever
existed before or since,"[5] and on August 6 moved to the Rock Ferry
Hotel, across the Mersey River, in pursuit of fresh air, Hawthorne said,
and a better prospect of surviving the "abominable weather." All the family except him had taken cold soon after landing, and he wrote Ticknor on
August 20 he doubted that his wife could bear the climate. On September
1 a further move, still in Rock Ferry, brought the family to a separate residence in Rock Park, a stone house of three stories and ample room, on
which the rent was £160 a year, furnished. A gateman charged a fee to
admit vehicles and by his presence discouraged passing in Rock Park.
Birkenhead Park gave both children and parents something of the air and
freedom they had left at the Wayside. Crossing the river was by steam
ferry to George's Dock every half hour until ten at night. Living in Rock
Park, Hawthorne said, would keep him out of "a good deal of nonsense,"
meaning social activities.[6] He might have said that the large house let him
invite acquaintances visiting Liverpool to be house guests.

After taking office on August 1, as planned, Hawthorne forwarded to
Washington an inventory and receipt for the government-owned books
and records left in his care and bought the office furniture from his predecessor. The two rooms occupied by the consulate were not "so splendid as
to indicate the assumption of much consular pomp," he wrote ten years
later in "Consular Experiences," an essay in *Our Old Home*. They were on
the first floor of the four-story Washington Building, located on Bruns-

wick Street, near the oldest docks. Entrance was by a narrow stairway and a hall leading to the outer office, in which the vice-consul and a clerk took care of most callers. The consul occupied the second room, the very sight of which Hawthorne afterward said he hated "from first to last." The two windows, looking out upon an "immense cotton warehouse, a plainer and uglier structure than ever was built in America," did not admit enough light to relieve the drab interior, which was painted imitation oak. On the walls were maps, a bust of Andrew Jackson, a lithograph of Zachary Taylor, and several engravings of American scenes; an eagle was painted on the mantel-piece. There were a few bookshelves, a barometer that all but never showed "Fair," and a worn and greasy New Testament for the swearing of oaths. The consul sat at a double desk facing the door, where one of the clerks brought documents to be signed or ushered in those callers requiring the attention of the highest officer. Julian Hawthorne remembered afterward the days when he went with his father to the office and at noontime walked to a baker's nearby for a lunch of rolls and butter, sometimes alone, sometimes with his father.[7]

Hawthorne set to work no less earnestly than as a customs officer and as a Brook Farmer. The employees of his predecessors stayed on, both experienced and faithful: the vice-consul, James Pearce, who could remember back to the appointees of George Washington, and the chief clerk, Henry J. Wilding, who possessed "English integrity, combined with American acuteness of intellect, quick-wittedness, and diversity of talent."[8] They conducted the technical business of the office and furnished the consul guidance based on experience he would not have accumulated even by the end of his term. Since mail to America had to wait for the departure of mail ships, short absences of his from the office did not necessarily delay official correspondence. There were nevertheless abundant matters requiring his personal attention, some of them complex or unpleasant or heartrending—or all together.

Four days after taking office, Hawthorne began his notebook; ten days later he noted that the demands of business had kept him from recording several notable scenes. In his third week he recounted an occurrence that would repeat itself with distressing frequency. With Wilding and an American ship-master he went to a boarding-house "in a mean street" to inventory the belongings of a deceased American ship captain, Wilson Auld. The landlady offered what she seemed to think a special privilege, a view of the corpse; he noted, "But, never having seen him during his lifetime, I declined to commence his acquaintance now." Attending the funeral the next day, he waited nearly an hour for others to arrive, took some wine, "for it seemed to be considered disrespectful not to do so," and followed the plumed hearse to the Cemetery of St. James. At the burial site, one of the coffin bearers stumbled, the coffin all but fell to the ground, and Hawthorne said he "really expected to see poor Captain Auld burst forth among us in his grave clothes." The notebook report of the funeral reveals the same mind that shows through the records Hawthorne had kept at North Adams and at the Isles of Shoals.[9] He was a speculative, ironic observer, alert to incongruities, with an eye to literary possibilities in the people he met and studied as he studied the characters of his fiction.

The day after the funeral Hawthorne wrote Captain Auld's widow the circumstances of the death and burial, assuring her that her husband received "the kindest treatment from those near him in his last moments." He sent her husband's effects by a ship captain, and he wrote her later that the money found in Captain Auld's trunk did not meet the expenses, "but the deficiency was supplied by a few friends." Those friends probably included no one but him, although the normal procedure would have been to seek donations from the sea captains in port. He said he still had three pounds for providing a "good plain stone," and added, "The Grave is in a very beautiful cemetery and will belong to the family."[10] This account drops no hint that Hawthorne saw a connection, but the pathetic end of Captain Auld could not fail to remind him of the death and burial of his own father in a strange port, and of the spare and unsatisfying reports that reached his widow.

The notebook entries show Hawthorne interested in the people who crowded the Mersey ferryboats and "the darker and dingier streets" he chose for the walks he took almost daily in the vicinity of the consulate. He always felt as if he would catch some disease in those streets; but he found in them "a bustle, a sense of being in the midst of life, and of having got hold of something real," which he did not find in the better streets (Aug. 20, 1853). On many pages of his notebooks he described and puzzled over the poverty he saw about him, and in *Our Old Home* he included an essay, "Outside Glimpses of English Poverty," that shows not only how persistently the subject occupied his mind, but also what conclusions it suggested about man and society.

Until his return to America in 1860, Hawthorne was in effect on an extended trip away from home, recording scenes and people in such a way as to understand them. Thinking it useless to describe scenery, he turned mainly to people and to buildings and monuments, as a rule seen against their historical backgrounds. After visiting the aged poet Leigh Hunt, he composed a notebook sketch which he thought of publishing separately, and did include in a revised version in the essay "Up the Thames" in *Our Old Home*. Thinking of England as the ancestral home, and often reminded of relations across the Atlantic, from the earliest crossings down to his own time, he saw comparisons to be made at every turn. He never forgot that he was an American, that the consulate was a major link in English-American relations, and that his observation extended from the upper levels of society and government to the dregs of both countries who came into the consulate. His earnest attempt to understand the two peoples separately and in their relations, his normal habits of skeptical inquiry into both individual character and social institutions, and his acute perception—these combined in the *English Notebooks, Our Old Home*, the fragmentary romances, and his letters to English and American correspondents, to produce a comparative presentation and interpretation perhaps not equaled elsewhere in the literature of either country.

Hawthorne soon discovered that, besides his normal duties at the consulate, there were other demands on him, both official and social. His predecessor in the consulate, Colonel Thomas Leonidas Crittenden (1819–93), called at once and soon had him for a dinner, which required the first of his many speeches. When representatives of the Liverpool Chamber of Commerce called on him at Mrs. Blodgett's boarding-house to pay their respects, he made his second speech. Before the end of his second week in office, he dined with the mayor at Town Hall, and again made a speech.

Four days after the Hawthornes arrived in Liverpool, Henry A. Bright (1830–84) and his father called, opening what would be one of Hawthorne's most satisfying relationships during his residence in England. The next day the father called again to invite the Hawthorne family to tea at Sandheys, the Bright home. The John Heywoods, relatives of the Brights who lived nearby at Norris Green in the summer and in London in the winter, were to entertain the Hawthornes and introduce them in both places. Henry Bright had met Hawthorne during a visit to America.[11] He was a university graduate with literary interests, who contributed occasionally to the *Westminister Review*, while engaged with his father in foreign trade. Tall, slender, and energetic, he was to Hawthorne thoroughly un-British in appearance and manner. Through his business experience and connections, he could furnish the consul with useful information and opinions. At Sandheys and at Norris Green, Hawthorne observed the kind of "appeased existence," in a phrase Henry James was to use later, that made life at an English country place so enviable and produced the type of English gentleman he was coming to admire. Henry Bright called often at the consulate, visited the Hawthornes frequently, and occasionally stayed overnight. He and Hawthorne talked much about literature and national traits, neither hesitating to challenge the other's opinions. The frank interchange they carried on, punctuated with banter that each knew the other would understand, enabled them to attack aspects of national policy and national character usually avoided when citizens of the two countries met, and provided Hawthorne a testing ground for the analysis and comparison he had begun when he first set foot in England.[12]

The Liverpool consulate had attracted Hawthorne in part because it would bring him to "our old home." All colonials, he said in "Old News," wanted to visit England, which they still called "their own home." It was his own experience that, in first visiting the church at Hatton, he "had a singular sense of having been there before." The church at Bebington was as familiar to him, when he first saw it, as the meeting-house he had known in his boyhood at Salem; the Poet's Corner in Westminister Abbey had always been a familiar spot to him. He soon thought of converting to literary use such real or imagined recollections as these, the longing for an earlier home, and the dream of returning to claim an ancestral inheritance.

Expecting to spend four years as consul, Hawthorne explored first Liverpool and its environs,. and postponed the more enticing regions in pleasant anticipation. He waited two years and two months to visit London. It was more than two months after landing at Liverpool that he made his first excursion out of the city. When W. D. Ticknor came to embark for America, Hawthorne accompanied him to Chester (Sept. 29), and afterward wrote in his notebook that he at last felt he had "a glimpse of Old England." The cathedral, the first he had seen, was impressive, he said, but "an American must always have imagined a better cathedral." On October 30, a Sunday, he returned to Chester with his wife and two oldest children. Not until July, 1854, did Hawthorne travel away from Liverpool again. His letters to America suggest that he thought surviving the English winter would be achievement enough.

Sophia wrote her father that in their visit to the Chester cathedral a dream of hers would be coming true: "For I always wished earnestly that the children might go to church first in a grand old cathedral, so that their

impression of social worship might be commensurate with its real sublim-
ity. And, behold, it will be so,—for they never yet have been to
church." During the sermon, "Julian gaped aloud, which so startled Mr.
Hawthorne that he exclaimed, 'Good God!' thus making the matter
worse." She could take comfort, however, presuming "that the same great
spaces which took up the canon's voice disposed of Mr. Hawthorne's
exclamation." The service affected her deeply, she said, it had been so
long since she had been to church, "—hardly once since Una was born!
You know I always loved to go to church, always supplying by my imagination what I did not find."[13] Her husband noted that the "magnificent
ceremonial" of the service was "the setting to a little meagre discourse,
which would not at all have past muster among the elaborate intellectual
efforts of New England ministers" (Nov. 5). At another time he remarked
that the dissenters, and particularly the Puritans, had been the ones who
gave the sermon its form and its importance.

Hawthorne and his wife had not attended church together in America;
and in Europe, except when they were attracted as tourists, their normal
procedure was the one they followed on a walk to Bebington Church, near
Rock Park, February 10, 1854, when Hawthorne continued to walk with
Julian while his wife and Una attended the service. From the following
October 22 onward, Sophia had within reach a church conducted by a
Unitarian minister from home, William Henry Channing (1810–84)—
Renshaw Street Chapel in Liverpool. The Hawthornes had a pew in the
chapel, and Sophia and the children attended. The father's absenting himself when the others attended church seems to have been a matter of understanding amusement in the family. While he and Julian lived at Mrs.
Blodgett's and the others were in Lisbon, he wrote Una (March 19, 1856)
that he had not been to hear Channing preach, but, "to make amends,"
had sent Julian every Sunday. Once in London later the same year, he accompanied his wife to the Essex Street Chapel when Channing was a visitor there. He was on friendly terms with the minister, who at least once
accompanied him home and spent the night and once borrowed £16 from
him.

An invitation to dine on August 7, 1853, at Poulton Hall, three miles
from Rock Ferry, took Hawthorne and his family by an old church which
answered to his "transatlantic fancies of English life." Poulton Hall also
realized some of his "fancies of English life": legends and ghost stories, a
martyr's chamber, and an "old black-letter library" in a room "shut,
barred, and padlocked." Dining with a wealthy merchant on October 1, he

met two sons of Robert Burns. One of them sang several of Burns's songs and his eyes glowed, Hawthorne wrote, "when he sang his father's noble verse—'The rank is but the guinea's stamp' etc. It would have been too pitiable if Burns had left a son who could not feel the spirit of that verse." Writing Ticknor a week later, Hawthorne said he had "got into great favor with" Burns's sons, partly because of the affection he showed for the whisky bottle. He was pleased by the "liberal tones of thinking" displayed on this occasion by his host and the other guests. At a dinner party the following March 26, he was not pleased because the family of the host, John Bramley-Moore, chairman of the Liverpool docks and formerly mayor, he found to be "virulent tories, fanatics for the Established Church." The host's purpose was to introduce the author of the satirical novel *Ten Thousand a Year*, Samuel Warren (1807–77), whom Hawthorne thought amusingly vain but agreeable.

Although Hawthorne's health had never been better than in the chill and fog of Liverpool, where he said "it never does rain, and it never don't rain,"[14] his wife suffered from colds and a threatening cough. The entire family had whooping-cough in the early summer of 1854; and when they were well, he proposed to give them a change of air. After an exploratory tour of Northern Wales he made with Henry Bright, July 8–10, he took them at the middle of July to the Isle of Man, which he pronounced the most interesting place he had yet seen. He held to his duties at the consulate, spending only a few days with his family during their fortnight there.

One of the house guests at Rock Park was the actress Charlotte Cushman (1816–76), who came on December 29, 1853. Before leaving America, Hawthorne had sat for a miniature which she wanted to take with her to England, and had met her as a consequence.[15] The next April, John Louis O'Sullivan and his family, including his mother, were guests for more than two weeks. He had been appointed minister to Portugal and was on his way to Lisbon. George P. Bradford, Hawthorne's associate at Brook Farm and afterward a guest at the Old Manse, came late in August and gave occasion for another visit to Chester and to Eaton Hall. On September 7, Sophia and the children went to Rhyl, on the north coast of Wales, where Hawthorne joined them two days later in the company of O'Sullivan, newly returned from Lisbon. After spending September 12–15 at the consulate, Hawthorne had three more days at Rhyl, and Sophia brought the children home on September 19. Another guest was Walter Murray Gibson (1823–88), an American adventurer who had missed his ship to America. Hawthorne invited him to spend the night, and afterward advanced money for his passage to America. In addition to his accounts of adventures in all quarters of the globe, Gibson interested Hawthorne with his claim that he was the heir to an English estate and expected to locate a lost portrait that would prove his claim. This was to Hawthorne "another instance of the American fancy for connecting themselves with English property and lineage" (Oct. 19, 1854). In transferring Gibson from the notebook to the essay "Consular Experiences," Hawthorne elaborated on the "wonderful eloquence" of his narratives, and said he thought the story of an English inheritance "wonderfully akin" to what might have been wrought out of his own head, "not unpracticed in such figments."

No more inclined in England than he had been in America to seek out celebrities, authors or others, Hawthorne was pleased nevertheless when English literary men called on him. The young poet William Allingham (1824–89), "not at all John Bullish," visited the consulate in February, 1854, and presented Hawthorne a volume of his own poems. Bryan Waller Proctor, who published poetry under the name Barry Cornwall, called the next June; Hawthorne pleased him by speaking of his popularity in America. At Norris Green on September 20, 1854, Hawthorne met Richard Monckton Milnes (1809–85), friend of Tennyson and Thackeray, poet, critic, and politician, who became Baron Houghton in 1863. When Milnes called at the consulate a week later, they agreed that Milnes should read some distinctively American books. Hawthorne ordered from America *The Biglow Papers* and *A Fable for Critics* by Lowell, *Walden* and *A Week on the Concord and Merrimac Rivers* by Thoreau, *Margaret* by Sylvester Judd, *Up-Country Letters* by Lewis W. Mansfield, *Passion Flowers* by Julia Ward Howe, and *Autobiography of an Actress* by Anna Cora Mowatt. Milnes reciprocated by sending his own books and three volumes of Keats he had edited.

Wishing to extend their acquaintance, Milnes wrote on November 8 for himself and Lord Crewe, urging Hawthorne to visit at Crewe Hall. Hawthorne declined, explaining that he was "an absurdly shy sort of person," and it was "too late to think of amendment." After having a renewed invitation declined also, Milnes still vowed to have him for a visit either in Yorkshire or in London.[16] Early in the year, Hawthorne had declined another invitation more whimsically but no less firmly. Mrs. Heywood had insisted that he attend a fancy-dress ball at Norris Green, but neither her urging nor that of her nephew Henry Bright, nor, presumably, the encouragement of Sophia, weakened his determination. He answered

Mrs. Heywood on February 10 that he was "in the position of an owl or a bat, when invited to take a pleasure-trip in the sunshine. . . . The truth is, Mr. H. has all his life been under a spell, from which it is now too late to free himself."

While feeling his way into his duties, Hawthorne was ready to accept both official and private invitations. When he was surer of his bearings in both areas, he was more selective. Even so, he participated in far more public functions than ever before, and in more social activities—alone or with his wife or with the children also—than at Salem or Lenox or Concord. The family had a sense of well-being, and for the first time their financial prospects offered a degree of certainty. On December 9, 1853, Hawthorne repaid the money George Hillard had given him from unidentified friends four years earlier. "This act of kindness," he wrote, "did me an unspeakable amount of good; for it came when I most needed to be assured that anybody thought it worth while to keep me from sinking." Although the money had come as a gift, his purpose to repay it had not been out of his mind "for a single day, nor hardly . . . for a single working hour." But he had remained quiet, for a reason that suggests his particular integrity: It would not have been right to declare that purpose before he was able to accomplish it; and he had waited until now to return the money because it would have been "selfish to purchase the great satisfaction" for himself by repaying it as long as there was a risk of leaving his "wife and children utterly destitute." [17]

After three days in the consulate Hawthorne wrote in his notebook that the pleasantest incident of the day was the appearance of the head clerk with the account books for the preceding day and "a little rouleau of the Queen's coin, wrapt up in a piece of paper." The coin, representing the fees collected for the services rendered by the consulate to merchant shippers, remained with the consul as his pay. The financial yield of the consulate was prominent in his letters—and in his mind—throughout his tenure. He reported the growth of his savings to Bridge and Ticknor and perhaps to others, and fretted that the accumulation was no faster. Fearing that the president would be persuaded to appoint a consular officer at Manchester, he had asked William Pike, soon after his own appointment was confirmed, to indicate an interest in that post, in order to serve as a screen against other applicants. The next year he urged Pike to accept a vice-consulship at Manchester, hoping in that way to push him toward the growth and achievement that had once seemed possible for him. But Pike remained at Salem and in 1857 became collector of the port. The post at

Manchester was not filled and its yield of £200 a year continued to be added to the income at Liverpool.[18]

It was commonly understood that the Liverpool consulate paid more than any other United States foreign post and that only the ambassadorship to Great Britain had greater prestige. Arthur Hugh Clough said a week after Hawthorne's appointment, no doubt reflecting what he had heard in Boston or Concord, that the pay would be $20,000 to $25,000 a year; Elizabeth Peabody had the figure $40,000, which Sophia corrected by saying that the total income in previous years had been only $10,000 to $12,000, and that shipping had decreased recently. Colonel Crittenden had spent $4,000 a year keeping himself and his wife in Mrs. Blodgett's boarding-house. Hawthorne was holding the cost for his family to a like sum, but he said he could do so only by renting a house and denying himself many things he "would gladly have."[19] But the accumulation was slow, and the prospects were unattractive. On November 25, 1853, Hawthorne wrote Ticknor that he wished he had his "whole pile, and were off to Italy." Two weeks later, when he had £300 to send, he said, "If it had been £3,000, I would kick the office to the devil, and come home again. I am sick of it, and long for my hillside, and—what I thought I never should long for—my pen! When once a man is thoroughly imbued with ink, he never can wash out the stain." He speculated as to how much he would have to save to be able to live on the income. On the next March 3 he exhorted Ticknor: "Invest—invest—invest! I am in a hurry to be rich enough to get away from this dismal and forlorn hole. If I can once see $20,000 in a pile, I shan't care much for being turned out of office." Immediately afterward, threats to his income appeared. A ruling by the secretary of the treasury in March, 1854, that consular certificates were no longer required for goods from Liverpool that would be trans-shipped from Boston to Canada, Hawthorne said would cut his income by one-fourth. In April he saw a greater threat in a bill introduced into Congress that would replace the fee system with fixed salaries for foreign service officers. The consul at Liverpool would receive $7,500, from which he would pay the salaries of his assistants, who must be American citizens, and would meet the other expenses of the office. Hawthorne was paying Pearce and Wilding $1,000 a year each, a third clerk $500, and a messenger $150; but much more would be needed, he said, to hire Americans of comparable efficiency. He multiplied and reiterated his objections: A consul would have nothing to give needy Americans who could receive no help from the government; the posts would be filled by rich men or rogues. The bill passed the House quickly; on the day it passed in the Senate, March 1, 1855, he wrote Charles Sumner on another matter, and added, "That Consular bill will soon prove itself an absurdity; but, meantime, it will have done my business." He thanked Bridge and Ticknor for their efforts to get the bill defeated, and, while continuing his protests, took a resigned but generally optimistic view, noting that his financial status was much better than five years earlier, and that money troubles as a rule did not bother him for long. At the end of his second year, his savings were near the minimum of $20,000 he had set; the greater security gave him greater tolerance for the duties of his office and the restriction on his income.

In writing the president on June 7, 1855, to urge that Albert Davy, consul at Leeds, be kept in the service if possible, Hawthorne added, "To my office, when I quit it, you must appoint either a rich man or a rogue;—no poor, honest, and capable man, will think of holding it." And he pitied his successor if he were not allowed to hire English clerks. "For heaven's sake," he continued, "do not let the next session pass without having this matter amended." Hawthorne's arguments, presented directly or through Ticknor and Bridge, may have had some influence on the new consular act passed on August 18, 1856, to take effect at the opening of 1857 (and not revised until 1906). It corrected many flaws of the 1855 act, and to the end of his term in the consulate, he was willing to say, even to Bridge and Ticknor, that he had no real quarrel about his income. When the revised act was in effect and he could see to the end of his term, he said that he could "count on the interest of nearly or quite $30,000," which he would think adequate, were it not for the expenses of the residence in Italy he planned. Because of those expenses, "the embroidery and trimmings" would have to come out of his inkstand.[20]

Late in the summer of 1855, Hawthorne had evidence that Pierce had his interest at heart. The president sent word through Bridge that he could become chargé d'affaires in Portugal if he wished. Although the pay would be only $4,500, the offer was attractive because Sophia was planning to spend the next winter in Lisbon as guest of the John Louis O'Sullivans, in the hope of escaping the lung infection the English climate had caused. Hawthorne had in mind taking her to Lisbon and foregoing his salary for whatever time he would be absent from Liverpool. He concluded, however, that, for the year or two he would hold any office, his present position was preferable to any other the president might offer.

Hawthorne appreciated Ticknor's urging him to protect his savings and was apologetic when he went against the advice. In preparing to lend Bridge $3,000 in 1854, he wrote to disarm Ticknor: "My relations with Bridge are of such a nature that I would lend him every cent I had, even if I were certain of never getting it again. . . . Let him have it, therefore, on any security which he may offer, or on no security, if he should offer none." Several times afterward he assured Ticknor that he would follow his advice not to lend any more money—as far as he could and ought, and once added, "But when the friend of half my lifetime asks me to assist him, and when I have perfect confidence in his honor, what is to be done? Shall I prove myself to be one of those persons who have every quality desirable in friendship, except that they invariably fail you at a pinch? I don't think I can do that; but, luckily, I have fewer friends than most men, and there are not a great many who can claim anything of me on that score." After two years, when Ticknor thought Bridge's loan was due, Hawthorne instructed him to let Bridge "have the money as long as he wants it, even should it be till the day of doom." On the same day he wrote Bridge, "You have stood by me, a true friend, for five and thirty years; and I believe there is nothing which friend can ask of friend, that either of us would not do for the other."[21]

It turned out that another loan of $3,000 was made to another friend, John Louis O'Sullivan. As surety, Hawthorne held a deed to property in New York which O'Sullivan continued to manage and intended to redeem. He sent Ticknor the deed on April 26, 1855, asking him to check the title and have the transfer recorded, provided it could remain secret. On the same subject he said later, "I have so little confidence in O'Sullivan's business qualifications (though entire confidence in his honor)." The parenthetical phrase suggests that Hawthorne was remembering the time almost twenty years earlier when Mary Silsbee had induced him to question his friend's honor. He assured Ticknor at intervals that he was satisfied for the loan to continue, and he tried through Pierce to win favor for O'Sullivan under the administration of President Buchanan.[22]

In the spring of 1854, Ticknor and Fields acquired the rights to *Mosses from an Old Manse* from Wiley and Putnam, and proposed to bring out a new edition. Sending Fields a copy of the work, "after a careful revision," Hawthorne wrote with his customary half-serious self-abnegation, and in a tone of remoteness: "Upon my honor, I am not quite sure that I entirely comprehend my own meaning in some of these blasted allegories; but I remember that I always had a meaning—or, at least, thought I had. I am a good deal changed since those times; and to tell you the truth, my past self is not very much to my taste, as I see myself in this book. Yet certainly there is more in it than the public generally gave me credit for, at the time it was written. But I don't think myself worthy of very much more credit than I got. It has been a very disagreeable task to read the book." He added the story "Feathertop," first published in 1852, and the preface to "Rappaccini's Daughter," omitted from the first edition of the *Mosses*. He remembered the framework narrative of the "Itinerant Story-teller" as written "quite up to the usual level of his scribblings," and added two sections from it under the titles "Passages from a Relinquished Work" and "Sketches from Memory."[23]

Hawthorne wrote in his notebook on December 28, 1854: "I think I have been happier, this Christmas, than ever before,—by my own fire-side, and with my wife and children about me. More content to enjoy what I had; less anxious for anything beyond it, in this life." His early life was perhaps a good preparation for his later years, "it having been such a blank that any possible thereafter would compare favorably with it." He told of a singular dream of his through the past twenty or thirty years, which was "probably one of the effects of that heavy seclusion" of his first twelve years after leaving college, when everybody moved onward and left him behind. In the dream, he was in college or school and, having failed to equal the progress of those about him, would meet them with shame and depression. The entry concludes, "How strange that it should come now, when I may call myself famous, and prosperous!—when I am happy, too!—still that same dream of life hopelessly a failure!"

By implication, Hawthorne did not think it strange that he had this dream twenty to thirty years ago, when he read and dreamed and wrote in the chamber under the eaves, and burned the manuscripts that failed to win publication or to meet his own high standards. Then, as he wrote Longfellow in 1837 and afterward wrote his fiancée, he had seen his college-mates moving ahead of him, and would have interpreted the dream as a bitterly ironic comment on his remaining "the obscurest man of letters in America," in spite of his ambition and his devotion to literature. His wife might have read the dream as a reflection of his demand for perfection and his modesty in evaluating his writings.

24

"Pegasus in a Yoke"

Neither of Hawthorne's objects in going to Liverpool—the pay and the foreign travel—demanded services beyond the minimum to be expected of a political appointee. His was nevertheless an efficient, prompt, orderly, and dependable administration. In the judgment of one well acquainted with his term as consul, his official correspondence was dignified and free of pettiness, and his management of official business "almost ideal."[1]

Knowing from earlier experience that he would not be able to write fiction while consul, he contented himself with storing materials in his mind and in his notebooks; and, although he lamented that his duties were heavy and unpleasant, he afterward took satisfaction in what he had accomplished. O'Sullivan once told Bancroft that appointing Hawthorne to a clerkship in Washington would be putting "Pegasus in a yoke."[2] If Hawthorne had been inclined to bemoan his lot, he might have cited his dispatch number 22 to argue that with him in the consulate Pegasus indeed had been put into a yoke. That dispatch, addressed to William L. Marcy, secretary of state, and dated July 12, 1854, contained 108 pages in his own handwriting, answering a series of queries received ten months earlier with information he had synthesized from many sources; and it enclosed books, pamphlets, papers, statistical compilations, and other documents related to the queries. The dispatch is testimony that the new consul took his office seriously and soon was familiar with such diverse matters as quarantine regulations, examinations for licenses issued by the

Marine Board, annual imports of cotton, prices of sails and sailcloth, the training of pauper children in industrial schools to become seamen, the number of seamen shipped and discharged at the Liverpool Sailors Home, the tonnage of coal shipped coastwise at each port of the district, the number and tonnage of North American vessels built and registered at Liverpool, and an improved form of anchor. Much of the information was not far different from what Hawthorne had recorded on previous travels in the past. He would have realized that collecting the materials from governmental and business offices, shipping firms, and a variety of informants was a good means of preparing himself to be consul, and to understand England and the English. Little wonder that, with this schooling, he spoke with some authority when he dealt with ship captains and seamen and government officials, and that he was not reluctant to advise the president of the United States, congressmen, two secretaries of state, two United States ambassadors to Great Britain, and various British officials. Understandably, when he was leaving the consulate, he was commended by the secretary of state for communicating from time to time "valuable information and suggestions relative to our commercial interests."[3]

Hawthorne was aware that preparing such dispatches as this and meeting the other demands of his office brought his literary work to a halt, but he might have said that even this drudgery helped stock the tank from which he would draw when he again took up his literary pen. Besides attending to routine matters at the consulate, he was alert to aspects of international relations that fell within his view, and he offered advice on the qualifications and the conditions of appointment and service of consular officers. His first weeks convinced him that "there are worse lives than that of an author."[4] The seamen and the officers he saw in a line or in groups at the entrance to the consulate represented intrusions into the privacy he had formerly maintained, or at least had controlled. He nevertheless put in full working days at his desk. As consul he came to know Americans better than before, he said; he had closer knowledge of acute human and social issues than at any time in the past; and he was in a position of greater responsibility and authority than ever before.

He wrote Horatio Bridge on March 30, 1854, that he wanted "to glide noiselessly through" his tenure at the consulate; before leaving the office, however, he had made considerable noise, though reluctantly, and had become an insistent advocate of reform in the merchant marine. At the time he wrote Bridge, he was smarting from a false newspaper report on his management of a situation he had faced. When 158 United States soldiers were brought to Liverpool from the wreck of the *San Francisco*, he supplied food and clothing on his own responsibility, although he had no authority to provide for the troops in any way; and, after James Buchanan, United States minister at London, had declined to direct further action, saying that he lacked authority, Hawthorne arranged for transporting the troops to America, chartering a ship that could depart at once and thus lessen the risk of having the soldiers switch to the British services. He had acted in the belief that the duty of an official, faced with such demands as had been made on him, "must be measured by the peculiar exigencies of the case, and by his utmost capacity to deal with them, and not by the narrow letter of his instructions, which were framed only to meet the ordinary routine of events." The *Portsmouth Journal of Literature and Politics* ran an editorial on March 4 under the title "A 'Scarlet' Mark," saying that the author of the life of Pierce had done nothing for the soldiers and that Buchanan was responsible for the relief provided, and concluding, "Should not Mr. Hawthorne have a 'scarlet letter' branded on his forehead?" Hearing of the false report, Hawthorne wrote Bridge an explanation and sent Ticknor a recital of the particulars, to be used in the newspapers if needed. He was glad his statement did not need to be printed, especially because it would have had to note Buchanan's refusal to have anything to do with the affair. Buchanan had visited him in Liverpool and struck him as "doubtless as honest as nine diplomatists out of ten."[5]

Within his first month in office, Hawthorne had shown initiative in protesting to Ambassador Buchanan that an American ship was being required to transport mail on a voyage from Liverpool to Australia, and at a rate fixed by the British Post Office. Drawing on arguments Hawthorne had sent him, Buchanan took the question up with Lord Clarendon, the British foreign secretary, noting that the same requirement might be made of British vessels clearing from United States ports. Lord Clarendon accepted the American view, and Hawthorne could feel satisfaction that all American ships would have the new freedom. In a series of dispatches in April and May, 1854, he reported his suspicions about three ships registered as owned by an American citizen, suggesting that they were British-owned and were registered as American so that they could enter the American trade with California and could sail as neutral vessels during the Crimean War. Whether or not his alertness was responsible, he was able to report later that all three ships had been registered anew as having English owners.[6]

Although Hawthorne had lost none of his skepticism in viewing causes and petitions and beggars, he found time to hear scores of those who appeared at his desk to plead their cases. Many of them interested him; and, as his notebooks show, some of them were candidates for admission to his sketches, tales, or romances. The consul ought to have funds to give those in need, he thought, and he had no choice but to use money of his own. He was sympathetic, as a rule kindly and forgiving, and he gave or lent money to the suppliants who came to his office, whether they were in need through their own fault or not. Since many of the loans he made were supposed to be repaid to his agent in America, he told Ticknor about them—he also defended what he had done and promised to exercise more discretion in the future. He saw a number of the suppliants more than once, studied them, and came to trust them to a degree he knew would astonish his banker.

An old man who came many times said he had been trying for twenty-seven years "to get home to Ninety-Second Street, Philadelphia"—just such a character, Hawthorne noted, as Herman Melville portrays in *Israel Potter*. His story seemed "almost as worthy of being chanted in immortal song as that of Odysseus or Evangeline," and the brief treatment Hawthorne gave him in "Consular Experiences" might have been expanded into at least a companion to his sketch "The Old Apple-Dealer." He decided not to give the old man passage money, thinking that to send him back to Ninety-second Street after twenty-seven years would be to usurp the role of God and perhaps to condemn the old man to a misery far beyond his present "gentle forlornness." Instead, the consul gave him alms time after time. He could never feel, Hawthorne explains, that he could "sufficiently comprehend any particular conjunction of circumstances with human character" to justify thrusting in his "awkward agency among the intricate and unintelligible machinery of Providence." As consul he had been compelled to give advice in "multifarious affairs" that did not personally concern him. "It is only one-eyed people who love to advise," he said. "When a man opens both his eyes, he generally sees about as many reasons for acting in any one way as in any other, and quite as many for acting in neither."

In dealing with a doctor of divinity, Hawthorne assumed the responsibility of advising, and of judging and condemning besides—and afterward realized his error. He reported the episode first in his notebook (May 24, 1855), next in a letter to Ticknor (May 27), and finally in "Consular Experiences." It has elements of a Hawthornesque tale, and fictional touches appear even in the notebook entry. Looking at the three versions together indicates something of the transformation factual materials underwent on their way to embodiment in his fictional works, and also something of the route his mind followed in exploring moral and psychological puzzles. He told Ticknor simply that he was sending to America a Dr. Richards, doctor of divinity, who had been brought to his office after a week's residence in a brothel, and he elaborated on the moral lecture he had given the wayward doctor. Parallels in language indicate that, with the notebook open before him when he wrote the later sketch, the author omitted several details not appropriate to his purpose, and added others. One addition in the final version is the narrator's taking the doctor home to dinner, and presumably greater intimacy between the two; another is his telling of the reverence he felt as a boy for a saintly clergyman he knew in Salem. The narrator can then refer to "the hereditary Puritan waxing strong" in his breast, before delivering his lecture in the expanded final scene. The author of this sketch in *Our Old Home* is given the same experiences and for the most part the same attitudes as Hawthorne, but he is also a literary character with traits best suited to the purpose of the book. It is this partially fictionalized narrator who presents the final sketch of the fallen doctor of divinity.

In the notebook account, Hawthorne delivered such a lecture as he had "never dreamed of having an opportunity to bestow on a Doctor of Divinity. It was really a very tragic scene." The entry closes, "Poor, Reverend Devil! Drunkard! Whoremaster [inked out in the manuscript]! Doctor of Divinity! He is very powerfully eloquent, I am told, in sermon and prayer." In the narrator's imaginative version of the later sketch, the conclusion is elaborated into a speculation on sin (the doctor's may have been less "vice than terrible calamity"); on the handicap clergymen have in knowing their own peccability; on the role of moral judge (in the future he would "operate upon sinners through sympathy, and not rebuke"); and on the effects of sin (the clergyman's flock probably "were thereafter conscious of an increased unction in his soul-stirring eloquence"). The sketch concludes by posing questions Hawthorne had raised in earlier fictional works: whether it was better for the doctor "thus to sin outright, and so to be let into the miserable secret what manner of man he was, or to have gone through life outwardly unspotted, making the first discovery of his latent evil at the judgment-seat"; and whether his dire calamity "might have been the only method by which precisely such a man as himself, and so situated, could be redeemed." A comparison of Hawthorne's three versions of the doctor of divinity episode suggests that, from the time actualities entered his awareness, they became the materials of metaphor and symbol and parable, and their transformation began even in his letters and his notebooks—if not earlier in his memory.

After nearly four years in the consulate, Hawthorne still accepted it "as a necessary expense of the office" to take care of needy Americans rather than to hand them over to "the charities of an English workhouse," even when he saw little chance of recovering his money or when he thought he was probably being gulled. During his last year as consul, he wrote Ticknor of loans to a musician, a painter, and a teacher, who he believed would repay sooner or later; to another whose father he thought would pay; to one whom he had advanced £30 with strong faith that he was an honest man. "I wonder what will become of all these vagabonds, when I quit the Consulate," he continued. "I have never relieved anybody except when it would have been harsh and inhuman not to do it." At another time he said he was thinking of his hill behind the Wayside, which he intended to "use pretty extensively" in the future. "I have received, and been civil to, at least 10,000 visitors since I came to England; and I never wish to be civil to anybody again."[7]

In helping one American who had fallen on bad times in England, Delia Bacon, Hawthorne showed particular generosity and tolerance and willingness to go far beyond any call of duty. When he answered her first letter, he had no way of knowing what the cost to him would be in money, time, and distress. Before he left America, Ralph Waldo Emerson had talked with him about Miss Bacon's theory that Francis Bacon and others wrote the plays attributed to Shakespeare, and had proposed to Elizabeth Peabody that "if Miss Bacon would really come to Concord, . . . we would make him listen, and she should make him believe."[8] Now, Hawthorne did listen to Miss Bacon and, though he did not believe, he gave her more help than either she or Emerson or Elizabeth Peabody could have expected. When Miss Bacon wrote Hawthorne on May 8, 1856,[9] she had been in England three years. She sought advice from him on publishing the fruits of her study. He replied on May 12 that he would help her publish her book, but would not be understood as having faith in her views; and he stated an opinion he was to hold through the trying days that followed: that the results of her devoted work deserved to be published.

Evidence was not slow to appear that helping the woman bent on sending the "old Player about his business," as she had stated her purpose in her first letter, would not be easy, for she had no money, her health was uncertain, relations with her family were strained, and there were indications that her mind had begun to fail her. On July 28, Hawthorne made his way to her lodging at 12 Spring Street, Sussex Gardens, the only time he was ever to see her. Already he had sent her ten pounds and had taken responsibility for an equal amount she had borrowed from the United States consul in London. After reading part of her manuscript, he had written her, "I feel that this is a most remarkable book, and I must own that you have carried me away with you, farther than I imagined possible."[10] He had told Elizabeth Barrett Browning about the theory, greatly to her horror. For his own part, he was willing to see truth in absurdity, and maintained that, in arguing her absurd case, she paid Shakespeare the high compliment of showing that he summed up his age with a fullness and an understanding achieved by no one else. The philosophy she had developed was itself a noble creation, and entitled to respect. During Hawthorne's visit, she told him she was sure that documents proving her theory were concealed in a hollow space in the underside of Shakespeare's gravestone. He concluded the notebook record of his visit, "Unquestionably, she is a monomaniac; this great idea has completely thrown her off her balance; but, at the same time, it has wonderfully developed her intellect, and made her what she could not otherwise have been." She believed that Providence had brought him forward at the "critical juncture." He would rather have had Providence employ "some other instrument," he noted, but he had "little or no scruple or doubt" about what he ought to do—he would give her every assistance he could.

He wrote her brother, the Reverend Leonard Bacon of New Haven, explaining that he would "dread the effect, on her mind" of any attempts to return her to America, and advising him to do whatever he could toward making her comfortable in England.[11] He had thought of asking Emerson's help toward publication in America, but decided not to write, remembering that three chapters of a manuscript of hers submitted through him to *Putnam's Monthly* had been lost. He explained to her, "If anything can be done, Mr. E. ought to feel himself bound to do it, that is, if he were a man like other men; but he is far more than that, and not so much."[12] In September, Hawthorne put the publishing arrangements for her book into the hands of his friend Francis Bennoch, saying that, if no better terms could be had, he would be responsible for the cost of an edition. "Only let it be done quickly; or this poor woman will kill herself— and worry me to death in the meanwhile."[13] He soon could write her that a publisher seemed to have been found, and offered his usual words of encouragement.[14] His wife had been reading the manuscript and had passed her enthusiasm along to the author, and also to him.

At this point the brightening sky grew dark, from unpredictable clouds in Delia Bacon's mind and will. She wrote Hawthorne a long, confidential letter, telling how she went to Shakespeare's grave, alone at night, intending to test her belief that beneath the gravestone were documents to prove her theory, but had postponed the test. She had intended to wait until her book was published before searching the tomb, and had changed her mind, so this distraught letter reveals, because of a letter in which her brother tried again to dissuade her from her theory and proposed that she turn her book into a novel. She was devastated by this letter, and Hawthorne's reply, intended to calm her feelings, had the opposite effect. She composed a letter to him over two days, vaguely and irrationally blaming him for her brother's attitude.[15]

When it was settled that T. Parker and Son would publish the book, provided Hawthorne would furnish a preface and would pay the cost, he asked Bennoch to make all necessary arrangements with Miss Bacon, and to give her for him the money she needed, disguised as the publisher's advance on royalties. He informed Ticknor that he was sending him 500 copies, half of the edition, for the American market; there had not been time to consult Ticknor in advance. He remarked to Bennoch: "betwixt her name and my own, my countrymen will feel a certain degree of interest in the book. How funny, that I should come in front of the stage-curtain, escorting this Bedlamite!" He was serving a special purpose, he told Bennoch, for Delia Bacon needed "somebody besides herself to wreak her mortification upon;—else she would tear herself to pieces." Before the end of January the book was printed, except for the preface, which was finished on February 10. It had been "painfully screwed out of a pre-occupied and unwilling mind," Hawthorne said in sending it to Bennoch the next day. "Thank Heaven, I have done with Miss Bacon and her book—that is, except paying the Printer's bill."[16]

So he thought until he received Delia Bacon's letter of February 14. She had taken a pair of scissors to his preface, cutting out every word he had quoted from an earlier introduction of hers which she now disowned. She saw that he did not appreciate her work as she thought he did, and she could "not consent to have this cloud thrown over" her. "You cannot come inside of this book, if you are going to throw doubt on the oracle. I consider myself a priestess of these Nine, and I don't allow of any skepticism or profane speeches within the lids of this book." Something of her mental state may be surmised from her reference to the nine Muses. If the publisher agreed, she would leave his name off the title page and would dedicate the book to him. Hawthorne opened his reply on February 19, "Dear Author of this Book, (For you forbid me to call you anything else)," and his preface as finally published employs the same substitute for her name. By March 13, she had accepted his preface, after deleting some paragraphs. But the Parkers had withdrawn their agreement to publish the book. Bennoch was able soon to engage Grombridge and Son to take over the book. Hawthorne furnished £25 for advertising, and reported to Ticknor that the printing had cost him more than £238, not including the binding, and added, " 'A fool and his money are soon parted.' However, I do not repent me what I have done." The book had grown larger, finally, by a hundred-page introduction Miss Bacon had added after the rest of it was in print. It was heavy "enough to swamp a ship of the line," Hawthorne wrote, and as if to assure Ticknor that he would not squander any more of his savings, he added, "However, this shall be the last of my benevolent follies, and I never will be kind to anybody again as long as [I] live." [17]

But he was still not through. When Miss Bacon's mind and health worsened, he guaranteed payment of costs on her account at Stratford-on-Avon for room and board and medical attention beyond what friends there furnished her; and he arranged for her to return to America, only to find that she was not well enough to travel. Finally, before he was ready to leave England at the end of 1857, he was satisfied that she would be looked after; a nephew of hers took charge and accompanied her to America in April, 1858. There was yet another ironic turn. The Reverend Leonard Bacon wrote on July 3, 1857, thanking Hawthorne for looking after his sister through her illness and deepening insanity, but showing himself unforgiving of those who had encouraged her to stay in England and pursue her study. Hawthorne was chief among these. One of the next generation, Miss Bacon's nephew and biographer Theodore Bacon, wrote of Hawthorne's role in the complex affair that "there is nothing in all his life or in all that he wrote more honorable than the noble generosity, the unwearying patience, the exquisite considerateness and delicacy, with which for two years he gave unstinted help, even of that material sort which she would not ask for, to this lonely countrywoman." [18]

Hawthorne kept so faithfully to his desk during his first two years at Liverpool that he saw little of the country. By the summer of 1855, he realized that, by coming to the office at intervals to sign documents and take care of matters requiring his attention, he could accomplish much of the travel he had planned. On June 18 he moved his family from Rock Park, in order to reduce living expenses and gain more freedom to travel. More than once in the next five years, before they were again at the Wayside, would he remark on their nomadic existence and the fact that the children were growing up without feeling they had a home or a country. They went first to Leamington for three weeks, from which they visited Stratford-on-Avon, Warwick, and Coventry. With first interest in literary connections, they sought out places of significance to authors and literary works. Hawthorne often encountered scenes that, from his reading, he felt had been familiar since childhood. In the same reading, he had become so steeped in history that scarcely a castle, a village, or a street failed to call up figures and events important in the development of the national character of Britain—and therefore important to the character of his own nation.

With some of the authors he felt a particular affinity, Samuel Johnson, for one. A notebook entry of July 4, 1855, tells of his going alone to Lichfield, and on to Uttoxeter, "on a purely sentimental pilgrimage." In the *Biographical Stories for Children* he had told of Johnson's standing with bared head in the jostling crowd of the market place at Uttoxeter, doing penance for his "pride and natural stubbornness" in disobeying his father half a century earlier. He recounted his own pilgrimage to the site in a sketch for the *Keepsake* of 1857 and in the essay "Lichfield and Uttoxeter" in *Our Old Home*. Following more than three weeks of thorough sightseeing in the Lake Country, he noted on July 30 that he had seen enough of the English lakes "for at least a year to come," and had concluded that "a man with children in charge cannot enjoy traveling."

At the first of August, the family took up temporary residence at the Rock Park Hotel. On August 23 Hawthorne was an overnight guest at Smithell's Hall, a few miles from Bolton. He had heard about the Bloody Footstep implanted on a stone at the base of a stairway in Smithell's Hall, and now he was pleased to see it and to learn the lore associated with it. He recorded full details of the ancient building and the legend of a martyr in Bloody Mary's time, which were to figure in the plans he soon began making for an English romance.

An invitation from the O'Sullivans in Lisbon would enable Sophia to escape the English winter. Before time for her to sail, the Hawthornes would make, finally, their first visit to London. On September 4 the entire family and the maid Fanny Wrigley took the train for Shrewsbury, spent the night there, and the next day proceeded to London. After putting up at 24 George Street, Hanover Square, Hawthorne and Julian, just before dark, "walked forth for the first time in London." Hawthorne wrote in his notebook, "It is long since I have had such a childish feeling; but all that I had heard, and felt, about the vastness of London, made it seem like swimming in a boundless ocean." The next day he wandered about alone, with no object in view but to lose himself, for the sake of finding himself among things he had always read and dreamed about. He returned to his lodgings at the end of the day, having seen no one he knew, except a man he had met casually once in Liverpool. After a month in London, he said he felt "more at home and familiar there, than even in Boston, or in Salem itself."[19] Sometimes he walked out with his wife, and at times with the two oldest children as well. After a visit to Westminster Abbey with his wife and Julian, who had become tired and hungry and, besides, was too young for such sightseeing, he confided to his notebook that he meant to go back by himself "—or, better, with Sophia alone." The added phrase seems to have been an afterthought, for his wife of course read his notebooks. His greatest enjoyment came when he explored the city alone, and he often sent his wife by cab back to Hanover Square and filled out the day in the wanderings that seemed never to tire him.

He was interested most in the London of those authors in the age of Queen Anne he had read. Again and again, when he had become lost in central London, St. Paul's Cathedral would stand ahead in the street he had just entered. The cathedral was a favorite of his, in its literal existence and in the metaphorical significance he saw in it. In Westminster Abbey, he found not one overpowering entity—within itself and as an embodiment of the nation—such as he found in St. Paul's, but countless artifacts, many of them objects of beauty and individual significance, and representing elements of the national character and history. Following a week in Liverpool at the middle of September, he resumed sightseeing in London. Once he went to a theater. His attempt to avoid society was largely successful, though calls were exchanged with the poet W. C. Bennett, General Robert B. Campbell, United States consul, and James Buchanan, minister to St. James. He and his wife were guests of the Buchanans one evening, and they dined with Russell Sturgis, friend of William Makepeace Thackeray and partner of the Barings, Hawthorne's bankers in London.

On October 7 the family took the train to Southampton, where the next day Sophia embarked with Una and Rose for Lisbon. Hawthorne called on the captain of the ship, the *Madrid*, and put his wife and daughters in his special care. His wife, he wrote in his notebook, "behaved heroically" at their parting. His entry for the day of her departure is reserved: "This is the first great parting that Sophia and I have ever had. . . . I was not depressed, (trusting in God's mercy, that we shall all meet again;) but yet the thought was not without a good deal of pain, that we were to be so long separated—so long a gap in life." His habit of watching for tokens prompted him to record that in the morning he saw a piece of rainbow and remembered that in the lore of seafaring such a sign told sailors to take warning. The weather late in the day seemed to support the warning, but sea captains told him the *Madrid* would have cleared the area ahead of the threatened winds. He recorded also Julian's suggestion that since his mother was away and he had no one else to depend on now, his father should be very kind to him. Stopping for the night at the Crown Hotel in Worcester, Hawthorne went to the smoking-room for a glass of whiskey and cold water, and made himself "as much at home as possible;—speaking to nobody, however, and spoken to by none, after the first civilities of offering a seat." Before retiring, he gave "a fatherly and motherly glance at Julian, in his separate chamber."

25

England and the English

As Hawthorne returned to Liverpool with Julian and took up residence at Mrs. Blodgett's, he was lonely and depressed. The consulate was more a prison than ever, and the gloomy days allowed him slight resilience. The glimpses he had into life on American merchant ships deepened the gloom. He took a deposition on November 15, 1855, from a sailor who had been beaten by the master of his ship; after the death of the sailor the next day, he wrote in his notebook, "There is a most dreadful state of things aboard our ships. Hell itself can be no worse than some of them; and I do pray that some New Englander, with the itch of reform in him, may turn his thoughts this way." It troubled him to realize that such conditions existed in an area for which he had at least partial responsibility.

He could not have failed to contrast Christmas this year with Christmas the preceding year, the happiest he had ever known. Report has it that he took only a reluctant part in the ceremony of kissing under the mistletoe in which the sea captains and the women of Mrs. Blodgett's household joined hilariously. His friend Henry Bright composed verses honoring the occasion, "Song of Consul Hawthorne," in the meter of Longfellow's *Hiawatha*, which had recently appeared and was the subject of wide comment. The verses tell of the maids who,

> Slyly laughing, softly stealing,
> Whisper, "Kiss me, Yankee Captain,—
> Kiss or shilling, Yankee Captain!"
> Slyly laughing, softly saying,
> "Kiss from you too, Consul Hawthorne!
> Kiss or shilling, Consul Hawthorne!"

The verses manage also to catch several aspects of Consul Hawthorne as his English friends knew him:

> Do you ask me, "Tell me further
> Of this Consul, of this Hawthorne"?
> I would say, he is a sinner,—
> Reprobate and churchless sinner,—
> Never goes inside a chapel,
> Says his prayers without a chapel!
> I would say that he is lazy,
> Very lazy, good-for-nothing;
> Hardly ever goes to dinners,
> Never goes to balls or soirées;
> Thinks one friend worth twenty friendly;
> Cares for love, but not for liking;
> Hardly knows a dozen people,—
> . . . .
> Hardly knows a soul worth knowing—
> Lazy, good-for-nothing fellow![1]

In his notebook on January 16, 1856, Hawthorne wrote that he had not suffered from such low spirits even in "the least auspicious periods" of his life, and supposed that his "desolate, bachelor condition" was the cause. His appetite was not good; he lay awake at night thinking sad thoughts and imagining somber things. His heart always sank as he climbed the stairs to his office, "from a dim augury of ill news—of black-sealed letters—or some such horrors." He sent Bridge, for passing on to Pierce, a request for leave of absence to be used if his wife's condition should require him to join her in Lisbon.

The essay "Outside Glimpses of English Poverty," in *Our Old Home*, includes an account based on Hawthorne's notebook record of his visit on February 27 to the West Derby Workhouse. He was already familiar with the streets of the poor, and in the early pages he engages in the kind of realistic portrayal touched with sympathy, irony, and moral condemnation which he found in Fielding and Dickens, both of whom he names. Considering the Englishman's policy of denying all beggars as unworthy against the opposed policy of buying "the little luxury of beneficence at a cheap rate," he declares, "The natural man cries out against the philosophy that rejects beggars. It is a thousand to one that they are imposters, but yet we do ourselves a wrong by hardening our hearts against them." Of the children in the mud and filth of the streets, he says, "Unless these slime-clogged nostrils can be made capable of inhaling celestial air, I know not how the purest and most intellectual of us can reasonably expect ever to taste a breath of it. The whole question of eternity is staked there."

His visit to the workhouse was a depressing experience, particularly because a child of six years, "wretched, pale, half-torpid," afflicted with scurvy, "took the strangest fancy to" him, smiled at him, held up its hands, and expressed in its face "such perfect confidence that it was going to be taken up and made much of, that it was impossible not to do it." He concluded his notebook account of the episode, "I wish I had not touched the imp; and yet I never should have forgiven myself if I had repelled its advances." In the essay on English poverty, he incorporates these and most of the other details in his notebook account, but does not identify himself as the man who took up the child. He uses the occasion, however, to analyze himself in the episode, pretending that it was another member of the party who picked up the child. "It was as if God had promised the poor child this favor on behalf of that individual, and he was bound to fulfil the contract, or else no longer call himself a man among men. Nevertheless, it could be no easy thing for him to do, he being a person burdened with more than an Englishman's customary reserve, shy of actual contact with human beings, afflicted with a peculiar distaste for whatever was ugly, and, furthermore, accustomed to that habit of observation from an insulated stand-point which is said (but, I hope, erroneously) to have the tendency of putting ice into the blood." It would not be easy to compose a better succinct statement of the way he saw himself—or the way he appears in the light of full biographical evidence.

Nor would it be easy to shape a clearer statement than the one, later in this essay, on brotherhood and individual liability for the universal guilt. The essayist is "seriously of opinion" that the one who took up the child performed "an heroic act, and effected more than he dreamed of towards his final salvation." It was no doubt the child's mission "to remind him that he was responsible, in his degree, for all the sufferings and misdemeanors of the world in which he lived, and was not entitled to look upon a particle of its dark calamity as if it were none of his concern; the offspring of a brother's iniquity being his own blood-relation, and the guilt, likewise, a burden on him, unless he expiated it by better deeds."

In another room at the workhouse he saw a baby which he said was the most horrible object he ever saw. The essay account of this baby, little altered in design and tone from that in the notebook, concludes by saying that the author lays the case, as far as he is able, "before mankind, on whom God has imposed the necessity to suffer in soul and body till this dark and dreadful wrong be righted." Though his heart had been wrenched on his visit to the workhouse, he acknowledged that answers were not clear or easy. He could say only that "the world, that requires such an establishment, ought to be ashamed of itself and set about an immediate reformation"; but he remained aware of incongruities. The paupers were better provided with food and other comforts than the laboring classes ordinarily had. He had gone to the workhouse with Mrs. Heywood, who had a kindly and humanitarian interest in the visit. At the country estate of the Heywoods for dinner afterward, he was shown the beautifully tended grounds. In his notebook he wondered "how many people live and die in the workhouse, having no other home, because other people have a great deal more home than enough!" The essay concludes with a lighter but a sober view of a mass wedding of poor couples performed in the Manchester Cathedral, followed at the same altar by a wedding at which wealth and class and the most favorable conditions were apparent. Less apocalyptically than in writing about the workhouse, the author says that one day "the gentlemen of England will be compelled to face" the question implicit in this contrast.

On March 20 Hawthorne took the train for London, leaving Julian with the Brights. Since the new consular regulations allowed an absence of only ten days in a quarter of the year without leave and loss of pay, he would beat his old Uncle at that game, he said, by absenting himself for twenty days overlapping two quarters. On this visit he often had some friend as guide; he was willing to be entertained; and he found it not unpleasant to be lionized.

He put up at 32 St. James's Place, where a young bachelor accountant named Bowman had secured him a room and would share his own drawing-room. Still in the shadow of his winter in Liverpool, he noted after his first day that the "shine and charm" had gone from the city since his previous visit. But his notebook report of a full day, March 23, at Hampton Court, and a walk of nearly fifteen miles with Bowman, regains the tone of his earlier excursions in the city and indicates that the spell of his winter gloom was broken. On his second day he called to see Francis Bennoch (1812–90), who had visited him at Rock Park soon after his arrival in Liverpool; and there followed a sequence of social engagements unlike anything he had ever experienced—or had ever thought likely for him, as he was handed from one dinner party to another, including the Lord Mayor's dinner, and heard his writings generously praised, often by authors and critics he respected.

Bennoch was a dealer in silk, a poet, and a friend of English and American authors. He took Hawthorne to see "some of the curiosities of old London," including the Greenwich Fair, where he was introduced to the game of Kissing in the Ring. Bennoch next took him to Aldershot Camp, where they observed a parade and a sham-battle, slept in the barracks, and otherwise sampled military life with the officers of the North Cork Rifles, which included dining, playing whist, and socializing until four one morning and two the next. Hawthorne's notebook account leaves no doubt that he enjoyed the experience and in particular the fraternizing "with these military gentlemen." The next stop on this whirlwind trip was with Martin Farquhar Tupper (1810–89) and his family at the village of Albury. Hawthorne found the author of the popular *Proverbial Philosophy* (1838) to be "a good soul, but a fussy little man."[2] At the Tuppers', a descendant of John Evelyn came in, bringing for the guests to see a volume of Evelyn's manuscript of his diary, the prayer-book supposedly taken by Charles I to the scaffold and stained with his blood, and a manuscript volume of letters and documents in Charles's hand. The journey continued to Tunbridge Wells, to Battle, the site of Battle Abbey and of lore descended from Norman times, and on to Hastings, where there was lunch with Theodore Martin and his wife, the actress Helen Faucit. Hawthorne was at once so pleased and so comfortable with them that he talked more, he thought, than at any other time since coming to London.[3]

Back in London at the mid-point of his visit, Hawthorne began ten days of lunches, dinners, and suppers at which he was all but suffocated with the incense burned under his nose, as he once put it, or had enough soft soap to last him a lifetime, or had molasses poured over his head, or heard himself praised so outrageously that he would not record the praise in his notebook, or was "besmeared . . . with such sweetness of laudation" that he felt "all over bestuck, as after handling sweetmeats or molasses-candy."[4] At Bennoch's previously he had met Newton Crosland and his wife, formerly Camilla Toulmin, who had published favorable criticism of his work and who now, he remarked in his notebook, March 25, "was awfully lavish in her admiration, preferring poor me to all the novelists of this age, or I believe, any other." At a dinner Bennoch gave at the Milton

Club on April 1, he saw Tupper again and met, among others, four who entertained him in the next few days: Samuel Carter Hall (1800–89), prominent author and editor; Dr. Charles Mackay (1814–89), editor of the *Illustrated London News;* Herbert Ingram (1811–60), founder and proprietor of the same journal and a member of the House of Commons from 1856 until his death; and Eneas Sweetland Dallas (1828–79), editorial writer for the *Times.* Dallas took him to his house for supper, following the dinner, and introduced his wife, the actress Isabella Dallas Glyn (1823–89). Dr. Mackay had him for dinner on April 3 at the Reform Club, where another guest was Douglas William Jerrold (1803–57), author of *Blackeyed Susan* (1829) and other plays. Two days later Dallas had Hawthorne for supper with half a dozen other guests, one of whom was the novelist Charles Reade (1814–84). The next day Bennoch and Dr. Mackay took Hawthorne to Firfield, Hall's place at Addlestone, where he planted a sumach tree in the lawn, for lack of the hawthorn that Hall had failed to provide. After dinner there were the usual toasts and what Hawthorne thought an outrageously long tribute to his genius.

The climax of Hawthorne's London visit came on April 7, at the Lord Mayor's dinner, the most imposing function he attended in England and the occasion of his most important speech. He knew before coming to Liverpool that speech-making would be required of him. Donald G. Mitchell reports that when Hawthorne was in Washington in the spring of 1853, contemplating this part of his consular duties "cast a leaden hue over his official sky, and over all his promise of European enjoyment."[5] In spite of an antipathy he vowed he had felt since his college days, he seems not to have thought of balking on any occasion, though for one reason or another he declined invitations to some of the dinners given by the mayor of Liverpool, when speeches would have been expected. Before he left England he showed on occasion, not only that he thought himself a successful speaker, but that he liked speaking. In his letters, his notebooks, and the essay "Civic Banquets," his adventures as an after-dinner speaker are treated with the varied mixtures of realism and fancy that occur in his imaginative works.

The notebook entries as a rule contain the self-abnegation and the ironic turns normal to accounts of his own activities. In his first effort, at the luncheon given by his predecessor, he was "perfectly self-possessed." When he received the delegation from the Chamber of Commerce, he "did not break down to an intolerable extent." At his first dinner with the mayor of Liverpool, his audience listened to his "nonsense with a great deal of rapping." Soon he was ready to generalize, as usual with tongue in cheek: "Any body may make an after-dinner speech, who will be content to talk onward without saying anything. . . . I hardly thought it was in me; but being once on my legs, I felt no embarrassment, and went through it as coolly as if I were going to be hanged."

He liked to write his friends about his speeches, with his usual eye to the details and phrasing for effect. After he had "mumbled some damned nonsense" in his first two speeches, he would have to mumble some more at the mayor's dinner. He took comfort, however, since he could not "cut a much more foolish figure than the Englishmen themselves," and continued, "For my part, I charge myself pretty high with champagne and port before I get upon my legs; and whether the business is to make a speech or be hanged, I come up to it like a man—and I had as lief it should be one as the other."[6] After a dinner given by the mayor of Liverpool, he said he had "tickled up John Bull's self-conceit (which is very easily done) with a few sentences of most outrageous flattery, and sat down in a general puddle of good feeling."[7] Another time he told of a reply he had made when Pierce had been toasted, "I had missed no opportunity of gulping down champagne, and so had got myself into that state of pot-valor which (as you and he know) is best adapted to bring out my heroic qualities."[8] The speeches became more difficult as English-American relations grew strained during 1855. In January of the next year he was to attend another Liverpool mayor's dinner—reluctantly, he said, "for my soul is in peril already with the lies I have told at the Mayor's dinner-table, in regard to the good feeling of America towards England." At one time near the end of his term as consul, he said, "I don't in the least admire my own oratory; but I do admire my pluck in speaking at all. I rather wonder at my coming off so well." At another time he generalized, "It is easy enough to speak when a man is cornered and *corned;* but I here make a vow never to raise my voice so as to be heard by more than six people, nor to speak more than a hundred words together, after quitting this Consulate."[9]

The reports Hawthorne sent his friends across the Atlantic were fore-studies for the full-blown account of his speechmaking in the essay "Civic Banquets," which reaches its climax at the Lord Mayor's dinner in London. His notebook report of the dinner sounds the same note of seriousness touched with lightness that characterizes the other entries for his London visit; but this was a more important occasion and suggested more ironic thrusts than usual. From the time he was announced by the footmen, who looked "something like American revolutionary generals, only far more splendid," until he had finished his speech and made his way back to his quarters, he attempted to sense the nature of the tradition-enshrouded ceremony, to grasp its meaning to the participants, and to see in proper perspective his own role in what he could not help thinking a comic performance. He sought help from his friend Samuel Carter Hall, realizing that he "could not have found a better artist in whip-syllabub and flummery."[10] His notebook reports that, among other preliminaries, the Lord Mayor paid some high compliments to his works. When the herald proclaimed that he was going to respond, the account runs, "I rose amid much cheering, so screwed up to the point that I did not care what happened next. The Lord Mayor might have fired a pistol, instead of a speech, at me, and I should not have flinched." Clothing some of Hall's flummery in his own words and interweaving two or three points of his own, he "tinkered up and amalgamated a very tolerable little speech." Cheers broke in between sentences, and afterward many praised his effort. But "I soon felt," he wrote, "—indeed, I have never ceased to feel—that I, like the other orators of the evening, had made a fool of myself, and that it is altogether a ridiculous custom to talk in one's cups."

What followed "this great event of the evening," his speech, as narrated in his notebook sums up his response to the whole affair. The consul of Liverpool, the speaker at the Lord Mayor's dinner, responding to a toast in behalf of the United States government and bespeaking friendly relations between the two nations at a troubled moment in their relations, afterward became obscured in the crowd, left the hall alone, and returned to his boarding-house by omnibus and on foot. It was Hawthorne's habit to see himself and his own actions as representational in the manner of character and plot in fiction; but he did not often see himself a central figure, as on this occasion, in such an ironic extravaganza of ancient tradition and major current issues.

The essay "Civic Banquets" reaches its peak in the dinner of the Lord Mayor of London, and the way is prepared for the dinner—and the disquisition on after-dinner speeches—to reach a climax in the Liverpool consul's speech. The Lord Mayor mentions the subject of English-American relations, inviting the American consul to speak the kind of reassurance most sought in the time of threatening possibilities. Hall has advised beginning with compliments to the Mayor. The essay then proceeds abruptly to its close, which is the close also of the volume *Our Old Home:*

> Thence, if I liked, getting flexible with the oil of my own eloquence, I might easily slide off into the momentous subject of the relations between England and America, to which his Lordship had made such weighty allusion.
>
> Seizing this handfull of straw with a death-grip, and bidding my three friends bury me honorably, I got upon my legs to save both countries, or perish in the attempt. The tables roared and thundered at me, and suddenly were silent again. But, as I have never happened to stand in a position of greater dignity and peril, I deem it a stratagem of sage policy here to close these Sketches, leaving myelf still erect in so heroic an attitude.

When "Civic Banquets" was being published in the *Atlantic Monthly*, Hawthorne said it was "a little funnier than befits the gravity and dignity of a man of consular rank," and that, if he had let his wife read it, she would not have let him print it.[11] But the anticlimactic ending of the consul's speech on this momentous occasion is a fitting conclusion for this essay and for the book of observations by the author, an American, on his ancestral home. It is a final reminder that, although the book reports his experiences and observations as reflected in his thoughtful analysis, the total has been given an imaginative literary character.

As usual, Hawthorne was displeased with the newspaper summaries of his speech; they exaggerated the theme of international friendship, which he thought he had himself expressed too strongly. He was "about half-seas over" when he got up to speak, but Bennoch would bear witness that he "spoke a devilish sight better" than the newspapers indicated.[12]

April 8 brought Hawthorne still a fuller day's schedule. After lunch with Bennoch, he went to the speakers' gallery of the House of Commons and listened to the debate. Later he had dinner in the refectory with a member of the House, Herbert Ingram. Bennoch took him next to a lecture by Albert Smith on the ascent of Mont Blanc, and afterward, joined by the lecturer, to an oyster house, and still later to Evans's Supper Rooms, "a rather rowdyish place," where he stayed until past one and where the superintendent said it had been "the dream and romance of his life" to have at one of his tables Hawthorne, Emerson, Channing, and Longfellow. Thus Hawthorne wrote Longfellow on April 12, saying also that he smiled to think of "such a party of roisterers drinking whisky-toddy or gin and water at one of his tables, smoking pipes or cigars, and listening to a bacchanalian catch from his vocalists." He had written Bennoch the day after his evening at Evans's that he had waked with a headache. Albert Smith was a trump, he said,

—the very ace of trumps—but he ought not to have come it quite so strong over my Yankee simplicity as to make me drink four!!!!—and upon my honor, I believe it was five!!!!!—five "goes" (is that the phrase?) of whisky toddy! Having never heard of this drink before, I naturally supposed that it was some kind of tee-total beverage; for in America, a lecturer (like Mr. Albert Smith) is looked upon as own brother to a clergyman, and is invariably a temperance-man. Do you think the respectable Mr. Evans could have deceived him by putting spirituous liquor in my tumbler? At any rate, I have a suspicion that hot whisky toddy, when taken in considerable quantities, has a slightly intoxicating quality. Please to tell Mr. Albert Smith so, and he will be on his guard how he gives it to his friends in future.

On Hawthorne's last evening in London, J. B. Davies, former American secretary of legation, took him for dinner with Henry Stevens, another American, who had a book brokerage house in London, several of the men he had met earlier, their wives, and several new acquaintances. It turned out to be the most tiresome of his evenings in the city, perhaps in part because he was tired from the preceding evening at Evans's Supper Rooms. It was ungracious, "even hoggish," not to be gratified with the interest expressed in him; but "one does not know what to do or to say," he wrote in his notebook. "I felt like the hippopotamus, or, to use a more modest illustration, like some strange bug imprisoned under a tumbler, with a dozen eyes watching whatever I did."

On this note ended his vacation. He wrote Bennoch before departing on April 10, "I shall return to Liverpool tomorrow, with such small remnants of a moral character as your evil guidance has left me," and the next day he wrote Ticknor that he had enjoyed himself gloriously and had "lived rather fast." On April 7 he had written his wife that the London people had found him out. If he stayed through the season, he would have two or three engagements a day. He had now as friends the three best actresses of London. "In short, I have been lionized, and am still being lionized; and this one experience will be quite sufficient for me. I find it something between a botheration and a satisfaction." The experience had been new to him, pleasant and flattering, but one he could hardly mention without smiling. He was glad his years of isolation had come before he had a wife and children, who would have had to share it; but comparing that life with the present seems to have left him with a haunting uncertainty as to which was real.

After three weeks in the consulate, Hawthorne spent the week of May 2–8 in Scotland, accompanied by Bowman, his London guide. They went

to Glasgow, Loch Lomond, the Trossachs, Edinburgh, Melrose and Dry-
burgh abbeys, Abbotsford, Newcastle, and York. The notebook record of
this tour was not written until he was back in Liverpool on May 8, and
consequently is little more than a routine travel narrative. He found the
Scottish people more like Americans and hence more attractive than the
English. At Edinburgh his greatest interest was in Mary Queen of Scots.
In the Trossachs and at the abbeys he was on the familiar ground of Sir
Walter Scott's romances, but at Abbotsford he was remorseful because he
could not find in Scott's home and surroundings "a single and great impression"; rather, it was like going to a museum; and one learned there
"that Scott could not have been really a wise man, nor an earnest one, nor
one that grasped the truth of life;—he did but play, and the play grew
very sad towards its close." Even so, he enjoyed the anticipation of reading all of Scott's novels again when back at the Wayside.

A telegram on June 9 brought Hawthorne word that his wife had
landed at Southampton. He and Julian took a late afternoon train the next
day, spent the night at Birmingham, and reached Southampton in the evening, re-uniting the family after eight months. For a week they lodged
with Mrs. Hume, a friend of Bennoch's, and with her as a guide visited
Salisbury and Stonehenge. The Salisbury Cathedral left Hawthorne with
the opinion that cathedrals were about the only things in the Old World
"to fill out" his ideal. From June 19 to 27 he was in Liverpool, and on July
2 he moved his family to the London suburb of Blackheath, where they
would occupy Bennoch's house during the two months he and his family
would spend on the Continent. Since the Bennochs were not ready to
leave until July 10, other quarters for the interim were rented for Una and
Rose and their nurse. Except for time spent in Liverpool July 14–26 and
August 8–26, Hawthorne resumed his sightseeing and moved again in the
circles to which he had been introduced in the spring. At Samuel Carter
Hall's with his wife on July 8, he saw the Lord Mayor and others he already knew; and he met for the first time several authors, artists, and
musicians, most notable among them Jenny Lind. Maunsell B. Field, who
had met Hawthorne in the Berkshires in 1850 and was present on this occasion, wrote that "Hawthorne's superb head was by all odds the finest in
the room. He looked genial, and *mirabile dictu* appeared at his ease. . . .
he talked brilliantly for half an hour, without exhibiting any of the
shyness which for years had made him a perfect recluse."[13] Field may
have been overstating the case, but there can be no doubt that Hawthorne's London admirers had drawn him forward. At a dinner given by

Mrs. Heywood the next day, Hawthorne met again Richard Monckton Milnes and his wife. In his notebook he implied the reason for the ease with which he conversed with Mrs. Milnes: she was "of noble blood, and therefore less snobbish than most English ladies," and reminded him of "the best-mannered American women." She assured him that Tennyson would be gratified to have him call—to which he replied that he would hardly venture to take such a liberty, "more especially as he might perhaps suspect me of doing it on the score of my own literary character." Her remarks on Charles Dickens caused him to note that he must see Dickens before leaving England.

On July 11 Hawthorne had what he recognized as his most important literary experience in England, a breakfast with Richard Monckton Milnes. Arriving too early from Blackheath and passing the time in exploring the streets, he became lost and, as if a perverse fate had taken charge, arrived too late to be introduced to anyone except the Marquess of Lansdowne and Elizabeth Barrett Browning, whom he was assigned to conduct to the table. The other lady present besides Mrs. Milnes was the mother of Florence Nightingale, who talked to him afterward about Lady Byron. During breakfast he concluded that a gentleman across the table was Thomas Babington Macaulay, and Robert Browning introduced himself after they had returned to the library. He already knew two other American guests, George Ticknor, the historian of Spanish literature, and John Gorham Palfrey, whom he had met through George Hillard. Hawthorne liked Mrs. Browning "very much—a great deal better than her poetry," which he "could hardly suppose to have been written by quite such a quiet little person as she." She belonged, he noted, to "that quickly appreciative and responsive order of women" with whom he could talk more freely than with men. She introduced the subject of spiritualism, and seemed to be a believer. He could not understand how "so fine a spirit as hers should not reject the matter, till, at least, it is forced upon her." This subject they would explore further when they were residents of Florence two years later.

While the re-united family was residing in Bennoch's house, Hawthorne spent some of the happiest hours he had known since leaving the Wayside. He could not say whether the "strange, vagabond, gypsy sort of life" they were leading would spoil them for any other, or would prepare them to enjoy more than ever the quiet of the Wayside when they returned to it. On August 30, he and his wife went to Oxford for six days with Bennoch, who had returned from the Continent. Hawthorne afterward expressed his gratitude to their host Richard James Spiers, former mayor of Oxford, by sending him a specially bound set of his works and by saying at the conclusion of the essay "Near Oxford" in *Our Old Home* that his host, unnamed, had "inseparably mingled his image with" his guests' "remembrance of the Spires of Oxford."

Hawthorne's probing of the American past had a logical extension to the ancestral home. He had only a mild interest in tracing his own origins, and in England did little more than note references to his family name that would supplement details he had earlier from Ebenezer Hawthorne and Susan Ingersoll. Soon after reaching Liverpool, he asked Fields to find out if he could where the first William Hawthorne came from, saying he would like to locate a gravestone with his name on it, though he would himself prefer to be buried in America. "The graves are too devilish damp here." Two years later he asked Ticknor to inquire of any genealogist he knew how he might learn about his English ancestors. Still later he had from his Salem friend David Roberts excerpts copied from William Hawthorne's will and a genealogical table for all the American genera- tions.[14] He learned from John Gorham Palfrey about a letter supposed to have been written by William Hawthorne in 1666 and was furnished a copy from the government archives in London. His interest in England was less in specifics than in generalities of likeness and difference, influ- ence, and attitude. Believing that any age is a product of past ages, and that an understanding of a nation, a region, or a family at any time de- pends on a knowledge of past times, he arrived in England ready to search out monuments and records of the English past and to observe in the present time the collateral descendants of the ancestors the English shared with Americans.

National affairs in both countries during Hawthorne's consulship, espe- cially the slavery issue in America and the Crimean War, caused him to register observations and judgments in letters, notebook entries, and the essays of *Our Old Home*. On September 23, 1853, two months after he ar- rived in Liverpool, the British fleet was ordered to Constantinople in a show of support for the Turkish forces. On October 3 the Turks declared war on Russia; the next March 28 Great Britain and France also declared war, and in September they landed troops in the Russian Crimea. The year-long siege of Sebastopol brought heavy losses to the British forces, of which the people were painfully aware. The charge of the Light Brigade at Balaklava on October 25, 1855, the subject two months later of a poem by the poet laureate, Tennyson, brought popular emotion to a high pitch.

Hawthorne was a close observer and recorder of the English response to these special strains, and he recorded especially intense feelings as relations grew so strained over soldier enlistments that war between England and America became a possibility. Hoping to lessen casualties to British troops, Parliament passed the Foreign Enlistment Act on December 23, 1854. Soon there was cumulative evidence that a program was being pursued in major American cities for encouraging—and paying—men to travel to Halifax, Nova Scotia, for enlistment in the British army; and it became clear that the central figure in the operations was the British minister at Washington, John F. T. Crampton (whom Hawthorne had known on the voyage from Boston to Halifax in 1853). Secretary Marcy on December 28, 1855, requested the recall of Crampton; and after receiving what seemed to be only a delaying reply, he acted in the name of President Pierce on May 28, dismissing Crampton and four British consuls.

Hawthorne's letters to America had been filled since his arrival with comments on England and the English. His liking for John Bull grew stronger on better acquaintance, but his admiration and respect decreased. He was sure that England's day was past, and he was thankful; he would like to have America annex England, as he thought would happen, though not in his time. During the controversy over the enlistment of American soldiers, he hoped America would "not bate an inch of honor for the sake of avoiding" war; "and if it does come, we have the fate of England in our hands. . . . I HATE England; though I love some Englishmen, and like them generally, in fact."[15] The "war cloud has blown over," he told Ticknor on December 7; but when he wrote the next February 15, he could not see how war could be avoided. His own attitude had stiffened: "I will disown Frank Pierce if he backs out one inch, (but I am sure he never will,) and I would rather see America sink (in which case I will come back and sink with her) than have her give up her just rights. But there is no danger of our sinking." It was quiet through Hawthorne's three weeks in London in March and April, 1856, but there was an undercurrent of uneasiness that no doubt accounted for the special attention paid him when he spoke, as at the Lord Mayor's dinner. Two decisive steps taken by President Pierce in May had Hawthorne's hearty approval—recognizing the Walker-Rivas government of Nicaragua, to the displeasure of the British, and dismissing Crampton. He did not agree with the popular view in England that George Mifflin Dallas, who had replaced Buchanan as ambassador, would be sent home, though he might wish he would be, "because it would be such a very foolish act on the part of the British

Government." On June 20 Hawthorne wrote both Ticknor and Bridge, challenging their gloomy estimates of American prospects and declaring his faith in the destiny of his country. Dallas had not been dismissed, he reminded Ticknor. "We have gained a great triumph over England, and I begin to like her better now; for, I can assure you, Englishmen feel that they have given up forever the pretensions to superiority, and the haughty tone, which they have hitherto held towards us. We have gone through a crisis, and come out right side up. Give Frank Pierce credit for this, at least; for it was his spirit that did it." To Bridge he summed up, "You cannot conceive how much the English are mortified and humbled by what has happened—so much, indeed, that I have not the heart to exult over my English friends, as I meant to do."

When Hawthorne received a copy of Ralph Waldo Emerson's new book, *English Traits*, he wrote him that it contained the "truest pages" yet written on England. He had found much to agree with in Emerson's assessment of the English: their "perfunctory hospitality," their "unaccommodating manners," and the "puissant nationality which makes their existence incompatible with all that is not English." He found in the book his own view that England was on a declining course and the United States on an ascending course, though he had not himself given the view a philosophical setting comparable to Emerson's cyclical theory of the history of nations. He nevertheless was not pleased to have Emerson credit the English with the qualities they valued most and deny them "only what they would be ashamed of, if they possessed it." He found the English comfortable to live among, but he felt "a certain malevolence and hostility . . . such as a man must necessarily feel, who lives in England without melting entirely into the mass of Englishmen." He had sympathized more with Russia than England in the Crimean War, and he concluded, "nothing has given me quite so much pleasure since I left home as the stoop which I saw in every Englishman's shoulders, after the settlement of the Enlistment question."[16] He had received Emerson's book when he was struggling to complete in behalf of Delia Bacon what he felt Emerson had left unfinished; consequently, his mood was to praise the book only with reservation and to speak of the English in the context of the recent tensions between England and America.

In praising Franklin Pierce for standing up to the British, Hawthorne was extending the defense of the president he had begun in the campaign biography. After coming to England, he had written his friend William Pike that the president was "entirely above any miserable vindictiveness,"[17] and he attempted again and again to counter the note of distrust he detected in Bridge's letters. "You and I are the two persons in the world whom he cares most about," he once wrote, and he urged Bridge to stay in Washington and be a friend and adviser to the president. At another time he explained that Pierce's position with regard to his friends was inconceivably difficult. "Do not mistrust him; and when we three come to sit down together, as old men, let there be no ugly recollections to disturb our harmony." Pierce was "truly glad to benefit his friends," he said, provided there was no compromise of his "very strong sense of official duty." To "suppositions" derived from what Bridge considered cold treatment by Pierce, Hawthorne replied that in Washington in the spring of 1853 he had met with the same kind of treatment as to public attention, Pierce inviting him only once to tea and once to go to a Methodist meeting, but that in their personal interviews Pierce had been as "free and kind" as in their college days.[18]

In Italy a few years later, when Pierce was no longer president, the two old friends grew closer together; and still later, back in America during the Civil War, when abolitionist sentiment against Pierce ran high, Hawthorne took occasion to affirm publicly and more staunchly than ever his confidence in Pierce.

26

Novelist as Consul

Hawthorne was determined that his family not be divided again. Unless his wife could face the winter of 1856–57 with some assurance, he intended to leave the consulate and move directly to Italy. She had returned in June with improved health, although the weather in Portugal had not been what she expected and a journey to Madeira with the O'Sullivan women in February had not been helpful. Another winter in Liverpool was out of the question. While at Liverpool late in the summer, Hawthorne visited first the picturesque town of Runcorn, going the fourteen miles from Liverpool by steamer in wind and rain that reminded him of the miserable hours he had spent crossing the Mersey; later he took the train twenty miles north along the coast to Southport, a town made up largely of lodging-houses for summer visitors. Although he had not seen "a drearier landscape, even in Lancashire," and the town was anything but attractive, he concluded that if his wife needed to reside by the sea, Southport might do as well as any.

On September 8 he and Julian returned to Liverpool from London; five days later his wife, "with all her train," joined them at Mrs. Blodgett's. They went to Southport on September 16, taking Fanny Wrigley with them as nurse, and took rooms in Brunswick Terrace, a stone house facing the beach. First intending to stay only a short while, they stayed on, and, since Sophia's health was better than at any time since she came to England, arranged for additional room and remained until July. On October

4 Hawthorne gave a dinner for Francis Bennoch and eight other guests at the Adelphi Hotel in Liverpool. He had wanted to entertain Liverpool friends and to reciprocate after Bennoch had invited him to Manchester the preceding May 22 and had introduced him to the poet and engraver Charles Swain and Alexander Ireland, publisher of the Manchester *Examiner*. Hawthorne stayed overnight at the hotel and the next day took Bennoch and Charles Swain to have dinner and spend the night at Southport.[1] Another guest at Southport, later, was Herman Melville.

After landing at Glasgow on October 26 and traveling in Scotland,[2] Melville called at the consulate on Monday, November 10. He went home with Hawthorne Tuesday afternoon and stayed until they returned to the city together on the noon train Thursday. Because the two had not met, and seemingly had not corresponded, since the unsuccessful attempt in the spring of 1853 to get Melville a consular appointment, Hawthorne "felt rather awkward at first," but "there was no reason to be ashamed," he wrote in his notebook, since he "failed only from real lack of power to serve him." They soon found themselves on pretty much their "former terms of sociability and confidence." Since becoming consul, Hawthorne had attempted again to help Melville to satisfactory employment. Commodore Matthew Calbraith Perry (1794–1858), returning from the voyage to the Orient on which he signed a commercial treaty between America and Japan, came to the consulate on December 28, 1854, to see whether Hawthorne would prepare an account of his voyage for publication. Hawthorne recorded at the time that he recommended Melville "and one or two others," but that Perry had "some acquaintance with the literature of the day, and did not grasp very cordially at any name" suggested. Melville looked "a little paler, and perhaps a little sadder." He had not been well, and no doubt had suffered from "constant literary occupation, pursued without much success." His late writings had "indicated a morbid state of mind." In these remarks Hawthorne seems to have been accepting the opinions of Melville's family—perhaps reported by Melville himself— as to the cause of his maladies. Since they last met, Melville had published *Pierre, Israel Potter*, and a series of stories in magazines that were collected in the volume *Piazza Tales. The Confidence-Man* was finished and would be published in the spring of 1857.

After their day at Southport, Hawthorne put into his notebook an estimate of Melville's condition, his mind, and his character, drawing on his knowledge of the man and his works over the past six years. They took a long walk and, sitting down in a hollow among the sand hills, smoked cigars.

> Melville, as he always does, began to reason of Providence and futurity, and of everything that lies beyond human ken, and informed me that he had "pretty much made up his mind to be annihilated"; but still he does not seem to rest in that anticipation; and, I think, will never rest until he gets hold of a definite belief. It is strange how he persists—and has persisted ever since I knew him, and probably long before—in wandering to-and-fro over these deserts, as dismal and monotonous as the sand hills amid which we were sitting. He can neither believe, nor be comfortable in his unbelief; and he is too honest and courageous not to try to do one or the other. If he were a religious man, he would be one of the most truly religious and reverential; he has a very high and noble nature, and better worth immortality than most of us.

On Friday Melville returned to the consulate, where Hawthorne endorsed his passport. Henry Bright took him to his club for lunch and guided him about the city. On Saturday Hawthorne took him for a full day at Chester. Melville called at the consulate on Monday and on Tuesday sailed for Constantinople.[3] On his return from the Holy Land, he reached Liverpool at noon, May 4, 1857, and embarked for home the next day. His diary reads, "Saw Hawthorne. Called on Mr. Bright. Got presents. Trunk. Packed." No entry for these days appears in Hawthorne's notebook.[4]

The analytical portrait of Melville, quoted in part above, resembles the character portraits in Hawthorne's fictional writings and, like them, reveals his own mind and outlook. In it he writes not personally, but authorially, with such even-handedness as appears in the portrait of Aylmer in "The Birthmark." Melville possesses "a very high and noble nature," as does Aylmer. He is "better worth immortality than most of us," and Hawthorne implies for him what he says of Aylmer: Had he "reached a profounder wisdom, he need not have flung away the happiness which would have woven his mortal life of the selfsame texture with the celestial."

Melville admired Hawthorne because he displayed "the power of blackness" and insisted "upon treating with all Powers upon an equal basis."[5] Hawthorne's example encouraged him to admit similar qualities to his own works from *Moby-Dick* onward and was a shaping influence on some of them. Both authors picture man as imperfect, with propensities for evil, and the victim of forces beyond his control; both see man also as aspiring toward perfection and capable of nobility and heroism. They differ in their views of man's position in the universe. Hawthorne accepted that position as he observed it. The characters in his fiction, responding to forces bearing on them from both within and without, are allowed choices, but every choice, every action, brings inescapable consequences. His characters are governed by psychological determinism; the universe and society are given, as is the iron necessity of consequences. Hence his romances and major tales move inexorably toward the resolution required by the characters and the circumstances under which they exist. Such was his meaning when he described the writing of *The Scarlet Letter*, and when he said of *The House of the Seven Gables* that it was "darkening damnably towards the close." He made it clear that in the last three chapters of the latter he consciously broke the chain of necessity.

Melville was impelled, not to accept, but to question man's relation to the universe and to continue seeking answers that eluded him. Hence the troubling uncertainty that remained with him to the writing of *Billy Budd* at the end of his life. He recognized of course that Hawthorne's sense of the blackness in human experience did not prevent him from accepting the universe, and it is likely that he thought of Hawthorne when such matters came into his writings, as in the Plotinus Plinlimmon section of *Pierre* and in some of the episodes in *The Confidence-Man*. He read and often annotated Hawthorne's later works as they appeared, and he re-read some of the earlier tales.

Julian Hawthorne's accounts of visiting Melville when writing the biography of his father and his mother say little that is definite, except that Melville was ill at ease during the interview and said he had destroyed Hawthorne's letters to him.[6] In saying he was convinced that there was some secret in Hawthorne's life not yet revealed, as reported by Julian, Melville gave the impression that Hawthorne had been much in his mind. He had felt rebuffed, it is clear, before the Hawthornes moved away from Lenox in 1851; and he had remained self-conscious, if not embarrassed. The long poem *Clarel* (1876) is constructed on a journey such as Melville took to the Holy Land (visiting Hawthorne on the way). The relations between the title character and the character Vine suggest that Melville was creating out of recollection and fantasy the interlude with Hawthorne, which had brought him perhaps the greatest exhilaration of his life and also the greatest disappointment. The poem entitled "Monody," published in the volume *Timoleon* in 1891 and possibly written much earlier, would seem to have Hawthorne as subject.

To have known him, to have loved him
   After loneless long;
And then to be estranged in life,
   And neither in the wrong;
And now for death to set his seal—
   Ease me, a little ease, my song!

By wintry hills his hermit-mound
   The sheeted snow-drifts drape,
And houseless there the snow-bird flits
   Beneath the fir-trees' crape:
Glazed now with ice the cloistral vine
   That hid the shyest grape.

On February 13, 1857, Hawthorne sent Ticknor his resignation for transmitting to President Buchanan, to become effective August 31.

On the night of February 18, burglars had entered the Hawthornes' residence by breaking a window and had taken some silver and clothing. Hawthorne reported the burglary to the police; the thieves were arrested in Liverpool; he identified the stolen articles; and on February 24 he attended a hearing. "I rather wished them to escape," he wrote, after learning that they were committed for trial. They were two brothers and were already known to the police. At their trial, March 25, they were convicted and sentenced to deportation.

With his wife and Julian, Hawthorne traveled, April 10–14, to Skipton, Bolton Priory, and York, and returned home by way of Manchester. On May 22 the same three made a more leisurely journey to Lincoln, Boston, Peterborough, Nottingham, Newstead Abbey, Matloch, and Manchester, and returned June 1. Three weeks later they set out again, and for a still longer journey: to Glasgow and its surroundings, to the Trossachs and on to Edinburgh, Abbotsford, and the abbeys, then to Durham, York, and Leeds, and home on July 14. Returning to Liverpool at intervals enabled Hawthorne to meet his normal obligations at the consulate and others as well. On April 15 he attended the laying of the cornerstone of the William Brown Free Library and replied to a toast proposed by Richard Monckton Milnes. He could not hear a word of Milnes's speech but, after reading it in the newspaper, wrote in his notebook that he did not see how he could have answered it better. He spoke "especially as the representative of the literature of America," and was happy that American authors had "returned something back of the great debt" owed to English authors. A reference to the recent strain on English-American relations prepared the audience to respond with great applause when he laid claim to Brown for America, because Brown had first entered business in America and had kept up various connections such as would promote good relations between the two countries.[7]

With his consular term all but over, Hawthorne moved his family from Southport in July. He had noted on May 10 that he regretted spending so many months "on these barren sands, when almost every other square yard of England contains something that would have been historically or poetically interesting." To search out some of those historic and poetic regions, he moved his family first to Manchester, where he undertook a systematic and leisurely study of the paintings and statues in the Arts Exhibition. He soon found the exhibition "fast becoming a bore," and on September 8 moved his family to Leamington. He had begun to weary of England; and the time he must remain in the country before finally getting free of the consulate would be trying on his patience. There was time enough, it turned out, for him to review and assess his career as consul.

He had met the responsibilities of his office and had gone far beyond those responsibilities in caring for individual Americans. The pathetic end of Captain Auld might be reckoned simply an episode in the chronicle of maritime life. In other instances, however, agents of evil were easy to identify, and Hawthorne could not rest in the simple role of closing out the affairs of the victims and extending sympathy to the bereaved. Men came to him often from American ships to complain of abuse or to report crimes, including murder. He at first lumped together "brutal shipmasters, drunken sailors, vagrant Yankees, mad people, sick people, and dead people" as responsible for the annoyances besetting him in the consulate. But as evidence accumulated, he saw that the ailments of the merchant marine—and hence the problems weighing heaviest on the consul—were not simple. His thinking on discipline at sea no doubt was influenced by the American sea captains he knew in Mrs. Blodgett's dining-room and smoking-room, who convinced him of their honesty and, for most of them, their earnest wish to reduce the abuses on their ships. At the consular office he did not generally see their best sides, but here he realized that "these men are alive, and talk of real matters, and matters which they know." Though not blameless, the masters were largely helpless, given the system and the caliber of men and officers under their command. By the time Hawthorne had reached this view, he realized that he was helpless to bring about any real improvement, though, as he declared in the essay "Consular Experiences," he "did the utmost that lay" in his power.

This essay, written several years after Hawthorne left the consulate, contains information and opinions he had only after his full term as consul. He had concluded that the base of the difficulty with the merchant marine, Hawthorne wrote in "Consular Experiences," was in the quality of the seamen. Only a small proportion of them were American. They were "the off-scourings and refuse of all the sea-ports of the world, such stuff as piracy is made of, together with a considerable intermixture of returning emigrants, and a sprinkling of absolutely kidnapped American citizens." Because there was a general shortage of hands, many crews included men who were not prepared to do the work expected, and consequently were likely to be abused by all regular seamen. In addition, Hawthorne observed that the mates were little if at all above the caliber of the seamen. He occasionally interceded for one of the mates, but he saw that the seamen were the ones most needing his help, and he spared no effort to bring them relief. He noted in "Consular Experiences" that the captains disliked any interference, and that they did not believe this consul—"a landsman, a bookman, and, as people said of him, a fanciful recluse"—could understand the difficulties they faced on board ship. But they did not appreciate "just that one little grain of hard New England sense, oddly thrown in among the flimsier composition of the Consul's character." More than one of them had occasion, nevertheless, to accept his interference.

In one area of the captain's relations to his crew, a specific regulation existed, and Hawthorne acted on it often: If a crewman was left in a foreign port against his wishes, the captain was subject to a fine of $500 and imprisonment up to six months; and if a crewman was dismissed in a foreign port because of sickness or the sale of the ship, he was due three months' pay, which the consul might be obliged to collect for him. Since American ships entering the harbor must deposit their papers with the consul, he could forward the papers to the secretary of state with a report of any infraction. Some of Hawthorne's requests to ship-masters were intentionally abrupt; some reflected moral indignation.[8] When he learned of seamen being required to take part of their discharge pay in clothing, he made his objection clear and reminded the captains that no discharge was legal without his approval. He was no less firm in demanding medical attention for crewmen. In one instance, when a seaman complained of not receiving the medical care he needed on his ship and the consul's request was ignored, he sent the seaman to the hospital, to stay at the ship's expense until other provisions were made. In another instance, he told a ship captain that if his request regarding the complaint of a seaman were not complied with, he would consider the seaman illegally forced on shore in a foreign port and leave the captain "to the action of the Governor."

Hawthorne could take satisfaction in his success in such instances as these; but there was little he could do to relieve the serious abuses or to bring to justice those accused of criminal acts. The Treaty of Washington, August 9, 1842, which governed the relations between England and the United States in the handling of criminal cases in the merchant marine, was far from adequate. It took account of no crime less than murder, assault with the intent to commit murder, or robbery; it provided no means for detaining witnesses or for arresting one accused while a warrant was secured for his arrest. In addition, the consul had to persuade a ship-master, who was normally reluctant, to transport the prisoner to America, and had to persuade witnesses to appear for the trial. In the case of Henry Norris Johnson, charged with stabbing a shipmate on July 10, 1855, aboard the *Cultivator*, Hawthorne followed out an elaborate skein of procedures which required more than six months. Finally, on January 18, 1856, the consul saw Johnson and a witness sail for America. The exasperating difficulties notwithstanding, Hawthorne sent other prisoners to the United States for trial. Not one to be easily defeated, he once asked the Liverpool police to prevent the escape of five accused of murder, one of whom was later sent to America for trial. In the case of a seaman who had died at sea after being beaten by two mates, he got the assurance that local authorities would not object, and hired officers to capture and hold the mates until authorization for their arrest could be secured.

By the midpoint in his four-year term, Hawthorne had concluded that drastic reform in the merchant marine was needed; and he intended to use his pen for that purpose, but he wrote nothing for print, finally, except the few pages in the essay "Consular Experiences," in which he says he "once thought of writing a pamphlet on the subject." Although he would not have admitted that he had "the itch of reform in him," he advocated in the highest offices of his country specific proposals for improvement. Moreover, he stretched the authority he had to provide what immediate relief he could. His efforts during his last months in office may have been encouraged by English protests. (He remarked that "nobody is so humane as John Bull, when his benevolent propensities are to be gratified by finding fault with his neighbor.") In his report on a case of great cruelty, he wrote the secretary of state that he had previously suggested a commission to study the matter and propose reforms. He wrote also to his friend

Charles Sumner, thinking he might bring conditions in the merchant marine to the attention of the United States Senate. Having been "thrust by Providence (and Pierce) into this consulate," he ought to try to do some good before leaving it. He told Sumner of "a free white citizen, a farmer of South Carolina, who had been absolutely kidnapped . . . , sent off to Liverpool as a seaman, and so abused by the captain and officers, during the voyage," that he died soon after the ship reached port; he told also of three instances brought before him in which sailors had been shot dead by their officers. After summarizing the system and the steps he thought should be taken, he continued, "If you will let slavery alone, for a little while, and attend to this business (where much good may, and no harm can possibly, be done) I think you will be doing our country a vast service." For a specific proposal, the "shipping-masters should be annihilated at once;—no slave-drivers are so wicked as they, and there is nothing in slavery so bad as the system with which they are connected."[9] Sumner took no notice of his letter.

Under a provocation that was in a measure personal, Hawthorne wrote on June 17, 1857, to General Cass, the secretary of state, giving the fullest statement he wrote anywhere on maritime reform, along with the firmest explanation and defense of his own efforts. The English newspapers had printed a letter from General Cass to Lord Napier, British minister to the United States, saying that existing laws were sufficient for the protection of the seamen—and implying that any abuses that might occur were due to laxness on the part of the consul. Hawthorne was writing in some detail, he remarked, since he had "bestowed much thought" on the matter and had "become practically acquainted." Since the first of the year, he might have said, the matter had been drawn to his attention almost daily. The Liverpool philanthropists, he wrote Ticknor, would like to have him "run a-muck with them against American ship-masters" and censured him for taking his own view of his duty, rather than becoming simply an agent for carrying out their programs. They would hardly succeed in crowding him off the track, though it was not to be denied that there was "nothing in this world so much like hell as the interior of an American ship." He wrote Bridge that there was nothing in slavery so bad as many things occurring on board American merchant ships. He forwarded to the secretary of state, with urgent comment of his own, a report by the Liverpool Society for the Relief of Foreigners and resolutions adopted at a meeting of American ship-masters. (On January 30 he had presided and made a speech at one such meeting.) "Something must be done, as our National character & commerce are suffering great damage." Again he recommended appointment of a commission. The "pernicious advance system" must be abolished; an international agreement must be reached for reclaiming deserters; British magistrates must be given jurisdiction in all cases below those covered by the Treaty of 1842, with the provision that the accused would have the right to trial by jury of his countrymen. Later he forwarded a report of the American Chamber of Commerce in Liverpool endorsing the resolutions of the American ship-masters; in a dispatch of May 8 he again urged upon Secretary Cass the main proposals he had made earlier.[10]

Thus Hawthorne was in no mood to read in the newspapers Secretary Cass's assertion that the existing laws were adequate. In "Consular Experiences" he wrote later that Cass had replied to Lord Napier "with perfectly astounding ignorance of the subject." He sent Ticknor a copy of a dispatch of his to Cass, "to be set afloat in the American papers," in order to enlighten the public and to show that he had been "zealous and faithful" in office. In this long dispatch, number 90, written in his own hand and dated June 17, he offered the secretary of state a full lesson. He believed that no one—owner, officer, or seaman—thought laws adequate under present conditions when not one crewman in ten was native-born or naturalized, and when most crews contained two antagonistic classes, the professional seamen and others who, of their own accord or induced by shipping-masters, were committed to work they were not qualified to do. After repeating what he had written in earlier dispatches about the difficulties of bringing criminals to trial, he noted the irony that, as he saw the problem, the first step toward restoring discipline and justice aboard merchant ships would be to restore flogging. The removal of this means of "judicious punishment" and the consequent substitution of ad hoc brutality administered by the mates was to be credited to the "wasted or destructive energy of philanthropists." So he wrote Secretary Cass and, in similar phrasing, Elizabeth Peabody. In summary, he thought the condition of the merchant marine a national emergency that could be relieved only by a program to create a class of American seamen. A statesman, knowing the condition, could ignore it only at his peril. Treaty arrangements to have lesser offenders tried in the English courts and to provide for the apprehension of deserting crewmen abroad would relieve part of the difficulty. But the fundamental need was to set up a program for recruiting, training, and regulating merchant seamen.

Turning finally to the bearing the secretary's letter to Lord Napier had upon "his own official character," Hawthorne declared that if he had possessed the power to punish the offenders and had not done so, his punishment should be severe. But, he continued, "If I am innocent—if I have done my utmost, as an executive officer, under a defective law, to the defects of which I have repeatedly called the attention of my superiors— then, unquestionably, the Secretary has wronged me by a suggestion pointing so directly at myself." The harm would be the greater because his leaving the consulate under this stigma would be construed as an admission of guilt. "Whether it is right that an honorable and conscientious discharge of duty should be rewarded by loss of character, I leave to the wisdom and justice of the Department to decide." A few days later, Hawthorne begged to inform Secretary Cass that he had no such power as a communication from the State Department said he had, and he enclosed documentation from British officials supporting his view. On September 24, three days before the new consul sailed from New York, the secretary sent Hawthorne one communication expressing satisfaction with his discharge of "the laborious and responsible duties" of the office of consul, and another, a reply to his dispatch 90, denying any intention of charging him with delinquency and commending him on "the prudent and efficient manner" in which he had discharged his duties.

Hawthorne had gone abroad consciously an American returning to the home of his ancestors, eager to compare Brother Jonathan to John Bull as to nature, habits, thoughts, present condition, and prospects. His *English Notebooks* contain the fullest and most dependable record of his running comparison of climate, mountains, parks, paths, vegetables, and fruits; lawyers, tailors, readers and writers of literature; houses, hotels, beds, ships, trains, gravestones; foods, drinks, manners; dinners and speeches. He found no fruits so flavorful as in America, no gingerbread so good; but in total his comparisons leave the two countries in something close to a balance. America he saw as good for the young; England, being delightfully sluggish, good for the older man and for the man of individuality and refinement. He could think of no life as admirable as that on English country estates; but those estates reminded him of the classes, the poverty, the slums, and the workhouses that had no parallels in America. The English had great loyalty, more awareness of their nation than was possible in America. He pronounced American merchants superior in honesty, Americans ten times as good readers as the English. In letters to America, he was inclined to overstatement under immediate provocation; in *Our Old Home* he synthesized impressions and judgments formed almost ten years earlier, and kept in mind his readers on both sides of the Atlantic. More than once he remarked while in England that his notes would make a good book, but were too full and frank to be published. He was thinking of English readers. When his English friends read *Our Old Home*, especially when they read the *English Notebooks* after his death, some of them thought his portraits, of individuals and of the nation, were unduly severe. Living abroad made him patriotic, as he said more than once, and most patriotic in the period of strained relations between England and America during the Crimean War. "Success makes an Englishman intolerable," he noted on October 6, 1854. "There is an account to settle between us and them for the contemptuous jealousy with which (since it has ceased to be unmitigated contempt) they regard us." No matter how many individual Americans an Englishman knew and liked, he would still feel hatred for the nation; an American would have reciprocal feelings. On May 24, 1856, Hawthorne introduced into his notebook Charles Watson, a merchant whom he met at Bennoch's dinner in Manchester, the only Englishman he had ever met "who fairly acknowledged that the English do cherish doubt, jealousy, suspicion, in short, an unfriendly feeling, towards the Americans." All Americans were aware of this feeling, but "no Englishman—except this sole Mr. Watson—" would confess it.

When writing his American friends, Hawthorne was often severe on his own country. It sickened him to think of the political bickering in America; he was ashamed of his native country; he might not return to America, but settle in Italy or elsewhere—were it not for the children, he usually added. He might say he felt rootless and without a home, but, if the Wayside entered the statement, it appeared somewhat less than satisfactory; if America was included, it would likely appear to be, as he once phrased it, a country he loved but did not like.

One subject of comparison, women, Hawthorne returned to again and again in his notebooks and dealt with at length in *Our Old Home*. Once when he met Jenny Lind, he objected to her speaking of American women as fragile and unhealthy because of improper exercising and eating; and it may be that his portrayal of English women in *Our Old Home* was intended in part as a rejoinder to such characterizations of American women. In the essay "Leamington Spa," he speaks first of "the comely, rather than pretty, English girls, with their deep, healthy bloom, which an American taste is apt to deem fitter for a milkmaid than for a lady," and proceeds to describe the English dowager such as he saw in many specimens on the Parade at Leamington:

. . . . it strikes me that an English lady of fifty is apt to become a creature less refined and delicate, so far as her physique goes, than anything that we Western people class under the name of woman. She has an awful ponderosity of frame, not pulpy, like the looser development of our few fat women, but massive with solid beef and streaky tallow; so that (though struggling manfully against the idea) you inevitably think of her as made up of steaks and sirloins. When she walks, her advance is elephantine. When she sits down, it is on a great round space of her Maker's footstool where she looks as if nothing could ever move her. She imposes awe and respect by the muchness of her personality, to such a degree that you probably credit her with far greater moral and intellectual force than she can fairly claim.

You can meet this figure in the street, and live, and even smile at the recollection. But conceive of her in a ball-room, with the bare, brawny arms that she invariably displays there, and all the other corresponding development, such as is beautiful in the maiden blossom, but a spectacle to howl at in such an overblown cabbage-rose as this.

This portrait leads the author to wonder "whether a middle-aged husband ought to be considered as legally married to all the accretions that have overgrown the slenderness of his bride." It was not easy for Henry Bright and Hawthorne's other English readers to realize that in this passage and others like it he was following his customary practice in adapting experience and observations to literary purposes.

Hawthorne wrote in his notebook for June 7, 1857, following a tour that included Boston, the origin of John Cotton and other early American Puritans: "Thus ended our tour; in which we had seen but a little bit of little England, yet rich with variety and interest. What a wonderful land! It is our forefathers' land; our land; for I will not give up such a precious inheritance." The author of the essay "Pilgrimage to Old Boston" in *Our Old Home* records the same tour and remarks on the "home-feeling and sense of kindred" he derived from the "hereditary connection" between old Boston and new Boston. He tells how, upon leaving old Boston, he fancied that the tower of St. Botolph's was bidding him farewell, "as it did Mr. Cotton, two or three hundred years ago."

The consulate was slow to release Hawthorne. Because the chief clerk, Henry Wilding, was sick the first week in August and again at the middle of September, Hawthorne did harder and steadier work at his desk than ever before—at a time when he had expected to be in Italy. At Leamington he was too far away for the commuting he had done from Manchester. In June President Buchanan had offered the post to J. W. Penney, who declined it; on August 18 he appointed Beverley Tucker, who did not sail from New York until September 27. When Hawthorne was relieved on October 12, he had put in almost a month doing the work of both the consul and the chief clerk. On November 10 he moved his family to 24 Great Russell Street in London, but the forced and indefinite waiting for his consular accounts to be closed left him in no mood to enjoy the city. Finally, on December 31, the accounts were closed, and on January 5 the Hawthorne entourage embarked at Folkestone for Boulogne.

Hawthorne had ceased to be an author and had spent nearly five years in a second career. Soon after entering the consulate, he had learned his duties and was prepared to give time and effort to insure an efficient administration. He brought to the office uncommon initiative, practical understanding, and independence of thought. He avoided taking matters directly to the president, but he sent analyses and suggestions to the secretary of state and to Senator Charles Sumner that were written with a frankness and an insistence not usual among foreign service officers. The tedious delay before his final release tended to dampen any feelings of satisfaction, and there was little evidence that he had accomplished much toward resolving the major difficulties. The essays in *Our Old Home* leave no doubt, however, that he took pride in looking back on his term at Liverpool. He had assisted scores of individuals in need; he had maintained his personal integrity throughout; and he had spoken forcefully in demands for justice and humanity, and for long-range programs to improve the maritime service. His achievements were far beyond what might have been expected of an officer appointed for political service, and especially an officer known primarily as a recluse who was most at home in the fairyland of his allegories and romances.

27

Art and Artists in Italy

The four months Hawthorne was kept in England for the closing of his consular accounts had proved anticlimactic and tedious. Snow fell during the train ride to Folkestone, and the weather kept him inside the station while waiting two hours for the Channel craft. He nevertheless lost none of his fondness for his ancestral home; and he encountered such miserable weather during the next several weeks that he longed for England, even in winter. The group that crossed the Channel on January 5, 1858, included Ada Shepard, who had come from America in the autumn to be companion and tutor for the children and to strengthen her own knowledge of languages. She had graduated from Antioch College, where the president was Horace Mann, and arrangements had been made through Mary Mann. She would receive no salary, but would have all her expenses paid. Hawthorne had shipped books and other belongings to America, but there remained a dozen trunks and half a dozen carpetbags he must look after at every move during the ensuing months.

France had scarcely entered Hawthorne's travel plans, and he declared he disliked the country even before touching French soil. At Boulogne the weather had grown colder, "in sunny France," in the ironic phrasing of his notebook, as the night set in "wickedly bleak and dreary."[1] He could not remember a more disagreeable short journey than the train ride to Amiens, where the party spent the night and the next day visited the cathedral. At five on the afternoon of January 6 they reached Paris and put

up at the Hôtel du Louvre. Hawthorne's view of France was no doubt
darkened by a nosebleed the first two days and a cold he did not shake off
until March. He had grown so English, he wrote Ticknor, that he had an
antipathy for everything French. After a week in Paris, he had the "dreary
and desperate feeling" which he said often came upon him when the sights
lasted longer than his capacity for viewing them, and he was glad to leave.
Continuing his habit of drawing international comparisons, he thought the
food "very delicate, and a vast change from the simple English system,"
but he was not sure English cookery was "not better for men's moral and
spiritual nature" than French cookery. He called on the United States
minister, and later the consul to have his passport put in order, and found
it "not half so pleasant to pay a consular fee as it used to be to receive it."

Taking the train southward on January 12, the Hawthornes spent the
night at Lyons, and the next three days at Marseilles. Their party had
been increased in Paris by the American astronomer Maria Mitchell
(1818–89), discoverer of a new comet in 1847 and professor at Vassar
College after 1865, who had asked to travel to Rome in their company.
After boarding the steamer *Calabrese* on January 17, they had one-day calls
at Genoa and Leghorn, and landed on January 20 at Civitavecchia (written
as two words by Hawthorne). The Cathedral of San Lorenzo at Genoa
gave Hawthorne his first glimpse of Italian church architecture and art. In
England he had tried to imagine the cathedrals as they were before Crom-
well's time, but he had never imagined anything approaching San
Lorenzo. Yet the cathedral was nothing in comparison with a church he
visited, which he noted had been built by "a pirate, in expiation of his sins,
and out of the profit of his rapine." In despair of describing it, he wrote
out a comparison that later appeared with but slight change in Chapter 38
of *The Marble Faun*. The journey from the port to Rome was by a four-
horse carriage which lumbered along under its "mountain of luggage."
Arriving at the Roman gate in a cold rain slightly before midnight,
Hawthorne "perpetrated unheard-of briberies on the custom-house
officers" and took lodging at Spillman's Hotel. After searching two or
three days he took a flat of ten rooms in the Palazzo Larazani, on the Via
Porta Pinciana.

Suffering from "a feverish influenza," he sat by the fireside much of the
first two weeks, with his thickest greatcoat over more clothes than he had
ever worn before. On the walks he sometimes took in the middle of the
day, he was warm only once, even in the sunshine. When he resumed his
notebook, he said he tried in vain "to get down upon paper the dreariness,

the ugliness, shabbiness, unhomelikeness of a Roman street." He had been in Rome nearly two months before writing a letter, except for one to his banker. If his pen would serve him as it had done of yore, he wrote Francis Bennoch, he would avenge himself by describing "this cold, rainy, filthy, stinking, rotten, rascally city. . . . I hate it worse than any other place in the whole world; and yet everybody assures me that I shall end with thinking it most delightful. We shall see." His wife, he noted, had "already made acquaintance with almost every temple and church in Rome."[2] He did see himself take delight in Rome; in time he took up his literary pen again; and before leaving Italy a year and a half later, he had written a draft of an Italian romance.

Early in February he was well enough to begin sightseeing and keeping his notebook. Often he elaborated on characters, incidents, places, or objects with such finish that they could be transferred to *The Marble Faun* with but slight revision. Before going to Italy, the whole family had read Macaulay, Gibbon, and Grote; Sophia was prepared to encourage and instruct in the study of ancient and recent art. A romancer impelled to explore the shadows of human nature and human history, and feeling the lack in his own country of suitable historical artifacts, Hawthorne found in Rome the tokens of man's glories interwoven with his guilt and suffering, dating back near the origin of recorded history. Every paving-stone, every fragment from a crumbled mosaic bore a history that could be discovered and interpreted through the play of his creative imagination. Thus he experienced a cumulative fascination in walking the streets of Rome, in returning many times to St. Peter's, the Coliseum, the Pantheon, and scores of other historical sites.

Occasionally he drew a comparison between Italy and America, but the span of Italian history—Etruscan, Roman, and Christian—was so great as to make comparisons inappropriate. In England his interest had been not in Americans, except for old friends who came his way, but in his new English acquaintances. In Italy he had no close associates among the Italians, but was sought out by Americans who could give him the guidance and instruction his English friends had furnished. He and his family moved in a circle of authors and artists he valued both professionally and personally. Among the authors were Fredrika Bremer and William Cullen Bryant, both of whom had called at the red house in the Berkshires, and later Robert and Elizabeth Barrett Browning. Most prominent of the artists was William Wetmore Story, whom he had known in Boston. Hawthorne called Story "the most variously accomplished and brilliant person, the fullest of social life and fire" he had ever seen; but he detected in Story "a pain and care, bred, it may be, out of the very richness of his gifts and abundance of his prosperity." He watched Story at work on the statue of Cleopatra, which he thought "a work of genuine thought and energy" and later introduced into *The Marble Faun*. On the same street as Story's apartments in the Barberini Palace was the studio of Cephas Giovanni Thompson, who had improved vastly, Hawthorne said, since painting his portrait in Boston in 1850. There was no other painter among the Americans in Rome "so earnest, faithful, and religious in his worship of art."[3]

Two young American women sculptors interested Hawthorne for the freedom and apparent safety in which they lived alone in Italy, practicing the art to which they were devoted. They became models for Hilda in *The Marble Faun:* Harriet Goodhue Hosmer (1830–1908), whose statue of Zenobia Hawthorne called "a high, heroic ode," and Maria Louisa Lander (1826–1923), a native of Salem, who for several months in 1858 was more intimately received into the Hawthorne family than anyone else in Italy. She called on January 25, two days after the Hawthornes had moved from the hotel to Porta Pinciana; on February 6, Hawthorne and his wife visited her studio, in the rooms formerly occupied by the Italian sculptor Antonio Canova (1757–1822); and on February 15 he began sittings in her studio, she having done him "the honor to request" him to sit for his bust. She seemed to have genuine talent, he wrote in his notebook that day. During the sitting, he talked a good deal, taking "a similar freedom with her moral likeness to that which she was taking" with his physical likeness. She lived "in almost perfect independence," going about the streets without fear, day and night, "with no household ties, no rules or law but that within her; yet acting with quietness and simplicity, and keeping, after all, within a homely line of right." The fascination Rome exercised on her and other artists was due, he thought, to "the peculiar mode of life, and its freedom from the enthralments of society, more than the artistic advantages" the city offered. Her dress, "a sort of pea-jacket, buttoned across her breast, and a little foraging-cap, just covering the top of her head," appears along with others of her characteristics in the character Hilda.

Hawthorne went for about twenty sittings, accompanied by his wife a few times. On March 31 Miss Lander declared the clay model finished, and a week later she "put the final touches" on it. She had dined with the Hawthornes at least three times, Hawthorne's pocket diary records, had called half a dozen evenings, and several times had accompanied them on excursions about the city. In the week before she departed for America, she called on them; they visited her studio; she spent an evening with them; Hawthorne paid her 20 scudi on the bust; she called one evening, he noted, after all but him had gone to bed, probably to ask for assistance in securing commissions for work during her visit to America, for the next day he wrote Ticknor in Boston to that purpose; and on April 15, she came for dinner, paying her last visit before departing. On May 17 Hawthorne deposited with his banker 100 scudi to pay the workmen as cutting of the stone progressed. He could hardly have made his letter to Ticknor a stronger personal and professional endorsement: Even his wife was delighted with the bust. Miss Bremer thought it "the finest modelled bust she ever saw." It had received the highest praise from all the sculptors in Rome, including the English sculptor Gibson. He hoped Ticknor and Fields would do what they could to bring her name favorably before the public. "She is a very nice person, and I like her exceedingly."

 Miss Lander appeared in Hawthorne's correspondence only once more, it seems, and in a far different light. He wrote from England on February 11, 1860, asking James T. Fields, then in Rome, to learn the amount still due on the bust and pay it for him, and added, "For reasons unnecessary to mention, I cannot personally communicate with the lady herself; but I should greatly regret to remain in her debt. . . . The bust, my friends tell me, is not worth sixpence; but she did her best with it."[4] Hawthorne's pocket diary for 1858[5] offers some clues to the break between Miss Lander and the Hawthornes. On October 17, 1858, the day after the Hawthornes arrived in Rome from their summer in Florence, he wrote in his diary, "Mr. Thompson called before dinner, and spoke of Miss Lander. What a pity!" Four days later he and his wife went to see his bust. His diary reads for November 9, "In the evening, Miss Lander and her sister (just from America) called, and were not admitted"; the next day, "Miss Lander sent in a card but was not seen"; three days later, "Wrote note to Miss Lander, and took it to the Bank"; on December 5, "A note from Miss Lander in the evening. Wrote an answer by bearer." Meanwhile letters brought by Miss Lander from America were received, some of them three days, others eight days after her first call. In a letter to her sister Elizabeth, Sophia mentioned Miss Lander in a way to indicate that her intimacy in the Hawthorne family was at an end. She said she thought all the letters brought by Miss Lander were now received, having "dropped out of her garments from time to time."[6] The information from Thompson that caused Hawthorne to exclaim "What a pity!" no doubt was about some indiscretion of hers that had made her socially unacceptable to members of the art colony.[7] In editing the Italian notebooks for publication in 1871, Sophia omitted Miss Lander's name entirely and left no trace of her association with the family except for Hawthorne's sitting for an unnamed sculptor.

Among the sculptors Hawthorne knew in Rome was Joseph Mozier (1812–70), who had left a business career in New York and in 1845 had joined the art colony in Rome. Hawthorne saw little merit in Mozier's work; and he set down a gossipy report of Mozier's on Margaret Fuller with the same implications of doubt he registered in recording apparently irresponsible comments by Mozier on C. G. Thompson.[8]

After going to Europe in August, 1846, to furnish travel letters for the *New York Tribune* and settling in Rome in the spring of the next year, Miss Fuller met Giovanni Ossoli and had a child by him in September, 1848; their marriage was announced when the child was a year old. They supported Mazzini in the unsuccessful Roman Revolution and on a voyage to America were lost when their ship went aground off Fire Island, New York, July 19, 1850. Mozier told Hawthorne that Ossoli's family, though technically noble, had "no rank whatever," and that Ossoli, lacking education and manners, but handsome, had "something to do with the care of" Margaret's apartments. Since Sophia normally read her husband's notebooks, his entry on this report can be read as another chapter in the debate they had carried on about Margaret Fuller since their courtship. As Margaret became more dedicated to the cause of women's rights, both of them grew impatient with her. After reading *Woman in the Nineteenth Century* in 1845, Sophia wrote her mother that the book left a disagreeable impression, and that even before she was married, she never felt the slightest interest in the movement for women's rights. A letter Mary Mann wrote Sophia after Margaret Fuller's death seems to be echoed in Hawthorne's notebook entry. She had learned from Mrs. Fuller and others that Margaret expected Ossoli to be out of place with her in America. Mary said she was not surprised that, even with her "vaulting ambition," Margaret's craving for affection was so great that she married "the first man who showed devoted love to her even if he were not particularly intellectual."[9] The solution to the riddle of Margaret's "total collapse . . . , morally and intellectually," Hawthorne wrote in his notebook, lay in her attempt to adorn her "strong and coarse nature" with "a mosaic of admirable qualities." But there remained "something within her that she could not possibly come at, to recreate and refine it; and, by and by, this rude old potency bestirred itself, and undid all her labor in the twinkling of an eye. On the whole, I do not know but I like her the better for it;—the better, because she proved herself a very woman, after all, and fell as the weakest of her sisters might." This analysis of Margaret Fuller has the frankness to be expected in Hawthorne's working out of the riddle she presented, written for only his wife and him to see, and with apparent overstatement at points to anticipate objections she might raise. He was subjecting Margaret to the kind of scrutiny he gave his fictional characters. The intellectual arrogance that others found in her was the pride he thought closest to the unpardonable sin. "There never was such a tragedy as her whole story." He could sympathize, but he could see in her death off Fire Island only the final step in the working out of inevitable consequences.[10]

Plans had been laid as early as March to spend the summer in Florence; and on May 23, the day before departing, Hawthorne had breakfast with the Storys, along with William Cullen Bryant and Harriet Hosmer. He noted that later he took Una for "a farewell walk in the Pincian Gardens to see the sunset." When they had walked in familiar streets of the city and along the Tiber, and had heard the great bell of St. Peter's, "Una spoke with somewhat alarming fervor of her love for Rome and regret at leaving it." Hawthorne acknowledged in his notebook the next day that he had a strange affection for the city and found it "very singular, the sad embrace with which Rome takes possession of the soul." A *vetturino* named Gaetano was engaged to drive the family to Florence, and the carriage "drove off under a perfect shower of anathemas." The female servant, Lalla, had been given three weeks' notice, but appeared, with her mother, to demand further pay; there also was a disagreement with the two men who loaded the baggage on the *vettura;* finally, Hawthorne continued in his notebook, they were "infested with beggars," and he was in no mood for almsgiving. When he thought someone proposed to take advantage of him, it was his habit to insist that the other party abide by the terms of the bargain, even if it meant a Lalla and her mother exploding "into a livid rage" and filling the streets with curses. Hawthorne wrote in his notebook every day of the journey, aware that delay would sacrifice freshness and exactness. The beauty of one scene left him miserable because he did not "know how to put it into words." He wrote about the people at the inns, along the road, and in the streets of the villages and towns. The beggars, displaying sundry deformities and infirmities, were a phenomenon he could neither understand nor get out of his mind; they belonged to the Old World and reminded him of their absence in America. They prompted him also to

self-analysis. Once he could not help giving something to a boy who held
out his hat with impudent certainty of being paid; it gave him a twinge to
recall that at the same time he had refused a man who looked sickly and
miserable. "But where everybody begs," he noted, "everybody, as a general rule, must be denied; and, besides, they act their misery so well, that
you are never sure of the genuine article." [11]

The week's journey had the novelty and mild adventure that pleased
Hawthorne in his travels. Though he now was cumbered by voluminous
luggage and several companions, the arrangements for the *vetturino* to furnish transportation, lodging, and meals relieved him of much responsibility. He took note of historical sites, such as the battlefield where Han-
nibal defeated the Roman army. At Assisi and Perugia there were art
collections to be seen, and at Arezzo he searched out Petrarch's birthplace;
and, prompted by the well which appears in one of Boccaccio's tales, he
wondered whether strangers would gaze at his "own town-pump in old
Salem" with such interest as he felt in Boccaccio's well. Of course they
would not, he thought. Still, although the Salem pump had long been
only an ordinary one, when he "grasped the handle, a rill gushed forth
that meandered as far as England, as far as India, besides tasting pleasantly in every town and village of our own country." He concluded, "I
like to think of this, so long after I did it, and so far from home, and not
without hope of some kindly local remembrance on this score." [12]

Upon arriving in Florence the last day of May, Hawthorne noted that
the journey had been "one of the brightest and most uncareful interludes"
in his life; the ensuing four and a half months before his return to Rome
extended the pleasant, largely undisturbed interlude into the most satisfying of his eighteen months in Italy. All members of the family were in
good health, and they found a comfortable social life, chiefly with the
Robert Browning and the Hiram Powers families in Florence and the
Story family in Siena. The Uffizi Gallery and the Pitti Palace, the
Duomo, and the various churches furnished ample works of art for study,
and yet spared Hawthorne something of the desperate feeling he had in
the presence of the artistic and historical abundance at Rome.

The American sculptor Hiram Powers had tentatively engaged living
quarters for the Hawthornes in the Casa del Bello, across the street from
his own residence and studio. The second floor would have sufficed, but
Hawthorne chose the first, which had a terrace and a garden, saying that
he wanted to make his family comfortable in their wandering life, "for just
this summer," and wanted to be comfortable himself, "after that

uncongenial life of the consulate" and before going back to his "own hard and dusty New England." His was the pleasantest of the rooms, all of which opened on a small inner court. He could, if he liked, "overflow into the summer-house or an arbor, and sit there dreaming of a story." His outlook remained pleasant. Five days after arriving in Florence, he had concluded that there could not "be a place in the world where life is more delicious for its own sake than in Florence." He was convinced that "the art of man has never contrived any other beauty and glory at all to be compared to" the cathedral. The windows in the dome prompted him to declare it "a pity anybody should die without seeing an antique painted window, with the bright Italian sunshine glowing through it." In a mood reminiscent of his early days at the Old Manse, he could say that the palaces on the banks of the Arno were "just as perfect in the tide beneath as in the air above,—a city of dream and shadow so close to the actual," and could add, "God has a meaning, no doubt, in putting this spiritual symbol continually beside us." [13]

On August 1 the Hawthornes moved for two months to the Villa Montauto, located on the hill Bellosguardo, a mile outside the Roman gate. The heat in the city had grown oppressive, and malaria was a threat; but living in the villa was especially attractive for the sense of adventure it would furnish. The house was "big enough to quarter a regiment," he wrote James T. Fields, with everyone, including each of the servants, having "a separate suite of apartments," and with "vast wildernesses of upper rooms" into which "exploring expeditions" had not yet been sent, and with also a "moss-grown tower, haunted by owls and by the ghost of a monk." He meant to take the villa "away bodily and clap it into" the romance which was in his head ready to be written out. In the villa were many reminders of history and legend. In the oratory adjoining Una's room was a life-size skull, fit reminder of the ambient ghostliness. Members of the family often climbed the shaky stairway to the tower, where they scanned the brown-dry terrain of the Arno Valley and picked out Galileo's tower, the convent of Monte Olivetto, and the Duomo; in the evening they watched the stars and the brilliant comet, and they heard the bells of Florence. On one of his last evenings in the villa, Hawthorne was loathe to descend from the tower "into the lower world," knowing that he would "never again look heavenward from an old tower top in such a soft calm evening." He had found the summer "a peaceful and not uncheerful one," and all members of the family would keep it in pleasant retrospect. [14]

On every hand in Rome and Florence were points where history and art intersected and fused. Hawthorne more than once noted that his wife and Ada Shepard and the children—including Rose, seven years old—were busy sketching. He set out dutifully to advance the study of art he had barely begun in England.[15] In the notes he wrote during his wife's absence in Portugal, he had stressed his lack of comprehension—having in mind that she would read his notebooks upon her return. He could say only that he was beginning to prefer some pictures to others, and thought that encouraging. At the British Museum one day, he had a sense of frustration as he identified the world of art with the burden of the past as he had viewed it in *The House of the Seven Gables*. He could wish that "the Elgin marbles and the frieze of the Parthenon were all burnt into lime. . . . We have not time, in our earthly existence, to appreciate what is warm with life, and immediately around us; yet we heap up all these old shells, out of which human life has long emerged." A few days later, however, he was at the National Gallery and fancied in himself "an increasing taste for pictures." After his wife had returned and he could rely on her as guide and tutor, he continued his self-examination, noting once that his comprehension had not yet reached the height of the old masters. His most intensive and, as he wrote more than once in his notebook, exhausting period of study was at the Manchester Arts Exhibition in the summer of 1857. At a London gallery where there were three full rooms of paintings, he gave them, on an average, one minute each. How absurd it would be to read poems at such a rate. "And a picture is a poem, only requiring the greater study to be felt and comprehended." He found some preliminary drawings by Raphael and Michelangelo better for his purpose than their finished pictures: "It is like looking into their brains, and seeing the first conception, before it took shape outwardly." As an artist, he wanted to see how other artists worked.

In Italy, Hawthorne occasionally acknowledged some satisfaction with his study of art, while declaring that he remained for the most part "a sturdy Goth." His notebooks often show him weary of the schooling he had undertaken, or depressed by the presumed obligation to appreciate all the artistic treasures of Italy, or self-conscious because of his wife's greater enthusiasm and understanding. He frequently noted that her receptivity was "unlimited and forever fresh," as his was not; he mentioned the contrast as a rule with self-deprecation and at times with a hint of resentment.[16] Many times he thanked Heaven for his escape when he had an excuse not to accompany her to an exhibit she was eager to see. His usual recourse was to wander about the streets, where his interest never flagged.

Though Hawthorne went to the art galleries to learn, and began by assuming the orthodox view to be correct, he kept his habit of questioning the existing cannons and relying finally on his own judgment. He tried to like the old masters but was never fully successful. He wondered "whether the pictorial art be not a humbug," noting that at times "the minute accuracy of a fly in a Dutch picture of fruit and flowers seems . . . something more reliable than the master-touches of Raphael." After Julian had condemned everything he saw at the Uffizi Gallery, his father wondered "whether we do not bamboozle ourselves in the greater part of the admiration we learn to bestow." At the Pitti Palace he found Andrea del Sarto's pictures "looking so much like first-rate excellence, that you inevitably quarrel with your own taste for not admiring them," and he thought "the splendor of the gilded and frescoed saloons . . . perhaps another bore"; but recalling that he was on one of his last visits to the gallery, he added, "my memory will often tread there as long as I live. What shall we do in America?" Because of his reluctance to accept any view without testing it in his own mind, he was far from passive in the galleries and in the Italian streets. He was accumulating and testing ingredients for *The Marble Faun:* the Roman Carnival, the Faun of Praxiteles, the Beatrice Cenci in legend and in Guido's painting, the interlinking of the artistic and the religious in St. Peter's and elsewhere, William Story's statue of Cleopatra, the artistic theories, speculations, and judgments he encountered in the studios of his friends, the paintings, statues, monuments, buildings, and people that filled his Italian days.[17]

While at Florence he found greater enjoyment in the art galleries than ever before. Much of this progress was due to the tutelage of Hiram Powers, with whom he spent many hours, listening to "the mill-stream of his talk" on artists and particular works, and on techniques and theories. After twenty years in Italy, Powers was a reservoir of information and opinions. He and Hawthorne "pervaded the whole universe" in the topics they discussed: the tones of bells and organs; whether a sculptor could model a blush or the smile of Mona Lisa; "instinct and reason, and whether the brute creation have souls, and, if they have none, how justice is to be done them for their sufferings here"; "other states of being" and the possibility that beings inhabit the earth contemporaneous with us but unknown to us. They explored the arguments about nudity and clothing for statues, tinted and pure white marble in sculpture, the old masters and the moderns, realism in Flemish paintings and symbolic idealization in classical art. With Powers, Hawthorne was probing the topics uppermost in his mind and was gaining the assurance fictional treatment would require.

Powers furnished an object lesson in the effects of prolonged residence abroad; he had "lost his native country without finding another." His long stay in Italy had made him unduly severe in judging America. Hawthorne had observed the same tendency in himself; and he feared that, when he finally returned home, life might have "shifted whatever of reality it had" to the country of temporary residence with the result that he could make himself "a part of one or the other country" only by laying his bones in its soil. Hawthorne felt pity and anxiety for a daughter of Powers, "lest she should never find a home anywhere." She had been born and had lived her nineteen years in Italy, but acknowledged no home but America.[18] Convinced, as always, that he could write best while in touch with his native soil, he had no serious thought of settling outside New England.

At Florence in the summer of 1858, Hawthorne renewed his acquaintance with Robert and Elizabeth Barrett Browning. At their home in Casa Guidi on June 8, Mrs. Browning impressed him as "a pale little woman, scarcely embodied at all." She and her son both seemed to be "of the elfin-breed." He found Browning exceedingly likable, "younger and handsomer" than when they met two years earlier at Milnes's breakfast in London, and he was surprised that Browning's "conversation should be so clear, and so much to the purpose of the moment; since his poetry can seldom proceed far without running into the high grass of latent meanings and obscure allusions." The most interesting topic discussed on this visit, as Hawthorne recorded the next day, was "that disagreeable and now wearisome one of spiritual communications, as regards which Mrs. Browning is a believer and her husband an infidel." The Brownings had attended a session of Daniel Dunglas Home's at which they saw and felt the "unearthly hands" he regularly displayed. "The marvelousness of the fact . . . melted strangely away" before Browning's logic, Hawthorne wrote in his notebook, "while his wife, ever and anon, put in a little gentle word of expostulation."[19]

Before leaving London, Hawthorne had met a firm believer in spiritualism, Dr. James John Garth Wilkinson (1812–99), who had treated the Hawthorne children when they had measles and had entertained the Hawthornes in his home. Wilkinson had seen and felt the "ghostly hands and arms" displayed by Home. Hawthorne had asked in his notebook whether he believed "these wonders," and had answered that of course he

did, for it was not possible to doubt Dr. Wilkinson. But he had added,
"Of course not; for I cannot consent to let Heaven and Earth, this world
and the next, be beaten up together like the white and yolk of an egg.
. . . I would not believe my own sight or touch of the spiritual hands."[20]

After the Brownings had left Florence, their friend Isabella Blagden was
often in the company of the Hawthornes. On August 24 Sophia attended,
with Ada Shepard, a spiritual session at Miss Blagden's and, before going
to bed, wrote out a report of the memorable day—for the first time she
had seen "spiritual manifestations." The six who were present had sat
around a table in a seance of two hours, but the table did not skip, and
there were no raps. Then Ada took a pencil and asked whether there were
any spirits present. First Mary Runnel wrote her name, followed by two
others; "but finally," the report continues, "one wrote 'Mother' and when
asked whose wrote 'Mrs. Hawthorne's.' I had not taken much interest or
notice till then, but I was deeply moved when with the utmost eagerness
and rapidity Ada's hand was seized to write 'My dear child, I am oftener
with you than with any one.' I wanted immediately to be alone with Ada,
so that the blessed spirit might say more to me, and so that I might ask
questions," but she did not care to do so while others were present.[21] In
writing her sister Elizabeth much the same account the next day, she
added that previously she "had kept aloof in mind, because Mr. Hawthorne has such a repugnance to the whole thing."[22] On the same day,
Hawthorne wrote in his diary, "Mamma and the children had communications with spirits through Miss Shepard, a writing medium. Flummery and delusion." In the next few days, Ada Shepard provided written
messages from Sophia's mother, father, two brothers, a sister who died in
infancy, and, among others, the wandering spirit named Mary Runnel.

Hawthorne could not force his mind to take an interest in these manifestations, and he was reluctant to give them the space they fill in his
notebook on September 1. Ada Shepard's integrity was "absolutely in-
dubitable," he said, and she disbelieved herself "the spiritual authenticity"
of her communications. She had written her sister to that effect on August
27. "I cannot help thinking," Hawthorne wrote, "that (Miss Shepard
being unconsciously in a mesmeric state) all the responses are conveyed to
her fingers from my wife's mind; for I discern in them much of her beautiful fancy and many of her preconceived ideas, although thinner and
weaker than at first hand. They are the echoes of her own voice, returning
out of the lovely chambers of her heart, and mistaken by her for the tones
of her mother."[23] Thus it might be that only the mind of the medium was

involved, in a mesmeric trance. In closing this long notebook entry, Hawthorne set down the conclusion to which his "soberest thoughts" tended:

> The whole matter seems to me a sort of dreaming awake, my wife being, in the present instance, the principal dreamer. It resembles a dream, in that the whole material is, from the first, in the dreamer's mind, though concealed at various depths below the surface; the dead appear alive, as they always do in dreams; unexpected combinations occur, as continually in dreams; the mind speaks through the various persons of the dream. . . . Mary Runnel is the only personage who does not come evidently from dreamland; and she, I think, represents that lurking scepticism, that sense of unreality, of which we are often conscious, amid the most vivid phantasmagoria of a dream.[24]

The acceptance of such "soberly attested incredibilities" as had been widespread since Home's visit to Florence prompted Hawthorne to remark that, "rather than receive a message from a dead friend through the organism of a rogue or charlatan," such as he understood Home to be, he would choose to wait till they met. His conclusions had not changed since he warned his fiancée against mesmeric treatments for her headaches. Even when presented facts acceptable to his understanding, he said, his inner soul did not admit them. A plan of creation would not be acceptable in which the integrity of a spirit, a soul, either embodied or disembodied, might be violated.

At six o'clock on the morning of October 1, the Hawthornes and Ada Shepard bade goodbye to their ghostly villa and to Florence, and took the train to Siena, where William Wetmore Story and his family were spending the summer at the Villa Belvedere. While his wife, Ada, and all three children were sketching at the Siena Cathedral, the best Hawthorne could do, he noted, was "try to preserve some memorial of this beautiful edifice in ill-fitting words that never hit the mark." He called the cathedral "a religion in itself." At the Institute of Fine Arts, he found Sodoma's fresco of Christ bound to the pillar "a thing to stand and weep at." This fresco appears in *The Marble Faun*. From his hotel window he watched "the specimens of human life" in the piazza below; and, after noticing twice that women at confession in the cathedral were "long about it," he thought how tedious it must be, listening to the "minute and commonplace iniquities of the multitude of penitents," and how rarely they would be "redeemed by the treasure-trove of a great sin." He may have had in mind already the "treasure-trove of a great sin" that would redeem Hilda's confession in *The Marble Faun*.[25]

Early on October 13, with a cold rain reminding them that the summer was past, the Hawthornes left Siena. Under an arrangement for Constantino Bacci to drive them to Rome, they resumed the travel they had enjoyed in May, returning by a different route and in only three and a half days. The town of Bolsena, site of a castle bearing marks left by the Etrurians, the Romans, and after them medieval occupants, Hawthorne described as "the very filthiest place . . . ever inhabited by man," and concluded, "No decent words can describe—no admissible image can give an idea—of this noisome place." He had not meant to write such an ugly description but thought it "well, once for all, to have attempted conveying an idea of what disgusts the traveller, more or less, in all these Italian towns." After entering Rome by the Cassian Way on October 16, he wrote in his notebook, "I had a quiet, gentle, comfortable pleasure, as if, after many wanderings, I was drawing near home, for, now that I have known it once, Rome certainly does draw into itself my heart, as I think even London, or even little Concord itself, or old sleepy Salem, never did and never will." Recalling the cold midnight of their first arrival in Rome, he was delighted to proceed, "in the noontide of a genial day," to the lodgings already engaged by C. G. Thompson at 68 Piazza Poli, "such a comfortable, cozy little house" as he had not thought existed in Rome.

The summer in Florence had been pleasant and satisfying to Hawthorne in part because he had become an author again. One piece of luggage brought from the Villa Montauto was a brown leather bag containing the rough draft of an Italian romance, which he planned to rewrite during the winter. The cheerful mood of the summer and the homecoming remained a few days, but on November 2 he wrote about "ugly, hopeless clouds, chill, shivering winds, drizzle, and now and then pouring rain. . . . It is extremely spirit-crushing, this remorseless gray, with its icy heart; and the more to depress the whole family, Una has taken what seems to be the Roman fever." He was not to have another bright day in Italy, and was not to write in his notebook again for four months.

28

The Marble Faun

Hawthorne's foreboding about Una's illness was borne out. She had indeed taken the Roman fever, which stayed with her six months; and twice she was given only the slightest chance of surviving. She suffered from the effects of the fever as long as she lived, and it was said that her father never recovered from the anguish her illness caused him. On November 21, Sophia wrote her sister Elizabeth that Una was in the care of Dr. Franco, "the most distinguished homeopathic physician in Italy—or perhaps in Europe," and told of watching through the night to administer quinine in the intervals between fever fits. The second and third of the fits had lasted twenty-four hours each, with only six hours between, and the doctor had said Una would die if there were not time to give enough quinine before a fourth fit. Her husband had not been told. She must examine Una constantly; it would be fatal to administer quinine after the fever had returned. Once she considered calling Hawthorne to help her decide when to give the quinine; but after resigning Una to God, she went on by herself. "The ninth powder was given at six o'clock," she wrote Elizabeth. "Una was then quiet and perfectly cool. I could not bear the revulsion of hope and joy alone, so I went to tell my husband close by. . . . On the fourteenth night I went to bed for the first time." [1]

Continuing her letter on November 27, she reported that the fever had returned, and that, although Una was again out of bed, even a slight cold might bring the fever back. Through the next four months, Una had fever

fits at intervals of a few days; she recovered enough occasionally to go outside, and to the John Lothrop Motleys' balcony several times in March to
see the Carnival. Ada Shepard was so ill the first fortnight of January that
Hawthorne did not expect her to live. The day after Sophia had joined the
invalids with a cold on January 17, Hawthorne wrote in his diary: "Mama
no better; Una tolerably; Miss Shepard well. Dr. F. came about 11. Mama
is to lie in bed during the day. Una has another chill and fever fit. It
begins to rain in the afternoon. I did not go out. Sat up till between 12
and 1 to give Una quinine." Ada had a relapse on January 23. Hawthorne
felt indisposed on February 8, lay in bed late, and took some powders Dr.
Franco left him on his daily call; he let the doctor be called two days later
and "received him in bed, the first time since" childhood. It was a week
before he dined with the family.

Early in April, after Una had not been out of bed for two weeks, fears
rose sharply and her father's pocket diary shows that she was rarely out of
his mind.[2] Dr. Franco began calling twice daily; on April 8 he seemed "to
have very little hope"; the best that could be said the next day was that he
seemed "not quite to despair"; a day later he brought a consulting doctor;
Ada Shepard and Elizabeth Hoar, Sophia's friend before the Hawthornes
were married and afterward at Concord, visited the consulting doctor; the
second doctor came with Dr. Franco twice more; on April 19 the doctors
thought Una much improved; two days later they found her still improving; that night Hawthorne wrote in his diary, "Mrs. Thompson came to
sit with Una; and Mama had a night's sleep—the first in five or six
weeks." Mrs. Story's woman sat up with Una the next night.

It was a comfort for Hawthorne to talk with his old friend Franklin
Pierce, who had arrived with his wife on March 10 and, until his departure on April 19, came almost every day and, when Una's condition was
worst, twice a day. On four days[3] Hawthorne took up in his notebook the
analysis of Pierce's character he had begun in the campaign biography and
had continued in letters to Horatio Bridge. "The more I see him, the more
I get him back, just as he was in our youth." Though not favored with
great political wisdom, Pierce was "endowed with a miraculous intuition
of what ought to be done just at the time for action." Hawthorne had not
known "what comfort there might be in the manly sympathy of a friend,"
and would "love him the better for the ministrations" during Una's illness.
Looking back over their long friendship, he remarked that each had done
"his best for the other as friend for friend." Una's improvement was so
steady that plans could be revived for leaving Italy. Earlier hopes had

been to accompany the Pierces when they departed for Venice; now the intention was to proceed as rapidly as Una's health would permit, by train to Civitavecchia and by ship to Marseilles.

Besides his voluminous Italian notebooks, Hawthorne brought away with him the draft of an Italian romance he expected to revise at the Wayside in the late summer. He had brought with him the idea and notes made in England for a story about the return of an American to reclaim an English inheritance; but since he had left his English notebooks with Henry Bright, he probably had not intended to do more in Italy than sketch out the new work. Two statues in the Villa Borghese in Rome pricked his interest, a dancing faun and a copy of the *Faun* of Praxiteles. The faun, characterized in his notebook on April 18, 1858, as "a natural and delightful link betwixt human and brute life, with something of a divine character intermingled," could not fail to suggest a use in fiction. The idea of such a creature had not been "wrought out in literature," and he envisaged "something very good, funny, and philosophical, as well as poetic" to be made of it. In the galleries of the Capitol he saw on April 22 another copy of the *Faun* of Praxiteles and envisaged more specific possibilities: the intermingling of the species with the human race, "the pretty, hairy ears" appearing in some of the descendants, and "the moral instincts and intellectual characteristics of the faun . . . picturesquely brought out." At the Capitol a week later, he wrote out a description of the *Faun* because the idea kept recurring to him "of writing a little romance about it." Two notebook entries his wife wrote on this statue suggest that she contributed to the fictional portrait taking shape in his mind.[4] In May Hawthorne saw in the Via Portoghese a battlemented tower and learned about the lamp burning constantly at its top before a shrine to the Virgin. From his first notebook entries in Rome, he had described scenes and paintings and statues with fictional use in mind, and soon he had fallen into his habit of musing and dreaming in preparation for composition.

At Florence on June 13 he wrote in his notebook, "I feel an impulse to be at work, but am kept idle by the sense of being unsettled, with removals to be gone through, over and over again, before I can shut myself into a room of my own, and turn the key. I need monotony, too—an eventless exterior life—before I can live in the world within." His room in the Villa Montauto had little in common with his chamber under the eaves on Herbert Street in Salem, which may have come to his mind, but he noted in his pocket diary on July 13, "Staid at home all day, principally employed in sketching plot of a Romance." Three days later he began a rough draft, and after two weeks he explained that whether the romance would come to anything was yet to be decided. By September 1 he had finished "planning and sketching out" the romance, and intended to spend the rest of his stay sightseeing in Florence. Two days later he wrote Fields that he had two romances planned, one to make use of the Villa Montauto and the other presumably to be set in England. The Italian atmosphere he found good to dream in, but he could not count on much progress in the writing; he needed the fogs of England or the east winds of Massachusetts to put him into "working trim." After ten days in Rome Hawthorne noted that he had begun writing his romance; he had only three more days of scribbling, as he phrased it, before Una became ill, and not until November 15 did he mention the romance again in his diary. From November 25 to January 23 he wrote on it every day, normally in the morning; a week later he had finished a draft. The pages had accumulated rapidly because on the days of Una's illness he had stayed close at home. One report has it that he sat for long periods before the fireplace parching leaves for her tea, having heard that the flavor would be improved.[5]

During the period in which the sketch and the draft were being written, Hawthorne's notebook had grown into a storehouse of description and analysis sufficiently polished for large sections to be moved directly into the romance. After the draft had been finished, he busied himself in sightseeing that would benefit his romance. He saw the carnival again, St. Peter's, the catacombs of St. Calixtus, the Coliseum, the Medici Gardens, and the Pincian Hill, all of which are prominent in *The Marble Faun*. He returned to Harriet Hosmer's studio, which became Miriam's studio, and to the Via Portoghese, where he saw again the original of Hilda's tower; also to the Capitol to see again the *Faun* and the *Dying Gladiator*, which appear in the first scene of the romance, and to Story's studio, the model of Kenyon's studio, where he saw the *Cleopatra* and watched the sculptor at work. He hoped the appearance of the *Cleopatra* in *The Marble Faun* would bring Story more recognition, and he mentioned also C. G. Thompson and Hiram Powers.[6] The notebook record skips the last week in March and the first two weeks in April when there was little hope that Una would survive. On April 13 Story and his wife drove Hawthorne outside the Porta Portese to see a recently unearthed Venus that was to appear in *The Marble Faun*. It was probably on this drive that Hawthorne supposedly had the carriage stopped so that he could better hear sounds that had reached his ears, and said, "I hear the wailings of former generations."[7] In his last few days in Rome, he went for a final look at Guido's *Beatrice*

Cenci, his third visit since returning from Florence, and wrote an analysis of the painting much like that he introduced into his romance. He went again to the Capuchin Church and again wrote on Guido's archangel.

The extent to which *The Marble Faun* draws on the author's observations for description and analysis of Italian art and architecture is suggested by one author who says, "Every writer who has since described Rome has consciously or unconsciously *plagiarized* from the rich mine of his incomparable romance";[8] and by another who says that, if the *Italian Notebooks* were indexed, they "would be the best guides to Rome ever published. . . . And *The Marble Faun* should receive the same close and studious attention."[9] An index to the contents of the romance would be a catalogue of the buildings, galleries, paintings, and statues in Rome and Florence and in several other cities and towns, and of the chief artists represented by the works. The journey of Kenyon and Donatello from the time they leave Montauto until they meet Miriam by appointment in Perugia includes much from the travels of the Hawthorne family between Florence and Rome. The residence of the spiritualist Kirkup in Florence and its occupants appear in Chapter 28 of *The Marble Faun.* But the romance does more than portray what the author observed in Italy; it incorporates his physical, intellectual, and emotional experience, as *The Blithedale Romance* incorporates his experience at Brook Farm. Prominent are the questions in artistic theory and criticism that had occupied his mind; the worth of the old masters and later artists, realistic detail in the Dutch painters, the merits of sculpture and of painting, nudity in art, tinted statues, Gothic and classical architecture, creative artists and copyists. He gave little thought to techniques; his characters say most about the works themselves, with particular attention to those which raise the questions of human character that attracted Hawthorne's speculation. To the aspects of sin and guilt he had dealt with earlier (the inevitable effects of sin, the weight of guilt from the past, the universality of sin, concealed sin and revealed sin, isolation and brotherhood, sin in the heart), he now added aspects which invited more intricate speculation.

In Rome Hawthorne saw on every hand support for his deterministic view of the weight of the past on the present. Mementoes of the long past were everywhere to be seen or to be heard in the "wailings of former generations." When Una's death seemed only a few hours away, he wrote Fields that he detested Rome; "I fully acquiesce in all the mischief and ruin that has happened to it, from Nero's conflagration downward."[10] Kenyon once remarks that in America, "that fortunate land, each generation has only its own sins and sorrows to bear."[11] More directly than in any of his previous writings, Hawthorne poses the question whether guilt does not bring with it an intellectual and emotional advance from an original state. Donatello is capable of love and devotion, and he senses evil as animals do. The killing of Miriam's model proceeds from his own emotional prompting supported by the approval he reads in Miriam's eyes, not from his will. In the aftermath of this fall, he evolves a sober awareness of good and evil—Kenyon observes in him the birth of a soul.[12] His future is not spelled out in the final chapter, but the implication is that he will serve a prison term and will afterward face an uncertain future with Miriam, to whom he is bound in love and guilt. When Hilda and Kenyon last see Miriam, before they return to America, Kenyon has just remarked, "Sin has educated Donatello, and elevated him. . . . Did Adam fall, that we might ultimately rise to a far loftier paradise than his?" Hilda exclaims, "O hush!" and he answers, "I never did believe it." But he pleads for guidance. Just then Miriam, who has been kneeling in the Pantheon, a penitent, extends her hands toward them, "with a gesture of benediction."—But the hands, "even while they blessed, seemed to repel, as if Miriam stood on the other side of a fathomless abyss, and warned them from its verge." One who has experienced the fall seems to be warning those whose experience has been only passive and vicarious.

The manuscript of *The Marble Faun*, given by the author to Henry Bright and now in the British Museum, seems to have ended at first after one further paragraph, which states that Kenyon and Hilda would return to America, "because the years, after all, have a kind of emptiness, when we spend too many of them on a foreign shore." Two additional paragraphs, which after a few lines continue on the back of the page, appear to have been written afterward. They tell of a bridal gift to Hilda, a bracelet "composed of seven ancient Etruscan gems, dug out of seven sepulchres, and each one of them the signet of some princely personage, who had lived an immemorial time ago." She has seen the bracelet in Miriam's possession and has heard her tell "a mythical and magic legend for each gem." Hawthorne had seen the original of this bracelet worn by Mrs. Story and had described it in his notebook as having the same components and the same history as Miriam's bracelet. It serves to bring Miriam and Donatello back to the reader's mind, in association with the immemorial past, which in Miriam's imagination is "characterized by a sevenfold gloom." To the author's query as to what the future of Miriam and Donatello would be, the answer of the last sentence is that "Hilda had a hopeful soul, and saw sunlight on the mountain-tops."

Hawthorne thus lessened the vagueness, and admitted a ray of light into the gloom of the close. He wrote Henry Bright on March 10, 1860, that his idea of Donatello was "an agreeable and beautiful one," but that presenting it to the reader was not easy. In his mind Donatello gained even in his loss of innocence. He would have seen no way, in truth to human experience, of eliminating the "old pain" that Longfellow found running through this and all his other writings.[13] His intention, first stated in his notebook, was to write a story about a faun "with all sorts of fun and pathos in it." Here, as usual, his intention did not bind him to substitute light and cheer for what he considered truth.

Hilda's visit to the confessional at St. Peter's (Chapter 39) introduces subtle aspects of guilt that Hawthorne had not explored in earlier works. In her mind, it was the guilt of others, not her own, that drove her to confess. Her cry that Miriam's deed has "darkened the entire sky" leads to the author's remark on the "terrible thought, that an individual wrong-doing melts into the great mass of human crime, and makes us . . . guilty of the whole." But the reader is led beyond Hilda's perception to see that her guilt lies in her failure to sympathize with Miriam. Kenyon has partaken of the same guilt in remaining "as cold and pitiless" as his own marble when Miriam came to his studio in Chapter 14. Consequently, as Kenyon and Hilda depart for a new life in America, their happiness is to be shaded by the awareness, not only of their friends' guilt, but also of their own guilt in withholding the brotherhood sought from them. Guido's painting of the Archangel Michael in battle with Lucifer is used to distinguish Miriam's view of good and evil from the more optimistic and less realistic view shared by Hilda and Kenyon. Hilda's unquestioning interpretation of the painting is challenged by Miriam, who says (Chapter 20) she could have told Guido better, and expands on the critique Hawthorne recorded in his notebook (May 15, 1859): instead of unruffled wings and a "prettily sandalled foot," Michael would have a third of his feathers torn from his wings; his sword would be hacked and bloody; and yet his visage would show "something high, tender, and holy." Even so, Miriam is "sadly afraid the victory would fall on the wrong side." In ironic representation of Hilda suffering for Miriam's sin, Hawthorne describes a portrait of her gazing in horror at a spot of blood on her white robe, to which the artist had affixed the title "Innocence, Dying of a Blood-stain" (Chapter 36).

Through Beatrice Cenci and Guido's portrait of her, Hawthorne speculates on the intricacies of guilt and sorrow. In bidding farewell to Guido's *Beatrice Cenci* on the eve of his departure from Rome, he was glad to leave it, he said, "because it so perplexed and troubled" him "not to be able to get hold of its secrets." When Miriam sees Hilda's copy of the portrait (Chapter 7), both recognize the elusiveness of Beatrice's glance described in Hawthorne's notebook, as if she were determined not to reveal her secret. Reminded that Beatrice was executed for the murder of her brutal father, Hilda is sure hers was nevertheless a "terrible guilt, an inexpiable crime"; Miriam reflects Hawthorne's bafflement in saying that she would give her life to know whether Beatrice "thought herself innocent, or the one great criminal since time began." As the facts and the ideas related to witchcraft and alchemy had furnished Hawthorne imagery for earlier works, so the objects of art and the related ideas he encountered in Italy served that purpose in *The Marble Faun*.

Whether or not Hilda's freedom and independence encouraged young American women to follow her example in Rome, as has been said,[14] her role caused later novelists to send innocent young American women to be tested in the society of the Old World, including Daisy Miller and successors of hers in the fiction of Henry James and Lydia Blood in William Dean Howells's *The Lady of the Aroostook*. One could imagine that James and Howells took up their pens after reading statements such as these about Hilda (Chapter 42): "In all her wanderings about Rome, Hilda had gone, and returned, as securely as she had been accustomed to tread the familiar street of her New England village. . . . Thus it is, that, bad as the world is said to have grown, Innocence continues to make a Paradise around itself, and keep it still unfallen." Hilda owed something to the author's wife—perhaps her courage and optimism, and surely her artistic talents. She is called Dove, Sophia's name in Hawthorne's love letters. In making her accept the role of copyist rather than strive for independent creativity, he is commenting on his wife, and also on women as artists—and as authors (Chapter 6). Hilda "lost the impulse of original design" and "ceased to aim at original achievement." Her custom was to concentrate her talents on "some high, noble, and delicate portion" of a master's painting, with the result that "the spirit of some great departed Painter now first achieved his ideal." There was "something far higher and nobler in all this. . . . Would it have been worth Hilda's while to relinquish this office, for the sake of giving the world a picture or two which it would call original; pretty fancies of snow and moonlight; the counterpart, in picture, of so many feminine achievements in literature."

If Sophia was less than pleased with his setting her limit at "pretty fancies of snow and moonlight," she seems to have left no record. With that qualification, he regularly paid her extravagant compliments. He said that her descriptions of art works surpassed his; and having Kenyon profit from Hilda's "delicate perceptions" was meant as a compliment to his wife. More than once he declared that his wife stood above all others as critic of what he wrote, and he said that she wrote better travel accounts than his. When James T. Fields asked her to contribute travel reports to the *Atlantic Monthly*, he replied on November 28, 1859, that he had read nothing so good as some of her narrative and descriptive letters to friends; but he doubted "whether she would find sufficient inspiration in writing directly for the public." In writing Bennoch the next day, he was obviously pleased to report Fields's invitation, but added that there was no danger of his having "a literary rival at bed and board," for she refused to be famous, and contented herself with being "the best wife and mother in the world." He was no doubt correct in saying that his wife refused to write for the *Atlantic*, for his view that authorship would be unbecoming, if not degrading, to a woman was so firm that proposing to write for a magazine would have been to her preposterous. In writing the next May 17 to her sister Elizabeth, who apparently had encouraged her to write for publication, she remarked that she did not need to print her notes to get money, and added that it was "enough to have one author in the family," giving Elizabeth room, it would seem, to understand more than was being said. A woman wrote well, in Hawthorne's view, only when she wrote with the devil inside her; most women wrote simply as weaker men.[15]

As Hawthorne planned a romance that would include a faun and would deal with subtle moral and psychological problems, he no doubt recognized a need for indefiniteness, if not shadow, in his presentation. As in his previous romances, no time is lost in introducing his main characters on the stage where they are to act and in suggesting also the mystery of Miriam's model, who in the third chapter appears appropriately in the catacombs and both deepens and darkens the mystery. The mystery surrounding Donatello required the lightness of touch and the genial fantasy present in "The Snow-Image" and the scene beside the brook in *The Scarlet Letter*. Through legends and episodes half-remembered by Donatello and ancient residents of his ancestral villa, Monte Beni, and by allusions to hazy beliefs that have come down from antiquity, Hawthorne conveys meanings without vouching for specific manifestations. The eight chapters set at Monte Beni came easily from Hawthorne's pen; they have the poetic, imaginative quality of his residence at the Villa Montauto. The mystery attached to the model was more troublesome, and additions made in the printer's copy indicate late attempts to remove the difficulty by deepening the shadows about him. The purpose was to show the model firmly linked to Miriam, and yet to encase both in such indefiniteness that the fancy of the reader would be left to fill in the unspecified evil and horror. The present Chapter 3 originally continued, it seems, through the first three or four pages of Chapter 4, and the remainder of that chapter was added later. The last two paragraphs of Chapter 4, which carry over to the back of the manuscript page, were a still later addition. In these additions, the indefiniteness and the mystery are augmented by wild speculations about the specter of the catacombs, and still more by the fantasies offered by Miriam herself, reinforcing the suggestions already offered in Chapter 3 as to her origin (one of them identifying her with the beautiful Jewish woman the author had seen at the London mayor's dinner and had described in his notebook).

The manuscript shows that until composition reached Chapter 30, Kenyon was named Graydon. (The additions in Chapter 4 were made before the name was changed.) Page numbers indicate that after writing Chapter 43, in which Hilda delivers a packet to the Palazzo Cenci for Miriam, Hawthorne turned back and wrote Chapter 11, in a further attempt to give substance to the past from which Miriam and her model come, without dispelling the haze surrounding it. This chapter, entitled "Fragmentary Sentences," is indeed fragmentary. It reports an interview between Miriam and the model, of which the author can hear only bits that resemble "fragments of a letter, which has been torn and scattered to the winds." The fragments make it clear that Miriam is resigned to her thralldom; that she and the model have a destiny they must fulfill together; and that she can foresee death as the necessary end. Hints come through the author's comment, but little clarification: "every crime is made to be the agony of many innocent persons, as well as of the single guilty one." "In their words, or in the breath that uttered them, there seemed to be an odour of guilt, and a scent of blood." To save his romance from becoming a tissue of absurdities, Hawthorne has Hilda state the case for indefiniteness. She says, "Nobody, I think, ought to read poetry, or look at pictures or statues, who cannot find a great deal more in them than the poet or artist has actually expressed. Their highest merit is suggestiveness."

On his last day in Rome, May 26, Hawthorne went early for a parting view of the Pincian Hill, the Borghese grounds, and St. Peter's. They "never looked so beautiful, nor the sky so bright and blue." He had no wish to see them again, although no other place had ever taken so strong a hold on his feelings. He had been miserable there, but he could not say he hated the city and "perhaps might fairly own a love for it." On the voyage northward, there was time to go ashore at Leghorn and visit Pisa, but he did not. At Marseilles on May 29 he wrote notes on his trip since leaving Rome; during a week at Avignon, he had "no spirit for description any longer; being tired of seeing things, and still more of telling" himself about them. He dutifully recorded his visits to Valence, Lyons, Geneva, Ville-neuve, Paris, and Le Havre. Only the Castle of Chillon did he report with the fullness or the interest of his earlier travel notes. From Paris he wrote Francis Bennoch on June 17 that he longed for England just as if he "were a native John Bull."

At Le Havre Ada Shepard sailed for America, and Hawthorne wrote his last notebook entry until the next February 5, except for a note on November 14. Crossing to Southampton on June 23 and reaching London the next day, he took lodgings Bennoch had reserved at 6 Golden Square. For the next three weeks his friends kept him in the kind of social whirl he had known in the spring of 1856. One morning he and Julian breakfasted with James T. Fields, who had brought his wife for a year in Europe. Henry Chorley, a literary critic who had reviewed his work since the 1830's, called and later invited him and his wife to dinner. Francis Ben-noch took charge from July 1 to 4, as he had done three years earlier, and took Hawthorne to Aldershot, to Brighton, where he made a speech, and elsewhere. Henry Bright came to London and on July 8 took Hawthorne to the House of Commons, to Richmond, to a private library, and to the Workingmen's College. They called on Senator Charles Sumner, whom Hawthorne had seen in Rome, and they had dinner with the Heywoods and breakfast with Monckton Milnes. Hawthorne also dined with Barry Cornwall, saw Leigh Hunt again, and several times saw Franklin Pierce, who had concluded his travels on the Continent.

Soon after returning to English soil, Hawthorne learned that Milnes was to bring up in the House of Lords the subject of abuses on the merchant ships crossing the Atlantic. At Henry Bright's request, he wrote Milnes on July 30, saying that "a better and more necessary thing could not be done" and that he thought England and America should confer on the matter. As consul he had been "utterly powerless either to protect the victims or punish the offenders," and had addressed his own government on the subject. He wanted it understood, he continued, that he thought American sea captains were eager to help eradicate the evils, and that he did not consider the character of his countrymen to be "solely or prin-cipally involved" in the offenses, since the perpetrators of the cruelties

Nathaniel Hawthorne, 1860; photograph by Mayall, London ("Motley"). Courtesy of the Essex Institute, Salem, Mass.

were in most cases not Americans. As he had done two years earlier, he made sure not to be drawn into a moral crusade by English reformers against American seamen and ship captains. The motion introduced by Milnes and adopted on August 2 called for public action of the sort

Hawthorne had urged on his own government, and it no doubt incorporated ideas deriving from him, directly or through Henry Bright.

An offer by the publishers Smith and Elder of £600 for the English rights to his new romance induced Hawthorne to cancel his earlier request for ship reservations on July 15 or August 1 and plan a year in England to finish the writing and secure an English copyright. In search of a place to live, the Hawthornes took a train on July 14 to Malton and the next day went on to Whitby; a week later they went to the village of Redcar and took lodgings at Mrs. King's, 120 High Street, on "as bleak and dreary a strip of sand" as they could have found, Hawthorne said, with "the gray German ocean" tumbling in upon them, twenty yards from their door. The next day, his diary states, he looked at the rough draft of his romance, and two days later he began writing in earnest. His schedule was to write from nine to three and after dinner to go for a walk, often with Julian. He had been so long away from the manuscript, he wrote Fields, that he made "many amendments," with the consequence that progress was slow. His family stayed close and had "not a single visitor or caller," Hawthorne said, during their two and a half months at Redcar. Sophia had half of the manuscript to read early in September, and after moving to Leamington on October 5, Hawthorne had a few chapters yet to write. His wife spoke rapturously of the new romance, he wrote Fields; "I, likewise, (to confess the truth,) admire it exceedingly, at intervals, but am liable to cold fits, during which I think it the most infernal nonsense. This happens to be the case just at the present moment."[16] On October 14 he wrote a preface; three days later he sent the publisher 429 pages; on November 9, the final 79 pages. The manuscript went to the printer at once; the first plan was to bring the work out before Christmas, but the date was postponed until February 28, in part because of delays in getting proof sheets to Boston for the American edition, which was out a week later.

When the title Hawthorne first proposed, "The Romance of Monte Beni," did not please Smith and Elder, he sent a dozen possibilities and at about the same time asked Ticknor to call the book in America "Saint Hilda's Shrine." He objected to the title Smith and Elder wanted, "Transformation; or the Romance of Monte Beni"; but when he realized that "Transformation" was one of the titles he himself had suggested, he accepted it for the English edition, and instructed Ticknor to entitle the work in America "The Marble Faun: A Romance of Monte Beni."

On March 4 Hawthorne wrote Bennoch that if a second edition were

printed, he would add "a few explanatory pages, in the shape of a conversation between the author and Hilda or Kenyon, by means of which some
further details may be elicited." He wrote the publisher of his intention,
saying "everybody complains that the mysteries of the Romance are not
sufficiently cleared up." Among those who complained was Henry Chorley.[17] Hawthorne told Henry Bright, however, that he preferred the book
as it stood, and explained, "The characters of the story come out of an
obscurity and vanish into it again, like the figures on the slide of a magic-
lanthern; but, in their transit, they have served my purpose, and shown
all that it was essential for them to reveal. Anything further, if you consider it rightly, would be an impertinence on the author's part toward his
reader." The new conclusion, he added, would show "how easy it is to
explain mysteries, when the author does not more wisely choose to keep a
veil over them." He told Bennoch that the book had as "one of its essential
excellencies that it left matters so enveloped in a fog."[18] His wife wrote
her sister Elizabeth that the postscript to the book was very saucy; "he
would not explain after all."[19] When Hawthorne was confronted with
criticism he could not accept, it was normal for him to undervalue his
achievement and to declare that he would write differently in the future—
but to hold saucily to his own views. He said that John Lothrop Motley
had half made *The Marble Faun* with his own imagination and had taken it
precisely as it was meant. He saw Motley as standing apart from "these
beer-sodden English beefeaters" who did not know how to read a romance. Motley had written that he liked "those shadowy, weird, fantastic,
Hawthornesque shapes flitting through the golden gloom," and "the misty
way in which the story is indicated rather than revealed."[20] Reviewers in
the *Westminster Review*[21] and the *North British Review*[22] wrote vaguely
grudging comments on the romance. The reviewer in the London *Times* of
April 7 knew how to read a romance, Hawthorne might have said, and he
did say that this reviewer "awarded the highest praise of all" the English
reviewers. He told Ticknor that in England the book might be called "a
successful affair"; the third edition was out, and "the good opinion of the
'Times' has great weight with John Bull."[23] The *Times* reviewer spoke of
the "airy conceptions" and said that Hawthorne possessed "more of this
rare quality than any living writer," a quality he found "so subtle as to
defy analysis."

The Marble Faun gave occasion for several essays which placed it among
Hawthorne's other works and assessed his total achievement. James Russell Lowell[24] and Richard Holt Hutton[25] found Shakespeare appropriate

for comparison, as Melville had tentatively suggested ten years earlier. Several writers agreed in calling Hawthorne primarily a psychological author. Lowell called him metaphysical also, and said, "Had he been born without the poetic imagination, he would have written treatises on the Origin of Evil." E. P. Whipple doubted that any living novelist was Hawthorne's equal.[26] Hutton and a reviewer in the *Universal Review*[27] for June spoke of Hawthorne's accumulation of details from real life and character to transform an allegorical ideal into a creation of vivid human experience.

With the conclusion provided for the second edition in both England and America, and with generally favorable reviews, Hawthorne entered several weeks of calm and for the most part pleasant waiting until time to embark for America. He was in a mood to estimate the worth of his past work and to make avowals of intentions for the future. This book was "an audacious attempt to impose a tissue of absurdities upon the public by the mere art of style and narrative," he wrote Fields, and added, "When I get home, I will try to write a more genial book; but the devil himself always seems to get into my inkstand, and I can only exorcise him by pensfull at a time."[28]

O'Sullivan, called by the children Uncle John, came for a visit, as did Francis Bennoch, who was happily recovering from his business failure two years earlier. At his host's request, Bennoch wrote a poem, "To Nathaniel Hawthorne. On the Anniversary of his Daughter Una's Birthday."[29] The family had moved on March 22 from Leamington to Bath, seeking the best region for Mrs. Hawthorne. She had suffered from the same bronchial irritation as in her other English winters, and early in May she was in the hospital.

Leaving his family at Bath, Hawthorne went to London May 16, where he was the house guest of first the John Lothrop Motleys and afterward the Bennochs. He accepted "a whole string of invitations" without a murmur, he wrote his wife on May 17; the stir of London life did him "a wonderful deal of good," and he felt better than for months past; but he added, "This is queer; for, if I had my choice, I should leave undone almost all the things I do." From May 24 to 28 he was in Cambridge with Henry Bright, who was there to receive the master's degree. Following a trip to Canterbury and farewell dinners given by the Bennochs and the Halls, he returned to Bath on May 31 and took his family to Liverpool. He had the pleasant task of acknowledging commendations of his new romance, including sonnets by W. C. Bennett honoring the author and his book. During these last weeks he wrote but little in his notebook, for he was simply marking time, eager to be at home. He thought soberly about the return to America. It might well be, he remarked more than once, that he would never be content to stay in one place, after seven years of nomadic existence, and he was sure he would long to see England again. The Hawthorne family sailed on the *Europa* June 16, accompanied by James T. Fields and his wife. They made port on the morning of June 28 and went directly to the Wayside.

29

The Wayside
after Seven Years

Hawthorne wrote John Lothrop Motley two months before sailing for America, "patriotic as you know me to be, you can conceive the rapture with which I shall embrace my native soil." He told Ticknor that America was "the healthiest and safest country to live in, in the world," and that he meant to "try to settle down into a respectable character" and had "serious thoughts of going to meeting every Sunday afternoon."[1] The captain of the *Europa* was the same Captain Leitch who had brought the Hawthornes to England seven years earlier on the *Niagara*. Fields reports that Hawthorne was cheerful during the voyage, and amused his companions by proposing fanciful delicacies for Fields, who was seasick, such as "stewed ibis, livers of Roman Capitol geese, the wings of a Phoenix not too much done, love-lorn nightingales cooked briskly over Aladdin's lamp." Fields reports also that Hawthorne said he "would like to sail on thus forever, and never come to land," implying something of a distaste for returning to America.[2] A report through his Bowdoin classmate Calvin Stowe and Harriet Beecher Stowe, who were also on the *Europa*, implies that he enjoyed the voyage—and the company—so much that he was sorry to land. More likely, both reports grew from the kind of sober comments Hawthorne normally made at important turns in his affairs.

The Wayside was ready for them when they arrived on June 28, having been occupied first by Sophia's brother Nathaniel Peabody and later by Mary Mann, after the death of Horace Mann in 1859. Bronson Alcott and

The Wayside (showing Nathaniel Hawthorne and his wife). From Julian Hawthorne, *Hawthorne and His Circle* (New York: Harper and Brothers, 1903)

his wife, who had moved back from Boston and lived near by, called the first evening; the next evening Emerson had a strawberries-and-cream party at his house to welcome Hawthorne home.[3] Ticknor and Fields gave a dinner in Boston, for which Fields had laid plans on the high seas. From July 14 to 17 Hawthorne visited Pierce at Concord, New Hampshire; early in September he joined Bridge at the seashore while Sophia was in the White Mountains. He still kept up his guard against imposition on his privacy. At least three times he declined invitations to lecture,[4] no doubt pleased to have no longer the obligation he had as consul to speak in public. While still abroad, he was elected to the Saturday Club, which had been founded in 1857 for literary discussion. When he attended the dinner meetings, held on the last Saturday of each month at the Parker House in Boston, he normally would travel from Concord with Emerson and Judge Rockwood Hoar, and would see his old friends Longfellow, Lowell, and Holmes.[5]

The presence of Franklin Pierce at the dinner given by Ticknor and Fields prompted Lowell to say that he had never seen anything funnier or more out of place.[6] Hawthorne of course knew the intensity of the abolitionists' feeling and the blame they attached to him for supporting Pierce. When the Saturday Club honored Governor John Albion Andrew late in 1860, Hawthorne wrote in advance that he would be absent, for he chose not to join in what he presumed to be "an acquiescent compliment to the Governor's public course, as well as his private character."[7] The governor was a firm abolitionist. The Hawthornes had many reminders that abolitionist sentiment was much stronger among their relatives and friends than seven years earlier. Both had protested against Elizabeth Peabody's writing them abroad as if she thought they supported slavery and were immoral in remaining friends with Franklin Pierce.[8] Sophia had written her mother more than once defending Daniel Webster, when her mother and sisters had joined in the emotional and irrational charges of disloyalty and personal immorality leveled at Webster because of his stand on the Compromise of 1850. It was Hawthorne's nature to distrust enthusiasm and to ask that advocates of social reform consider the full and ultimate effects of the action they proposed. This he thought the radical abolitionists failed to do. It was in such a context that he wrote Elizabeth Peabody from England, August 13, 1857, in returning an abolitionist essay of hers she had sent him in manuscript: "No doubt it seems the truest of truth to you; but I do assure you that, like every other Abolitionist, you look at matters with an awful squint, which distorts everything within your line of vision; and it is queer, though natural, that you think everybody squints except yourselves. Perhaps they do; but certainly *you* do." Any day's news might bring up issues on which the Hawthornes held views divergent from those generally expressed in Concord and in the Saturday Club.

Reports of meetings of the Saturday Club agree in stressing Hawthorne's reclusiveness. The elder Henry James tells of an occasion when Hawthorne foiled the efforts of another at the dinner table to draw him into conversation. After remarking that "the world is breaking up on all hands"—this was in January, 1861—James added, "the glimpse of the everlasting granite I caught in Hawthorne shows me that there is stock for fifty better."[9] Hawthorne was present on September 16, 1861, when Anthony Trollope was entertained by the Saturday Club, and on June 3 of the next year he submitted the name of James T. Fields for membership. He normally placed himself next to Longfellow in club meetings, or Lowell. In 1861, after the death of his wife in a household fire, Longfellow ceased to attend.

Bronson Alcott's journal records one overture after another that Hawthorne received coolly. Alcott had offered to help (in his "rustic way," which Hawthorne knew to be indeed rustic) with improvements to be made at the Wayside. A year and a half after the Hawthornes returned to Concord, Hawthorne paid his second call, Alcott wrote, and sat "for half an hour, but diffidently, and as if he were wishing to rise and leave at the first easy pause in the conversation."[10] How different were Alcott's relations with another Concord neighbor: "Emerson comes, and we look about my garden and grounds. He tastes of my apples and carries away some of them, and mint, to Edith. Invites me to supper, and we discuss the Platonic genius, the *Atlantic* Club, his essay in the *Monthly* on 'Culture.'" Alcott said he got only glimpses of Hawthorne, "dodging about amongst the trees on his hilltop as if he feared his neighbor's eyes would catch him as he walked." He probably had read in "The Custom-House" that even the permanent inspector was desirable "as a change of diet, to a man who had known Alcott." Still, he found "nothing sullen or morose" about the avoidances of his neighbor, "a coy genius," who excited "a pitying affection" because of his impulse to solitude and study. "There was a soft sadness in his smile and a reserve in his glance that told how solitary he was. He never seemed to be one of his company while with it." In these notes, Alcott probably reflects the way in which Hawthorne impressed most of his neighbors after returning to Concord. Hawthorne's amused tolerance of Alcott appears in verses he composed for the pleasure of his children, about the "airy Sage of Apple Slump," who, given a plate of vegetables and "raw apples to hold on his knees," would "prate of the Spirit as long as you'd please."[11]

Mrs. Hawthorne called Henry David Thoreau "Concord itself in one man," writing to Annie Fields on May 7, 1862, the day after his death. Of all those who resided in the town or were in some degree identified with it, Hawthorne enjoyed the company of Thoreau most. Valuing his individuality and his originality, and recognizing also his quirks and his narrowness, Hawthorne produced, in his various comments taken together, perhaps the best balanced portrait of Thoreau left by his contemporaries.

Thoreau appears in Hawthorne's notebook from his first entry at the Old Manse, August 5, 1842. He came to play his music box for the

Hawthornes, sold Hawthorne his boat, taught him how to row, introduced him to the streams and paths in the neighborhood, and was his authority for much information he thought worth recording. Hawthorne spoke of Thoreau's fondness for Indians and the Indian quality in his outlook—without indicating his own view; but he declared once that the Old Manse was worth a score of tepees. On September 1, the day after Thoreau first dined at the Manse, Hawthorne wrote the first in a series of analyses, in which he said that Thoreau had lived so close to nature that she had seemed to "adopt him as her especial child" and to show him secrets few others ever witnessed. In sending an article Epes Sargent had requested for *Sargent's New Monthly Magazine*, he recommended Thoreau to Sargent for a series of articles on natural history such as he had published recently in the *Dial*, and also for his poems, "which seem to be very careless and imperfect, but as true as bird-notes. The man has stuff in him to make a reputation of."[12] Two years later, Hawthorne urged Evert Duyckinck to seek from Thoreau a volume for the series he was editing in which *Mosses from an Old Manse* would appear. Feeling that he could speak frankly to Duyckinck without being misunderstood, he wrote, "He is the most unmalleable fellow alive—the most tedious, tiresome, and intolerable—the narrowest and most notional—and yet, true as all this is, he has great qualities of intellect and character."[13] Hawthorne recognized that Thoreau's quirky intolerance and his absolute scorn of anything he did not approve were essential qualities of his mind and character. He would have agreed with his wife's statement that conversation with Thoreau would have been more pleasant if he did not talk like one who thought he was saying something important. But Thoreau's integrity, his independence of thought, and his determined reliance on his own judgment counted enough with Hawthorne to offset the annoyances.

After Thoreau had been to Staten Island in 1843–44 as teacher for the children of Emerson's brother William, he and Hawthorne were together less; and not until he lectured at the Salem Lyceum in 1848 were they brought together again. At that time Hawthorne wrote Longfellow, accepting an invitation to dinner and proposing to bring Thoreau, "a man of thought and originality, with a certain iron-pokerishness, an uncompromising stiffness in his mental character, which is interesting, though it grows rather wearisome on close and frequent acquaintance."[14] It may be that, when Hawthorne moved back to Salem in 1852, he avoided the weariness of frequent exposure to Thoreau's "mental character"; he once noted that Emerson seemed to find Thoreau an uncomfortable household resident. Both Hawthorne and Thoreau were conscious by

then of their divergent political views and actions. Hawthorne's appointment to the Liverpool consulate prompted Thoreau to write in his journal,
"Better for me to go cranberrying this afternoon . . . to get but a pocket-
ful and learn its peculiar flavor . . . than to go consul to Liverpool and get
I don't know how many thousand dollars for it, with no such flavor."[15]

When Hawthorne undertook to introduce his English friend Richard
Monckton Milnes to some of the best American books, he chose Thoreau's
Walden and *A Week on the Concord and Merrimack Rivers* as written by "a
very remarkable man." Replying later to a letter from Milnes, he sent a
thumbnail sketch of Thoreau:

> He is an excellent scholar, and a man of most various capacity; insomuch
> that he could make his part good in any way of life, from the most barba-
> rous to the most civilized. But there is more of the Indian in him, I think,
> than of any other kind of man. He despises the world, and all that it has
> to offer, and, like other humorists, is an intolerable bore. I shall cause it
> to be made known to him that you sat up till two o'clock, reading his
> book; and he will pretend that it is of no consequence, but will never
> forget it. I ought not to forbear saying that he is an upright, conscien-
> tious, and courageous man, of whom it is impossible to conceive any-
> thing but the highest integrity. Still, he is not an agreeable person; and in
> his presence one feels ashamed of having any money, or a house to live
> in, or so much as two coats to wear, or of having written a book that the
> public will read—his own mode of life being so unsparing a criticism on
> all other modes, such as the world approves. I wish anything could be
> done to make his books known to the English public; for certainly they
> deserve it, being the work of a true man and full of true thought.

Thoreau was not a particular friend of his, Hawthorne told Milnes; they
had never been intimate, although they had been neighbors a good many
years. He added that he did not speak of his friends with quite this
freedom.[16] He presented copies of Thoreau's books to another English
friend, Charles Mackay (1814–89), editor of the *Illustrated London News*,
recommending them as "full of new and peculiar thought."[17]

It was the story of a deathless man Thoreau told that gave Hawthorne
the idea for a romance about the search for an elixir of life. He first intended to introduce that romance, which remained the fragment *Septimius
Felton* at his death, with a sketch of Thoreau; he later planned to write an
autobiographical introduction like "The Old Manse" and "The Custom-
House," in which Thoreau would be woven into the life about the Wayside. Our understandings of both Thoreau and Hawthorne are the less
because he did not carry out either of these plans.

The Hawthorne children, Una, Julian, and Rose, in 1860. Courtesy of Manning Hawthorne

The Hawthorne children were at ages, when they returned to Concord, to establish social ties of their own, with the Emersons, the Alcotts, Aunt Mary Mann's family, and the Fieldses in Boston. There were picnics and parties, and in June, 1862, a dance at the Wayside, when the furniture was removed from three downstairs rooms to accommodate the forty dancers. Hawthorne came down, and shook hands with the guests as they departed. In September Julian began schooling under Frank Sanborn, who had moved to Concord in 1855 and had taught the three sons of Mary Mann. Una studied with George Bradford, her father's associate at Brook Farm, and Rose also attended private school. Sophia once wrote Sanborn that she and her husband were opposed to the association of the sexes in his co-educational school, particularly in the dancing (the American rather than the Spanish type of waltz). When the time approached for Julian to apply for admission to Harvard, his father decided that Sanborn's teaching had been inadequate, especially because it followed Julian's years without formal schooling in Europe; and he sent Julian to Cambridge for additional tutoring.[18] Hawthorne remarked to more than one of his correspondents that he had expected to leave one member of his family in Europe, meaning Una. She experienced in September, 1860, the relapse the doctors had said might occur, and her father's spirits rose and fell with her health during the ensuing weeks. He wrote Pierce the details: Una had suffered mental derangement but had responded to the electrical shock administered by a Mrs. Rollins, so that after two days she required "no further restraint," and he was ready to recommend medical electricity for all diseases. There need be "no apprehension of future mental disturbance," for, as he had phrased it to Ticknor earlier, her case had "yielded at once to the incantations of a certain electrical witch."[19]

Additions to the Wayside—rooms above two existing rooms and a tower at the back that would include a third-story workroom for Hawthorne—cost more than $2,000 instead of the $500 he first had in mind, and it cost him also disquiet and exasperation that kept him away from his desk beyond the end of the year 1860. After the work was finished, he wrote the humorist Donald G. Mitchell, "Ik Marvel," that the carpenter had taken the matter into his own hands and had produced "the absurdest anomaly you ever saw; . . . an unimaginable sort of thing." His intention being to imitate the extravagance of Mitchell's writing, he added, "If it would only burn down! But I have no such luck."[20] He had remarked as the work progressed that the house was taking a good appearance, and there is no evidence that he was displeased with his "sky-parlour," though he conceded in writing Francis Bennoch that it was "not quite so high as the tower of Monte Beni."[21]

William Dean Howells's account of visiting New England in the summer of 1860 furnishes a glimpse of Hawthorne in the literary community of Concord, Cambridge, and Boston. Howells went to the Wayside bearing a letter of introduction from James Russell Lowell, dated August 5. As he recalled this occasion in 1894, his visit with Hawthorne was more satisfying than with anyone else he met. In an hour on the hill back of the Wayside, his host smoked a cigar, asked questions about the West, and displayed a quiet naturalness that contrasted with the role-playing he found in Lowell, Holmes, Thoreau, and Emerson. He remembered Hawthorne as "sombre and brooding," "full of dark repose," possessed of a "quiet, patient intelligence." In summary, Howells wrote, Hawthorne had been as cordial as so shy a man could be, and revealed, "with the repose that nothing else can give, the entire sincerity of his soul." Hawthorne sent his visitor to Emerson with a note: "I find this young man worthy." Emerson displayed what Howells was coming to see as a New England trait, totally lacking in Hawthorne, the habit of enunciating precepts and showing oneself as an example to be emulated. Emerson had read *The Marble Faun*, apparently, and casually called it "mere mush." Howells was so overwhelmed with a sense that he had failed in his visit to Emerson that he thought of returning to Hawthorne and confessing his failure, confident of being understood.[22]

As Hawthorne's carefully written notebooks accumulated in England, he thought of them as something more attractive than the kind of literary drudgery he had often considered in the past. He mentioned to Ticknor that he "could easily make up a couple of nice volumes," except that "unluckily, they would be much too good and true to bear publication." His London journal, he said, "would be worth a mint of money to you and me, if I could let you publish it." Several times afterward he spoke of publishing his journals if they were not "too spicy" and "too full and free" and written with too "free and truth-telling a pen." Before going to Italy in 1858, he told Fields he had thought of sealing his journals for a hundred years, and he did seal the seven volumes before leaving them with Henry Bright, saying that they were not to be opened until the year 1900, by which time, he said in a remark typical of his bantering with Bright, England would probably be "a minor Republic, under the protection of the United States."[23]

One sketch from the journals appeared in the *Keepsake* for 1857, "Uttox-

eter," which tells about the "purely sentimental pilgrimage" Hawthorne
made in July, 1855, to the scene of Samuel Johnson's penance; and by the
summer of 1860 he had acceded to Fields's urging that he publish additional sketches. He first looked at his notes on Leigh Hunt, which he had
thought of publishing at the time he wrote them; but a sketch of his visit
to the Burns country looked more manageable, in a short time, since it
would be "of the photographic kind."[24] "Some of the Haunts of Burns"
came out in the October *Atlantic Monthly;* a year passed before the second
sketch appeared; three more came out in 1862, and five in 1863. The installments were popular; Fields increased the author's pay from $100 each
to $150, and then to $200. Having in mind the autobiographical sketches
used as introductions to *The Scarlet Letter* and *Mosses from an Old Manse,*
Hawthorne wrote "Consular Experiences" and kept it for initial publication as the first in a collection of the sketches, *Our Old Home.* The earlier
article on Johnson's penance was expanded under the title "Lichfield and
Uttoxeter," bringing the number of sketches to twelve. The book was
published on September 18, 1863. Fields had arranged with Smith and
Elder for an English edition, for which £150 would be paid.

Hawthorne had voiced his usual doubts as he shaped the essays and
sent them to the *Atlantic.* Fields was writing unrestrained praise of every
article; and Hawthorne's doubts about the worth of the essays were in a
measure his modest acknowledgment of praise. He did concede that the
sketch entitled "Consular Experiences" had "some of the features that attract the curiosity of the foolish public, being made up of personal narrative and gossip, with a few pungencies of personal satire," and he stressed
the truthfulness throughout.[25] In answering a reader who had written
him, he declared the sketch of the doctor of divinity to be "entirely true
and neither overdrawn nor overcolored," and he wrote also what is in effect a statement on his literary method: "Though a professed man of fiction, I am scrupulous in whatever purports to be matter of fact. . . . I
narrated the fact because it was in itself so striking, and because it illustrated the liability of those who stand highest among us to fall into the
depths of error and iniquity."[26]

When English protests against *Our Old Home* reached Hawthorne, he
expressed surprise; but he could not have expected this volume to be
much more acceptable to English readers than he had supposed the notebooks would be. In his letter of dedication he had predicted—or indeed
had invited—protests. Although he had felt "hereditary sympathies" with
the English and had seldom met one "without beginning to like him" or

without afterward having his "favorable impressions wax stronger with the progress of the acquaintance," it was nevertheless undeniable, he said, that an American was "continually thrown upon his national antagonism by some acrid quality in the moral atmosphere of England." The English thought "so loftily of themselves, and so contemptuously of everybody else," that it required more generosity than he possessed to stay in a good humor with them. It might be that he had moved from his notebook to these pages "little acrimonies of the moment" that would not belong in a profound portrait of the national character; but he was convinced that all elements of his portrait contained "more or less of truth," and if they were true, there could be no reason not to say them. "Not an Englishman of them all ever spared America, for courtesy's sake or kindness." It would be a mistake, he continued, to think the English as sensitive as the Americans in this regard, and he hoped that Americans were growing less sensitive.[27]

The earliest reviews Hawthorne read were in the English journals. The reviewer in the *Reader* declared the book to be "pervaded from beginning to end by an anti-English feeling." After reading this comment, Hawthorne wrote Fields, October 18, that, whenever he drew a comparison, he almost invariably favored the English. The reviewers as a rule complimented the author and his previous works; even the writer of a sarcastic tribute in *Punch* to this "Liverpool Lovelace, Nathaniel Hawthorne," as a lady-killer among English girls and matrons, this master of "caricatures and libels upon English folk," allowed himself to praise the prose style. In seeking to explain how such a genial and gifted author had turned to what he called the "perpetual carping and much virulence" of this book, the writer in *Blackwood's Magazine* found an explanation in the resentment generated in the Northern states by the English sympathy for the Confederate cause. Edward Dicey, who had visited Hawthorne at Concord, published a sympathetic and mainly understanding essay, in which he blamed the war and political alignments for Hawthorne's severity on the English, but concluded that the English had been far too harsh in attacking the book.[28]

English sensitivity showed up in others besides the reviewers, and in some instances long afterward. The Scottish physician and author John Brown wrote Fields twenty years later that *Our Old Home*, rather than truth, was a caricature of truth. But he credited Hawthorne with "a marvelous weird, Rembrandtish power of light and shadow."[29] Matthew Arnold wrote in the same year, when he could look back on experiences of his own in exchanging charges and counter-charges across the Atlantic, that *Our Old Home* is "the work of a man chagrined." Arnold remarked, in an explanation thoroughly in character for him, that Hawthorne had associated mainly with English Philistines, who Arnold said can be trying.[30] Henry James found the book provincial, as he did Hawthorne's total work, in this instance "exquisitely provincial"; but he found in it also "more charming and affectionate things than . . . had ever before been written about a country not the writer's own."[31]

Henry Bright reviewed *Our Old Home* and also wrote the author a private comment. In print he spoke of the grace and beauty, pathos, and humor of the book, but said that the author "saw things as an American with strong prejudices." He kept the review on a half-serious level, saying, for example, that Hawthorne was so fond of England that he envied the English for having it.[32] It was in keeping with his and Hawthorne's frank and bantering but largely serious exchanges about national traits for him to send his severest criticism in a letter. "Don't think me ungrateful for my abuse of your abuse of English ladies," he said; "an inevitable lance had to be broken, both for the fun of it and the truth of it." If he were writing his review now, he said, his lance would be sharper and his thrust more vigorous, for he had just become "the happy father of a little girl who promises to be a typical Englishwoman."[33] Bennoch wrote to put Hawthorne right about things English: "We won't be put down as to the quality of our fruit, but challenge all creation." And as to English beauty, "This won't do! For either grace or loveliness, good bearing or refined gentleness, I'll back England's daughters against the world."[34]

When Hawthorne wrote Fields that he did not care to see any more English reviews of *Our Old Home*, he meant that he expected the national bias to be reflected over and over. He was no less aware when he published the essays than when he wrote the entries in his notebook that his portrayal of the English would stir resentment. He may have thought there was some truth, moreover, in the assertions of the English reviewers that events of the war had sharpened his barbs. Before *Our Old Home* went to press, he had faced a major decision on a dedication for the volume. The decision depended on his answer to questions about national politics and the Civil War that had distressed him since he returned to America.

30

A Divided Nation
and Divided Minds

In the Liverpool consulate, Hawthorne's mind turned often to the future of his country, particularly in the summer of 1856. The international tension at that time bolstered his patriotism, and in letters to Ticknor and Bridge he urged them to be less gloomy about America. He said he regretted that Bridge thought of the Union so despairingly, for he would like "to hold on to the old thing," even if the states were "too various and too extended to form really one country." Yet he sympathized with the Northern feeling, and thought it time to make a stand. If he had to choose, he would go for the North, though he had "no kindred with nor leaning towards the Abolitionists."[1] As early as the debate over the annexation of Texas, Sophia wrote her mother that Hawthorne said "he should be glad of the separation of the South from the North, for then he should feel as if he had a country, which he can never do while that weight of slavery hangs on our skirts."[2]

After leaving the Liverpool consulate, Hawthorne had less news from America, but when he was in Concord again, national affairs were much in his mind. Writing friends in England required him to formulate his opinions on current matters. He sent Henry Bright assurances late in 1860 that he was prepared for whatever might come, for "New England will still have her rocks and ice"; and for a time he continued his customary playful manner of speaking about national and international affairs. In proposing that Bright come to America on his honeymoon, he wrote, "If you come soon enough, you will have the pleasure (and I know it will be a great one, to your wicked English heart) of seeing the Union in its death-throes, and of triumphing over me in revenge for all the uncivil things I used to say about England and her institutions." Might not England be induced to take the New England states back? Or might not Canada, New England, and Nova Scotia be lumped together as a kingdom for Prince Alfred? He would gladly exchange the South for Canada, and, if such an arrangement were made, he would "claim to be made a peer for having been the first to suggest it." Still, it would not surprise him if the Americans, as a result of the stress, became "a better and a nobler people than ever heretofore. As to the South," he continued, "I never loved it. We do not belong together; the Union is unnatural, a scheme of man, not an ordinance of God, and as long as it continues, no American of either section will ever feel a genuine thrill of patriotism, such as you Englishmen feel at every breath you draw."[3]

On April 13, 1861, Sophia wrote in her pocket diary "WAR!!" and noted the firing on Fort Sumter. Her notes the following day indicate how seriously the family took the news; they held morning service in the chapel in the Wayside, and at noon she went with her husband on the hill back of the house, where he normally went alone and was not to be disturbed. He repeated to Bridge on May 26 his previous statements in the new context: "What ever happens next, I must say that I rejoice that the old Union is smashed. We never were one people, and never really had a country." But he still had his life-long habit of seeing more than one side, of moderating any certainty, surely any enthusiasm, in the skeptical processes of his mind. To share in the heroic sentiment and to feel that he had a country seemed to make him young again. It was a regrettable matter that he was too old to shoulder a musket; a joyful thing that Julian was too young. Although he approved the war as much as anyone, he did not quite understand what the fighting was for, or what result could be expected. If the South were defeated, it should be cut adrift. The annihilation of slavery might be a wise object, and would be the only one consistent with a restoration of the Union. With that object in view, he continued, "we should see the expediency of preparing our black brethren for future citizenship by allowing them to fight for their own liberties, and educating them through heroic influences." As news arrived from the battlefields, he allowed himself emotional responses. After the Battle of Bull Run, he wrote James Russell Lowell on another matter and concluded, "last evening's news will dull the edge of many a northern appetite; but if it puts all of us into the same grim and bloody humour that it does me, the South had better have suffered ten defeats than won this victory."[4] He was conscious of writing to an abolitionist; in writing Francis Bennoch at about the same time, he included a note of puzzlement as to what those in different sections of the country would say they were fighting for: in the South, "for State rights, liberty and independence"; in the Midwest, for the Union; in the North and East, for the annihilation of slavery. But he said also, "When I hear the drums beating, and see their banners flying, and witness their steady marching, I declare were it not for certain silvery monitors hanging by my temples suggesting prudence, I feel as if I could catch the infection, shoulder a musket, and be off to the war myself."

He wrote Henry Bright late in 1861 that the war had drawn his "thoughts wholly to itself," and his letters recorded his growing depression. Statements that ultimately the war would do the country good, chiefly in letters to England, gave way to assertions that "no nation ever came safe and sound through such a confounded difficulty as this of ours." He was not "bigoted to the Union," as he said Pierce was; he "would fight to the death for the Northern slave-states," and then "cast off the extreme Southern States, and giving them a parting kick, let them go to perdition in their own way." It would be absurd for the North to spend all her strength, "for the next generation, in holding on to a people who insist on being let loose." The conflict continued to haunt his mind until he had visited Washington and had written an essay stating conclusions he had reached with enough assurance to free his mind of the war, except for the "infinite weariness" he felt.[5]

Early in 1862, he had an invitation to visit Horatio Bridge in Washington. After first demurring, he left Boston on March 7 with W. D. Ticknor, stopped in New York and Philadelphia, and arrived on the tenth. Through the management of Bridge and others, he followed a schedule that included a call on President Lincoln, visits to Alexandria, Fort Ellsworth, Harper's Ferry, Manassas, Fortress Monroe, and Newport News. He went aboard the *Monitor* and other warships; he observed General McClellan reviewing his troops; he had a close view of Union soldiers in camp, Confederate prisoners, and slaves fleeing northward. He took notes and used the occasion to clarify his opinions on questions that had troubled him. The essay "Chiefly about War Matters," which appeared in the July *Atlantic*, is among the most helpful of his writings toward an understanding of his views on the current scene and on broad human and social issues as well, and toward an understanding of how his mind worked and how he adapted the materials of observation to literary use. More than in any other of his works, he is dealing here with immediate and momentous questions, on which his relatives and associates had positive and divergent opinions, and on which he felt a moral obligation to reach defensible conclusions of his own. Conspicuous throughout the essay is the play of his skeptical, ironic, and symbolic mind on materials that can be known from other sources for comparison with his treatment.

The article went to Fields, along with the author's statement that he was omitting a great deal—"else it would have grown into a book"—and that he "found it quite difficult not to lapse into treason continually; but . . . made manful resistance to the temptation." He included "some editorial footnotes" which he hoped Fields would "have no hesitation in adopting, they being very loyal." Fields sent the manuscript to the printer unread, and went to New York without seeing the proof-sheets. Hawthorne therefore wrote Ticknor that he wanted someone's judgment as to the "expediency of publishing two or three passages" of the essay. He had already "half-spoilt it by leaving out a great deal of spicy description and remark, and whole pages of freely expressed opinion," which he "doubted whether the public would bear." He could see no room for objection to anything that remained, but he did not want to foist an article on the magazine that might damage it. Still, he would be known as the author and would be "willing to take the responsibility of much worse things" than this article. Besides, he thought the "political complexion" of the *Atlantic* had been "getting too deep a black Republican tinge," for which the publishers would soon be sorry. The politics of the magazine suited Massachusetts "tolerably well (and only tolerably) but it does not fairly represent the country at large"; and he believed "it would be good policy to be preparing to respond to another, and wiser, and truer mood of public sentiment." Ticknor wrote on the envelope of this letter that it was not answered.[6]

After reading the proof, Fields wrote on May 21 that he liked the article hugely, but would ask Hawthorne not to call the President "Uncle Abe" and not to describe his "awkwardness and general uncouth aspect." He did not like the way the essay spoke of the Southerners and wanted to strike out the expressions that he thought would "outrage the feelings of many Atlantic readers."[7] Hawthorne replied after two days, acquiescing in part, but allowing Fields little room to be proud of his victory. He thought Fields wrong, but was complying with his requests. Since he could not alter his account of the interview with Uncle Abe, he was omitting it, though he believed it had historical value and was "the only part of the article really worth publishing." He had made the other changes and could not conceive of any further objection. "What a terrible thing it is," he added, "to try to let off a little bit of truth into this miserable humbug of a world! If I had sent you the article as I first conceived it, I should not so much have wondered." He wanted a proof-sheet of the article before the alterations; for, in any future reprinting, he would "insert it in all its original beauty." He had been able to see Lincoln because he was invited to join a Massachusetts delegation which had an appointment to present a riding whip. Fields may have supposed the *Atlantic* readers would dislike as much as anything else the remarks that the gift of a whip was "a suggestive and emblematic one" and that "the President's Yankee aptness and not-to-be-caughtness stood him in good stead" when he said that he "accepted the whip as an emblem of peace, not punishment."

Even with the omissions and amendments made at Fields's behest, "Chiefly about War Matters" remained thoroughly Hawthornean. In 1871 Fields published the deleted passages and they appeared in subsequent printings of the essay.[8] Since he had concluded, the author says at the beginning, that "there is a kind of treason in insulating one's self from the universal fear and sorrow, and thinking one's idle thoughts in the dread time of civil war," he had left the "unsubstantial business" usual with him and had given his full attention to the war. On the prospect of eliminating all war in the future, he echoes the conclusion stated in his earlier sketch "Earth's Holocaust" (1844) that the Millennium probably "will advance to the sound of trumpets." The thought comes to him in this connection that after the war "One bullet-headed general" will "succeed another in the Presidential chair." But the thought has another facet, that such a political succession might "substitute something more real and genuine" than the shams on which office-seekers normally base their claims. Thus the author establishes at once the tone of his essay; he will present matters of utmost national importance with enough whimsy and irony to prompt, he hopes, the reconsideration he believes needed in the public and among public officials.

Again and again Hawthorne displays two edges where his reader expects only one. Fort Ellsworth ought to be preserved, for it will "afford fit soil for poetry to root itself in," and the richer will be "the daily life that feeds upon the past." Observing "a party of contrabands, escaping out of the mysterious depths of Secession," he knows not what to wish in their behalf, but feels sure that whoever might benefit from the results of the war, it will not be the present generation of Negroes, "who must hence-forth fight a hard battle with the world, on very unequal terms." He can-not escape his conviction that consequences are inevitable. His quarrel with reformers has been that they are too likely not to envisage and pro-vide for all the results of their efforts. His recent observations have shown him that men "are as ready to slaughter one another now, after playing at peace and good will for so many years, as in the rudest ages, that never heard of peace societies. . . . it is odd, when we measure our advances from barbarism, and find ourselves just here!" A footnote supposedly by the magazine editor voices surprise at "this outbreak in favor of war from the Peaceable Man," but adds that "the justice of our cause makes us all soldiers at heart," and that twenty Quakers have been reported fighting in one unit of a Pennsylvania regiment. Hawthorne's visit to Alexandria, across the Potomac from Washington, has caused him to try "to imagine how very disagreeable the presence of a Southern army would be in a sober town of Massachusetts," and has lessened his wonder at the "sullen demeanor" shown by the Virginians in the presence of Union soldiers. Since a Southerner must be a traitor to either his country or his state, and since the country is "too vast by far to be taken into one small human heart," leaving a citizen no unit except his state or his section for which he can have a love comparable to that of an Englishman for England, the au-thor urges, "If a man loves his own State, therefore, and is content to be ruined with her, let us shoot him, if we can, but allow him an honorable burial in the soil he fights for." Again a footnote calls this remark repre-hensible in tone and impolitic at the time. While Hawthorne was in Wash-ington, General McClellan was in great disfavor following the early Union losses and his slowness to move against the Confederate forces in northern Virginia. Taking note of the "bitter outcry, and detraction loud and low," Hawthorne declares that he will not give up his "faith in McClellan's sol-diership until he is defeated, nor in his courage and integrity even then." It was never difficult for him to enter reservations against the clamor of the mob.

In recounting his journey to Harper's Ferry (in a party that included the essayist N. P. Willis and the English journalist Edward Dicey),[9] Haw-thorne notes that Virginia towns are shabby but would appear less so, in contrast to those of New England, if the Southerners "were as much in the habit of using white paint," which is "prodigiously efficacious in put-ting a bright face upon bad matter." Thus he approaches the subject of John Brown. He will "not pretend to be an admirer of old John Brown," nor does he expect ever "to shrink so unutterably from any apophthegm of a sage, whose happy lips have uttered a hundred golden sentences, as from that saying (perhaps falsely attributed to so honored a source), that the death of this blood-stained fanatic has 'made the Gallows as venerable as the Cross!' " On June 22, 1862, Hawthorne answered a letter from Horatio Woodman, a fellow member of the Saturday Club, saying that he was sorry he had misquoted the "apophthegm of a sage," Emerson, and that he knew only the sentence that had reached him in England. The *New York Daily Tribune* of November 8 and the *Liberator* of November 11, 1859, had reported the speech Emerson made in Boston on November 7, and both had contained the sentence, "The Saint, whose fate yet hangs in suspense, but whose martyrdom, if it shall be perfected, will make the gallows as glorious as the cross." Hawthorne said the version Woodman sent him made "a considerable difference, as allowing the reader or auditor (if he pleases) to put John Brown at a somewhat lower elevation than Jesus Christ. But, as a mere matter of taste, surely, it had better never have been said." The essay continues, "Nobody was ever more justly hanged," and "any common-sensible man, looking at the matter unsentimentally, must have felt a certain intellectual satisfaction in seeing him hanged, if it were only in requital of his preposterous miscalculation of possibilities." A footnote exclamation at this point reads, "Can it be a son of old Massachusetts who utters this abominable sentiment? For shame!"

The Confederate prisoners confined at Harper's Ferry Hawthorne says are "peasants, and of a very low order," who have not a single trait in common with the Northern rural population. The next statement takes an unexpected direction: They are more respectful "than a rustic New Englander ever dreams of being towards anybody except perhaps his minister." And one of the prisoners has been called to his attention as one who "absolutely trampled the soul out of a wounded Northern soldier who had sought his assistance." This is "a wild beast of a man," Hawthorne's account runs, a "fiend, if you prefer to call him so, though I would not advise it, . . . a wild beast, as I began with saying,—an unsophisticated wild beast,—while the rest of us are partially tamed, though still the scent of blood excites some of the savage instincts of our nature. What this wretch needed, in order to make him capable of the degree of mercy and benevolence that exists in us, was simply such a measure of moral and intellectual development as we have received." These sentences were hardly calculated to support emotional dedication to a war by partially tamed beasts against untamed beasts. For the Confederate prisoners, "all truly valuable things are dependent on our complete success." A parenthetical statement is less assuring: "For ourselves, the balance of advantages between defeat and triumph may admit of question." The concluding sentences in this sequence are no less sweeping: "No human effort, on a grand scale, has ever yet resulted according to the purpose of its projectors. The advantages are always incidental. Man's accidents are God's purposes. We miss the good we sought, and do the good we little care for."

As if in relief from such weighty, if not disturbing, considerations as these, the essay presents an interlude before its conclusion. As a member of a "commission to proceed to Fortress Monroe and examine into things in general," the author went aboard various ships, including the *Monitor*, the "gigantic rat-trap" which had recently demonstrated its superiority over conventional ships. But he was affected "with far profounder emotion" by seeing the masts of two sunken vessels, the *Congress* and the *Cumberland*. (In writing his son Julian on March 27 about the *Cumberland*'s refusing to surrender to the *Merrimac* and firing its last shot after its decks were awash, he had said, "A braver thing was never done, and I only wish I could write a song about it—or you either." Henry Wadsworth Longfellow did write a poem about it, "The Cumberland," in the December *Atlantic*.) This interlude also expands the whimsical proposition Hawthorne had explained to Francis Bennoch earlier: no one under fifty years of age would be accepted for training; no soldier would be allowed to volunteer for the most dangerous duty under the age of seventy. "Methinks there would be no more Bull Runs; a warrior with gout in his toe, or a rheumatism in his joints, or with one foot in the grave, would make a sorry fugitive!"

Concluding his essay with observations at Willard's Hotel in Washington, Hawthorne pictures the Peace Democrats, those who wanted to end the war and restore the Union as it formerly existed. If the matter is looked at generously, he says, theirs is "no unpardonable crime." Still, he can see "no way but to go on winning victories, and establishing peace and a truer union in another generation, at the expense, probably, of greater trouble, in the present one, than any other people ever voluntarily suffered." His conclusion that the present generation must pay heavily for a truer union in the future prepares for his concluding sentence: "Or, if we stop short of that blessed consummation, heaven was heaven still, as Milton sings, after Lucifer and a third part of the angels had seceded from its golden palaces,—and perhaps all the more heavenly, because so many gloomy brows and soured, vindictive hearts had gone to plot ineffectual schemes of mischief elsewhere." In the longest of his footnotes, he allows the editor, supposedly, to have his say: "The war can never be allowed to terminate, except in the complete triumph of Northern principles. . . . We should be sorry to cast a doubt on the Peaceable Man's loyalty, but he will allow us to say that we consider him premature in his kindly feelings towards traitors and sympathizers with treason." Referring to the author's supposition that "a common-sensible man" might take satisfaction in seeing John Brown hanged, the editor asserts, "There are some degrees of absurdity that put Reason herself into a rage, and affect us like an intolerable crime,—which this Rebellion is, into the bargain." Fields, the editor supposed to be writing these notes, could take little pleasure in the portrait of him thus drawn by implication.

After spending a month in Washington and writing "Chiefly about War Matters," Hawthorne had satisfied himself on the issues that had distressed him for two years. His outlook afterward was no less gloomy, but his remarks reflected acceptance and resignation to what he had come to see as inevitable. He wrote Bennoch late in 1862 that the war was "the most inevitable event that ever happened." The next January he wrote Fields that he expected the close of the war to bring "utter ruin—at all events, so dark a gloom that nobody can see to read in it." In March he wrote Bright that he felt chiefly "a sense of infinite weariness." He wanted "the end to come, and the curtain to drop, and then to go to sleep." He had been "publicly accused of treasonable sympathies"; if he had any wishes, they were "that New England might be a nation by itself." Even "the most uncompromising opponents of the war" were beginning to see "the impossibility of ever bringing it to an end except by completest victory or direst defeat." Members of the Saturday Club all favored continuing the war. Emerson was "as merciless as a steel bayonet"; earlier Hawthorne had told Bright that Emerson was breathing fire, but had softened the remark by adding, "like the rest of us."[10] In recent letters to his friends in England, he had said little about the war, but had made it clear that he was disappointed in the English attitude. After reading an article by Harriet Beecher Stowe in the *Atlantic* for January, 1863, in which she chided the English women for statements from England, which she quoted, sympathetic to the Confederacy, he wrote her that John Bull was "a hardened and villainous hypocrite," caring "nothing for or against slavery, except as it gave him a vantage-ground on which to parade his own virtue and sneer at our iniquity."[11]

Nathaniel Hawthorne, 1862; photograph by Mathew B. Brady. Courtesy of the Essex Institute, Salem, Mass.

Hawthorne's decision to dedicate *Our Old Home* to Franklin Pierce was the only one open to him, given his loyalty to friends and his unwillingness to be drawn into the camp of the abolitionists on this occasion, out of what might seem to be deference to his neighbors and relatives and to his own financial interests. The issues were the same he had faced in deciding to write Pierce's campaign biography, but now they were more sharply and more emotionally conceived. With most of the manuscript completed, he enumerated for Fields on May 3 the three possibilities he saw: a dedication to Pierce, or to Francis Bennoch, or no dedication. When Fields later asked for the prefatory matter if there was to be any, Hawthorne replied, "It requires some little thought and policy in order to say nothing amiss at this time; and I intend to dedicate the book to Frank Pierce, come what may."[12] He delivered the manuscript on July 3 and went on to Concord, New Hampshire, where the next day he sat on the platform when Pierce addressed a Democratic Party meeting on the theme that "efforts to maintain the Union by force of arms" were futile. Hawthorne wrote Pierce afterward that "some spiteful Abolitionist" had sent him a compendium of bitter newspaper attacks following the speech, which he tossed away without reading.[13] In sending the proofs of the prefatory matter, Fields wrote that it was the opinion of wiser men than he in the trade that the dedication would ruin the sale of the book. He continued, "You must decide whether you will risk the sale of 'Our Old Home' by putting a friend's name to it. . . . Rough days we live in. . . . Last night we had blood in the streets."[14]

If Fields had understood Hawthorne better, he would have said less about the threat to the sale of the book and less about the rough days as arguments against the dedication. Hawthorne wanted time to "ponder deeply on" the advice. Moreover, he responded, "I have no fancy for making myself a martyr when it is honorably and conscientiously possible to avoid it; and I always measure out my heroism very accurately according to the exigencies of the occasion, and should be the last man in the world to throw away a bit of it needlessly." He would rewrite the last paragraph in such a way that, while doing justice to his friend, it would contain "not a word that ought to be objectionable to any set of readers." But "it would be a piece of poltroonery" to withdraw the dedication or the dedicating letter. The book had been made possible by Pierce; and, Hawthorne added, "if he is so exceedingly unpopular that his name is enough to sink the volume, there is so much the more need that an old friend should stand by him." He would not alter his purpose "merely on account of pecuniary profit or literary reputation," and if he were to tear out the dedication, he would "never look at the volume again without remorse and shame." The literary public must take his book as he thought best for it, or let it alone. "If the public of the North see fit to ostracize me for this, I can only say that I would gladly sacrifice a thousand or two of dollars rather than retain the good will of such a herd of dolts and mean-spirited scoundrels." [15] He bowed to Fields's urging enough to say in the revised final paragraph that he was dedicating his book "to the Friend" and would "defer a colloquy with the Statesman till some calmer and sunnier hour." But he left unchanged his avowal that he needed no assurance that Pierce continued "faithful forever to that grand idea of an irrevocable Union." [16]

Hawthorne had supposed that the question of the dedication was between him and his publisher; his wife did not know what he intended, nor did Pierce. So he wrote Elizabeth Peabody. She had written him at the behest of Ellery Channing, who had been enlisted by Fields in an effort to dissuade him from dedicating the book to Pierce. [17] His reply gave fuller statements of the arguments he had sent Fields, and also was his first attempt, he said, to write down ideas that had previously existed only "in a gaseous state" in his mind: Although he had always believed that the war should have been avoided, he had "longed for military success as much as any man or woman of the North." The war would "only effect by a horrible convulsion the self-same end that might and would have been brought about by a gradual and peaceful change." He would as lief see his grandfather's ghost as have the Union revive, and he wanted the North to retain only as much Southern soil as could be digested into freedom in another century. At the time he was fearful that, with the North never caring much for "the negro-question," the Peace Democrats and the Southern officials would reach an agreement for preserving the old Union and slavery also. [18]

General Ethan Allen Hitchcock (1798–1870), military adviser to President Lincoln throughout the Civil War, visited in Concord and corresponded with residents of the town, including Elizabeth Peabody, Mary Mann, and Mrs. Hawthorne. A student of hermetic philosophy and a voluminous writer on literary and philosophical topics, he had been a favorite of Mrs. Hawthorne's from the time he called at the Wayside on September 9, 1862. In the letters they exchanged afterward, aspects of the war appeared often. She sent him the full endorsement of his belief "that God's law would without fail have removed slavery without this dreadful convulsive action. . . . It always seems to me that Man is very arrogant in taking such violent measures to *help God*. . . . I find no one in Concord or hardly in Boston to whom I can utter such sentiments without exciting fiery indignation. My sisters cannot hear me speak a word. They believe alone in instant vengeance on the slave owner. . . . To my husband only can I speak." Late in 1863 Hitchock wrote her and her sister Mary Mann asking advice on a problem that had come to him as commissioner in charge of the exchange of prisoners of war: Support was growing in Washington for a policy of retaliation against Confederate soldiers in prison, the justification being reports that captured Union soldiers were underfed and mistreated in Southern prisons. Mrs. Hawthorne replied in a long letter reiterating her exclamation, "No retaliation of any kind!" Her husband, she said, was entirely of her opinion as to retaliation, and he was surprised to learn that Emerson had joined Mary Mann in favoring such a policy— so surprised, in fact, that he called on Emerson and was assured that there had been a misunderstanding, that Emerson did not agree with Mary Mann. Mrs. Hawthorne wrote Hitchcock in haste to correct what she had said, and added, "Mr. Emerson had used so many *ifs* in talking to my sister, that in effect he differs from her, while she is deceived by the *ifs*."[19]

Hawthorne held to his views, stated them when there was a proper occasion, as in "Chiefly about War Matters," and even challenged Emerson on the question of retaliation against prisoners. Whether he could "look serenely on opposing forces and do justice to each," as his wife wrote Hitchcock he could, there is no evidence that he was embittered toward his neighbors. His severest comments on them that have been preserved are in his published works. Yet he would not have failed to know how far he stood on current issues from Emerson, Thoreau, and Alcott. During his earlier residence at Concord he had taken little part in the community routine of visiting and conversing, but he was more secluded during his last years at the Wayside than he had been at any time since his years under the eaves on Herbert Street in Salem. The depression he experienced because of the war was increased, no doubt, because he realized that those around him had different opinions from his on the greatest issue of his time.

31

Romances in Fragments

In December, 1863, Hawthorne's wife said that in the past four or five years he had lost the "zest of life he used to have," that "the splendor and pride of strength" in him had succumbed.[1] It was her habit to say that his body and spirit were inseparable, and that he had never recovered from the fear and sorrow he suffered during Una's illness in Rome.

While consul at Liverpool, Hawthorne had said repeatedly and with a note of pride that his health had never been better. His rage against the colds that plagued him in Rome suggests that the misery was a new experience; his lack of interest in sightseeing and his distaste for notebook writing on the journey from Rome to London in 1859 had implications of poor health. The scenery along the Rhone River, he remarked in his notebook on June 11, would interest him if he were not weary of being interested. "Rest, rest, rest! There is nothing else so desirable; and I sometimes fancy, but only half in earnest, how pleasant it would be to be six feet under ground, and let the grass grow over me." He lacked "energy to seek objects of interest, curiosity even so much as to glance at them, heart to enjoy them, intellect to profit by them." In the same long entry he added, "It may be disease; it may be age; it may be the effect of the lassitudinous Roman atmosphere; but such is the fact." During the year he remained in England, he concentrated on completing *The Marble Faun*, and had little interest beyond that, except to say farewell to his English friends and take the ship for home.

Soon after returning to America, he began to show himself aware of health and age. He wrote to David Roberts, his card partner of the 1830's, that they had reached the age "when old friends ought to make the most of each other," and continued, "I cannot say that I feel a great deal older than when we parted, though seven years of vicissitude cannot have passed without a good deal of wear and tear."[2] He invited Roberts to pay him a long visit in the summer, adding the warm invitation of his wife, which seems out of keeping with her coldness toward Roberts in earlier years. Events later in the summer indicate that she saw a need for help in drawing her husband out of his retirement. He and Julian went to Pride's Crossing, West Beach, near Beverly. Lodging at a farmhouse, they walked in the woods with Aunt Ebe, who lived nearby, fished and swam and picked berries; and the father recalled for his son his own boyhood acquaintance with the region. At the end of the day he left home, July 27, his wife recorded her sense of his "depressed energies and spirits"; of all trials, the heaviest for her was to see him "so apathetic, so indifferent, so hopeless, so unstrung." She had operated with a deft hand to get off to the seashore, by leading him to believe that, as he wrote James Russell Lowell, Julian needed "sea-air and change." And she urged him to stay, for her health as well as his: ". . . stay, at Pride's Crossing, or somewhere where there is sea, with a happy and easy mind; and we shall all be in health for it."[3]

Hawthorne had told Ticknor in February, 1861, that he had begun spending two or three hours a day in his tower, but that nothing important had resulted; in the autumn he said he was planning a romance, but wanted it announced only conditionally. On October 12 he wrote Bridge he was "blotting successive sheets of paper, as of yore." A month later he confessed to Henry Bright that his health had not been as good as in England; the next February 13 he told Bridge he was "not very well, being mentally and physically languid." While he was visiting Bridge in Washington in the spring of 1862, his wife urged that he make such visits more often, for his spirits would get "below concert pitch" when he stayed too long in one place. She had no "purer pleasure and completer pleasure" than when she got him "fairly away from Concord influences."[4] He took Julian to West Gouldsboro, on the coast of Maine, and took lodgings in a farmhouse for the last three weeks in August. They kept a joint notebook, in which Hawthorne wrote sketches[5] of people he met, as he had done over the past thirty years. In October he wrote Bennoch that he did not expect ever to see England again. On December 11 his wife wrote Una,

who was visiting Aunt Ebe, "Papa . . . eats no dinners except a little potato. But he is trying to write, and locks himself into the library and pulls
down the blinds."

During the winter of 1862–63 Hawthorne declined invitations even to
Boston and noted that his friends there did not visit him often. He wrote
Ticknor: "I don't know whether I shall ever see you again; for I have now
staid here so long that I find myself rusted into my hole, and could not get
out even if I wished." He promised Fields to come to Boston in the spring
but added, "I have now been a hermit so long that the thought affects me
somewhat as it would to invite a lobster or a crab to step out of his shell."
Near the end of May, he accepted Lowell's invitation to visit him after a
meeting of the Saturday Club and stay until Monday. He hoped he would
not drink and smoke too much and fill his pipe too often in Lowell's
study, as he had done the last time. But on Friday he wrote Lowell that
he had "a cold and derangement of the stomach" that would not let him
leave home. In June he thought he would put off going to Boston until the
autumn, but he went on July 3, on his way to visit Pierce and to sit on the
platform during his address on the Fourth. He and Pierce laid plans for an
excursion in the mountains, which had to be canceled on account of Mrs.
Pierce's illness. In asking Ticknor later in the month for $300 from his ac-
count, Hawthorne remarked that he expected to outlive his means and die
in the alms-house. He must try to get his "poor blunted pen at work again
pretty soon," especially because Fields threatened that nobody would buy
Our Old Home on account of the dedication.[6] Mrs. Hawthorne had written
Ticknor on May 15 that, although Hawthorne was unwell, she could not
persuade him to drink some wine he had—he said it was expensive and
should be saved for guests. "He feels so poor now, and is so accustomed to
go without everything he wants himself." She did succeed in getting him
off to the beach in September, to Rockport this time, on the coast north of
Salem, and with Una.[7]

Late in 1863, prompted by growing fears that his savings would be inadequate and ignoring the threats of poor health, Hawthorne resumed the
attempt to write a final romance that had defied him for more than three
years. After returning to the Wayside in 1860, he had taken up again the
idea of an English romance he had laid aside in Italy to write *The Marble
Faun*. At Liverpool in January, 1855, he had written Ticknor of plans for
a romance that would be set in England and would be "all the better for
ripening slowly"; he did no more with the plans than make a few notebook
jottings the following April, until the spring of 1858 in Rome, when he

wrote out the twenty-one copybook entries under dates from April 1 to May 19 that were published after his death as *The Ancestral Footstep*.[8] The bloody footstep at Smithell's Hall would be a central image and have a function in the return of an American to claim an English heritage. The sketches included also a hospital which he noted would be "pretty literally copied after Leicester's" (XII, 88) with its twelve ancient pensioners; they included also the ceremony of the loving cup he had observed at the London mayor's dinner.

Hawthorne had in mind, as he indicated in the last of these sketches, introducing the romance with a sketch similar to "The Old Manse" and "The Custom-House." The romance, he said, would be "an integral and essential part" with his introduction, which would give "a pleasant and familiar summary" of his life in the consulate at Liverpool. He would develop one of the strange Americans who had come to the consulate obsessed with the thought of an ancestral heritage, and would describe him with touches that would puzzle the reader to decide whether it was not an actual portrait. Part of this character's story might be told in the introduction, or it might be kept for the romance proper (XII, 87–88). In either instance, he would be fusing the actual and the imagined in the method he had followed with Surveyor Pue in "The Custom-House," Judge Pyncheon in *The House of the Seven Gables*, and characters in *The Blithedale Romance*.

Notes for the character Alice in the sketches indicate that she was to be modeled in part on Maria Louisa Lander, who was at work on the bust of Hawthorne at the time he wrote these sketches. Alice would be a sculptor interested particularly in busts and displaying the independence of thought and action, along with the courage and self-sufficiency that he saw in Miss Lander and Harriet Hosmer as distinctly American traits (XII, 86). In one sketch, Alice is not an American and voices the same charges Hawthorne heard from Jenny Lind, that American women were frail and unhealthy, for want of proper food and exercise. The character Middleton offers in the sketch the same defense of American women the author had offered Miss Lind and something of the same characterization of English women that appears in *Our Old Home* (XII, 70–71).

When the carpenter had left the Wayside late in 1860 and Hawthorne could begin writing in "the sky-parlour" of his tower, he first expanded the earlier sketches on the return of an American to reclaim his English inheritance, and then he wrote what would be the first part of the romance, set in the Peabody house beside the graveyard on Charter Street in Salem.

He stopped the narrative at intervals during composition and interjected analyses of the difficulties he was having. After giving up the first draft in exasperation, he started again and rewrote the American part of the romance before he abandoned it for good. From the two drafts, his son Julian put together a work he published in 1882 as *Doctor Grimshawe's Secret*. *The American Claimant Manuscripts*, Volume XII of the Centenary Edition, prints from the manuscripts *The Ancestral Footstep* and the two later drafts, which are given the titles *Etherege* and *Grimshawe*, from the names borne by the chief character in the two versions.

From his English experiences Hawthorne had abundant materials interesting enough and developed fully enough in his notebook to be readily adaptable to fictional use. He wanted to continue the international comparison that had filled his notebooks and his letters while he was in England, and to satirize the flaws and the foibles the comparison highlighted in the characters of both peoples. *The Blithedale Romance* had drawn extensively on his immediate observations and had incorporated social comment. But in that romance the focus is on the moral and psychological dimensions of the characters. Similarly in "Ethan Brand" the literal, realistic portrayal of the scene and the people the author knew at North Adams is subordinated to the idea of an unpardonable sin and the effects that idea has in Ethan Brand's mind. The bloody footstep might have served as the central image of an English romance; but Hawthorne found no way to give it the psychological context or the moral significance required by his method and his purpose. Perhaps he came to see that his English materials were producing no more than a romance of a retrieved heritage freighted with social comment. Perhaps the dreaming and thinking he must do to write fiction had been impossible while his mind was occupied so distressfully by the war.

If Hawthorne concluded that his English romance lacked the moral and psychological implications to leaven the mass of realistic and Gothic detail to be included, he saw better possibilities for a romance about the search for an elixir of life. Such a theme would have conventional thought on immortality as background, while exploring the concept of earthly immortality achieved by man's own efforts. At the death of his mother in 1849, he had written in his notebook that her forty years of widowhood and her death were arguments enough for immortality. And the idea of earthly immortality, or at least a greatly extended life on earth, had fascinated him as he encountered it in his reading—in stories of the Wandering Jew, for example, and the Flying Dutchman, and in the lore of alchemy. The idea of noble undertakings, as in reform efforts or artistic production, cut short by death, came to his mind often. Owen Warland, in "The Artist of the Beautiful," feels thwarted by the time limits enforced by his mortality. A notebook entry of January 20, 1855, suggests the puzzlement with which Hawthorne speculated on the subject: "God himself cannot compensate us for being born, in any period short of eternity. All the misery we endure here constitutes a claim for another life;—and, still more, all the happiness involves something more than the earth owns, and something more than a mortal capacity for the enjoyment of it."

His chief stimulus toward writing a story about an elixir of life came from what Henry David Thoreau told him at about the time he moved into the Wayside in 1852. A former resident of the house "was resolved never to die." Hawthorne said he could almost swear that the ghost of this predecessor frequented the Wayside in his own time. And while in Europe, he "mused and meditated, . . . and tried to make out what manner of man this might be, that deemed it within his power to subvert the usual conditions of humanity. How did he mean to do it? Had he discovered, as he might suppose, the great secret which philosophers used to seek for?" So Hawthorne wrote in a sketch at about the time in 1861 when he laid out his plan for James T. Fields, as they walked on the hill back of the Wayside.[9] When he began writing in earnest, these questions remained unanswered, and he had reached no clear views on the idea of an extended life. The elixir might be sought for unworthy reasons and might be given a ludicrous slant, as in the story "Dr. Heidegger's Experiment," or it might be sought for noble purposes. As with the story of the lost English heritage, he abandoned a romance for which he had produced voluminous manuscript, leaving a series of sketches and fore-studies and two unfinished drafts. One of the drafts was edited by his daughter Una, with assistance from Robert Browning, and published in 1872 as *Septimius Felton*. Volume XIII of the Centenary Edition, *The Elixir of Life Manuscripts*, prints the two unfinished drafts of this romance under the titles *Septimius Felton* and *Septimius Norton*, which represent the names of the main character in the two versions.

When Hawthorne returned to his desk in the autumn of 1863, hoping to complete a final romance that would be his best, and determined at least to supplement his dwindling savings, he took up again the story of the search for an elixir of life. He would modify the theme by giving a character the ability to stop aging and also to grow young again. He noted in an early sketch that the character must have "some clear connection with human sympathies in the particular object of this desire." He must aim at "something that shall give a substance to all his life," so that, after it is accomplished, he will feel "as if he could die willingly, and with a sense of completeness." In another sketch the character would want to live for the sake of the child of a friend who had sacrificed his own life to save his. Another purpose might be "to study the new order of things that seems to be opening on the world." [10] Persuaded by Fields, he went against his better judgment and allowed the new romance to be announced and the first installment scheduled for the *Atlantic* early in 1864. It did not appear, however, until July, after his death. Two additional segments, not continuous, were later published, one in the magazine the next January, and another when the three were combined under the title *The Dolliver Romance* in 1876. These three fragments, along with several fore-studies and draft fragments, are included in *The Elixir of Life Manuscripts* (XIII, 449–97, 530–53).

The fragments Hawthorne left at his death afford a glimpse into his workshop. Since they were a series of attempts that he was unable to finish, they show him repeating himself from one to another far more than in others of his works. A number of characters, situations, events, and ideas appear in more than one of the manuscripts: the bloody footstep, an American making a claim to an English inheritance, the comparisons between the two countries, flowers growing from a grave, the effects of Indian blood, the medicinal efficacy of spider webs, the wizard ancestor, the potion of which all ingredients are known except one. In the unfinished manuscripts the sources of these materials are identifiable, as are other elements drawn from the author's own outlook and experience. Because he was trying to assemble and combine materials from various other sources without a dominant idea of sufficient weight and an image impressive enough to fuse the whole into a Hawthornean romance, the separate components and the marks of the author's hand are recognizable. When he realized the reason for his failure, as he seems to have done before making a new start on *The Dolliver Romance*, he realized also that to complete the work he had begun would be impossible.

32

"Nearer to
the Way-Side Inn"

A poem in the *Atlantic Monthly* for November, 1863, seemed to Hawthorne "profoundly touching." It was Henry Wadsworth Longfellow's poem "Weariness," which says in the first stanza: "I, nearer to the way-side inn/ Where toil shall cease and rest begin,/Am weary. . . ." Hawthorne wrote Fields, "I too am weary, and begin to look ahead for the Wayside Inn." He opened the next sentence, "Meantime. . . ."

Two or three chapters of his new romance were ready to be written, he said, but he was "not yet robust enough to begin" and felt that he "should never carry it through." Were it not for his need of money, he doubted that he would write even the first chapter. He had warned Fields earlier that he could not say when the first installment would be ready, if ever, and had added, "There is something preternatural in my reluctance to begin. I linger at the threshold, and have a perception of very disagreeable phantasms to be encountered, if I enter. I wish God had given me the faculty of writing a sunshiny book."[1] In letter after letter, he had to ask for more time. On November 8 he saw no hope of getting the first chapter in by the fifteenth, but would have it ready by the end of the month, for the February number, if it turned out "fit for publication at all." He had agreed to let this romance be serialized in the *Atlantic*, and now proposed that the title be simply "Fragments of a Romance," so that he could "exercise greater freedom as to the mechanism of the story," and later could "fill up the gaps, and make straight the crookednesses, and christen it with a fresh title" for book publication. Even in more favorable circumstances he no doubt would have been cautious with "this untried experiment of a serial work."

Because Thoreau had given him the idea for the story of a deathless man, Hawthorne first intended to preface the new romance with a sketch of Thoreau; but he soon decided to make the sketch autobiographical, with Thoreau mixed up in the life of the Wayside. Such a sketch would be pleasant to write and would not infringe upon his "proper privacy." On the matter of privacy, he told Fields of receiving a letter from one who said he had read the introductions to the *Mosses* and *The Scarlet Letter* and felt he knew their author better than he knew his closest friends. Hawthorne added, "I think he considerably overestimates the extent of his intimacy with me." In a playful justification of including Thoreau in the proposed sketch, he remarked that it is "the duty of a live literary man to perpetuate the memory of a dead one," and continued, "but how Thoreau would scorn me for thinking *I* could perpetuate him." The gloom of Hawthorne's letters continued to be relieved by touches of ironic, at times sardonic, humor. Once he wrote that, if he should "subside into the Alms House" before his intellectual faculties were extinguished, he thought he "could make a very pretty book out of it." And, if he alone were concerned, he would have no "great objection to winding up there."[2]

Later Hawthorne said he hoped to have "a chapter or two of absurdities" ready for the February number, and on December 4 he delivered the first chapter of a work he said he would never finish. His wife had described for Annie Fields the conditions under which that chapter was written. In the night of November 23 her husband had been "more ill than ever in his life." After she had administered homeopathic treatment, he could sit up at intervals. He was able once to go "on the hill" and the next day vowed he would "go into his study and write," in order to have the chapter ready as he had promised.[3] After attending the funeral of Franklin Pierce's wife in Andover, Massachusetts, he went home with Pierce. At the graveside Pierce is reported to have turned up Hawthorne's coat collar against the cold. Spending the night with the Fieldses on his return trip, Hawthorne talked about his boyhood in the Maine woods and said that he first got his "cursed habits of solitude"[4] there. Encouraged by Fields to continue with his romance, he asked for the first chapter back, so that he could write the rest of the first installment "in a similar strain," but said it would not be ready for the February number. He wished Providence thought him worthy of possessing a pen he could write with, but

James T. Fields, Nathaniel Hawthorne, W. D. Ticknor; photograph, 1862–63. Courtesy of the Essex Institute, Salem, Mass.

was glad his "labor with the abominable little tool" was drawing to a close. Fields sent pens and paper and the first chapter, already in type. Hawthorne replied that, though really not well, he would set about finishing the first installment, with such "terrible reluctance" as he had never felt before.[5]

In writing Longfellow to commend his new book, *Tales of the Wayside Inn,* and to say he was gratified to find his own name in the verse (lines 65–66 of the prelude), as if he had detected his features in the moon, Hawthorne said that he did not know what ailed him, but was inclined to conclude that he would "have little more to do with pen and ink." It had been a notion of his, he said, that his last book would be his best, "full of wisdom about matters of life and death," but it would be "no deadly disappointment" if he had to drop it. In a remark reminiscent of statements he had put into the mouths of the Story-Teller and Oberon thirty years earlier, he said Longfellow could tell better than he "whether there is ever anything worth having in literary reputation—and whether the best achievements seem to have any substance after they grow cold." It might be noted that the file of Hawthorne's letters shows him still complying with requests for autographs. He wrote Ticknor that he felt enough better to "begin to be conscious of an inclination to resume the pen." After ten days he was "not quite up to writing yet"; his mind had "lost its temper and its fine edge."[6] During January and February he continued his self-diagnosis in letters intended to provoke a smile while revealing his worsening health. And in writing Fields on February 25, he said that it could not be pleasant for "an author to announce himself, or to be announced, as finally broken down as to his literary faculty," but that his presentiment was proving true: he would never finish the romance.

> Say to the Public what you think best, and as little as possible;—for example—"We regret that Mr. Hawthorne's Romance, announced for this Magazine some months ago, still lies upon its author's writing-table; he having been interrupted in his labor upon it by an impaired state of health."—or—"We are sorry to hear (but know not whether the Public will share our grief) that Mr. Hawthorne is out of health, and is thereby prevented, for the present, from proceeding with another of his promised (or threatened) Romances, intended for this Magazine"—or—"Mr. Hawthorne's brain is addled at last, and, much to our satisfaction, he tells us that he cannot possibly go on with the Romance announced on the cover of the Jany Magazine. We consider him finally shelved, and shall take early occasion to bury him under a heavy article, carefully summing up his merits (such as they were) and his demerits, what few of them can be touched upon in our limited space."—or—"We shall commence the publication of Mr. Hawthorne's Romance as soon as that gentleman chooses to forward it. We are quite at a loss how to account for this delay in the fulfilment of his contract; especially as he has already been most liberally paid for the first number."
>
> Say anything you like, in short, though I really don't believe that the

Public will care what you say, or whether you say anything. If you choose, you may publish the first chapter as an insulated fragment, and charge me with $100 of overpayment. I cannot finish it, unless a great change comes over me; and if I make too great an effort to do so, it will be my death; not that I should care much for that, if I could fight the battle through and win it, thus ending a life of much smoulder and scanty fire in a blaze of glory. But I should smother myself in mud of my own making.

Hawthorne had to defer meeting Pierce in Boston on March 10, but he said he had new hope for reasonable improvement. He walked very feebly, his wife said, and for the first time she read to him. In writing Pierce for him, cancelling their engagement to meet at Andover, she used the occasion to advance plans for a journey he had agreed to take with Ticknor and Pierce.[7] Hawthorne had said more than once that living abroad again or returning to the Isles of Shoals would restore his health. His wife had urged him in past summers to go to the seashore, to Washington, or elsewhere; and their friends were ready to forward his plans for travel. It was Hawthorne's intention, his wife said, to make a covenant with his companions that on this trip they "not introduce him to any persons, especially not any ladies." He did not wish to be a guest anywhere, or to visit Pierce or travel alone with him, lest he be oppressed by Pierce's low spirits and delicate health. After Pierce had withdrawn from the plans, Hawthorne made a trip to Boston for a trial of his strength. He was resolved to start on the trip with Ticknor on March 23 but delayed because of a whitlow on his finger. He went on March 27, spent the night with Fields, and the next evening took the train with Ticknor for New York. The intention was to go wherever whim might dictate, possibly to Havana. A storm prevented travel by sea, and they had bad weather during a week's stay at the Astor House in New York. Ticknor's letters to Hawthorne's wife chronicled their doings. The day after they reached New York, Hawthorne did not leave the hotel, on account of the weather, but he seemed to be improving. The next day he took a morning walk, rested after lunch, and slept before dinner. He said he intended to write home, but apparently did not. A driving rain on April 2 prevented any further travel. He slept well and took a morning walk. He began to read the newspapers the next day and took a drive with Ticknor in Central Park. Moving on to Philadelphia April 4, they found it rainy on shore and too stormy to go to sea; Ticknor took a severe cold. Hawthorne did not go out on April 5, a rainy and windy day; Ticknor went out only briefly. There was sunshine on the sixth; they called on publishers and a bookseller and were driven to Fairmont Park and Girard College. Hawthorne wrote his first letter to his wife since leaving home.[8] He was tired and went to bed before nine, but at breakfast the next morning he felt much better.

They were thinking of going to Baltimore, but on Friday morning, April 8, Ticknor suffered what Hawthorne called a severe bilious attack. The next day it fell to Hawthorne to furnish a report. He wrote Fields that Ticknor had sent for a physician, seemingly Friday night, and had fallen "into the hands of an allopathist, who of course belabored [him] with pills and powders of various kinds, and then proce[e]ded to cup, and poultice, and blister, according to the ancient rule of that tribe of savages. The consequence is, that poor Ticknor is already very much reduced, while the disease flourishes as luxuriantly as if that were the Doctor's sole object." Since they were in adjoining rooms, he could step in at any moment; but, he continued, "that will be of about as much service as if a hippopotamus were to do him the same kindness. Nevertheless, I have blistered, and powdered, and pilled him, and made my observations on medical science and the sad and comic aspects of human misery. . . . As regards myself, I almost forgot to say that I am perfectly well. . . . You would be surprised to see how stalwart I have become in this little time." It would have been surprising indeed to Fields, or to anyone else who had seen him recently, to see Hawthorne rise like the phoenix and become the stalwart nurse that Ticknor had been a few hours earlier. His remark afterward was that you do what you have to do.

In the morning of April 9 the doctor had the hotel manager telegraph a report to Boston, and thus relieved Hawthorne of deciding whether to send a message. As Dr. W. B. Atkinson told members of Ticknor's family afterward, Ticknor refused to take any more stimulants that evening and was convinced he would die before morning. At five-fifteen the next morning, April 10, he died. An editorial writer in the *Philadelphia Press* of April 11, on whom Ticknor and Hawthorne had made a call on April 6, reported that Hawthorne, "who never left him from the time he was taken ill, held his hand at the moment he breathed his last," and was "deeply affected by the severe blow. . . ."[9] Hawthorne telegraphed Ticknor's family and called an undertaker. George William Childs, one of those Hawthorne and Ticknor had visited on April 6, recalled afterward that he went to the hotel and found Hawthorne distraught, Ticknor's body having been removed already. Ticknor's son Howard came and on April 11 accompanied the body to Boston. Burial was at the Auburn Cemetery on April 15.[10]

Hawthorne returned to Boston and spent the night with Fields, "in a very excited and nervous state," according to Fields, "and talked incessantly of the sad scenes he had just been passing through."[11] Taking the train home the next day and seeing no carriage at the Concord station, he walked to the Wayside. When he arrived, Sophia wrote later, "his brow was streaming with a perfect rain—so great had been the effort to walk so far." She had never seen him "so haggard, so white, so deeply scored with pain and fatigue was his face. . . . It relieved him somewhat to break down" as he spoke of Ticknor's death. He lay "in a kind of uneasy somnolency not wishing to be read to even—not able to attend or fix his thoughts at all." On April 18 he walked outside, but for only ten minutes. He had not smiled since he came home until she "made him laugh with Thackeray's humor in reading to him. . . . An infinite weariness" filmed his eyes. He thought of the Isles of Shoals, and his wife considered having Ada Shepard, now Mrs. Badger, stay with Una and Rose while she accompanied him.[12]

General Pierce, recovered from his own illness, came forward with a plan, which might include a visit to the Isles of Shoals. He would drive Hawthorne by carriage, starting at Concord, New Hampshire, and continuing as their wishes might direct. Hawthorne's letter to Pierce on May 7, the last to come from his pen, is evidence of his lessened faculties: "I have received yours of Friday last, I believe, but have not it now by me to refer to. I am rejoiced to hear of your well being, and shall do my best to join you at Bromfield House on Wednesday next. My own health continues rather poor, but I shall hope to revive rapidly when once we are on the road. Excuse the brevity of my note, for I find some difficulty in writing." As the day for departure approached, Mrs. Hawthorne could see little hope for much improvement, though she hoped the "boy-associations" with Pierce would refresh her husband. She wrote Fields that Hawthorne's steps were uncertain and his eyes were uncertain too. He seemed quite bilious and had a restlessness that was infinite. She asked Fields to arrange for Oliver Wendell Holmes to see him "in some ingenious way." She would not have him "take any of the allopathic drugs for the world," for he was sure "he could not survive calomel, blue pill and such horrors."[13] Una later wrote Fields they had learned that her father's absolute refusal to see a doctor applied "only to a homeopathic physician." Supposing that learned doctors such as Dr. Holmes did "not drug their patients as absurdly as they did in old times," she and her mother were eager for Dr. Holmes to see him.[14] These statements resemble in tone

Hawthorne's comments on allopathy when he wrote about Ticknor's illness in Philadelphia and his teasing references in years past to his wife's belief in homeopathy; but they do little to clarify his views on medical practice at the time. They do make it clear that he refused to see a doctor, and they suggest that he had made a diagnosis of his own in which he had confidence.

Hawthorne and his wife took the train for Boston at 8:30 on the morning of May 11. Bronson Alcott noted in his journal afterward that his neighbor had looked too feeble to undertake a journey.[15] Holmes called at the Bromfield House, where Hawthorne was to meet Pierce, and found him greatly "changed from his former port and figure! . . . He seemed to have shrunken in all his dimensions, and faltered along with an uncertain, feeble step, as if every movement were an effort." During half an hour's walk, as Holmes wrote afterward in the *Atlantic Monthly*, he learned that Hawthorne experienced boring pain in his stomach, distension, difficult digestion, and "great wasting of flesh and strength," that he was depressed but showed no failing in his conversational powers. Holmes was glad not to make a formal examination, for he thought it best for the patient not to have explicit knowledge of his ailment. He did no more by way of treatment than to give practical hints for the journey with Pierce.[16]

Later in the day Hawthorne met Pierce at the Bromfield House, and the next morning they took the train to Andover, where they stopped for a visit with Mrs. Aiken, sister of Mrs. Pierce. Because of unfavorable weather they delayed at Pierce's home at Concord, New Hampshire, until Monday, May 16, to set out on their carriage journey to the lakes, along the Pemigewasset Valley, and possibly on beyond the White Mountains to the wild region of the Dixville Notch, or possibly westward to Saratoga Springs. They would leave plans to develop as they proceeded and might be gone several weeks. Monday night they were at Franklin; on the road to Laconia the next day, they talked about Horatio Bridge, Hawthorne saying, "We have, neither of us, met a more reliable friend."[17] Before they reached Centre Harbor late that afternoon, Pierce saw that his friend "was becoming quite helpless." For more than a year, he wrote afterward, Hawthorne had been "more or less infirm," and his strength had clearly diminished during the past few months. "He walked with difficulty, and the use of his hands was impaired." Hawthorne had said earlier that his sight was seriously affected, and it was obviously affected during their journey together. Partial paralysis of the lower extremities had been apparent for weeks and had increased since they left Boston, until he found it difficult to move without aid. He complained of being stupid; his mind was sluggish, but clear when roused. Before they left Boston, Pierce had concluded that "the seat of the disease . . . was in the brain or spine, or both," and that it was incurable.

After a restless night at Centre Harbor, Hawthorne ate a slight breakfast and toward midday enjoyed an hour on the piazza. He was weak but was not suffering from pain. To Pierce's suggestion that they not travel for a day or two, he replied that he preferred to go on—seeing the region would be pleasant; the ride would not fatigue him; and he would be more comfortable in the carriage alone with Pierce than anywhere else. They talked little during the afternoon's drive. After asking and learning that Pierce had read an account of William Makepeace Thackeray's death, Hawthorne "remarked in a low, soliloquizing tone—what a boon it would be, if when life draws to its close one could pass away without a struggle!" Thackeray had died in his sleep the preceding December. Before they reached the Pemigewasset House at Plymouth, just as the sun was setting, Pierce had determined to send the next day for Mrs. Hawthorne and Una to join them there.

Hawthorne took a cup of tea and toast in the evening and, after sleeping an hour or more on the sofa, awoke and retired for the night. Pierce retired in his adjoining room soon after ten, having arranged the lamp so that through the open door he could see Hawthorne, no more than five or six feet from his own bed. Between one and two o'clock, he awoke and observed Hawthorne lying "in a perfectly natural position, like a child, with his right hand under his cheek." Awaking again between three and four and seeing that Hawthorne was in the same position, and that "no change had come over his features," he investigated and discovered that "the great, generous, brave heart beat no more—The boon of which he spoke in the afternoon had before morning's dawn been graciously granted to him. He had passed from natural sleep to that from which there is no earthly waking—without the slightest struggle—evidently without moving a muscle." Oliver Wendell Holmes said that he had probably died of fainting, as is likely "in any disease attended with such debility" as Hawthorne had experienced.[18]

Pierce telegraphed the news to Boston; he wrote Fields an account and began a letter to Mrs. Hawthorne that he did not finish. On May 20 he met Julian in Boston and went with him to Concord; Elizabeth Hawthorne wrote Una that her health would not permit her to come for the funeral. The next day the body reached Concord. Hawthorne's infirmity had developed so rapidly that others besides Holmes and Pierce realized that nothing could restore him. On April 28 Una had written her cousin Horace Mann in Hawaii that she was preparing herself "if a dark time comes." Mary Mann wrote Horace, after Hawthorne's death, that he had "actually come to that period which he hoped never to see, for he was fast losing the power of helping himself." Holmes had concluded, she said it had been learned, that "the shark's tooth was upon him."[19] Holmes had said also, it seems, that Hawthorne had fears of mental deterioration; for on May 20 the widow wrote a distressed plea to Fields that he "refrain from saying a word" to her sisters about her husband's saying that he was afraid he might cease to be himself, "because on any such suggestion I fear my sister would talk of it to others and inevitably exaggerate and I wish to guard him from a word being said that would have grieved him here—and you know his mind had not yet a shadow—Oh I wish Dr. Holmes would not say he feared it." Una sent a note along with her mother's letter: "You see this agony is almost too great for Mamma to bear. The thought that a shadow should fall on his clear mind is an arrow all poison in her heart."

The evidence available in statements by Pierce, Holmes, Hawthorne himself, and his wife indicates that he died of a brain tumor. The symptoms he observed in his last weeks—the wasting away of his body, the boring pain within, the restlessness, and finally the lessened control over his eyes and his limbs—would indicate a systemic malignancy that at last reached the brain. The symptoms convinced him, it seems clear, that treatment would be useless, and may have encouraged him to set out on the carriage journey with Pierce as a way of saving his family from experiencing his death with the immediacy with which he had experienced his mother's.

Although Mrs. Hawthorne said that she and her husband had never spoken of the contingency that one would leave the other,[20] she could not have failed to see his death as certain weeks in advance. She nevertheless drew on inner resources that let her maintain her lifelong self-discipline and optimism. A broadside was printed with the title "Hawthorne's Wife on His Death: A Letter Copied in Mrs. J. T. Fields's Diary," probably distributed by the Fieldses, with Mrs. Hawthorne's approval, or at her instigation. It begins, "When I see that I deserved nothing, and that my Father gave me the richest destiny for so many years of time to which eternity is to be added, I am struck dumb with an ecstasy of gratitude, and let go my mortal hold with an awful submission and without a murmur. I stand hushed into an ineffable peace, which I cannot measure nor understand. . . . Do not fear for my 'dark hours.' I think there is nothing dark for me henceforth. . . . I have no more to ask, but that I may be able to comfort all who mourn as I am comforted. If I could bear all sorrow, I would be glad, because God has turned for me the silver lining."[21] Una wrote to Annie Fields that she would like to wear black in mourning but that her mother did not approve. "She thinks Papa would not have liked it." Of her mother she added, "Nothing could be imagined more angelically lovely. It is a triumph of the most vivid faith I ever saw."[22]

The funeral, at one o'clock on May 23, was held in the Congregational Church of Concord; burial was in Sleepy Hollow, beneath the pine trees on a hill frequented often by Hawthorne and his wife when they lived at the Old Manse. "The corpse was unwillingly shown," Emerson wrote in his journal, "—only a few moments to this company of his friends. . . . A large company filled the church and the grounds of the cemetery."[23] The Boston *Journal* of the next day reported "such a convocation of mourners as is seldom gathered to the obsequies of an American citizen."

Many of those present recorded what they observed and what they thought. The occasion was rich in symbols, readily discernible to those who knew the symbolic richness of Hawthorne's writings. The orchards were in blossom; the church was filled with white flowers; and the birds sang all the way from the church to the grave. There was "a pomp of sunshine and verdure, and gentle winds," Emerson said. To Holmes "The sun shone brightly, and the air was sweet and pleasant, as if death had never entered the world"; he said to Emerson that "it looked like a happy meeting." Longfellow marked this "one bright day/In the long week of rain!" and wrote Charles Sumner that the village was "all sunshine and blossoms and the song of birds." The manuscript of the unfinished *Dolliver Romance* lay on the coffin. Beside the hearse from the church to Sleepy Hollow walked a group whom Mrs. Hawthorne called "ideal pallbearers." Of Hawthorne's three closest friends over the past forty years, from his college days, Horatio Bridge was confined after an accident in Washington; Longfellow was among the pallbearers; and Pierce was with Hawthorne's widow and her children. Louis Agassiz picked a bunch of violets and dropped them in the grave; other members of the Saturday Club also dropped flowers.

The services in the church and at the graveside were read by James Freeman Clarke, who had married the Hawthornes twenty-two years earlier and had not seen Hawthorne since. He said, in the report of the *Boston Evening Transcript* the next day:

> Our friend has fallen asleep; he has done his work; he has finished all that
> God gave him to do. . . . if ever one received and developed his powers
> faithfully, it is the friend whom we have here. All who knew him, knew
> that his thought was his own, his fame his own, his work his own. God
> placed him here to glorify New England life and pour over it the poetical
> beauty which was in his heart. I know no other thinker or writer who
> had so much sympathy with the dark shadow, that shadow which the
> theologian calls sin, as our friend. He seemed to be the friend of all sin-
> ners, in his writings. He felt his way through the dark passages always to
> draw love over them, never to censure. His books were full of sun-
> shine.[24]

In the phrasing of Emerson's journal notes, Clarke said that Hawthorne
had done "more justice than any other to the shades of life, shown a sympathy with the crime in our nature, and, like Jesus, was the friend of sinners." When others had left the cemetery and the carriage bearing the
widow had reached the gate, Julian Hawthorne recalled, Longfellow,
Holmes, Whittier, Lowell, Pierce, Emerson, and half a dozen more stood
with uncovered heads as it passed.[25]

Holmes wrote for the July *Atlantic* a tribute, along with an account of
his last interview with Hawthorne and diagnosis of his final ailment, saying in conclusion that in Hawthorne's works he had "left enough to keep
his name in remembrance as long as the language in which he shaped his
deep imaginations is spoken by human lips."[26] Lowell declared afterward
that Hawthorne's was "the rarest creative imagination of the century, the
rarest in some ideal respects since Shakespeare."[27] Longfellow sent Mrs.
Hawthorne a poem, to be published in the *Atlantic* for August, with the
title "Concord, May 23, 1864," in which he echoes their forty years of
mutually generous friendship and his recognition of what he had called,
when he read *The Marble Faun*, "the old, dull pain . . . that runs through
all Hawthorne's works." With a glance at the manuscript Hawthorne had
left unfinished, and a reference to the hand that "let fall the pen,/And left
the tale half told," the poem concludes:

> Ah! who shall lift that wand of magic power,
>   And the lost clew regain?
> The unfinished window in Aladdin's tower
>   Unfinished must remain.

The poet hears from

The hill-top hearsed with pines

. . . .

Their tender undertone,
The infinite longings of a troubled breast,
The voice so like his own.[28]

Emerson returned from the funeral to his journal and recorded the same
puzzlement he had felt over the past twenty-five years. Devotee of conversation and founder of clubs for discussion among the like-minded, he
thought Clarke's funeral sermon might have "more fully rendered" the
"painful solitude of the man," which, he supposed "could not longer be
endured and he died of it." He continued, "It would have been a happiness, doubtless to both of us, to have come into habits of unreserved intercourse. It was easy to talk with him,—there were no barriers,—only, he
said so little, that I talked too much, and stopped only because, as he gave
no indications, I feared to exceed." Emerson said he had felt that he could
wait Hawthorne's time—"his willingness and caprice—and might one day
conquer a friendship." His journal entry continues, "Now it appears that I
waited too long." Herman Melville, the one of all Hawthorne's literary associates who had experienced the broadest affinity for him, was "much
shocked" at hearing of his death, his wife reported.[29] It was soon afterward, probably, that Melville recorded in the poem "Monody" the dull
pain of having "loved him/After loneless long," and then being "estranged
in life,/And neither in the wrong."

Notes

A Note on Citations

References to Hawthorne's writings are to the Centenary Edition of the Works of Nathaniel Hawthorne, edited by William Charvat, Roy Harvey Pearce, and Claude M. Simpson, 13 volumes to the present (Columbus: Ohio State University Press, 1962–), unless indicated otherwise, and may be designated, in the notes or in the text, by only volume and page. References to Hawthorne's *American Notebooks* are to Volume VIII of this edition or to *Hawthorne's Lost Notebook, 1835–1841*, edited by Barbara S. Mouffe (University Park, Pa., 1978). Citations of the *English Notebooks* are given by date and can be located in Randall Stewart's edition (New York, 1941), in which the entries appear in chronological order.

Letters by Hawthorne are designated by addressees and dates, in the text or in the notes. Quotations from these letters follow the texts established for the Centenary Edition. Other letters are cited by writer, addressee, and date. Letters and documents of the Hawthorne and the Manning families, unless otherwise noted, are in the extensive Hawthorne-Manning Collection at the Essex Institute, Salem, Massachusetts. Letters by members of the Peabody family are in the Berg Collection, New York Public Library, unless otherwise noted.

1. The Hawthorne Beginnings

1. To Horatio Bridge, Jan. 15, 1857; to W. D. Ticknor, Feb. 16, 1861; to Henry Bright, March 8, 1863.
2. "The Custom-House," in *The Scarlet Letter*, Centenary Edition of the Works of Nathaniel Hawthorne (Columbus, Ohio, 1962), I, 8, 11, 44–45.
3. The novelist adopted the spelling "Hawthorne" at about the time his writings

were first published, apparently to insure the pronunciation he preferred. (The fact that college-mates called him "Hath" indicates that they gave the *a* the same sound as in "Nathaniel.") According to Horatio Bridge, Hawthorne began signing the changed form only after 1830 and explained that he had found it in records of his early ancestors. Bridge to Richard C. Manning, Feb. 14, 1871 (at the Essex Institute). The spelling "Hathorne" had become normal in the family, but the form including *w* had occurred among a variety of spellings in both England and America. In fact, the baptism of Hawthorne's father at the First Church of Salem was registered with *w* in the name. See Hubert Hoeltje, "Captain Nathaniel Hawthorne: Father of the Famous Salem Novelist," *Essex Institute Historical Collections* (*EIHC* in subsequent references), LXXXIX (Oct., 1953), 331; and Edward C. Sampson, "The 'W' in Hawthorne's Name," *EIHC*, C (Oct., 1964), 297–99. Hawthorne's sisters, Elizabeth and Maria Louisa, followed him in spelling the name with *w*. In the following pages the name is spelled "Hawthorne" for all members of the family, in the novelist's own time or earlier.

4. See Vernon Loggins, *The Hawthornes: The Story of Seven Generations of an American Family* (New York, 1951), pp. 205–6; and Hubert Hoeltje, *Inward Sky: The Mind and Heart of Nathaniel Hawthorne* (Durham, N.C., 1962), p. 26.

5. See *Ship Registers of the District of Salem and Beverly, Massachusetts, 1789–1900*, copied by A. Frank Hitchings, with annotations by Stephen Willard Phillips (Salem, 1906); Robert E. Peabody, *Merchant Venturers of Old Salem* (Boston, 1912), p. 37; and Joseph B. Felt, *Annals of Salem*, 2 vols. (Salem, 1845), II, 268.

6. The ballad was printed in *Graham's Magazine*, XXI (Oct., 1842), 227, and in *Poets and Poetry of America* (Philadelphia, 1842) and *Curiosities of American Literature* (New York, 1843), both edited by Rufus Wilmot Griswold. See Gardner Weld Allen, *Massachusetts Privateers of the Revolution* (Boston, 1927), p. 102, and Ralph D. Paine, *The Ships and Sailors of Old Salem: The Record of a Brilliant Era of American Achievement* (Boston, 1927), p. 459. The *Salem Gazette* of April 19, 1796, reports the honors paid Captain Hawthorne at his death.

7. See William Bentley's *Diary*, 4 vols. (Salem, 1905–14), II, 360. Bentley was minister of the East Church, or Second Church, of Salem. His diary is in effect a gossipy history of the town from the time he became a resident in 1783 until his death in 1819.

8. See Henry Wyckoff Belknap, "Simon Forrester of Salem and His Descendants," *EIHC*, LXXI (Jan., 1935), 17–64; Loggins, *The Hawthornes*, pp. 171–72; Marianne Silsbee, *A Half Century in Salem* (Boston, 1887), pp. 86–87.

9. See Manning Hawthorne, "Parental and Family Influences on Hawthorne," *EIHC*, LXXVI (Jan., 1940), 9.

10. See *Ship Registers of the District of Salem and Beverly*, p. 8: James Duncan Phillips, *Salem and the Indies: The Story of the Great Commercial Era of the City* (Boston, 1947), p. 185.

11. Captain Nathaniel Silsbee's own narrative of this encounter is printed in his "Biographical Notes," *EIHC*, XXXV (Jan., 1899), 22–24. See also Edward Stanton Maclay, *A History of American Privateers* (New York, 1899), pp. 220–22; and Paine, *The Ships and Sailors of Old Salem*, pp. 294–95.

12. An entry in Bentley's *Diary* (II, 323) may afford a glimpse of the couple between the time the verses were written and their wedding: On November 13,
1799, he rode to a neighboring town with "Capt. Harthorne and the Misses
Manning." Or this "Capt. Harthorne" may not have been Nathaniel, who apparently was not yet a ship captain, but his brother Daniel, who was. The
Misses Manning would have been Elizabeth and her older sister Mary, both
active members of Bentley's congregation.

13. James T. Fields, *Yesterdays with Authors* (Boston, 1871), pp. 42–43. See also
Horatio Bridge, *Personal Recollections of Nathaniel Hawthorne* (New York, 1893),
p. 38, and George Parsons Lathrop, *A Study of Hawthorne* (Boston, 1876), p.
62.

14. Loggins, *The Hawthornes*, pp. 200–1, says that Hawthorne was on a voyage to
Sumatra and Java from December, 1801, to early 1803 on the *Astrea*, once
owned by Elias Hasket Derby of Salem but later owned in Boston. Among
the Hawthorne papers at the Essex Institute is a document signed by J. T.
Slade dated April 18, 1802, acknowledging payment for sugar, pepper, and
coffee loaded on board the *Astrea*.

15. When the ship sailed from France on October 24, 1805, on its return to
Salem, Robert Brookhouse was master, and Hawthorne was not listed in the
ship's complement (Hoeltje, "Captain Nathaniel Hawthorne," p. 3). At the
Essex Institute is a bill to "Captain Hawshorn," for medicine, dated January
11, 1806, at Batavia. A likely possibility is that in a French port Hawthorne
transferred to a ship bound for Batavia. The *Hannah*, the *Mary and Eliza*, and
the *Neptune*, the three ships on which he had sailed in succession, all had
Joseph White as owner or part owner. The likelihood that his voyage to
France was extended as master of another vessel bound for the Orient has support in a letter of September 10, 1806, in which his wife's sister Maria Manning wrote to her sister Mary, then absent from Salem, "Eliza is anxious to hear
from her husband." A preserved business record of October 10, 1806, shows
Captain Hawthorne in the French port of Nantes, again master of the *Neptune*.

16. The *Nabby* carried a private venture of $124.30 at the risk of Robert Manning,
brother of the captain's wife.

17. This final balance sheet showed Captain Hawthorne due $24.88 in wages
(after deductions for an advance and other amounts), $427.02 as his four per-
cent on the *Nabby*'s cargo from Cayenne in 1807, and $423.28 as his percent-
age on the cargo of his final voyage. Debits to his account were $16.70 paid by
the ship owners in duty on his private venture on the voyage from Cayenne
and $285.08 for his final expenses in Surinam.

18. Hoeltje, "Captain Nathaniel Hawthorne," p. 352.

19. Lathrop, *A Study of Hawthorne*, pp. 61–62. To J. T. Fields, March 6, 1851.
The miniature is reproduced in Julian Hawthorne, *Nathaniel Hawthorne and
His Wife*, 2 vols. (Boston, 1885), I, 36.

20. *Ibid.*, I, 96–98.

21. See *ibid.*, I, 177, and Norman Holmes Pearson, "Elizabeth Peabody on
Hawthorne," *EIHC*, XCIV (July, 1958), 262–63.

22. In saying that the house was built by his grandfather Daniel Hawthorne, the
novelist may have been misinformed or may have purposely shortened his

statement in order to emphasize what he particularly wanted to say: that it was his grandfather who disposed of the land passed down in the family from the initial settlement and moved to Union Street. See the autobiographical notes furnished Richard Henry Stoddard in 1853 (J. Hawthorne, *Nathaniel Hawthorne and His Wife*, I, 95).

23. Abbott Lowell Cummings, "Nathaniel Hawthorne's Birthplace: An Architectural Study," *EIHC*, XCIV (July, 1958), 196–204. This house, without the wing and the lean-to that were added about 1745, has been restored and located at the foot of Turner Street on the grounds of the House of the Seven Gables. The lot on which the house stood measured 143 feet on Union Street and extended 100 feet to Herbert Street. In 1816 the heirs of Daniel Hawthorne released the Hawthorne property to Simon Forrester; when it was conveyed to Forrester's widow after his death the next year, the lot had been reduced to 85 feet on the street and 45 feet in depth.

2. The Manning Years

1. Among the Manning papers is a receipt signed by Miriam Manning for the Manning estate, crediting Captain Hawthorne's widow with $1,638.00 paid for the board of her children ($2.00 a week for Elizabeth, $1.50 for Nathaniel, $1.00 for Louisa) from July 1, 1808, to July 1, 1815. Another receipt, dated March 1, 1808, shows Robert Manning paying his father $3.00 a week for board.

2. Norman Holmes Pearson, in "Hawthorne and the Mannings," *EIHC*, XCIV (July, 1958), 170–90, stresses the importance of Hawthorne's maternal relatives during his early years.

3. Since entries in the *English Notebooks*, ed. Randall Stewart (New York, 1941), are arranged chronologically, references to them in the text or in the notes are by date only. The last word on John seems to have been an indirect report in 1814 that he had gone to the Lakes to work. Many times the Reverend William Bentley of the East Church was asked to pray for the Manning son at sea. See his *Diary*, 4 vols. (Salem, 1905–14), IV, 163–64, 211, 522.

4. The land had been granted in 1690 to Captain William Raymond and members of his company for service in Indian warfare. Raymond's company was from Beverly, adjoining Salem on the north, and it was from their heirs that Manning bought titles to land in the original grant. See Bentley's *Diary*, III, 7–8; IV, 163–64, 584–85.

5. Aunt Ruth Hawthorne long afterward recalled Nathaniel as "a little boy, with his rosy cheeks, and bright eyes, and his golden curls waving as he ran about." Maria Louisa Hawthorne to Una Hawthorne, May 7, 1844 (Berg Collection).

6. See the quatrain in Richard E. Peck, *Nathaniel Hawthorne: Poems* (Charlottesville, Va., 1967), p. 4.

7. For reports on Hawthorne's childhood, see Randall Stewart, "Recollections of Hawthorne by His Sister Elizabeth," *American Literature*, XVI (Jan., 1945), 316–31; Maurice Bassan, "Julian Hawthorne Edits Aunt Ebe," *EIHC*, C (Oct., 1964), 274–78; Manning Hawthorne, "Hawthorne's Early Years,"

EIHC, LXXIV (Jan., 1938), 1–21, and "A Glimpse of Hawthorne's Boyhood," *EIHC*, LXXXIII (April, 1947), 178–84; Norman Holmes Pearson, "Elizabeth Peabody on Hawthorne," *EIHC*, XCIV (July, 1958), 256–76; Julian Hawthorne, *Nathaniel Hawthorne and His Wife*, 2 vols. (Boston, 1885), I, 99; George Parsons Lathrop, *A Study of Hawthorne* (Boston, 1876), pp. 63–64, and *Tales, Sketches, and Other Papers by Nathaniel Hawthorne* (Boston, 1883), p. 454; James T. Fields, *Yesterdays with Authors* (Boston, 1871), pp. 9–11.

8. Probably Oliver Kitteredge, physician of the Mannings, but possibly Jacob Kitteredge, who had recently opened an office in Salem. The physician first consulted was Dr. Gideon Barstow, husband of Nathaniel's cousin Nancy Forrester. See Russell Leigh Jackson, "Physicians of Essex County," *EIHC*, LXXXIV (Jan., 1948), 84–85.

9. Priscilla Manning to Robert Manning, Aug. 29, 1814.

10. Lathrop, *A Study of Hawthorne*, p. 68. Worcester published in 1817 the first of several compilations from his pen, a two-volume *Geographical Dictionary, or Universal Gazetteer, Ancient and Modern*, which he long afterward sent Hawthorne in a later edition (to Worcester, April 14, 1861).

11. Other receipts at the Essex Institute show that Nathaniel was taught by Miss Carlton in the following two years, by Francis Moore in 1810 and 1811, and by Worcester in 1813.

12. See M. Hawthorne, "Hawthorne's Early Years," pp. 8–9.

13. The cost of his dancing lessons was by no means negligible—he paid at Turner's Dancing School $5 on entrance and $9 a quarter. See "Notes on Old Times in Salem. . . . Master Turner's Dancing School. . . . From Notes of Francis H. Lee," *EIHC*, LXXIV (Oct., 1938), 365–72.

14. See Robert Cantwell, *Nathaniel Hawthorne: The American Years* (New York, 1948), pp. 42–44; also Leonard B. Chapman, "Recalling Days When Hawthorne Went to School," *Portland Sunday Times*, Feb. 14, 1909; and Nathan Gould, "Parson Bradley and Hawthorne," No. 28 of "Portland Sketches" (clipping in the Bowdoin College Library).

15. Symmes was an illegitimate mulatto who grew up in the Raymond community, followed the sea for twenty-five years, and was a detective during the Civil War. He showed himself acquainted with Hawthorne and with Raymond and reported that the diary had come to him, through intermediaries, ultimately from the Raymond house of Richard Manning. In 1902 Pickard threw doubt on the authenticity of the diary, for he had learned that one incident recounted in it had occurred in 1828. "Is 'Hawthorne's First Diary' a Forgery?" *Dial*, XXXIII (Sept. 16, 1902), 155. Reversing his position again in 1910, Pickard said that his earlier suppression of the book was a hasty act, and he was sure that Hawthorne "*must* have written most of the items" (in a letter of January 27, 1910, which Pickard had inserted in all copies of the *First Diary* he could locate).

16. Fields, *Yesterdays with Authors*, p. 113.

17. *Hawthorne's First Diary*, pp. 4–5.

18. Randall Stewart, "Recollections of Hawthorne by His Sister Elizabeth," *American Literature*, XVI (Jan., 1945), 322.

19. J. Hawthorne, *Nathaniel Hawthorne and His Wife*, I, 101.
20. Longfellow to Horatio Bridge, Dec. 12, 1875. Horatio Bridge, *Personal Recollections of Nathaniel Hawthorne* (New York, 1893), pp. 54–55.

3. Preparing for College

1. To Robert Manning, March 24 and May 16, 1819.
2. To Robert Manning, July 26; to Louisa Hawthorne, Sept. 28, 1819. Long afterward Hawthorne recalled playing with his cousin Benjamin, somewhat older than he, son of Benjamin and Amstis Foster, who lived on a farm at the base of Browne's Hill, across the North River. The *American Notebooks* contain accounts of his return to the site in 1837 and again in 1847 (VIII, 158–61, 274–78); and in writing the sketch "Browne's Folly" in 1860, he drew on the notebook entries open before him and on pleasant childhood memories to describe the region again, stressing the ruins of the pre-Revolutionary mansion that had given the locality its fame, and saying that as a boy he used to be brought there to see his "country cousin."
3. When Simon Forrester's widow, Aunt Rachel, died in 1823, she provided in her will for her unmarried sisters Eunice and Ruth and her widowed sister Sarah Crowinshield, but nothing for her brother Nathaniel Hawthorne's widow or his three children. See Henry Wyckoff Belknap, "Simon Forrester of Salem and His Descendants," *EIHC*, LXXI (Jan., 1935), 17–64.
4. For an announcement of Oliver's school, see the *Salem Gazette*, May 7, 1813. See also the sketch of an older Benjamin Lynde Oliver (1760–1835) in the *EIHC*, LXVIII (Jan., 1932), 1–4.
5. See Pat M. Ryan, Jr., "Young Hawthorne at the Salem Theatre," *EIHC*, XCIV (July, 1958), 243–55.
6. For the constitution and the proceedings of the Pin Society, see Elizabeth Chandler, ed., "Hawthorne's *Spectator*," *New England Quarterly*, IV (April, 1931), 289–330.
7. The full contents are printed in *ibid*.
8. Julian Hawthorne, *Nathaniel Hawthorne and His Wife*, 2 vols. (Boston, 1885), I, 95.
9. See *Vital Records of Salem, Massachusetts, to the End of the Year 1820*, 2 vols. (Salem, 1916, 1918). The two younger daughters, Maria and Priscilla, also left the East Church, but joined the Evangelical Tabernacle Church.
10. To Elizabeth C. Hawthorne, March 9, 1820; to Robert Manning, July 21, 1819.

4. Bowdoin College

1. Letters Hawthorne wrote from Bowdoin are printed in Manning Hawthorne's article "Nathaniel Hawthorne at Bowdoin," *New England Quarterly*, XIII (June, 1940), 246–79.
2. Horatio Bridge proposed long afterward that the stream in which he and Hawthorne used to fish be named Hawthorne Brook. *Brunswick Herald*, Aug. 23, 1882.

3. Because the question of what to do with the house Mrs. Hawthorne had occupied was not answered for several years, members of the family called it "Manning's Folly." It was leased for a time as a tavern, and in 1827 Richard thought of donating it to the Congregational Society for a parsonage. Later it was given to the community for public use in an arrangement that continues today.

4. Horatio Bridge, *Personal Recollections of Nathaniel Hawthorne* (New York, 1893), p. 51.

5. See "Hawthorne's Bowdoin College Bills," *EIHC*, LXXVI (Jan., 1940), 13.

6. Allen's letter is printed in M. Hawthorne, "Nathaniel Hawthorne at Bowdoin," p. 260.

7. See *ibid.*, pp. 267, 271.

8. To Louisa Hawthorne, Aug. 11, 1824.

9. See Julian Hawthorne, *Nathaniel Hawthorne and His Wife*, 2 vols. (Boston, 1885), I, 113; and M. Hawthorne, "Nathaniel Hawthorne at Bowdoin," p. 266. This dissertation, entitled "De Patribus Conscriptis Romanorum," appears in the appendix of George Parsons Lathrop, *A Study of Hawthorne* (Boston, 1876), pp. 237–39.

10. To W. D. Ticknor, Jan. 31, 1857.

11. The card signed by Wells in February, 1825, admitting Hawthorne to the lectures, is preserved at the Essex Institute. See Hubert H. Hoeltje, "Hawthorne as Senior at Bowdoin," *EIHC*, XCIV (July, 1958), 207–10.

12. Lathrop, *A Study of Hawthorne*, p. 111.

13. G. T. Packard, "Bowdoin College," *Scribner's Monthly*, XII (May, 1876), 47–61.

14. Alpheus S. Packard, *History of Bowdoin College* (Boston, 1882), 302–3.

15. From Jonathan Cilley, Nov. 17, 1836, in J. Hawthorne, *Nathaniel Hawthorne and His Wife*, I, 144.

16. See Harriet S. Tapley, "Hawthorne's 'Pot-8-O Club' at Bowdoin College," *EIHC*, LXVII (July, 1931), 225–32.

17. Quoted in George Lowell Austin, *Henry Wadsworth Longfellow* (Boston, 1883), pp. 68–69.

18. See M. Hawthorne, "Nathaniel Hawthorne at Bowdoin," p. 270.

19. Bridge, *Personal Recollections of Nathaniel Hawthorne*, pp. 34–37, 41–42.

20. "The Ocean," in the *Salem Gazette*, Aug. 26, 1825, signed C. W.; "The Moon," in the *Independent Chronicle and Boston Patriot*, Aug. 16, 1826.

21. Two poems signed "Hawthorne" in *Scenes in the Life of the Saviour by the Poets and Painters* (Philadelphia, 1845), edited by Rufus W. Griswold, "Walking on the Sea" and "The Star of Calvary," have been attributed to Hawthorne, no doubt by mistake. See Joy Bayless, *Rufus Wilmot Griswold* (Nashville, Tenn., 1943), p. 83. Preserved manuscripts contain several humorous poems written by Hawthorne for the amusement of his children. In *Nathaniel Hawthorne: Poems* (Charlottesville, Va., 1967), Richard E. Peck collects the poems and fragments.

22. *The Life of Franklin Pierce* (Boston, 1852), pp. 16–17. See also Roy Franklin Nichols, *Franklin Pierce* (Philadelphia, 1931), pp. 23–25.

23. Bridge, *Personal Recollections of Nathaniel Hawthorne*, p. 4. A number of Haw-

thorne's literary acquaintances of later years searched for words to describe his eyes: Charles Reade: "an eye like a violet with a soul in it" (Theodore F. Wolfe, *Literary Shrines: The Haunts of Some Famous American Authors* [Philadelphia, 1896], p. 159); Richard Henry Stoddard: "the most wonderful eyes in the world, searching as lightning and unfathomable as night" (J. Hawthorne, *Nathaniel Hawthorne and His Wife,* I, 460); Bayard Taylor: "the only eyes he had ever known flash fire" (*ibid.,* p. 121); Fredrika Bremer: "wonderful, wonderful eyes. They give, but receive not" (Rose Hawthorne Lathrop, *Memories of Hawthorne* [Boston, 1897], p. 200); Julia Ward Howe: "the beauty of those eyes, which I could compare to nothing but tumulous saphires" (*The Hawthorne Centenary at the Wayside, Concord, Massachusetts, July 4–7, 1904* [Boston, 1905], p. 38); T. W. Higginson: "great gray eyes, with a look too keen to seem indifferent, too shy to be sympathetic" (*ibid.,* p. 4); Moncure D. Conway: "No one who ever saw Hawthorne can forget his wonderful eyes. They were search-lights, but soft ones,—the look not that of curiosity, but of interest and attentiveness" (*ibid.,* p. 127).

24. George Parsons Lathrop, "Biographical Sketch," in *Tales, Sketches and Other Papers by Nathaniel Hawthorne* (Boston, 1883), p. 463.

25. Bridge, *Personal Recollections of Nathaniel Hawthorne,* p. 5.

26. J. Hawthorne, *Nathaniel Hawthorne and His Wife,* I, 96.

27. *Ibid.,* p. 112.

28. To Elizabeth or Louisa Hawthorne, Oct. 1, 1824.

29. Long afterward Hawthorne had occasion to speak of Simon Forrester and his family. After reading the novel *The Morgesons* by Elizabeth Drew Stoddard (1823–1902), he wrote her husband, Richard Henry Stoddard (1825–1903), January 8, 1863, commending the novel, in which he found "a sort of misty representation" of Salem and "half-revealed features of people" he had known. Referring to the children of Simon Forrester, he said, "those respectable individuals in the novel were my cousins." He wrote Mrs. Stoddard on January 26, "I thank Heaven I am not a Forrester," noting that Forrester "drank terribly through life," and passed the tendency on to his sons. Mrs. Hawthorne had written Annie Fields on the preceding June 19 about the claim to aristocratic lineage advanced by the Forresters, and cited a statement by her husband that "the only claim to position they had was from connection with the Hawthornes" (in the Boston Public Library).

30. To Elizabeth Hawthorne, July 14, 1825.

31. A senior project was for class members to have silhouettes made. G. T. Packard states in his article "Bowdoin College" in *Scribner's Monthly,* XII (May, 1876), 46–61, that Hawthorne refused to have his profile cut. Horatio Bridge says that Hawthorne refused to appear in the "College Golgotha," and that he too refused (*Personal Recollections of Nathaniel Hawthorne,* pp. 4–5). Bridge is not in the collection preserved by a class member, George Snell, and now at the Bowdoin College Library; Hawthorne is present, but with a difference. Beneath every other silhouette, the graduate signed his full name in ink; beneath his is only "Hath," in dim ink or pencil. It may be that Bridge remembered correctly, and that Hawthorne's silhouette was added to Snell's

collection at some time after graduation. A letter of Hawthorne's to Louisa on May 4, 1823, no doubt refers to a silhouette of himself: "I do not believe you can tell whose profile the enclosed is."

5. The Chamber under the Eaves

1. Julian Hawthorne, *Nathaniel Hawthorne and His Wife*, 2 vols. (Boston, 1885), I, 106–8. George Parsons Lathrop quotes (*A Study of Hawthorne* [Boston, 1876], p. 83) from a letter on the same subject which Elizabeth Peabody said was once in her possession but no longer existed: "I do not want to be a doctor and live by men's diseases, nor a minister to live by their sins nor a lawyer and live by their quarrels. So, I don't see that there is anything left for me but to be an author. How would you like some day to see a whole shelf full of books, written by your son, with 'Hawthorne's Works' printed on their backs?" Since no letter has come to light containing this passage, it seems likely that Elizabeth Peabody was remembering Hawthorne's letter of March 13, 1821, to his mother.
2. Horatio Bridge, *Personal Recollections of Nathaniel Hawthorne* (New York, 1893), p. 67.
3. Others of the Manning heirs agreed that there had never been any expectations that Mary or the Hawthorne family would be charged for board. (Richard Manning to Robert Manning, Feb. 8, 1827.)
4. Another document of the same day shows the portion of the Manning estate to which each of the remaining heirs was entitled: Mrs. Hawthorne, 28/84 (⅓); Mary, 25/84; Robert, 16/84; and Priscilla, 15/84. William had earlier liquidated his interest.
5. At the Essex Institute are Robert Manning's account books and a file of letters received. Sketches of his life appear in *History of the Massachusetts Horticultural Society, 1829–78* (Boston, 1880), pp. 48–49, and in the *Dictionary of American Biography* (1933), XII, 252–53.
6. The character Fanshawe owed something also to Nathaniel Mather, who died in 1688 at the age of nineteen, and the reader is told in the final chapter (III, 460) that part of the inscription on Fanshawe's tomb "was borrowed from the grave of Nathaniel Mather, whom, in his almost insane eagerness for knowledge and in his early death, Fanshawe resembled."
7. J. Hawthorne, *Nathaniel Hawthorne and His Wife*, I, 123–24.
8. *Yesterdays with Authors* (Boston, 1871), p. 65; and Randall Stewart, "Recollections of Hawthorne by His Sister Elizabeth," *American Literature*, XVI (Jan., 1945), 323.
9. Lathrop, *A Study of Hawthorne*, pp. 134–35.
10. J. Hawthorne, *Nathaniel Hawthorne and His Wife*, I, 124. Bridge, *Personal Recollections of Nathaniel Hawthorne*, p. 68.
11. Elizabeth P. Peabody, "The Two Hawthornes," *Western: A Journal of Literature, Education and Art*, n.s. I (June, 1875), 353–54.
12. Bridge, *Personal Recollections of Nathaniel Hawthorne*, pp. 67–68.
13. To J. T. Fields, Jan. 12, 1851.

14. In Cotton Mather's *The Wonders of the Invisible World* (London, 1862; first published in 1693), p. 91—or in another source—Hawthorne would have known an account by Erasmus of a devil or witch who first threatened and then carried out the threat to scatter ashes from the top of a chimney and burn the town.

15. Lathrop (*A Study of Hawthorne*, p. 156) quotes Oberon interchangeably with Hawthorne in recounting the burning of the manuscripts.

16. Father Ralle in "Bells" (*American Magazine of Useful and Entertaining Knowledge*, May, 1836) and "A Bell's Biography"; King Philip in "Martha's Vineyard" (*ibid.*, April, 1836) and "The Gray Champion."

17. "The Birchen Canoe" and "Lovellspond" for "Roger Malvin's Burial"; "Soldier of Hadley" for "The Gray Champion." For other appearances of the Hadley episode in history and literature, see G. Harrison Orians, "The Angel of Hadley in Fiction," *American Literature*, IV (Nov., 1932), 257–69.

18. Hawthorne spoke to the same purpose in reviewing a book by William Gilmore Simms in 1846. The themes suggested by Simms and treated in his method, Hawthorne wrote, "would produce nothing but historical novels, cast in the same worn out mould that has been in use these thirty years, and which it is time to break up and fling away." Randall Stewart, "Hawthorne's Contribution to the *Salem Advertiser*," *American Literature*, V (Jan., 1934), 331–32.

19. Samuel Griswold Goodrich, *Recollections of a Lifetime, Or Men and Things I Have Seen*, 2 vols. (New York, 1856), I, 270. In the *History of Bowdoin College*, which was begun by Nehemiah Cleaveland and was completed and published by Alpheus S. Packard, Cleaveland cites an avowedly uncertain report that it was at the urging of George Barrell Cheever, a Bowdoin classmate, that Hawthorne approached Goodrich; but since Cheever did not move to Salem until 1832, any such urging probably came later than 1829 (p. 304).

20. J. Hawthorne, *Nathaniel Hawthorne and His Wife*, I, 131–32.

21. If Goodrich printed in *The Token* for 1831 the second contribution Hawthorne said he was sending, the most likely piece is an anecdote entitled "The Haunted Quack." It has little in common with his known early tales and sketches, but it has the care and finish of language usual with him, and it includes a journey on the Erie Canal such as he may have taken by 1830.

22. Hawthorne returned to Dunton afterward; he drew the *Life and Errors* (London, 1705; reprinted in 1818) from the Salem Athenaeum on September 6 and 10, 1833.

23. The reliance Hawthorne put on his sources is suggested by his citing John Dunton to bear out his saying that Phipps closed a military drill with a prayer.

6. Of Puritans, Quakers, and Witches

1. Hawthorne wrote in his notebook for August 22, 1837, that the family seat was Wigcastle, Wigton, Wiltshire (VIII, 153), apparently relying on information from his Aunt Rachel Forrester. For other references to his English ancestors, see Randall Stewart, ed., *The English Notebooks by Nathaniel Hawthorne*

(New York, 1941), pp. 40, 61–62, 395. For genealogical details from wills and other documents preserved in Berkshire, see Robert S. Rantoul, "An Account of the First Reunion of the Descendants of Major William and John Hawthorne . . . ," *EIHC*, XLI (Jan., 1905), 77–92.

2. For an account of William Hawthorne's activities, see Vernon Loggins, *The Hawthornes: The Story of Seven Generations of an American Family* (New York, 1951), pp. 23–95; for a detailed assessment of his influence on the colony, see Richard P. Gildrie, *Salem, Massachusetts, 1626–1683: A Covenant Community* (Charlottesville, Va., 1975).

3. Joseph B. Felt, *Annals of Salem*, 2 vols. (Salem, 1845), II, 535.

4. This copy, bearing a note by Hawthorne, is in the Berg Collection. See Stewart, ed., *The English Notebooks*, pp. 383–84; also Caleb H. Snow, *History of Boston* (Boston, 1827), pp. 146–48.

5. In May, 1827, Hawthorne borrowed from the Salem Athenaeum Library *History of New England*, by Daniel Neal, 2 vols. (London, 1720), which recounts in detail the Quakers' defiance of the progressively severe laws (I, 302–3). He read also the Quaker historian William Sewell, who reported many of the same events as Neal, from the Quaker point of view (*A History of the Rise, Increase, and Progress of the Christian People Called Quakers*, 2 vols. [Philadelphia, 1832], I, 247, borrowed by Hawthorne from the Salem Athenaeum in 1828 and 1829 in a Burlington, N.J., edition of 1774).

6. Neal, *History of New England*, I, 324–25. Cotton Mather records in the *Magnalia Christi Americana*, 2 vols. (Hartford, 1855; first published in 1702), that two Quaker women came naked before the congregation in church (II, 527).

7. I, 364–65. Sewell adds that, before the Quakers came, William Hawthorne had opposed "compulsion for conscience." The law required a magistrate to specify the number of stripes and the towns, not to exceed three.

8. For a discussion of changes Hawthorne made after the first printing of this story, see Seymour L. Gross, "Hawthorne's Revision of 'The Gentle Boy,'" *American Literature*, XXVI (May, 1954), 196–208.

9. Hawthorne's tale "Edward Randolph's Portrait" (1838) presents Randolph as suffering "the awful might of a people's curse."

10. See Robert Calef, *More Wonders of the Invisible World*, in George Lincoln Burr, ed., *Narratives of the Witchcraft Cases* (New York, 1914; reprinted in 1970), pp. 358, 369.

11. Burr, *Narratives of the Witchcraft Cases*, p. 361; see also p. 244.

12. "History and Influence of the Puritans," in *The Miscellaneous Writings of Joseph Story*, ed. W. W. Story (Boston, 1852), p. 468.

13. See Calef, *More Wonders of the Invisible World*, in Burr, *Narratives of the Witchcraft Cases*, p. 351.

14. *The Wonders of the Invisible World*, in *ibid.*, pp. 250–51. In his two-volume *Salem Witchcraft* (Boston, 1867), Charles W. Upham reinforced his earlier indictment of Cotton Mather; and after a writer in the *North American Review* had charged him with unfairness to Mather, he published *Salem Witchcraft and Cotton Mather: A Reply* (Morrisania, N.Y., 1869), in which he remarked that other writers had taken the same view of Cotton Mather as he. He likely had

Hawthorne in mind as one such writer. In the same work he noted that John Hawthorne "did not often, if ever, sit as a judge" (p. 16).

15. For an account of Joseph Hawthorne's life, see Loggins, *The Hawthornes*, pp. 142–67.

16. Joseph B. Felt, *The Annals of Salem, from the First Settlement* (Salem, 1827), p. 353.

7. "The Story-Teller"

1. See Manning Hawthorne, "Hawthorne and the Man of God," *Colophon*, n.s. II (Winter, 1937), 266–68.

2. This letter is known only in the undated portion of it included in George Parsons Lathrop, *A Study of Hawthorne* (Boston, 1876), pp. 143–44.

3. To Louisa Hawthorne, Aug. 17, 1831.

4. Elizabeth Peabody's account appears in Moncure D. Conway, *Life of Nathaniel Hawthorne* (London, 1890), p. 32.

5. To Elizabeth Peabody, Aug. 13, 1857. See an editorial note in the *New-England Magazine*, VI (Dec., 1834), 515–16; and Buckingham's *Personal Memoirs and Recollections of Editorial Life*, 2 vols. (Boston, 1852), I, 74. For exploration and speculation on the fate of the "Story-Teller" collection, see Nelson F. Adkins, "The Early Projected Works of Nathaniel Hawthorne," *Papers of the Bibliographical Society of America*, XXXIX (First Quarter, 1945), 119–55; and Alfred Weber, *Die Entwicklung der Rahmenerzählungen Nathaniel Hawthornes: "The Story Teller" und anders frühe Werke (1825–1835)* (Berlin, 1972).

6. The name of the tobacco pedlar in this story suggests Hawthorne's habit of giving persons and events from real life existence in his fiction that is half real and half imagined. Keziah Dingley, a sister of Hawthorne's Aunt Susan who taught school at Raymond, seems to have been teased about trying to marry Dominicus Jordan, one of the original settlers at Raymond. In the *Spectator* Hawthorne announced that they were to be married, and some time later they were. Dominicus Pike marries the school-mistress and settles in the Story-Teller's hometown.

7. See Seymour L. Gross, "Hawthorne's 'Vision of the Fountain' as a Parody," *American Literature*, XXVII (March, 1955), 101–5.

8. Samuel T. Pickard (*Hawthorne's First Diary* [Boston, 1897], p. 46) remarks that "The Vision of the Fountain" contains reminiscences of Hawthorne's term in Caleb Bradley's school. The student is fifteen years old, lives in the home of the teacher, who is a minister, and in January leaves for home, a hundred miles distant—details that apply also to Hawthorne.

9. Two of these scraps had been cut from the manuscript of "My Visit to Niagara." In XI (Centenary Edition), the two paragraphs, "A sound of . . . their hands," pp. 320–22, originally preceded the last paragraph beginning on p. 283; the two paragraphs, "on reaching . . . in shadow," pp. 319–20, followed p. 288. "An Afternoon Scene," published in December, 1835, as one of the "Sketches from Memory," is the first paragraph, omitting the opening sentence, of "My Return Home" in "Fragments from the Journal of a Solitary

Man," XI, 322–23. Parts of these "Fragments" in quotation marks are from Hawthorne's pen. Benjamin probably did not remember exact details from the early installments, it seems, and did not feel a need to make the Oberon who returned home consistent with the Story-Teller who had departed earlier. See David W. Pancost, "Evidence of Editorial Additions to Hawthorne's 'Fragments from the Journal of a Solitary Man,' " *Nathaniel Hawthorne Journal 1975*, pp. 210–26.

10. The following tales and sketches probably appeared in the frame narrative at the points designated by volume, page, and line of the Centenary Edition: In "The Canal Boat": "Monsieur du Miroir" (X, 435.18), "The Maypole of Merry Mount" (X, 433.32), and "Night Sketches beneath an Umbrella" (X, 438.29); in "A Night Scene": "Young Goodman Brown" (XI, 305.12); in "My Visit to Niagara": "The Haunted Mind" (XI, 285.12); in "Fragments from the Journal of a Solitary Man": "The Devil in Manuscript" (preceding XI, 312.1), "Graves and Goblins" (XI, 317.21), "The Wedding Knell" (XI, 318.28), "Little Annie's Ramble" (XI, 321.11), "The Vision of the Fountain" (XI, 322.3). The last two of these were originally in the framework account of the visit to Niagara; see note 8 in this chapter.

11. In the Norman Holmes Pearson Collection at Yale University.

8. *Twice-Told Tales*

1. When Bradford resumed the editorship after Hawthorne's term, he published in the September number (III, 1) a note saying that he had left the magazine because the owners were changed and they had chosen another editor "from among their particular friends." See Arlin Turner, ed., *Hawthorne as Editor: Selections from His Writings in the American Magazine of Useful and Entertaining Knowledge* (University, La., 1941); Manning Hawthorne, "Nathaniel and Elizabeth Hawthorne, Editors," *Colophon*, III (Sept., 1939), 35–46.

2. Julian Hawthorne, *Nathaniel Hawthorne and His Wife*, 2 vols. (Boston, 1885), I, 133–34.

3. To Louisa Hawthorne, Jan. 21; to Elizabeth Hawthorne, Jan. 25, 1836. The *Athenaeum* of November 7, 1835, recommended his three tales in the *Token* for 1836 and quoted excerpts from "The Maypole of Merry Mount."

4. Wayne Allen Jones has printed Hawthorne's review, along with notes on his relations with Goodrich at the time ("Hawthorne's First Published Review," *American Literature*, XLVIII (Jan., 1977), 492–500.

5. To Elizabeth Hawthorne, Jan. 25, March 22, 1836.

6. J. Hawthorne, *Nathaniel Hawthorne and His Wife*, I, 125.

7. Fessenden's volume of satiric verse, *Terrible Tractoration and Other Poems, by Christopher Caustic*, had appeared in a new edition, thirty-three years after first publication. After Fessenden's death, Hawthorne published a sketch of his life and works in the *American Monthly Magazine* for January, 1838.

8. J. Hawthorne, *Nathaniel Hawthorne and His Wife*, I, 140, 142, 146.

9. *Ibid.*, p. 146.

10. *Ibid.*, p. 139.

11. This account follows that in Bridge's *Personal Recollections of Nathaniel Hawthorne* (New York, 1893), pp. 78–81, which prints Goodrich's letter of October 20. Goodrich wrote in *Recollections of a Literary Life*, 2 vols. (New York, 1856), II, 269–73, that he "recommended Mr. Hawthorne to publish a volume" and later persuaded the Stationers' Company to undertake it, but only after he had relinquished his copyrights on the tales he had published and had "joined a friend of his in a bond to indemnify them against loss." Goodrich could recall important ways in which he assisted Hawthorne's literary career; in 1856, when he wrote his memoirs and Hawthorne was a renowned author, he may have remembered that his assistance on this occasion was greater than it was.

12. May 14, 1836 (J. Hawthorne, *Nathaniel Hawthorne and His Wife*, I, 136).

13. The reconciliation between Hawthorne and Benjamin mentioned by Bridge early in 1837 probably followed an estrangement growing out of Benjamin's publishing sections of "The Story-Teller." He had printed only one sketch in 1836, "Old Ticonderoga"; after the reconciliation he published "Fragments from the Journal of a Solitary Man" and "The Three-Fold Destiny," both in the *American Monthly Magazine*. In Horace Greeley's weekly *New-Yorker* and in his own weekly the *New World* he continued to publicize Hawthorne's works, reprinting a number of the stories, informing readers of new work as it appeared, and publishing full-scale reviews. See my article "Park Benjamin on the Author and the Illustrator of 'The Gentle Boy,'" *Nathaniel Hawthorne Journal 1974*, pp. 85–91.

14. To Elizabeth Peabody, Aug. 13, 1857.

15. J. Hawthorne, *Nathaniel Hawthorne and His Wife*, I, 144–45, 147, 149.

16. Hawthorne wrote Bridge on April 13, 1850, that he had recently come across these notices in the *Age* and thought nothing better had been said about the book since.

9. Duels: Comic and Tragic

1. For these letters of Bridge and Pierce, see Julian Hawthorne, *Nathaniel Hawthorne and His Wife*, 2 vols. (Boston, 1885), I, 152–64.

2. In preparing Hawthorne's notebooks for publication, his widow had this earliest one in her hands, but omitted about one-third of its contents, especially the passages related to his early acquaintance with the Peabody family and his courtship. This manuscript notebook was lost for more than a hundred years, until it was discovered by Mrs. Barbara Mouffe, who has published it in facsimile and transcription: *Hawthorne's Lost Notebook, 1835–1841* (University Park, Pa., 1978), with a Foreword by Charles Ryskamp and an Introduction by Hyatt H. Waggoner. See also Hyatt H. Waggoner, "A Hawthorne Discovery: The Lost Notebook, 1835–1841," *New England Quarterly*, XLIX (Dec., 1976), 618–26. The text of the *Lost Notebook* is followed in all quotations of passages that appear in it, including those that are also in the Centenary Edition.

3. These details are drawn largely from two accounts based on Elizabeth Hawthorne's recollections: (1) James T. Fields, *Yesterdays with Authors* (Boston,

1871), pp. 65–67, corrected by Randall Stewart, "Recollections of Hawthorne by His Sister Elizabeth," *American Literature*, XVI (Jan., 1945), 316–31; and (2) Julian Hawthorne, *Nathaniel Hawthorne and His Wife*, I, 127–28, modified by Maurice Bassan, "Julian Hawthorne Edits Aunt Ebe," *EIHC*, C (Oct., 1964), 274–78. Randall Stewart tells of information reaching him from Martha's Vineyard that Hawthorne proposed marriage to one Eliza Gibbs after traveling on the island (*Nathaniel Hawthorne: A Biography* [New Haven, Conn., 1948], pp. 43–44). His visit to Martha's Vineyard could not have been later than 1835, for a sketch in the *American Magazine* of April, 1836 (II, 341–44), was based on a month's visit. A notebook reference to Edgartown between September 7 and October 17, 1835, suggests that he had recently been to Martha's Vineyard, probably between the dates of two other entries, June 22 and August 31. See *Hawthorne's Lost Notebook, 1835–1841*, ed. Barbara Mouffe, pp. 7–15.

4. See VIII, 3–6, 17, 162–65; also Walter Strange, "Hawthorne's 'Footprints on the Seashore,' " *Boston Suburban*, Aug. 25, 1904.

5. A revision for inclusion in the second edition of *Twice-Told Tales* in 1842 lessens the earthiness of the toll-gatherer's view, possibly in deference to the author's fiancée.

6. A relative of Miss Ainsworth wrote in later years that it was understood in the family that she could have married Hawthorne if she had wanted "such a queer fellow." Carroll A. Wilson, *Thirteen Author Collections of the Nineteenth Century*, ed. C. S. Wilson and D. A. Randall, 2 vols. (New York, 1950), I, 131–32.

7. In a letter from O'Sullivan to Henry A. Wise, Nov. 24, 1843. See the London *Athenaeum*, No. 3225 (Aug. 17, 1889), p. 225; and Norman Holmes Pearson, "Hawthorne's Duel," *EIHC*, XCIV (July, 1958), 240.

8. The story appears in J. Hawthorne, *Nathaniel Hawthorne and His Wife*, I, 167–75. The notes Julian Hawthorne kept after talking with his aunt in 1882, now in the Pierpont Morgan Library, are printed in Pearson, "Hawthorne's Duel," pp. 232–33.

9. See *ibid.*, pp. 234–35; and Horatio Bridge, *Personal Recollections of Nathaniel Hawthorne* (New York, 1893), pp. 5–6.

10. In an editorial note introducing Hawthorne's essay on Cilley in the *Democratic Review*, III (Sept., 1838), 68.

11. Bridge, *Personal Recollections of Nathaniel Hawthorne*, pp. 19–22.

12. See, for example, the *Salem Gazette*, March 2, 6, 9, 13, 17, Sept. 4, 1838; *New-Yorker*, March 24 (V, 13), Sept. 29, 1838 (VI, 29); *New York Review*, July, 1838 (III, 268–70); *New World*, May 7, 1842 (IV, 305).

13. Hawthorne's assessment of the duel was borne out in the report of a select committee of the House of Representatives (25th Congress, 2nd Session, Report No. 825). The committee offered resolutions that Graves, his second, and Cilley's second be dismissed from the House. Two motions to table the resolutions were defeated; a third was passed. A summary of this report was printed in the *Democratic Review*, IV (Nov. and Dec., 1840), 196–200.

14. Mouffe, ed., *Hawthorne's Lost Notebook, 1835–1841*, pp. 58–59.

15. See J. Hawthorne, *Nathaniel Hawthorne and His Wife*, I, 145; Pearson, "Hawthorne's Duel," p. 232.

10. The Peabodys

1. Manuscript notes of Jullian Hawthorne, "Biography of Nathaniel Hawthorne/ Extracts from a letter of E. P. P.," in the Berg Collection.
2. See Lindsay Swift, *Brook Farm: Its Members, Scholars, and Visitors* (New York, 1908), pp. 259–60; George Haven Putnam, *George Palmer Putnam: A Memoir*, 2 vols. (New York, 1903), I, 68; and Van Wyck Brooks, *New England: Indian Summer* (New York, 1940), p. 20.
3. Moncure D. Conway, *Life of Nathaniel Hawthorne* (London, 1890), p. 10; *Emerson at Home and Abroad* (New York, 1882), p. 261.
4. George Parsons Lathrop, *A Study of Hawthorne* (Boston, 1876), pp. 167–70; Julian Hawthorne, *Nathaniel Hawthorne and His Wife*, 2 vols. (Boston, 1885), I, 177–82. Norman Holmes Pearson, "Elizabeth Peabody on Hawthorne," *EIHC*, XCIV (July, 1958), 256–76, has published Julian Hawthorne's manuscript record of what Elizabeth Peabody told him.
5. This quotation and the others from Elizabeth Peabody's account are from Pearson, "Elizabeth Peabody on Hawthorne," pp. 256–76.
6. Rose Hawthorne Lathrop, *Memories of Hawthorne* (Boston, 1897), pp. 4 ff.
7. The entries for this period are in Barbara Mouffe, ed., *Hawthorne's Lost Notebook, 1835–1841* (University Park, Pa., 1978), pp. 56–65.
8. J. Hawthorne, *Nathaniel Hawthorne and His Wife*, I, 165–67.
9. This essay is included in my article, "Elizabeth Peabody Reviews Twice-Told Tales," *Nathaniel Hawthorne Journal 1974*, pp. 75–84.
10. Elizabeth Peabody's letter, to which her sister Mary appended and signed a postscript, and Mann's reply on March 10 are printed in Wayne Allen Jones, "Sometimes Things Just Don't Work Out," *Nathaniel Hawthorne Journal 1975*, pp. 11–26.
11. Sophia Peabody to Elizabeth Peabody, April 23, 29, May 1, June 1, 1838. Extracts from letters exchanged between Sophia and Elizabeth Peabody during the summer appear in Rose Hawthorne Lathrop, *Memories of Hawthorne*, pp. 13–21, 22–26; and in J. Hawthorne, *Nathaniel Hawthorne and His Wife*, I, 183–94.
12. Mouffe, *Hawthorne's Lost Notebook, 1835–1841*, pp. 62–64.
13. Sophia Peabody to Elizabeth Peabody, April 27, May 14, 1838.
14. Quoted in Norman Holmes Pearson, *Hawthorne's Two Engagements* (Northampton, Mass., 1963), p. 11.
15. VIII, 169–78, and Mouffe, *Hawthorne's Lost Notebook, 1835–1841*, pp. 65–78.
16. Between November 18, 1837, and the next July 28, the *Mirror* printed a dozen sketches by "Jonathan Oldbuck." Only "The Journey of the Moon" could be considered a product of Hawthorne's pen. The reprinting of the sketch by Hawthorne's friend Caleb Foote in the *Salem Gazette* might be taken to argue for Hawthorne's authorship.
17. Mouffe, *Hawthorne's Lost Notebook, 1835–1841*, pp. 74, 77–78.

18. J. Hawthorne, *Nathaniel Hawthorne and His Wife*, I, 192.
19. Writing in 1893, Bliss Perry said that among the residents of North Adams were some who remembered Hawthorne's visit. ("Hawthorne at North Adams," in *The Amateur Spirit* [Boston, 1904], pp. 117–39.)
20. From Sophia Peabody, Dec. 6, 1838.
21. Mouffe, *Hawthorne's Lost Notebook*, p. 81.
22. See Caroline Healey Dall to Mr. Niles, Jan. 24, 1894, in Carroll A. Wilson, *Thirteen Author Collections of the Nineteenth Century*, ed. C. S. Wilson and D. A. Randall, 2 vols. (New York, 1950), I, 131–32; "Peter Gilsey's Collection," *New York Times*, Sept. 27, 1902; and Julian Hawthorne, Letter to the Editor, *New York Times*, Oct. 4, 1902.

11. Port-Admiral

1. Barbara Mouffe, ed., *Hawthorne's Lost Notebook, 1835–1841* (University Park, Pa., 1978), p. 85.
2. Norman Holmes Pearson, "Elizabeth Peabody on Hawthorne," *EIHC*, XCIV (July, 1958), 267. George O. Holyoke, whose mother was a friend of the Peabodys, recalled more than sixty years later that as a boy five or six years old, he was the model for Ilbrahim, posing on a bolster on the floor in Sophia's room. Letter of November 10, 1901, in the Berg Collection.
3. These notices are reprinted in my article, "Park Benjamin on the Author and the Illustrator of 'The Gentle Boy,' " *Nathaniel Hawthorne Journal 1974*, pp. 85–91.
4. Sophia to her father, Jan. [9], Feb. 9–13, 1839. Diary letters such as these, written over several days and sometimes bearing a sequence of dates, appear often in the Peabody family correspondence.
5. Rose Hawthorne Lathrop, *Memories of Hawthorne* (Boston, 1897), pp. 29–32.
6. Published by the Society of the Dofobs, 2 vols. (Chicago, 1907); reprinted by C. E. Frazer Clark, Jr. (Washington, 1972).
7. To Sophia Peabody, July 15, 1839.
8. To Sophia Peabody, Dec. 1, 4, 1839; April 22, 1840.
9. To Sophia Peabody, May 19, 1840.
10. To Sophia Pebody, June 9, 1842; Sept. 17, 1841.
11. The *Common School Journal* announced on January 1, 1840, that a volume of Hawthorne's *New-England Historical Sketches* was to be published by the firm of Marsh, Capen, and Lyon. See Roy Harvey Pearce, "Historical Introduction," *True Stories from History and Biography*, Centenary Edition, VI, 291.
12. At about this time Hawthorne wrote George P. Morris that he intended to write for this series, which he said promised to be more profitable than "any other line of literary labor." George Haven Putnam, *George Palmer Putnam: A Memoir*, 2 vols. (New York, 1903), I, 338.
13. See my article, "Hawthorne and Longfellow: Abortive Plans for Collaboration," *Nathaniel Hawthorne Journal 1971*, pp. 3–11.
14. A report coming through Horace Conolly on the origin of the idea and the title of *Grandfather's Chair* probably has some basis in fact. Conolly said

Hawthorne wrote him in May, 1840, about going in March with David Roberts to visit Susan Ingersoll and having her ask why he did not write something. To his reply that he had no subject, she countered: "Oh, there are subjects enough,—write about that old chair in the room; it is an old Puritan relic, and you can make a biographical sketch of each old Puritan who became in succession the owner of the chair." See Manning Hawthorne, "Hawthorne and 'The Man of God,' " *Colophon*, n.s. II (Winter, 1937), 269.

15. To Sophia Peabody, July 5, 1839; March 17, April 3, May 29, 1840.
16. To Sophia Peabody, Sept. 9, 1839; and Charles T. Copeland, "From Concord to Concord in Hawthorne's Life," *Hawthorne Centenary Celebration at the Wayside* (Boston, 1905), p. 18.
17. To Sophia Peabody, March 18, 1840.

12. Mr. Ripley's Utopia

1. See Caroline Healey Dall, *Margaret Fuller and Her Friends* (Boston, 1895; reprinted in 1972), and Joel Myerson, "Caroline Dall's Reminiscences of Margaret Fuller," *Harvard Library Bulletin*, XXII (Oct., 1974), 414–28.
2. At the time Hawthorne decided to join in Ripley's venture, Emerson was slowly—and he would "almost say penitentially"—deciding not to join. In the mixture of lowly and lofty images that was common with him, he said he chose not to "raise the siege of this hencoop and march baffled away to a pretended siege of Babylon" and thus deny his "long trumpeted theory . . . that a man is stronger than a city." See *The Journals and Miscellaneous Notebooks of Ralph Waldo Emerson, Volume VII: 1838–1842*, ed. A. W. Plumstead and Harrison Hayford (Cambridge, Mass., 1969), p. 408; *The Letters of Ralph Waldo Emerson*, ed. Ralph L. Rusk, 6 vols. (New York, 1939), II, 364–65, 368–71. Margaret Fuller had concluded that Ripley's aim was worthy but that he did "not take time to let things ripen in his mind," and that there was nothing for her to do "at present, except to look on and see the coral insects work." See T. W. Higginson, *Margaret Fuller Ossoli* (Boston, 1884), p. 180.
3. To Sophia Peabody, April 4, 13, 14, 16, 1841.
4. Both of these letters, Elizabeth Peabody's dated April 26 and Sophia Ripley's dated May 4, were to John Sullivan, who joined the Brook Farm community the following November. These and other letters related to Brook Farm are printed in Zoltan Haraszti, *The Idyll of Brook Farm: As Revealed by Unpublished Letters in the Boston Public Library* (Boston, 1937), pp. 14, 17–18.
5. To Sophia Hawthorne, April 16, 1841.
6. This letter, in the Berg Collection, is one that escaped the fire when Hawthorne burned her letters before going abroad in 1853. Sarah Clarke recalled afterward that Sophia visited her in Newton, four miles from Brook Farm, and that Hawthorne came there to see Sophia. See Joel Myerson, "Sarah Clarke's Reminiscences of the Peabodys and Hawthorne," *Nathaniel Hawthorne Journal 1973*, p. 132. For comment on the plan for individual cottages at Brook Farm, see Joel Myerson, " 'A True & High Minded Person': Transcendentalist Sarah Clarke," *Southwest Review*, LIX (Spring, 1974), 169–70.

7. To Sophia Peabody, Aug. 12, 18, 1841.

8. These letters are printed in Julian Hawthorne, *Nathaniel Hawthorne and His Wife*, 2 vols. (Boston, 1885), I, 229–35.

9. On October 24 he walked to the highest spot on the farm, the gray pudding-stone outcropping known as Eliot's Pulpit, where tradition had it that John Eliot preached to the Indians. Here the first house built by the Brook Farmers, the Eyrie, was finished in 1842.

10. See George Ripley to Charles A. Dana, Dec. 8, 1845, in the Boston Public Library. On October 7, 1842, Ripley and Dana signed a note for $524.05 (principal and interest for a year, less nineteen days) when Hawthorne turned in the share of stock he held as surety for the $500 advanced toward a house. In 1845 he had George Hillard enter a suit to collect the note; he was awarded a judgment but seems to have collected nothing. See Robert F. Metzdorf, "Hawthorne's Suit Against Ripley and Dana," *American Literature*, XII (May, 1940), 235–41.

11. See Alice E. McBride, *From Utopia to Florence: The Story of a Transcendental Community in Northampton, Mass., 1830–1852* (Northampton, Mass., 1947); and Manning Hawthorne, "Hawthorne and Utopian Socialism," *New England Quarterly*, XII (Dec., 1939), 726–30.

13. Eden Revisited

1. Hawthorne's father, a member of the society, was required to furnish its museum the logs of his voyages and curious articles he might collect in distant lands. A Bowdoin classmate, Malthus A. Ward, was superintendent of the museum from 1825 to 1831; Hawthorne took Franklin Pierce and Samuel Dinsmore there when they visited him on March 22, 1832, as he did Evert and George Duyckinck when they sought him out on July 2, 1838—the first time, he afterward said, such a compliment was paid his writings. See Leland Schubert, "A Boy's Journal of a Trip into New England in 1838," *EIHC*, LXXXVI (April, 1950), 97–105; and C. E. Goodspeed, "Nathaniel Hawthorne and the Museum of the East India Marine Society," *American Neptune*, V (Oct., 1945), 266–85.

2. *The Letters of Ralph Waldo Emerson*, ed. Ralph L. Rusk, 6 vols. (New York, 1959), III, 50.

3. Elizabeth Hawthorne's letters of May 23 and June 15 are in the Berg Collection.

4. Dec. 13, 1875. In the Bancroft Library, University of California, Berkeley. After Hawthorne's death his wife found in his diary a bequest to his sister Elizabeth.

5. To Sophia Peabody, June 26, 1842.

6. This journal, from which Hawthorne's portions are included in the *American Notebooks*, is at the Pierpont Morgan Library, New York.

7. Sophia Peabody to her mother, Elizabeth Peabody, Aug. 5; her mother to Sophia Peabody, Aug. 8, 1842. These letters are printed in Julian Hawthorne, *Nathaniel Hawthorne and His Wife*, 2 vols. (Boston, 1885), I, 251, 264–66.

8. Barbara Mouffe, ed., *Hawthorne's Lost Notebook, 1835–1841* (University Park, Pa., 1978), p. 84.

9. Manuscript joint notebook, 1842–43, p. 5.

10. John McDonald has published a separate journal kept by Sophia Hawthorne from December 1, 1843, to the next January 5: "A Sophia Hawthorne Journal," *Nathaniel Hawthorne Journal 1974*, pp. 1–30. This quotation is from p. 4.

11. Manuscript joint notebook, 1843–44, p. 8.

12. *The Journals and Miscellaneous Notebooks of Ralph Waldo Emerson, Volume VIII: 1841–1843*, ed. William H. Gilman and J. E. Parsons (Cambridge, Mass., 1970), pp. 271–74.

13. *Ibid., Volume VII: 1838–1842*, ed. A. W. Plumstead and Harrison Hayford (Cambridge, Mass., 1969), p. 21, June 6, 1838.

14. *Ibid.*, p. 465, Sept. 4, 1842.

15. F. B. Sanborn, *Henry David Thoreau* (Boston, 1882), p. 137.

16. Manuscript joint notebook, 1842–43, p. 95 (April 23, 1843).

17. *Ibid.*, p. 113 (May 23).

14. Calm Summer of Heart and Mind

1. Manuscript joint notebook, 1842–43, p. 92, at the Pierpont Morgan Library.

2. See Sophia to her mother, Dec. 29, 1842.

3. John McDonald, "A Sophia Hawthorne Journal," *Nathaniel Hawthorne Journal 1974*, p. 15.

4. Rose Hawthorne Lathrop, *Memories of Hawthorne* (Boston, 1897), p. 73.

5. To Louisa Hawthorne, March 15, 1844.

6. Manuscript joint notebook, 1844–54, p. 9.

7. McDonald, "A Sophia Hawthorne Journal," p. 19.

8. To Margaret Fuller, Feb. 1, 1843.

9. To Horatio Bridge, May 3, 1843, April 1, 1844.

10. To W. B. Pike, March 19, 1840.

11. See "Memoir of Benjamin Frederick Browne Read Monday, Feb. 15, 1875," *EIHC*, XIII (April, 1875), 81–89; "Hawthorne's 'Privateer' Revealed at Last," *Literary Digest*, XCIII (April 9, 1927), 48–49. Clifford Smyth published in 1926 *The Yarn of a Yankee Privateer Edited by Nathaniel Hawthorne* (New York), reprinting the chapters from the *Democratic Review* and adding one not previously published.

12. Sophia to her mother, Jan. 9, 1844; see also letters of April 5 and September 3, 1843.

13. VIII, 222–26. He had observed a similar pedlar in North Adams in the summer of 1838 (VIII, 108–9).

14. See Rose Hawthorne Lathrop, *Memories of Hawthorne*, pp. 24, 26, 29–30; and Edwin Gittleman, *Jones Very: The Effective Years, 1833–1840* (New York, 1967), pp. 161, 282–87.

15. See *The Complete Works of Edgar Allan Poe*, ed. James A. Harrison, 17 vols. (New York, 1902), XIII, 142–43; Sophia to Louisa Hawthorne, April 17, and to her mother, April 20, 1843 (in Julian Hawthorne, *Nathaniel Hawthorne and*

His Wife, 2 vols. [Boston, 1885], I, 273). In April, 1843, James Russell Lowell relayed to Hawthorne Poe's request for a contribution and also an engraving to appear in the first number of the *Stylus*, the magazine he intended to found. Hawthorne agreed to both requests, but the *Stylus* remained only a dream in Poe's mind.

16. To Sophia Peabody, April 21, 1840.
17. Barbara Mouffe, ed., *Hawthorne's Lost Notebook, 1835–1841* (University Park, Pa., 1978), pp. 30–31; VIII, 21.
18. Mouffe, *Hawthorne's Lost Notebook*, p. 32. Within the tale Hawthorne refers to the bosom serpent in Southey's *Roderick, the Last of the Goths*, but he might have cited other instances in literature and in the magazines and newspapers of his own time. See, for example, Daniel R. Barnes, " 'Physical Fact' and Folklore: Hawthorne's 'Egotism; or The Bosom Serpent,' " *American Literature*, XLIII (March, 1971), 117–21; Sargent Bush, Jr., "Bosom Serpents Before Hawthorne: The Origins of the Symbol," *American Literature*, XLIII (May, 1971), 181–99; George Monteiro, "A Nonliterary Source for Hawthorne's 'Egotism: or The Bosom Serpent,' " *American Literature*, XLI (Nov., 1970), 575–77.
19. Mouffe, *Hawthorne's Lost Notebook*, p. 17; VIII, 20–21. See William Bentley, *Diary*, 4 vols. (Salem, 1905–14), IV, 462–63, July 5, 1817.
20. Sophia to her mother, Jan. 9, 1844.
21. In "Howe's Masquerade" is a reference to Deacon Drowne, a "cunning carver of wood," whom Hawthorne might have learned about in Caleb H. Snow's *History of Boston* (Boston, 1827), p. 245, as the one who carved the Indian figure on the cupola of the Province House.
22. Mouffe, *Hawthorne's Lost Notebook*, p. 2; VIII, 184.
23. *Ibid.*, pp. 56, 46, 86; VIII, 165, 158, 184.
24. *Ibid.*, p. 85; VIII, 184.

15. The Expulsion

1. Some ten years later, the English poet Arthur Hugh Clough, then in America, wrote, on the authority of Henry Wadsworth Longfellow, that Hawthorne and his wife had lived one year at the Manse for a hundred dollars, subsisting on potatoes and apples. Clough, *Correspondence*, ed. Frederick L. Mulhauser, 2 vols. (Oxford, 1957), II, 369.
2. To George Hillard, March 24, 1844.
3. To Horatio Bridge, May 3, 1843.
4. To Sophia, March 16, 1843.
5. To George Hillard, May 14, Aug. 19, 1844.
6. To Sophia, Dec. 2, 1844.
7. To Louisa Hawthorne, Nov. 25, 1842.
8. To Horatio Bridge, March 25, 1843.
9. To Evert Duyckinck, Nov. 28, 1843.
10. This letter is at the Maine Historical Society.
11. To Horatio Bridge, Nov. 29, 1844.
12. *Ibid.*

13. To Evert Duyckinck, April 7, 1845.

14. The correspondence of George Bancroft, including letters from Hillard and others related to the appointment of Hawthorne to the Salem custom-house, is at the Massachusetts Historical Society. See also Horatio Bridge, *Personal Recollections of Nathaniel Hawthorne* (New York, 1893), pp. 94–104; and Julian Hawthorne, *Nathaniel Hawthorne and His Wife*, 2 vols. (Boston, 1885), I, 284–85.

15. *Ibid.*, I, 281.

16. VIII, 267–70. See Bridge, *Personal Recollections of Nathaniel Hawthorne*, pp. 108–10.

17. To Sophia, May 31, Dec. —, 1844.

18. Hawthorne wrote George William Curtis that he had spent the happiest years of his life at the Manse, but would leave "cheerfully and contentedly." See Gordon Milne, *George William Curtis and the Genteel Tradition* (Bloomington, Ind., 1956), p. 29.

19. Sophia to her mother, Sept. 7, 1845 (J. Hawthorne, *Nathaniel Hawthorne and His Wife*, I, 286–87.)

20. On January 19, 1848, Hawthorne replied to a letter from C. G. Ripley, son of Samuel Ripley, from whom the Old Manse had been rented, saying that he could not pay the amount due but would give his note. L. Neal Smith, who called this letter to my attention, believes that Hawthorne made payment within a few days from money borrowed from Francis George Shaw of Boston. See Shaw's letter to Hawthorne, Jan. 26, 1848, in the Berg Collection.

21. To Sophia, Nov. 10, 13, 19, 1845; Jan. 19, 1846.

22. See J. Hawthorne, *Nathaniel Hawthorne and His Wife*, I, 284–85.

23. An undated letter to General James Miller, collector of customs at Salem, probably was used to help persuade Hoyt and his supporters to accept the appointment of Howard as naval officer. The letter endorses Hoyt for some office in the Salem custom-house in the control of the collector, and is signed by Hawthorne and five of his friends in the local Democratic Party organization: William B. Pike, Horace L. Conolly, Zachariah Burchmore, Benjamin F. Browne, and John D. Howard. (This letter is in the Bancroft Library, University of California, Berkeley.)

24. To Evert Duyckinck, April 7, May 2, July 1, 1845; Jan. 24, Feb. 22, April 15, 1846. John J. McDonald has published two valuable articles on Hawthorne's years at the Old Manse: " 'The Old Manse' and Its Mosses: The Inception and Development of *Mosses from an Old Manse*," *Texas Studies in Literature and Language*, XVI (Spring, 1974), 77–108; and "A Guide to Primary Source Materials for the Study of Hawthorne's Old Manse Period," *Studies in the American Renaissance 1977*, pp. 261–312.

25. To Horatio Bridge, Oct. 20, 1846.

26. Sophia Hawthorne to her mother, Nov. 17, 1846; April 23, Sept. 10, 1847. J. Hawthorne, *Nathaniel Hawthorne and His Wife*, I, 310–14.

27. To Evert Duyckinck, April 1, 1847. See Randall Stewart, "Hawthorne's Contributions to *The Salem Advertiser*," *American Literature*, V (Jan., 1934), 327–41.

28. To H. W. Longfellow, Nov. 11, 1847; Feb. 10, 1848.

29. Hawthorne offered "Ethan Brand" for Elizabeth Peabody to include in the volume *Aesthetic Papers* (Boston, 1849), which she was editing. He feared that it might not be suitable for the volume, and Sophia, in sending the manuscript, indicated that she had the same fear: "It is tremendous truth, written, as he often writes truth, with characters of fire, upon an infinite gloom,—softened so as not wholly to terrify, by divine touches of beauty,—revealing pictures of nature, and also the tender spirit of a child." (J. Hawthorne, *Nathaniel Hawthorne and His Wife*, I, 330–31.) Instead of this tale, "Main Street" appeared in *Aesthetic Papers*, pp. 145–84.

16. "Decapitation"

1. The events in the removal of Hawthorne were reported by two of the main Whig participants: John Chapman in a letter of June 30, 1849, and Charles W. Upham in a memorial written about ten days later, both addressed to William M. Meredith, secretary of the treasury. These and other letters and documents related to the episode are in the National Archives. A number of them are printed by Winfield S. Nevins, "Nathaniel Hawthorne's Removal from the Salem Custom House," *EIHC*, LIII (April, 1917), 97–132.
2. John Chapman to William M. Meredith, June 30, 1849.
3. To keep her parents informed of developments, Sophia wrote them on June 8, 10, 15, 17, 21, and July 4. See Rose Hawthorne Lathrop, *Memories of Hawthorne* (Boston, 1897), pp. 93–101.
4. This letter is printed in Nevins, "Nathaniel Hawthorne's Removal from the Salem Custom House," pp. 125–27.

17. *The Scarlet Letter*

1. Sophia to her mother, Sept. 2, 1849. Julian Hawthorne, *Nathaniel Hawthorne and His Wife*, 2 vols. (Boston, 1885), I, 353–54.
2. From Sophia, July, 1847. Rose Hawthorne Lathrop, *Memories of Hawthorne* (New York, 1897), p. 88.
3. See accounts by Julian Hawthorne in *Nathaniel Hawthorne and His Wife*, I, 340, *Hawthorne and His Circle* (New York, 1903), pp. 3–4, and "The Making of the 'Scarlet Letter,'" *Bookman*, LXXIV (Dec., 1931), 401–11; and by Moncure Conway in *Life of Nathaniel Hawthorne* (London, 1890), p. 117, and *Emerson at Home and Abroad* (Boston, 1882), p. 268.
4. Sophia to Mary Mann, Dec. 5, 1847.
5. Sophia to her mother, Nov. 25, 1849.
6. J. Hawthorne, *Nathaniel Hawthorne and His Wife*, I, 335, 353.
7. See Whittier to Hawthorne, Feb. 22, 1850, in *ibid.*, I, 355–56.
8. Rose Hawthorne Lathrop, *Memories of Hawthorne*, p. 117. Two years earlier Hawthorne had borrowed from Shaw, apparently to pay the amount still due for rent on the Old Manse. See note 20, Chapter XV.
9. J. Hawthorne, *Nathaniel Hawthorne and His Wife*, I, 354–55.

10. J. R. Lowell to Duyckinck, in Horace Elisha Scudder, *James Russell Lowell: A Biography*, 2 vols. (Boston, 1901), I, 283–84.

11. See Harold Blodgett, "Hawthorne as Poetry Critic: Six Unpublished Letters to Lewis Mansfield," *American Literature*, XII (May, 1940), 173–84.

12. See Hawthorne to J. T. Fields, Jan. 12; to B. F. Browne, Jan. 13; J. T. Fields to Hawthorne, Jan. 14, 1851 (in the Berg Collection).

13. June 12, 1849, four days-after Hawthorne knew of his removal from office. See Benjamin Lease, "Hawthorne and *Blackwood's* in 1849: Two Unpublished Letters," *Jahrbüch für Amerikastudien*, XIV (1969), 152–54.

14. James T. Fields, *Yesterdays with Authors* (Boston, 1871), pp. 49–51. In a letter of Sophia's to Fields on January 27, 1851, there seems to be authentication for his return to Mall Street after reading the fragment of *The Scarlet Letter;* she was sending him from Lenox the manuscript of *The House of the Seven Gables* and wished he lived closer, she said, "so that I might again see you come in with such a radiant expression of delight as when you had read the Scarlet Letter." She wrote to Richard Manning on February 12, 1871, after the quarrel had developed between her and Fields over royalty payments, that it was absurd for Fields to say that "he was the sole cause of the Scarlet Letter being published!!!! . . . It was Mr. Whipple . . . who came to Salem with Mr. Fields, and told him what a splendid work it was—and then Mr. Fields begged to be the publisher of it."

15. *The Annals of Salem from Its First Settlement* (Salem, 1827), p. 455.

16. It is reported that, when Hawthorne was asked once for a glimpse of the scarlet "A," he replied that he had it until recently, when the children got their hands on it and threw it into the fire. Edward Waldo Emerson, *The Early Years of the Saturday Club: 1855–1870* (Boston, 1918), p. 209.

17. Burchmore preserved Hawthorne's letters and released some of them for publication in the *Boston Gazette*, Aug. 5, 12, 19, 26, Sept. 2, 15, 30, Oct. 7, 1883.

18. To Fields, March 7, 1850.

19. March 23, 1850, in J. Hawthorne, *Nathaniel Hawthorne and His Wife*, I, 364–66. One who remembered after half a century the response to "The Custom-House" in Salem said it was a daughter of Lee who talked about cowhiding Hawthorne. George O. Holyoke to G. M. Williamson, Nov. 10, 1901, in the Berg Collection. See Benjamin Lease, "Hawthorne and 'a Certain Venerable Personage': New Light on 'The Custom-House,'" *Jahrbüch für Amerikastudien*, XV (1970), 201–7.

20. Carroll A. Wilson, *Thirteen Author Collections*, ed. C. S. Wilson and David A. Randall, 2 vols. (New York, 1950), I, 154. Upham owned an inscribed copy of *The Gentle Boy: A Thrice Told Tale*, now at the Bowdoin College Library.

21. For an account of the relations between Conolly and Hawthorne, see Manning Hawthorne, "Hawthorne and 'The Man of God,'" *Colophon*, n.s. II (Winter, 1937), pp. 262–82, in which this letter is printed in full. The "infernal drafts from Philadelphia" probably represented loans to Conolly. In a scrapbook for 1839, Hawthorne noted that Conolly owed him $53.39, when O'Sullivan owed him $550.00. See Claude M. Simpson, "A Manuscript Mystery: Hawthorne's 1839 Scrap-Book," *Nathaniel Hawthorne Journal 1975*, pp. 28–33.

22. For a discussion of history in this romance, see Charles Ryskamp, "The New England Sources of *The Scarlet Letter*," *American Literature*, XXXI (Nov., 1859), 257–72.

23. Reviews of *The Scarlet Letter* have been reprinted in J. Donald Crowley, ed., *Hawthorne: The Critical Heritage* (New York, 1970); Arlin Turner, ed., *Studies in The Scarlet Letter* (Columbus, Ohio, 1970). See also Bertha Faust, *Hawthorne's Contemporaneous Reputation: A Study of Literary Opinion in America and England 1828–1864* (Philadelphia, 1939).

24. To J. T. Fields, Jan. 27, 1851; to Lewis Mansfield, March 19, 1850; to Miss M. A. A. Dawson, Sept. 29, 1851.

25. See Rose Hawthorne Lathrop, *Memories of Hawthorne*, pp. 121–22.

18. In the Berkshires

1. To Horace Mann, Aug. 8, 1849; to Zachariah Burchmore, April 18, May 13; to Horatio Bridge, April 13; to Louisa Hawthorne, May [16], 1850.

2. April 26, 1850. See Horatio Bridge, *Personal Recollections of Nathaniel Hawthorne* (New York, 1893), pp. 117–18.

3. Sophia to her mother, June 9, 1850.

4. To Zachariah Burchmore, June 9, 1850; to G. W. Curtis, April 21, 1851; to G. P. R. James, June 16, 1851.

5. Sophia to her mother, June 9, 23–25, 1850.

6. *Ibid.*, Aug. 1, Oct. 27, 1850.

7. Bridge, *Personal Recollections of Nathaniel Hawthorne*, pp. 120–23.

8. Rose Hawthorne Lathrop, *Memories of Hawthorne* (Boston, 1897), p. 162.

9. Passages from this letter and reports by several who attended this picnic are included in Jay Leyda, *The Melville Log* (New York, 1951), pp. 382–86, 922–26 (in the supplement added in a new edition of 1969), and in Eleanor Melville Metcalf, *Herman Melville, Cycle and Epicycle* (Cambridge, Mass., 1953), pp. 85, 89–92. In a three-part sketch, "Several Days in Berkshire," in the *Literary World* of August 24, 31, September 7, Cornelius Mathews narrated the events playfully. In *Yesterdays with Authors* (Boston, 1871), pp. 52–53, James T. Fields gives Hawthorne a less restrained role than he has in the reports written at the time, saying that on the picnic "Hawthorne was among the most enterprising of the merry-makers" and at the dinner "rayed out in a sparkling and unwonted manner" and "stoutly" opposed Holmes's comparison of Englishmen and Americans.

10. In a letter to her sister Elizabeth, Aug. 8, 1850, in Metcalf, *Herman Melville, Cycle and Epicycle*, p. 86.

11. Pertinent excerpts from Evert Duyckinck's letters are printed in Leyda, *The Melville Log*.

12. Part of this letter is printed in Metcalf, *Herman Melville, Cycle and Epicycle*, p. 85.

13. *Ibid.*, pp. 91–92; Leyda, *The Melville Log*, pp. 924–25.

14. *The Letters of Herman Melville*, ed. Merrell R. Davis and William H. Gilman

(New Haven, Conn., 1960), p. 113. Subsequent references to Melville's letters are to this edition, in which they are arranged chronologically.

15. Metcalf, *Herman Melville, Cycle and Epicycle*, pp. 91–92.
16. *Ibid.*, pp. 89–90.
17. Raymond M. Weaver, *Herman Melville, Mariner and Mystic* (New York, 1921), p. 24.
18. Metcalf, *Herman Melville, Cycle and Epicycle*, pp. 91–92.
19. Theodore F. Wolfe, *Literary Shrines: The Haunts of Some Famous American Authors* (Philadelphia, 1895), pp. 190–91. Hawthorne brought as a gift the four-volume set of *The Mariner's Chronicle* that had come to him in 1832 from his Uncle Richard Manning's library (Leyda, *The Melville Log*, p. 408).
20. See Perry Miller, *The Raven and the Whale: The War of Words and Wits in the Era of Poe and Melville* (New York, 1956), pp. 281–311.
21. Sophia Hawthorne to her sister Elizabeth Peabody, May 7, Oct. 4, 1851.

19. *The House of the Seven Gables*

1. In the Berg Collection.
2. Sophia to her mother, Jan. 27, 1851.
3. To J. T. Fields, March 6, 1851.
4. *Ibid.*, Jan. 12, 1851.
5. To Evert Duyckinck, April 27, 1851.
6. To J. T. Fields, May 23, 1851.
7. *Ibid.*, Feb. 22 and Jan. 27; to Horatio Bridge, March 15, 1851.
8. To Louisa Hawthorne, July 10; to James T. Fields, July 20, 1851.
9. To James T. Fields, July 15, 1851.
10. To H. T. Tuckerman, June 20, 1851, printed in part in Tuckerman, "Nathaniel Hawthorne," *Littell's Living Age*, LXXXI (June 11, 1864), 518.
11. To J. T. Fields, May 23, 1851. To one of the descendants who protested also that another ancestor of his, Andrew Oliver, had appeared in *Grandfather's Chair*, Hawthorne sent a firm reply on May 3: In telling how Andrew Oliver, the first tax officer after passage of the Stamp Act, was hanged in effigy, Grandfather was reporting history; a descendant of the illustrious Oliver family would surely not want them omitted from history. Hawthorne would have thought of the two earliest American ancestors in his paternal line, in whom he took pride at the same time he said he took shame on their account. See Norman Holmes Pearson, "The Pynchons and Judge Pyncheon," *EIHC*, C (Oct., 1964), 235–55.
12. May 3, 1851, in Julian Hawthorne, *Nathaniel Hawthorne and His Wife*, 2 vols. (Boston, 1885), I, 438.
13. Sept. 17, 1850.
14. Henry James, *Hawthorne* (London, 1879), p. 125.
15. See Carroll A. Wilson, *Thirteen Author Collections of the Nineteenth Century*, ed. C. S. Wilson and D. A. Randall, 2 vols. (New York, 1950), I, 131.
16. See VIII, 234–37, 426–31, 80–91, 96–97, 66–68. See pages 92–93 of this volume and Thomas Morgan Griffiths, *Maine Sources in "The House of the Seven Gables"* (Waterville, Maine, 1945).

17. Vernon Loggins (*The Hawthornes: The Story of Seven Generations of an American Family* [New York, 1951], pp. 169–70) records that in 1765 Captain Daniel Hawthorne, the novelist's grandfather, together with a brother and two sisters, undertook to initiate court proceedings in an effort to gain title to this land. No trial was held, but the eastern land claim remained in family lore. Julian Hawthorne refers to the family tradition of a lost deed to Maine land and suggests a connection with *The House of the Seven Gables* (J. Hawthorne, *Nathaniel Hawthorne and His Wife*, I, 26).

18. Manning Hawthorne, "Hawthorne and the Man of God," *Colophon*, n.s. II (Winter, 1937), 268–69. Claims have been advanced also for the Philip English house, built in 1685 and torn down in 1833, and for the Curwin house, built in 1642, later known as the "Witch House." James Russell Lowell supposed the Curwin house was Hawthorne's original and bragged, he said, that he was descended from the man who built it. See J. Hawthorne, *Nathaniel Hawthorne and His Wife*, I, 390–92.

19. Charles W. Upham's *Lectures on Witchcraft* (Salem, 1832, p. 100) includes this report and adds a further note from Thomas Hutchinson's *History of Massachusetts*, which Hawthorne read, that "there was a tradition among the people, and it has descended to the present time, that the manner of Mr. Noyes' death strangely verified the prediction." See Joseph B. Felt, *Annals of Salem*, 2 vols. (Salem, 1845), II, 24, 587, 590; John Farmer, *A Genealogical Register of the First Settlers of New-England* (Lancaster, Mass., 1829), p. 192.

20. A remark Elizabeth Hawthorne made in old age suggests the way in which members of the family kept the inherited curse in mind while not believing in it. She wrote Una Hawthorne that if Julian became a successful author, he might lift the family curse. She then added that she should not speak of a curse, since their ancestors had bequeathed them "the best brains in the world." See J. Hawthorne, *Nathaniel Hawthorne and His Wife*, I, 9, 24.

21. See Harold Blodgett, "Hawthorne as Poetry Critic: Six Unpublished Letters to Lewis Mansfield," *American Literature*, XII (May, 1940), 173–84.

22. To J. T. Fields, April 7, 1851.

23. To Washington Irving, July 16, 1852.

24. Rose Hawthorne Lathrop, *Memories of Hawthorne* (Boston, 1897), p. 167.

25. Quoted in James T. Fields, *Yesterdays with Authors* (Boston, 1871), p. 52.

26. To Evert Duyckinck, April 27, 1851; to W. B. Pike, July 24, 1851.

27. To W. B. Pike, Sept. 2, 1851.

20. *The Blithedale Romance*

1. To E. P. Whipple, May 2, 1852.

2. To W. B. Pike, July 24, 1851.

3. Sophia to her mother, June 10, 1850. See also page 180 of this work.

4. It has been plausibly suggested that "Feathertop" owed something to Ludwig Tieck's "Die Vogelscheuche," which probably was the story Hawthorne said he struggled to read in German in April, 1843. See two articles by Alfred A. Kern: "The Sources of Hawthorne's 'Feathertop,' " *PMLA*, XLVI (Dec.,

1931), 1253–59; and "Hawthorne's 'Feathertop,' and R. L. R.," *PMLA*, LII (June, 1937), 503–10.

5. From Fields, July 7, 1852; Sophia to ——, spring, 1852.

6. VIII, 261–67, first published in Julian Hawthorne, *Nathaniel Hawthorne and His Wife*, 2 vols. (Boston, 1885), I, 295–303. For information on Martha Hunt, see George William Curtis, "Hawthorne," in *Literary and Social Essays* (New York, 1895), pp. 55–59.

7. See also to ——, Oct. 16, 1852. In sending a copy of *The Blithedale Romance* to George William Curtis, who had lived at Brook Farm for two years, Hawthorne instructed him, "Do not read it as if it had anything to do with Brook Farm (which essentially it has not)" (July 14, 1852).

8. See my article, "Autobiographical Elements in Hawthorne's *The Blithedale Romance*," *Texas Studies in English*, XV (1935), 40–62, and my introduction to *The Blithedale Romance* (New York, 1958).

9. London *Athenaeum* (July 10, 1852), 741–43.

10. *Westminster Review*, LVIII (Oct., 1852), 592–98.

11. *Brownson's Quarterly Review*, VI (Sept., 1852), 561–64.

12. *Graham's Magazine*, XLI (Sept., 1852), 333–34.

13. *New York Tribune*, April 6, 26, 1852.

14. For other reviews see the *Southern Quarterly Review*, n.s. VI (Oct., 1842), 543; the *Christian Examiner*, LV (Sept., 1852), 292–94; and the *American Whig Review*, XVI (Nov., 1852), 417–24. John Humphrey Noyes, himself associated with similar undertakings, wrote in 1870 that Hawthorne joined the Brook Farm community "only to jilt it" and had "given the world a poetico-sneering romance about it" (*History of American Socialisms*, Philadelphia, 1870, p. 107).

15. In J. Hawthorne, *Nathaniel Hawthorne and His Wife*, I, 432–33.

16. Sophia to Louisa Hawthorne, Feb. 25, 1852.

17. Sophia to her mother, June 6; also 13, 14, 1852; excerpts are printed in Rose Hawthorne Lathrop, *Memories of Hawthorne* (Boston, 1897), pp. 189–97.

18. To G. P. Putnam, April 14, 1852.

19. To Evert Duyckinck, June 15, 1852.

20. *Ibid.*, and to G. W. Curtis, July 14, 1852.

21. Maria L. Hawthorne to Sophia, August —, 1850, in J. Hawthorne, *Nathaniel Hawthorne and His Wife*, I, 437.

22. Sophia to her mother, July 30, 1852.

23. *Ibid.*, Aug. 5, 1852.

24. Elizabeth Hawthorne to Sophia, Nov. 24, 1864.

25. Sophia to her mother, Aug. 5, 1852.

21. "We Are Politicians Now"

1. A report supposedly originating with Pierce seems to have no authenticity but has the sound of truth: Seeing Pierce the first time after his nomination, Hawthorne "sat down by him on a sofa, and after a melancholy silence, heaving a deep sigh, said, 'Frank, *what* a pity!' Then, after a pause, 'But, after all, this world was not meant to be happy in—only to succeed in!' " (M. A.

DeWolfe Howe, *American Bookmen* [New York, 1898], p. 216.) Another version of this account has Hawthorne exclaim, "Frank, I pity you! Indeed I do, from the bottom of my heart!" (Maunsell B. Field, *Memories of Many Men and Some Women* [New York, 1874], pp. 159–60.)

2. Roy Franklin Nichols, *Franklin Pierce* (Philadelphia, 1931), p. 208.
3. Rose Hawthorne Lathrop, *Memories of Hawthorne* (Boston, 1897), p. 203.
4. To Franklin Pierce, June 28, 1832. See Zoltán Haraszti, "Hawthorne Forecasts Franklin Pierce's Career," *Bulletin of the Boston Public Library*, III (Jan., 1951), 83–86.
5. Rose Hawthorne Lathrop, *Memories of Hawthorne*, p. 203. The report by Frank B. Sanborn (*Hawthorne and His Friends: Reminiscence and Tribute* [Cedar Rapids, Ia., 1908], p. 7) that Hawthorne had Pierce come to Concord in order to recommend his candidacy among the local residents may have reference only to this visit.
6. To Horatio Bridge, Oct. 18, 1852.
7. Sophia to her mother, Sept. 19, 1852.
8. See Louis C. Hatch, *The History of Bowdoin College* (Portland, Me., 1927), pp. 253–54.
9. For the notebook account of the visit on the Isles of Shoals, see VIII, 511–43.
10. To J. T. Fields, Nov. 14, 1852.
11. In an *Atlantic Monthly* essay of August, 1869, "Among the Isles of Shoals," and in a book with the same title in 1873, Celia Thaxter recounts legends of the Isles, including some of those she and her husband told Hawthorne in 1852. In a letter to Annie Fields, James T. Fields's wife, on May 4, 1869, she sought to identify a poem entitled "The Grave" which Hawthorne had said he thought "the most powerful thing in modern poetry." *Letters of Celia Thaxter*, ed. A. F. and R. L. (Boston, 1895), p. 42. The author of the poem was Caroline Wigley Clive (Mrs. Archer Clive), who in 1840 included it in a volume entitled *IX Poems by V.* It opens, "I stood within the grave's o'ershadowing vault," and in sixteen quatrains marshals the sweep of humanity within the vast tomb. The Isles of Shoals in Hawthorne's observation, and in the history and lore he learned during his visit, apparently recalled this poem to his mind; it may have recalled also the poems he wrote in his youth on similar topics.
12. Sophia to her mother, Aug. 13, Oct. 31, 1852; Sophia's notebook, Sept. 2, 1852. Excerpts are printed in Julian Hawthorne, *Nathaniel Hawthorne and His Wife*, 2 vols. (Boston, 1885), I, 481–85.
13. Louisa Hawthorne to Elizabeth M. Hawthorne, July 18, 1852.
14. From Elizabeth M. Hawthorne, Sept. 23, 1852.

22. Prime Minister

1. To Sophia, March 15, 1840.
2. Pike is delineated by Randall Stewart in "Hawthorne and Politics," *New England Quarterly*, V (April, 1932), 237–63. Unless otherwise indicated, the letters exchanged between Hawthorne and Pike are printed in this article.

3. At the Pierpont Morgan Library.
4. To H. W. Longfellow, May 8, 1851.
5. To W. B. Pike, March 27, 1857.
6. To Zachariah Burchmore, July 15, 1851. Aspects of the relations between Hawthorne and Burchmore are discussed in Stewart, "Hawthorne and Politics."
7. To G. B. Loring, Jan. 9, 1853.
8. To Zachariah Burchmore, May 31, 1853.
9. *Ibid.*, July 15, 1851.
10. To Horatio Bridge, Oct. 18, 1852.
11. See letters to Charles Peaslee, March 21, April 13, 1853; to J. I. (?) Lee, May 2, 1853.
12. To R. H. Stoddard, March 16, 1853; to E. P. Whipple, March 29, 1853.
13. *Herman Melville: A Biography* (New York, 1951), pp. 202–3.
14. Julian Hawthorne, *Nathaniel Hawthorne and His Wife*, 2 vols. (Boston, 1885), I, 475.
15. Eleanor Melville Metcalf, *Herman Melville: Cycle and Epicycle* (Cambridge, Mass., 1953), p. 147. Hawthorne may have had Melville in mind the next February 16 when he asked Ticknor to find out whether the chargé-ship at Rome would be available, saying that he had a friend who wanted to apply. A week before going to Washington, he wrote Ticknor that, while there, he would like to be of service to a friend to whom he was "indebted for many kindnesses." This may have been a reference to Melville, or to Ellery Channing, who had written on March 29 asking to be recommended to "our friend" for appointment to Rome (in the Berg Collection, brought to my attention by L. Neal Smith).
16. To R. H. Stoddard, March 16, 1853.

23. Return to Our Old Home

1. *Love Letters of Nathaniel Hawthorne*, 2 vols. (Chicago, 1907).
2. Samuel Longfellow, *Life of Henry Wadsworth Longfellow with Extracts from His Journals and Correspondence*, 2 vols. (Boston, 1886), II, 234. See Arthur Hugh Clough, *Correspondence*, ed. Frederick L. Mulhauser, 2 vols. (Oxford, 1957), II, 450.
3. Julian Hawthorne, *Nathaniel Hawthorne and His Wife*, 2 vols. (Boston, 1885), II, 15; Rose Hawthorne Lathrop, *Memories of Hawthorne* (Boston, 1897), p. 219.
4. Lathrop, *Memories of Hawthorne*, pp. 222–24.
5. J. Hawthorne, *Nathaniel Hawthorne and His Wife*, II, 18.
6. To W. B. Pike, Sept. 13, 1853.
7. J. Hawthorne, *Nathaniel Hawthorne and His Wife*, II, 19–22.
8. *Our Old Home*, Centenary Edition, V, 44. See Hawthorne's letter to Henry Bright recommending Wilding, Jan. 4, 1858.
9. *The English Notebooks by Nathaniel Hawthorne*, ed. Randall Stewart (New York, 1941), pp. 13–16. Citations of the *English Notebooks* will be given by date, in the text or in notes, and may be located in this edition, in which the entries are in chronological order.

10. To Mrs. Wilson Auld, Aug. 24, Oct. 31, 1853.

11. H. W. Longfellow to Hawthorne, Sept. 21, Oct. 3, 1852, in *The Letters of Henry Wadsworth Longfellow*, ed. Andrew Hilen (Cambridge, Mass.), IV (1972), 355–57.

12. Henry Bright appears in the essay "Consular Experiences" as "a young English friend, a scholar and a literary amateur," for whom the author had an affectionate regard. He is not named but is identified in a hint, "Bright was the illumination of my dusky little apartment, as often as he made his appearance there."

13. Lathrop, *Memories of Hawthorne*, pp. 250–51.

14. To W. D. Ticknor, Sept. 13, 1853.

15. Lathrop, *Memories of Hawthorne*, pp. 250–51, 261–62.

16. *Ibid.*, p. 310.

17. This letter was published in the *Athenaeum*, no. 3225 (Aug. 17, 1889), p. 225.

18. See Randall Stewart, "Hawthorne and Politics," *New England Quarterly*, V (April, 1932), 237–63.

19. *The Correspondence of Arthur Hugh Clough*, ed. F. L. Mulhauser, 2 vols. (Oxford, 1957), II, 409; J. Hawthorne, *Nathaniel Hawthorne and His Wife*, II, 30–31; to Pike, Sept. 13, 1853; Sophia to her father, April 14, 1854.

20. To W. D. Ticknor, March 18, 1857.

21. To W. D. Ticknor, March 30, 1854, Jan. 19, 1855, June 20, 1856; and to Horatio Bridge, June 20, 1856.

22. To W. D. Ticknor, Oct. 26, 1855, June 20, 1856, March 13, 1857.

23. To J. T. Fields, April 13, June 7, 1854.

24. "Pegasus in a Yoke"

1. John Bell Osborne, "Nathaniel Hawthorne as American Consul," *Bookman*, XVI (Jan., 1903), 461–64. A book-length study of Hawthorne as consul being written by James O. Mays reaches much the same conclusions as Osborne. "Consular Dispatches of Nathaniel Hawthorne," in *EIHC*, CXIII (Oct., 1977), 239–322, edited by John R. Byers, Jr., prints selections from Hawthorne's dispatches to the secretary of state, including the two long ones in Hawthorne's own hand, No. 22 and No. 90.

2. J. L. O'Sullivan to George Bancroft, May 31, 1844. See p. 167 of this volume.

3. Dispatches from Hawthorne's term as consul are in the National Archives.

4. To W. D. Ticknor, March 30, 1854.

5. To Horatio Bridge, March 30, 1854; to W. D. Ticknor, March 30, April 30, 1854.

6. See Samuel Flagg Bemis, ed., *The American Secretaries of State and Their Diplomacy* (New York, 1928), VI, 236–62.

7. To W. D. Ticknor, April 9, July 30, 1857.

8. See Vivian Hopkins, *Prodigal Puritan: A Life of Delia Bacon* (Cambridge, Mass., 1959), p. 169; Theodore Bacon, *Delia Bacon: A Biographical Sketch* (Boston, 1888), p. 55.

9. This and other letters from Delia Bacon to Hawthorne are printed in Theodore Bacon, *Delia Bacon: A Biographical Sketch.*

10. To Delia Bacon, July 10, 1856.

11. To Leonard Bacon, Aug. 14, 1856.

12. To Delia Bacon, July 12, 21, 1856.

13. To Francis Bennoch, Sept. 2, 1856.

14. To Delia Bacon, Oct. 6, 1856.

15. From Delia Bacon, Oct. 16, 22–23, 1856.

16. To W. D. Ticknor, Nov. 6; to Francis Bennoch, Oct. 27, Dec. 2, 1856, Feb. 11, 1857.

17. To W. D. Ticknor, April 9, May 20, 1857. The title page of the book reads: *The Philosophy of the Plays of Shakespeare Unfolded. By Delia Bacon. With a Preface by Nathaniel Hawthorne, Author of "The Scarlet Letter," etc.* (London and Boston, 1857).

18. Theodore Bacon, *Delia Bacon,* pp. 170–71.

19. To W. D. Ticknor, Nov. 23, 1856.

25. England and the English

1. Julian Hawthorne, *Nathaniel Hawthorne and His Wife,* 2 vols. (Boston, 1885), II, 78–80.

2. In publishing the *English Notebooks,* Hawthorne's widow omitted the account of the visit to Tupper, but in *Nathaniel Hawthorne and His Wife* (II, 108–16) Julian Hawthorne included part of it—enough to cause Tupper to indicate in *My Life as an Author* (London, 1886), pp. 246–47, that he was hurt and resentful. Hawthorne recorded in his notebook for August 31, 1856, that Bennoch had told him "something about Tupper that gives him an aspect of pathos and heroic endurance. . . . The thing is not to be recorded; but Tupper is a patient, tender, Christian man."

3. In his book *Helen Faucit* (London, 1900), p. 259, Martin tells about this visit and other meetings with Hawthorne, declaring that he and his wife reciprocated his warm friendship.

4. To Sophia, April 7, 1856.

5. *American Lands and Letters,* 2 vols. (New York, 1897–99), I, 249.

6. To W. D. Ticknor, Aug. 6, 1853.

7. To J. T. Fields, Aug. 19, 1853.

8. To Horatio Bridge, April 17, 1854.

9. To W. D. Ticknor, Jan. 17, 1856, April 24, Jan. 31, 1857.

10. In his *Retrospect of a Long Life,* 2 vols. (London, 1883), II, 202, Hall gives his recollection of the occasion, no doubt modified by the elapsed years and his high regard for Hawthorne.

11. To J. T. Fields, July 18, 1863.

12. To W. D. Ticknor, May 10, 1856.

13. *Memories of Many Men and Some Women* (New York, 1874), pp. 144–45.

14. To J. T. Fields, Sept. 16, 1853; to W. D. Ticknor, March 16, 1855; from David Roberts, Sept. 16, 1856, Feb. 14, 1857. Roberts's letters are in the Bancroft Library, University of California, Berkeley.

15. To J. T. Fields, Sept. 13, 1855; to W. D. Ticknor, Sept. 13, Oct. 12, 26, Nov. 9, 1855.
16. To R. W. Emerson, Sept. 10, 1856. Hawthorne could endorse Emerson's views particularly in Chapter 13, "Result."
17. To W. B. Pike, Jan. 6, 1854.
18. To Horatio Bridge, March 30, May 1, June 9, 1854.

26. Novelist as Consul

1. Manuscript pocket diary kept by Hawthorne in 1856, in the Pierpont Morgan Library. In a letter to Ticknor on October 10, Hawthorne listed the guests and enclosed the itemized bill for the dinner, totaling twenty pounds.
2. For Melville's visits in November and the following May, see *Journal of a Visit to Europe and the Levant, October 11, 1856–May 6, 1857,* ed. Howard C. Horsford (Princeton, N.J., 1955), pp. 61–64, 261–62; and Jay Leyda, *The Melville Log* (New York, 1951, 1969), pp. 526–31, 533, 577, 929–41.
3. See Leyda, *The Melville Log,* p. 533.
4. See *ibid.,* pp. 617, 674, 694, 696, 782. For studies of the personal and literary relations between Hawthorne and Melville, see Randall Stewart, "Melville and Hawthorne," *South Atlantic Quarterly,* LI (July, 1952), 436–46; Henry Bamford Parkes, "Poe, Hawthorne, Melville: An Essay in Sociological Criticism," *Partisan Review,* XVI (Feb., 1949), 157, 165; Charles N. Watson, Jr., "The Estrangement of Hawthorne and Melville," *New England Quarterly,* XLVI (Sept., 1973), 380–402; Luther Stearns Mansfield, "Melville and Hawthorne in the Berkshires," in *Melville and Hawthorne in the Berkshires,* ed. Howard P. Vincent (Kent, Ohio, 1968), pp. 4–21.
5. See Melville's essay "Nathaniel Hawthorne and His Mosses" and his letter to Hawthorne, April 16, 1851.
6. See Jay Leyda, *The Melville Log,* 782–83.
7. Hawthorne's speech is printed by C. E. Frazer Clark, Jr., in "An Exhibition Commemorating Nathaniel Hawthorne in England: Liverpool, England, 15–20 July 1971," *Nathaniel Hawthorne Journal 1972,* pp. 208–9.
8. Hawthorne's official correspondence, in the National Archives, includes letters to ship captains, other consuls, the United States Ambassador to Great Britain, British officials, and some other individuals, as well as dispatches to the State Department and to the Treasury Department.
9. To Charles Sumner, May 23, 1855.
10. To W. D. Ticknor, Jan. 31; to Horatio Bridge, Feb. 13; to the secretary of state, Feb. 13, March 27, May 8, 1857.

27. Art and Artists in Italy

1. The entry for January 6, 1858, written in Paris, begins Hawthorne's French and Italian notebooks. Quotations from these notebooks follow the text established for the Centenary Edition, in which they can be located by date, since the arrangement is chronological.

2. To Francis Bennoch, March 16, 1858.

3. Notebook entries, Feb. 14, March 11, 1858.

4. Julian Hawthorne asserts that the bust was spoiled when an unnamed American instructed the workmen to make alterations in cutting the stone (*Nathaniel Hawthorne and His Wife*, 2 vols. [Boston, 1885], II, 183).

5. In the Bancroft Library, University of California, Berkeley.

6. See Sophia to Elizabeth Peabody, Nov. 21, 1858, in the Mary K. and Harry L. Dalton Collection, Duke University.

7. See John L. Idol, Jr., and Sterling Eisiminger, "Hawthorne Sits for a Bust by Maria Louisa Lander," *EIHC*, CXIV (Oct., 1978), 207–12, and Wayne Craven, *Sculpture in America* (New York, 1968), p. 332.

8. Notebook entries, April 3 and Oct. 21, 1858.

9. Letter of July 19, 1850, in the Berg Collection.

10. Hawthorne's widow copied the notebook entry on Mozier and Margaret Fuller (her manuscript pages 178–81, in the Berg Collection), but did not publish it. Julian Hawthorne included the entry in *Nathaniel Hawthorne and His Wife*, I, 259–62. There followed protests against the publication of the material, as in the *Critic*, n.s. III (Jan. 17, 24, 1885), 30, 147, and against Hawthorne's analysis of Miss Fuller's character, as in an article by a nephew of hers, Frederick T. Fuller, "Hawthorne and Margaret Fuller," *Literary World*, XVI (Jan. 10, 1885), 11–15. Emerson quoted in his journal for 1851 an excerpt from a letter in which Elizabeth Peabody indicated aspects of Margaret Fuller's character similar to those Hawthorne described later. She quoted Hawthorne as saying that knowing James Lloyd Fuller, Margaret's youngest brother, whom he had known at Brook Farm, "explained the faults of Margaret." She concluded characterization of Lloyd thus: "He was sent, perhaps, as a sign what original ugliness could be overcome by a glorious spirit, which had a vision of the good & true & beautiful, with a will & determination to conquer. Margaret's life was the result of this strange association[."] Emerson, *Journals and Miscellaneous Notebooks, Volume XI, 1848–1851*, ed. A. W. Plumstead and others (Cambridge, Mass., 1975), p. 440.

11. Notebook entry, May 27, 1858.

12. *Ibid.*, June 2, 1858.

13. *Ibid.*, June 4, 5, 1858.

14. To J. T. Fields, Sept. 3, 1858; notebook entry, Sept. 28, 1858.

15. For Hawthorne's study of art in England, see entries in the *English Notebooks*, March 23–27, June 17, Aug. 2, 5, 1856; Sept. 5, 1856, July 24–Sept. 6, 1857.

16. See notebook entry, Feb. 23, 1858.

17. Notebook entries, June 30, Sept. 10, 25, 1858.

18. Powers appears in notebook entries for June 7, 27, July 8, 28, Sept. 29, 1858. He had been commissioned by the United States government for a statue to be placed in the national capitol. Because the $25,000 appropriated had never become available, he was bitter toward Franklin Pierce and others he thought responsible. Hawthorne spoke to Pierce about the matter, and concluded that he was sure Powers "acted fairly in his own eyes."

19. Ada Shepard wrote her sister Kate, August 27, 1858, that the Brownings were

"entirely antagonistic to each other" on this subject. Copies of her letters are in the Norman Holmes Pearson Collection.

20. Dec. 20, 1857.

21. Notebook dated July 3–Oct. 8, 1858, in the Berg Collection. See also Hawthorne's pocket diary for 1858, Aug. 24.

22. Rose Hawthorne Lathrop, *Memories of Hawthorne* (New York, 1897), pp. 397–98.

23. Not surprisingly, Mrs. Hawthorne omitted from the printed notebooks the last sentence quoted and the part of the previous sentence following the semicolon.

24. Julian Hawthorne tells of finding the name Mary Rondel in a copy of Sidney's *Arcadia* in which he concluded that she and Daniel Hawthorne, the novelist's grandfather, had exchanged love notes. He adopts this name in place of Mary Runnel in the reports of both Hawthorne and his wife and adds the statement, not in their reports, that Mary Rondel wanted the sympathy of Nathaniel Hawthorne. For statements by Julian Hawthorne, see *Nathaniel Hawthorne and His Wife*, I, 30–35; *Memoirs*, ed. Edith Garrigues Hawthorne (New York, 1938), p. 205; and "Books of Memory," *Bookman*, LXI (July, 1925), 567–69.

25. Notebook entries, Oct. 5, 9, 12, 1858.

28. *The Marble Faun*

1. This letter is in the Mary K. and Harry L. Dalton Collection, Duke University.

2. Hawthorne's pocket diary for 1859 is in the Essex Institute.

3. March 11, 15, 23, April 19, 1859.

4. The notebooks containing these descriptions, dated February 14–March 15, 1858, and October 9–12, 1858, are in the Berg Collection.

5. Reported by Mrs. Story to Moncure D. Conway, *Life of Nathaniel Hawthorne* (London, 1890), p. 79.

6. See the preface to *The Marble Faun* and Chapter 13.

7. Conway, *Life of Nathaniel Hawthorne*, p. 179.

8. Maude Howe Elliott, "Hawthorne in Italy," *The Hawthorne Centenary Celebration at the Wayside* (Boston, 1905), pp. 100–1.

9. Lawrence Hutton, *Literary Landmarks of Rome* (New York, 1897), pp. 60–61.

10. To J. T. Fields, Feb. 3, 1859.

11. Chapter 33.

12. Chapter 29.

13. *Life of Henry Wadsworth Longfellow with Extracts from His Journals and Correspondence* (Boston, 1886), II, 351.

14. See Elizabeth Dickinson Rice Bianciardi, *At Home in Italy* (Boston, 1884), pp. 21–22; Nathalia Wright, *American Novelists in Italy: The Discoverers, Allston to James* (Philadelphia, 1865), particularly the chapters on Hawthorne, Howells, and James and the chapter "The Young American in the Italian Life School."

15. Mrs. Hawthorne's volume of *Notes in England and Italy* (1869), published after her husband's death, suggests that he spoke for himself more than for her in

declining Fields's invitation. At least when she had less need to be "the best wife and mother in the world," she did write for publication, but she wrote as if in awe of her departed husband, saying almost nothing about herself or her family and restricting herself almost entirely to descriptions of artistic subjects—as if she were aiming at only "pretty fancies of snow and moonlight."

16. To Francis Bennoch, July 23; to J. T. Fields, Aug. 6, Oct. 10, 1859.
17. In the *Athenaeum* (March 3, 1860), pp. 296–97.
18. To Smith and Elder, March 7, 1860. To Henry Bright, March 10, April 4, 1860; to Francis Bennoch, March 24, 1860. Hawthorne echoes in these statements the advice he had written the poet Lewis Mansfield ten years earlier (February 10, 1850): In a particular type of story, it might be "allowable, and highly advisable, . . . to have as much mist and glorified fog as possible, diffused on all sides, but still there should be a distinct pathway to tread upon—a clue that the reader shall confide in, as being firmly fastened somewhere." But the readers will not proceed far unless they "know—or, at least, begin to know, or fancy they are about knowing—something of the matter in hand."
19. Sophia to Elizabeth Peabody, May 17, 1860.
20. From J. L. Motley, March 29; to Motley, April 1, 1860.
21. LXXIII (April, 1860), 624–27.
22. XXXII (Aug., 1860), 87–98.
23. To J. T. Fields, April 26; to W. D. Ticknor, April 19, 1860.
24. *Atlantic Monthly*, V (April, 1860), 509–10.
25. *National Review*, XI (Oct., 1860), 458–81.
26. *Atlantic Monthly*, V (May, 1860), 614–22.
27. III (June, 1860), 742–71.
28. To J. T. Fields, April 26, 1860.
29. In Bennoch's *Poems, Lyrics, Songs, and Sonnets* (London, 1877), pp. 265–67.

29. The Wayside After Seven Years

1. To J. L. Motley, April 1, 1860; to W. D. Ticknor, April 6, 19, 1860.
2. James T. Fields, *Yesterdays with Authors* (Boston, 1871), pp. 92–93.
3. See *The Journals of Bronson Alcott*, ed. Odell Shepard (Boston, 1938), p. 328.
4. To Henry W. Bishop, Jr. (Young Men's Christian Association, Chicago), Oct. 16, 1860; to William C. Bryant (Buffalo, N.Y.), Oct. 12, 1861; to Charles S. Smith (Young Men's Association of Albany, N.Y.), March 12, 1863.
5. Edward Waldo Emerson, *The Early Years of the Saturday Club* (Boston, 1918), p. 235; Charles Francis Adams, "Hawthorne's Place in Literature," *The Hawthorne Centenary Celebration at the Wayside* (Boston, 1905), p. 45.
6. See James Russell Lowell to Jane Norton, July 12, 1860, in *Letters of James Russell Lowell*, ed. Charles Eliot Norton, 2 vols. (New York, 1893), I, 302.
7. To Horatio Woodson, Nov. 5, 1860.
8. Sophia to Elizabeth Peabody, Nov. 27, 1858, in the Mary K. and Harry L. Dalton Collection.
9. See Edward Waldo Emerson, *The Early Years of the Saturday Club*, pp. 215,

331–32; F. B. Sanborn, *A. Bronson Alcott: His Life and Philosophy*, 2 vols. (Boston, 1893), II, 465–68; *The Hawthorne Centenary Celebration at the Wayside*, pp. 193–95.

10. This and the following quotations are from Shepard, *The Journals of Bronson Alcott*, pp. 341, 329, 335–36, 411–12.

11. Richard E. Peck, ed., *Nathaniel Hawthorne: Poems* (Charlottesville, Va., 1967), p. 28.

12. To Epes Sargent, Oct. 21, 1842.

13. To Evert Duyckinck, July 1, 1845.

14. To H. W. Longfellow, Nov. 21, 1847.

15. *The Writings of Henry David Thoreau*, ed. Bradford Torrey, 20 vols. (Boston, 1909), XV, 37.

16. To Richard Monckton Milnes, Nov. 13, 18, 1854.

17. To Charles Mackay, June 26, 1956.

18. In the Bancroft Library, University of California, Berkeley, are notebooks and sketchbooks from Julian's years in Europe.

19. To W. D. Ticknor, Sept. 27, 1860. The senior Henry James wrote his brother the Reverend William James, December 21, 1860, urging him to try galvanic treatment, and saying that by galvanic treatment Mrs. Rollins had "cured Hawthorne's eldest daughter *Una* in two days of one of the most fearful attacks of *dementia* ever suffered. She reduced her *in two hours* from a condition of fury dangerous to every body and everything about her to a state of tranquil rationality like health itself." This letter is in the Houghton Library, Harvard University.

20. To Donald G. Mitchell, Jan. 16, 1864. See Mitchell, *American Lands and Letters*, 2 vols. (New York, 1897–99), I, 249–51.

21. To Francis Bennoch, Dec. 17, 1860.

22. "My First Visit to New England," published in 1894 and included in the autobiographical volume *My Literary Friends and Acquaintance* (New York, 1900).

23. To Ticknor, May 23, June 5, 20, 1856; to J. T. Fields, Sept. 9, 1857; to Elizabeth P. Peabody, Aug. 13, 1857; to Henry Bright [Jan. 2], 1858, in J. Hawthorne, *Nathaniel Hawthorne and His Wife*, 2 vols. (Boston, 1885), II, 168–69.

24. To J. T. Fields, July 19, 1860.

25. To J. T. Fields, Oct. 5, 1862; April 30, 1863.

26. To Samuel H. Emory, Nov. 6, 1863.

27. In the essay "On a Certain Condescension in Foreigners" (1869), James Russell Lowell voiced the same hope.

28. *Reader*, II (Sept. 26, 1863), 336–38; *Punch*, LXXIX (Oct. 17, 1863), 339–40; *Blackwood's Magazine*, XCIV (Nov., 1863), 610–23; *Macmillan's Magazine*, X (July, 1864), 241–46.

29. June 25, 1884; in the Boston Public Library.

30. *Macmillan's Magazine*, L (May, 1884), 1–13.

31. Henry James, *Nathaniel Hawthorne* (New York, 1879), p. 145.

32. *Examiner*, No. 2907 (Oct. 17, 1863), pp. 662–63.

33. From Henry Bright, Oct. 20, 1863, in the Berg Collection.

34. J. Hawthorne, *Nathaniel Hawthorne and His Wife*, II, 307–8.

30. A Divided Nation and Divided Minds

1. To Horatio Bridge, Jan. 15, 1857.
2. Sophia to her mother, March 6, 1845.
3. To Henry Bright, Dec. 17, 1860.
4. To J. R. Lowell, July 23, 1861.
5. To Henry Bright, Oct. 12, Nov. 14; to Horatio Bridge, Oct. 12, 1861, Feb. 13, 1862, March 8, 1863.
6. To J. T. Fields, May 7; to W. D. Ticknor, May 17, 1862.
7. James C. Austin, *Fields of the Atlantic: Letters to an Editor, 1861–1870* (San Marino, Calif., 1952), pp. 218–19.
8. In *Atlantic Monthly*, XXVII (April, 1871), 510–12.
9. See Henry A. Beers, *Nathaniel Parker Willis* (Boston, 1885), p. 345; and Edward Dicey, "Nathaniel Hawthorne," *Macmillan's Magazine*, X (July, 1864), 241–46, and *Six Months in the Federal States*, 2 vols. (London, 1863).
10. To Francis Bennoch, Oct. 12, 1862; to J. T. Fields, Jan. 8, 1863; to Henry Bright, March 8, 1863, Nov. 14, 1862.
11. To H. B. Stowe, Jan. 7, 1863.
12. To J. T. Fields, May 3, July 1, 1863.
13. See Roy F. Nichols, *Franklin Pierce* (Philadelphia, 1931), pp. 522–23.
14. Austin, *Fields of the Atlantic: Lecture to an Editor, 1861–1870*, pp. 230–31.
15. To Fields, July 18, 1863.
16. Whether or not the dedication and the prefatory letter "To a Friend" hurt the sale of *Our Old Home* is a matter of speculation. The early sales were about as large as for any of the romances before *The Marble Faun;* the sales in England were good. It might be that the sales in America gained, ultimately, as a result of the feelings stirred by the dedication. For information on publication and sales, see Claude M. Simpson's introduction to *Our Old Home* in the Centenary Edition, V, xxvi–xxxi. When Ralph Waldo Emerson's copy of the book arrived, he "cut out the dedication and letter." M. A. DeWolfe Howe, *Memories of a Hostess* (Boston, 1922), p. 15. See Randall Stewart, "Hawthorne and the Civil War," *Studies in Philology*, XXXIV (Jan., 1937), 98–106.
17. As Elizabeth Peabody explained in a letter of June 4, 1884, to Horatio Bridge (in the Bowdoin College Library) after Hawthorne's letter to her had been published in the *New York Post*, presumably from a copy Channing made when she showed him the letter.
18. To Elizabeth Peabody, June 20, 1863.
19. Sophia to E. A. Hitchcock, Aug. 9, Nov. 16, 22, 1863. Her letters to General Hitchcock are in the Manuscript Division of the Library of Congress, and are used with permission of the Director, Dr. John C. Broderick. See E. A. Hitchcock to Sophia Hawthorne, Aug. 31, Nov. 24, 1863. In the Berg Collection.

31. Romances in Fragments

1. Sophia to Una Hawthorne, Dec. 19, 1863.
2. To David Roberts, Jan. 29, 1861.

3. To J. R. Russell, July 23; from Sophia, July 30, 1861.
4. Rose Hawthorne Lathrop, *Memories of Hawthorne* (Boston, 1897), p. 436.
5. Excerpts are printed in Julian Hawthorne, *Nathaniel Hawthorne and His Wife* (Boston, 1885), II, 315–21.
6. To W. D. Ticknor, Jan. 6, June 7, July 27; to J. T. Fields, Feb. 14; to J. R. Lowell, May 26, 29, 1863.
7. Sophia to W. D. Ticknor, May 15, 1863.
8. In *The American Claimant Manuscripts*, Centenary Edition, XII, 3–89; first published in the *Atlantic Monthly*, 1882–83. See also "Historical Commentary," XII, 491–521; and Edward H. Davidson, *Hawthorne's Last Phase* (New Haven, Conn., 1949).
9. XIII, 499–500; see James T. Fields, *Yesterdays with Authors* (Boston, 1871), p. 96.
10. XIII, 531, 534.

32. "Nearer to the Way-Side Inn"

1. To J. T. Fields, Oct. 24, 18, 1863.
2. *Ibid.*, Nov. 6, 8, 1863.
3. Sophia to Annie Fields, Nov. 29, 1863; in the Boston Public Library.
4. James T. Fields, *Yesterdays with Authors* (Boston, 1871), pp. 112–13; and *Biographical Notes and Personal Sketches* (Boston, 1881), p. 85.
5. To J. T. Fields, Dec. 9, 15, 1863.
6. To H. W. Longfellow, Jan. 2; to W. D. Ticknor, Jan. 7, 1864.
7. To Franklin Pierce, March 9; Sophia to W. D. Ticknor, March 10, and to Franklin Pierce, March 13, 1864.
8. Caroline Ticknor, *Hawthorne and His Publisher* (Boston, 1913), p. 319. This letter seems not to have been preserved.
9. Reprinted in the *Boston Transcript* of April 12. See also the *Boston Daily Advertiser* of the same day.
10. See the *Boston Journal*, April 16.
11. Fields, *Yesterdays with Authors*, p. 118.
12. Sophia to Annie Fields, April 18, 21, 1864; in Fields, *Yesterdays with Authors*, pp. 118–20.
13. Sophia to J. T. Fields, May 6, 1864, in Fields, *Yesterdays with Authors*, pp. 120–21.
14. Una to J. T. Fields, May 8, 1864; in James C. Austin, *Fields of the Atlantic Monthly: Letters to an Editor, 1861–1870* (San Marino, Calif., 1953), p. 236.
15. *The Journals of Bronson Alcott*, ed. Odell Shepard (Boston, 1938), p. 363.
16. "Hawthorne," *Atlantic Monthly*, XIV (July, 1864), 98–101.
17. Franklin Pierce to Horatio Bridge, May 21, 1864; in Bridge, *Personal Recollections of Nathaniel Hawthorne* (New York, 1893), pp. 176–79. In a letter to Sarah Webster of March 18, 1868 (at the University of Virginia Library, printed in part in Sidney Webster, *Franklin Pierce and His Administration* [New York, 1892], pp. 24–28), Pierce covered much the same ground as in writing Bridge and added several details incorporated here.

18. "Hawthorne," *Atlantic Monthly*, XIV (July, 1864), 100.

19. For the reports sent to Horace Mann in Hawaii, see my article "Hawthorne's Final Illness and Death: Additional Reports," *Emerson Society Quarterly*, XIX (2nd Quarter, 1973), 124–27.

20. In a letter to Horace Mann, Oct. 30, 1864, in the Mary K. and Harry L. Dalton Collection, Duke University Library.

21. A copy of this broadside is in the Huntington Library. It is published in J. T. Fields, *Biographical Notes and Personal Sketches*, pp. 92–95. Another letter to Mrs. Fields, "written by Mrs. Nathaniel Hawthorne while her husband lay dead," appears in M. A. DeWolfe Howe, *Memories of a Hostess* (Boston, 1922), pp. 70–72.

22. Undated letter in the Boston Public Library.

23. Emerson wrote about the funeral on July 24. *Journals of Ralph Waldo Emerson*, ed. Edward Waldo Emerson and Waldo Emerson Forbes, 10 vols. (Boston, 1914), X, 39–41.

24. Reprinted in the *Nathaniel Hawthorne Journal 1972*, pp. 259–61.

25. Julian Hawthorne, *Nathaniel Hawthorne and His Wife*, 2 vols. (Boston, 1885), II, 348.

26. "Hawthorne," *Atlantic Monthly*, XIV (July, 1864), 101.

27. *My Study Windows* (Boston, 1871), p. 196.

28. From Longfellow's Journal, quoted in Edward Waldo Emerson, *The Early Years of the Saturday Club* (Boston, 1918), p. 213.

29. Jay Leyda, *The Melville Log* (New York, 1951, 1969), p. 669.

Index